T0340131

Foundations for a Disequilibrium Theory of the Business Cycle

Building on *The Dynamics of Keynesian Monetary Growth* by Chiarella and Flaschel (2000), this book is a key contribution to business cycle theory, setting out a disequilibrium approach with gradual adjustments of the key macroeconomic variables. Its analytic study of a deterministic model of economic activity, inflation and income distribution integrates elements in the tradition of Keynes, Metzler and Goodwin (KMG). After a qualitative analysis of the basic feedback mechanisms, the authors calibrate the KMG model to the stylized facts of the business cycle in the US economy, and then undertake a detailed numerical investigation of the local and global dynamics generated by the model. Finally, topical issues in monetary policy are studied in small macro-models as well as for the KMG model by incorporating an estimated Taylor-type interest rate reaction function. The stability features of this enhanced model are also compared to those of the original KMG model.

CARL CHIARELLA is Professor of Quantitative Finance in the School of Finance and Economics at the University of Technology, Sydney.

PETER FLASCHEL is Professor of Economics at the University of Bielefeld.

REINER FRANKE is a member of the Ludwig Boltzmann Institute for Monetary Economics at the Vienna University of Technology.

Foundations for a Disequilibrium Theory of the Business Cycle

Qualitative Analysis and Quantitative Assessment

Carl Chiarella

School of Finance and Economics, University of Technology, Sydney

Peter Flaschel

Faculty of Economics, University of Bielefeld

Reiner Franke

Ludwig Boltzmann Institute for Monetary Economics, Vienna University of Technology

CAMBRIDGE
UNIVERSITY PRESS

CAMBRIDGE UNIVERSITY PRESS
Cambridge, New York, Melbourne, Madrid, Cape Town,
Singapore, São Paulo, Delhi, Tokyo, Mexico City

Cambridge University Press
The Edinburgh Building, Cambridge CB2 8RU, UK

Published in the United States of America by Cambridge University Press, New York

www.cambridge.org
Information on this title: www.cambridge.org/9780521369923

First published 2005
First paperback edition 2011

A catalogue record for this publication is available from the British Library

ISBN 978-0-521-85025-4 Hardback
ISBN 978-0-521-36992-3 Paperback

Contents

Figures

Tables

Foreword

The authors of this book, Carl Chiarella, Peter Flaschel and Reiner Franke, have been engaged in a major research programme in macroeconomic analysis for an extended period of time, arguably dating from the mid-1980s if not earlier. This has resulted in a series of papers and books by them and several others in various combinations, including Willi Semmler, Toichiro Asada, Gang Gong, and still more. This group is scattered in various parts of the globe, principally in the cities of Bielefeld, Beijing, New York, Sydney and Tokyo. While the output of this group is the result of visits to each other's institutions (particularly those of Flaschel to the University of Technology, Sydney) and meetings at various international conferences, the intellectual centre of their enterprise has been the Faculty of Economics at Bielefeld University. It is here that Flaschel, Franke and Semmler are, or have been at various times, located, and where the group has held an almost annual workshop on their developing research agenda over the last decade. Hence I feel it is appropriate to neologize here and dub the results of their collective efforts to constitute an emerging school of macroeconomic thought 'the Bielefeld School'. This book can then be characterized as representing a significant phase in the development of this Bielefeld School.

The authors themselves have in earlier work provided their own label for the core model they have developed and studied: the 'Keynes–Metzler–Goodwin' (KMG) model. This book more directly compares this model to other macroeconomic approaches, both those of a more New-Classical orientation as well as most substantially with those of various New-Keynesian formulations, especially the recently emerging synthesis due to Michael Woodford along with Glenn Rudebusch and Lars Svensson. At one point, in reference to James Tobin's later work, they suggest that their model could be considered to be derived from an 'Old-Keynesian' perspective, and it does draw on the basic IS-LM framework still used by many policymakers, with an added aggregate supply component. However, they generally stick to their use of the KMG label in describing it.

The basic elements in this approach involve allowing for substantial real effects to arise from financial markets, which they argue is the Keynes part. The Metzler part involves allowing an important role for inventory adjustments, something that is much less common in many current macroeconomic models. Finally, the Goodwin part emphasizes the importance of income distribution, particularly wage dynamics operating through a modified Phillips curve setup. In sharp contrast to both the New-Classical and New-Keynesian approaches they abjure the rational expectations assumption in modelling inflationary expectations. They do allow inflation expectations to play a central role in their model, but view them as operating in a more generalized 'inflation climate' that gradually adjusts over time. Rather than just a trend-chasing adaptive expectations mechanism they also assume a tendency for reversion to a normal level over time, a pattern they label 'regressive expectations'. These are models fundamentally of disequilibrium dynamics with gradually adapting processes.

Another central element that distinguishes their approach from many others is the assumption of nonlinearity in the investment function. While this may further separate them from many of the New-Classical and Keynesian modellers, this draws upon the influence of earlier economists who worked at the time of Keynes, such as Kalecki or – in his aftermath – such as Kaldor and Hicks, with both Metzler and Goodwin part of that group as well. This links them with the more general literature on models of complex dynamics arising from nonlinear models, which both Chiarella and Franke have separately contributed to in the past. In this KMG approach, instability arises from the nonlinearities being sufficiently great to trigger Hopf bifurcations and resulting endogenous limit cycle behaviour. However, these nonlinearities also provide bounds to the dynamics of the system.

There are two principal extensions that this book presents. The first is an effort to reach out more directly to policymakers by an effort to calibrate their model to fit parameter values relevant to the US economy. The second (in the final two chapters) is the introduction of a Taylor rule to endogenize policy feedback and the determination of interest rates. In this they are directly confronting the efforts of Woodford, and also of Rudebusch and Svensson, who have seen the Taylor rule as a way to eliminate indeterminacy in their models. They label this extension of their basic model the KMGT model.

Their final chapter examines the stability characteristics of this KMGT model. There they de-emphasize the nonlinearity of the investment function, which allows for endogenous cycles no longer to arise from a Hopf bifurcation. They even consider the matter of cycles due to exogenous shocks on an otherwise stable system in a Frischian manner. A final curious implication from this model is a heightened importance of the Metzlerian aspect of the system in determining the pattern of its dynamics.

At this point I would like to raise a point about a lacuna in this otherwise generally comprehensive book. This is the relationship of this Bielefeld School to those of the various branches of Post-Keynesian macroeconomics. They do not directly draw upon or cite any of the current prominent Post-Keynesian economists. However, it can be argued that their approach can be viewed as a sophisticated formulation of certain Post-Keynesian elements or trends. Certainly, Goodwin as well as Kalecki have been much admired by many Post-Keynesians, and the idea that money has real effects is an idea accepted by most Post-Keynesians. However, they do not obviously focus on endogenous money per se as do Paul Davidson and Basil Moore, even though their use of a Taylor rule effectively makes money endogenous. Also, they have been more precisely mathematical than have been many of the Post-Keynesians. Nevertheless, certain Post-Keynesians have developed models that have some definite similarities to what this school does, with Philip Arestis and Peter Skott coming to mind most particularly, notably in combining financial models with real effects with distributional shares dynamics that can generate endogenous cycles. Thus, I have no problem describing the Bielefeld School as representing effectively a highly sophisticated Post-Keynesian approach. Certainly, there is no doubt that they belong to the more general Keynesian approach, arguably much more so than the New-Keynesians, who use the questionable rational expectations assumption.

Thus the authors of this book should be applauded. They have moved a distinctive and policy-relevant approach to macroeconomic analysis forward decisively. Their careful synthesis of realistic dynamic elements and their careful analysis of the sensitivity and stability characteristics of their model in a policy context is much to be admired. In this book the Bielefeld School achieves a genuine culmination of great depth and breadth.

J. BARKLEY ROSSER, JR.
James Madison University
Harrisonburg, Virginia

October 2004

Preface

In this book we build on a theoretical approach the foundations for which were laid in the work *The Dynamics of Keynesian Monetary Growth: Macrofoundations* by two of the present authors. In that work we considered a hierarchically structured sequence of macrodynamic models, starting from Tobinian neoclassical monetary growth and its historical counterpart, the Keynes–Wicksell monetary growth models, leading then via Keynesian IS-LM growth dynamics to a model type that has been labelled the Keynes–Metzler–Goodwin (KMG) growth dynamics. In the present book we will extend the baseline KMG model in various directions, analysing it in a much more detailed way than in previous work and, most importantly, studying it also from the empirical and the numerical point of view. Special emphasis is placed on the dynamic feedback relationships and on endogenously generated business cycle fluctuations in a growth context. In the initial stages the study concentrates here on the private sector and, essentially, abstracts from policy issues. Gaining thereby basic insights into the stabilizing and destabilizing forces in the economy, modern discussions of monetary policy are also integrated later.

As shown in the work by Chiarella and Flaschel, the KMG model type manages to avoid a variety of problems associated with the traditional IS-LM growth model, such as the boundedness in the responsiveness of aggregate demand, multiple IS-LM equilibria, or discontinuities in phase space dynamics. The model achieves this by allowing for disequilibrium on the goods market, taking the implied inventory changes into account and introducing gradual adjustments towards desired inventories as well as the concept of expected sales. All this is formulated along Metzlerian lines and so constitutes the M-component of the KMG approach. From the higher-dimensional viewpoint of the Metzlerian disequilibrium adjustment process, the problems that many advanced IS-LM models are facing appear, in fact, rather misleading. Our model's Metzlerian component can thus be regarded as a useful or even indispensable device for the general modelling architecture, though its mechanisms are not at the heart of the economy.

The outstanding theoretical features of the KMG approach to macrodynamics are the relationships to Keynes' (1936) *General Theory* and to Goodwin's (1967) seminal paper on the interaction of growth and income distribution; these are the K- and G-components in the model. Concerning the K-component, the present book is still close to traditional macroeconomics in its description of consumption and investment behaviour. In a first stage, the interest rate is also determined by a familiar LM equilibrium condition, where the money supply is assumed to grow at a constant rate. It can in this respect be said that, while government and a central bank are present in the model, they conduct a neutral policy, so that the private sector can be studied in a kind of vacuum. In a second stage, we take up the recent New-Keynesian research agenda and follow the modern practice of studying monetary policy rules – i.e. interest rate rules of a Taylor type.

The real innovation of our modelling framework lies, nevertheless, in a new approach to the wage-price spiral as an extension of both Keynes' and Goodwin's views on this matter. As it is formulated and combined with aggregate demand, this building block can be usefully compared to the traditional Keynesian AS-AD dynamics (Old Neoclassical Synthesis) as well as to the currently fashionable New-Keynesian theory of staggered wage and price settings (New Neoclassical Synthesis). Underlining the agents' gradual reactions to the disequilibria they perceive, the wage-price dynamics in our model are, however, radically different from the Neoclassical Syntheses (Old and New), with respect to modes of operation and the implications for the macrodynamic system into which it is embedded. The role of an elaborate wage-price spiral in the course of the business cycle is thus one major focus of interest in this book, from the theoretical point of view as well as empirically, where in our numerical simulations we seek to calibrate the model's cyclical behaviour to the stylized facts of the business cycle fluctuations observed in the world's major economy, namely the US economy.

In sum, the book takes up the work begun in Chiarella and Flaschel (2000a) and provides detailed qualitative, quantitative and empirical studies of a mature version of the traditional Keynesian approach, which were then still out of reach. As an alternative to the New-Keynesian macroeconomics, it puts forward an approach to disequilibrium dynamics that aims to shed light on the study of demand-constrained modern market economies that, in particular, are subject to sometimes more and sometimes less virulent adjustments in wages and prices.

A number of professional colleagues deserve special thanks. There are, first of all, our co-authors in several related published and unpublished works, Toichiro Asada, Willi Semmler and Peter Skott, who in many ways have contributed to the present project through stimulating discussions on various aspects of the subject matter of this book as well as on related research projects. We furthermore thank Richard Day, Duncan Foley and Reinhard Neck for a variety of stimulating comments at various stages in the development of the present work and related topics. We are grateful for comments and criticisms we have received from numerous participants at presentations of aspects of the material of this book at international conferences and research seminars. Of course, none of the aforementioned is responsible for the remaining errors in this work, neither with respect to form nor substance. We are indebted to three anonymous referees who read the original version of the manuscript (chapters 2 to 6) and offered many, even detailed, suggestions for its improvement. We also wish to acknowledge the sustained financial support for this project from the School of Finance and Economics at the University of Technology, Sydney. Finally, we would like to thank Chris Harrison and Lynn Dunlop of CUP for all that they have done to make the publication process go as smoothly as it has.

CARL CHIARELLA
School of Finance and Economics
University of Technology, Sydney

PETER FLASCHEL
Faculty of Economics
University of Bielefeld

REINER FRANKE
Ludwig Boltzmann Institute for Monetary Economics
Vienna University of Technology

September 2004

Notation

Steady-state or trend values are indicated by a superscript 'o'. When no confusion arises, letters F, G, H may also define certain functional expressions in a specific context. A dot over a variable $x=x(t)$ denotes the time derivative, a caret its growth rate: $\dot{x} = dx/dt$, $\hat{x} = \dot{x}/x$. In the numerical simulations, flow variables are measured at annual rates.

As far as possible, the notation tries to follow the logic of using capital letters for level variables and lower-case letters for variables in intensive form, or for constant (steady-state) ratios. Greek letters are most often constant coefficients in behavioural equations (with, however, the notable exceptions being π, ω, ξ and ϕ).

B outstanding government fixed-price bonds (priced at $p_b = 1$)

C real private consumption (demand is generally realized)

E number of equities

F neoclassical production function in chapter 2; otherwise generic symbol for functions defined in a local context

G real government expenditure (demand is always realized)

I real net investment of fixed capital (demand is always realized)

I_N^d desired real inventory investment

$\mathcal{J}$ Jacobian matrix in the mathematical analysis

K stock of fixed capital

L employment – i.e. total working hours per year (labour demand is always realized)

L^s labour supply – i.e. supply of total working hours per year

M stock of money supply

N inventories of finished goods

N^d desired stock of inventories

S total real saving: $S = S_f + S_g + S_h$

S_f real saving of firms (unintended inventory changes)

S_g real government saving

S_p real saving of private households

T total real tax collections

T^c real taxes of asset holders

W real wealth of private households

Y real output

Y^d real aggregate demand

Y^e expected real aggregate demand

Y^n output at normal use of capacity: $Y^n = y^n K$

a_y abbreviates a sum of coefficients in chapter 6, section 3, sub-section 3: $a_y = c_p + \gamma + s_c \delta - (1 - s_c)\theta_c$

c_p consumption coefficient of agents without income from economic activities; see chapter 4, section 2, subsection 1, eq. (4.4)

e employment rate (w.r.t. hours): $e = L/L^s$

f_x functional relationship representing the determination of variable x, $\dot{x}$ or $\hat{x}$

f_{xy} partial derivative of function f_x with respect to variable y

g^o steady-state growth rate of real variables

g_ℓ growth rate of labour supply: $g_\ell = \hat{L}^s$ (a constant)

g_m growth rate of money supply: $g_m = \hat{M}$ (a constant)

g_z growth rate of trend labour productivity: $g_z = \hat{z}^o$ (a constant)

i nominal rate of interest on government bonds; federal funds rate in chapters 8 and 9

k^s fixed capital per (efficiency units of) labour supply: $k^s = K/z^o L^s$

ℓ labour intensity (in efficiency units): $\ell = z^o L/K = 1/k^s$

m real balances relative to the capital stock: $m = M/pK$

n inventory–capital ratio: $n = N/K$

p price level

p_e price of equities

q return differential: $q = r - (i - \pi)$

r rate of return on fixed capital, specified as $r = (pY - wL - \delta pK)/pK$

s_c propensity to save out of capital income on the part of asset owners

s_h households' propensity to save out of total income (in chapters 2 and 3)

u rate of capacity utilization: $u = Y/Y^n = y/y^n$

v wage share (in gross product): $v = wL/pY$

w nominal wage rate per hour

x_m auxiliary variable in chapter 2: $x_m = z^o M/wK$

y output–capital ratio: $y = Y/K$; except in chapter 1, section 3, where y denotes the output gap

y^d ratio of aggregate demand to capital stock: $y^d = Y^d/K$

y^e ratio of expected demand to capital stock: $y^e = Y^e/K$

y^n normal output–capital ratio (a constant; no recourse to a neoclassical production function)

z labour productivity – i.e. output per working hour: $z = Y/L$

z^o trend value, or 'normal' level, of labour productivity

α marginal product of capital in chapter 2: $\alpha = \alpha(y) = F_K(K, z^o L)$; symbol for policy parameters in Taylor rule in chapters 8 and 9

α_i coefficient measuring interest rate smoothing in the Taylor rule

α_p coefficient on inflation gap in the Taylor rule

α_u coefficient on output gap in the Taylor rule

β_x generically, reaction coefficient in an equation determining x, $\dot{x}$ or $\hat{x}$

β_y adjustment speed in adaptive sales expectations

β_π general adjustment speed in revisions of the inflation climate

β_{xy} generically, reaction coefficient related to the determination of variable x, $\dot{x}$ or $\hat{x}$ with respect to changes in the exogenous variable y

β_{Iq} responsiveness of investment (capital growth rate) to changes in q

β_{Iu} responsiveness of investment to changes in u

β_{nn} stock adjustment speed

β_{ny} desired ratio of inventories over expected sales

β_{pu} reaction coefficient of u in price Phillips curve

β_{pv} reaction coefficient of $(1+\mu)v - 1$ in price Phillips curve

β_{we} reaction coefficient of e in wage Phillips curve

β_{wv} reaction coefficient of $(v - v^o)/v^o$ in wage Phillips curve

β_{zu} responsiveness of (procyclical) labour productivity to changes in u

γ government expenditures per unit of fixed capital: $\gamma = G/K$ (a constant, except for chapter 7, section 6, subsection 3)

δ rate of depreciation of fixed capital (a constant)

$\eta_{m,i}$ interest elasticity of money demand (expressed as a positive number)

κ coefficient in reduced-form wage-price equations: $\kappa = 1/(1 - \kappa_p \kappa_w)$

κ_p parameter weighting $\hat{w}$ vs. π in price Phillips curve

κ_w parameter weighting $\hat{p}$ vs. π in wage Phillips curve

κ_{wp} same as κ_w, in chapter 5

κ_{wz} parameter weighting $\hat{z}$ vs. $\hat{z}^o$ in wage Phillips curve (only chapter 5)

κ_π parameter weighting adaptive expectations vs. regressive expectations in revisions of the inflation climate

μ actual markup rate in chapter 5; same as μ^o otherwise

μ^o target markup rate over unit labour costs

ξ relative excess demand: $\xi = (Y^d - Y)/Y$

π general inflation climate; except in chapter 1, section 3, where π denotes inflation

θ same as θ_c (in chapters 2 and 3)

θ_c tax parameter for T^c (net of interest): $T^c - iB/p = \theta_c K$

τ_w tax rate on wages

ϕ flexibility term in the nonlinear investment function in chapters 6 and 8: $\phi = \phi(u, q)$

ω real wage rate, deflated by trend productivity: $\omega = (w/p)/z^o$

1 Competing approaches to Keynesian macrodynamics

1.1 Introduction

1.1.1 General methodological remarks

This book proposes a view of dynamic macroeconomic modelling that stresses the non-market-clearing approach. Here the focus is very much on dynamic adjustment processes amongst the principal markets and agents of the macroeconomy and the dynamic linkages between these. Our starting point is the *Keynes–Metzler–Goodwin* (KMG) model developed in earlier work of the authors together with other collaborators. The label is meant to highlight the key macroeconomic mechanisms introduced by the great economists referred to. The 'Keynes' refers to the causal nexus from financial to real markets, 'Metzler' to inventory dynamics and 'Goodwin' to the dynamics of distributive shares. It is our view that these are the core mechanisms which need to be at the heart of descriptive models of the macroeconomy.

An important aim of our analysis is to understand the dynamic interplay between these core driving mechanisms of the macroeconomy, in particular which are stabilizing and which destabilizing, and which parameters have the most influence in moving the economy back and forth between the regions of stability and instability. In the shock-driven models of modern macrodynamics a stabilizing effect is one that reduces the variance of some important state variables; however, here we are almost exclusively concerned with deterministic systems, and so the terms 'stability' and 'instability' are used in the sense that they refer to the local properties of the steady state.

For the KMG model that we work with, it can be mathematically proved that parameter variations that bring about instability are associated with a Hopf bifurcation. We will not be so concerned with regard to the details of this phenomenon but, rather, take it mainly as an indication that over a wider range of parameter values the dynamics are basically of a cyclical nature. Here, we are specifically interested in oscillations that occur at business cycle frequencies. For these investigations, however, we will need to resort to a numerical analysis.

Of course, oscillations in linear deterministic models will die out if the equilibrium is stable. This equally holds true if, as in the most elementary specifications of our building blocks, the model is (not linear but) 'quasi-linear'. On the other hand, the intrinsic nonlinearities (such as a multiplication of two variables) are also not sufficient to bound the explosive motion if the steady state is locally unstable. Hence, in order to generate persistent and bounded cyclical behaviour, we employ parameter combinations that imply instability and then introduce an extrinsic nonlinearity that takes effect in the outer regions of the state space, so that locally the system is spiralling outward and further away from the steady state it is spiralling inward. Since the KMG model, despite the various feedbacks from wage-price and inventory dynamics, is essentially still an investment-driven model, we will in this book focus concretely on a suitable nonlinearity in the investment function.

The present book adds two features to earlier work of the authors on the KMG model. First, it undertakes a very careful calibration of the model to the stylized business cycle facts of US data. The dynamic properties of the resulting calibrated model are studied in detail, especially stability regions in the space of key parameters. Second, in the final two chapters we take the LM block of versions of the model hitherto developed and replace it with a Taylor-type interest rate rule. This type of rule has, of course, become a – if not the – major policy tool of central banks worldwide, so in the interests of realism any model of the modern business cycle needs to incorporate it. To the resulting model we give the label *Keynes–Metzler–Goodwin–Taylor* (KMGT). The model could be taken by economists and policymakers inclined to the non-market-clearing approach and used as the basis of policy experiments and further empirical studies.

With its stress on the underlying macroeconomic forces of the economy and their interaction, the authors have characterized their approach in previous works as *macrofounded*. The authors still contend that this is the major advantage of the approach to business cycle modelling that they are advocating in this and other work. The approach thus stands in contrast to other currently more fashionable approaches, in particular real business cycle theory and the New-Keynesian approach. The common element of these two frameworks is the insistence on deriving all dynamic equations from microfoundations. In a pure form, this involves a representative agent solving an intertemporal expected utility-maximizing problem. The corresponding Euler equation, the market-clearing assumptions and the hypothesis of rational expectations yield the dynamic structure of these models. Models of this kind still amount to a Robinson Crusoe economy, progress perhaps being that Friday has joined as his companion.[1] In a less pure form, these models are enriched by modifying the Euler equation or combining it with elements that intuitively or plausibly are meant to capture additional features such as, for example, other sectors in the economy or so-called backward-looking, boundedly rational agents. These models are microfounded in spirit, but no longer in all explicit details.[2]

Whilst it is, of course, good to obtain microfoundations for the postulated behavioural relationships, this approach carries with it certain disadvantages, in our view. Most importantly, the nature of the solution procedures for stochastic intertemporal optimization models makes it very difficult, if not impossible, to understand clearly the dynamic linkages and feedbacks between the various sectors and agents of the economy. It may in this respect be worth referring to the points made by Romer (2000) about the relevance of the IS-LM-AS model for analyzing short-run fluctuations, a model that in our terms could be viewed as a macrofounded model (though we emphasize that Romer himself does not employ that term). Romer sees two important advantages. First, prices do not adjust instantaneously to disturbances, and this seems to be a necessary feature of any model purporting to describe economic reality. Second, the microfounded approach does not at the end of the day lead to models that are more realistic than those based on intuitive or so-called 'ad hoc' arguments. As Romer (2000, pp. 7f.) summarizes it,'The tradeoff [when moving from the ad hoc assumption in IS-LM-AS to a relatively simple formulation based on intertemporal optimization] is similar for grounding the analysis of investment demand, money demand, price rigidity, and soon more strongly in microeconomic foundations: even the easiest models are dramatically harder than their IS-LM-AS counterparts, and not obviously more realistic.'

One might also go one step further and scratch at the halo of the expression 'microfoundations' as it has been used in the last three

---

[1] For example, Friday may be a rule-of-thumb consumer, as in the New-Keynesian models by Amato and Laubach (2003) or Gal et al. (2004).

[2] As a consequence, the conventional jump-variable techniques of this literature are less obvious in these models than in a purely optimizing framework. We recall that, in the early stages of the development of the jump-variable techniques for solving rational expectations models, some concerns were expressed about the lack of any theory to explain the jump in economic variables as well as about the arbitrariness in the selection of jump variables in larger-scale models. Some of these issues were articulated by Burmeister (1980). A nice quotation is also the following side remark by Blanchard (1981, p. 135) in his application of the jump-variable technique to the value of the stock market: 'Following a standard if not entirely convincing practice, I shall assume that q always adjusts so as to leave the economy on the stable path to equilibrium.'

decades against 'ad hoc' model building. We feel, in fact, sympathetic to Solow in his summary of the contemporarily predominant methodological approach: 'One could even question whether a representative agent model qualifies as microfoundation at all' (Solow, 2004, p. 660).[3]

A more specific point where we certainly depart from current fashions is in the handling of expectations. For almost three decades the rational expectations assumption has been accepted almost as an article of faith in some quarters. Interestingly, its hold on the economics profession has loosened over the last decade, with many papers on boundedly rational and heterogeneous agents appearing in a range of journals and books. Nevertheless, the grip of the rational expectations assumption is still almost vice-like in the reigning business cycle paradigms. However, we remain to be convinced that it is useful to build models of the economy where agents have the information and computational ability to form rational expectations or behave 'as if' they had such abilities. We believe that such an assumption is so far from reality that it does not serve even as some sort of baseline around which the economy moves. Rather, the formation of expectations under conditions of incomplete information, bounded rationality and limited computational ability is part of economic reality.

Apart from this negative judgement, four points should be mentioned with regard to the treatment of expectations in this book. First, we join the common – in fact, almost exclusive – practice in macrodynamic modelling of concentrating on the rate of inflation as the one and only variable about which expectations are formed.[4] Second, we will avoid the expression 'expected rate of inflation'. We, rather, introduce a variable π that in an uncertain environment the agents conceive as some average over a longer time in the future; it is not just the rate expected for the next period. Therefore, we prefer to use the term 'inflation climate' for π.

From this point of view it becomes, third, reasonable to consider the changes in π as revisions of a currently held opinion, which are made in a gradual manner in light of the most recent information about inflation.

---

[3] It would by no means inappropriate if we filled the next pages by quoting all the methodological remarks from this paper, which is an obituary of James Tobin where Solow reminds us of his seminal paper 'A general equilibrium approach to monetary theory' from thirty-five years ago. On this occasion we may say that we see ourselves in the tradition of Tobin's approach, about which Solow, to provoke contradiction we suppose, fears 'that it may soon be extinct, like some obscure Melanesian language whose native speakers are dying off (Solow, 2004, p. 659)

[4] Though it is hardly ever mentioned as a problem, we consider this a most serious shortcoming. Keynes' famous 'animal spirits' that are guiding entrepreneurs certainly refer to other, or at least additional, economic variables. Thus, in future work, we intend to take up the notion of a 'state of confidence' or a general 'business climate' as the expectational variable that should be centre stage in macrodynamic modelling. A first attempt in this direction was Franke and Asada (1994).

Formally (but only formally, we stress), this mechanism can be described as adaptive expectations. Though this adjustment principle has a bad reputation in some quarters, there is indeed widespread evidence from economics and the behavioural sciences that it is by no means that foolish and that it is indeed widely used by real economic agents (Flaschel et al., 1997, pp. 149–62 or, more extensively, Franke, 1999, give a compilation of such arguments). For the purposes of the present discussion, the following short citation from Mankiw (2001, p. C59) is illuminating enough. After noting how odd it is to assert that expectations about inflation are formed without incorporating all the news events that are so readily available in the modern world, he adds, 'Yet the assumption of adaptive expectations is, in essence, what the data are crying out for.'[5]

The fourth point is that we combine the 'adaptive expectations' with another relevant mechanism. While the former could also be characterized as chasing a trend, we additionally draw on a general idea from the asset markets, a fundamentalist view, so to speak, according to which the variable is expected to return to its normal level after some time. The adjustment mechanism that we will propose for our inflation climate π will thus be a weighted average of 'adaptive expectations' and these, as we call them, regressive expectations.

Returning to our interest in business cycle dynamics, we may also point out that the microfounded models are limited in the type of cyclical behaviour they can generate. The solution procedures usually involve a (log-)linearization of the Euler equations, otherwise it may be difficult to apply the solution methodology required to operationalize the rational expectations assumption.

Since linear dynamic models can make economic sense only in their regions of stability, exogenous stochastic processes are needed to generate persistent cycles. Attempts to calibrate these types of models often come down to tuning various types of exogenous stochastic processes. This problem is similar in kind to that of introducing suitable nonlinear mechanisms into our deterministic models to bound the explosive

---

[5] In our view, agents in the real world are not 'forward-looking', which is just another expression for rational expectations. They are 'backward-looking', to take up this currently fashionable term, in that they have only data from the past on the basis of which they can form expectations about the future. On the other hand, agents are sufficiently sophisticated to make use of econometric methods. While, being univariate, the adaptive expectations method is a particularly simple one, it would be more appropriate to assume that the agents adopt vector autoregressions to forecast future inflation. Then, in order to reduce at least the computational effort, one might try to short-circuit this general device by some simplified adjustment formulae where, however, reference is made not only to current inflation but also to some measure of the output gap, and perhaps the interest rate too.

motion. If this device may be viewed as the ad hoc feature of the macro-founded approach, then it may equally be argued that the open choice of exogenous stochastic processes may be seen as the ad hoc feature of the microfounded approach.

A final argument that we may give for developing further the macro-founded approach that we are advocating is that it still seems to be at the heart of the explicit or implicit modelling framework used by many policymakers. This is, no doubt, due to the fact that the microfounded approaches leave obscure the linkages between the different sectors and agents of the economy. But it is precisely these linkages that are of importance to policymakers.

1.1.2   A historical perspective

After elaborating on the many aspects of his new and, as he emphasized (Keynes, 1936, p. 3), *general* theory about the most fundamental macroeconomic relationships, Keynes (p. 313) purports in chapter 22 of *The General Theory* that this work should also be useful for a better understanding of the fluctuations that are summarized as business cycles, or, in his words, the trade cycle. The definite article 'the' already indicates that it is viewed as a systematic phenomenon (pp. 313f.):

By a *cyclical* movement we mean that as the system progresses in, e.g. the upward direction, the forces propelling it upwards at first gather force and have a cumulative effect on one another but gradually lose their strength until at a certain point they tend to be replaced by forces operating in the opposite direction; which in turn gather force for a time and accentuate one another, until they too, having reached their maximum development, wane and give place to their opposite. We do not, however, merely mean by a *cyclical* movement that upward and downward tendencies, once started, do not persist for ever in the same direction but are ultimately reversed. We mean also that there is some recognisable degree of regularity in the time-sequence and duration of the upward and downward movements.

Hence, there must be deeper causes for this kind of cyclical behaviour. The most important cause Keynes identifies is investment and its key determinant, the marginal efficiency of capital (p. 313). The other two pillars of his theory are the marginal propensity to consume and the state of liquidity preference. Once these 'three main gaps in our existing knowledge' are filled, the complementary 'theory of prices [and wages] falls into its proper place as a matter which is subsidiary to our general theory' (pp. 31f.).

This approach to a theory of the trade cycle has not received full attention in the discussions that developed after the appearance of *The*

General Theory, which in the main is probably due to the strong psychological factors that are penetrating the dynamic feedback mechanisms. So the concepts just mentioned provided only a loose theoretical frame for the more formal versions of Keynesian theory. In its striving for a rigorous design, modern macrodynamic modelling started out from more precise, and more limited, behavioural assumptions. This holds point in the 1950s and 1960s, as well as for the progress that the contemporary New-Keynesians claim to have made. In the remainder of this chapter we give a brief overview of these approaches from our point of view, and then locate our own approach with respect to these traditions. Since, in particular, price and wage formation are here not just a 'subsidiary' component, we emphasize the different assumptions and specifications concerning perfectly flexible or more sluggish prices and wages. It should also be remarked that this discussion – not only because of its brevity – loses sight of the systematic cyclical movements that Keynes had in mind. We will, however, return to this topic in the analysis of our own models later in the book.

We start, therefore, in the next section with a reconsideration of the old Neoclassical Synthesis, which we date as Stage I. Based initially on Patinkin's micro-oriented approach to macrodynamics and then further refined, this blend of Keynes and the Classics considered the original debate from the perspective of a larger modelling framework where all building blocks of the Keynesian approach are present, together with Classical and later Friedmanian supply-side arguments (marginal cost determination of the price level and an expectations-augmented money wage Phillips curve). A rigorous and almost canonical formulation was given to it by Sargent's advanced textbook (1979, chaps. 1–5). At the one end of the synthesis, the Classical version of the working of the macroeconomy was obtained by assuming enough flexibility in the real markets, in the first instance fully flexible wages and prices, while at the other end the Keynesian version emerged when real markets became less perfect and at least money wages were assumed to adjust in a delayed manner.

In section 1.3 we subsequently consider the basic components of the New-Keynesian approach, which we perceive as the Neoclassical Synthesis, State II. In section 1.4, still in a highly stylized fashion, the main ingredients of our own modelling framework are discussed. Here, the preceding sections 1.2 and 1.3 prove to be useful in two respects. First, the best perspective from which to understand and evaluate our work is to view it as introducing disequilibrium elements into the AS-AD setting of the Neoclassical Synthesis, Stage I, in order to remove certain central theoretical weaknesses. We will thus present our approach as a matured Keynesian macroeconomic model of disequilibrium dynamics. If it were not so risky in the overall competition for catchy and marketable labels, we might even be tempted to call it defiantly an Old-Keynesian approach.[6]

Second, the discussion of the Neoclassical Synthesis, Stage II, is useful since, interestingly, the reduced and sketchy way in which we try to characterize it allows us to recognize a close correspondence between our and the New-Keynesian modelling of, in particular, the wage-price and output dynamics. When stripped down to the bones, at first sight only the period-dating of these variables in the postulated relationships seems to be different. It will, however, also be worked out that this leads to radically different conclusions regarding the working of the economy.

1.2   Neoclassical Synthesis, Stage I: traditional AS-AD dynamics

We reconsider in this section what constituted the core of Keynesian macroeconomic theory until the beginning of the 1970s. This was, of course, the Neoclassical Synthesis, and we have already announced that, thirty years later and with a view to our discussion further below, we will also occasionally refer to it more precisely as the Neoclassical Synthesis, Stage I (NCS I). This body of theory organizes the description of a closed economy into three major building blocks: the IS and LM relationships for the goods and money market, which in combination yield the so-called AD curve; an AS curve derived from the marginal productivity principle for labour; and demand facing supply on the labour market. In its basic equilibrium formulation, prices (p) as well as nominal wages (w) are perfectly flexible, so that the economy is on its steady-state growth path.[7] For easier reference, let us denote this approach as NCS I(p, w). More recently it has found expression in the New-Classical economics and the equilibrium business cycle theory.

The agents' out-of-equilibrium behaviour has always been discussed verbally and also often formalized in small models, which, however, have mostly concentrated on selected issues. A first and most influential attempt to introduce disequilibrium adjustments into a complete macroeconomic model of NCS I was undertaken by Sargent (1979, chap. 5). We therefore find it appropriate to begin our review of Keynesian macrodynamics at this point.

---

[6] Inspired by the title of Tobin's (1992) article on the sense and meaning of less than perfect price flexibility.

[7] For a detailed presentation, see, e.g., Sargent (1979, chap. 2).

For a better comparison with the New-Keynesian models later on and their emphasis on monetary policy, it should be mentioned at this stage that all versions of NCS I that we are going to consider assume a neutral policy of Friedmanian type – that is, money supply is exogenous and grows at a constant rate.

1.2.1   Keynesian AS-AD dynamics with rational expectations

Sargent's (1979, chap. 5) economy comprises three sectors: households, firms and the government. The behavioural assumptions he employs are a good compromise between richness, where in some parts partial microfoundations are also provided, and parsimony, where stylized assumptions serve to keep the model analytically tractable. In particular, Sargent takes account of the budget equations for savings and asset accumulation; flows and stocks are thus explicitly related in a consistent manner.

The model departs from NCS I in only one respect: the assumption of perfectly flexible money wages w is abandoned and replaced with gradual adjustments. They are represented by an ordinary expectations-augmented wage Phillips curve, which is formulated in continuous time. Denoting inflationary expectations by π^e, measuring the demand pressure on the labour market by the deviations of the actual rate of employment $e = L/L^s$ from its exogenously given NAIRU level e^o (L is labour demand and L^s the labour supply), and specifying the speed of adjustment by a positive coefficient β_{we}, the wage Phillips curve reads

$$\hat{w} = \pi^e + \beta_{we}(e - e^o) \tag{1.1}$$

($\hat{w} = \dot{w}/w$ is the growth rate of w). Regarding expectations, π^e in (1.1) is viewed as capturing the price changes in the near future, even over the next short period, so to speak. If sluggish wages are to be the only departure from the equilibrium formulation of NCS, myopic perfect foresight has to be assumed in this respect. In the continuous-time setting we therefore have, for p the price level and $\hat{p}$ the current rate of inflation,

$$\pi^e = \hat{p} \tag{1.2}$$

To be precise, $\hat{p}$ has to be thought of as the right-hand time derivative; cf. Sargent (1987, p. 120).[8] Prices themselves, the perfect flexibility of

---

[8] In a further departure from NCS I(p, w), Sargent (1987, chap. 5.1) assumes gradual adjustments for expected inflation π^e, too. As will be worked out in chapter 2, section 4, this model has still some peculiar features, which can be seen as a weak reflection of the peculiar features that will arise in the presence of (1.2).

which is maintained, are supposed to be determined within a standard AS schedule based on marginal wage costs. Accordingly,

$$p = w/F_L(K, L) \tag{1.3}$$

where K is the capital stock, $F = F(K, L)$, the neoclassical production function (without technical progress), and $F_L = \partial F/\partial L$, the marginal product of labour.

The most important feature of the IS part of the model, which goes slightly beyond a principles textbook, is that (net) investment is no longer a function of the interest rate alone. Sargent instead conceives it as an increasing function of a return differential q, which is the difference between the real rate of return, r, of firms on their capital stock and the real rate of interest $i - \pi^e$ (i being the nominal interest rate).[9] With the neoclassical production function, r is given by the marginal product of capital $F_K = \partial F/\partial K$ minus the rate of depreciation of the capital stock. For the other other components of aggregate demand it is convenient to assume suitable fixed proportions to the capital stock as trend term (as they are detailed in chapter 2, section 2, of this book, for example). This leads to a simple multiplier relationship for output Y of the kind $Y = (1/s)(I + K)$, where I is investment and s the constant propensity to save of private households. Together, the model's IS block in intensive form is described by

$$y = (1/s)(I/K + \text{const.}) \tag{1.4}$$

$$I/K = f_I(q), \quad f_I' > 0 \tag{1.5}$$

$$q = r - (i - \pi^e) \tag{1.6}$$

$$r = F_K(K, L) - \delta \tag{1.7}$$

On the other hand, the LM equilibrium condition for the exogenous money supply M in a growing economy can be posed as

$$M = pY \, f_m(i), \quad f_m' < 0 \tag{1.8}$$

As far as the evolution of money, capital and the labour supply is concerned, it considerably eases the exposition if we here neglect the capacity effects of investment and assume that the capital stock K grows at the

---

[9] Sargent (1987, pp. 11–14) demonstrates that this expression is indeed close to Tobin's (average) q.

same constant rate g^o as the labour supply L^s, to which in turn the money supply adjusts:[10]

$$\hat{M} = \hat{K} = \hat{L}^s = g^o \tag{1.9}$$

Of course, long-run equilibrium inflation must be zero then, $\hat{p}^o = (\pi^e)^o = 0$, and g^o is the real as well as nominal steady-state growth rate (the steady-state values are generally indicated by a superscript 'o'). In sum, eqs. (1.1) to (1.9) constitute a model of the Neoclassical Synthesis, Stage 1, with perfectly flexible prices (p) and gradual wage adjustments ($\hat{w}$), though in a somewhat simplified form. For short, it may be referred to as NCS I($p, \hat{w}$).

The analysis of system (1.1) to (1.9) decomposes into two major steps. In the first step, we reveal the far-reaching implications of the marginal productivity principle for labour in eq.(1.3). Define, to this end, the labour–capital ratio $\ell = L/K$ and write the production function in intensive form, $f_y(\ell) := F(1, \ell) = F(1, L/K) = Y/K = y$, where $f_y'(\ell) = \partial F(1, L/K)/\partial(L/K) = \partial(KF(1, L/K))/\partial L = \partial F(K, L)/\partial L = F_L(L, K) > 0$ and $f_y''(\ell) < 0$. Inverting the function f_y gives the relationship $\ell = \ell(y) := f_y^{-1}(y)$, with the derivative $\ell'(y) = 1/f_y'[\ell(y)] > 0$.

Next, let ℓ^o be the labour intensity associated with full employment and notice that $\ell^s := L^s/K = \text{const.}$ by (1.9), and $\ell^s = \ell^o$ more specifically. This allows us to write the employment rate as $e = L/L^s = \ell/\ell^s = \ell(y)/\ell^o$.

From the manipulations above it is also seen that eq.(1.3) itself can be written as $p = w/f_y'[\ell(y)]$ in intensive form. Solving the equation for the real wage rate $\omega := w/p$, we have $\omega = f_y'[\ell(y)] = f_y'(e\ell^o)$, which in turn can be inverted as $(f_y')^{-1}(\omega) = e\ell^o$. The employment rate can thus be conceived as a function of the real wage, $e = e(\omega)$. The derivative of $(f_y')^{-1}$ being given by $d(f_y')^{-1}/d\omega = 1/f_y'' < 0$, we know that the employment rate is inversely related to the real wage, $e'(\omega) < 0$.

Now substitute this function and the hypothesis of myopic perfect foresight (1.2) into the wage Phillips curve (1.1). With $\hat{\omega} = \hat{w} - \hat{p} = \hat{w} - \pi^e$, we then get the upshot of the first step of the analysis, a scalar differential equation in the real wage rate ω alone,

$$\dot{\omega} = \omega\beta_{we}\left[e(\omega) - e^o\right], \quad \text{where } e'(\omega) < 0 \tag{1.10}$$

Equation (1.10) has a unique stationary point ω^o that brings about full (or normal) employment, $e(\omega^o) = e^o$, which is obviously globally asymptotically stable. Since we can recover from ω the employment

---

[10] Sargent (1987, chap. 5.2) allows for, in our notation, $\hat{K} = I/K = f_I(q)$. This makes the analysis more technical, while the main conclusions are preserved.

rate e, labour intensity ℓ and the output–capital ratio y, the stability property applies to the whole real sector of the economy. Note in addition that this holds regardless of what may happen to the nominal variables, and that the IS relationships (1.4) to (1.7) have played no role so far. Hence three conclusions emerge: (1) the model dichotomizes into a real and a nominal part; (2) the real sector is completely determined by the supply-side of the economy; and (3), as will be generally expected in mainstream approaches to economic theory, the real sector is a global shock absorber.

The second step of the analysis must be concerned with the nominal magnitudes, goods prices p and money wages w. To simplify the presentation, suppose the dynamics has already settled down on its steady-state values. Since Y, by (1.9), will then constantly grow at the same rate as M, the ratio M/Y stays put and the only remaining variable on which the LM rate of interest in (1.8) depends is the price level p. Of course, the interest rate increases with p, so that we have

$$i = i_{LM}(p) \quad \text{where } i'_{LM} > 0 \tag{1.11}$$

Observe, furthermore, that the return rate r in (1.7) is dependent on real variables only. The steady-state assumption for the real sector makes it therefore a constant, $r = r^o$. Since $f_I(q) = I/K = \hat{K} = g^o$ in this equilibrium, the return differential q must also attain a fixed value q^o.[11] It follows that $q = r^o - i_{LM}(p) + \pi^e = q^o$.

Finally, we return to the myopic perfect assumption in (1.2), $\hat{p} = \pi^e$, and substitute it in the previous equation. Solving for $\hat{p} = \dot{p}/p$ and multiplying the result by p, the price level is seen to be governed by the differential equation

$$\dot{p} = p[q^o - r^o + i_{LM}(p)], \quad \text{where } i'_{LM} > 0 \tag{1.12}$$

This equation, too, has a unique equilibrium value p^o. Unlike eq. (1.10), however, it is unstable; since the right-hand side of (1.12) is strictly increasing in p, the price level dynamics are explosive. Such an unstable economy would, of course, not be meaningful.

Recognizing this, two alternative conclusions can be drawn. Either the model is not well enough designed and some building blocks should be respecified, or the description of the model is not yet complete. The usual reception of similar models, or models with similar properties,

---

[11] q^o may well be positive, which could be interpreted as a risk premium of fixed investment, which yields the return r, vs. purchasing government bonds, which yields $i - \pi^e$ as its real rate of return.

leans towards the second conclusion, understanding it as calling not for another behavioural relationship to be built into the model but for an additional assumption to be invoked. This is the assumption of rational expectations, which in a somewhat related framework has been introduced by Sargent and Wallace (1973). For our present purpose, the *rational expectations hypothesis* may be summarized as follows.

Looking into the future, the agents in a dynamic economic system behave in such a way that, among the a priori possible solutions of the formal equations, all eventually unbounded trajectories fail to realize.

The postulate takes effect in the initial conditions of the dynamics, where it implies that not all variables can be treated as predetermined at starting time $t = 0$, say. Some of the variables are instead permitted to take on special values that ensure the boundedness of all state variables if the system starts from there. These variables are commonly said to 'jump' onto a suitable set (a stable manifold often) that contains this value. If these variables and their jumps make economic sense, then the model is still considered to be well defined. For example, a capital stock cannot jump within or at the beginning of a short period, but an expectational variable may.

The procedure itself, and thus implicitly the theoretical assumption from which it derives, is also raised to the status of a 'technique'. Accordingly, we now have to subject our system to the 'jump variable technique'.

Regarding the unstable differential equation (1.12), where the real sector was supposed to be already in its equilibrium position, the jumping procedure is trivial. There is only one dynamic variable left, the price level p, and the only possibility to keep it within bounds is to let it directly jump to its equilibrium values p^o, from which the system has come to rest.

Things are more complicated if the real sector is out of equilibrium and adjustments are still taking place there. We can here refer to Sargent (1987, p. 122), who, assuming a suitable log-linearity in the LM equation (1.8), is able to compute the time path of p in explicit terms. He arrives at an equation that expresses the current price level as a function of the entire *future* paths of the money supply and other variables of the real sector, where, as he adds in parentheses (p. 122), 'we are again imposing a terminal condition' that formally suppresses a monotonically diverging term like const. $\cdot e^{\alpha t}$ ($\alpha = $ const. > 0). This corresponds to the situation of an n-dimensional linear differential equations system that has one unstable and $n-1$ stable eigenvalues λ_i (with Re $\lambda_i > 0$ and Re $\lambda_i < 0$, respectively); and, given the $n-1$ initial values of the predetermined variables, the price level, as prescribed by Sargent's formula, jumps onto the system's $(n-1)$-dimensional stable manifold. Note that, since the real wage ω is a predetermined variable, the money wage rate w is a jump variable too (though it need not show up in the mathematical analysis).

It is worth pointing out that in this type of model, NCS I$(w, \hat{p})$, money is neutral not only in the long run but also in the short run, the latter in the sense that an unanticipated permanent shock to the money supply leaves the real sector unaffected if the price level jumps immediately by the same percentage as the change in M. Besides, it is remarkable that the inflation thus occurring in the economy goes unnoticed by the private agents, since they are exclusively concerned with $\pi^e = \hat{p}_+$, the right-hand derivative $(p_{t+h} - p_t)/hp_t$ of the price level with $h \to 0$, which in our simplified setting can always remain at zero.

Somewhat polemically, this type of jump experiment might also be considered to be a static equilibrium argument in dynamic disguise. In any case, the behaviour of jump variables is more appealing if the sudden change in the money supply is anticipated. Say, in a stationary economy ($g^o = 0$ for simplicity), the central bank announces at time $t = 0$ that at time $T > 0$ it will raise the money supply from M_o to M_1, which increases the equilibrium price level from p_o to p_1 (omitting superscript 'o' for a moment). The point is that, under these circumstances, the price level does not jump, at $t = T$, from p_o to p_1.

In general terms, this would enable some agents to make capital gains, a possibility that would be realized by other agents, who, in turn, would exploit this situation themselves – and so on. Consistency then requires the price level to jump at an earlier time, already at $t = 0$ when the change in M was announced, and by a lesser amount; from then on the price level steadily increases until it reaches the new equilibrium value at precisely $t = T$.[12] Hence, the economy experiences inflation before anything has happened to the money supply, and no more inflation at all after the change has taken place. This attractive feature for a theory that invokes the Rational Expectations Hypothesis (and additional arbitrage arguments) is illustrated in figure 1.1.

Nevertheless, the kind of jumps occurring in NCS I$(p, \hat{w})$ look quite strange from a Keynesian perspective. Recall that money wage adjustments are governed by the wage Phillips curve (1.1), and that this relationship was introduced to take account of an empirical regularity. The latter observation means that, unlike in the New-Keynesian versions,

---

[12] See Turnovsky (1995, p. 73) for a formal reasoning.

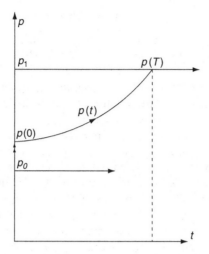

Figure 1.1: An anticipated monetary policy shock in NCS I$(p, \hat{w})$

this type of Phillips curve is still, in modern terms, backward-looking. In discrete time with an adjustment period of length h it would read

$$(w_{t+h} - w_t)/w_t = h[\pi_t^e + \beta_{we}(e_t - e^o)]$$

where all variables dated t are given. This makes clear that, at the time when NCS I$(p, \hat{w})$ was designed, the money wage rate w was, or should have been, thought of as a predetermined variable.

On the other hand, in the experiment described above the money wage rate had to jump, because the price level had to jump while the level of the real wage rate had to be preserved. It follows that the discontinuity in w has its reason outside the wage Phillips curve; in an ad hoc manner, we might say, the Phillips curve was cancelled in one point in time. It is in this sense that the model and the jump variable technique applied to it exhibit an inconsistency.

A deeper conceptual explanation of this failure of NCS I$(p, \hat{w})$ can be sought in the feature that it, within a framework that admits some sluggish adjustments in the nominal variables, attempts to integrate the assumption of demand-constrained firms with the assumption that firms are price takers. Essentially, this type of model falls back on the Neoclassical Synthesis that is operated under the assumption that prices and wages are both perfectly flexible; that is, we are essentially back in NCS I(p, w).[13]

---

[13] Further details of the anomalies that rational expectations may give rise to in models with IS-LM-AS plus Phillips curve, where the real wage remains a predetermined variable, can be found in Flaschel et al. (1997, chap. 8 & 9).

1.2.2   Further scenarios of the wage-price dynamics

Introducing dynamic elements into the equilibrium formulation of the Neoclassical Synthesis, Stage I, as it was done in NCS I($p, \hat{w}$), is, according to our evaluation in the previous subsection, not a very promising step towards modelling Keynesian disequilibrium dynamics. The first unsatisfactory feature was that the economy dichotomizes into real and nominal sectors. Since this is mainly due to the assumption that prices at every point in time are determined by the marginal productivity principle for labour, it is straightforward to ask if a more plausible model results if the assumption is relaxed, while nevertheless maintaining the principle as a benchmark case. In this way we get an alternative version of NCS I where not only wages but also prices are supposed to adjust in a gradual manner. Hence, in this respect, prices and wages are now put on equal footing. Even without a deeper analysis, this seems more reasonable than their methodologically unequal treatment in NCS I($p, \hat{w}$).

The basic idea is that the price level p is predetermined in the short period, and firms raise it in the next period when it is currently below its natural reference value, which is still given by nominal marginal wage costs, or the competitive price p_c,

$$p_c = w/F_L(K, L) \tag{1.13}$$

Conversely, firms tend to reduce prices if p exceeds p_c. In meanwhile obvious notation, we refer to this type of model with gradual adjustments in both p and w as NCS I($\hat{p}, \hat{w}$).

In the precise specification of this idea we cannot maintain the myopic perfect assumption $\pi^e = \hat{p}$ from (1.2) and at the same time use the same expression for reference inflation, namely π^e, as in the wage Phillips curve (1.1). $\hat{p}$ would then show up on the left-hand side as well as on the right-hand side of such a relationship, which would not be meaningful in the present setting. Rather, we already let ourselves be guided by a common device in the New-Keynesian Phillips curve literature. Combining, as it is called, forward-looking and backward-looking elements in discrete time and neglecting the discount factor (which occurs if the price Phillips curve is explicitly derived from microeconomic fundamentals), it reads

$$\hat{p}_t = \phi_p \hat{p}_{t+1} + (1-\phi_p)\hat{p}_{t-1} + \beta_p \cdot \text{demand pressure}$$

where, retaining the symbol, $\hat{p}_t = (p_t - p_{t-1})/p_{t-1}$ and ϕ_p $(0 \leq \phi_p \leq 1)$ measures the weight of the forward-looking inflation component. Here we still disregard this kind of forward-looking behaviour and set $\phi_p = 0$, so that only the first difference $\hat{p}_t - \hat{p}_{t-1}$ remains. For our purpose we translate it directly into the time derivative of the rate of price inflation. The role of the demand pressure is taken over by the percentage deviation of nominal marginal wage costs from the current price p. With a constant adjustment speed β_p, gradual price (or, rather, inflation) adjustments are therefore described by

$$d\hat{p}/dt = \beta_p(p_c/p - 1) \tag{1.14}$$

In order to give real wages a more direct bearing on investment and thus (negatively) on aggregate demand, we slightly respecify the real rate of return r in (1.7). We drop the marginal product of capital there and define r now as the rate of profit $r = (pY - wL - \delta pK)/pK$. Recalling that labour intensity $\ell = L/K$ was shown to be an increasing function of the output–capital ratio, $\ell = \ell(y)$ with $\ell'(y) > 0$, the profit rate can be written as

$$r = y - \omega\ell(y) - \delta \tag{1.15}$$

Lastly, the dimension of the model can be reduced if it is assumed that the money supply M grows in line not with real capital K as in (1.9) but with price-valued capital pK. The proportions being already those of the steady-state ratio m^o, we have

$$M/pK = m^o \quad (= \text{const.}) \tag{1.16}$$

Our simplified version of NCS I$(\hat{p}, \hat{w})$ is thus complete. In sum, it is given by eqs. (1.1), (1.2), (1.4) to (1.6), (1.8), (1.9) and (1.13) to (1.16) (eq. (1.9) now without the first equality, of course).

The stability analysis has to begin with the model's IS-LM part. By (1.16), the LM equation becomes $m^o = yf_m(i)$, from which it is clear that the LM interest rate is an increasing function of the output–capital ratio, $i = i(y)$ with $i'(y) > 0$. Plugging this together with (1.5), (1.6) and (1.15) into the goods market equilibrium equation (1.4) gives $y = (1/s)f_I[y - \omega\ell(y) - \delta - i(y) + \hat{p}]$ as the condition for the output–capital ratio in the IS-LM equilibrium. It is easily seen that the solution y is a function of the real wage rate and the rate of inflation, and that (at least near the long-run equilibrium position) the partial derivatives have the expected sign:[14]

$$y = y(\omega, \hat{p}), \quad y_\omega = \partial y/\partial\omega < 0, \quad y_\pi = \partial y/\partial\hat{p} > 0$$

---

[14] Note that in the long-run equilibrium, where the marginal productivity principle holds, $\partial(y - \omega\ell(y))/\partial y = 0$; see the remarks leading to eq. (1.10). Hence $f_I[..]$ unambiguously decreases with y.

From the analysis in the previous subsection we know that $p_c = w/F_L = w/f'_y(\ell)$, where $f_y = F(1, L/K)$ with $f'_y > 0$, $f''_y < 0$. Hence $p_c/p = \omega/f'_y(\ell)$. On the other hand, (1.1) and (1.2) give rise to $\hat{\omega} = \hat{w} - \hat{p} = \pi^e + \beta_{we}$ $(e - e^o) - \hat{p} = \beta_{we}(e - e^o)$, and we also know that the employment rate is an increasing function of the output–capital ratio, $e = e(y)$. NCS I$(\hat{p}, \hat{w})$ can therefore be reduced to a two-dimensional differential equations system. Abbreviating $\ell(\omega, \hat{p}) = \ell[y(\omega, \hat{p})]$ and $e(\omega, \hat{p}) = e[y(\omega, \hat{p})]$,

$$\hat{\omega} = \omega \beta_{we}[e(\omega, \hat{p}) - e^o] \tag{1.17}$$

$$d\hat{p}/dt = \beta_p\{\omega/f'_y[\ell(\omega, \hat{p})] - 1\} \tag{1.18}$$

It is clearly seen that the real wage impacts on the rate of inflation and vice versa. Thus, making both prices as well as wages a dynamic variable has overcome the dichotomy of NCS I$(p, \hat{w})$. In this sense, NCS I$(\hat{p}, \hat{w})$ is a superior variant of Keynesian dynamic modelling.

It is easily established that system (1.17), (1.18) has a unique equilibrium position ω^o, $\hat{p}^o$. Evaluating the Jacobian $\mathcal{J}$ at that point, three entries are unambiguously signed. The sign of the fourth entry j_{21} is given by the sign of the expression $f'_y - \omega f''_y \ell' y_\omega = \omega(1 - y_\omega f''_y/f'_y)$. We limit the discussion to the most relevant case of a positive sign. It results if the curvature of the production function is shallow enough, or if the IS-LM output response y_ω is sufficiently weak, which in turn can be caused by sufficiently weak investment reactions, f'_I small. The Jacobian of (1.17), (1.18) then has the following sign pattern:

$$\mathcal{J} = \begin{bmatrix} j_{11} & j_{12} \\ j_{21} & j_{22} \end{bmatrix} = \begin{bmatrix} - & + \\ + & + \end{bmatrix}$$

Since $\det \mathcal{J} < 0$, the equilibrium of (1.17), (1.18) is a saddle-point. This indicates that, again, the jump variable technique might be used in order to place the dynamics on the stable manifold. Notice, however, that in contrast to NCS I$(p, \hat{w})$, it would now be applied to the rate of inflation and no longer to the price level itself. Nevertheless, we have already pointed out in the methodological remarks that this is not a convincing design for a Keynesian disequilibrium dynamics.

The local instability result can be understood against the background of the traditional Keynesian feedback mechanisms: the Keynes effect, the Mundell effect and the real wage (or Rose) effect. They are discussed in detail as the book proceeds, especially in chapter 2, section 7, chapter 3, section 8, chapter 7, section 3, subsection 2, and chapter 7, section 4, subsection 2. A graphical exposition of the latter two effects is given in figures 3 and 4 further below. Briefly, we may mention that the simplifying assumption (1.16) has cancelled the stabilizing Keynes effect (which involves real balances effects from changes in the price level and their impact on the LM interest rate and aggregate demand). So we can summarize that, while the real wage effect is stabilizing (reflected by $j_{11} < 0$ in the Jacobian), it is dominated by the destabilizing Mundell effect (entry $j_{22} > 0$ in $\mathcal{J}$), irrespective of the adjustment speed β_{we} and β_p.

This interpretation also gives a hint as to how the instability could alternatively be dealt with. We could try to build a suitable nonlinearity into the investment function that is able to tame the explosive tendencies in the outer regions of the state space. In this way the dynamics would be confined to a compact region and persistent fluctuations would be obtained.[15]

Another route of research is to find conditions for local stability by changing one or two assumptions in the model, while still preserving the basic structure; in particular, the treatment of wages and prices. To begin with, an immediate approach is to drop the assumption of myopic perfect foresight, $\pi^e = \hat{p}$, and assume a gradual adjustment of π^e towards current inflation (which we will argue at another place can indeed be meaningful). As already mentioned, this was another model of the NCS I(p, $\hat{w}$) variety that was put forward by Sargent (1987, chap. 5.1), which we will carefully reconsider in chapter 2. A typical result in this and many other small-scale models with the same mechanism is that local stability prevails if the adjustments of π^e are sufficiently sluggish. In this book we will, moreover, encounter the result in the model of chapter 3, which – going beyond Sargent – could be classified as an elaborated NCS I($\hat{p}$, $\hat{w}$) textbook model.[16] Interestingly, in the more advanced model studied in Part II, the stability result will then have to be somewhat qualified.

To indicate quite another approach to the stability issue that maintains the myopic perfect foresight assumption, the present economy could also be stabilized by a more active monetary policy. In anticipation of the discussions of the Taylor rule, assume the central bank changes the money supply in such a way that the interest rate rises or falls if the rate of inflation rises or falls, respectively. The response may even be supposed to be so strong that the same holds true for the real rate of interest $i - \pi^e = i - \hat{p}$. Accordingly, the LM equation (1.8) is dismissed and the interest rate is represented by a function of the inflation rate, $i = i(\hat{p})$ with $di/d\hat{p} > 1$.

This interest rate policy undermines the Mundell effect, in that an increase in $\hat{p}$ directly diminishes investment $I/K = f_I[r - (i - \hat{p})]$. As a

---

[15] Although it has to admitted that the present model might be too small to achieve this feature in a reasonable manner.

[16] Examples of the same kind of result from the literature (in a Tobinian vein) are Hadjimichalakis (1971), Benhabib and Miyao (1981) and Hayakawa (1984).

consequence, the IS-LM equilibrium response $\partial y/\partial \hat{p}$ is now negative, and so are the entries j_{12} and j_{22} in the Jacobian $\mathcal{J}$ of the resulting economy, which ensures a positive determinant of $\mathcal{J}$ and a negative trace. The equilibrium is therefore stable.

Apart from the purely Classical situation with perfectly flexible prices and wages, we have so far considered gradual wage adjustments combined with perfectly flexible prices and the case where both wages and prices react gradually to a perceived disequilibrium. For systematic reasons a fourth case remains to be considered, namely the combination of gradual price adjustments with perfectly flexible wages, or NCS I($\hat{p}$, w). Besides, this version can be conceived as a prelude to the contemporary New-Keynesian baseline model, which assumes continuous clearing of the labour market and staggered price setting by firms.

In the present framework, with a given normal rate of employment e^o, labour market equilibrium means that the output–capital ratio is already at its steady-state level y^o, which equals $f_y(\ell) = f_y(e^o \ell^o)$ (recall that, generally, $e = \ell/\ell^o$). The IS-LM equilibrium output relationship then degenerates to $y^o = (1/s)f_I[y^o - \omega \ell(y^o) - \delta - i(y^o) + \hat{p}]$. Since the argument of the function f_I must be constant, too, we get $\hat{p} - \omega \ell(y^o) =$ const., implying that the real wage moves in line with the rate of inflation, $\omega = \omega(\hat{p})$ and $d\omega/d\hat{p} > 0$. In this way eq. (1.18), which drives the rate of inflation, becomes

$$d\hat{p}/dt = \beta_p[\omega(\hat{p})/f_y'(e\ell^o) - 1] \qquad (1.19)$$

and this is the only law of motion left in the economy.

Clearly, eq. (1.19) is purely explosive. As in NCS I(p, $\hat{w}$) above, it follows that to obtain stable dynamics one would have to resort to the jump variable technique. However, even if we had no objections to this procedure as a matter of principle, the model is still conceptually questionable for two other reasons. First, it is not only the rate of price inflation that would have to jump but, with it, the level (!) of real wages as well. Second, given that the labour market is supposed to be in equilibrium all the time irrespective of possible shocks to real wages and inflation, what variable is then to be viewed as clearing this market? We conclude from these observations that NCS I($\hat{p}$, w) is also an unsatisfactory, if not inconsistent, approach to Keynesian dynamics.

Focusing on the determination of wages and prices in the economy, table 1.1 summarizes the four scenarios of the Neoclassical Synthesis, Stage I, that we have considered. Within our small models stripped down to two dimensions, it has been argued that only the two versions on the diagonal of the table appear to be a useful basis for a further analysis of

Table 1.1: *Four variants of the Neoclassical Synthesis, Stage I (NCS I)*

	Equilibrium prices	Gradual price adjustments
Equilibrium wages	NCS I(w, p) Classical AS-AD version	NCS I$(w, \hat{p})$ Later: New-Keynesian baseline model
Gradual wage adjustments	NCS I$(\hat{w}, p)$ Textbook Keynesian AS-AD version	NCS I$(\hat{w}, \hat{p})$ Later: mature Keynesian models

traditional AS-AD growth dynamics. We uphold our negative evaluation of NCS I$(w, \hat{p})$ in the upper right corner, but have also indicated that it has later been revived in a microfounded and appreciably refined form that led to a standard and now orthodox model of contemporary macroeconomics, the New-Keynesian baseline model. This approach can even be viewed as the Neoclassical Synthesis, Stage II. Avoiding all the technical effort a full-fledged analysis would require, we will therefore try to reveal its basic mechanisms in the next section.

The classical AS-AD equilibrium version in the first diagonal entry of table 1.1 has later developed into the New-Classical economics and the equilibrium business cycle theory, a theoretical framework that we will not be concerned with here. The lower diagonal entry alludes to the version of NCS I that with its dynamic adjustments of both prices and wages will be most fruitful for us. In fact, all the models studied from chapter 3 onwards can be construed as arising from this approach – in a much more elaborated and appropriate form, of course, as we will claim. Hence the brief characterization that NCS I$(\hat{w}, \hat{p})$ provides the basis for our (and perhaps other) 'mature' Keynesian models. A first introduction to the wage-price dynamics that will be underlying Parts II and III of the book, as they emerge from the discussion in the present section, is given in section 1.4 below.

1.3   Neoclassical Synthesis, Stage II: New-Keynesian macrodynamics

Starting out from the concepts of the Neoclassical Synthesis at the beginning of the 1970s, the preceding section has discussed four model versions that distinguish perfectly flexible wages and/or prices vs. gradual adjustments of wages and/or prices. One of these versions could be seen as a first analogue of the present and topical New-Keynesian view on macrodynamics. Apart from the specific building blocks that we will have to discuss, in general three features may be mentioned that make this approach stand out: the state-of-the-art, mathematically rigorous microfoundations; the 'forward-looking' elements; and its close connection to issues of monetary policy. The reformulation of the traditional Keynesian AS-AD dynamics along these lines has by now gained so much popularity that we have classified it as the Neoclassical Synthesis, Stage II (NCS II).

A survey of its achievements and problems can, for example, be found in Galì (2000) and King (2000). Walsh (2003, chaps. 5 & 11) provides an advanced textbook presentation of the New-Keynesian baseline model, including an extensive discussion of monetary policy matters. The stress on monetary policy is even stronger in Woodford's (2003) book, which contains the most detailed analysis of this, as it may also be called, Neo-Wicksellian type of modelling.

In the present section we take up the New-Keynesian baseline model and a certain type of extension. In the baseline model, goods prices are determined in a staggered fashion while wages are assumed to clear the labour market instantaneously. On the other hand, the extended version studied by us allows for both gradual price and wage adjustments. These models are formulated in a most elementary way that, in particular, abstracts from the otherwise important stochastic perturbations. We can therefore discuss immediately their basic implications, their potential and weaknesses, without great technical effort.

The simplified presentation also permits us to relate the models to the deterministic and continuous-time modelling of the matured Keynesian macrodynamics that will be the main subject of the book. For convenience, a direct comparison can be made to a stripped-down version of the book's dynamic AS-AD approach, which will be put forward in section 1, subsection 4.

We limit ourselves to an assessment of the basic properties of the private sector in the different frames of reference, largely in isolation from any policy interference. For each model version we will therefore also consider a perfectly neutral monetary policy, which means here that the (nominal) interest rate is pegged at its steady-state value. As a rule, economies in the New-Keynesian theory exhibit quite unsatisfactory features, a finding that strongly emphasizes the role of monetary policy in the current macrodynamic literature. In contrast to the Neoclassical Synthesis, Stage I, with its exogenous money supply, it has to be noted that now monetary policy, which sets out to remedy the possible shortcomings, takes the form of an interest rate reaction function (mostly a version of the famous Taylor rule). This means that the interest rate itself becomes a policy variable; the money supply and the LM curve can even completely disappear from the scene.

1.3.1   The baseline model with perfect wage flexibility

Following the presentation in Walsh (2003, chap. 11.1), the New-Keynesian baseline model is made up of three components. The demand side is obtained from a log-linear approximation to the representative household's Euler condition for optimal consumption. This gives rise to an expectational output relationship, where, however, fixed investment by firms is still absent.[17] Equations of this kind are often referred to as a dynamic IS curve in the literature. Next, the supply-side of the economy is represented by inflation adjustments occurring in a setting of monopolistic competition, where individual firms adjust prices in a staggered overlapping fashion. This yields the New-Keynesian Phillips curve. The third component is monetary policy in the form of an interest reaction function. We postpone this issue a little while and provisionally assume that the nominal interest rate is simply pegged at its steady-state value i^o.

To be in line with the New-Keynesian standard notation, we slightly change the meaning of two symbols in this section (temporarily). Thus, π at present denotes the rate of price inflation itself (not expected inflation), while (instead of the output–capital ratio) y stands for the output gap, the percentage deviation of output from its equilibrium level.[18] Furthermore, let E_t be the expectation operator based on information available at time t, and β a discount factor, $\beta \leq 1$.[19] With $\varepsilon_{y,t}$ and $\varepsilon_{p,t}$ being stochastic demand and supply shocks, respectively, the first two components of the baseline model can be written as

$$y_t = E_t y_{t+1} - \beta_{yi}[i_t - E_t \pi_{t+1} - (i^o - \pi^o)] + \varepsilon_{y,t} \qquad (1.20)$$

$$\pi_t = \beta E_t \pi_{t+1} + \beta_{py} y_t + \varepsilon_{p,t} \quad [\pi_t = (p_t - p_{t-1})/p_{t-1}] \qquad (1.21)$$

---

[17] Investment can be incorporated, but this complicates the model considerably (showing that an extension of the most elementary microfoundations is no easy matter); see Woodford (2003, chap. 5.3, pp. 352ff.). A clear and concise summary of a more ambitious private sector is also given in section 3 by Smets and Wouters (2003).

[18] Since Walsh himself confines the analysis to a stationary economy, the equilibrium level Y^o of output can be normalized at unity and we have $y = (Y - Y^o)/Y^o \approx \ln Y - \ln Y^o = \ln Y$.

[19] Interpreted as the representative household's discount factor, β (the usual notation, which we maintain) is strictly less than unity. However, as Mankiw (2001, pp. C51f.) derives the New-Keynesian Phillips curve from staggered price setting along the lines of Calvo (1983), β can also be equal to one.

It goes without saying that these equations presuppose rational expectations. As the shocks are normally distributed around zero, the steady-state values of inflation and the output gap are $\pi^o = 0$, $y^o = 0$. From the dating convention for the rate of inflation π_t of period t it can, moreover, be inferred that, if the model treats π_t as a jump variable, this is tantamount to treating the price level of period t as a jump variable. Since the current price level is the control variable of the optimizing firms, π_t should indeed be a jump variable. Similarly, the output gap is directly determined by private consumption, which is the control variable of the optimizing household. Hence y_t, too, should be a jump variable.

To reveal the basic dynamic properties of this private sector it suffices to study the deterministic counterpart of (1.20), (1.21). Solving (1.21) for $\pi_{t+1} = E_t \pi_{t+1} = (\pi_t - \beta_{py} y_t)/\beta$, substituting it in (1.20) and using $\pi^o = 0$, we get

$$y_{t+1} - y_t = \beta_{yi}(i_t - i^o) - (\beta_{yi}/\beta)(\pi_t - \beta_{py} y_t)$$
$$\pi_{t+1} - \pi_t = (1/\beta - 1)\pi_t - (\beta_{py}/\beta)y_t$$

Before investigating this system we should, however, pause for a moment and consider the inflation adjustments that derive from the New-Keynesian Phillips curve (1.21), for this purely forward-looking determination of the inflation rate has undergone severe empirical criticism. Mankiw (2001, p. C52) summarizes it in a particularly strong statement: 'Although the New Keynesian Phillips curve has many virtues, it has also one striking vice: It is completely at odds with the facts.'

The basic problem of the New-Keynesian Phillips curve can be seen without much econometrics. Neglecting the discount factor in the inflation adjustment equation, i.e. putting $\beta = 1$, we have the relationship $\pi_{t+1} - \pi_t = -\beta_{py} y_t$. It predicts that the rate of inflation rises if output is below its natural (or trend) level, and vice versa. This kind of reaction may appear counter-intuitive. Actually, it contradicts the basic principles taught in macroeconomic textbooks. For example, Taylor's (2001, chap. 24) discussion of his inflation adjustment rule can be readily formalized as

$$\pi_{t+1} - \pi_t = \tilde{\beta}_{py} y_t \tag{1.22}$$

with no minus sign on the right-hand side. Taylor supports the relationship by a diagram (on p. 569), the message of which he sums up as: 'The data show that inflation falls when real GDP is below potential GDP, and inflation rises when real GDP is above potential GDP.' Blanchard (2000, chap. 8, p. 154) calls a relationship like (1.22) an 'accelerationist' Phillips curve. He illustrates its validity in another diagram that (instead of the output gap) refers to the unemployment rate. He also provides a straightforward estimation that for annual inflation changes in the United States between 1970 and 1998 gives the equation $\pi_t - \pi_{t-1} = 6.5\% - 1.0 \cdot \text{unemployment}_t$. These elementary observations suffice to explain Mankiw's verdict.[20]

It may be added that (1.22) implies countercyclical (!) motions of the price level (relative to its trend). This feature is by now an established stylized fact of the business cycle, not only in the United States. We will deal with it in chapter 5; to anticipate, the countercyclicality in the time series of the price level is nicely brought out in figure 2.

After this brief critical evaluation of the New-Keynesian Phillips curve, we return to the two-dimensional difference equations system in y_t and π_t. Its analysis and that of the other systems below is simplified if we consider their continuous-time analogues, where we replace only the difference operator with the time derivative.[21] The private sector specified so far is then succinctly described by the two differential equations

$$\dot{y} = \beta_{yi}(i - i^o) + (\beta_{py}\beta_{yi}/\beta)y - (\beta_{yi}/\beta)\pi \quad (\text{where } i = i^o) \quad (1.23)$$

$$\dot{\pi} = -(\beta_{py}/\beta)y + (1/\beta - 1)\pi \quad (1.24)$$

According to the remark on (1.20), (1.21), y and π should be both jump variables, which requires both eigenvalues of the Jacobian of (1.23), (1.24) to have positive real parts. In this deterministic setting both variables would then directly jump into the equilibrium point of the system. Thus, $y^o = 0$, $\pi^o = 0$ constitute the uniquely determined starting point of the optimal solution path. The trajectory itself is here rather uninteresting since, without shocks, output and prices remain at their initial levels.

It is, however, straightforward to show that the Jacobian of (1.23), (1.24) is negative, so that the equilibrium point of this system is a saddle

---

[20] Mankiw (2001, pp. C54ff.) takes a slightly different angle and formulates his argument in terms of impulse-response functions to a monetary contraction. One reply from the New-Keynesian side to this kind of criticism is that here the output gap is specified as deviations from a smooth trend, which is an ad hoc measure with no theoretical justification. It would be more appropriate to conceive it as output minus the concept of flexible price output (which is unsmooth and quite volatile), though this variable is neither observable nor does it constitute the present New-Keynesian notion of the output gap. This problem, in turn, can be solved (as it is claimed) by returning to the more fundamental version of the Phillips curve, which refers to marginal wage costs instead of an output gap; see Galì and Gertler (1999) and Galì et al. (2001).

[21] Hence, the differential equations thereby obtained should not be interpreted as the limit of a sequence of discrete-time economies with adjustment period h, where h shrinks to zero. Though deterministic and continuous-time formulations are absent in the New-Keynesian references given above, they are occasionally found useful at other places. An example is Fuhrer and Moore (1995).

where one eigenvalue is negative and the other positive.[22] As a consequence, the system could start anywhere on the one-dimensional stable manifold to get to $y^o = 0$, $\pi^o = 0$. In other words, we have a situation of indeterminacy. In this sense, the model turns out to be ill-defined. To be more precise, a stochastic framework could handle indeterminacy by invoking the concept of 'sunspot equilibria'. But indeterminacy is certainly an undesirable feature for an elementary model at the beginning of a theory.

We can, therefore, sum up that a basic New-Keynesian model with neutral monetary policy holding the nominal interest rate constant is as inconsistent as its forerunner NSC I($\hat{p}$, w) set up in the preceding subsection, where in the presence of the LM curve the real balances ratio M/pK was supposed to remain fixed.

The incompatibility of the number of unstable eigenvalues and the number of jump variables in (1.23), (1.24) is the place where monetary policy can be seen to set in. Suitable reactions of the interest rate to deviations of output and inflation from equilibrium can help the model economy out of the dilemma. Specifically, this is achieved by a (now standard) Taylor rule, which – parameterizing Taylor's (1993a, p. 202) formulation – we write down as[23]

$$i = (i^o - \pi^o) + \pi + \alpha_\pi (\pi - \pi^o) + \alpha_y\, y \qquad (1.25)$$

Zero policy coefficients, $\alpha_\pi = \alpha_y = 0$, pursue a policy of a constant real rate of interest, while with $\alpha_\pi > 0$ the central bank increases not only the nominal but also the real interest rate as inflation rises. A positive output gap coefficient, $\alpha_y > 0$, is another facet of a central bank leaning against the wind.

Plugging the interest rate rule (1.25) into (1.23) and taking account of $\pi^o = 0$ transforms the dynamic IS curve into

$$\dot{y} = \beta_{yi}(\alpha_y + \beta_{py}/\beta)y + \beta_{yi}(1 + \alpha_\pi - 1/\beta)\pi \qquad (1.26)$$

The optimality conditions for the changes in y and π are now given by (1.26) and (1.24). The Jacobian $\mathcal{J}$ of this system has a positive trace, since both diagonal entries are positive. The determinant is calculated as

$$\det \mathcal{J} = \beta_{yi}[\alpha_y(1 - \beta) + \alpha_\pi \beta_{py}]/\beta$$

---

[22] The original discrete-time system can also be shown to be a saddle-point; so the simpler continuous-time system leads to no distortion.

[23] Of course, π^o, which is here zero, corresponds to the target rate of inflation, which Taylor sets at 2 per cent. For the policy coefficients he chooses the well-known values $\alpha_\pi = \alpha_y = 0.50$.

which is positive as soon as $\alpha_y > 0$ or $\alpha_\pi > 0$. As the latter can be taken for granted, the New-Keynesian baseline model with the Taylor rule (1.25) has a uniquely determined optimal solution trajectory. This kind of monetary policy has indeed succeeded in ruling out indeterminacy. It may, furthermore, be stressed that the outcome that the private sector is not workable by itself is a general result in New-Keynesian baseline approaches. King (2000), Walsh (2003) and Woodford (2003) provide a variety of examples where a Taylor-type rule is employed in order to get determinacy. And also, conversely, monetary policy is in this theoretical field the only device that is considered to take care of determinacy if it is endangered.

While the model is now consistent, one may nevertheless question its usefulness. It has already been remarked about eqs. (1.23), (1.24) that the dynamic trajectories are rather dull. In the deterministic setting nothing else happens after the agents have chosen the optimal levels of inflation and output (the latter via consumption). Some motions would be observed in a stochastic setting, but the shocks are purely transitory there: as soon as the random noise stops, inflation and the output gap would immediately jump back to their steady-state values. In the New-Keynesian baseline model there is thus no inertia at all, so the macroeconomic dynamics are still quite poor.

It might at first appear surprising that a model in which the concept of staggered prices has originally been set out to capture inertial pricing behaviour cannot generate persistence. Following Mankiw (2001, p. C53), the puzzle resolves if the distinction between inertia in the price level and inertia in the inflation rate is made. Because individual prices are adjusted intermittently in the New-Keynesian models, the price level adjusts slowly to shocks. But the rate of inflation – the change in the price level – can adjust instantly (just as the capital stock adjusts slowly, while net investment may be a jump variable that can change immediately to changing conditions).

1.3.2   Staggered wages and prices

One extension of the New-Keynesian baseline model is particularly important for us. In light of the central role that the real wage rate has played in the Neoclassical Synthesis, Stage I, wage formation may also be here made explicit. In fact, wage-setting agents can be, and have been, incorporated into the model analogously to the treatment of the goods market, by way of assuming monopolistic competition among suppliers of differentiated types of labour. Erceg et al. (2000) and, following them, Woodford (2003, chap. 4.1) combine this idea of wage determination with an advanced version of the earlier price determination (see also Walsh, 2003, chap. 5.5). Apart from an interest in extensions of the New-Keynesian workhorse model as such, it will also be informative to compare the resulting wage and price Phillips curve relationships with the Phillips curves that we employ in the book's mature Keynesian models, which will be subsequently briefly introduced in section 1.4.

After the dust of processing the microeconomic foundations of staggered wage and price setting has settled, Woodford (2003, p. 225) comes up with the following two equations that the joint evolution of wages and prices must satisfy:

$$\pi_t^w = \beta E_t \pi_{t+1}^w + \beta_{wy} y_t - \beta_{w\omega}(\ln \omega_t - \ln \omega_t^n) \tag{1.27}$$

$$\pi_t^p = \beta E_t \pi_{t+1}^p + \beta_{py} y_t + \beta_{p\omega}(\ln \omega_t - \ln \omega_t^n) \tag{1.28}$$

where π_t^w denotes wage inflation, $\pi_t^w = (w_t - w_{t-1})/w_{t-1}$, and π_t^p price inflation (the superscript 'p' has now been added for a more pronounced contrast to wage inflation). The output gap enters the determination of price as well as wage inflation, since in this framework there is no room for unemployment.

What is most remarkable in these relationships is the influence of the real wage rate $\omega = w/p$, i.e. its percentage deviations from the natural real wage (the equilibrium real wage when both wages and prices are fully flexible). Observe that ω has a negative bearing on wage inflation and a positive bearing on price inflation.

The full model is given by eqs. (1.27), (1.28), the Euler condition of the private households (1.21) and the Taylor rule (1.25).[24] The previous two jump variables y_t and $\pi_t = \pi_t^p$ are thus joined by π_t^w, which is likewise a jump variable. As this is tantamount to treating the price level p_t and the nominal wage rate w_t as jump variables (cf. the remark on (1.21) above), the real wage rate ω_t is a jump variable too. In other words, the model still includes no predetermined variable. This means that the critical remark at the end of the preceding subsection continues to apply: also, this extended New-Keynesian model will not be able to generate dynamics with some meaningful persistence in the time series (apart from persistence in the exogenous random shocks).

The rest of the present subsection is thus exclusively concerned with consistency: is the model's determinacy ensured? To avoid the technical

---

[24] The explicit introduction of wages does not affect the condition for optimal consumption of households; see Erceg et al. (2000, p. 291).

subtleties, the analysis is again similarly sketchy as above. To begin with (1.27), (1.28), in a deterministic setting with rational expectations we have

$$\pi_{t+1}^w = [\pi_t^w - \beta_{wy}y_t + \beta_{w\omega}(\ln\omega_t - \ln\omega_t^n)]/\beta$$
$$\pi_{t+1}^p = [\pi_t^p - \beta_{py}y_t - \beta_{p\omega}(\ln\omega_t - \ln\omega_t^n)]/\beta$$

To ease the exposition, let us now directly work with $\beta = 1$. This has the advantage that the first differences of the inflation rates, $\pi_{t+1}^a - \pi_t^a$ ($a = w, p$), depend merely on y_t and $\ln\omega_t$. Neglect furthermore exogenous variations of the natural real wage and put $\chi_t = \ln\omega_t - \ln\omega_t^n = \ln\omega_t - \ln\omega^n$. The continuous-time analogue of (1.27), (1.28) then reads

$$\dot{\pi}^w = -\beta_{wy}y + \beta_{w\omega}\chi \tag{1.29}$$

$$\dot{\pi}^p = -\beta_{py}y - \beta_{p\omega}\chi \tag{1.30}$$

The change in χ derives from its definition. The change in y is obtained from substituting (1.25) and the above expression for π_{t+1}^p in the Euler condition $y_{t+1} - y_t = \beta_{yi}(i_t - i^o) - \beta_{yi}\pi_{t+1}^p$. Thus,

$$\dot{y} = \beta_{yi}[(\alpha_y + \beta_{py})y + \alpha_\pi\pi^p + \beta_{p\omega}\chi] \tag{1.31}$$

$$\dot{\chi} = \pi^w - \pi^p \tag{1.32}$$

Together, the economy's dynamic first-order conditions translated into continuous time are described by the Jacobian matrix $\mathcal{J}$ of (1.29) to (1.32), which has a simple determinant:

$$\mathcal{J} = \begin{bmatrix} 0 & 0 & -\beta_{wy} & \beta_{w\omega} \\ 0 & 0 & -\beta_{py} & -\beta_{p\omega} \\ 0 & \beta_{yi}\alpha_\pi & \beta_{yi}(\alpha_y + \beta_{py}) & \beta_{yi}\beta_{p\omega} \\ 1 & -1 & 0 & 0 \end{bmatrix} \tag{1.33}$$

$$\det\mathcal{J} = -\alpha_\pi\beta_{yi}(\beta_{p\omega}\beta_{wy} + \beta_{py}\beta_{w\omega})$$

Since all variables are jump variables, the determinacy of the model's optimal solution path requires that all four eigenvalues of $\mathcal{J}$ have positive real parts. To check this, factorize the characteristic polynomial $P(\lambda)$ with respect to the four eigenvalues $\lambda_1, \lambda_2, \lambda_3, \lambda_4$. We get the following equation that an eigenvalue λ must satisfy:

$$P(\lambda) = \lambda^4 + a_3\lambda^3 + a_2\lambda^2 + a_1\lambda + a_o = (\lambda - \lambda_1)(\lambda - \lambda_2)(\lambda - \lambda_3)(\lambda - \lambda_4) = 0$$

Consider first the case $\alpha_\pi = 0$, which implies $\lambda_1 = 0$ because of det $\mathcal{J} = 0$. It is well known that the term a_1 in the polynomial is given by $a_1 = -\sum_k \mathcal{J}_k$, where $\mathcal{J}_k$ are the four third-order principal minors. Multiplication in $P(\lambda)$ then gives for the coefficient associated with $\lambda = \lambda^1$

$$-\lambda_2 \lambda_3 \lambda_4 = a_1 = -(\mathcal{J}_1 + \mathcal{J}_2 + \mathcal{J}_3 + \mathcal{J}_4) > 0$$

The positive sign obtains because $\mathcal{J}_1 < 0$, $\mathcal{J}_2 < 0$, $\mathcal{J}_3 = \mathcal{J}_4 = 0$. Hence, at least one eigenvalue has a negative real part. Again, as in the baseline model, the economy would be ill-defined in the absence of monetary policy, when $\alpha_\pi = \alpha_y = 0$.

Similarly, as before, we therefore ask: can the Taylor rule with $\alpha_\pi > 0$ and $\alpha_y \geq 0$, or at least with a suitable choice of the two policy coefficients, ensure determinacy? This time the answer is a definite 'no'. The impossibility result follows directly from the negative sign of the determinant of $\mathcal{J}$ as $\alpha_\pi > 0$. For then we have $\lambda_1 \cdot \lambda_2 \cdot \lambda_3 \cdot \lambda_4 = $ det $\mathcal{J} < 0$, implying that at least one eigenvalue continues to have a negative real part.

Erceg et al. (2000) treat the problem of monetary policy in terms slightly different from indeterminacy. They include random errors in their model, but only shocks to the Pareto-efficient steady-state values. The main proposition (on pp. 296ff.) states that, however the interest rate is set, no more than one of the three variables output gap, price inflation and wage inflation can have zero variance when the exogenous shocks have non-zero variance. The reason is that the output gap would remain at zero and wage and price inflation would remain constant only if the aggregate real wage rate were continuously at its Pareto-optimal level. The latter, however, moves in response to each of the exogenous shocks considered.

The significance of this result is accentuated by a complementary proposition that examines the limiting cases of perfectly flexible wages and prices, respectively. It says that, with staggered price contracts and perfectly flexible wages, monetary policy can completely stabilize price inflation and the output gap, thereby attaining the Pareto-optimal social welfare level. And, conversely, monetary policy can achieve the same goal in the presence of staggered wage contracts and perfectly flexible prices (Erceg et al., 2000, p. 298).

At a general level, the following quote from Erceg et al. (2000, pp. 305f) is a good conclusion of the discussion on the extended baseline model: 'While considerations of parsimony alone might suggest an exclusive focus on either staggered price setting or staggered wage setting, the inclusion of both types of nominal inertia makes a critical difference in the monetary policy problem.' The way in which the difference becomes 'critical' and the continual prevalence of the parsimonious formulations cast serious doubts, in our view, on the usefulness of hard-core New-Keynesian theory, an approach entirely based on agents who, in accordance with the intertemporal infinite-horizon optimization problems they are supposed to solve, are purely forward-looking – as was, for example, specified in eqs (1.27), (1.28) above.

1.3.3   Combining forward-looking and backward-looking behaviour I

Empirical criticism, such as Mankiw's (2000) verdict quoted above on the New-Keynesian Phillips curve with its purely forward-looking expectations, has fostered the idea that inertia in the rate of interest may be generated if some – as they are called – backward-looking elements are introduced. One idea is to augment the microfoundations by a backward-looking indexation of prices (or wages) that takes the form $\ln p_t = \ln p_{t-1} + \gamma_p \pi^p_{t-1}$, where γ_p is the indexation rate for prices that are not reoptimized ($0 \le \gamma_p \le 1$; see Woodford, 2003, p. 234). Equation (1.28) thus becomes

$$\pi^p_t - \gamma_p \pi^p_{t-1} = \beta E_t(\pi^p_{t+1} - \gamma_p \pi^p_t) + \beta_{py} y_t + \beta_{p\omega}(\ln \omega_t - \ln \omega^n_t) \qquad (1.34)$$

(and likewise for wages). Obviously, the formal analysis can remain perfectly the same as before if we introduce the auxiliary variable $\tilde{\pi}^p_t := \pi^p_t - \gamma_p \pi^p_{t-1}$, which is again a jump variable. However, even if, for example, after a purely transitory shock to inflation at $t = 0$ this variable immediately returns to its zero equilibrium value at $t = 1$, this does not yet hold true for the inflation rate π^p_t itself. Now it exhibits some persistence since $\pi^p_1 = \tilde{\pi}^p_1 + \gamma_p \pi^p_o = 0 + \gamma_p \pi^p_o$ and, repeating this argument forward in time, $\pi^p_t = \gamma^t_p \pi^p_o$. Hence, the higher the indexation rate the higher the degree of persistence in inflation.[25]

More common in the literature on optimal monetary policy in particular is another specification that is almost, but not exactly, identical to (1.34). It starts directly from the New-Keynesian Phillips curve (1.21), and makes no more explicit reference to the underlying microfoundations. The combination of forward-looking and backward-looking elements is, rather, formulated in a straightforward manner as a weighted

---

[25] The IS curve can be treated in a similar way as (1.34) if the terms $u(C_t)$ in the representative household's intertemporal utility function are replaced with $u(C_t - \eta C_{t-1})$, where the parameter η measures the degree of 'habit persistence' ($0 \le \eta < 1$).

average of the two corresponding inflation rates. The device is likewise applied to the IS equation (1.20). Together we thus have[26]

$$y_t = \phi_y E_t y_{t+1} + (1 - \phi_y) y_{t-1} - \beta_{yi} [i_t - E_t \pi_{t+1} - (i^o - \pi^o)] + \varepsilon_{y,t} \quad (1.35)$$

$$\pi_t = \phi_p \beta E_t \pi_{t+1} + (1 - \phi_p) \pi_{t-1} + \beta_{py} y_t + \varepsilon_{p,t} \quad (1.36)$$

The weights ϕ_y, ϕ_p determine the extent to which behaviour looks forward and backward $(0 \le \phi_y, \phi_p \le 1)$.[27] Clearly, with $\phi_y = \phi_p = 1$, we are back to the New-Keynesian baseline model (1.20), (1.21). At the other end, $\phi_y = \phi_p = 0$, agents are said to to be purely backward-looking (except for the expectations $E_t \pi_{t+1}$ in (1.35), if they are maintained).

Generally with hybrid expectations, $0 < \phi_y, \phi_p < 1$, forward-looking and backward-looking agents are conceived to coexist. It is, however, not clear what the microfoundations look like in such a world and why these relationships should lead to just the equations as they are specified in (1.35), (1.36), though they might appear fairly appealing. Why should the naive, backward-looking agents survive at all? Why are they not outperformed and ousted by the fully rational forward-looking agents?[28] The view on these issues is usually pragmatic, unless agnostic. The following quote from Leeper and Zha (2001, p. 85) is certainly representative for applications of (1.35), (1.36): 'We are less concerned with whether backward-looking behavior can be sensibly rationalized in an optimizing framework than we are with extracting the model's implications.' Is it unfair to say that the hybrid specification (1.35), (1.36) has only 'soft' microfoundations?

It is a priori not obvious, either, which variables should be regarded as predetermined in (1.35), (1.36), and it is also not always explicitly stated in the presentation of these equations. Nonetheless, the consequence

---

[26] Wages are again neglected in this subsection, as they are in almost all the literature that integrates forward-looking and backward-looking behaviour by similar principles as in eqs. (1.35) and (1.36). In the following we therefore return to the previous notation $\pi_t = (p_t - p_{t-1})/p_{t-1}$ for the rate of price inflation, dropping the superscript 'p' of section 1.3.2.

[27] Note that Woodford's equation (1.34) can be rearranged as (omitting the superscript 'p') $\pi_t = \phi_{p1} \beta E_t \pi_{t+1} + \phi_{p2} \pi_{t-1} + \beta_{py}/(1 + \beta \gamma_p) y_t + \cdots$, but unless $\beta = 1$ the two coefficients ϕ_{p1} and ϕ_{p2} do not exactly add up to unity as in (1.36).

[28] Besides habit persistence in the scientific community, this is precisely Milton Friedman's (1953, especially pp. 21f.) defence of rational expectations as a positive hypothesis about observable behaviour: agents need not consciously formulate and solve complex optimization problems and make sure in sophisticated ways that their beliefs and decisions are mutually consistent. The vision is, rather, that evolutionary pressure and imitation induce them to act as if they did meet the epistemic conditions of the rational expectations hypothesis, while other behaviour will be driven out of the market.

appears to be that now y_t and π_t are treated as predetermined, and $E_t y_{t+1}$ and $E_t \pi_{t+1}$ are jump variables.[29]

One approach to obtaining the time paths of (1.35), (1.36), after an interest rate rule has been incorporated, is a suitable transformation of these equations such that the changes in the predetermined variables are described by an ordinary (backward-looking) difference equation of the form

$$\begin{bmatrix} y_{t+1} \\ \pi_{t+1} \end{bmatrix} = P \begin{bmatrix} y_t \\ \pi_t \end{bmatrix} + Q \begin{bmatrix} \varepsilon_{y,t} \\ \varepsilon_{p,t} \end{bmatrix} \tag{1.37}$$

The problem, of course, is to derive the two matrices $P, Q \in \mathbb{R}^{2 \times 2}$ of the reduced form from the structural equations, where determinacy of the model prevails if P turns out to be stable (both eigenvalues within the unit circle). There are (at least) two procedures to determine P and Q, both of which require so much effort that, as a rule, one has to resort to numerical methods. One procedure, for example, amounts to finding the solution of a quadratic matrix equation for P. This also shows that the structural coefficients in (1.35), (1.36) enter the reduced-form solution (1.37) in complicated (and 'unpredictable') ways. The appendix to chapter 8 presents more details of how (1.35), (1.36) and P in (1.37) can be dealt with.

Definite results on (1.35), (1.36) in combination with the Taylor rule are not too difficult to obtain if all agents are assumed to be backward-looking: $\phi_y = \phi_p = 0$. Even if the expectations $E_t \pi_{t+1}$ in (1.35) are maintained, the structural equations can be transformed into (1.37) without sophisticated methods. The resulting entries of the matrix P are, however, so unwieldy that we omit this case. To illustrate the stabilizing potential of monetary policy when inflation and the output gap are predetermined, it suffices to suppose a lagged influence of output in the Phillips curve, which proves to be more convenient, while the forward-looking element in (1.35) can be preserved. Thus, we set up the following deterministic version of a dynamic IS curve and an accelerationist Phillips curve, combined with the Taylor rule:

$$y_t = y_{t-1} - \beta_{yi}[i_t - E_t \pi_{t+1} - (i^o - \pi^o)] \tag{1.38}$$

$$\pi_t = \pi_{t-1} + \beta_{py} y_{t-1} \tag{1.39}$$

$$i_t = (i^o - \pi^o) + \pi_t + \alpha_\pi (\pi_t - \pi^o) + \alpha_y y_t \tag{1.40}$$

---

[29] One often learns this from elaborations in a technical appendix of a working paper. For example, we have found such a clear and direct statement in Ellingsen and Söderström (2004, p. 15). Incidentally, this paper demonstrates that more advanced models may look more than one period ahead in the future; see our sketches in the appendix to chapter 8.

What the Taylor rule (1.40) should achieve in this case is that, whatever values of y_t, π_t are given by history (and demand and supply shocks) in period $t = 0$, in the absence of further shocks the economy will eventually return to its steady-state position $(y^o, \pi^o) = (0, 0)$. Correspondingly, with exogenous shocks imposed on (1.38) to (1.40), the variances of y_t and π_t would remain finite.

After a few elementary manipulations, the reduced-form equations of (1.38) to (1.40) result as

$$\begin{bmatrix} y_{t+1} \\ \pi_{t+1} \end{bmatrix} = \mathcal{J} \begin{bmatrix} y_t \\ \pi_t \end{bmatrix} = \begin{bmatrix} (1 - \alpha_\pi \beta_{yi} \beta_{py})/h(\alpha_y) & -\alpha_\pi \beta_{yi}/h(\alpha_y) \\ \beta_{py} & 1 \end{bmatrix} \begin{bmatrix} y_t \\ \pi_t \end{bmatrix} \quad (1.41)$$

where $h(\alpha_y) := 1 + \beta_{yi}(\alpha_y - \beta_{py})$. The stability of $\mathcal{J}$ can be examined with the aid of the Schur criterion. Defining and computing

$$a_1 := -\text{trace } \mathcal{J} = -1 + (\alpha_\pi \beta_{yi} \beta_{py} - 1)/h(\alpha_y)$$

$$a_2 := \det \mathcal{J} = 1/h(\alpha_y)$$

the criterion states that the two eigenvalues of $\mathcal{J}$ are inside the unit circle if and only if[30]

$$1 - a_1 + a_2 > 0, \quad 1 + a_1 + a_2 > 0, \quad 1 - a_2 > 0$$

The second inequality is satisfied unambiguously, the third one if $\alpha_y - \beta_{py} > 0$, and a sufficient (but by no means necessary) condition for the first inequality to be satisfied is $1 - \alpha_\pi \beta_{yi} \beta_{py} > 0$. It can thus be concluded that the central bank can stabilize the economy if it adopts the Taylor rule (1.40) with a sufficiently small (!) inflation gap coefficient: and a sufficiently large output gap coefficient: $\alpha_\pi < 1/\beta_{yi}\beta_{py}$ and $\alpha_y > \beta_{py}$.

Obviously, the time paths generated by (1.41) will then also exhibit a certain degree of persistence. The economy (1.38)–(1.40) is in this respect far more satisfactory than the New-Keynesian baseline model and its wage-price extension we have considered, though it does not meet the New-Keynesian standards regarding the microeconomic underpinnings. Using an estimated model with more lags from the literature, we will actually argue in chapter 8, section 4, that models of this type even produce too much persistence – mainly in the rate of inflation, which is due to the accelerationist specification of the Phillips curve in (1.39).

As has been indicated in the remark on (1.35), (1.36) concerning the predetermined variables, mixed forward-looking and backward-looking

---

[30] In this convenient form the criterion is quoted in Gabisch and Lorenz (1989, p. 45). a_1 and a_2 are the coefficients of the characteristic polynomial $\lambda^2 + a_1\lambda + a_2$, which are known to be given by $-\text{trace } \mathcal{J}$ and $\det \mathcal{J}$, respectively.

systems are much more difficult to handle. We must therefore content ourselves with giving a brief impression that these economies may have meaningful properties. To this end, we again resort to a continuous-time approximation. As it is still more heroic than before, it may be taken as a purely heuristic device. The result that the analysis of the mixed economies is more involved than in the New-Keynesian baseline model also makes itself felt in the fact that the continuous-time approximation will no longer be two-dimensional but four-dimensional. In this respect, the basic structure of the discrete-time economy with its two predetermined and two jump variables still shines through.

Thus, consider the deterministic version of (1.35), (1.36). To avoid clumsy expressions, set $\beta = 1$ in (1.36) right at the beginning. Rearranging the terms and letting Δ denote the (backward) difference operator, the two equations can be written as

$$\phi_y(\Delta y_{t+1} - \Delta y_t) = (1 - 2\phi_y)\Delta y_t + \beta_{yi}[i_t - \pi_{t+1} - (i^o - \pi^o)]$$

$$\phi_p(\Delta \pi_{t+1} - \Delta \pi_t) = (1 - 2\phi_p)\Delta \pi_t - \beta_{py} y_t$$

The heroic approximation, now, is to replace the second-order differences with the second-order time derivatives (which is only meaningful for $0 < \phi_y, \phi_p < 1$). In addition, in the first equation we substitute for π_{t+1}, which equals $\Delta \pi_{t+1} + \pi_t$, the term $\dot{\pi} + \pi$.[31] Substituting the Taylor rule for i_t, we get

$$\ddot{y} = [\alpha_y \beta_{yi} y + (1 - 2\phi_y)\dot{y} + \alpha_\pi \beta_{yi} \pi - \beta_{yi}\dot{\pi}]/\phi_y$$

$$\ddot{\pi} = [(1 - 2\phi_p)\dot{\pi} - \beta_{py} y]/\phi_p$$

The equations can be transformed into a four-dimensional first-order differential equations system by setting $x = \dot{y}$ and $\rho = \dot{\pi}$. It then reads

$$\begin{bmatrix} \dot{y} \\ \dot{x} \\ \dot{\pi} \\ \dot{\rho} \end{bmatrix} = \mathcal{J} \begin{bmatrix} y \\ x \\ \pi \\ \rho \end{bmatrix} = \begin{bmatrix} 0 & 1 & 0 & 0 \\ \alpha_y \beta_{yi}/\phi_y & (1 - 2\phi_y)/\phi_y & \alpha_\pi \beta_{yi}/\phi_y & -\beta_{yi}/\phi_y \\ 0 & 0 & 0 & 1 \\ -\beta_{py}/\phi_y & 0 & 0 & (1 - 2\phi_p)/\phi_p \end{bmatrix} \begin{bmatrix} y \\ x \\ \pi \\ \rho \end{bmatrix}$$

$$(1.42)$$

---

[31] It appears more appropriate to solve (1.36) for $\pi_{t+1} = (1 - \phi_p)\Delta \pi_t/\phi_p - \beta_{py} y_t/\phi_p - \pi_t$ and make use of this expression. We nevertheless prefer the other option, since it yields a zero determinant of the Jacobian matrix for the benchmark coefficient $\alpha_\pi = 0$. This is not only helpful for the subsequent analysis but also, perhaps, more trustworthy. (The determinant in the alternative case has the same sign as $\alpha_\pi + 2$.)

Of course, y and π must maintain their role as predetermined variables. While in the original (deterministic) model y_{t+1} and π_{t+1} are jump variables, this part can here be taken over by the time derivatives $\dot{y} = x$ and $\dot{\pi} = \rho$. Hence, determinacy requires that the matrix $\mathcal{J}$ has two eigenvalues with negative and two with positive real parts.

From the sign of the determinant, det $\mathcal{J} = \alpha_\pi \beta_{yi}\beta_{py}/\phi_y\phi_p$, it can be inferred immediately that indeterminacy prevails if monetary policy is inactive – that is, if the interest rate is fixed at $i = i^o$: this case corresponds to $\alpha_\pi = -1$, so that det $\mathcal{J} < 0$ and the relation $\lambda_1\lambda_2\lambda_3\lambda_4 = $ det $\mathcal{J}$ for the four eigenvalues tells us that the number of eigenvalues with positive real parts cannot be even.

Suppose for the rest of the analysis that forward-looking behaviour has a greater weight in the economy, so that $\phi_y > 1/2$, $\phi_p > 1/2$. Consider first the special case $\alpha_\pi = 0$, where the determinant vanishes and one eigenvalue λ_1 is zero. Three of the principal third-order minors are zero, the fourth is unambiguously positive, $\mathcal{J}_3 = \beta_{yi}[\beta_{py} - \alpha_y(1-2\phi_p)]/\phi_p > 0$. By the same argument as in the preceding subsection this gives us the condition $-\lambda_2\lambda_3\lambda_4 = -(\mathcal{J}_1 + \mathcal{J}_2 + \mathcal{J}_3 + \mathcal{J}_4) < 0$ for the other three eigenvalues. Assuming without loss of generality that $\lambda_2 > 0$, both λ_3 and λ_4 have either positive or negative real parts. From $\lambda_1 + \lambda_2 + \lambda_3 + \lambda_4 = $ trace $\mathcal{J} < 0$ it follows that they are negative.

The real parts of $\lambda_2, \lambda_3, \lambda_4$ do not change their sign when α_π is slightly increased above zero. Since det $\mathcal{J} > 0$ then the equation $\lambda_1\lambda_2\lambda_3\lambda_4 = $ det $\mathcal{J}$ now tells us that λ_1 is real and positive. In sum, two eigenvalues of $\mathcal{J}$ have positive and two have negative real parts. We can therefore conclude that, at least if $\phi_y > 1/2$, $\phi_p > 1/2$ and the central bank's inflation gap coefficient α_π is not too high, determinacy of the economy is ensured.

Basically, models with hybrid expectations are still in line with he New-Keynesian baseline model in that they preserve the feature of jumping variables. On the other hand, an important conceptual change to observe is that the output gap and the rate of inflation turn from jump variables into predetermined variables. Interestingly, in the original discrete-time and stochastic formulation of the hybrid expectations model, the meaning of the term 'jump variable' becomes somewhat eroded, in particular if, for computing the time paths of the economy, one refers to the reduced-form presentation (1.37) that governs the dynamics of – exclusively – the predetermined variables.

The great advantage of the hybrid expectations over the baseline model is that, by allowing the key variables output and inflation to be predetermined (without introducing additional variables such as the capital stock), it provides much greater scope for a reasonable persistence in the time series. This explains the fact that the vast majority of New-Keynesian-oriented models on monetary policy issues with an empirical background (however remote) disregard the baseline model and work with some version of hybrid expectations.

1.3.4 Combining forward-looking and backward-looking behaviour II

While introducing a weighted average of forward-looking and backward-looking components into the New-Keynesian framework considerably widens the scope for gaining satisfactory trajectories, these models, even in their less advanced versions, are already fairly complex. One may therefore look for simplifications that preserve the basic concepts but make the model easier to analyse. Such simplifications could also be more readily accepted now since, as we have already indicated, the microfoundations of the hybrid expectations models are not as 'firm' as in the New-Keynesian baseline model.

A useful simplification one occasionally finds in the literature does not change the variables entering eqs. (1.35) and (1.36) in the preceding subsection but does change the time index of some of them. Specifically, the output gap in the IS equation and the rate of inflation in the Phillips curve are shifted one period forward in time, on the left-hand side as well as on the right-hand side of the equations. Presupposing also $\beta = 1$ and, of course, $\phi_y, \phi_p < 1$, we have

$$y_{t+1} = \phi_y E_t y_{t+1} + (1 - \phi_y) y_t - \beta_{yi}[i_t - E_t \pi_{t+1} - (i^o - \pi^o)] + \varepsilon_{y,t} \quad (1.43)$$

$$\pi_{t+1} = \phi_p E_t \pi_{t+1} + (1 - \phi_y) \pi_t + \beta_{py} y_t + \varepsilon_{p,t} \quad (1.44)$$

The prevailing view seems to be that this modification of (1.35), (1.36) does not need a comprehensive justification. In Lansing and Trehan (2003, p. 250), for example, it is understood that equations such as (1.43) and (1.44) serve 'to loosely approximate some commonly-used specifications in the literature'. In the precursory working paper (2001, p. 4), the authors speak of a timing convention that, with respect to inflation, changes a New-Keynesian Phillips curve to a 'Neoclassical'-style Phillips curve.[32] The undogmatic attitude of papers employing (1.43) and (1.44) is also exemplified by remarks that the same or other authors have obtained similar results on the basis of the New-Keynesian dating, where the advantage of (1.43) and

---

[32] For further details on the two Phillips curve setups, reference is made to Roberts (1995). The modified dating is also mentioned in Woodford (2003, p. 150).

(1.44) is that they are simpler and may even admit an analytical treatment.[33]

The first gain from eqs. (1.43), (1.44) is that they relieve the user of any further thoughts about predetermined variables; inflation π_t and output gap y_t are definitely predetermined. After a few manipulations, the system is seen to be equivalent to the following ordinary stochastic difference equations:[34]

$$y_{t+1} = y_t - \frac{\beta_{yi}}{1-\phi_y}\left[i_t - \pi_t - \frac{\beta_{py}}{1-\phi_p}y_t - (i^o - \pi^o)\right] + \varepsilon_{y,t} \qquad (1.45)$$

$$\pi_{t+1} = \pi_t + \frac{\beta_{py}}{1-\phi_p}\pi_t + \varepsilon_{p,t} \qquad (1.46)$$

Obviously, once y_o, π_o are given at time $t = 0$, these equations can be directly iterated forward and there is also no more necessity to think about 'jump' variables. The feature is, of course, maintained if the Taylor rule $i_t = i(\pi_t, y_t)$ from (1.40) is applied to the interest rate.

A nice property of (1.43), (1.44) is also that one can immediately see the bearing that forward-looking expectations have on the economy. An increase in the forward-looking component, represented by rising weights ϕ_y and ϕ_p in the reduced-form equations (1.45), (1.46), reinforces the reactions of y_{t+1}, π_{t+1} to the deviations of y_t, π_t from equilibrium. The reactions would even tend to infinity as the weights approach unity. The effects of ϕ_y and ϕ_p may be similar in the New-Keynesian setting of (1.35), (1.36), but this is much harder to verify there.

The fact that we can obtain the time paths of (1.43), (1.44) without any sophisticated methods does not yet mean that this economy (as a linear system) is meaningful. In this respect, it still has to be checked that the deterministic counterpart of (1.45), (1.46) is asymptotically stable. However, an analysis of these difference equations is certainly easier than in the New-Keynesian case of hybrid expectations, where first a matrix such as P in (1.37) would have to be computed. To illustrate the strong prospects of (1.43), (1.44) for stability, it here suffices for us to consider the (deterministic and) continuous-time analogue of (1.45), (1.46). Substituting the Taylor rule (1.40) into (1.45), putting the first

---

[33] Lansing and Trehan can explicitly compute the policy coefficients α_π and α_y that minimize an intertemporal loss function of the central bank.

[34] The derivation is based on the rule that an equation such as $z_{t+1} = \phi E_t z_{t+1} + \beta x_t + \varepsilon_t$ (with $E_t \varepsilon_t = 0$ and β and x being row and column vectors, respectively) can be transformed into $z_{t+1} = \beta x_t/(1-\phi) + \varepsilon_t$. To see this, take expectations of both sides of the structural equation, solve it for $E_t z_{t+1}$, which yields $E_t z_{t+1} = \beta x_t/(1-\phi)$, and substitute this expression back into the original equation.

differences of y and π on the left-hand side, replacing them with the time derivatives and abbreviating $\tilde{\beta}_{py} = \beta_{py}/(1 - \phi_p)$, we get

$$\begin{bmatrix} \dot{y} \\ \dot{\pi} \end{bmatrix} = \mathcal{J} \begin{bmatrix} y \\ \pi \end{bmatrix} = \begin{bmatrix} -\beta_{yi}(\alpha_y - \tilde{\beta}_{py})/(1 - \phi_y) & -\alpha_\pi \beta_{yi}/(1 - \phi_y) \\ \beta_{py}/(1 - \phi_p) & 0 \end{bmatrix} \begin{bmatrix} y \\ \pi \end{bmatrix}$$

(1.47)

Again, the private sector on its own with the interest rate fixed at $i = i^o$ is not viable (as a linear system), since the equilibrium of (1.47) is then a saddle point. Just note that this case is captured by setting $\alpha_\pi = -1$, which renders entry j_{12} positive and so leads to det $\mathcal{J} = 0 - j_{12}j_{21} < 0$.

On the other hand, $\alpha_\pi > 0$ yields $j_{12} < 0$ and thus a positive determinant, while $\alpha_y > \beta_{py}/(1 - \phi_p)$ takes care of a negative trace of $\mathcal{J}$. It follows that, by adopting the Taylor rule in a reasonable way (i.e. choosing a positive inflation gap coefficient and a sufficiently strong response to the output gap), the central bank can stabilize the economy. It may also be observed that this holds for any degree to which the agents are forward-looking; only the output gap coefficient α_y must sufficiently increase as ϕ_p, the weight in the Phillips curve, increases towards unity.

Convergence of the deterministic economy is ensured, but it takes time after a shock until the two state variables y and π reach their steady-state values. In other words, the model generates inertia in inflation and the output gap. It thus shares this property with the hybrid expectations as they were specified in (1.35), (1.36), whereas the analysis of the reduced-form system (1.47) requires far less effort than that of the four-dimensional system (1.42).

With the neoclassical dating convention, there is also some scope to drop the assumption of perfectly flexible wages and reintroduce the nominal wage adjustments from the New-Keynesian framework of subsection 1.3.2. In contrast to the impossibility result there obtained, monetary policy may now be able to stabilize an economy with uniquely determined time paths. The range of the policy coefficients α_π and α_y achieving this might even be established analytically.

Thus, reconsider the (deterministic) New-Keynesian Phillips curves (1.27) and (1.28) for wage and price inflation (π^w and π^p) and subject them to the neoclassical dating. Setting $\beta = 1$ and assuming that the natural real wage ω^n is time-invariant, the equations become

$$\pi_{t+1}^w = \phi_w E_t \pi_{t+1}^w + (1 - \phi_w)\pi_t^w + \beta_{wy}y_t - \beta_{w\omega}(\ln \omega_t - \ln \omega^n) \quad (1.48)$$

$$\pi_{t+1}^p = \phi_p E_t \pi_{t+1}^p + (1 - \phi_p)\pi_t^p + \beta_{py}y_t + \beta_{p\omega}(\ln \omega_t - \ln \omega^n) \quad (1.49)$$

Besides (1.48), (1.49), the economy is described by the neoclassical-type IS equation (1.43), the Taylor rule (1.25) and a definitional equation determining the changes in the real wage rate. Certainly, wage inflation and the real wage are predetermined too, so that we have four dynamic equations for the four predetermined variables π^w, π^p, y and $\chi = \ln \omega - \ln \omega^n$. To set up the deterministic continuous-time counterpart, solve (1.49) for π^p_{t+1} and substitute this in (1.43). The time derivatives for π^w, π^p, y are then computed in the same way as before, and the one for χ is just eq. (1.32). Together, the following four-dimensional system of ordinary differential equations is obtained:

$$\dot{\pi}^w = (\beta_{wy}y - \beta_{w\omega}\chi)/(1 - \phi_w) \tag{1.50}$$

$$\dot{\pi}^p = (\beta_{py}y + \beta_{p\omega}\chi)/(1 - \phi_p) \tag{1.51}$$

$$\dot{y} = -\beta_{iy}[(\alpha_y - \tilde{\beta}_{py})y + \alpha_\pi \pi - \tilde{\beta}_{p\omega}\chi]/(1 - \phi_y) \tag{1.52}$$

$$\dot{\chi} = \pi^w - \pi^p \tag{1.53}$$

where $\tilde{\beta}_{pa} := \beta_{pa}/(1 - \phi_a)$, $a = y$, ω in (1.52). It is instructive to compare this system to the equations (1.29) to (1.32), which approximate the original New-Keynesian model with staggered wages and prices. The difference in the first three constituent equations is plain too see: in all three of them a sign reversal has taken place.

The purely forward-looking New-Keynesian approach has therefore been changed in two fundamental respects. First, the introduction of hybrid expectations with their backward-looking component transforms jump variables into predetermined variables. Second, the neoclassical dating convention relates the same variables and their time derivatives to each other as in the baseline approach, where, however, we find that a negative impact turns into a positive effect and vice versa.

In the remainder of this subsection we examine whether the present system (1.50)–(1.53) differs from the New-Keynesian wage-price baseline model in a third respect as well. Analysis of the New-Keynesian system (1.29)–(1.32) (and other results from the literature) has revealed that there was no way in this model for monetary policy to bring about determinacy. The corresponding question for the predetermined variables in (1.50) to (1.53) is whether, with a suitable choice of the policy coefficients in the Taylor rule, the central bank can ensure the asymptotic stability of the equilibrium point.

A stability analysis of (1.50)–(1.53) has to study the Jacobian matrix of this system. It exhibits the same pattern of entries as the matrix $\mathcal{J}$ in (1.33) from the New-Keynesian economy, except that, as we have just seen, most of the signs are reversed. Although it is a 4×4 matrix, the many zero entries still make it possible to apply the Routh–Hurwitz stability conditions and get out definite results.[35] On the other hand, here we prefer to save ourselves the admittedly tedious calculations and concentrate on the essential distinction from the New-Keynesian case. For this purpose we can content ourselves with a numerical demonstration that the central bank can, in fact, succeed in stabilizing (1.50)–(1.53).

There are not too many parameters to which numerical values are to assigned. From the estimated (purely backward-looking) model by Rudebusch and Svensson (1999), which we shall discuss in chapter 8, section 4, we borrow $\beta_{yi} = 0.09$ and $\beta_{py} = 0.15$. Deliberately, we set β_{wy} slightly higher than β_{py}, choosing $\beta_{wy} = 0.20$. The real wage effect in the two Phillips curve, we feel, should not be very strong, so put $\beta_{p\omega} = \beta_{w\omega} = 0.05$. Since in subsection 1.3.3 we were almost forced to assume $\phi_y > 1/2$, $\phi_p > 1/2$ (in order to have a negative trace for $\mathcal{J}$ in (1.42)), we here choose a lower degree to which the agents are forward-looking; let us say $\phi_y = \phi_p = \phi_w = 0.25$.

It remains to choose two values for the policy coefficients α_π and α_y, compute the eigenvalues of system (1.50)–(1.53) and note whether they imply stability or not. Doing this for a great many combinations of the two parameters, the (α_π, α_y) policy parameter plane is subdivided into two areas: a region containing the pairs α_π, α_y entailing stability, and the parameters in the rest of the plane, which imply instability. The outcome is shown in figure 1.2.[36]

The stability conditions acquired from figure 1.2 appear quite plausible. For every value of α_π that is not too large, sufficiently high values of α_y guarantee stability. On the other hand, for $\alpha_\pi \geq 0.20$ roughly, α_y must not be too large, either. Incidentally, Taylor's proposed coefficients $\alpha_\pi = \alpha_y = 0.50$ are contained within the stability region. Varying the forward-looking weights, it is furthermore found that a greater influence of the forward-looking agents has a certain destabilizing tendency: the stability region shrinks as ϕ_y, ϕ_p, ϕ_w are uniformly increased. The stability region even tends to vanish as the weights approach unity. Non-uniform variations of the three weights (especially ϕ_w) can produce additional interesting effects.[37]

The main point we wish to make, however, is that, in contrast to the purely forward-looking version of the New-Keynesian approach, the present combination of output and wage-price dynamics constitutes a

---

[35] The pattern of zero entries is not much different from the 4×4 Jacobian matrix to which the Routh–Hurwitz conditions were successfully applied in Franke and Asada (1994, pp. 280ff., 293f.).

[36] Pairs in the dotted area induce local stability; instability prevails outside.

[37] A salient feature of our parameter setting is that, with equal weights ϕ_p and ϕ_w, the coefficient β_{wy} exceeds β_{py}. Stability is still possible if β_{wy} falls short of β_{py}, but the stability regions have another shape then.

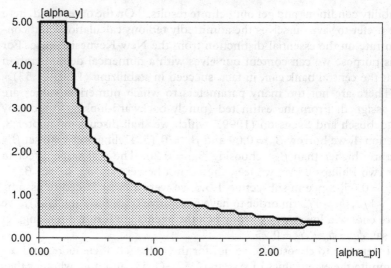

Figure 1.2: The parameter diagram of (α_π, α_y) for system (1.50)–(1.53)

model with a reasonable scope for inertial behaviour and for monetary policy.

1.4   Keynesian DAS-AD dynamics and the wage-price spiral

1.4.1   The D(isequilibrium)AS-AD approach to the wage-price spiral

Our approach to Keynesian wage-price dynamics is rooted in the Neoclassical Synthesis, Stage I; in the version that advances both a Phillips curve for money wages and a Phillips curve for changes in the price level. Originally, marginal pricing still served as a benchmark, but it was no longer required to apply in every instant of time. In other words, firms were allowed to be off their supply curve; hence, the approach can be characterized as a disequilibrium AS approach, designated by the acronym DAS for short.

A simple model of this type was put forward for illustrative purposes in subsection 1.2.2, and in table 1.1 in the same subsection we indicated that it could be seen as a precursor to later, as we called them, 'mature' Keynesian models. In fact, the wage and price Phillips curves that we will widely employ in this book have been developed over the years from these beginnings. Nevertheless, we leave the genesis by which we arrived at the present specification to one side. After the discussion of the New-Keynesian treatment of wage and price formation and, in particular, the neoclassical dating convention, it is instead expedient to refer to the two New-Keynesian Phillips curves from the preceding subsection. For convenience they are reproduced here:

$$\pi_{t+1}^w = \phi_w E_t \pi_{t+1}^w + (1 - \phi_w)\pi_t^w + \beta_{wy}y_t - \beta_{w\omega}(\ln \omega_t - \ln \omega^n) \qquad (1.48)$$

$$\pi_{t+1}^p = \phi_p E_t \pi_{t+1}^p + (1 - \phi_p)\pi_t^p + \beta_{py}y_t + \beta_{p\omega}(\ln \omega_t - \ln \omega^n) \qquad (1.49)$$

Our own approach can be presented as starting out from these equations and then modifying them in six respects.

(1) According to eq. (1.48), the anticipation of next period's inflation entering the determination of the change in money wages is the rate of wage inflation itself. In contrast, we hold that price inflation is the relevant term here. That is, we replace $E_t \pi_{t+1}^w$ in (1.48) with $E_t \pi_{t+1}^p$. On the other hand, we continue to assume that these future inflation rates are perfectly foreseen, so that we can directly substitute π_{t+1}^p for $E_t \pi_{t+1}^w$.

(2) Analogous reasoning applies to the price Phillips curve, which means that π_{t+1}^w is substituted for $E_t \pi_{t+1}^p$ in (1.49).

(3) The idea of the entries π_t^w and π_t^p in (1.48), (1.49) was to represent backward-looking behaviour. This was even more clearly expressed in the original hybrid expectations (1.36), where in the price Phillips curve this rate was dated $t-1$. Here we introduce a new variable π^c, which we conceive as a general *inflation climate*, and substitute π_t^c for both (!) π_t^w in (1.48) and π_t^p in (1.49). The climate is predetermined in period t and is later supposed to change between the periods in a way that can be described as gradual adjustments towards the current rate of inflation (a target that is possibly combined with other reference rates of inflation). As the story is currently told, the replacement of π_t^w and π_t^p with π_t^c can be viewed as being motivated by the fact that, in modern terminology, adjustments of this kind are called backward-looking.

(4) Regarding the key terms in the Phillips curve, our perspective is that wage and price inflation are influenced by the demand pressure on the respective markets. The corresponding measure for the labour market is (not the output gap but) the rate of employment e_t – i.e. its deviation from the NAIRU level e^o (which we assume to be exogenously given and fixed).

(5) The output gap (denoted by y) in the price Phillips curve could be retained in this respect. In the models we consider it is, however,

more appropriate to employ the output–capital ratio as a proxy for the demand pressure on the goods market, which we likewise, from now on and in the rest of the book, denote by the letter y. That is, we refer to the deviations of y_t from its equilibrium level y^o. In the small model below it is assumed to be fixed, for simplicity.[38]

(6) Lastly, the role and the signs of the influence of real wages is maintained, except that we drop the logarithm and identify the natural real wage rate ω^n, which in principle may vary, with the fixed value of the real wage ω^o that prevails in the steady state.

In sum, these remarks give rise to the following version of a wage and a price Phillips curve, where, obviously, κ_w and κ_p are the two weights $(0 \le \kappa_w, \kappa_p \le 1)$ corresponding to ϕ_w and ϕ_p in (1.48), (1.49):

$$\pi^w_{t+1} = \kappa_w \pi^p_{t+1} + (1 - \kappa_w)\pi^c_t + \beta_{we}(e_t - e^o) - \beta_{w\omega}(\omega_t - \omega^o) \quad (1.54)$$

$$\pi^p_{t+1} = \kappa_p \pi^w_{t+1} + (1 - \kappa_p)\pi^c_t + \beta_{py}(y_t - y^o) + \beta_{p\omega}(\omega_t - \omega^o) \quad (1.55)$$

It goes without saying that, as in the New-Keynesian specification (1.48), (1.49) of hybrid expectations under the neoclassical dating convention, the two rates of inflation π^w_t and π^p_t are treated as predetermined. However, because the same variable π^c_t is supposed to enter the price and the wage Philips curve, eqs. (1.54) and (1.55) cannot encompass the former, not even in the most special case when $\kappa_w = \kappa_p = 0$ and the determination of the inflation climate degenerates to identifying it with current inflation. For $\pi^c_t = \pi^w_t$, (1.54) is then identical to (1.48), but not (1.55) with (1.49); and the other way round for $\pi^c_t = \pi^p_t$.

The important thing to note in (1.54), (1.55) is that income distribution is supposed to have a bearing on both the changes in prices and money wages. To be in line with (1.48), (1.49), income distribution is here represented by the real wage rate. Later in the book, from chapter 3 onward, in the context of our reasoning there we will find it more reasonable to employ the wage share for the same purpose. The sign of the impact of real wages is the same as in (1.48), (1.49): negative in the wage Phillips curve and positive in the price Phillips curve.[39]

Since in particular the additional influence of a wage term in the two Phillips curves, with the postulated signs, is not a standard feature in the literature, it should first be checked that the approach of eqs. (1.54) and

---

[38] Generally also the concept of potential output may be taken as a benchmark, which in models with a neoclassical production function is given by the output level that maximizes short-run profits and so is varying with labour intensity $\ell = L/K$.

[39] We will later also replace the output–capital ratio y with the rate of capacity utilization u. This is, however, rather inessential, since with our specification of the latter y and u will differ only by a proportionality factor.

(1.55) is not outright counter-factual. In Chen et al. (2004) the equations have therefore been subjected to an econometric test, combining them with two adjustment equations for the utilization of capital (u_t, taking the role of y_t, in a dynamic IS equation) and of labour (e_t, being directly coupled with u_t). The inflation climate was simply specified in a backward-looking manner, as a moving average over the past twelve quarters with linearly declining weights. Though these four equations are a relatively small system compared to an unrestricted VAR with twelve lags, it was found that the null hypothesis of imposing these structural restrictions cannot be rejected in favour of the latter. Hence, the small system can also be econometrically defended as one parsimonious representation (among several or many others, of course) of the true data-generating process. The estimation of its wage-price part, on the basis of quarterly data for the US economy from 1965 to 2000, resulted in the following numerical equations, where the role of the real wage ω_t is here supposed to be taken by the wage share, denoted as v_t:[40]

$$\pi^w_{t+1} = 0.65\pi^p_{t+1} + 0.40\pi^c_t + 0.11(e_t - e^o) - 0.09(v_t - v^o)$$

$$\pi^p_{t+1} = 0.35\pi^w_{t+1} + 0.67\pi^c_t + 0.03(u_t - u^o) + 0.07(v_t - v^o)$$

Two features of the estimates are worth pointing out. First, although the coefficients on the first two terms of the equations were unrestricted, they are not only positive but also their sum is not significantly different from one. This justifies their interpretation as weights in setting up a rate of benchmark wage and price inflation, $\kappa_w\pi^p_{t+1} + (1-\kappa_w)\pi^c_t$ and $\kappa_w\pi^w_{t+1} + (1-\kappa_w)\pi^c_t$, respectively. Second, all coefficients come out with the theoretically required signs and are, furthermore, significant. In particular, this holds for the impact of the wage share. Thus these non-standard terms, too, are corroborated by the data. In sum, the estimation lends confidence to the concept of our two Phillips curves in (1.54), (1.55) and their additional reference to a wage term.

So far, the Phillips curves have been considered in their structural form. Here it has to be taken into account that they cannot be directly used to gauge the impact of the gap variables $e_t - e^o$, etc., on the two inflation rates. For example, though not being present in (1.54), the demand pressure on the goods market $y_t - y^o$ still has a bearing on wage inflation, via its influence on π^p_{t+1}, which in turn enters the determination of π^w_{t+1}. These effects can be made explicit, and their relative strength can be assessed, if we compute the reduced form of (1.54), (1.55). To

---

[40] Actually, in the models from chapter 3 on we ourselves will employ the wage share rather than the real wage.

this end it has to be ruled out that the weights κ_w and κ_p are both unity. Substituting (1.55) in (1.54) and solving the resulting equation for π_{t+1}^w, and correspondingly so to obtain π_{t+1}^p, the reduced-form equations for wage and price inflation are seen to read,

$$\pi_{t+1}^w = \pi_t^c + \kappa[\beta_{we}(e_t - e^o) + \kappa_w\beta_{py}(y_t - y^o) + (\kappa_w\beta_{p\omega} - \beta_{w\omega})(\omega_t - \omega^o)]$$

(1.56)

$$\pi_{t+1}^p = \pi_t^c + \kappa[\beta_{py}(y_t - y^o) + \kappa_p\beta_{we}(e_t - e^o) + (\beta_{p\omega} - \kappa_p\beta_{w\omega})(\omega_t - \omega^o)]$$

(1.57)

$$\kappa := 1/(1 - \kappa_w\kappa_p)$$

These two Phillips curve relationships are clearly traditional in their dependence on demand pressure and the inflation climate. Regarding the latter, note that it corresponds to what defines an expectations-augmented Phillips curve and is there usually called expected inflation. With a view to its (still outstanding) determination in a backward-looking manner, we have preferred to call it a general inflation climate, which, being in a non-perfect world with less than perfect foresight, we think of as being adopted by boundedly rational agents.

On the other hand, eqs. (1.56) and (1.57) are more advanced than the usual reduced-form Phillips curves, in that there are two separate curves the dependent variables of which are each determined by the conditions on both the labour and the goods market. Apart from that, we have the additional influence of the real wage rate (or the wage share later in the book). Whether eventually π_{t+1}^w and π_{t+1}^p are negatively or positively affected by that variable is contingent on the relative size of the coefficients $\beta_{w\omega}$, $\beta_{p\omega}$, κ_w, κ_p.

Relating (1.56), (1.57) to the New-Keynesian specifications discussed in subsection 1.3.4, it may be observed that no current rate of inflation enters the right-hand side, neither π_t^w nor π_t^p. This means that our approach does not include, even as a special case, the accelerationist-type Phillips curves that result from the neoclassical dating; see eqs. (1.50), (1.51) for the continuous-time formulation in the same subsection. As we have remarked on (1.54), (1.55), under exceptional conditions either the wage or the price Phillips curve might be of an accelerationist type, but not both.

The actual wage-price dynamics could nevertheless come close to what would be generated by accelerationist Phillips curves, depending especially on the adjustment rules that are supposed to govern the changes of the inflation climate. To some extent this issue will be investigated in the calibrations of chapter 5, where a common wage Phillips curve

(1.54) is combined with a simple accelerationist price Phillips curve, on the one hand, and with the price Phillips curve of eq. (1.55) on the other hand. It will there be shown that these two building blocks can produce very similar cyclical features of wages, prices and income distribution.

1.4.2   Feedback-guided stability analysis: example 1

Clearly, two separate Phillips curves for wages and prices imply a theory of income distribution, at least as far as real wages are concerned.[41] In this respect it is a great advantage of our approach that, although the inflation climate π^c has an important bearing on the rates of inflation, income distribution remains unaffected by it. Passing over to continuous time and again writing $\hat{w}$ for π^w, $\hat{p}$ for π^p, it is immediately seen from the reduced-form equations (1.56), (1.57) that π^c cancels out in the determination of the changes in the real wage, $\hat{\omega} = \hat{w} - \hat{p}$. Specifically, we get

$$\dot{\omega} = \omega\kappa\{(1 - \kappa_p)[\beta_{we}(e - e^o) - \beta_{w\omega}(\omega - \omega^o)] - (1 - \kappa_w)[\beta_{py}(y - y^o)$$
$$+ \beta_{p\omega}(\omega - \omega^o)]\} \tag{1.58}$$

If the coefficients $\beta_{w\omega}$, $\beta_{p\omega}$ are positive and κ_w, κ_p less than one, eq. (1.58) yields a negative feedback of ω directly on itself – that is, a stabilizing effect. We note that this effect is different from what is implied by the New-Keynesian laws of motion (1.29), (1.30), (1.32) in subsection 1.3.2. Ignoring the output gap for this kind of partial argument, we there obtain a second-order differential equation for $\chi = \ln \omega - \ln \omega^n$, namely $\ddot{\chi} = \dot{\pi}^w - \dot{\pi}^p = (\beta_{w\omega} + \beta_{p\omega})\chi$. Since the two roots of the characteristic polynomial $\lambda^2 + (\beta_{w\omega} + \beta_{p\omega}) = 0$ are purely imaginary, Re $\lambda_{1,2} = 0$, the direct auto-feedback of real wages is neutral.

The traditional argument regarding real wage effects is a bit more indirect. It says that an increase in ω reduces aggregate demand and so output and employment, which in turn lowers price as well as wage inflation. It thus depends on the relative flexibilities of wages and prices whether the real wage rate in the second stage, so to speak, rises or falls. These flexibilities are usually seen to be represented by the slope coefficients in the two Phillips curves, by β_{we} and β_{py} in our notation. Equation (1.58), however, demonstrates that the seemingly innocent weights κ_w and κ_p also take effect.

Reconsidering the discussion of the Neoclassical Synthesis, Stage I, we can build a small model reflecting these stability effects. If we abstract

---

[41] The wage share is additionally influenced by possible variations of labour productivity over the cycle, which we will account for from chapter 3 on.

from other dynamic feedbacks, they are even decisive. In setting up the IS-LM part of the model, it will be understood that the expected rate of inflation in the specification of the real interest rate is now replaced with the inflation climate, so that the return differential in (1.6) reads $q = r - (i - \pi^c)$. The other equations we here employ are (1.4), (1.5) and (1.15), while the interest rate is determined in the LM equation (1.8) under the additional assumption $\hat{M} = \hat{K}$ for the money supply, or we simply peg it at $i = i^o$. In the former case we have $pyf_m(i) = M/K = $ const. in (1.8), which shows that the interest rate is an increasing function of the output–capital ratio, $i = i(y)$ with $i' > 0$; otherwise $i' = 0$, of course.

Freezing furthermore the inflation climate at its steady-state value $\pi^o = 0$, temporary equilibrium on the goods market is described by the condition $y = (1/s)f_I[y - \omega\ell(y) - \delta - i(y) + \pi^o]$ (recall that $\ell = L/K$ is labour intensity, a rising function $\ell = \ell(y)$ of the output–capital ratio). It has already been observed in subsection 1.2.2 that $\partial(y - \omega\ell(y))/\partial y = 0$ in the steady-state position. This ensures that (at least locally) output is inversely related to the real wage, $y = y(\omega)$ with $y_\omega = \partial y/\partial \omega < 0$.

The employment rate $e = L/L^s = \ell/\ell^s = \ell[y(\omega)]/\ell^s$ is a function of $\ell^s = L^s/K$ and the real wage, and so likewise responds negatively to an increase in ω – i.e. $e = e(\omega, \ell^s)$ with $e_\omega = \partial e/\partial \omega = \ell' y_\omega/\ell^s < 0$. Regarding the denominator of e, we assume that the labour supply grows at a constant rate equal to the real growth rate in long-run equilibrium, g^o. Thus, $\hat{\ell}^s = \hat{L}^s - \hat{K} = g^o - I/K = g^o - f_I$, or, more explicitly,

$$\dot{\ell}^s = \ell^s\{g^o - f_I[y(\omega)] - \omega\ell[y(\omega)] - \delta - i[y(\omega)] + \pi^o]\} \tag{1.59}$$

Substituting $y = y(\omega)$ and $e = e(\omega, \ell^s)$ in (1.58) and solving it for the time derivative $\dot{\omega} = \hat{\omega} \cdot \omega$, we have a differential equations system in the two (predetermined, of course) variables ω and ℓ^s. Evaluated at the steady state, the Jacobian is easily computed as

$$\mathcal{J} = \begin{bmatrix} \omega\kappa[-(1-\kappa_p)\beta_{we}|e_\omega| + (1-\kappa_w)\beta_{py}|y_\omega| - \tilde{\beta}_\omega] & -\omega\kappa(1-\kappa_p)\beta_{we}/\ell^s \\ \ell^s f_I'(1 - |y_\omega|i') & 0 \end{bmatrix}$$

$$= \begin{bmatrix} ? & - \\ + & 0 \end{bmatrix}$$

where $\tilde{\beta}_\omega := (1-\kappa_p)\beta_{w\omega} + (1-\kappa_w)\beta_{p\omega} \geq 0$; besides $\kappa_p < 1$, we have in the sign pattern assumed that the interest rate reactions to output changes are not too extreme, so that $i' = di/dy < 1/|y_\omega|$ ($i' = 0$ if i is fixed at i^o).

As det $\mathcal{J} > 0$ under these circumstances, the steady state is stable if and only if trace $\mathcal{J} < 0$ – that is, if entry j_{11} is negative. Hence, stability prevails if the composite term $\tilde{\beta}_\omega$, representing the direct real wage auto-feedbacks, is dominant, or already if $(1-\kappa_p)\beta_{we}$ exceeds $(1-\kappa_w)\beta_{py}$.

In the present setting we are told that higher wage flexibility in the form of a steeper slope β_{we} in the wage Phillips curve is favourable for stability, whereas higher price flexibility in the form of a steeper slope β_{py} in the price Phillips curve tends to be destabilizing. Of course, this can only be a very preliminary message. An immediate objection is that we have limited ourselves to just one channel through which real wages affect aggregate demand, namely its negative impact on investment demand. If differentiated savings propensities of 'capitalists' and workers are allowed for, then rising wages would raise consumption on the part of workers, which could well dominate the other negative effect(s). We would thus obtain a different sign pattern in the Jacobian.

Another aspect is of general significance. It has to be realized that results on the, say, stabilizing effect of a parameter increase may not necessarily carry over to more comprehensive models. The reason is that β_{we}, β_{py}, etc. could also reinforce or weaken a second or third stabilizing or destabilizing mechanism. To anticipate two central results from this book's extensive numerical stability investigation, the characterization (suggested here) of β_{we}, $\beta_{w\omega}$, $\beta_{p\omega}$ as stabilizing and β_{py} as destabilizing may be compared with our final and succinct summary of parameter stability effects in the full Keynes–Metzler–Goodwin model, which is table 7.3 (chapter 7, section 5, subsection 3) for the version with LM curve, and table 9.6 (chapter 9, section 5, subsection 3) for the version with a Taylor-type interest rate reaction function.[42]

Besides, chapter 7, section 3, designs and studies carefully another two-dimensional submodel that concentrates on real wage effects, but discards IS and instead includes elements of the Metzlerian goods market disequilibrium part. The stability results there obtained are then directly confronted with the corresponding findings in the full KMG model. These remarks may give a first impression that we wish to understand basic feedback mechanisms and their consequences for economic stability, whereas we are at the same time aware that we cannot rely too much on them if the theoretical framework is extended. In this way, however, we also learn more about what is important, or peculiar, in the richer model economy.

1.4.3 Feedback-guided stability analysis: example 2

Other feedback mechanisms that, besides the real wage effects, will be dealt with at various places in the book are the Keynes effect and the Mundell effect. The Keynes effect is well known for its stabilizing potential, which

---

[42] The counterpart of coefficient β_{py} is there β_{pu}.

involves the price level and its impact on real balances in the LM curve. As high prices above normal are tantamount to relatively low real balances, they raise the nominal interest rate and diminish investment (and perhaps consumption). Reinforced through the multiplier, this decreases output and finally puts downward pressure on the price level to return to normal.[43]

The Mundell effect works through expected inflation, or, in our framework, the general inflation climate. An increase in π^c reduces the real rate of interest and so increases investment. The induced increase in output raises inflation rates, which, perhaps with some delay, causes the inflation climate to move upward. Taken together, a positive feedback loop comes into being. In particular, the destabilizing effect will be stronger, and therefore tend to outweigh the stabilizing Keynes effect, the more rapidly the inflation climate adjusts to actual inflation.

To identify these effects within a small model in pure form, we cancel the real wage dynamics. For example, if we put $\kappa_w = 1$ and $\beta_{we} = \beta_{wv} = 0$, the real wage in (1.58) remains constant, $\hat{\omega} = 0$. Regarding its level, we assume $\omega = \omega^o$.

To make the role of the price level more pronounced, let the money supply move one to one with real capital, $\hat{M} = \hat{K}$. The LM condition (1.8) then becomes $p y f_m(i) = M/K = \text{const.}$, from which it can be immediately inferred that the LM interest rate is an increasing function of both the output–capital ratio and the price level, $i = i(y, p)$ and $i_y > 0$, $i_p > 0$ for its partial derivatives. Inserting this in the IS equilibrium condition, $y = (1/s) f_I [y - \omega^o \ell(y) - \delta - i(y, p) + \pi^c]$, and once again recalling that $\partial(y - \omega \ell(y))/\partial y = 0$ in the steady state, it is readily seen that the IS-LM output–capital ratio is a function of p and the inflation climate π^c, $y = y(p, \pi^c)$, with $y_p = \partial y/\partial p < 0$ and $y_\pi = \partial y/\partial \pi^c > 0$. These signs have just been verbally described as the output link in the chain of the Keynes and Mundell effects, respectively.

Substituting the output function in the continuous-time expression of the reduced-form price Phillips curve (1.57), we obtain

$$\dot{p} = p[\pi^c + \psi(p, \pi^c)], \quad \psi(p, \pi^c) := \kappa \beta_{py}[y(p, \pi^c) - y^o] \qquad (1.60)$$

Obviously, $\psi_p = \partial \psi/\partial p < 0$ and $\psi_\pi = \partial \psi/\partial \pi^c > 0$.

Concerning the adjustments of the inflation climate, we assume gradual adjustments of π^c towards current price inflation,

$$\dot{\pi}^c = \beta_\pi (\hat{p} - \pi^c) = \beta_\pi \psi(p, \pi^c) \qquad (1.61)$$

---

[43] In essence, this mechanism has already been pointed out by Keynes in chapter 19 of *The General Theory*, which was devoted to a discussion of 'Changes in money wages'. Indeed, it is the only mechanism that Keynes recognized as being of any significance to the alleged benefits of flexible prices.

where β_π measures the speed of these adjustments. The principle of (1.61) is commonly referred to as 'adaptive expectations', a term that, with our interpretation of π^c as a general climate variable, we consider to be not quite precise. In fact, in a disequilibrium context there are a number of theoretical and empirical arguments pointing out that partial adjustments towards a moving target are not as foolish as they are mostly held to be (see Flaschel et al., 1997, pp. 149–62 or, more extensively, Franke, 1999, for a compilation of such arguments). As we have already referred to Mankiw's (2001) paper on the Phillips curve, it is also interesting to quote his evaluation of adaptive expectations in this context. After noting that these expectations are formed without taking important news into account that is available everywhere, he adds to this observation: 'Yet, the assumption of adaptive expectations is, in essence, what the data are crying out for' (p. C59).

Equations (1.60) and (1.61) make up an autonomous system in the two variables p and π^c, the Jacobian of which is given by

$$\mathcal{J} = \begin{bmatrix} p\psi_p & p(1+\psi_\pi) \\ \beta_\pi\psi_p & \beta_\pi\psi_\pi \end{bmatrix}$$

Entry $j_{11} = -p|\psi_p| < 0$ reflects the stabilizing Keynes effect. Its strength depends, in particular, on the responsiveness of the LM interest rate to price variations, which in combination with the IS equilibrium condition is here integrated in the derivative $\psi_p < 0$. The other diagonal entry $j_{22} = \beta_\pi\psi_\pi > 0$ represents the destabilizing Mundell effect, the strength of which is directly measured by the adjustment speed β_π.

In the present model these two effects are actually decisive for stability, since the determinant of the Jacobian is unambiguously positive, $\det \mathcal{J} = \beta_\pi p|\psi_p| > 0$, so that the stability condition reads $\mathrm{trace}\,\mathcal{J} = \beta_\pi\psi_\pi - p|\psi_p| < 0$. Perfectly in line with the above argument, stability therefore prevails if the destabilizing Mundell is sufficiently weak in comparison to the stabilizing Keynes effect. The condition is especially satisfied if the adjustment speed β_π is sufficiently low.

At the end of the preceding subsection we did, however, warn against premature conclusions from such small-scale submodels. In fact, in the more advanced models in the book, the wage share terms in the two Phillips curve, which replace the present real wage terms, become relevant and may spoil the nice picture just obtained. There are two reasons. First, although indirectly, these terms are also affected by output variations, the link being labour productivity Y/L, as $wL/pY = (w/p)/(Y/L)$. Second, corresponding to Okun's law, labour productivity (relative to its trend) will be assumed to move procyclically.

On the whole, it then turns out that the response of inflation to output changes can be different from what holds true in the present limited model. The consequence will even be opposite stability effects: the Mundell effect can be stabilizing and the Keynes effect can be destabilizing. The conditions for and the likelihood of this to happen are discussed in great detail in chapter 3, section 8, and chapter 7, section 4, subsections 2 and 3. Again, we may emphasize that the results at which we will arrive in these more elaborated models can be better assessed against the background of the traditional and elementary feedback mechanisms here expounded.

Lastly, it should be considered what becomes of the Keynes effect in a modern framework (Part III of the book) that dispenses with the traditional determination of the interest rate through the LM curve and instead employs the concept of an interest rate reaction function. In a strict sense, there is then no more room for this effect. Alternatively, the notion of the Keynes effect might be extended: first, in that it relates to the rate of inflation rather than the price level; and, second, in that it is now directly and intentionally the central bank, and not 'the money market', that increases the interest rate in response to rising inflation.

1.4.4   D(isequilibrium)AS-D(isequilibrium)AD modelling

The notion of temporary goods market equilibrium is a useful tool to keep the dimensionality of models low. It comes with an assumption, however, that, at least in more ambitious models, is not unproblematic. The assumption, of course, is that of a downward-sloping IS curve. It is usually validated by the practically equivalent assumption of ultra-short-run stability of an underlying quantity adjustment process, which allows for the inequality of demand and supply, and for firms correspondingly changing their production levels. These activities are supposed to take place at the beginning of a period, within virtually no time at all and involving no inventory changes when output and demand are not matching. The process must therefore be viewed as a hypothetical, tâtonnement-like adjustment process.

Specifically, the assumption corresponds to Keynes' requirement that the marginal propensity to consume be less than unity. More generally, aggregate demand D may positively depend on m variables x^k, $D = D(x^1, \ldots, x^m)$, which in their turn are (directly or indirectly) increasing functions of output, $x^k = x^k(Y)$. Regarding $D = D[x^1(Y), \ldots, x^m(Y)]$, ultra-short-run stability then demands that, as Y rises, D rises less; formally, $\sum_k (\partial D / \partial x^k)(dx^k / dY) < 1$.

So, the first problem with IS equilibrium is the justifying background story of the ultra-short-run quantity adjustment process, which, when one comes to think about it, is conceptually not very convincing. On the other hand, it has become a convention and might be accepted as just that, especially when it serves to make a model analytically tractable.

The other problem is the stability condition itself. Leaving the realm of general mathematical analysis and passing over to concrete numerical issues, it may be found that the required boundedness of the term(s) $\partial D/\partial x^k$ is in fact too restrictive. One point is that a low responsiveness may imply unpleasant properties in numerical simulations. As a matter of fact, in Part I of the present book, which still works with the notion of IS-LM, our simulations of the cyclical dynamics we are interested in typically yield cycles with periods that are much too long to permit the interpretation of business cycles (see chapter 2, section 8, and chapter 3, section 10). Our view is that stronger output reactions would shorten the expansion and contraction phases, and that these faster reactions should, in the first instance, be brought about by a higher responsiveness of investment to the return differential (a higher coefficient f'_I in the notation above). Unfortunately, this is precluded by the ultra-short-run stability assumption, which we therefore experience as a straitjacket for this approach.

Other models may have problems with other implications of the boundedness requirement. It is already the case that a back-of-the-envelope calculation can often show that, a priori, the admitted order of magnitude is implausibly low. Generally, we conclude that as Keynesian models, or the topics that are studied by numerical methods, become more detailed and more ambitious it becomes increasingly desirable to get rid of the IS device. In other words, a disequilibrium AD part of such models becomes desirable.

Abandoning the IS concept means allowing for goods market disequilibrium to prevail over one or several short periods. Recognizing that goods are non-perishable and that rationing is not a universal phenomenon in the economy, the imbalances of output and demand have to be buffered by inventories. So an inventory dynamics is added to the model. On the other hand, production by firms adjusts gradually now, not instantaneously, to demand. For these decisions firms have to form sales expectations, and they have to take into account the deviations of the actual stock of inventories from an optimal or desired level. A new model building block incorporating these features will be designed later in chapter 4, section 2, subsection 2, and will then be underlying in the rest of the book, Parts II and III.

According to the remarks above, and in extension of the title of section 1.4, the modelling framework that thus emerges can be classified as a DAS-DAD approach to Keynesian modelling, where the additional letter 'D' stands for 'disequilibrium'. Alluding to the expression used in table 1.1 (subsection 1.2.2) on the four variants of the Neoclassical Synthesis, Stage I, this will then really be a 'mature' Keynesian model.

1.5   Plan of the book

1.5.1   Part I: Textbook Approaches

Part I of the book begins, in chapter 2, by reconsidering (and slightly extending) Sargent's (1979, 1987) textbook model of the conventional AS-AD growth dynamics, which integrates into a consistent whole what has been – and still is – regarded by many economists as being representative of Keynesian macroeconomic theory. The key features of this model are: savings and investment are independent decisions; an interest-bearing financial asset is explicitly considered; the rate of monetary expansion is a control variable; goods and financial markets are in continuous temporary equilibrium; employment of labour is determined by output meeting aggregate demand and so will generally differ from the level of labour supply; firms are nevertheless always on their supply curve – that is, the marginal productivity principle for labour applies and serves to determine the price level and, a fortiori, the rate of inflation; the rise of nominal wages is governed by an expectations-augmented Phillips curve; and inflationary expectations are formed by a combination of adaptive and regressive expectations.

The analysis of this chapter completes Sargent's rather sketchy treatment of the dynamic system thus defined. The ensuing study of the local dynamics, in particular, overturns Sargent's general optimism concerning the stability of the steady-state growth path. Moreover, singling out three basic feedback mechanisms and investigating their relative strength by means of numerical simulations, the system's potential for cyclical dynamics is demonstrated.

From chapter 3 on, the book dispenses with the marginal productivity principle for labour because of its counter-factual implications in a business cycle context. An alternative representation of the production technology allows for variations in capacity utilization and for procyclical fluctuations in (detrended) labour productivity. While, in the short term, firms produce to satisfy current demand, prices remain invariant and are changed only between these periods. Their adjustments are described by a second Phillips curve relationship. A novel feature here is that price inflation reacts not only to a measure of demand pressure but also to deviations of the present markup on average cost from a target markup rate. The influence of this second factor, which involves the wage share and later turns out to be of some consequence for the usual (Keynes and Mundell) effects on stability, is justified a priori on theoretical grounds as well as by referring to the cyclical implications for the real wage dynamics.

After a conceptual discussion and the mathematical investigation of local stability conditions, a numerical stability analysis is performed, which is based on a partial (here still back-of-the-envelope) calibration of the model's key parameters. A sensitivity analysis shows that, despite being only three-dimensional, the model is already so complex that a number of important reaction coefficients cannot always be unambiguously identified as being either stabilizing or destabilizing. A more careful analysis of the basic feedback loops also reveals that the effects more or less known from the literature do not suffice to explain stability or instability; there are more circuitous mechanisms involving certain cross-effects of the state variables that can play a major role in this respect. In these interactions one can also identify the forces that may bring an economic expansion to an end, so that typically the system exhibits cyclical behaviour. Lastly, a global simulation run sketches the resulting comovements of the key economic variables.

1.5.2   Part II: Analytical Framework: Theory and Evidence

Part II of the book is an extensive study of our Keynes–Metzler–Goodwin model. As is introduced in chapter 4, the model emerges from that presented in chapter 3 with the addition of some specification details; in particular, it also includes an influence of the wage share in the wage Phillips curve. The major conceptual innovation, however, is that now goods market disequilibrium is allowed for. The rationale for this extension is based on certain theoretical reasoning and the fact that the IS temporary equilibrium design in the previous chapters puts severe restrictions on some numerical coefficients. The demand for finished goods is assumed to be satisfied from current production and existing inventories. The latter means that the model also has to keep track of the accumulation of stocks, and that firms' decisions about the level of production and inventory investment have to be newly specified (which constitutes the 'Metzlerian' component of the model). Apart from that, special care is taken of the model's accounting consistency in the macro context. Although in other respects the modelling is rather parsimonious, the reduced form of the dynamic system is already six-dimensional.

It may also be mentioned that the LM part and the assumption of a constant growth rate of the exogenous money supply is maintained throughout Part II. This conception has, in the meantime, become somewhat dated, and it will be abandoned in Part III. Our reasons for not immediately giving it up are explained in the next subsection.

The first achievement of the investigation of the KMG model is that a mathematical analysis can still set up economically meaningful conditions for local stability. The method of proof rests on a general principle, which begins with a suitable 3×3 submatrix of the system's Jacobian matrix and then constructs a cascade of stable submatrices of increasing order. The method may also have some interest beyond the present context, as it may equally be applied to other, and perhaps even more encompassing, disequilibrium models. In addition, it can be proved that if the system loses stability upon variations of a parameter then this occurs via a Hopf bifurcation. We take this result as an indication of the general potential of the KMG model for cyclical behaviour. A global analysis of this phenomenon, however, again requires a numerical approach, to which the ensuing chapters are devoted.

Chapter 5 concentrates on numerical simulations of the wage-price dynamics. Within a business cycle context, three alternative theories of inflation are combined with the extended money wage Phillips curve already mentioned and with adjustments of inflationary expectations. The first approach, almost directly, amounts to countercyclical motions of the price level; the second utilizes the extended price Phillips curve of the KMG model; the third considers formalized adjustments of a variable markup on unit labour costs. Assuming exogenous stylized sine wave oscillations of capacity utilization and the capital growth rate as the driving force, we are here interested in the cyclical features that the three modules imply for, in particular, the motions of the real wage rate, the wage share and the (detrended) price level. The corresponding cyclical statistics should come close to the stylized facts of the business cycle – that is, to the leads, lags and amplitudes of these variables that we gather from the empirical data of the US economy.

We find that in all three model variants this goal can be achieved by an appropriate choice of the numerical parameters. Hence, all three of them are suitable candidates for being incorporated into more comprehensive models of the business cycle.[44]

Chapter 6 combines the wage-price module of the KMG model with the other components of that model. Regarding their calibration, it is very

---

[44] In a comparison of the cyclical properties, the variable markup approach could be said to have a slight edge over the other two models, but this marginal advantage may easily be offset by arguments put forward by other model builders.

helpful that, as long as the motion of utilization and the capital growth rates are treated as exogenous, the former model part is independent of the dynamics of the latter (but not vice versa). The numerical values of the second module of chapter 5 can be taken over unaltered. On this basis, the rest of the KMG model is calibrated to the empirically observed fluctuations of the variables that are determined here. This completes the first stage of our calibration study, which also requires most of the effort. In the second stage, the sine wave motions of our two exogenous variables are replaced with their noisier empirical fluctuations. It turns out, nevertheless, that the main cyclical characteristics of the model variables are preserved, which confirms the usefulness of the stage 1 approach.

Finally, in stage 3, capacity utilization and the capital growth rate are endogenized, to which end the investment function is now included in the model. At medium levels of utilization, the influence of its two determinants (utilization and the return differential, profit rate minus real interest rate) is specified in a linear manner, whereas at higher rates of under- or overutilization the weights of the two determinants are plausibly shifting. This, on the whole, nonlinear function is numerically described by four parameters, and we are able to find values for them that achieve all that we want – not perfectly so, but to a satisfactory degree: (1) the model generates endogenous cycles around an unstable equilibrium that are bounded and persistent; in fact, the trajectories converge towards a globally unique limit cycle; (2) the oscillations occur at a business cycle frequency (a period of around eight years); (3) the variability and comovements of the variables are similar to those in stages 1 and 2.

The whole set of these numerical parameters constitutes our base scenario. Although, beginning with the fact that we are concerned with a deterministic economy, our calibration procedure is different from the methods of the real business cycle school, the results concerning a satisfactory match of the cyclical characteristics of the data can absolutely stand comparison with what has been obtained by this competitive equilibrium approach to business cycle modelling.

Chapter 7 performs a sensitivity analysis in a narrow and a wider sense. To begin with the latter, three two- or three-dimensional submodels are considered and their stability properties are related to those of the full KMG model. These submodels focus on the Metzlerian inventory dynamics, the wage-price dynamics, and the dynamics of the nominal variables. We identify the basic feedback mechanisms and examine their bearing on stability and instability in the submodel and then in the six-dimensional KMG model. At a general level, our findings here warn against premature stability conclusions from the low-dimensional models; not always, but occasionally, they may not carry over to the full model, even qualitatively. A more specific feature to which we should draw attention is that our calibration implies a negative output–inflation nexus, which is at first sight counter-intuitive. A more careful analysis seeks to reconcile it with intuition, or the habitual way of thinking.

The sensitivity analysis in a narrow sense investigates the impact of parameter variations on local stability. In order to provide a definite and concise message, our final aim is to classify thirteen central reaction coefficients or adjustment speeds as either stabilizing, destabilizing or ambiguous. Lastly, the effects of parameter changes on some selected topics of the global dynamics are looked into.

1.5.3   Part III: Monetary Policy

The earlier chapters assume a neutral monetary policy, in the form of a constant growth rate of the money supply. In modern macroeconomic modelling, however, central bank behaviour is increasingly described by an interest rate reaction function. To incorporate these recent developments, Part III reverses the causality of money and the rate of interest, and specifies a Taylor rule with interest rate smoothing. Accordingly, the interest rate undergoes partial adjustments in response to deviations of inflation and capacity utilization from their target values. Adding in this way the Taylor rule to the KMG model makes it a Keynes–Metzler–Goodwin–Taylor, or KMGT, model.

A Taylor rule in some form or another is certainly an appropriate modelling tool for the sake of realism. It might therefore be asked why it has not already been introduced in Part II of the book. We are well aware that the assumption of an exogenously growing money supply that, via LM, determines the rate of interest can be regarded as counterfactual. We have, nevertheless, maintained it in KMG for the following reason. A constant money growth rate is not only of interest as a historical (Friedmanian) recommendation to policymakers, it is also a most natural specification of a neutral monetary policy (that's why it was recommended, of course). Since the KMG model treats government spending and tax collections in a similar vein, the government sector as a whole, while being present in the model, behaves in a neutral manner. It is only the agents in the private sector that react to disequilibrium, so the KMG model is seen to study the private sector in a kind of vacuum. It makes sense to begin with such a theoretical construct in order to get an understanding of the basic stabilizing and destabilizing forces in the economy.

Moreover, if we subsequently reconsider the same effects, their strength and their direction, in the KMGT model and compare them to the effects in the KMG model, we get a better understanding of the general validity of these effects, on the one hand, and of the scope for an active monetary policy in the form of Taylor rules on the other.

After discussing the concept and estimation results of the Taylor rule, chapter 8 first seeks to reveal its logic and its stabilizing potential in a more elementary setting, with and without interest rate smoothing. We therefore temporarily leave the KMG framework altogether and put forward four low-dimensional prototype models in continuous time, consisting of an IS relationship, an accelerationist price Phillips curve and a version of a Taylor rule. Subsequently, an estimated quarterly 'backward-looking' model is studied. Originally put forward by Rudebusch and Svensson, it is well known in the literature and can be viewed as a discrete-time extension of the fourth of the prototype models with various lags. As they should be, the results from a numerical stability analysis of this ten-dimensional system are very compatible with the stability properties of the prototype models. As the Rudebusch–Svensson model is linear and the estimated parameters imply stability, demand and supply shocks serve to keep the economy going. For later comparison with our KMGT model, we note the most important dynamic properties, including the features of an impulse-response function.

An appendix sketches the kinds of problems that arise if such a backward-looking model is turned into a (hybrid) New-Keynesian 'forward-looking' model with the accompanying rational expectations hypothesis. Besides a compact introduction as to how linear rational expectations models can be treated, the appendix can be viewed as substantiating our evaluation of the New-Keynesian models in the methodological subsection 1.1.1, to the effect that 'the nature of the solution procedures ... makes it very difficult, if not impossible, to understand the dynamic linkages and feedbacks' in the economy.

Chapter 9 returns to KMG and incorporates the Taylor rule into it. The mathematical analysis in the KMGT model established in this way is more limited than in the KMG model. In particular, we find that a loss of stability as a parameter varies is no longer necessarily associated with a Hopf bifurcation.

For the numerical analysis the estimated policy coefficients of the Rudebusch–Svensson model for the Taylor rule are adopted (suitably adjusted to our continuous-time version). The numerical parameters from the calibration of the KMG model are maintained except for the coefficients of the nonlinear investment function (and one other parameter). Resetting them in an appropriate way makes the steady state unstable, and the system again generates endogenous, bounded and persistent oscillations with very similar cyclical statistics as in the KMG base scenario. In addition, we also consider an alternative set of investment coefficients that stabilize the steady state. Augmenting this system by demand and supply shocks comparable to those in the Rudebusch–Svensson model, the KMGT model can be more directly related to the Rudebusch–Svensson model and its dynamic properties. The richer structure of KMGT indeed pays off, in that some of its features prove to be more satisfactory than in that reference model.

Incidentally, this section also demonstrates that cyclical behaviour in KMG and KMGT is not necessarily dependent on an unstable equilibrium and extrinsic nonlinearities in some behavioural function(s). It can be generated (and match the data) just as well as in the orthodox business cycle models by employing the Frisch paradigm – i.e. imposing random shocks on an otherwise stable system.

After thus calibrating the KMGT model, we study the effect of changes in the three policy coefficients of the Taylor rule, in both the stable and unstable cases. Of course, we are also interested in the stability effects of the behavioural parameters of the private sector. In the end, we again arrive at a succinct characterization of these parameters as stabilizing, destabilizing or ambiguous. Finally, they are compared to the same characterization for the KMG model.

This brief overview of KMG and KMGT has summarized the positive results we reach. We will not conceal the fact that the properties of our model, even if the present framework is basically accepted, are not in every respect perfect, which is not too surprising since the dynamic feedbacks it takes into account are still limited. In particular, we would have liked more robustness in the variations of two or three parameters. To uncover more about these imperfections, however, the reader will have to investigate the fine detail of our analysis.

Part I

Textbook Approaches

2   AS-AD growth theory: a complete analysis of the textbook model

2.1   Introduction

As indicated in the previous overview chapter, the hierarchy of disequilibrium growth theories discussed in this book starts with a supply-side model at a textbook level, which has originally been put forward by Sargent (1979, 1987, chap. 5). Being rooted in the neoclassical synthesis and conventional AS-AD growth theory, it is a prototype model that integrates into a consistent whole what has been – and still is – regarded by many economists as being representative of Keynesian macroeconomic theory. It can, in particular, be considered a first complete Keynesian model, insofar as it includes dynamic interactions between all three of the main market groups: the markets for goods and labour, and financial markets.

The model ensemble is impressive in its purposeful and parsimonious design. However, although the building blocks are most elementary, Sargent's subsequent investigation of the resulting dynamic system remains incomplete and inconclusive. Besides slightly extending Sargent's framework, the present chapter identifies what is missing in his treatment and sets out to provide a full analysis of the local dynamics of this model.[1]

While the models in the chapters to follow are more demand-oriented and also, as we believe, in many respects more satisfactory, it is nevertheless useful to begin with a careful study of Sargent's contribution. The reason is that his system already exhibits a variety of properties that will later be encountered in our more advanced model variants as well. Because of the lower dimensionality of Sargent's model, the feedback and propagation effects can be better isolated here, and the dynamic phenomena are easier to recognize and to understand. Thus, Sargent's model is an important and, in setup and dynamic properties, extremely

---

[1] The chapter draws on Franke (1992a). By comparison, this journal article is much more compact in its presentation and deals only with Sargent's original and simpler version. In addition, the present numerical analysis is entirely new.

stimulating forerunner to what we consider a proper Keynesian theory of economic fluctuations and growth.

The model that Sargent advances can be seen in the tradition of Keynes–Wicksell models.[2] This type of model possesses five crucial characteristics:

(1) the separation of the acts of investment and savings decisions;
(2) the explicit consideration of an interest-bearing financial asset;
(3) the stock of capital is endogenously determined and growing over time;
(4) the inflation rate is also an endogenous variable; and
(5) the rate of monetary expansion is a control variable.

The formulation of Sargent distinguishes itself by the following additional features:

(6) continuous temporary equilibrium on the goods and financial markets;
(7) full employment of the capital stock – that is, firms are always on their supply curve and the marginal productivity principle for labour applies;
(8) the employment of labour is determined by these output decisions and so will generally differ from the level of labour supply;
(9) the rise of nominal wages is governed by an expectations-augmented Phillips curve;
(10) the price level and, *a fortiori*, the rate of inflation are determined by the marginal productivity principle for labour and goods market equilibrium; and
(11) expectations of inflation are formed adaptively.

In addition, we extend this framework by including Harrod-neutral exogenous technological progress and by mixing the adaptive expectations with regressive expectations. With a suitable notation, the first point leaves the laws of motion unaffected. The second point is a modest step in the direction of more appropriate expectation formation mechanisms.

The long-run equilibrium notion of the model has classical properties and supports the basic tenet of monetarist theory, according to which the growth rate of money supply is the main determinant of price inflation and the evolution of the 'real economy' is fully determined by 'real factors'. However, allowing for disequilibrium and the agents' gradual

---

[2] Cf. Stein (1982, pp. 19–22, 163, 191), while the term 'Keynes–Wicksell' itself was introduced in Stein (1969). Stein inspired and actually did most of the work along these lines. In some details, however, there are significant differences between the formulation of Sargent and the relationships studied by Stein over the years.

responses to it poses the problem of the stability of this steady-state position. In sketching the dynamics that set in after the steady state has been disturbed by a sudden increase in the stock of money, Sargent identifies movements of output and the interest rate back to the steady state, but he also observes an overshooting phenomenon and the possibility of cyclical behaviour resulting from it. At this point he stops the analysis and just postulates, by way of an (implicit) assumption, that the cycles will eventually die out.

This optimism concerning stability is difficult to comprehend since a number of less elaborated dynamic Keynesian models developed around the same time had already clearly demonstrated that stability cannot be taken for granted. More specifically, these models had shown that the high speed at which the expected rate of inflation adjusts to current inflation is strongly destabilizing.[3] As a matter of fact, it will be found that in Sargent's model the adjustment speed plays a similar role, while, as may be expected, regressive expectations have a stabilizing influence. We will also have more to say on the conditions giving rise to cyclical dynamics.

The remainder of this chapter is organized as follows. Section 2 introduces the growth model, which originally refers to level variables. To prepare the grounds for a mathematical analysis, it is reformulated in intensive form in section 3. Section 4 sets up the steady-state position, gives the (as it is conveniently called) IS-LM analysis and completes the formulation of section 3 by making sure that the actual rate of inflation is well defined. In this way the model is reduced to three state variables, the motions of which are governed by three differential equations. Section 5 presents the local stability analysis, which is supplemented in section 6 by a numerical investigation. For a better understanding of the inherent stabilizing and destabilizing tendencies, section 7 singles out three basic feedback loops. These mechanisms and their relative strength in generating cyclical behaviour are illustrated by a dynamic simulation of the system in section 8. Section 9 concludes.

2.2   The modelling equations

Input-output relationships in the production sector are described by a standard neoclassical production function with exogenous, purely labour-augmenting technical progress. Thus, let K denote the stock of fixed capital and L employment, and let z^o represent the current state

---

[3] For example, a result of this type has been found in the generalized Tobin models studied by Hadjimichalakis (1971), Benhabib and Miyao (1981) and Hayakawa (1984), or in the Tobin-Buiter model simulated by Smith (1980).

of technology – i.e. a trend term of labour productivity, such that $z^o L$ is labour input in efficiency units.[4] Y being total output, the production function reads

$$Y = F(K, z^o L) \qquad (2.1)$$

Certainly, $F_K = \partial F/\partial K > 0$, $F_L = \partial F/\partial(z^o L) > 0$, $F_{KK} < 0$, $F_{LL} < 0$ (the latter in obvious notation).

On this basis, the textbook approach follows Keynes in that it accepts the first fundamental postulate of the classical theory of employment. That is, paraphrasing Keynes (1936, p. 17), the 'vital fact' is not disputed that, 'in a given state of organisation, equipment and technique, the real wage earned by a unit of labour has a unique (inverse) correlation with the volume of employment'. More precisely, 'the wage is equal to the marginal product of labour' (p. 5). With technical progress, real wages are to be deflated by the trend term of labour productivity, so that the marginal productivity principle for labour takes the form

$$F_L(K, z^o L) = (w/p)/z^o \qquad (2.2)$$

Even if (2.2) is an elementary and well-established formulation, the relationship between the variables deserves a closer look. The classical interpretation is that, besides capital K and the state of technology z^o, the price level p and the nominal wage w are historically given in the short period. Eq. (2.2) then determines the demand for labour L and via (2.1) the level of production Y, as it is the first-order condition for maximizing short-run profits, $pF(K, z^o L) - wL$, with respect to the employment of labour.

This point of view implies that the price level is responsible for bringing about temporary equilibrium on the output market, while firms remain continuously on the aggregate supply curve (2.2). The consequence is explicitly pointed out by Sargent (1987, p. 58) in his discussion of the ultra-short-run adjustments on the goods market. However, as it turns out, there is no component of real demand that depends on the price level directly; p enters only indirectly through the interest rate in

---

[4] Strictly speaking, labour productivity is specified as output per working hour. However, in this book variations in hours worked per labourer are neglected, so that L (number of workers employed) can be identified with L^h (total working hours per year), and the same holds true for labour productivity and labour supply. That z^o is indeed a trend level of labour productivity follows from the linear homogeneity of the production function. Dividing through by $z^o L$ and rearranging terms yields $Y/L = z^o F(K/z^o L, 1)$ in eq. (2.1) below, where the argument $K/z^o L$ solely reflects substitution effects (the ratio will be constant on a steady-state growth path).

investment demand, which, in response to adjustments on the money market, varies with real money balances M/p. In our opinion, grounding the notion of market clearing on these conceptually weak links between goods demand and prices is not fully satisfactory, which would become even more apparent in disequilibrium extensions of the model that allow for sluggish price reactions.

On the other hand, according to the usual Keynesian IS interpretation the goods market is cleared through adjustments in output Y, where in the simple textbook treatments the price level is fixed. In this perspective, eq. (2.2) could be viewed as endogenizing p by reversing the classical causality. That is to say, given w, L and therefore Y, (2.2) serves to determine the price level. The problem is, on the basis of what rationale, as a first-order condition for what maximization problem, should firms set prices in this way? These sceptical remarks are put forward here to indicate our desire for a more convincing price theory. In the present chapter, however, we still work with the standard formulation (2.2), in whatever interpretation, and postpone the issue of alternative pricing rules until later.

In any case, it is assumed that the demand for labour deriving from (2.1) or (2.2) can always be realized. The terms 'employment' and 'labour demand' can therefore be used interchangeably.

The next four equations give the components of real demand and a simple rule for tax collections:

$$C = (1 - s_h)[Y + iB/p - \delta K - T], \quad 0 < s_h < 1 \qquad (2.3)$$

$$I = f_I[F_K(K, z^o L) - \delta - (i - \pi)] \cdot K, \quad f_I' > 0 \qquad (2.4)$$

$$G = \gamma K \qquad (2.5)$$

$$T = \theta K + iB/p \qquad (2.6)$$

Neglecting wealth and direct interest rate effects, consumption in (2.3) increases proportionately with a proxy for real disposable income: iB/p are real interest payments to households, i being the nominal rate of interest and B government fixed-price bonds outstanding (their price being normalized at unity); δ is the rate of capital depreciation, T real taxes, and s_h households' average propensity to save. The argument in the (net) investment demand schedule in (2.4), where π is expected price inflation, can be interpreted as being close to Tobin's q (i.e., average q; see Sargent, 1987, pp. 11–14). Alternatively, since with eq. (2.2) the identity $(pY - wL - \delta pK)/pK = F_K - \delta$ holds true,[5] investment decisions

---

[5] By virtue of Euler's Theorem on homogeneous functions together with eq. (2.2), one has $Y = F_K K + F_L z^o L = F_K K + (w/p)L$, from which the identity easily follows.

of firms can be seen as comparing the rate of profit with the (expected) real interest rate. Eqs. (2.5) and (2.6) state that government expenditures as well as real taxes net of interest payments remain in a fixed proportion to the capital stock ($\gamma, \theta \geq 0$). These specifications are made for convenience. In particular, the lump-sum taxes in (2.6) allow Sargent to eliminate bonds from the stage again, which by saving one dynamic state variable will simplify the analysis considerably.

Eqs. (2.7) and (2.8) formulate the conditions for the clearing of goods and financial markets. M in eq. (2.8) is the money supply controlled by the monetary authorities; the right-hand side of (2.8) is an ordinary money demand function.

$$Y = C + I + \delta K + G \tag{2.7}$$

$$M = pYf_m(i), \quad f'_m < 0 \tag{2.8}$$

Eqs. (2.1) to (2.8) constitute a temporary equilibrium position of the economy, which is brought about by variations in eight variables: output, Y; employment, L; consumption, C; investment, I; government spending, G; real taxes, T; the price level, p; and the nominal interest rate, i. The temporary equilibrium depends on a number of other variables, which are predetermined in the short period and change only from one short period to another, so to speak. Correspondingly, the temporary equilibrium is shifted when the statically exogenous, or dynamic, variables are moving. These are: the state of technology, z^o; the capital stock, K; money balances, M; the nominal wage rate, w; and expected inflation, π. In addition, the supply of labour, L^s, has to be considered since the employment rate feeds back on wages. The evolution of the dynamic variables, formulated in continuous time, is governed by the following set of differential equations:

$$\hat{z}^o = g_z \tag{2.9}$$

$$\hat{L}^s = g_\ell \tag{2.10}$$

$$\hat{M} = g_m \tag{2.11}$$

$$\dot{K} = I \tag{2.12}$$

$$\hat{w} = \pi + g_z + f_w(L/L^s), \quad f_w(1) = 0, f'_w > 0 \tag{2.13}$$

$$\dot{\pi} = \beta_\pi[\kappa_\pi(\hat{p} - \pi) + (1 - \kappa_\pi)(\pi^o - \pi)], \quad 0 \leq \kappa_\pi \leq 1 \tag{2.14}$$

$$\pi^o = g_m - g_\ell - g_z \tag{2.15}$$

According to (2.9) and (2.10), technology and labour supply grow at exogenous and constant rates. Eq. (2.11) postulates a simple Friedmanian policy rule that keeps the money supply on a steady growth path at a constant rate, g_m. We take this assumption as an expression of neutral monetary policy, so that the stabilizing and destabilizing tendencies we will find can, basically, be attributed to the private sector.

Equation (2.12) incorporates the capacity effect of investment expenditures, by keeping track of the resulting change in the capital stock. Nominal wage adjustments are described by (2.13), which is an expectations-augmented Phillips curve. The key variable is the employment rate L/L^s, where employment at $L/L^s = 1$ is to be understood not as maximal employment but as 'normal' employment. Thus, as has already been indicated above, $L > L^s$ is a viable situation for some time.[6] Since this puts an upward pressure on wages, it will be expected that overemployment will be gradually reduced after a while, which, however, must turn out to be a property of the model in its entirety. Similarly the other way round, when unemployment $L < L^s$ reigns. At normal employment, $L/L^s = 1$, nominal wages increase in step with expected inflation and technological progress. Including also trend productivity growth g_z as a reference term in the Phillips curve makes it possible that the share of wages in national income will remain constant in a long-run equilibrium.

Though all the building blocks are firmly rooted in the textbook literature, we would like to emphasize a certain dissonance in the design of the wage-price sector. It should be noted that wages and prices are treated on an unequal footing: the wage rate is a dynamic variable that changes from one short period to another but remains fixed over the short period itself, whereas the price level is a statically endogenous variable that is determined within the short period. (The adjustment concepts would be brought more clearly to the fore in a discrete-time setting.) This observation might at present be deemed of secondary importance, and the uneasiness we express just an aesthetic and hypersensitive feeling. It will, however, be seen later that the different treatment of wages and prices could give rise to somewhat peculiar features in the reactions of the rate of inflation (see chapter 2, section 4, below).

The last dynamic variable is the expected rate of inflation. The basic idea of eq. (2.14) is borrowed from Groth (1988, p. 254). Here the revisions of π are a combination of two rules with weighting factor κ_π, where the adjustments take place at a general speed of adjustment β_π. The polar case $\kappa_\pi = 1$ represents adaptive expectations. After the intellectual triumph of the rational expectations hypothesis, working with this principle has become something of a heresy. However, in a

---

[6] If, conforming to footnote 4, L and L^s are conceived in working hours, this situation may also mean overtime work for the already employed.

disequilibrium context there are a number of theoretical and empirical arguments that demonstrate that adaptive expectations make more sense than is usually attributed to them (see Flaschel et al., 1997, pp. 149–62; or, more extensively, Franke, 1999). The other extreme case $\kappa_\pi = 0$ is a regressive mechanism. In a growth equilibrium, the growth rate of the real sector would be given by the population growth rate plus the rate of technological progress. Subtracting them from the growth rate of money balances yields the equilibrium rate of inflation, here denoted as π^o in eq. (2.15). Similarly to fundamentalist traders on speculative asset markets, the public may perceive a certain tendency of actual inflation to return to that value. Taken on its own, each principle ($\kappa_\pi = 0$ or $\kappa_\pi = 1$) appears rather mechanical. A combination of them, $0 < \kappa_\pi < 1$, is a first step, still at a very elementary or introductory level, towards a greater flexibility in modelling the formation of macroeconomic expectations.

Eqs. (2.1) to (2.15) make up the dynamic model that is to be investigated in this chapter. It has, however, to be noted that these equations do not yet form a well-defined mathematical system. The problem is actual inflation $\hat{p}$ in eq. (2.14). While the level of p can be readily determined within the temporary equilibrum part (2.1)–(2.8) as a function of some other variables, this is much more complicated for its instantaneous rate of change. Preparations for solving the problem are made in the next section, among other things; the solution itself is presented in the section after it.

2.3   The model in intensive form

For further analysis, the model has to be reformulated in intensive form by suitably scaling down the level variables, which are growing in the long run. In this way an equivalent system of differential equations is set up with the property that a stationary point of it represents the balanced growth path of the original economy. The present section takes the first steps in this direction. In particular, some equations are substituted into others, such that the temporary equilibrium of eqs. (2.1) to (2.8) is more succinctly described by two equations resembling the familiar IS-LM equations. In addition, we indicate, in a preliminary way, the three dynamic variables and their laws of motion to which the entire system (2.1)–(2.15) can finally be reduced.

To begin with, let $y = Y/K$ be the output–capital ratio and $\ell = z^o L/K$ labour intensity in efficiency units. By virtue of its linear homogeneity, the production function (2.1) can be rewritten as

$$y = f_y(\ell) := F(1, \ell) = F(1, z^o L/K) \qquad (2.16)$$

with derivatives $f_y'(\ell) > 0$, $f_y''(\ell) < 0$.[7] Reverse the dependency in (2.16) and let $\ell = \ell(y)$ denote the inverse function of f_y, which means $\ell = \ell(y)$ if and only if $y = f_y(\ell)$. From the inverse function theorem one has

$$\ell'(y) = 1/f_y'(\ell(y)) > 0 \qquad (2.17)$$

For later use we also compute the second derivative of the labour intensity function, which is also positive:

$$\ell''(y) = -f_y''(\ell(y))\ell'(y)/[f_y'(\ell(y))]^2 > 0 \qquad (2.18)$$

Since, as explicitly stated in the previous footnote, $F_L(K, z^oL) = f_y'(\ell)$, the marginal productivity condition for labour in eq. (2.2) now reads $1/\ell'(y) = (w/p)/z^o$. In the next section we will have recourse to its solution for the price level,

$$p = (w/z^o)\ell'(y) \qquad (2.19)$$

Regarding the marginal product of capital, note that $F_K(K, z^oL) = \partial F(K, z^oL)/\partial K = \partial[KF(1, z^oL/K)]/\partial K = \partial[Kf_y(z^oL/K)]/\partial K = f_y(\ell)$ $+K \cdot f_y'(z^oL/K) \cdot (-z^oL/K^2)$. Thus,

$$F_K(K, z^oL) = \alpha(y) := y - \ell(y)f_y'(\ell(y)) \qquad (2.20)$$

For the numerical analysis in sections 6 and 8 below, we add that, if F is Cobb–Douglas, $F = AK^\alpha(z^oL)^{1-\alpha}$ and $\alpha = \text{const.}$, the expression $\alpha(y)$ in (20) simplifies to $\alpha(y) = \alpha \cdot y$ (A is just a scaling factor). Taking (2.17) and the remark on the sign of f_y'' in (2.16) into account, the function $\alpha(\cdot)$ can be shown to be increasing in y:

$$\alpha'(y) = -\ell(y)f_y''(\ell(y))\ell'(y) > 0 \qquad (2.21)$$

We are therefore ready to turn to the temporary equilibrium on the goods market and describe it in intensive form. Using (2.5), substituting (2.6) into (2.3) and (2.20) into (2.4), and dividing (2.7) through K leads to the condition

$$y = (1 - s_h)[y - \theta - \delta] + f_I[\alpha(y) - \delta - (i - \pi)] + \delta + \gamma \qquad (2.22)$$

---

[7] Differentiating both sides of the identity $F(K, z^oL) = K \cdot F(1, z^oL/K)$ with respect to labour L gives $F_L(K, z^oL) \cdot z^o = K \cdot F_L(1, z^oL/K) \cdot (z^o/K) = F_L(1, \ell) \cdot z^o$; hence $f_y'(\ell) = F_L(1, \ell) = F_L(K, z^oL) > 0$. The negative sign of the second derivative follows from $f_y''(\ell) = dF_L(1, \ell)/d\ell = F_{LL}(1, \ell) < 0$.

As it is written, (2.22) looks like an ordinary IS equation with $y = Y/K$ as the market-clearing variable (i.e. Y varies and K remains fixed in the short period). In particular, with real balances in the consumption function being neglected, the price level does not show up. Recall, however, the underlying marginal productivity principle for labour and the brief discussion on the causality in eq. (2.2) in the preceding section. If equality in (2.22) were supposed to be brought about by variations of Y, and p only to adjust to its changes in a second step such as to satisfy (2.2), then the rationale for this pricing rule was already said to be an open question. It therefore seems necessary to consider p as the market-clearing variable in (2.22). In this version, y (or Y, respectively) must be regarded as a function of p – that is, $y = y(p)$ is determined by eqs. (2.2) (which determines L) and (2.1) (which subsequently determines Y). This is, in fact, the aforementioned treatment by Sargent (1987, p. 58).

These interpretational problems notwithstanding, it facilitates the analysis of the model if the goods market equilibrium is dealt with in the form of eq. (2.22), where y is determined first and p, via (2.19), only afterwards. Interestingly, in his later presentation of the dynamic Keynesian model in chapter 5 of his book, Sargent (1987, p. 115) follows the same procedure and does not even mention his previous theoretical underpinning of the market-clearing process.

Once the role of y in the short-run analysis is accepted, money market equilibrium can be represented in an LM-like fashion. In order to express it in intensive form, we define the auxiliary variable

$$x_m := z^o M/wK \tag{2.23}$$

Usually, at this point, a variable such as $m = M/pK$ is introduced and then used as a dynamic state variable (in fact, m will show up in the subsequent chapters). Reference to m is purposeful if the price level is driven by a dynamic law. In the present chapter, however, p is directly and, so to speak, statically determined by eq. (2.19), so that m would become $m = z^o M/w\ell'(y)K = x_m/\ell'(y)$. Since y, as part of a temporary equilibrium solution, will itself be a function of other variables, it would be quite cumbersome to set up a differential equation for m. Neglecting the term $\ell'(y)$ in the specification of a dynamic monetary variable and, instead, working with x_m will turn out much more convenient in this respect.

Dividing (2.8) by the capital stock, substituting (2.19) for p and rearranging terms, the clearing of the money market can now be reformulated as

$$x_m = y\ell'(y)f_m(i) \tag{2.24}$$

The temporary equilibrium part (2.1)–(2.8) is thus characterized by a pair (y, i) of the output–capital ratio and the interest rate that fulfills eqs. (2.22) and (2.24). Though conceptually not fully warranted, (2.22) and (2.24) may be termed the model's IS and LM equations, for convenience. They depend on two statically exogenous variables: the expected rate of inflation, π, and the auxiliary variable, x_m.

Next, the dynamic part (2.9)–(2.15) of the model has to be suitably accommodated. The expectation mechanism for π can be taken over unaltered as specified in (2.14). A description of the motions of x_m, however, needs to refer to a third variable, namely $k^s = K/z^o L^s$, fixed capital per head of (in efficiency units) labour supply. k^s enters the scene through the employment rate $L/L^s = (z^o L/K)(K/z^o L^s) = \ell(y)k^s$ in the Phillips curve (2.13), which in turn appears in the logarithmic differentiation of x_m, via $\hat{x}_m = \hat{z}^o + \hat{M} - \hat{w} - \hat{K}$. The evolution of k^s itself is given by $\hat{k}^s = \hat{K} - \hat{z}^o - \hat{L}^s$. In sum, using (2.9) to (2.14) in combination with (2.4) and (2.20), the three dynamic variables k^s, x_m and π obey the following laws of motion:

$$\hat{k}^s = f_l[\alpha(y) - \delta - (i - \pi)] - g_z - g_\ell \tag{2.25}$$

$$\hat{x}_m = g_m - \pi - f_w[\ell(y)k^s] - f_l[\alpha(y) - \delta - (i - \pi)] \tag{2.26}$$

$$\dot{\pi} = \beta_\pi[\kappa_\pi(\hat{p} - \pi) + (1 - \kappa_\pi)(\pi^o - \pi)] \tag{2.27}$$

where it has to be taken into account that y and i are the IS-LM solutions, $y = y(x_m, \pi)$, $i = i(x_m, \pi)$, of conditions (2.22) and (2.24). In particular, it is only through this channel that the monetary variable x_m feeds back on the motions of the system.

For the special case of purely regressive expectations, $\kappa_\pi = 0$, eqs. (2.25) to (2.27) are obviously a well-defined set of differential equations. In order to show that the same holds true in the general case incorporating adaptive expectations, $\kappa_\pi > 0$, a functional relationship still has to be established between the three state variables and the realized rate of inflation, such that $\hat{p} = \hat{p}(k^s, x_m, \pi)$. Obviously, it should be derived from eq. (2.19). In the present, continuous-time framework this is, however, a somewhat lengthy procedure, which, to be exact, requires an analysis of the IS-LM equilibria. These topics are dealt with in the next section.[8]

---

[8] The questions of what the state variables of a reduced and well-defined dynamic system are and how they determine actual inflation $\hat{p}$ are totally missing in the treatment by Sargent (1979, 1987). The shortcoming has previously been pointed out by Flaschel (1985, p. 139), together with a brief proposal of how to address the problem.

2.4   IS-LM analysis and completion of the dynamic system

Before turning to the temporary equilibrium analysis and the determination of the rate of inflation, it is appropriate to set up the steady-state position of the economy. Its existence and uniqueness is straightforward and can be demonstrated in a number of successive steps. The steady-state values of the variables are denoted by a superscript 'o'.

(1) Setting the right-hand side of (2.25) equal to zero gives the equilibrium growth rate of the real sector, $g^o = (I/K)^o = (f_I)^o = g_z + g_\ell$.

(2) Solving the IS equation (2.22) for the steady-state value of the output–capital ratio yields $y^o = [g^o + \gamma + \delta - (1 - s_h)(\theta + \delta)]/s_h$.

(3) Logarithmic differentiation of (2.19) provides us with $\hat{p}^o = \hat{w} - \hat{z}^o$. Substituting this in $0 = \hat{x}_m = \hat{z}^0 + \hat{M}^o - \hat{w}^o - \hat{K}^o$ and taking account of specification (2.15) leads to $\hat{p}^o = g_m - g^o = \pi^o$.

(4) Setting (2.27) equal to zero, one subsequently makes sure that expected inflation in the steady state is in fact given by π^o as defined in (2.15).

(5) From (2.26) and (2.15) we get $0 = g_m - \pi^o - (f_w)^o - g^o = -(f_w)^o$; hence, the argument of f_w is equal to unity, which in turn implies $(k^s)^o = 1/\ell(y^o)$.

(6) The equilibrium real rate of interest, $(i - \pi)^o$, is determined (possibly implicitly so) as the solution of the investment equation $g^o = (f_I)^o = f_I[\alpha(y^o) - \delta - (i - \pi)^o]$. It is unique since the function $f_I(\cdot)$ is strictly increasing. The nominal interest rate is then obtained as $i^o = \pi^o + (i - \pi)^o$.

(7) Finally, the steady-state value of the auxiliary variable x_m is directly given by (2.24), $x_m^o = y^o \ell'(y^o) f_m(i^o)$.

It goes without saying that the parameters and the shapes of the functions involved are assumed to give rise, in this way, to economically meaningful values.

For the following representation of the inflation rate to go through without further qualifications, the analysis must be confined to the vicinity of the steady-state position. Correspondingly, we also consider the IS and LM curves in such a neighbourhood – that is, the geometric locus of the pairs (y, i) satisfying (2.22) and (2.24), respectively, with respect to given values of x_m and π.

First, it is readily verified that the LM curve has a positive slope; by virtue of (2.18) a rise in y increases the expression $y\ell'(y)$ in (2.24), so the interest rate i has to increase, too, in order to restore equality in (2.24). Second, whether an increase in the interest rate causes the IS output–capital ratio to rise or fall depends on the sign of the term $s_h - \alpha' f_I'$

(differentiate (2.22) with respect to y), which is generally ambiguous since $\alpha' > 0$ by (21). We follow Sargent (1987, p. 115) and work with the familiar downward-sloping IS curve. Hence the following assumption.

Assumption 1
Evaluated at the steady-state values, the responsiveness in fixed investment is so restrained that $f_I' < s_h/\alpha'$.

It is also easily checked that a *ceteris paribus* increase in $x_m = z^o M/wK$ produces a downward shift in the LM curve. Note that in the short-run, with w, z^o and K fixed, this change is tantamount to a rise in the money supply. Since wealth effects are absent in the goods demand functions, the IS curve remains unaffected and the point of intersection of the IS and LM curves shifts south-east (y on the horizontal, i on the vertical axis). Regarding the other statically exogenous variable and, in particular, its impact on investment demand, an increase in the expected rate of inflation π here has the opposite effect of a rise in the interest rate. This means that the IS curve shifts upward, while this time the LM curve remains unaffected. Thus, the point of intersection of the two curves shifts north-east. Besides, it can be shown analytically that the interest rate rises less than *pari passu* with π, so that the real interest rate $i - \pi$ falls as expected inflation increases. Despite the conceptual problems with the marginal productivity principle that were indicated above, all this is much in line with the comparative-static exercises in an ordinary IS-LM framework with a fixed price level. The results are summarized in the following proposition.

Lemma 1
Let Assumption 1 apply. Then, for all x_m and π close to their steady-state values x_m^o and π^o, a (locally) unique solution $y = y(x_m, \pi)$ and $i = i(x_m, \pi)$ exists with (continuous) partial derivatives

$$\partial y/\partial x_m > 0, \quad \partial i/\partial x_m < 0, \quad \partial y/\partial \pi > 0, \quad 0 < \partial i/\partial \pi < 1.$$

Proof: Referring to eqs. (2.22) and (2.24), define the two functions F_1 and F_2 by

$$F_1 = F_1(y, i, \pi) := -s_h y + f_I - (1 - s_h)(\theta + \delta) + \gamma$$

$$F_2 = F_2(i, y, x_m) := y\ell'(y)f_m(i) - x_m$$

The IS output–capital ratio $y_{IS} = y_{IS}(i, \pi)$ is given by that value of y which, with respect to i and π given, brings about $F_1(y, i, \pi) = 0$. Similarly, the LM interest rate $i_{LM} = i_{LM}(y, x_m)$ is given by that value of i

which, given y and x_m, brings about $F_2(i, y, x_m) = 0$. The partial derivatives of y_{IS} and i_{LM} can be computed by making use of the implicit function theorem in dimension $n = 1$,

$$\partial y_{IS}/\partial v = -(\partial F_1/\partial v)/(\partial F_1/\partial y), \quad \text{where } v = i, \pi$$

$$\partial i_{LM}/\partial v = -(\partial F_2/\partial v)/(\partial F_2/\partial i), \quad \text{where } v = y, x_m$$

Assumption 1 states that $\partial F_1/\partial y < 0$. It is helpful in the detailed calculations to work with $\eta_{m,i}$ for the expression $-f'_m i/f_m$ which is the interest elasticity of the demand for money, conceived as a positive number.

Then, define the function $F = F(y, x_m, \pi) := F_1[y, i_{LM}(y, x_m), \pi]$ (in the present limited context there will be no confusion with the notation for the production function). Given (x_m, π), a solution $y = y(x_m, \pi)$ of $F = 0$, together with $i = i(x_m, \pi) := i_{LM}[y(x_m, \pi), x_m]$, constitutes an IS-LM equilibrium. The partial derivatives of these functions are again obtained by application of the implicit function theorem.

With $F_y := \partial F/\partial y = \partial F_1/\partial y + (\partial F_1/\partial i)(\partial i_{LM}/\partial y) < 0$, one computes $\partial y/\partial \pi = -(\partial F/\partial \pi)/F_y = -f'_I/F_y > 0$, and $\partial y/\partial x_m = -(\partial F/\partial x_m)/F_y = (i/x_m \eta_{m,i})(\partial y/\partial \pi) > 0$. Subsequently, $\partial i/\partial \pi = (\partial i_{LM}/\partial y)(\partial y/\partial \pi) > 0$. One also easily verifies that $1 - \partial i/\partial \pi = (\partial F_1/\partial y)/F_y > 0$. Lastly, $\partial i/\partial x_m = (\partial i_{LM}/\partial y)(\partial y/\partial x_m) + \partial i_{LM}/\partial x_m = (-i/x_m \eta_{m,i})[1 - \partial i/\partial \pi] < 0$.

$$\text{QED}$$

On the basis of the IS-LM temporary equilibrium functions, we can finally address the problem of the determination of the actual rate of inflation, $\hat{p}$, which enters the differential equation (2.27) for expected inflation (if the coefficient κ_π exceeds zero). To simplify notation, define the functional expressions

$$H_1 = H_1(x_m, \pi) := f_I\{\alpha[y(x_m, \pi)] - \delta - i(x_m, \pi) + \pi\} \qquad (2.28)$$

$$H_2 = H_2(k^s, x_m, \pi) := f_w\{\ell[y(x_m, \pi)] \cdot k^s\} \qquad (2.29)$$

$\hat{p}$ is obtained from differentiating the marginal productivity condition (2.19) with respect to time. Using (2.9), (2.13), (2.26) and (2.27), we get

$$\hat{p} = \hat{w} - \hat{z}^o + \ell''(y)\dot{y}/\ell'(y)$$

$$= \pi + H_2 + \frac{\ell''(y)}{\ell'(y)}\left\{\frac{\partial y}{\partial x_m}\dot{x}_m + \frac{\partial y}{\partial \pi}\dot{\pi}\right\}$$

$$= \pi + H_2 + \frac{\ell''(y)}{\ell'(y)}\left\{\frac{\partial y}{\partial x_m}x_m[g_m - \pi - H_2 - H_1]\right. \qquad (2.30)$$

$$\left. + \frac{\partial y}{\partial \pi}\beta_\pi[\kappa_\pi(\hat{p} - \pi) + (1 - \kappa_\pi)(\pi^o - \pi)]\right\}$$

To solve the equation for $\hat{p}$, define

$$\phi = \phi(\beta_\pi, \kappa_\pi; x_m, \pi) := 1 - \beta_\pi \kappa_\pi \frac{\ell''(y)}{\ell'(y)} \frac{\partial y}{\partial \pi} \qquad (2.31)$$

$$H_3 = H_3(k^s, x_m, \pi)$$

$$:= H_2 + \frac{\ell''(y)}{\ell'(y)} \left[\frac{\partial y}{\partial x_m} x_m (g_m - \pi - H_2 - H_1) \right.$$

$$\left. + \beta_\pi (1 - \kappa_\pi) \frac{\partial y}{\partial \pi} (\pi^o - \pi) \right] \qquad (2.32)$$

where the output y is evaluated at $y = y(x_m, \pi)$. Presupposing that $\phi \neq 0$, the rate of inflation can then be written as

$$\hat{p} = \hat{p}(k^s, x_m, \pi) = \pi + \frac{H_3(k^s, x_m, \pi)}{\phi(\beta_\pi, \kappa_\pi; x_m, \pi)} \qquad (2.33)$$

Equation (2.33) reveals that, mediated by a larger number of economy-wide repercussion effects, actual inflation depends not only on expected inflation, which is fairly natural, but also upon the two parameters κ_π and β_π in the adjustment equation for π, which seems more peculiar. In particular, fix $\kappa_\pi > 0$ and consider a situation with $H_3 > 0$. Since by virtue of (2.17), (2.18) and Lemma 1 the coefficient of $\beta_\pi \kappa_\pi$ in (2.31) is positive, one has $\hat{p} > \pi$ if β_π is low enough. Faster revisions of inflationary expectations, by contrast, switch the sign of ϕ and lead to $\hat{p} < \pi$. Moreover, there is a critical range of parameter values of β_π that lets ϕ nearly vanish and so generates hyperinflation – or 'hyperdeflation', for that matter. But notice that, *ceteris paribus*, this phenomenon subsides again if β_π is further increased. The critical range may, moreover, shift if (x_m, π) varies and with it the terms $\ell'(y)$, $\ell''(y)$, $\partial y / \partial \pi$ in the definition of ϕ. Hence neither the sign nor the size of the difference $\hat{p} - \pi$ is very robust.[9]

The problem with the model's implied theory of inflation is that these features can hardly be explained by any transparent economic mechanism. The reduced-form equation for $\hat{p}$ is just the outcome of several mathematical manipulations. Their formal complications reflect the fact that, in the determination of the rate of inflation, too many effects are

---

[9] It may be mentioned that these effects would be less dramatic in a discrete-time version of the model; say, in a quarterly model. But this observation should only reinforce our uneasiness with the model design.

simultaneously interacting. To be more precise, wages and prices share the property that their rates of change are mutually interdependent: $\hat{w}$ is influenced by expected inflation, and π in turn is influenced by $\hat{p}$ (see eqs. (2.13) and (2.14)); while the price level is proportionally related to the wage level in (2.19), which entails that $\hat{p}$ depends on $\hat{w}$. This kind of interrelationship is a bit complicated but still fully 'tolerable'. What is really significant, however, is the different specifications in which output (in its intensive form) $y = Y/K$ impacts on wage and price inflation. Whereas $\hat{w}$ depends on the *level* of y in $f_w = f_w[\ell(y)k^s]$, price inflation $\hat{p}$ was seen to depend on the *rate of change* of y. As the output–capital ratio is a statically endogenous variable, this conceptual difference instigates very many feedback effects in (2.33) and makes the underlying computations highly interlaced.[10] Equation (2.30) even demonstrated that, in this way, $\hat{p}$ feeds back on itself.

The somewhat strange features of the reduced-form equation (2.33) motivate us in the subsequent chapters to put prices and wages on an equal footing, which will mean that the marginal productivity principle is dropped and $\hat{p}$ is regarded as being governed by a similar type of adjustment mechanism as $\hat{w}$ in (13). Unfortunately, the price of this greater conceptual clarity is that, in the end, an additional state variable comes into being. On the other hand, some important qualitative properties can already be encountered in the present model. So, despite our basic criticism of Sargent's wage-price sector, the model is nevertheless quite useful in other respects. We therefore proceed with the analysis.

After eq. (2.33) has been established, it only remains to substitute $\hat{p}$ in (2.27). Taking account of definitions (2.29)–(2.32), we arrive at the following set of three differential equations as the intensive-form representation of the original equations (2.1) to (2.15):

$$\dot{k}^s = k^s[H_1 - g_z - g_\ell] \tag{2.34}$$

$$\dot{x}_m = x_m[g_m - \pi - H_2 - H_1] \tag{2.35}$$

$$\dot{\pi} = \beta_\pi[\kappa_\pi H_3/\phi + (1 - \kappa_\pi)(\pi^o - \pi)] \tag{2.36}$$

(Evaluation of the terms H_1, H_2, H_3, ϕ is obvious.) System (2.34)–(2.36) is well defined, at least locally in a neighbourhood around the steady state, if $\phi = \phi(\beta_\pi, \kappa_\pi; x_m^o, \pi^o) \neq 0$.

---

[10] It is thus also seen that things would be quite similar if the price theory were less neoclassical and the price level determined by some markup on a term that varies with the level of output.

2.5   Local stability analysis

It has already been intimated that Sargent is much more informal in the presentation of his model than our preceding treatment. He is, nevertheless, able to get some preliminary insights into the working of the model by considering the shifting IS and LM curves in the (y, i)-plane (Sargent, 1987, pp. 117–20). In a simplified version, he first fixes expected inflation at the steady-state level. Assuming that the system is thrown out of equilibrium by a sudden jump in the money supply, he recognizes an 'overshooting' phenomenon in the motions of y and i, which suggests a cyclical dynamics. He subsequently restores eq. (2.14) (in our notation, where $\kappa_\pi = 1$) and thus permits π to respond to the evolution of actual inflation. These additional effects seem to accentuate the overshooting tendencies. The problem of stability, however, is not addressed: Sargent contents himself with the mere supposition that the system is dynamically stable (p. 119). This leads him to state that 'the final effect of the once-and-for-all jump in M, once the system has returned to its steady state, is to leave all real variables unaltered and to increase the price level and the money wage proportionately with the money supply'. He summarizes, '[T]hough this model is clearly Keynesian in its momentary or point-in-time behavior, its steady state or long-run properties are 'classical' in the sense that real variables are unaffected by the money supply' (p. 119).

In this section we investigate the margin for such a conclusion to be warranted, at least locally around the equilibrium growth path. It was for just this purpose that Sargent's economy had to be reformulated and transformed to a well-defined dynamic system. A full-fledged stability analysis rests on the Jacobian matrix, $\mathcal{J}$, of eqs. (2.34)–(2.36), evaluated at $((k^s)^o, x_m^o, \pi^o)$. To set it up, we refer to the expressions H_1, H_2, H_3 in (2.28), (2.29) and (2.32) and abbreviate

$$H_{ik} = \partial H_i / \partial k^s, \quad H_{ix} = \partial H_i / \partial x_m, \quad H_{i\pi} = \partial H_i / \partial \pi \qquad (2.37)$$

The fact that all evaluations are at the steady-state values (which will henceforth be understood) facilitates the computations, since it makes several terms in the partial derivatives of the right-hand sides of (2.34)–(2.36) vanish. We get

$$\mathcal{J} = \begin{bmatrix} 0 & k^s H_{1x} & k^s H_{1\pi} \\ -x_m H_{2k} & -x_m(H_{2x} + H_{1x}) & -x_m(1 + H_{2\pi} + H_{1\pi}) \\ \dfrac{\beta_\pi \kappa_\pi}{\phi} H_{3k} & \dfrac{\beta_\pi \kappa_\pi}{\phi} H_{3x} & \beta_\pi \left[\dfrac{\kappa_\pi}{\phi} H_{3\pi} - (1 - \kappa_\pi) \right] \end{bmatrix} \qquad (2.38)$$

The entries in the first two rows are unambiguously signed, as the next lemma asserts. The calculations are straightforward, so a detailed proof can be omitted.

Lemma 2
Suppose that Assumption 1 holds and define

$$\eta_{m,i} := |f'_m(i^o)| i^o / f_m(i^o),$$

the interest elasticity of money demand at the equilibrium rate of interest. Then the partial derivatives of the functional expressions H_1 and H_2 are given by

$$H_{1\pi} = f'_I [\alpha'(\partial y / \partial \pi) + 1 - \partial i / \partial \pi]$$

$$H_{1x} = H_{1\pi} i / x_m \eta_{m,i}$$

$$H_{2\pi} = f'_w \ell'(y) k^s (\partial y / \partial \pi)$$

$$H_{2x} = H_{2\pi} i / x_m \eta_{m,i}$$

$$H_{2k} = f'_w \ell(y)$$

and all of them are positive.

Lemma 2 is already sufficient to handle two special cases. In the first one, we take up Sargent's procedure mentioned above and freeze expected inflation at the equilibrium rate π^o. This dynamics is described by the two differential equations (2.34) and (2.35), the Jacobian of which is given by the upper-left (2×2) submatrix on the diagonal of $\mathcal{J}$. Since it has a negative trace and a positive determinant, local (asymptotic) stability prevails in this truncated system irrespective of the size of the behavioural parameters. In particular, the overshooting phenomenon observed by Sargent is not strong enough to destabilize this economy.

In the second case, eq. (2.36) is revived but expectations are supposed to be purely regressive – i.e. $\kappa_\pi = 0$. This renders entries j_{31} and j_{32} zero in $\mathcal{J}$, while $j_{33} = -\beta_\pi$ on the diagonal. One easily infers the three eigenvalues of $\mathcal{J}$: two of them coincide with those of the two-dimensional special case, which both have negative real parts, while the third eigenvalue equals $-\beta_\pi$. It can thus be concluded that, under regressive inflationary expectations as well, the system is unambiguously locally stable.

Let us then turn to the general case that includes adaptive expectations, $\kappa_\pi > 0$. The most important information to assess stability in the unrestricted system is provided by the sign of the determinant of $\mathcal{J}$.

Though the matrix looks quite complicated at first sight, its determinant is rather uninvolved.

Lemma 3

Suppose that Assumption 1 holds. With respect to $0 < \kappa_\pi \leq 1$, define the following expressions

$$H_4 = H_4(\beta_\pi) := \frac{1 + (1 - \kappa_\pi)H_5\beta_\pi}{1 - \kappa_\pi H_5\beta_\pi} + \frac{1 - \kappa_\pi}{\kappa_\pi}$$

$$H_5 = \frac{\ell''(y)}{\ell'(y)}\frac{\partial y}{\partial \pi}$$

$$\beta_\pi^c = 1/\kappa_\pi H_5.$$

Then

$$\det \mathcal{J} = -k^s x_m H_{1x} H_{2k} \kappa_\pi \beta_\pi H_4(\beta_\pi)$$

and $0 < \beta_\pi < \beta_\pi^c$ entails $\det \mathcal{J} < 0$, while $\det \mathcal{J} > 0$ if $\beta_\pi > \beta_\pi^c$.

Proof: The determinant can be computed by a number of successive elementary row operations: (1) factorize, row by row, k^s, $(-x_m)$, and $\beta_\pi \kappa_\pi / \phi$; (2) add $iH_5/\eta_{m,i}$ times the second row to the third row; (3) subtract the third row from the second row. This leads to $j_{11} = j_{21} = 0$, and steps 2 and 3 leave the value of the determinant unaltered. Expanding the matrix thus obtained by the first column results in the expression given in the lemma.

Differentiating H_4 with respect to β_π and observing that $H_5 > 0$, it is easily checked that $H_4(\cdot)$ is increasing everywhere where the function is defined. Furthermore, $H_4(\beta_\pi) \to \infty$ as β_π approaches β_π^c from below, $H_4(\beta_\pi) \to -\infty$ as β_π approaches β_π^c from above, $H_4(0) = 1/\kappa_\pi$, and $H_4(\beta_\pi) \to 0$ as $\beta_\pi \to \infty$. H_{1x} and H_{2k} being positive by Lemma 2, the second statement of the lemma follows.

QED

The finding that the determinant of $\mathcal{J}$ changes sign as β_π increases beyond the critical value β_π^c (at which the system is not defined) disproves Sargent's stability optimism. Since $\det \mathcal{J} < 0$ is well known to be a necessary stability condition, it is immediately seen that the long-run equilibrium is unstable if inflationary expectations adjust so rapidly that $\beta_\pi > \beta_\pi^c$.

On the other hand, the fact that $\det \mathcal{J} < 0$ and the off-diagonal entries j_{31} and j_{32} in the third row tend to zero as $\beta_\pi \to 0$, in connection with the stability of the truncated two-dimensional system, enables us to draw the quick conclusion that the steady state becomes locally stable then. (Rigorously, this stability is a direct consequence of the more general

'Lemma' that is stated and proved in chapter 4, section 4.) These and the previous results are summarized in the following proposition.

Proposition 1
Under Assumption 1, the following statements hold true.

(1) *The truncated system (2.34), (2.35) with expected inflation frozen at the equilibrium value π^o is locally asymptotically stable.*
(2) *The full system (2.34)–(2.36) is locally asymptotically stable if inflationary expectations are purely regressive, $\kappa_\pi = 0$, or, given $0 < \kappa_\pi \leq 1$, if the adjustments of inflationary expectations are sufficiently slow - i.e. if β_π is sufficiently small.*
(3) *Given $0 < \kappa_\pi \leq 1$, the steady state of system (2.34)–(2.36) is unstable if $\beta_\pi > \beta_\pi^c$ (the latter as defined in Lemma 3).*

Because of Lemma 3 and the inequality $\det \mathcal{J} < 0$ as a necessary stability condition, it was natural to concentrate on variations of the adjustment speed β_π in the stability analysis. Given a positive weight of adaptive expectations, $\kappa_\pi > 0$, the statement of Proposition 1 is, however, limited to high and (sufficiently) low values of β_π, which leaves out an intermediate range. It would, in fact, be quite tedious to provide a full analytical characterization of the regions in the (κ_π, β_π) parameter plane that entail local stability and instability. While we can do this numerically in the next section, here we just point out that, for values β_π falling short of the critical value β_π^c, the steady state may also be unstable. Besides the stability issue, this property is of special interest since it will allow us to infer the existence of cyclical dynamics.

Thus, consider the entry j_{33} of the Jacobian matrix (2.38). Referring to the terms in Lemma 3, the expression $H_{3\pi}$ reads in greater detail,

$$H_{3\pi} = H_{2\pi} - [1 + H_{1\pi} + H_{2\pi}]H_5 i/\eta_{m,i} - \beta_\pi(1 - \kappa_\pi)H_5$$

Lemmata 1 and 2 tell us that the single terms are all positive, hence $H_{3\pi}$ may well also be positive.[11] If, furthermore, $\kappa_\pi = 1$ or close to 1, j_{33} will grow beyond all bounds as β_π approaches β_π^c from below, so that ϕ in (2.31) tends to zero. Since the other diagonal entries are independent of β_π, the trace of $\mathcal{J}$ will eventually become positive, which implies that the equilibrium is unstable. Fixing all parameter values except β_π, it follows that there exists a threshold value β_π^H of this adjustment speed, smaller

---

[11] For example, if κ_π is close to unity, f_w' large enough and f_I' small enough. The latter, in particular, takes care that $\partial y/\partial \pi$ in the definition of H_5 is limited; see the proof of Lemma 1.

than the other critical value β_{π}^c, where with an increase of β_{π} the system changes from being locally convergent to locally divergent.[12]

The significance of this observation derives from the fact that, by virtue of Lemma 3, the determinant of $\mathcal{J}$ is nonzero at $\beta_{\pi} = \beta_{\pi}^H$, and so are the three eigenvalues. There is consequently a pair of conjugate complex eigenvalues of the Jacobian that, as β_{π} rises beyond β_{π}^H, moves from the left half to the right half of the complex plane, crossing the imaginary axis at $\beta_{\pi} = \beta_{\pi}^H$. The third eigenvalue being a negative real number, we can conclude that, for all β_{π} in the vicinity of β_{π}^H, the trajectories of the system will typically display oscillatory behaviour.

The potential for cyclical dynamics is an additional important analytical result for this chapter's Keynes–Wicksell textbook model. Moreover, the variations of the eigenvalues just discussed are also the key condition for a Hopf bifurcation to occur (therefore the superscript H). The corresponding mathematical theorem establishes that, over a certain range of parameter values β_{π} close to β_{π}^H (but generally different from it), even strictly periodic orbits exist. (A precise formulation of the Hopf bifurcation theorem, including its meaning and our view on it, is given in the appendix to this chapter.) We can therefore additionally conclude that the loss of stability that is found as expectations adjust more rapidly is associated with the emergence of persistent but bounded regular cyclical motions of the variables of system (2.34)–(2.36).

Proposition 2
Suppose that $H_{2\pi} > [1 + H_{1\pi} + H_{2\pi}] H_5 i / \eta_{m,i}$ in the steady state. Then for all values κ_{π} sufficiently close to unity there exists a value β_{π}^H of the adjustment speed of inflationary expectations at which system (2.34)–(2.36) undergoes a Hopf bifurcation with respect to variations in β_{π}.

As for a proof it suffices to mention that, according to the discussion of the eigenvalues above, the conditions that are listed in the appendix are obviously satisfied.

It may be added that, for a linear differential equations system, periodic orbits exist only for the bifurcation value itself, though there are infinitely many of them. If the system is nonlinear, there is a whole interval of the varying parameter such that for each such value the corresponding system has one periodic orbit. If, however, the nonlinearities are weak, as (perhaps somewhat surprisingly) proves to be the case in the present economy, then the range of parameter values giving rise to periodic orbits

---

[12] For a slightly simpler economy and the special case $\kappa_{\pi} = 1$, a (in practical terms not very restrictive) condition that ensures the uniqueness of such a β_{π}^H is spelled out in Franke (1992a, p. 250).

will be very narrow. This is one reason why the emergence of strictly periodic orbits from a Hopf bifurcation should not be overemphasized.

Another point is that the version of the Hopf bifurcation theorem to which we refer does not indicate whether the so-called subcritical case prevails – i.e. periodic orbits arise for $\beta_\pi < \beta_\pi^H$ – or whether the supercritical case applies, where periodic orbits arise for $\beta_\pi > \beta_\pi^H$. Given that the third root is negative (at least for β_π close to β_π^H), the periodic orbits would be repelling in the first case and locally attracting in the second case. While these features are certainly of general interest, the condition from which subcriticality and supercriticality could be inferred is extremely complicated. Entering this condition are composed expressions of third-order derivatives of the behavioural functions, which, at least in the present economy, would lack any economic rationale. Moreover, even if we were able to ascertain – numerically – which case prevails, a slight respecification of one or two functions could easily overthrow the previous result. On these grounds we do not consider it worthwhile to enquire any more deeply into the issue of whether the periodic orbits are attracting or repelling.

In sum, the Hopf bifurcation property is here not exploited in full. Instead we content ourselves with the information deriving from it, that over a certain range of the adjustment speeds β_π the economy exhibits cyclical behaviour, at least locally in a neighbourhood of the equilibrium path.

2.6   A numerical stability analysis

While the range of parameter values encompassed by Propositions 1 and 2 is somewhat limited, the scope for local stability vs. instability, and cyclical vs. monotonic behaviour can be further explored by means of a numerical analysis. We start by specifying the aggregate production technology as a Cobb–Douglas function,

$$Y = AK^\alpha (z^o L)^{1-\alpha}, \quad A = y^o \tag{2.39}$$

It is well known that, under the marginal productivity principle for labour, the exponent α represents the profit share. Accordingly, the wage share (in gross income) remains constant, being given by $v = wL/pY = 1 - \alpha$. A is no more than a scaling factor. To simplify some of the formulae in the computational work, it is convenient to set it equal to y^o. In particular, the function $\ell = \ell(y)$ of labour intensity in efficiency units is then $\ell(y) = (y/y^o)^{1/(1-\alpha)}$, so that $\ell(y^o) = 1$ in equilibrium.[13]

---

[13] As the model is set out, we can neglect the minor drawback of this 'normalization' that, in the steady state, where $y = y^o$, actual labour productivity $z = Y/L$ differs from what we designate z^o.

In setting up the steady-state position, care should be exercised that the coefficients and ratios are broadly compatible with the magnitudes empirically observed. We base the steady state on the following numerical values, where the underlying flow variables are measured at annual rates:

$$y^o = 0.70 \quad v^o = 70\% \quad \delta = 9.5\%$$

$$g_z = 2\% \quad g_\ell = 1\%$$

$$\pi^o = 3\% \quad i^o = 5\% \quad (M/pY)^o = 0.20$$

$$(G/Y)^o = 11\% \quad \theta_y := [(T - iB/p)/Y]^o = 10\%$$

To check the data we used the package of empirical time series of the US economy that is provided by Ray C. Fair on his home page.[14] We, in particular, appreciate that it contains a capital stock series of the nonfinancial firm sector. With regard to the output–capital ratio, the ratio of the empirical real magnitudes, Y/K, is in the region of 0.90. The price ratio p_y/p_k of the output and capital goods is, however, systematically different from unity. It remains around 0.75 until the early 1980s and then steadily increases up to around 1 by the end of the 1990s. Correspondingly, the nominal output–capital ratio, $p_y Y/p_k K$, first varies around 0.65 and then steadily increases up to 0.90. On the grounds that in a two- or multi-sectoral version of the model the relevant ratio, in an IS-like equation, for example, would be $p_y Y/p_k K$, we prefer to make reference to the nominal magnitudes and choose an equilibrium value $y^o = 0.70$, which is slightly higher than 0.65.

If employer social security contribution is included in the definition of the wage rate, then $v = wL/pY \approx 0.70$ results as the time average between 1952 and 1998. Insofar as wages are a cost on the part of firms, entering the definition of profits, this is an obvious convention. Insofar as receipts from social insurances at the same time generate demand, it is then implicitly assumed that, in a revolving procedure, these are treated like the other income categories (which are not differentiated in the consumption function).

The physical depreciation rate of the capital stock given by Fair is lower than the value of δ here proposed. However, what Fair calls (nominal) 'capital consumption' in his identity for profits in the firm sector yields a higher ratio when related to the nominal capital stock $p_k K$. In this way we decide on $\delta = 9.5\%$. Note that the equilibrium (gross) rate of return on real capital implied so far is $r^o = (1 - v^o)y^o - \delta = 11.5\%$, which does not appear too unreasonable.

---

[14] The URL (at the time of this chapter being written) is http://fairmodel.econ. yale.edu.

With respect to the velocity of the circulation of money, 0.20 is roughly the time average of M1 to nominal output in the last twenty years, when this ratio was relatively stable (as compared to the steady decline until the end of the 1970s). $g^o = g_z + g_\ell = 3\%$ is the order of magnitude of the average growth rate of real output between 1960 and 1998. $(G/Y)^o = 0.11$ is inferred from the average ratio (again) of nominal government demand to output over the same period (though the ratio varies considerably over different subperiods). The inflation rate, the nominal rate of interest and, especially, the tax rate θ_y are set freehand.

The other parameter and steady-state values are now residually determined. To begin with, we have

$$\alpha = 1 - v^o = 0.30$$

$$\gamma = G/K = (G/Y)^o \cdot y^o = 0.077$$

$$\theta = (T - iB/p)/K = \theta_y \cdot y^o = 0.070$$

$$g_m = \pi^o + g^o = \pi^o + g_z + g_\ell = 6\%$$

The equilibrium value of k^s has already been derived as $(k^s)^o = 1/\ell(y^o)$ in section 2.4, while $\ell(y^o) = 1$ has just been noted. To obtain x_m^o, we use the decomposition $x_m = z^o M/wK = (pY/wL) \cdot (z^o L/K) \cdot (M/pY) = (1/v) \cdot \ell(y) \cdot (M/pY)$. Hence

$$(k^s)^o = 1, \quad x_m^o = 0.286$$

We can then turn to the coefficients in the behavioural functions. The savings propensity s_h in the consumption function (3) can no longer be set at will. It is implied by the previous parameters, since the goods-market-clearing condition has to be taken into account. In detail, divide the condition $Y = C + I + \delta K + G$ by Y and use $(I/Y)^o = g^o(K/Y)^o$, which yields the steady-state consumption ratio $c^o := (C/Y)^o = 1 - (g^o + \delta)/y^o - (G/Y)^o = 0.711$. Dividing (3) by Y gives the relationship $c^o = (1 - s_h)[1 - \theta_y - \delta/y^o]$, from which the public's savings propensity is obtained as

$$s_h = 1 - \frac{c^o}{1 - \theta_y - \delta/y^o} = 1 - \frac{0.711}{0.764} = 0.069$$

It may be noticed that the feasible size of the tax rate θ_y is rather limited, because the denominator must not fall short of c^o.

Besides β_π and κ_π for revising the inflationary expectations in eq. (2.14), three reaction coefficients remain. They are set as follows:

$$\eta_{m,i} = 0.25 \quad f_w' = 0.30 \quad f_I' = 0.20 \tag{2.40}$$

The interest elasticity of money demand is chosen on the basis of the empirical estimates reported in Goldfeld (1976) and the short compilation by Boorman (1976, pp. 328–35). To get a feeling for the slope coefficient of the Phillips curve (13), we consider a 5 per cent increase of the output–capital ratio. With $L/L^s = (z^o L/K) \cdot (K/z^o L^s) = \ell(y) \cdot k^s$, this raises the employment rate from unity up to $(1.05)^{1/(1-\alpha)} = 1.072$ if simultaneous changes in k^s are neglected. The latter is legitimate since the variations in k^s take place at a very low scale.[15] If, furthermore, $f_w(\cdot)$ is a linear function and we have the intuition that, from this source, the nominal wage rate in (2.13) is pushed upward by, say, 2 per cent, then we get the back-of-the-envelope estimate $f'_w \cdot 0.072 = 0.02$ for f'_w – i.e. $f'_w = 0.278$.

Investment reactions with $f'_I = 0.20$ may seem rather sluggish. They are, however, constrained by Assumption 1, $f'_I < s_h/\alpha'$. With the Cobb–Douglas production function, the marginal product of capital in eq. (2.20) is given by $F_K = \alpha(y) = \alpha \cdot y$, so that $\alpha'(y) = \alpha = 0.30$ and the condition reads $f'_I < 0.23$.

Thus, the stage is set to study variations of the parameters β_π and κ_π, where β_π represents the general speed of adjustment in inflationary expectations and κ_π the weight of adaptive expectations vs. regressive expectations. Laying a grid (of sufficiently small size) over the parameter plane, for each pair (β_π, κ_π) of the grid the eigenvalues of the Jacobian matrix (2.38) are computed. The results are summarized in figure 2.1.[16]

First, for each value of κ_π the corresponding critical value $\beta^c_\pi = \beta^c_\pi(\kappa_\pi)$ defined in Lemma 3 is obtained. It is depicted as the outer bold line in figure 2.1. Since we know that (saddle-point) instability prevails if $\beta^c_\pi > \beta^c_\pi(\kappa_\pi)$, it suffices to concentrate on the area to the left of this borderline. The diagram shows that the line $\beta^c_\pi = \beta^c_\pi(\kappa_\pi)$ separates the stable from the unstable case as long as regressive expectations are strong enough, for $0 \leq \kappa_\pi \leq 0.595$. In addition, convergence for $\beta^c_\pi < \beta^c_\pi(\kappa_\pi)$ is always monotonic then, because all eigenvalues of the Jacobian are real.

On the other hand, when more weight is attached to adaptive expectations, $0.60 \leq \kappa_\pi \leq 1.00$, instability can occur to the left of the curve $\beta^c_\pi = \beta^c_\pi(\kappa_\pi)$. It is over this interval of κ_π that Proposition 2 takes effect. Accordingly, for all κ_π in the interval a value $\beta^H_\pi = \beta^H_\pi(\kappa_\pi)$ exists at which, with respect to *ceteris paribus* variations in β_π, the system undergoes a Hopf bifurcation. The value β^H_π is also found to be unique. The Hopf

---

[15] By contrast, the 7 per cent increase in the employment rate appears quite exaggerated. This would be (just) one argument against working with a neoclassical production function in a business cycle context.

[16] Dotted area indicates local stability. MC and CC designate monotonic and cyclical convergence, CD and MD cyclical and monotonic divergence, respectively.

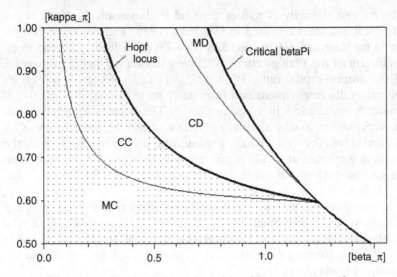

Figure 2.1: The local dynamics arising from parameters (β_π, κ_π)

bifurcation locus is the inner bold line in figure 2.1, until it hits the curve $\beta_\pi^c = \beta_\pi^c(\kappa_\pi)$ at a value of κ_π slightly less than 0.60. Hence, the steady state is unstable for all pairs (β_π, κ_π) to the right of the Hopf locus, and it is locally asymptotically stable to the left of it.

The other reason why we are interested in the Hopf locus is the fact that, in a neighbourhood of it, the system exhibits cyclical behaviour. The full range of the cyclical dynamics is identified by the regions CC and CD, which indicate cyclical convergence and cyclical divergence, respectively.[17] Nevertheless, divergence can be monotonic, too; see region MD. For the case of cyclical divergence this means that with rising values of β_π, while κ_π is being fixed, the imaginary part of the complex eigenvalues shrinks to zero, from which it is seen that these cycles become infinitely long as β_π approaches the MD region.[18]

In short, figure 2.1 provides the following information, which partly corroborates the statements of Propositions 1 and 2, and partly goes

---

[17] Convergence is cyclical if two eigenvalues $\lambda_{1,2}$ are complex and their real part exceeds the third real eigenvalue λ_3. If Re $\lambda_{1,2} < \lambda_3$, oscillations may still arise but are generally transitory (except for a fluke). However, in the dynamic simulations of the model, under the initial conditions to be reported in the next section, we observe a tendency for the monotonic regime to take over only when the economy has already come very close to its equilibrium position. On this evidence, a pair (β_π, κ_π) is classified CC when it gives rise to $\lambda_3 < 0$, Re $\lambda_{1,2} < 0$ and, still, Re $\lambda_{1,2} < 3 \cdot \lambda_3$.

[18] With respect to complex eigenvalues $\lambda_{1,2} = a \pm ib$, the period T of the oscillations is given by $T = 2\pi/b$.

beyond them. Regressive expectations (low values of κ_π) are stabilizing. They also tend to induce monotonic dynamics. The same applies to slow adjustments of inflationary expectations in general – i.e. low values of the adjustment speed β_π. While high values of β_π are destabilizing, a medium range exists that generates cyclical trajectories. Though cyclical dynamics is not a universal phenomenon, the scope for it is still considerable. Saying this, it should furthermore be pointed out that similar diagrams of the (β_π, κ_π)-plane are obtained when the underlying parameters, particularly those in (2.40), are varied.[19]

One last numerical phenomenon may be reported. Over an extremely wide range of the model's parameter values, one real eigenvalue always turns out to be in the region of -0.035, quite irrespective of the admittedly very large variations of the other two eigenvalues. As a consequence, even if the steady state is stable and the other two eigenvalues have a smaller real part, convergence is relatively slow. Imagining that the economy is perturbed from the steady-state growth path and then again left to itself, the leading term d_t that measures, in per cent, the remaining distance to the equilibrium position after t years is given by $d_t = e^{-0.035 \cdot t}$. Hence, for example, $d_t = 0.70$ for $t = 10$, and $d_t = 0.50$ for $t = 20$. That is, after ten years the economy-wide adjustments have bridged 30 per cent, and after twenty years they have bridged just half of the gap. It is remarkable that this low speed at which the system can, at best, approach the equilibrium is affected only insignificantly by variations in all of the reaction parameters.

2.7   Basic feedback loops

The previous sections were concerned with a consistent formulation of the model, its mathematical analysis and a numerical exploration of the conditions for local stability and cyclical behaviour. In the present section we have a closer look at the dynamic mechanisms involved. To this end three feedback loops are isolated that are recognizable as stabilizing or destabilizing. These are a real wage effect, the Mundell effect and the regressive expectations effect.

It may be noted that the Keynes effect, known from traditional Keynesian textbook analysis, cannot be discussed in the present framework. The Keynes effect starts out from considering an increase in the price level, the resulting increase in real balances, and its impact on the

[19] One difference is that, if a lower value of f_l' or f_w' is underlying, a *ceteris paribus* reduction of β_π at low values of κ_π may take us from MC to CC. That is, CC also prevails at values of κ_π below that value at which the Hopf locus hits the β_π^c-curve, though the period of the cycles tends to become rather long then.

nominal rate of interest. This is not possible here since the price level is directly determined by the marginal productivity principle for labour and therefore is not, either formally or conceptually, an independent variable. Similarly, the model contains no variable like M/p or M/pK. Nevertheless, the interest rate effects in the feedback chain that constitutes the Keynes effect will show up in what we summarize as the real wage effect.

(1) *The real wage effect.* Let $\omega = (w/p)/z^o$ denote the real wage rate deflated by the trend term of labour productivity. Owing to the marginal productivity principle, in the form of eq. (2.19), ω is tied to the output–capital ratio by the relation $\omega = 1/\ell'(y)$, where $\ell = \ell(y)$ is labour intensity in effciency units, $\ell = z^o L/K$, if firms, with the existing capital stock K, produce output $Y = yK$ (see eq. (2.16)). Since the function $\ell(\cdot)$ is convex, (see eqs. (2.17) and (2.18)), ω and y are inversely related. Of course, this is nothing other than the first fundamental postulate, formulated in intensive form, of the classical theory of employment, as already mentioned at the beginning of section 2.2.

Then, suppose that the real wage is above its equilibrium value, $\omega > \omega^o$, which is tantamount to an output–capital ratio below equilibrium, $y < y^o$. The latter implies, at least in a *ceteris paribus* argument, a certain degree of unemployment, as $L/L^s = (z^o L/K)(K/z^o L^s) = \ell(y)k^s < 1$, which via the Phillips curve (2.13) puts downward pressure on nominal wages. In contrast to many other textbook models, however, this has no direct effect on the goods market. One reason is that consumption demand derives from total income in the economy and does not separate out workers' consumption. The other reason is that the real rate of return entering the investment function is the marginal product of capital, and not some average rate of profit that would directly be influenced by nominal wage costs.

In the present model, lower wages impact on the economy via the marginal productivity principle (2.19) and through the channel of the money market (or bond market, respectively). In the latter respect, the reasoning is similar to that in the Keynes effect. The (relative) decline in wages lets the price level decline *pari passu*, by eq. (2.19). This raises real balances, which diminishes the rate of interest (the LM curve in the (y, i)-plane shifts south-east). The difference between the marginal product of capital and the real interest rate increases, as does investment demand and, through multiplier effects, output as a whole.

In the model's notation, a relative decline in nominal wages increases the auxiliary variable $x_m = z^o M/wK$. The IS-LM analysis in Lemma 1 assures us that, after the multiplier effects have worked out, the output–capital ratio increases too. By the marginal productivity principle, this means a reduction of the real wage ω. Thus, in sum, we have a chain of effects that takes care that high real wages are corrected downward. That is, the real wage effect as it is here singled out is a stabilizing mechanism.

(2) *The Mundell effect.* The initial link in the feedback loop of the Mundell effect is an increase in expected inflation, π. The decrease in the real interest rate thus brought about leads to higher investment and, reinforced through the multiplier, a higher output–capital ratio. Via the Phillips curve, the corresponding rise in the employment rate increases wage inflation, which carries over to goods prices via (2.19). The higher rate of inflation affects the adaptive expectations component of eq. (2.14) if $\kappa_{\pi} > 0$, causing a further increase in the expected rate of inflation. The Mundell effect is, therefore, a positive feedback effect, which tends to destabilize the economy.

(3) *The regressive expectations effect.* This effect is almost trivial. Since in this part of their expectation formation process agents expect that inflation will eventually return to normal, the effect is stabilizing by definition. Formally, $\pi > \pi^o$ induces directly $\dot{\pi} < 0$ in eq. (2.14).

Taking for granted that no other crucial destabilizing mechanism has been overlooked, it is now immediately clear why the steady state is stable if inflationary expectations are purely regressive: $\kappa_{\pi} = 0$ puts to rest the only positive feedback loop. Furthermore, the Mundell effect is activated if adaptive expectations are given sufficient weight vs. the regressive expectations – i.e. if κ_{π} is high enough. Then, the Mundell effect gains in strength if inflationary expectations adjust more rapidly – i.e. if the adjustment speed β_{π} increases. In fact, the Mundell effect also dominates the stabilizing real wage effect if β_{π} is sufficiently high. These elementary observations explain the stability–instability information in Proposition 1 and figure 2.1.

Regarding the other reaction parameters (the interest elasticity of money demand $\eta_{m,i}$, the slope of the Phillips curve f'_w and the responsiveness of investment f'_I), we are not able to attribute a similarly obvious stabilizing or destabilizing effect to them, since all three parameters are involved in the real wage effect as well as in the Mundell effect. A numerical investigation reveals that lower values of $\eta_{m,i}$, which intensify the reactions of the rate of interest, are stabilizing. A similar statement holds true for lower values of f'_w. The effects of the responsiveness f'_I are not so easy to assess. It may be said that a reduction of f'_I is (very) weakly stabilizing, while enlarging somewhat the scope for cyclical motions.

Though it is not our subject here, the effects of f'_w should not go completely unnoticed. Conventional wisdom has it that part of the problem of unemployment is due to wage rigidity, suggesting that higher wage flexibility favours the return to full (or 'normal') employment. In the present context, higher wage flexibility is represented by a steeper slope of the Phillips curve, i.e. a higher coefficient f'_w. Hence, what we infer from the analysis of Sargent's model is that more flexible wages are destabilizing, rather than stabilizing! We will have to take up this issue again in later parts of the book.

2.8 A representative simulation run

In the preceding section, stabilizing and destabilizing feedback loops have been worked out. From the local analysis we know that their interactions may give rise to·cyclical behaviour. It is quite difficult, however, to describe these cyclical motions in general terms. In particular, a purely verbal reasoning about the turning points could easily become ambiguous. To gain a clearer insight into the relative strength of the feedback mechanisms here involved, we conclude the investigation of the Sargent model with a dynamic simulation of the system.

In addition to the production function, we then also have to specify the form of the behavioural functions f_I, f_m and f_w in eqs. (2.4), (2.8) and (2.13). For our purpose linear functions will do. Taking account of $F_K = \alpha \cdot y$ for the marginal product of capital of the Cobb–Douglas production function (2.39) (see the remark on eq. (2.20)), we thus have

$$f_I = f_I[F_K - \delta - (i - \pi)] = \beta_{Io} + \beta_{Iq}(\alpha y - \delta - i + \pi) \tag{2.41}$$

$$f_m = f_m(i) = \beta_{mo} - \beta_{mi}i \tag{2.42}$$

$$f_w = f_w(L/L^s) = \beta_w(L/L^s - 1) \tag{2.43}$$

where $\beta_{Iq}, \beta_{mi}, \beta_w > 0$. The two coefficients β_{Iq} and β_w are equal to, respectively, $f'_I = 0.20$ and $f'_w = 0.30$ in (2.40). β_{Io} in (2.41) is subsequently determined by the steady-state condition $f^o_I = g^o$ for the real growth rate. β_{mi} in (2.42), of course, corresponds to the interest elasticity of money demand. Given $\eta_{m,i} = 0.25$, two equations are needed to compute the slope β_{mi} and the intercept β_{mo} in (2.42) as residuals. Both being evaluated at the steady-state values, these are the definition of the elasticity, $\eta_{m,i} = f'_m i^o / f_m(i^o) = \beta_{mi} i^o / (\beta_{mo} - \beta_{mi} i^o)$, and the LM equation (2.24), which reads $x^o_m = y^o \ell'(y^o) f_m(i^o) = (\beta_{mo} - \beta_{mi} i^o)/(1 - \alpha)$.[20] They are solved as $\beta_{mi} = x^o_m \eta_{m,i}(1 - \alpha)/i^o$ and $\beta_{mo} = x^o_m(1 - \alpha)(1 + \eta_{m,i})$.

---

[20] Taking up the remark on eq. (2.39) and the inverse function $\ell(y)$ deriving from this Cobb–Douglas production function, one has $\ell'(y^o) = 1/[y^o(1 - \alpha)]$.

A few words may be added on our view on the simulations of economic adjustments formulated in continuous time. It goes without saying that simulations on a digital computer can only be an approximation of the continuous-time system. However, rather than using a more·or less sophisticated discretization procedure (of Runge–Kutta type, say) of the three differential equations (2.34)–(2.36), we consider it more meaningful to go back to the original formulation (2.1)–(2.15) and conceive of this economy as a sequential, discrete-time economy with a market, or adjustment, period of length h.

Accordingly, we take time t as the beginning of 'month' $[t, t + h)$. The dynamic variables z^o, L^s, M, K, w, π are predetermined and remain fixed over this interval. They determine the corresponding temporary equilibrium, which is solved by means of a straightforward iteration mechanism (the details of which can be omitted here). Subsequently, the dynamic variables for the next 'month' are obtained by computing the discrete-time one-step analogues of (2.9)–(2.14). For example, $K_{t+h} = K_t + h \cdot (f_t K_t)$ in eq. (2.12), or, taking (2.13) as another example,

$$w_{t+h} = w_t \{ 1 + h \cdot [g_{w,t} + f_w(L_t / L_t^s)] \} \tag{2.44}$$

This equation also illustrates that, occasionally, a little care has to be taken with the growth rates involved. Here it is the reference growth rate $g_{w,t}$, which, in the continuous-time framework of (2.13), is simply given by $g_w = \pi_t + g_z$. Making proper use of the discrete-time relationships, the expression becomes more cumbersome and includes a mixed term: $g_{w,t} = \pi_t + g_z + h(\pi_t g_z)$.[21] A more extensive discussion of our method to set up a discrete-time sequential economy for the numerical simulations, which relates there to the main model studied in this book, is given in the appendix to chapter 4. It also contains the source code of the core of the computer program, which in its essence is not very different from the present example.

Regarding the revision of π, it is appropriate here to adopt the rate of inflation that has just been observed. That is, eq. (2.33) can be disregarded and $\hat{p} = \hat{p}_t$ in the right-hand side of (2.14) is directly defined

---

[21] The reason is that $g_w = g_{w,t}$ is based on a composed variable, since g_w is the reference growth rate of nominal wages, which, when prevailing, would ensure that the productivity-deflated nominal wage rate, w/z^o, grows at the rate of expected inflation. It thus has to satisfy $(1 + hg_w)/(1 + hg_z) = 1 + h\pi$. Solving this condition for g_w yields the expression in the text. Similar respecifications are necessary for the steady-state growth rates deriving from the composed variables $k^s = K/z^o L^s$ and $x_m = z^o M/wK$. The requirement that these variables are constant on the equilibrium path implies the conditions $(1 + hg^o)/(1 + hg_z)(1 + hg_\ell) = 1$ and $(1 + hg_z)(1 + hg_m)/(1 + hg_w^o)(1 + hg^o) = 1$, respectively.

backwards, as $\hat{p}_t = (p_t - p_{t-h})/hp_t$. Quite agreeably, this also avoids the possible problems that may arise with the pole in (2.33).

The length of the market period is a priori unspecified. It will, of course, be expected that the dynamic behaviour of the discrete-time economy is close to that of the continuous-time system if h is chosen small enough. The idea is indeed supported by formal work.[22] In our case it proves sufficient to set $h = 1/12$, so that we literally simulate a monthly model.

As for the two coefficients in the formation of inflationary expectations, it simplifies the discussion of the cyclical motions if we concentrate on adaptive expectations. Furthermore, the speed of adjustment is set such that it generates slowly dampened oscillations. Given the other numerical parameters from section 2.6, this behaviour is brought about by

$$\kappa_\pi = 1.00, \quad \beta_\pi = 0.23$$

It remains to specify the initial conditions. A usual procedure is to start the system in its equilibrium position, perturb it by a one-time shock and then leave it to itself again. Sargent (1987, p. 117) assumes a sudden jump in the money supply. The disadvantage of this device in a numerical exercise is that either the effects are rather minor or otherwise the change in M has to be quite large, which creates an unpleasant discontinuity. We consider it more reasonable to distribute the shock effects over a longer period.

In detail, the economy is supposed to be on its steady-state growth path and to stay there until $t = 1$. At this point in time, the growth rate of the money supply is temporarily increased by three percentage points, from (approximately; cf. the remark on (2.44)) $g_m = \pi^o + g_z + g_\ell = 6\%$ to $g_m + \Delta g_m = 9\%$. This pace of the expansion of M is maintained for one year, and at $t = 2$ the money growth rate is set back to its original level. Figure 2.2 shows the reactions of four central variables: the output–capital ratio y, the interest rate i, the inflation rate $\hat{p}$ and the expected rate of inflation π which is shown as the dotted line in the bottom panel of the time series diagram.

The immediate effect of the higher growth rate of the money supply, at $t = 1 + h = 1 + 1/12$, is an increase in $x_m = z^o M/wK$ (the x_m series is not shown). According to the IS-LM result of Lemma 1, this raises the output–capital ratio and diminishes the rate of interest. The decline in i, however, cannot be discerned in figure 2.2 as it is rather small, and,

---

[22] For an investigation of the precise relationship between differential equations systems and their one-step discretization, with respect to Lyapunov stable points or sets, see Kloeden and Lorenz (1986).

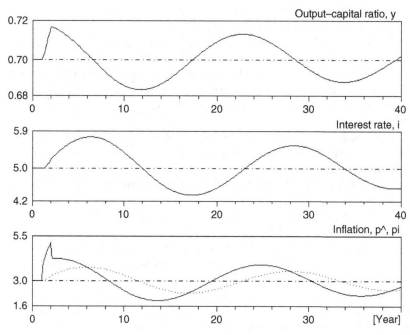

Figure 2.2: Time paths of y, i, $\hat{p}$ and π in response to a monetary shock

from the next market period $t = 1 + 2/12$ on, the interest rate begins to increase, although x_m continues to grow.

The upturn in i is due to the simultaneous change in inflation. The higher output–capital ratio increases the employment rate above unity, which induces a faster growth of nominal wages in the Phillips curve. With the rise of w as well as y in the marginal productivity equation (2.19), the price level rises even more rapidly. As a result, the expected rate of inflation in (2.14) starts rising as well. Despite the moderate changes in π, this positive effect on the interest rate still dominates the negative effect from the rising x_m. On the other hand, the additional positive impact of π on y reinforces the increase in the output–capital ratio.

The evolution goes on until the end of the transition period at $t = 2$. As the money growth rate attains its previous level, x_m begins to fall. Expected inflation keeps on rising, but, regarding y, here it is x_m (with a now negative impact on y) that turns out to dominate the positive effect from π. That is, from $t = 2$ on the output–capital ratio is falling, too.

This also reduces inflation, but only gradually so. Hence $\hat{p}$ still exceeds π, so that expected inflation rises further.

When $x_m = z^o M/wK$ is back at its initial value after a short while (at $t \approx 3.8$), the adjustment is by no means complete. In the meantime, wage inflation has risen significantly above its equilibrium value, and the same applies to the capital growth rate, though the latter effect is rather small (see below). x_m consequently continues its descent below the equilibrium level.

At the same time, the rise in expected inflation decelerates as the gap between $\hat{p}$ and π narrows. Eventually $\hat{p}$ falls below π, from when π, in following $\hat{p}$, decreases. At this stage of the process both x_m and π are falling, and they work together in steadily reducing the output–capital ratio, down to y^o and beyond.

Why, then, does the contraction not go on for ever, and why is y able to recover after $t = 12$? It may be noted, first, that the changes in the capital stock relative to the labour supply are quantitatively so small that $k^s = K/z^o L^s$ remains very close to unity all the time.[23] The employment rate $L/L^s = \ell(y)k^s$ therefore follows the motion of y quite directly. The downswing of L/L^s and the start of a fall in expected inflation reduce wage inflation in a progressive manner, which is the main reason why $x_m = z^o M/wK$ eventually reaches a lower turning point at about $t = 9$, and then starts rising again.

The rise in x_m corresponds, albeit not exactly, to a rise in real balances. Via the financial markets, we thus have a negative impact on the rate of interest. In fact, the interest rate has reached a maximum value before, shortly after π has reached its peak value. While the formal argument, which refers to Lemma 1 and the IS-LM 'multipliers' $\partial y/\partial x_m > 0$, $\partial y/\partial \pi > 0$, is somewhat different and more technical, we may emphasize this interest rate channel as a central mechanism wherein the seeds to overcome a recession are to be found. The basic elements involved here had already been discussed in the identification of the real wage effect in the previous section.

Inflation does not move in synchrony with economic activity y but follows it with something of a lag. It results from the continued decline in expected inflation, which delays the rise in $\hat{w}$ in the Phillips curve. Via (2.19), this carries over to actual inflation $\hat{p}$.

With the economic expansion after $t = 12$, we obtain a mirror image of the pattern just described. In this way the economy enters a fairly

[23] This phenomenon is primarily due to the reaction coefficient $f'_l = \beta_{Iq} = 0.20$, a value which in the context of the motions of $\alpha y - (i - \pi)$ turns out to be very small. On the other hand, it has already been mentioned in section 2.6 that we are not allowed to increase f'_l much further. This order of magnitude is indeed one serious limitation to a more satisfactory 'calibration' of the model.

regular, oscillatory motion, which is seen to be weakly dampened over time. We may stop the numerical analysis at this point, since we are not interested here in sustained cyclical behaviour as such, and content ourselves with pointing out some crucial cycle-generating propagation mechanisms.

It may finally be observed that, with a view to 'realism', the present investigation can only be preliminary. As one 'realistic' feature of a business cycle model, we would demand a cycle duration of less than ten years, whereas the oscillations shown in figure 2.2 exhibit a period of more than twenty years. The most effective parameter to shorten the cycles is an increase in the slope of the Phillips curve, f'_w. This change must, however, be considerable, which would bring us in conflict with the argument for setting $f'_w = 0.30$ in eq. (2.40). We note that this argument had to invoke the Cobb–Douglas production function. The problems indicated here are one reason, though by no means the only one, why from the next chapter on we will leave any neoclassical production function behind us.

2.9   Conclusion

In this chapter we have reconsidered, and slightly extended, a Keynesian supply-side model as it was advanced by Sargent (1979, 1987) in his well-known macroeconomics textbook. In a first step, a full and mathematically consistent formulation was given, which led to a three-dimensional system of differential equations. Subsequently the conditions for local stability were investigated. It was found that Sargent's stability statements are overly optimistic and that, especially when agents become more 'rational', in the sense that they react more rapidly in adjusting their expected rates of inflation, the equilibrium growth path will become unstable. In addition, cyclical behaviour was identified, which was also illustrated by means of a typical simulation run.

Regarding Sargent's concern, that, in the long run, the growth rate of money supply determines only price inflation and has no real effects, it follows that his model is not quite apt to support the monetarist position – since this claim presupposes the asymptotic stability of the steady state. We take it as a neat irony that, to the contrary, the model and the elementary insights it provides may be taken as a starting point for a theory of endogenous and persistent cyclical behaviour (which would also reintroduce a scope for active fiscal and monetary policies).

Nevertheless, with respect to the oscillatory motions of the aggregate key variables, more attention should be paid to the most important 'stylized facts' that we gather from reality. In the next chapter this will induce us to abandon the marginal productivity principle for labour and a neoclassical production function altogether. As a consequence, we will have to put forward an alternative price theory – that is, a theory of price adjustments. As a matter of fact, the setting of prices will be the only essential difference from Sargent's model; his other building blocks may perhaps be slightly modified, but all of them will be easy to recognize.

2.10   Appendix: The Hopf bifurcation theorem

The version of the Hopf bifurcation theorem that we prefer to employ derives as a special case from Theorem A in Alexander and Yorke (1978, pp. 263–6). We have chosen it since it avoids, as far as possible, the technical subtleties entering other variants of (the complex of) the theorem.[24] In exchange, it contents itself with the mere existence of periodic orbits and has nothing to say about their stability or instability. Accordingly, the present version does not distinguish the often mentioned subcritical and supercritical cases, which are tantamount to repelling and attracting periodic orbits, respectively.

Our limitation may be accepted on economic grounds, since the condition for orbital stability or instability involves higher-order derivatives of the right-hand side of the differential equations system and is so complicated that in most applications it lacks any economic interpretation. The argument that the (composed) expressions of the higher-order derivatives could be computed in numerical simulations is not fully convincing, since their robustness to slight respecifications of the behavioural functions usually remains entirely unclear. Hence any result that might be thus obtained should not be overrated.

The formulation of the theorem requires a few definitional preliminaries. With respect to I, an open interval of the real line, and M, an open subset in $\mathbb{R}^n$, let $F: I \times M \to \mathbb{R}^n$ be a differentiable function. Consider the family of autonomous differential equations systems parameterized by $\mu \in I$,

$$\dot{x} = F(\mu, x) \tag{2.45}$$

Denote by $\Phi(\mu, t, x) \in \mathbb{R}^n$ the solution of (2.45) at time t, given μ, which at time zero starts out from $x(0) = x$. The pair (x, μ) is called *stationary* if $\Phi(\mu, t, x) = x$ for all $t \geq 0$. (x, μ) is called *periodic* if it is not stationary and

---

[24] These include higher-order derivatives and the requirement that the critical pair of complex eigenvalues passes the imaginary axis at a positive speed. A standard reference is Marsden and McCracken (1976); see, in particular, pp. 65 & 81.

there exists $T > 0$ such that $\Phi(\mu, T, x) = x$. If (x, μ) is periodic, all positive T for which $\Phi(\mu, T, x) = x$ are called *periods*, while the smallest positive period is called the *least period*. The theorem then reads as follows.

The Hopf bifurcation theorem

Suppose that

(1) $x^o \in M$ is a stationary point of (2.45) for all μ – i.e. $F(\mu, x^o) = 0$ for all $\mu \in I$;

(2) the functions $F(\mu, \cdot)$ are continuously differentiable;

(3) the Jacobian matrix $\mathcal{J}(\mu)$ of (2.45) at (μ, x^o), $\mathcal{J}(\mu) = \partial F(\mu, x^o)/\partial x \in \mathbb{R}^{n \times n}$, is continuous in μ;

(4) at a parameter value μ^H the Jacobian $\mathcal{J}(\mu^H)$ is non-singular and has a conjugate pair of purely imaginary eigenvalues $\pm i\beta$, while all other eigenvalues have nonzero real parts;

(5) for μ close but not equal to μ^H, no eigenvalue has zero real part.

Then for all $\varepsilon > 0$ there exists a triple $x = x(\varepsilon) \in M$, $\mu = \mu(\varepsilon) \in I$, $T = T(\varepsilon) \in \mathbb{R}$ such that $(x(\varepsilon), \mu(\varepsilon))$ is periodic with least period $T(\varepsilon)$ and all points of the orbit $\{\Phi(\mu(\varepsilon), t, x(\varepsilon)) : t \geq 0\}$ are of distance less than ε from point x^o. In addition, $x(\varepsilon) \to x^o$, $\mu(\varepsilon) \to \mu^H$, $T(\varepsilon) \to 2\pi/\beta$ as ε approaches zero.

Note that, regularly, either $\mu(\varepsilon) > \mu^H$ or $\mu(\varepsilon) < \mu^H$ for all (small) $\varepsilon > 0$. A degenerate case occurs, $\mu(\varepsilon) = \mu^H$ for all $\varepsilon > 0$, if the functions $F(\mu, \cdot)$ are linear.

Generally, in this book, we see a Hopf bifurcation as a useful tool to establish that, over a certain range of the parameter μ under investigation, the trajectories of the economy are at least locally of a cyclical nature, convergent and divergent ones alike. Stronger statements on the existence and stability of strictly periodic orbits are possible but of limited significance. As a matter of fact, the Hopf bifurcation theorem is, basically, still a local proposition. Insofar as we are interested in endogenous, persistent and bounded growth cycles within a deterministic setting, we consider it a more fruitful approach to study the global dynamics, where the steady-state position may be unstable and the divergent tendencies in the outer regions of the state space are tamed by some suitable non-linearities. In this perspective, the local analysis – along with a Hopf bifurcation result – serves us as a first piece of information about the economy's general potential for oscillatory behaviour. It thus provides a firm basis for a subsequent global analysis, which from three dimensions on will soon have to resort to computer simulations.

3 Disequilibrium growth: the point of departure

3.1 Introduction

Sargent's Keynesian textbook model of economic growth, which we studied in chapter 2, was basically a supply-side model. Accordingly, firms' production is determined by the solution of their short-run profit maximization problem, with no quantity constraints involved. In connection with the standard neoclassical production function, this amounts to the marginal productivity principle for labour. We have on several occasions expressed our uneasiness with the implications of this hypothesis. This unease is so profound that, as has already been announced, we now drop it completely. In doing this, three components of the model have to be conceived anew: (a) the production technology, (b) firms' output, and (c) firms' price setting. The rest is, essentially, taken over from the Sargent model, perhaps adjusted slightly to fit the modified context, or extended slightly.

The usual alternative to the neoclassical production function is a fixed-coefficients technology. In point (a) we accept this supposition as far as long-run equilibrium growth is concerned, but allow for variations in capacity utilization as well as for procyclical fluctuations in (detrended) labour productivity. Regarding (b), we employ the concept that the output of firms satisfies current demand. In familiar parlance, the model may thus be termed a Keynesian demand-side model. More formally, the short-run time horizon of goods and financial markets is specified in IS-LM fashion, where, in contrast to the Sargent model, the price level is predetermined. Regarding the third component (c), prices remain invariant within the (infinitesimally) short period and are changed between these periods. The adjustments are governed by a Phillips curve relationship. The model will therefore exhibit two Phillips curves, one for nominal wages and one for goods prices. It is important to note that prices will be assumed to react not only to a measure of demand pressure but also to any deviations of the current markup on average cost from a target markup rate.

In this perspective, the model can be thought of as a disequilibrium extension of the Sargent model. In a brief summary, which may be compared with that in chapter 2, section 1, it is characterized by the following features:

(1) separation of the acts of investment and savings decisions;
(2) explicit consideration of an interest-bearing financial asset;
(3) endogenous determination of the stock of capital, which is growing over time;
(4) the inflation rate is an endogenous variable;
(5) the rate of monetary expansion is a control variable;
(6) continuous IS-LM temporary equilibrium on the goods and financial markets;
(7) over- and underutilization of productive capacity;
(8) employment of labour (by taking a procyclical productivity component into account) is determined by the output decisions in (6) and so will generally differ from labour supply;
(9) the rise of nominal wages is governed by an expectations-augmented Phillips curve;
(10) the rise of the price level is governed by an expectations-augmented Phillips curve, which includes demand pressure as well as deviations from a target markup; and
(11) inflationary expectations are governed by a combination of adaptive expectations and regressive expectations.

Besides these introductory remarks, the presentation and investigation of the model is organized into ten sections. In the next section we discuss stylized facts concerning the comovements of real wages and labour productivity. They lead us to reject not only the marginal productivity principle for labour but also the neoclassical production function as such. In addition, they motivate our alternative specification of the production relationships. The presentation of the model is completed in section 3. To prepare it for the later analysis, it is subsequently reformulated in intensive form in section 4. In this way the economy is reduced to a three-dimensional differential equations system.

Section 5 is devoted to a mathematical investigation of local stability conditions for the steady-state position. Section 6 reverts to the aforementioned stylized facts. Here numerical values for the parameters involved in the wage-price sector are sought which ensure that the real wage dynamics implied by the modelling equations are broadly consistent with the empirical observations. These parameter values are the basis for the ensuing numerical stability analysis in section 7. The main task in this section is to characterize a number of important reaction coefficients as stabilizing or destabilizing. In particular, it points out that these effects are not always unambiguous.

While section 7 is still concerned with information about the system's local behaviour that can be inferred from the Jacobian matrix, the next sections investigate the dynamic relationships more directly. Section 8 seeks to reveal basic feedback loops, which, again, are either stabilizing or destabilizing. It is found that the effects already largely known from the literature do not suffice to explain the system's (in)stability; more circuitous mechanisms involving certain cross-effects of the state variables play a greater role in this respect.

Section 9 enquires into the reasons for nonmonotonic behaviour. By studying the cyclical pattern of the key variables in a simulation run, it identifies the sources that eventually cause an economic expansion to come to an end. Section 10 starts out from the fact that the steady state is, typically, locally unstable, and that the trajectories continue to spiral outward globally if the behavioural functions are specified in a linear way. To contain the centrifugal forces within reasonable bounds, we propose a straightforward procedure that makes the adaptive expectations mechanism for the rate of inflation more flexible. A numerical simulation illustrates how the nonlinearity thus introduced fulfils its task. Section 11 concludes.

3.2   An alternative to the neoclassical production function

While a neoclassical production function – together with the marginal productivity principle for labour – may be a useful tool in a study of the determinants of long-run economic growth, this concept must be critically reconsidered when it comes to its implications in a business (growth) cycle context. A few points have already been hinted at in the previous chapter. Thus, in section 2.2, it was mentioned that the marginal productivity principle is not without conceptual problems if it is combined with an IS-like temporary equilibrium condition on the goods market. In section 2.4 it was further pointed out that the resulting determination of the rate of inflation is rather mechanical and economically not very transparent. Judging by these unsatisfactory features, a more convincing price theory was thought to be desirable.

Apart from these considerations, it is well known that the marginal productivity principle gives rise to a countercyclical real wage rate. For the production function (2.1) with technological progress, $Y = F(K, z^o L)$, this can be readily shown as follows. Note, first, that the stages of the business cycles are usually characterized by the output gap – i.e. the percentage deviations of total output or GDP from some trend line – and that these motions are highly correlated with the output–capital ratio (perhaps similarly corrected for some low-frequency changes). Now, eqs. (2.16) and (2.17) have established that labour intensity in efficiency units, $\ell = z^o L/K$, can be expressed as an increasing function of the output–capital ratio, y. Writing $\omega = (w/p)/z^o$ for the real wage rate deflated by the trend term of labour productivity, eq. (2.19) reformulated the marginal productivity principle as $\omega = 1/\ell'(y)$. Since $\ell''(y) > 0$ by (2.18), the real wage is inversely related to the measure of the business cycle that is convenient here, the output–capital ratio.

Very soon after the publication of Keynes' *General Theory*, Dunlop (1938) and Tarshis (1939) described empirical evidence that they interpreted as failures to confirm the countercyclical pattern predicted by the standard theory (which Keynes had accepted). These contributions aroused a lively debate among economists, which even nowadays flares up occasionally. The diverse findings are somewhat conditional on precisely how the real wage is constructed, depending on the price index chosen and on whether the nominal wage includes various compensation items. For a succinct summary of the controversy it nevertheless seems fair to say that real wages, if anything, are procyclical rather than countercyclical.

We may support this assessment by having a look ourselves at the (quarterly) data.[1] This is done in figure 3.1. The upper series is the deviation (in per cent) of the output–capital ratio from a smooth line that was obtained by employing the standard Hodrick–Prescott (HP) filter.[2] The second panel displays the real wage rate detrended by the same procedure.[3] A quick glance suffices to see that, in any case, real wages are not countercyclical. Rather, there appear to be certain positive comovements

[1] As mentioned in chapter 2, section 6, we made use of Ray C. Fair's package offered on his home page, http://fairmodel.econ.yale.edu, which, in particular, includes a capital stock series.

[2] Regarding the smoothing parameter, the standard value for quarterly data, $\lambda = 1600$, was adopted; see Hodrick and Prescott (1997). Though the cyclical features of Y/K are clearly visible in the raw series itself, the HP filter was used to eliminate the weakly declining (until the beginning of the 1980s) and then weakly increasing tendency in the ratio. The resulting pattern in figure 3.1 is indeed very similar to the output gap obtained from (the log of) Y or GDP, where the growing log series is detrended by HP or a band pass (6,32) filter; see, for example, King and Rebelo (1999, p. 933 fig. 1) or Stock and Watson (1999, p. 13 fig. 2.5) and the surrounding discussion.

[3] That is, it displays the series $100 \cdot (\ln(w/p) - \ln(w/p)^o)$, where $\ln(w/p)^o$ is the HP trend line. To be precise, w/p in figure 3.1 is the product wage, the denominator being the price index for total output. The nominal wage rate in the numerator includes overtime payment. This means that the (base) wage rate is multiplied by Fair's rule-of-thumb measure $(HN + 1.5 \cdot HO)/(HN + HO)$, where HN and HO are the average number of non-overtime and overtime hours, respectively, paid per job in the firm sector. Besides, the procyclical effect from HO is not very dramatic and detrending the unmodified wage rate yields a quite similar picture.

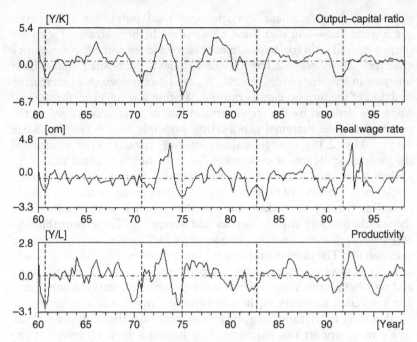

Figure 3.1: Percentage deviations of empirical time series from an HP trend line

with the output–capital ratio, at least until 1990. In fact, the correlation coefficient between the two series between 1960:1 and 1998:2 is 0.51. The statistic rises slightly to 0.56 if the shorter period 1960 to 1992 is considered. If we concentrate on the selected subperiods 1960 to 1983 or 1970 to 1982, it even increases up to 0.70 or 0.77, respectively.

Although the empirical evidence against countercyclical wage movements suggests dropping the marginal productivity principle, one might still argue for sticking to a standard production function as a purely technological representation of the relationship between aggregate inputs and outputs. Uneasiness with the device as such, however, was first noted in chapter 2, section 6, where it was observed that a 5 per cent increase in the output–capital ratio raises the employment rate by as much as 7.2 per cent, which seems a rather unlikely order of magnitude. In addition, the example demonstrates that average labour productivity would thus decrease in an economic expansion. The crucial point is that this property is not restricted to the Cobb–Douglas function of our numerical exercise but that it holds true in general.

To see this, let L be hours worked (per year) and $z = Y/L$ average labour productivity, and use the linear homogeneity of a production function

$Y = F(K, z^o L)$, which yields $1 = Y/Y = F(K/Y, z^o L/Y) = F(1/y, z^o/z)$. Obviously, if the first entry falls in the last functional expression, the second entry must rise to maintain the identity. Hence, if y increases, labour productivity relative to its trend, z/z^o, decreases. In short, a neoclassical production function predicts countercyclical labour productivity.

Again, the theoretical outcome may be confronted with the data. In the notation just introduced, the bottom panel of figure 3.1 exhibits the empirical series $(z - z^o)/z^o$ (in per cent, where z^o is obtained from the same HP filter as above).[4] Very similar to the real wage rate, we can immediately conclude that average labour productivity is, at any rate, not countercyclical. One may furthermore recognize a certain procyclical pattern, though perhaps weaker than with real wages. Quantitatively, this is brought out by the correlation coefficients as follows. Over the periods 1960 to 1998, 1960 to 1992 and 1960 to 1983, respectively, they are computed as 0.42, 0.44 and 0.47. The connection is stronger if, motivated by the troughs in 1969, 1974 and 1990, a two-quarter lead in productivity is taken into account; here the coefficients result as 0.54, 0.58 and 0.61. With our interest in features of business cycle modelling, this evidence should be strong enough to dismiss a (deterministic) neoclassical production function altogether.

Saying this, an alternative representation of production has to be put forward, which should also improve upon a purely fixed-coefficients technology. We distinguish two aspects. First, we allow for under- and overutilization of productive capacity. It is only for the latter concept that fixed coefficients are assumed, in the form of a constant output–capital ratio y^n that would prevail under 'normal' conditions. With respect to a given stock of fixed capital K, productive capacity (or 'normal' output, synonymously), which we denote as Y^n, is then defined by

$$Y^n = y^n K \qquad (3.1)$$

Incidentally, note that fixing y^n implies Harrod-neutral technological progress in a long-run equilibrium.

Actual production Y will later be determined on the goods market such that it generally differs from Y^n. Accordingly, capacity utilization

$$u = Y/Y^n = y/y^n \qquad (3.2)$$

will generally be different from unity.

The second point concerns labour input, where we refer to hours, L. On the one hand, they depend on the current scale of technology.

---

[4] As before, the panel shows the log differences $100 \cdot (\ln z - \ln z^o)$ as the usual approximation of percentage deviations from trend.

We proxy this level by the labour productivity z^o that would prevail under, once more, normal conditions. That is, z^o (like the capital stock) is predetermined in the short period and production $Y = Y^n$ requires $L = Y/z^o$ hours of work. For disequilibrium utilization $u \neq 1$, however, variable labour productivity is admitted, so that, if Y deviates from Y^n, L deviates from Y/z^o.

We draw our inspiration from the empirical observation of a more or less procyclical pattern of productivity. For simplicity, we neglect the various dynamic adjustment mechanisms and possible lags that will be involved here and postulate a direct and tight relationship between productivity z (i.e. its deviation from the trend level z^o) and capacity utilization u. Introducing a strictly increasing real function $f_z = f_z(u)$, it reads

$$z = z^o f_z(u), \quad f_z(1) = 1, f_z' > 0 \tag{3.3}$$

Hence, to produce output Y when the state of technology is z^o and productive capacity is Y^n, firms must employ workers spending $L = Y/[z^o f_z(u)] = Y/[z^o f_z(Y/Y^n)]$ hours of work. Instead of working hours, we may more conveniently proceed to speak of, simply, labour or employment.

How can a relationship such as (3.3) be explained? Leaving aside the option of (suitably scaled and autocorrelated) random shocks to the technology, two standard arguments on procyclical productivity are labour hoarding and overhead labour. Labour hoarding, in the first instance, relates to blue-collar labour. When firms experience a downturn they keep more production workers than are technologically necessary to meet the current regular output and operation requirements. Part of this excess employment could be justified by the value of other work, such as maintenance, cleaning, training and so on, that is completed in a recessive phase. Another part could be classified as being hoarded in the strict sense: when the contraction is not too severe or expected to be only temporary, firms seek to avoid the costs associated with the layoffs, and with the search and training costs for the newly employed when the recovery sets in (apart from the anticipation that segments of the labour market might soon tighten then).[5]

Overhead labour, on the other hand, can be conceived of in much the same way as we regard excess capacity. Because of their quasi-fixed nature, it is clear that the productivity of the overhead labour force goes up as output rises. Moreover, if there is a large surplus of overhead

---

[5] For the typical plant over a trough quarter, Fay and Medoff (1985, p. 638) estimate total blue-collar labour hoarding at 8 per cent, with 4 per cent falling into the category of strict hoarding, as we have expressed it.

labour relative to the amount that is normally required for an initial level of production labour, more production workers can be employed, with the labour force being 'spread out' over them. Therefore, an increase of the production man-hour input could possibly even reduce output per production man-hour – since this negative effect may well be dominated, nevertheless, by the rising productivity of the overhead labour force, such that average productivity over the whole labour force continues to increase (relative to trend productivity).

Certainly, any more detailed discussion of the employment decisions of firms in a cyclical (and uncertain) environment would teach us that a dynamic theory is needed. This, however, is a field of research in its own right, the results of which would go far beyond what could reasonably be integrated into the models of the type considered in this book. To maintain their tractability, eq. (3.3) short-circuits the many problems lurking here. On the positive side, we contend that this simple approach to integrating the variability of labour productivity is at least more realistic than the two polar cases of a neoclassical production function and a fixed-coefficients technology.

In concluding this section, a word may be in order concerning the implication of eq. (3.3) for the employment rate. The problem is that the positive employment effect from a higher output level goes along with a negative effect from rising productivity. More formally, we refer to an employment rate in hours, $e = L/L^s$, where L^s are the total hours that the number of workers in supply would normally work. Defining, as in chapter 2, $k^s = K/z^o L^s$, the employment rate can be decomposed as $e = L/L^s = z^o(L/Y)(Y/Y^n)(Y^n/K)(K/z^o L^s) = (z^o/z)uy^n k^s = y^n k^s u/f_z(u)$. Neglecting the (comparatively) small changes in k^s, e rises in an expansion if the cyclical component of labour productivity, $f_z(u)$, rises less than utilization itself. That is, around normal utilization $u = 1$, e rises if $f_z' < 1$.

The condition $f_z' < 1$, on the other hand, can certainly be taken for granted. It suffices to note that the oscillations of the percentage trend deviations of $z = Y/L$ in figure 3.1 are significantly lower than those of $y = Y/K$ (observe that, by eq. (2), $(y - y^n)/y^n = u - 1$). In the numerical explorations later on we will, in fact, argue that $f_z' = 0.50$ is a reasonable coefficient. With $f_z' < 1$ it is also clear that the employment rate will be less variable than the rate of capacity utilization.

3.3   The remainder of the model

As the technological side of production is set out, the supply of goods could be said to be given by the level of productive capacity, Y^n, of firms. The concept of over- and underutilization, $u \neq 1$, in eq. (3.2) has already indicated that actual output generally differs from Y^n. In this sense, firms will be in disequilibrium. In fact, they are assumed to adjust their output to the demand currently directed to them.

At the same time, firms fix the price for their output at the beginning of the short period, so that p is a dynamic, and in this respect predetermined, variable. Hence, the organizing principle for the goods market is the usual Keynesian IS temporary equilibrium. The disequilibrium possibly arising on the part of firms, $Y \neq Y^n$, prompts them to change the output price in the next period (though, in common parlance, it is infinitesimally short in a continuous-time model).

The components of real demand are much the same as in the previous chapter. The equations for consumption and government demand, together with Sargent's convenient tax rule, are taken over unaltered from section 2.2:

$$C = (1 - s_h)[Y + iB/p - \delta K - T], \quad 0 < s_h < 1 \tag{3.4}$$

$$G = \gamma K \tag{3.5}$$

$$T = \theta K + iB/p \tag{3.6}$$

To recall, s_h is households' average propensity to save, B government (fixed-price) bonds, δ the rate of capital depreciation, T real tax collections and G government demand.

Net investment in section 2.2, eq. (2.4), was supposed to be an increasing function of the difference between the marginal product of capital minus δ and the real interest rate. Having dismissed the neoclassical production function, the first rate of return is no longer available. In commenting on (2.4) it was, however, remarked that $F_K - \delta$ coincides with the rate of profit, $r = (pY - wL - \delta K)/pK$, if the marginal productivity principle applies. In the present context it is therefore only natural to replace $F_K - \delta$ in this investment function with r:

$$I = f_I[r - (i - \pi)] \cdot K, \quad f_I' > 0 \tag{3.7}$$

(π being the expected rate of inflation). Referring to the output–capital ratio y and the wage share $v = wL/pY$, the rate of profit can be written as $r = (1 - v)y - \delta$, which, taking account of (3.1), becomes

$$r = (1 - v)uy^n - \delta \tag{3.8}$$

For the mathematical analysis later on it is appropriate to express the wage share in terms of the real wage rate deflated by trend productivity,

$\omega = (w/p)/z^o$. Decomposing v as $v = (w/pz^o) \cdot (L/Y) \cdot z^o = \omega \cdot (z^o/z)$ and using (3.3), we have

$$v = \omega/f_z(u) \tag{3.9}$$

The presentation of the real sector is completed by the market-clearing condition

$$Y = C + I + \delta K + G \tag{3.10}$$

On the basis of the money supply set by the monetary authorities, equilibrium on the financial markets is restated from eq. (2.8),

$$M = pYf_m(i), \quad f_m' < 0 \tag{3.11}$$

Equations (3.1) to (3.11) constitute the temporary equilibrium part of the economy. The main difference from Sargent's model in chapter 2, section 2, is the specification of the production technology and the fact that the price level is now treated as a predetermined variable in the short period. The other predetermined variables are, again, z^o as the state of technology, K the capital stock, M the money supply, π expected inflation, w the nominal wage rate, and the thus induced real wage rate $\omega = (w/p)/z^o$.

The temporary equilibrium itself comprises the following eleven endogenous variables: productive capacity, Y^n; actual production, Y; utilization, $u = Y/Y^n$; labour productivity, $z = Y/L$; consumption, C; investment, I; government spending, G; real taxes, T; the nominal interest rate, i; the rate of profit, r; and the wage share, v. The analysis in the next section will reduce (3.1)–(3.11) to two IS-LM equations in intensive form, with u and i as the market-clearing variables.

In addition, the dynamic laws for K, L^s (labour supply in normal working hours), z^o, M and π, complemented by the specification for the (correctly perceived) trend rate of inflation π^o, are exactly the same as in the previous chapter, where the growth rates g_z, g_ℓ and g_m are exogenous constants:

$$\dot{K} = I \tag{3.12}$$

$$\hat{L}^s = g_\ell \tag{3.13}$$

$$\hat{z}^o = g_z \tag{3.14}$$

$$\hat{M} = g_m \tag{3.15}$$

$$\dot{\pi} = \beta_\pi[\kappa_\pi(\hat{p} - \pi) + (1 - \kappa_\pi)(\pi^o - \pi)], \quad 0 \le \kappa_\pi \le 1 \tag{3.16}$$

$$\pi^o = g_m - g_\ell - g_z \tag{3.17}$$

The wage Phillips curve (3.18) that we put up next differs from its predecessor (2.13) in two respects. First, (2.13) is slightly extended in that the reference term for inflation is not just expected inflation, π, but a weighted average of the expected and the actual rate of inflation, $\kappa_w \hat{p} + (1 - \kappa_w)\pi$ (of course, $0 \leq \kappa_w \leq 1$). The idea behind this combination is the following. The role of π is to define the (*ex ante*) real interest rate $i - \pi$ that enters the investment function (3.7). Since investment in fixed capital involves a longer time horizon, π could be viewed as an expected time average of inflation over the next few years.[6] By contrast, the expected rate of inflation underlying a wage-bargaining process relates to a shorter time horizon of, say, one year or so. Correspondingly, these inflationary expectations will be comparatively more influenced by actual inflation $\hat{p}$. Introducing the weighted average $\kappa_w \hat{p} + (1 - \kappa_w)\pi$ is a straightforward device, which allows us to refer to two conceptually different rates of expected inflation but to proceed with the modelling with just one such expectational variable.

The other difference of the present wage Phillips curve from (2.13) is a slight limitation. In (2.13) the growth rate of nominal wages reacted to the employment rate. In the present context we can save one state variable if, instead, the rate of utilization is employed for this purpose. Substituting u for the rate of employment is justified by the empirical observation that the time series of the employment rate (proxied by the deviations of total working hours from trend) and utilization (or the output gap) exhibit strong comovements.[7] In sum, the modified wage Phillips curve reads

$$\hat{w} = g_z + \kappa_w \hat{p} + (1 - \kappa_w)\pi + f_w(u), \quad f_w(1) = 0, f_w' > 0 \tag{3.18}$$

The specification $f_w = f_w(u)$ in (3.18) reduces the role of labour supply to a minimum; only the growth rate g_ℓ determined in (3.13) will remain, which makes itself felt in the specification of the trend rate of inflation in

---

[6] We are aware that this interpretation is not fully consistent, because a similar reasoning should then apply to the nominal interest rate and the rate of profit in (3.7). These problems are, however, completely neglected in the modelling literature. In order not to go astray, we follow the usual habit and adopt the current rates of interest and profit in (3.7) rather than the expected ones.

[7] See, for example, the juxtaposition of hours and output in King and Rebelo (1999, p. 936, fig. 3). A more direct statement concerning empirical estimates of (reduced-form price) Phillips curves is found in Brayton et al. (1999, p. 4): 'Movements of the utilization and unemployment rates are sufficiently similar over the past forty or so years that the goodness of fit of equations on one is quite similar to the fit of equations based on the other.' The state variable that we save, already known from the Sargent model, is $k^s = K/z^o L^s$. If wages were assumed to react to the employment rate L/L^s, then k^s would reappear by way of the decomposition $L/L^s = (z^o L/Y)(Y/Y^n)(Y^n/K)(K/z^o L^s) = [1/f_z(u)]u \, y^n k^s$, which has already been mentioned in the previous section.

eq. (3.17). We return to this subject in the discussion of the steady-state notion.

The final dynamic variable to be considered is the price level p. As announced in chapter 2, it is now put on an equal footing with the wage rate w. In detail, we postulate

$$\hat{p} = \kappa_p(\hat{w} - g_z) + (1 - \kappa_p)\pi + f_p(u, v) \tag{3.19}$$

$$f_p(u, v) = f_{pu}(u) + f_{pv}[(1 + \mu)v - 1],$$

$$f_{pu}(1) = 0, \quad f_{pv}(0) = 0, \quad f'_{pu}, f'_{pv} > 0 \tag{3.20}$$

The term for benchmark inflation parallels that in (3.18) and may be explained by a similar line of reasoning. Here it is a weighted average of the expected inflation rate π and wage inflation corrected for technological progress. It may furthermore be noticed that the special combination $\kappa_p = \kappa_w = 1$ of the weights κ_w and κ_p in (3.18) and (3.19) would lead to a circular specification. This case has to be ruled out by assumption. The exclusion is only natural, however, since $\kappa_p = \kappa_w = 1$ would mean that inflationary expectations are completely ignored in the wage-price sector.

The adjustment function $f_p = f_p(u, v)$ combines two principles. With the concept of output adjusting to demand, it is clear that utilization u can also be seen as representing the demand pressure in percentage terms. Therefore, the component f_{pu} signifies a demand-pull term. On the other hand, the component f_{pv} is another cost-push term, besides the impact of the wage increases upon the variable representing benchmark inflation. f_{pv} may even be called a cost-push term proper. The reason is that μ in the argument of this function is a target markup rate over unit labour cost. Price increases thus exceed benchmark inflation if labour costs are so high that, at current prices, $p < (1 + \mu)wL/Y$ (which is equivalent to $(1 + \mu)wL/pY - 1 = (1 + \mu)v - 1 > 0$).

Taking account of labour costs in a price Phillips curve also has some empirical support. Brayton et al. (1999, pp. 22–27) find that adding the markup of prices over trend unit labour costs to the other explanatory variables is significant in all versions of their estimations. The variable itself has the implication that, when the price level is high relative to trend unit labour costs, downward pressure is exerted on inflation. To relate this result to our framework, observe that trend unit labour costs are given by $w(L)^o/Y = w/z^o$, and the markup rate $\tilde{\mu}$ over this expression by the equation $p = (1 + \tilde{\mu})w/z^o$. Hence, p is high relative to trend unit labour costs and impacts negatively on the rate of inflation if $p/(w/z^o)$ or, equivalently, $\tilde{\mu}$ is high.

Since $p/(w/z^o) = 1/\omega = 1/vf_z(u)$ (the latter equality by virtue of (3.9)), it is seen that a *ceteris paribus* increase in the wage share v or, via procyclical productivity, in capacity utilization u has a positive effect on $\hat{p}$. Since in Brayton et al. (1999) utilization (or, equally effectively, the unemployment rate) is already included among the independent variables of the regression equations, it can be assumed that the wage share taken on its own also contributes significantly to an explanation of price inflation, in the same direction as stated in eqs. (3.19) and (3.20).

Another argument for the approach in (3.20) is the real wage dynamics implied by (3.18) and (3.19), with and without the function f_{pv}. This topic will be later discussed in an extra section. Lastly, it may be mentioned that the function f_{pv} is also 'needed' to make income distribution determinate in the steady state – i.e. the wage share or the real wage rate.[8]

With regard to the theoretical consistency of the cost-push term f_{pv}, a note of caution should be added. By setting the target markup μ, firms simultaneously determine the wage share $v^o = 1/(1+\mu)$ in a long-run equilibrium position. Certainly, income distribution is not completely at the mercy of firms, but is also influenced by other economic and social factors. Employing the concept of a given target markup implicitly assumes that this level is compatible with the long-run balance of power between workers and capital owners. The latter relationship is to be distinguished from the struggle over income distribution in the course of a business cycle, the fierceness of which is here characterized by the reaction coefficients f'_{pu}, f'_{pv} and f'_w in the wage-price sector. The present model contents itself with studying these medium-term fluctuations of the current wage share v around the equilibrium level v^o.

Nevertheless, the target markup μ need not be fixed but could itself be subjected to a slow adjustment process, when firms perceive that it contradicts some other economic factors. We forgo this more appropriate modelling option for the sake of simplicity.

3.4   The model in intensive form

To be analytically tractable, the model has to be reformulated in intensive form. This procedure is much easier than it was with Sargent's model in chapter 2. As the building blocks have been specified, the entire model

---

[8] Concretely, this can be seen in the next section from point 4 in the derivation of the steady-state values; the argument given there would break down if f_{pv} were missing in (3.20). Indeterminacy of the steady state for $f_{pv} = 0$ is also reflected by the fact that the Jacobian matrix $\mathcal{J}$ of the reduced differential equations system would be singular, $\det \mathcal{J} = 0$, if $f'_{pv} = 0$; see Lemma 2 in section 3.5.

can be transformed to three ordinary differential equations in three state variables. These are $m = M/pK$, real balances scaled down by the capital stock; $\omega = (w/p)/z^o$, the productivity-deflated real wage rate; and π, the expected rate of inflation.[9]

To begin with, the temporary equilibrium part (3.1)–(3.11) of the economy can be compactly summarized by two equations that represent the market-clearing conditions (3.10) and (3.11) in intensive form. Dividing (3.10) by K and (3.11) by pY yields

$$f_I[(1 - \omega/f_z(u))uy^n - \delta - (i - \pi)]$$
$$+ (1 - s_h)(uy^n - \theta - \delta) + \delta + \gamma - uy^n = 0 \qquad (3.21)$$
$$f_m(i) - m/uy^n = 0 \qquad (3.22)$$

Clearly, (3.21) and (3.22) are an IS and LM equation, respectively, without any further qualification, as in chapter 2 for the corresponding equations (2.22) and (2.24). Utilization u is the variable clearing the goods market in (3.21), while the nominal interest rate i clears the money market in (3.22). This temporary equilibrium solution varies with the statically exogenous variables m, ω and π. The existence and uniqueness of such functions $u = u(m, \omega, \pi)$ and $i = i(m, \omega, \pi)$ will be formally established in the next section.

Thus we can turn to the dynamic variables m, ω and π. To describe their motions it must first be observed that the structural wage-price equations (3.18) and (3.19) are interconnected, since $\hat{p}$ shows up on the right-hand side of the $\hat{w}$ adjustments, and $\hat{w}$ on the right-hand side of the $\hat{p}$ adjustments. A little calculation is required to convert these equations to the so-called reduced form, where $\hat{p}$ and $\hat{w}$ are eliminated from the right-hand side. Assuming, as already mentioned before, that at least one of the weights κ_p and κ_w falls short of unity, and defining $\kappa := 1/(1 - \kappa_p\kappa_w) > 0$, we obtain

$$\hat{p} = \pi + \kappa[\kappa_p f_w(u) + f_p(u, v)] \qquad (3.23)$$
$$\hat{w} = \pi + g_z + \kappa[f_w(u) + \kappa_w f_p(u, v)] \qquad (3.24)$$

Note the cross Phillips curve effects in the two equations: price inflation is also influenced by the central term f_w from the wage Phillips curve, and wage inflation by the central term f_p from the price Phillips curve (provided κ_p and κ_w are not zero).

---

[9] Looking back at the analysis in chapter 2, section 3, it may be said that m takes the role of the composed variable $x_m = z^o M/wK$; see the remark on eq. (2.23).

The rates of change of m, ω and π can now readily be derived as follows. Logarithmic differentiation of $m = M/pK$ and $\omega = w/pz^o$ gives $\hat{m} = \hat{M} - \hat{p} - \hat{K}$ and $\hat{\omega} = \hat{w} - \hat{p} - \hat{z}^o$, respectively. Subsequently, substitute (3.23) for $\hat{p}$, here as well as in eq. (3.16) for $\dot{\pi}$. Taking (3.12), (3.14) and (3.15) into account, we arrive at

$$\dot{m} = m\{g_m - \pi - \kappa[\kappa_p f_w(u) + f_p(u, v)]$$
$$-f_l[(1 - v)uy^n - \delta - (i - \pi)]\} \tag{3.25}$$

$$\dot{\omega} = \omega\kappa[(1 - \kappa_p)f_w(u) - (1 - \kappa_w)f_p(u, v)] \tag{3.26}$$

$$\dot{\pi} = \beta_\pi\{\kappa_\pi\kappa[\kappa_p f_w(u) + f_p(u, v)] + (1 - \kappa_\pi)(\pi^o - \pi)\} \tag{3.27}$$

where it is understood that $v = \omega/f_z(u)$, and $u = u(m, \omega, \pi)$ and $i = i(m, \omega, \pi)$ are the IS-LM solutions of (3.21) and (3.22).

Having reduced the model to a set of differential equations, next it has to be demonstrated that system (3.25)–(3.27) possesses a uniquely determined equilibrium point (m^o, ω^o, π^o). Since it implies constant income shares and proportional growth of the real and financial sector, and also of the level variables within the real sector itself, it is obvious that (m^o, ω^o, π^o) constitutes a steady-state position of the economy. A supplementary analysis will then be concerned with its stability properties.

The steady-state investigation is subdivided into two main parts. We first construct such a position, and subsequently argue for its uniqueness. Regarding the first step it should be pointed out right away that, in order for the equilibrium to be meaningful and consistent with the functional specifications chosen, an assumption on a suitable parameter combination will have to be introduced.

It is certainly expected from a long-run equilibrium position that actual labour productivity z grows at the given rate $\hat{z}^o$ of technological progress, and that employment and labour supply move in step. Using (3.13), (3.14) and writing g^o for the equilibrium real rate of growth, this postulate amounts to $g^o = \hat{Y} = \hat{L}^h + \hat{z} = \hat{L}^{hs} + \hat{z}^o = g_\ell + g_z$. Admittedly, (3.13) was not involved in deriving eqs. (3.25)–(3.27). So, strictly speaking, the equation is imposed on them from the outside. On the other hand, it is a postulate that is needed to support the specification of π^o in (3.17) as a relevant reference rate of inflation for the regressive expectations in eq. (3.16).

Taking the relationship $(f_I)^o = g^o = g_\ell + g_z$ for granted, the steady-state values of the other variables can be computed in a unique way. This is done in a number of successive steps.

(1) $(f_I)^o = g_\ell + g_z$ and (3.25) = 0 together with (3.17) imply $\kappa[\kappa_p f_w + f_p] = g_m - g_\ell - g_z - \pi = \pi^o - \pi$. Substituting this in (3.27) = 0 gives

$\kappa_\pi(\pi^o - \pi) + (1 - \kappa_\pi)(\pi^o - \pi) = 0$. Hence, expected inflation in the growth equilibrium is indeed equal to π^o as defined in (3.17) (thus justifying the slight slip in the notation for equilibrium inflation above).

(2) There are now two equations determining f_w and f_p: $\kappa_p f_w + f_p = 0$ from (3.25) = 0, and $(1 - \kappa_p)f_w - (1 - \kappa_w)f_p = 0$ from (3.26) = 0. With $1 - \kappa_p \kappa_w \neq 0$, the two equations are independent. Hence, there is no other solution besides the obvious $f_w = 0, f_p = 0$.

(3) From $f_w = 0$ one concludes $u^o = 1$; see (3.18).

(4) $f_p = 0$ and its decomposition in (3.20), together with (3.9) and (3.3), yields $\omega^o = \omega^o/f_z(u^o) = v^o = 1/(1 + \mu)$.

(5) The nominal interest rate i^o is given by that value of i which fulfils the equation $f_I[(1 - v^o)u^o y^n - \delta - i + \pi^o] = (f_I)^o$. It is unique since the investment function $f_I(\cdot)$ is strictly increasing.

(6) Lastly, m^o is obtained from the LM equation (3.22), $m^o = u^o y^n f_m(i^o)$.

There is, however, a problem with this derivation of the steady state, since the IS equation (3.21) has been completely ignored so far. To maintain it, we must suppose that the parameters s_h, y^n, θ, δ and γ are so well suited to each other that, given $f_I = (f_I)^o = g_\ell + g_z$ and $u = u^o = 1$, they bring about equality in (3.21). Doing this, $u(m^o, \omega^o, \pi^o) = u^o$ and $i(m^o, \omega^o, \pi^o) = i^o$ for the IS-LM functions is ensured.

Presumably, the assumption on the parameters appears quite artificial at first sight. It may nevertheless be justified by taking a slightly higher point of view.[10] From this perspective, a more satisfactory consumption function would be desirable, which distinguishes the different saving propensities of workers and rentier households (we will actually introduce this differentiation in the next chapter). With such a function, the real wage rate would show up outside the investment function f_I in eq. (3.21). We could then modify the argument in step 4 above and argue that, given $f_I = (f_I)^o$, the equilibrium real wage rate is (formally) determined by means of this IS equation.

This approach also clarifies the role of the target markup rate μ. It has already been indicated at the end of the previous section that firms, in order to be consistent with long-run income distribution, must adjust the level of μ such that $1/(1 + \mu) = v^o = \omega^o/f_z(u^o) = \omega^o$. In a more elaborate modelling version, firms might be supposed to vary μ over time in response to some perceived disequilibrium phenomena. This device would indeed be the most appropriate solution to arrive at a consistent, meaningful and truly endogenous determination of the steady-state position.

---

[10] In particular, we do not think of a neoclassical 'solution', which might propose making the normal output–capital ratio y^n an endogenous variable.

Accepting the equilibrium values m^o, ω^o, π^o as they stand, it remains to consider their uniqueness. That is, it has to be shown that no other stationary point $(\tilde{m}, \tilde{\omega}, \tilde{\pi})$ of (3.25)–(3.27) exists, not even one that violates the initial postulate $(f_I)^o = g_\ell + g_z$. First of all, the triple (m^o, ω^o, π^o) is locally unique. This directly follows from the fact, to be established in the ensuing local stability analysis, that the Jacobian matrix of (3.25)–(3.27) has a nonzero determinant and is thus invertible.[11]

But, globally as well, (m^o, ω^o, π^o) is most likely to be the only equilibrium. To see this, suppose that another equilibrium $(\tilde{m}, \tilde{\omega}, \tilde{\pi})$ exists in which utilization is $\tilde{u}$ (it does not matter whether $\tilde{u} = 1$ or $\tilde{u} \neq 1$). In detail, $(\tilde{m}, \tilde{\omega}, \tilde{\pi})$ can be reconstructed by the following procedure. Putting the right-hand side of (3.26) equal to zero determines the equilibrium wage share $\tilde{v}$ and, by eq. (3.9), the real wage $\tilde{\omega}$. Subsequently, $\tilde{\pi}$ is obtained from setting (3.27) $= 0$. On this basis, the real growth rate $\tilde{g} = f_I[\ldots]$ can be computed by setting (3.25) $= 0$. The equality $f_I[(1 - \tilde{v})\tilde{u}y^n - \delta - (i - \tilde{\pi})] = \tilde{g}$ allows one to determine the equilibrium rate of interest. With $\tilde{\omega}$ and $\tilde{\pi}$ already being given, this interest rate is brought about by a suitable value $\tilde{m}$, via the IS-LM function for i.

However, for a thus derived triple $(\tilde{m}, \tilde{\omega}, \tilde{\pi})$ to constitute a steady state of the model, the IS-LM utilization function is required to yield the same level $\tilde{u}$ from which we have started out, i.e. $u(\tilde{m}, \tilde{\omega}, \tilde{\pi}) = \tilde{u}$. If $(\tilde{m}, \tilde{\omega}, \tilde{\pi}) \neq (m^o, \omega^o, \pi^o)$, this could happen only by a fluke.

3.5   Local stability results

In a similar manner to chapter 2, the investigation of local stability is preceded by the IS-LM analysis of eqs. (3.21) and (3.22). It is, again, easily checked that the LM curve is unambiguously upward-sloping – i.e. the market-clearing interest rate i is an increasing function of capacity utilization u; and, again, the IS curve is required to have the usual negative slope, according to which the interest rate has a negative impact on the level of utilization that satisfies the current demand for goods. The latter property is achieved by the following supposition, the analogy of which to Assumption 1 in chapter 2, section 4 is obvious.

Assumption 1
Evaluated at the steady-state values, the responsiveness in fixed investment is so restrained that $f_I' < s_h/[1 - v^o(1 - f_z')]$.

---

[11] The property that $\det \mathcal{J} \neq 0$ implies the local uniqueness of the system's equilibrium point is connected to the implicit function theorem – or, more precisely, the inverse function theorem, on which it is mathematically grounded.

A *ceteris paribus* increase in the money supply, or $m = M/pK$, for that matter, shifts the LM curve downward. Since the goods market is not concerned and so the IS curve does not move, utilization increases and the interest rate declines. The underlying economic mechanisms are the same as in the familiar undergraduate textbook story.

By contrast, expectations of higher inflation π leave the LM curve unaffected and act on the IS curve only. The corresponding fall in the real rate of interest and the higher investment thus brought about, which is also known as the Tobin effect, produces an upward shift in the IS curve. Hence utilization increases, at the 'cost' of a nominal interest rate that also rises. The mathematical argument, however, reveals that the real rate of interest $i - \pi$, after the market adjustments have all worked out, is still lower than before. It may be noted in passing that u may also increase if Assumption 1 is (mildly) violated, but that then i would rise more than π, which does not seem reasonable. In this sense the constraint on the responsiveness f_I' is a necessary assumption to make.

While in the simple IS-LM model versions there is no role for distribution, in eq. (3.21) distribution enters the investment function in the form of the real wage rate, via the rate of profit. The effects of a rise in ω are therefore a mirror image of a decline in π; they reduce both u and i. Lemma 1 collects up all these results. More detailed computations, which will be used repeatedly in the ensuing stability analysis, can be found in the proof.

Lemma 1
Let Assumption 1 apply. Then for all m, ω and π close to the steady state, a (locally) unique IS-LM solution $u = u(m, \omega, \pi)$ and $i = i(m, \omega, \pi)$ of (3.21) and (3.22) exists. The (continuous) partial derivatives satisfy

$$\partial u/\partial m > 0 \quad \partial u/\partial \omega < 0 \quad \partial u/\partial \pi > 0$$

$$\partial i/\partial m < 0 \quad \partial i/\partial \omega < 0 \quad 0 < \partial i/\partial \pi < 1$$

Proof: The basic approach is the same as in the proof of Lemma 1 in chapter 2, section 4. Referring to eqs. (3.21) and (3.22), define the two functions F_1 and F_2 by

$$F_1 = F_1(u, i, \omega, \pi) := -s_h u y^n + f_I[(1 - \omega/f_z(u))uy^n - \delta - i + \pi] + \text{const.}$$

$$F_2 = F_2(u, i, m) := f_m(i) - m/uy^n$$

IS utilization $u_{IS} = u_{IS}(i, \omega, \pi)$ is given by that value of u which, with respect to i, ω, π given, brings about $F_1(u, i, \omega, \pi) = 0$. Likewise, the LM interest rate $i_{LM} = i_{LM}(u, m)$ is determined by that value of i which, given

u and m, brings about $F_2(u, i, m) = 0$. The partial derivatives of u_{IS} and i_{LM} are obtained from the implicit function theorem, which yields

$$\partial u_{IS}/\partial a = -(\partial F_1/\partial a)/(\partial F_1/\partial u), \quad \text{where } a = i, \omega, \pi$$

$$\partial i_{LM}/\partial a = -(\partial F_2/\partial a)/(\partial F_2/\partial i), \quad \text{where } a = u, m$$

Assumption 1 states that $\partial F_1/\partial u < 0$. Again, in the detailed calculations it is helpful to work with the interest elasticity of money demand, $\eta_{m,i} = -f_m' i^o/f_m$.

Defining the function $F = F(u, m, \omega, \pi) := F_1[u, i_{LM}(u, m), \omega, \pi]$, utilization in the IS-LM temporary equilibrium is determined by a value $u = u(m, \omega, \pi)$ that satisfies $F = 0$ (m, ω, π being given). The corresponding IS-LM interest rate $i = i(m, \omega, \pi)$ results from $i_{LM}[u(m, \omega, \pi), m]$. Applying the implicit function theorem and observing that $F_u := \partial F/\partial u = \partial F_1/\partial u + (\partial F_1/\partial i) \cdot (\partial i_{LM}/\partial u) < 0$, one computes $u_\pi := \partial u/\partial \pi = f_I'/(-F_u) > 0$, $\partial u/\partial m = (i/m\eta_{m,i})u_\pi > 0$, and $\partial u/\partial \omega = -y^n u_\pi < 0$.

Subsequently one gets $\partial i/\partial \pi = (\partial i_{LM}/\partial u)(\partial u/\partial \pi) > 0$ and, analogously, $\partial i/\partial \omega < 0$. It is also readily checked that $1 - \partial i/\partial \pi = (\partial F_1/\partial u)/F_u > 0$, and $\partial i/\partial m = (\partial i_{LM}/\partial u)(\partial u/\partial m) + \partial i_{LM}/\partial m = (i/m\eta_{m,i})[(\partial i_{LM}/\partial u)(\partial u/\partial \pi) - 1] = (i/m\eta_{m,i}) (\partial i/\partial \pi - 1) < 0$.

QED

The partial derivatives of the lemma enter the Jacobian matrix of system (3.25)–(3.27). To set it up, we abbreviate

$$H_w = H_w(m, \omega, \pi) := f_w(u)$$

$$H_p = H_p(m, \omega, \pi) := f_{pu}(u) + f_{pv}[(1 + \mu)\omega/f_z(u) - 1]$$

$$H_I = H_I(m, \omega, \pi) := f_I[(1 - \omega/f_z(u))uy^n - \delta - i + \pi]$$

with, of course, $u = u(m, \omega, \pi)$, $i = i(m, \omega, \pi)$. Write furthermore

$$H_{ab} := \partial H_a/\partial b, \quad a = w, p, I \text{ and } b = m, \omega, \pi$$

for the partial derivatives of the H functions (evaluated at the steady-state position) and collect terms as follows, where $b = m, \omega, \pi$:

$$H_{1b}(\kappa_p) := \kappa \kappa_p H_{wb} + \kappa H_{pb} + H_{Ib}$$

$$H_{2b}(\kappa_p, \kappa_w) := (1 - \kappa_p)H_{wb} - (1 - \kappa_w)H_{pb}$$

$$H_{3b}(\kappa_p) := \kappa(\kappa_p H_{wb} + H_{pb})$$

The Jacobian then reads

$$J = \begin{bmatrix} -mH_{1m}(\kappa_p) & -mH_{1\omega}(\kappa_p) & -m[1 + H_{1\pi}(\kappa_p)] \\ \omega\kappa H_{2m}(\kappa_p, \kappa_w) & \omega\kappa H_{2\omega}(\kappa_p, \kappa_w) & \omega\kappa H_{2\pi}(\kappa_p, \kappa_w) \\ \beta_\pi \kappa_\pi H_{3m}(\kappa_p) & \beta_\pi \kappa_\pi H_{3\omega}(\kappa_p) & \beta_\pi[\kappa_\pi H_{3\pi}(\kappa_p) - (1 - \kappa_\pi)] \end{bmatrix} \quad (3.28)$$

Before studying the local dynamics of the full system (3.25)–(3.27), let us follow the procedure of chapter 2, section 5, and consider the same two simplified cases. First, freeze the expected rate of inflation at its equilibrium value π^o. The Jacobian of the corresponding dynamics of eqs. (3.25), (3.26) is given by the upper-left (2×2) submatrix of J. Though the single entries of this matrix are rather complicated, its determinant is unambiguously positive. On the other hand, unlike the analogous case in section 2.5, there exist parameter combinations that render the trace positive, so that now the truncated dynamics might already be unstable.

The second simplified case includes inflationary expectations and their motions in eq. (3.27), but confines them to be purely regressive. With $\kappa_\pi = 0$, the entries j_{31} and j_{32} in J vanish, while $j_{33} = -\beta_\pi$. Hence, two eigenvalues are the same as before and the third one is $-\beta_\pi$. This system is thus locally stable if, and only if, the truncated two-dimensional system is stable. The stability condition itself is given in an extra proposition.

Proposition 1
Consider the truncated two-dimensional dynamics (3.25), (3.26) with π frozen at π^o, or the case of purely regressive expectations $\kappa_\pi = 0$ in the full system (3.25)–(3.27). Then, under Assumption 1, the long-run equilibrium is locally asymptotically stable if

$$iH_1 f_I' / \eta_{m,i} + (1 - \kappa_w)\kappa f_{pv}' + \kappa u_\pi [\kappa_p i / \eta_{m,i} + (1 - \kappa_p) y'' \omega] f_w'$$
$$+ \kappa u_\pi [(1 - \kappa_w) y'' \omega - i / \eta_{m,i}](f_z' f_{pv}' - f_{pu}') > 0$$

where $H_1 := y''(1 - v + v f_z')u_\pi + (1 - i_\pi) > 0$, and $u_\pi = \partial u / \partial\pi$, $i_\pi = \partial i / \partial\pi$ (all derivatives evaluated at the steady-state values). Instability prevails if the inequality is reversed.

Proof: Denote the upper-left (2×2) submatrix of J by $J^{(2)}$. The proposition follows from the stability conditions for the two-dimensional case, $\det J^{(2)} > 0$, $\operatorname{trace} J^{(2)} < 0$, and the remark in the text. The computations are straightforward, though quite tedious and space-consuming.

We content ourselves with a few hints. The partial derivatives H_{ab} result as follows:

$$H_{w\pi} = f'_w u_\pi \qquad H_{p\pi} = (f'_{pu} - f'_z f'_{pv}) u_\pi$$

$$H_{wm} = (i/m\eta_{m,i}) H_{w\pi} \qquad H_{pm} = (i/m\eta_{m,i}) H_{p\pi}$$

$$H_{w\omega} = -y^n H_{w\pi} \qquad H_{p\omega} = (1+\mu)f'_{pv} - y^n H_{p\pi}$$

$$H_{I\pi} = f'_I H_1 \qquad H_{Im} = (i/m\eta_{m,i}) H_{I\pi} \qquad H_{I\omega} = -y^n H_{I\pi}$$

Several of these terms cancel out in the computation of the determinant. We finally obtain

$$\det \mathcal{J}^{(2)} = (i\omega\kappa(1+\mu)f'_{pv}/\eta_{m,i})(u_\pi f'_w + (1-\kappa_w)H_1 f'_I) > 0$$

The inequality in the proposition collects and rearranges the terms in the condition $-\text{trace}\,\mathcal{J}^{(2)} > 0$. Given $\det \mathcal{J}^{(2)} > 0$, it is necessary and sufficient for the eigenvalues to have negative real parts.

QED

Instability of the steady state becomes possible if the last term on the left-hand side of the inequality in Proposition 1 is negative and also dominates the other three terms. It may be felt that only some extraordinary parameter combinations can bring this about. As a matter of fact, the numerical coefficients influencing the real wage dynamics that will be discussed in the next section imply that the questionable term itself is already positive, since both expressions $(1 - \kappa_w)y^n \omega - i/\eta_{m,i}$ and $f'_z f'_{pv} - f'_{pu}$ are positive (if for y^n, ω, i, $\eta_{m,i}$ the values of chapter 2, section 6, are taken over). Without going into further computational details, it can be believed that the stability condition on the whole is robust against a wide range of parameter variations.

Leaving artificial reaction coefficients aside, the most 'natural' way to construct instability is manipulating the weights κ_w and κ_p in the wage-price adjustment equations. For example, instability would prevail if the numerical parameters specified in the next two sections are maintained and the weights are set at $\kappa_w = 1$ and $\kappa_p = 0.70$ (or higher). It may be observed that this source of instability has no counterpart in the Sargent model. There we have (implicitly) $\kappa_w = 0$ in the wage Phillips curve (2.13), while a price Phillips curve where κ_p could enter does not exist. If, instead, the determination of the price inflation rate in (2.33) is considered for a comparison, then the weighting factor would read $\kappa_p = 0$. In other words, if in this respect we want to be conceptually close to the Sargent model by setting $\kappa_w = \kappa_p = 0$, then in the present framework as well local stability would be the normal case when inflationary expectations are neutralized.

Besides, it is interesting to note that the most important destabilization comes from a combination of two coefficients that appear innocent at first sight; in an a priori guess of which of the many coefficients are the most likely to be capable of bringing about instability, κ_w and κ_p would probably not be given high priority.

To revive the adaptive expectations mechanism for π and turn to the general three-dimensional dynamics, the key information to assess its stability is the sign of the determinant of the Jacobian matrix. In contrast to chapter 2, section 5 (Lemma 3), it is here unambiguously signed.

Lemma 2
Referring to the positive expression H_1 defined in Proposition 1, the determinant of the Jacobian $\mathcal{J}$ in (3.28) is given by

$$\det \mathcal{J} = -(i/\eta_{m,i})\kappa\beta_\pi f'_{pv}(u_\pi f'_w + (1-\kappa_\pi)(1-\kappa_w)H_1 f'_I) < 0.$$

Proof: The calculations of $\det \mathcal{J}$ proceed in seven steps. For reasons of space, once more only a few hints will be given.

(1) Assume $\kappa_\pi > 0$ in $\det \mathcal{J}$ and factorize, row by row, $-m$, $\omega\kappa$, $\beta_\pi\kappa_\pi$.
(2) Subtract the third row from the first row.
(3) Assume $\kappa_w < 1$ and add $\kappa/(1-\kappa_w)$ times the second row to the third row.
(4) Define $H_2 := (1-\kappa_p)f'_w + (1-\kappa_w)(f'_z f'_{pv} - f'_{pu})$ and use the formulae for the derivatives of H_{ab} in the proof of Proposition 1. $\det \mathcal{J}/(-m\omega\kappa\beta_\pi\kappa_\pi)$ is then equal to the determinant of the matrix

$$\begin{bmatrix} if'_I H_1/m\eta_{m,i} & -y''f'_I H_1 & f'_I H_1 + 1/\kappa_\pi \\ iu_\pi H_2/m\eta_{m,i} & -(1-\kappa_w)(1+\mu)f'_{pv} - y''u_\pi H_2 & u_\pi H_2 \\ \dfrac{if'_w u_\pi}{m\eta_{m,i}(1-\kappa_w)} & \dfrac{-y''f'_w u_\pi}{1-\kappa_w} & \dfrac{f'_w u_\pi}{1-\kappa_w} - \dfrac{(1-\kappa_\pi)}{\kappa_\pi} \end{bmatrix}$$

(5) Subtract $u_\pi f'_w/(1-\kappa_w)H_1 f'_I$ times the first row from the third row. The effect is that the first two entries in the third row vanish. The 33-diagonal element is $H_3 := -(1-\kappa_\pi + u_\pi f'_w/(1-\kappa_w)H_1 f'_I)/\kappa_\pi$.
(6) The determinant of the upper-left 2×2 submatrix of the matrix obtained in step 5 is computed as $H_4 := -i(1-\kappa_w)(1+\mu)H_1 f'_I f'_{pv}/m\eta_{m,i}$.

(7) It remains to multiply H_4 with H_3 and $-m\omega\kappa\beta_\pi\kappa_\pi$. Observing that, in the steady state, $\omega^o(1+\mu) = v^o/v^o = 1$, the expression given in the lemma results. Since $\det \mathcal{J}$ varies continuously with the coefficients κ_π and κ_w, the formula is also valid for the limiting cases excluded before, $\kappa_\pi = 0$ and $\kappa_w = 1$.

QED

Accepting the local stability of the two special dynamics as discussed above, this property carries over to the general case if inflationary expectations, especially the adaptive expectations component, are sufficiently sluggish; that is, if the adjustment speed β_π is sufficiently low. The formal argument is the same as for the stability proposition in chapter 2, section 5. It is based on the fact that the determinant of $\mathcal{J}$ in (3.28) and the determinant of its upper-left (2×2) submatrix have opposite signs (see Lemma 2 and the proof of Proposition 1), and that the entries j_{31} and j_{32} in $\mathcal{J}$ tend to zero as $\beta_\pi \to 0$. Given that the truncated two-dimensional system is stable, the full system (3.25)–(3.27) is likewise locally stable if β_π is small enough.

By contrast, the steady state is unstable – at least – if trace $\mathcal{J} > 0$. This condition will be fulfilled if the term $H_{3\pi}(\kappa_p)$ in the entry j_{33} is positive, κ_π sufficiently close to unity and then β_π sufficiently large. Hence, if adaptive expectations are sufficiently important vs. regressive expectations, fast adjustments of inflationary expectations can again be destabilizing.

Under these circumstances, there will, moreover, be (at least) one critical value $\beta_\pi = \beta_\pi^H$ of the adjustment speed where, with β_π rising, the system changes from being locally convergent to locally divergent. Since $\det \mathcal{J} \neq 0$ throughout, this gives rise to a Hopf bifurcation. Just as with the Sargent model, therefore, the present economy too has a certain potential for cyclical motions. For further details we may refer to the discussion surrounding Proposition 2 in chapter 2, section 5. These results and, in particular, a more explicit instability condition are summarized in the second theorem.

Proposition 2
Given Assumption 1, the following statements hold true.

(a) *The equilibrium point of system (3.25)–(3.27) is locally asymptotically stable if the inequality in Proposition 1 is satisfied and the adjustment speed β_π is sufficiently low.*

(b) *Suppose that $\kappa_p f_w' - (f_z' f_{pv}' - f_{pu}') > (1 - \kappa_\pi)/\kappa\kappa_\pi(\partial u/\partial\pi)$. Then the equilibrium is unstable for all β_π sufficiently large.*

(c) For all ceteris paribus *variations of a single parameter, a Hopf bifurcation occurs at that value of the parameter where the equilibrium changes from being locally stable to unstable, or vice versa.*

Proof: Referring to the definition of $H_{3\pi} = \kappa(\kappa_p H_{w\pi} + H_{p\pi})$ and the computation of $H_{w\pi}$, $H_{p\pi}$ in the proof of Proposition 1, the inequality in part (*b*) restates the condition $\kappa_\pi H_{3\pi} - (1 - \kappa_\pi) > 0$ in the entry j_{33} in (3.28). The remainder has been discussed in the main text.

QED

Unfortunately, the condition in part (*b*) of the proposition is not very far-reaching. For example, it is typically not satisfied when $\kappa_p = 0$. On the other hand, it should be emphasized that it is by no means necessary to obtain instability for high values of β_π. An analytical treatment that invokes the other conditions of a full-fledged mathematical investigation (the Routh–Hurwitz theorem) is, however, rather cumbersome. To check the generality of this type of instability statement, as well as for an assessment of the stabilizing and destabilizing tendencies of the other reaction coefficients, a numerical stability analysis is more informative. This equally holds true for evaluating the scope for cyclical dynamics and their finer details. The remaining sections of the chapter are thus devoted to these numerical issues.

3.6   A tentative calibration of the real wage dynamics

The model is already so rich that a numerical stability analysis has to deal with a considerable number of parameter values. This especially concerns the wage-price sector, which in eqs. (3.18) to (3.20) comprises five coefficients directly, namely κ_w, f'_w, κ_p, f'_{pu} and f'_{pv}, and indirectly (as will become clear in a moment) the coefficient f'_z from eq. (3.3). Because estimations of empirical Phillips curve relationships are fraught with difficulties that are certainly beyond the scope of this book, we take another path to obtain some hints as to what might be reasonable orders of magnitude here. In contrast to econometrics, our approach amounts in essence to what is called a 'calibration' of a model. That is, we ask for the *implications* that these coefficients have for the cyclical evolution of the main variable of the wage-price sector, the (deflated) real wage rate ω.

In the present section we still content ourselves with a rather sketchy and tentative procedure. Against the background of this book's main model, the Keynes–Metzler–Goodwin model that is put forward in the next chapter, the subsequent chapter 5 carries out a much more systematic calibration of the wage-price dynamics.

Looking at the differential equation (3.26) for ω and recalling that by (3.9) the wage share v can be expressed as $v = \omega/f_z(u)$, it is seen that, apart from the auto-feedback, the motion of ω is solely governed by the time path of the utilization rate u; it is quite helpful that expected inflation cancels out and takes no effect. Thus, we posit a stylized cyclical motion of u, with an amplitude of ± 4 per cent, and study the impact of different parameter values on the resulting time path of the real wage. Judging from the empirical series of ω exhibited in figure 3.1 above, and more formally from the cross-correlations with u and the fact that the standard deviation of the percentage trend deviations of ω is about half that of u, the artificial series of ω is required to meet two demands: it should move more or less procyclically with u, and the amplitude should be some ± 2 per cent around its equilibrium value. In addition, we shall have an eye on the cyclical characteristics of the wage share.

Four functions are therefore involved in this context: $f_z = f_z(u)$, $f_w = f_w(u)$, $f_{pu} = f_{pu}(u)$ and $f_{pv} = f_{pv}(v)$. We specify them as linear functions of their arguments. Taking the equilibrium constraints in (3.3), (3.18) and (3.20) into account, they read

$$f_z(u) = 1 + \beta_{zu}(u - u^o) \tag{3.29}$$

$$f_w(u) = \beta_{wu}(u - u^o) \tag{3.30}$$

$$f_{pu}(u) = \beta_{pu}(u - u^o) \tag{3.31}$$

$$f_{pv}(v) = \beta_{pv}[(1 + \mu)v - 1] \tag{3.32}$$

Certainly, $u^o = 1$ and the β coefficients are all positive. Accepting eqs. (3.3) and (3.29) as they stand, i.e. $(z - z^o)/z^o = \beta_{zu}(u - 1)$, a value for the coefficient β_{zu} can be obtained right away from the data. Though a simple regression of $(z - z^o)/z^o$ on $u - 1 = (y - y^n)/y^n$ suggests itself (see (3.2) for the latter equality), it is not useful since the predictions thereby obtained do not trace out the peak and trough values of the actual series; the regression coefficient comes out too low in this respect. Instead, we take the standard deviations σ_z and σ_u of the two series and approximate β_{zu} by the ratio σ_z/σ_u. Depending on the sample period, the ratio varies between 0.46 and 0.51.[12] We thus put $\beta_{zu} = 0.50$.

Taking up the discussion at the end of section 3, we can next argue that the function $f_{pv}(\cdot)$ is a necessary prerequisite for a nearly procyclical real

---

[12] As indicated in section 2, the underlying trend of z and y is obtained from the standard Hodrick–Prescott filter. A value near 0.50 likewise comes about if one measures the peak and trough values of $(z - z^o)/z^o$ and $(y - y^n)/y^n$ and computes the average of the respective ratios.

wage dynamics. To see this, suppose $\beta_{pv} = 0$ and, using (3.30), (3.31), write down eq. (3.26), which gives rise to the differential equation

$$\dot{\omega} = \omega\kappa[(1 - \kappa_p)\beta_{wu} - (1 - \kappa_w)\beta_{pu}](u - u^o) \qquad (3.33)$$

Clearly, under these circumstances a regular cyclical motion of u induces oscillations of ω, which, depending on the sign of the expression in square brackets, lags or leads utilization by a quarter of a cycle. Hence, the coefficient β_{pv} may not be too small if we are to hope for procyclical real wages. By the same token, the weighting coefficient κ_w should fall significantly short of unity in (3.26). This supposition is, however, intelligible since it means that the wage-bargaining process underlying eq. (3.18) refers to expectations about future price inflation and not to the current rate of inflation alone.

As for the growth rate of nominal wages above their benchmark value, we have the intuition that it is between 0.25 per cent and 0.50 per cent if utilization is 1 per cent above normal. We then take 0.40 as a specific slope coefficient in the wage Phillips curve. Because of the lack of any clue in this direction, we furthermore treat the weights of inflationary expectations in the wage and price Phillips curves symmetrically and assume that they are somewhat more important than the direct 'cost terms' ($\hat{p}$ and $\hat{w} - g_z$ in (3.18) and (3.19)). Let us set these weights at 3/4. The values of the remaining two coefficients β_{pu} and β_{pv} are motivated by their effects in our little simulation experiment. Taken together, we choose

$$\begin{aligned} \kappa_w &= 0.25 & \kappa_p &= 0.25 & \beta_{zu} &= 0.50 \\ \beta_{wu} &= 0.40 & \beta_{pu} &= 0.20 & \beta_{pv} &= 2.00 \end{aligned} \qquad (3.34)$$

The stylized motion of utilization itself as the driving variable is conveniently conceived of as a sine wave, the period being eight years. Initializing the real wage rate at its steady-state value (numerically the same as in chapter 2, section 6), $\omega = \omega^o = 0.70$ at $t = 0$, the wage rate and the wage share soon enter a periodic motion. Figure 3.2 shows the result.

The parameter values in (3.34) yield a lag in real wages of rather more than two quarters and an amplitude of ± 2.19 per cent of the equilibrium value. With u attaining its maximum at $t = 26.00$, the precise peak value of real wages (with $\omega = 0.71532$) occurs at $t = 26.58$ (incidentally, measured at four digits we have $\omega = 0.7153$ over the time interval [26.50, 26.67], since the resulting (quasi-) sine wave in ω is rather flat around its turning points). The wage share lags utilization by about a quarter of a cycle, the maximum value being $v = 70.68\%$ at $t = 28.08$.

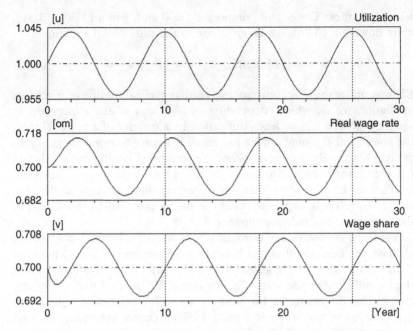

Figure 3.2: Stylized motions of u, ω and v induced by (3.34)

It will perhaps be expected that a weaker, or even negative, influence of u in the real wage dynamics could achieve a further reduction of the lag in ω. This is not true, however. For example, setting $\beta_{pu} = \beta_{wu} = 0$ (or any other value) does not affect the lag at all and depresses the amplitude of ω only to ± 0.0127. Emphasizing the price adjustments and putting $\beta_{pu} = 0.40$, while $\beta_{wu} = 0$, does not change the lag either.

Without diminishing the amplitude of ω too much, the lag can be shortened by invoking the wage share coefficient β_{pv}. A *ceteris paribus* increase up to $\beta_{pv} = 5.00$ reduces the lag to three months, the maximum real wage now being $\omega = 0.7150$ at $t = 26.25$. The 'price' to be paid for this 'success' is an extremely small amplitude of the wage share; it just rises to $v = 70.29\%$ at $t = 27.75$ (which explains the apparently high numerical value of β_{pv} that acts on v). It should by now also be clear that lowering *pari passu* the weights κ_w and κ_p has a similar effect; quantitatively, $\kappa_w = \kappa_p = 0$ implies a lag in ω of 0.25 years, with maximum values of ω and v at 0.7159 and 70.59 per cent, respectively.

On the basis of our a priori given values of β_{zu} and β_{wu}, we conclude from this discussion that the other four parameter values for β_{pu}, β_{pv}, κ_w and κ_p in (3.34) provide a sensible compromise between a lag in ω

that is not too long and an amplitude of the wage share that is not too small.[13]

We note finally that the rate of profit leads utilization by about three quarters. Recalling its definition in (3.8), $r = (1 - v)uy^n - \delta$, it is immediately seen that after $t = 26$, say, both the decreasing utilization rate u and the increasing wage share v exert a downward pressure on r. Hence, r necessarily begins to fall before u reaches its peak, at a time when the rise in u slows down and v begins to increase more rapidly (in relative terms) than u.

3.7   Numerical stability analysis

In mathematically establishing that high adjustment speeds β_π of inflationary expectations are destabilizing, at least if the weight of adaptive expectations κ_π is sufficiently high, Proposition 2(b) has relied on the condition $\kappa_p f'_w - (f'_z f'_{pv} - f'_{pu}) > (1 - \kappa_\pi)/\kappa\kappa_\pi(\partial u/\partial \pi)$. If we now adopt the coefficients of the wage-price sector proposed in (3.34), the left-hand side of the inequality becomes $\kappa_p \beta_{wu} - (\beta_{zu}\beta_{pv} - \beta_{pu}) = 0.10 - 0.80 < 0$. Independently of the rest of the model, the basis for Proposition 2(b) is thus undermined (recall that $\partial u/\partial \pi > 0$). The first goal of the numerical investigations undertaken in this section is to demonstrate that, despite this, the destabilizing potential of β_π is normally preserved.

To set up the steady-state relationships for the numerical analysis, the proportions from chapter 2, section 6, can be taken over. Following the presentation in that section, only two further reaction coefficients are to be fixed: the interest elasticity of money demand, $\eta_{m,i}$; and the responsiveness to invest, f'_I. We choose

$$\eta_{m,i} = 0.25 \quad f'_I = 0.08 \tag{3.35}$$

The value for $\eta_{m,i}$ is the same as before in (2.40). Regarding f'_I, we are constrained by Assumption 1. The savings propensity being $s_h = 0.069$ and the equilibrium wage share $v^o = 0.70$, it reads $f'_I < s_h/[1 - v^o(1 - \beta_{zu})] = 0.106$. $f'_I = 0.08$ keeps a moderate distance to this upper bound. Although the order of magnitude for f'_I appears rather low, the implications for the IS-LM reactions of utilization and the interest rate are not too implausible. With (3.35) one computes that a *ceteris paribus* increase in expected inflation by one percentage point raises the utilization rate by

[13] Direct empirical evidence on systematic cyclical features of the wage share is not without problems, in particular because the structural changes are so severe that the usual Hodrick–Prescott detrending procedure leads to strong variations in the trend line itself. Employing this filter despite such reservations yields an amplitude of the trend deviations that is indeed rather limited.

2.86 per cent and the rate of interest by 0.57 per cent (see the formulae for $\partial u/\partial \pi$ and $\partial i/\partial \pi$ in the proof of Lemma 1).[14]

Accepting (3.34), (3.35) together with the steady-state values of chapter 2, section 6, we again ask how the local dynamics of the economy is affected by variations of the two remaining parameters in the expectations adjustment mechanism, κ_π and β_π. The counterpart of figure 2.1 in section 2.6 is the (β_π, κ_π) diagram in figure 3.3,[15] which subdivides the parameter plane into the regions of cyclical convergence (CC), cyclical divergence (CD), monotonic divergence (MD) and monotonic convergence. The latter occurs for extremely small β_π values, to the left of the vertical solid line in the dotted area.[16] The congruence between figure 3.3 and the aforementioned parameter diagram of the Sargent model is evident. Neglecting the region where the 3×3 Jacobian matrix (2.38) of the Sargent model has a positive determinant, which for the present $\mathcal{J}$ in eq. (3.28) is ruled out by Lemma 2, both diagrams reveal similar dynamic properties of the economies to which they refer. Insofar as the diagrams are numerically comparable, it might only be said that the present model has a somewhat greater scope for (convergent) cyclical behaviour.

Although the cyclical tendencies pointed out in figure 3.3 are a basic characteristic of the model advanced here, it cannot yet be claimed that the corresponding fluctuations are of a business cycle nature. Two reasons suffice to warn against premature conclusions. First, one may focus on parameter combinations near the stability frontier, the bold line in figure 3.3. Computing the imaginary parts of the complex eigenvalues, it turns out that the pairs (β_π, κ_π) in a vicinity of the Hopf bifurcation locus give rise to oscillations that typically exhibit an overly long period. Thus, the (unique) Hopf bifurcation value of β_π that is associated with $\kappa_\pi = 0.90$ is given by $\beta_\pi^H = 0.2137$ (rounded) and leads to cycles that extend over $T = 33.43$ years. Reducing κ_π, which strengthens regressive expectations and their tendency for returning directly to the equilibrium value of π, shortens the cycles. To give another example, $\kappa_\pi = 0.50$ induces $\beta_\pi^H = 2.1675$ with $T = 14.57$. The point is not so much that this period is still too long but that, even if we are able to detect other parameter combinations implying a more satisfactory cycle period (which

---

[14] To assess the influence of the investment coefficient, we also give the multipliers for a value close to the upper bound. Setting $f_i' = 0.10$ yields $\partial u/\partial \pi = 4.37$ and $\partial i/\partial \pi = 0.87$. For a low coefficient such as $f_i' = 0.04$, a case that will be considered below, $\partial u/\partial \pi = 1.05$ and a weak interest rate effect $\partial i/\partial \pi = 0.21$ are obtained.

[15] Dotted area indicates local stability.

[16] Monotonic convergence is additionally encountered for medium and large values of β_π, if κ_π is close to zero.

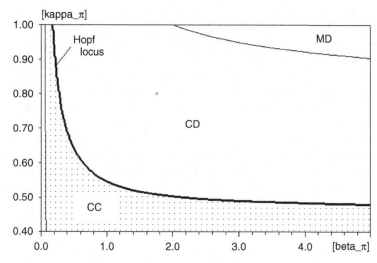

Figure 3.3: The local dynamics arising from parameters (β_π, κ_π)

we briefly indicate below), these two examples will raise serious doubts about the robustness of such a result.

Besides, lowering κ_π any further in figure 3.3 soon yields excessively high bifurcation values β_π^H. Also, fixing β_π and diminishing κ_π does not decrease T over the whole range; reducing κ_π beyond a certain threshold reverses the relationship with T.

The second argument against business cycle interpretations at the present stage of the analysis starts out from the point of view that not too much should depend on the (perhaps) benevolent effects of suitably weighted regressive expectations; all the more since other Keynesian models in a similar vein work with adaptive expectations (possibly slightly modified) as the only expectations mechanism. Hence, weights such as $\kappa_\pi = 1$ or $\kappa_\pi = 0.70$ should be regarded as equally admissible. Taking this for granted, extremely low adjustment speeds β_π are needed to contain the local dynamics. Consequently, if for reasons of a priori plausibility we want to employ medium-sized speeds of adjustment, then significant nonlinearities have to be introduced in the global dynamics in order to keep the system within bounds.[17] A discussion of these points, which goes beyond the present context, is postponed until section 10.

---

[17] To be exact, the differential equations system (3.25)–(3.27) is already nonlinear, even if in addition to (3.29)–(3.32) the functions $f_m(\cdot)$ and $f_l(\cdot)$ are linear too. However, the other nonlinearities inherent in (3.25)–(3.27) are weak, so that the global dynamics in fact resembles the local dynamics. This is intuitively clear, and we have also checked it by computer simulations.

The (β_π, κ_π) parameter diagram in figure 3.3 can also serve as a frame of reference for the second topic in this section, an investigation of the stabilizing or destabilizing potential of the single parameters in the model.[18] To this end we change the parameters, one at a time, and compare the resulting stability regions in the (β_π, κ_π) diagram with that of figure 3.3. This is done in figure 3.4,[19] where the base scenario (3.34), (3.35) is varied, in turn, by a *ceteris paribus* change in the coefficients f'_{wu}, f'_{pu}, κ_w, f'_{pu}, f'_l and $\eta_{m,i}$. In all six panels the bold line is the stability frontier that separates the region of cyclical convergence (CC, the dotted area) from that of cyclical convergence (CD).[20] The thin solid line is the stability frontier as it was obtained in figure 3.3, so that by comparing the areas south-west of the two frontiers we can tell whether the parameter change is stabilizing or destabilizing.

The upper-left panel in figure 3.4 relates to the wage Phillips curve (3.18). It shows that higher wage flexibility, in the form of a steeper slope of the curve, is destabilizing. More precisely, it is largely destabilizing. At high values of κ_π near unity, wage flexibility is (very) weakly stabilizing, since here the stability frontier shifts slightly to the right – a phenomenon that is hardly visible in this diagram. We return to this ambiguity shortly.

A rise in the corresponding coefficient in the price Phillips curve, f'_{pu} in the upper-right panel, shifts the stability frontier slightly outwards. Hence, higher price flexibility with respect to the pressure of demand is stabilizing, though only weakly so. A reverse statement applies to the responsiveness of price adjustments in the direction of the target markup as captured by the coefficient f'_{pv}; see the middle-right panel.

A second coefficient in the wage Phillips curve (3.18) is κ_w, which in the specification of the benchmark rate of inflation is the weight attached to the current inflation rate $\hat{p}$, vis-à-vis the rate of expected inflation π. As this parameter measures no reaction to some perceived disequilibrium, it may be felt that it is of secondary importance. The middle-left panel disproves this surmise. Adopting current inflation as benchmark inflation, $\kappa_w = 1$ is destabilizing. Compared to the other reactions, the effect is actually quite strong. By contrast, the corresponding weight κ_p

---

[18] To be explicit, we call a parameter change stabilizing if it widens the scope for local stability. This notion has to be distinguished from the discussion of stochastic models in the literature, where stabilization means a lower variance in the time series of (some of) the state variables. According to this approach, either the deterministic part of these models is locally stable anyway, or, in models with rational expectations exhibiting saddle-point instability, the agents are assumed always to be on the stable manifold.

[19] The thin solid line indicates the Hopf locus in the base scenario as shown in figure 3.3.

[20] The region of monotonic convergence is here ignored since it is too small to be clearly discernible.

in the price Phillips curve has a similarly weak effect (not shown) to the coefficients f'_{pu} and f'_{pv}, also not in a unique direction.

The two panels in the bottom row of figure 3.4 are concerned with parameters in the IS-LM part of the model. They illustrate that both a slower responsiveness of fixed investment, f'_I, as well as a lower interest elasticity of money demand, $\eta_{m,i}$, are stabilizing. Interestingly, regarding f'_I the stabilizing effect works through the channel of inflationary expectations, where it requires a certain weight of regressive expectations,

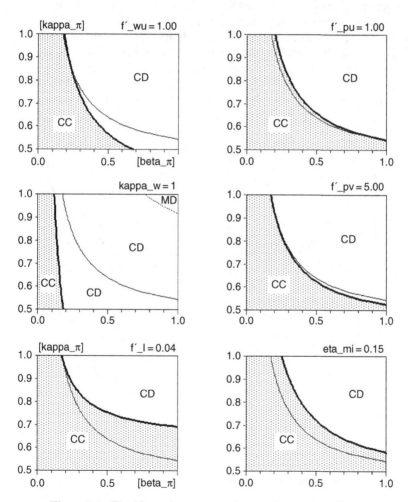

Figure 3.4: The (β_π, κ_π) parameter plane under *ceteris paribus* parameter variations

$\kappa_\pi < 1$. The stabilization of a lower $\eta_{m,i}$ succeeds independently of this parameter.

Insofar as the same, or very similar, parameters are also present in the Sargent model, we can in sum conclude that the effects of their *ceteris paribus* variations go in the same direction. These parameters are β_π, κ_π, f'_w, f'_I and $\eta_{m,i}$, and in both models lower values of them tend to favour local stability. Nonetheless, in the present model some qualifications occasionally have to be made, to which we now turn for the remainder of this section.

Departing more or less from the base scenario, the phenomenon of stability or instability 'reswitching' may show up. By this we mean that, as a parameter is increased, the system changes from being locally stable to being locally unstable, and then, after a further increase, changes back to stability again; likewise with instability. A number of selected examples are presented in figure 3.5.[21] In addition to eqs. (3.33), (3.35), the parameter κ_π is here fixed at $\kappa_\pi = 0.90$, giving a dominating role

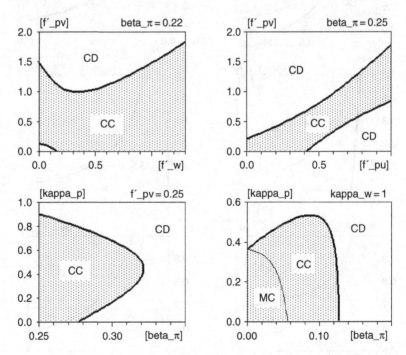

Figure 3.5: Reswitching phenomena in selected parameter diagrams

[21] Underlying is $\kappa_\pi = 0.90$; other parameters, except those in the title, are as in the base scenario.

to the, possibly destabilizing, adaptive expectations in the inflationary expectations. Apart from this, only one parameter is set different from the base scenario, at the value given in the respective title line of the four panels.

The upper-left panel exemplifies the fact that higher wage flexibility can be destabilizing (the normal case in figure 3.4) as well as stabilizing. At a value such as $f'_{pv} = 1.30$, we have local stability for low coefficients f'_w, instability for medium values and, once more, stability for high values of f'_w. The panel also shows that, as found before, lower values of the parameter f'_{pv} can stabilize the system. However, for extremely small values of f'_w the system again becomes unstable if f'_{pv} is similarly small. The same kind of reswitching for f'_{pv} is seen in the upper-right panel, given a value of f'_{pu} that exceeds 0.42; and horizontally for the other price adjustment coefficient f'_{pu}, if f'_{pv} is not too high and not too low.

With respect to a minor influence of the cost-push reactions (proper) in the price Phillips curve, i.e. a very low coefficient f'_{pv}, the lower-left panel shows the reswitching of instability for the weight parameter in this Phillips curve, κ_p. This can happen if β_π is small enough, but not too small.

Perhaps the most astounding result is obtained in the lower-right panel. Setting $\kappa_w = 1$ and considering a suitable range of κ_p, the steady state can in the familiar way be stabilized by sufficiently lowering the adjustment speed β_π. However, instability prevails again if β_π is further diminished and becomes extremely small.

The Hopf locus in this diagram is also remarkable for another point, namely the associated cycle period, T. Fixing $\kappa_p = 0.50$ and increasing β_π from zero yields a first Hopf bifurcation at $\beta_\pi = 0.0548$. A cycle is here as short as $T = 7.77$ years. The second Hopf bifurcation occurs at $\beta_\pi = 0.1082$, the period having then mildly increased to $T = 9.92$ years, which would still be acceptable as a business cycle frequency. Nevertheless, as indicated above, these frequencies should not be overemphasized, since the weights κ_p, κ_w and κ_π appear rather special and, even worse, the adjustments of inflationary expectations are unreasonably slow.

While, according to figure 3.4, a decrease in the investment parameter f'_I is clearly stabilizing, the (β_π, f'_I) diagrams in figure 3.6[22] reveal that this mechanism may also be disturbed. The figure furthermore demonstrates that it depends crucially on the, seemingly innocuous, parameter κ_w whether f'_I acts as a stabilizer or destabilizer. In all four panels the base scenario with, again, $\kappa_\pi = 0.90$ is underlying; however, κ_p is now increased to $\kappa_p = 0.50$. The upper-left panel of figure 3.6, with

---

[22] Underlying is the base scenario with $\kappa_\pi = 0.90$ and κ_p changed to $\kappa_p = 0.50$.

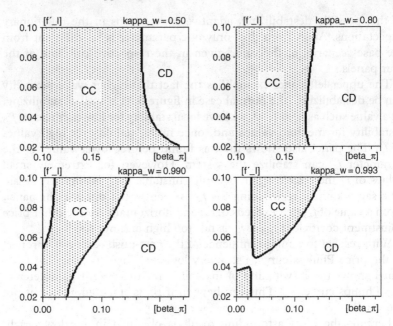

Figure 3.6: (β_π, f_I') parameter diagrams under variations of κ_w

$\kappa_w = \kappa_p = 0.50$, corresponds to what is similarly encountered in the base scenario (where $\kappa_w = \kappa_p = 0.25$): presupposing that β_π is not already too large, a decrease in f_I' is unambiguously stabilizing.

Raising κ_w up to $\kappa_w = 0.80$ affects the entire shape of the stability frontier. Over a small range of β_π in the upper-right panel, the steady state can be stable at a high responsiveness f_I' (that is, high with respect to the upper bound $f_I' = 0.106$ from Assumption 1) and unstable as f_I' is diminished. Possibly a further reduction of f_I' restores local stability, in which case the panel is another example of stability reswitching.

Increasing the weight κ_w further and setting it close to the polar case, at $\kappa_w = 0.990$ in the lower-left panel, broadens the range of β_π over which a reduction of f_I' is destabilizing. In exchange for the reswitching phenomenon, which is no longer present, a new instability region emerges, at larger values of f_I' and very small values of β_π. We thus have one more instability reswitching phenomenon for β_π, albeit of a slightly different nature from the one in the lower-right panel in figure 3.5.

As κ_w approaches unity, the 'topology' of the parameter diagram is very sensitive to small variations of κ_w. Setting κ_w slightly higher than 0.99, at $\kappa_w = 0.993$, now disconnects the stability region. This phenomenon is exhibited in the lower-right panel. Lastly, the small stability region in the south-west corner of this panel disappears as we put $\kappa_w = 1.00$. Then a combination of both small f_I' and β_π brings about instability, in stark contrast to the only marginally lower values of $\kappa_w < 1$.

The properties illustrated by figures 3.5 and 3.6 may be seen from two sides. First, the discussion shows that there are several parameters that may have ambiguous effects regarding the system's stability. For example, higher wage flexibility (f_w') or a higher investment responsiveness (f_I') are mostly destabilizing, but in certain subregions of the parameter space they may instead become stabilizing. In particular, this property depends on such an inconspicuous weighting factor as κ_w in the wage Phillips curve. Hence, even if a parameter is established to be mostly, say, destabilizing, these exceptions make it difficult to find out the mechanisms that are primarily responsible for this effect. The model already seems too complex for simple statements on stability issues. This is perhaps the main message of the 'counter-examples' in figures 3.5 and 3.6.

On the other hand, although the richness of these results is appealing, they should not be overestimated. In all of them the adjustment speed β_π was too low to be credible. While it may then be argued that similar effects could possibly be achieved by putting more weight on regressive expectations (i.e. choosing lower values of the underlying κ_π), this direction of proceeding with the analysis is problematic. As remarked before, not too much should depend on selected values of this parameter. These considerations lead us to accept the 'unfavourable' assumption of higher values of κ_π, as well as a medium or fast adjustment speed β_π. Local instability is consequently admitted as a normal, or at least non-negligible, case to consider. It requires studying the global dynamics and the introduction of certain nonlinearities into the model. This subject is dealt with in section 10, after an investigation of the central dynamic feedback mechanisms and the cyclical pattern to which they give rise.

3.8   Basic feedback loops

The local stability analysis in the previous section has shown the existence of many opposing forces in the model that vary in strength, to some extent in a very complicated manner, as a single parameter is changed. To go beyond merely enumerating which of the parameters are stabilizing, under what circumstances or with what exceptions, we now turn to the underlying dynamic mechanisms. In a similar manner to chapter 2, section 7, we begin by identifying dynamic feedback loops that can be recognized as stabilizing or destabilizing. Following what is discussed in the literature, or what is obvious, there are four of them.

Three effects – or, rather, their names – are already known from the Sargent model: the regressive expectations effect the real wage effect and the Mundell effect. The first one acts in the same simple way as before. The real wage effect is conceptually different, but the outcome is similar. By contrast, due to the present version of the price Phillips curve, the Mundell effect will be easily reversed. The fourth feedback effect is the Keynes effect, which did not apply in the Sargent model. It will be seen that this effect, too, does not work in the familiar direction.

(1) The regressive expectations effect. In this part of their expectation formation process, agents expect inflation to tend to return to normal. Thus, the effect is stabilizing by definition; $\pi > \pi^o$ directly induces a downward adjustment of π in the second component of eq. (3.16).

(2) The Keynes effect. This effect is well known for its stabilizing potential. The argument usually starts out from the price level. Say it is below normal: the low level raises real money balances, decreases the nominal rate of interest on the bond market and increases investment and/or consumption expenditures. The subsequent rise in production and employment has a positive impact on money wages. Given that output prices are positively linked to the wage bill and/or to capacity utilization, the price level moves upward as well, back to normal. A similar reasoning applies to changes in the price level, so that a negative feedback loop in inflation comes into being. For easier reference, we may call the chain of reactions from output changes to changes in inflation the *output-inflation nexus*.

Let us then reconsider the argument with regard to the present model. Suppose inflation is below its equilibrium value, $\hat{p} < \hat{p}^o = \pi^o$. As a consequence, $m = M/pK$ tends to rise (since $\hat{m} = \hat{M} - \hat{p} - \hat{K}$). By way of the IS-LM mechanism, this increases utilization u ($\partial u/\partial m > 0$ by Lemma 1). Higher utilization means faster growth of money wages in (3.18), which in turn has a positive impact on the inflation rate in (3.19) if $\kappa_p > 0$. In addition, utilization impacts directly on $\hat{p}$ in the price Phillips curve, which is captured by the functional expression $f_p = f_p(u, v)$, with $\partial f_p/\partial u = f'_{pu} > 0$. Here, however, it must not be forgotten that utilization also affects the wage share, owing to the procyclical variability of labour productivity. As can be seen from the identity $v = \omega/f_z(u)$ in eq. (3.9), the rise in utilization exerts a downward pressure on the wage share. Hence, in addition to the previous two positive effects, we also get a negative effect on $\hat{p}$. To sum up, if procyclical productivity is taken into account ($f'_z > 0$) and the target markup is included in the price Phillips curve

$(\partial f_p/\partial v = f'_{pv} > 0)$, the output-inflation nexus is generally ambiguous, and so is the Keynes effect.

Having already proposed a calibration of the wage-price sector, we are at this point certainly interested in its consequences for the output-inflation nexus: whether the calibration renders the positive or negative feedback dominant. To this end the reduced form of inflation in eq. (3.23) can be used, where the effects just mentioned are found again in the derivative of the function

$$h(u) := \kappa_p f_w(u) + f_p[u, \omega/f_z(u)] \tag{3.36}$$

Evaluated at the steady-state values (observing that $f_z(u^o) = 1$ and $(1 + \mu)\omega^o = 1$ for the component f_{pv} of the function f_p), one obtains

$$
\begin{aligned}
dh/du &= \kappa_p f'_w + f'_{pu} + f'_{pv}(1 + \mu)\omega^o(-f'_z) \\
&= \kappa_p f'_w + f'_{pu} - f'_z f'_{pv} \\
&= 0.25 \cdot 0.40 + 0.20 - 0.50 \cdot 2.00 = -0.70
\end{aligned}
\tag{3.37}
$$

Thus, an increase in utilization depresses inflation and, on the whole, low inflation rates tend to be further reduced. That is, accepting the numerical parameters in (3.33) and (3.34) for the wage-price sector, the Keynes effect turns out to be *destabilizing*!

It is worth mentioning that the Keynes effect is also to some degree reflected in the Jacobian matrix (3.28), in the sense that $j_{11} > 0$ is a sufficient condition for the Keynes effect to be destabilizing. To see this, consider the relationship $\hat{m} = \hat{M} - \hat{p} - \hat{K} = g_m - \hat{p} - \hat{K}$ and notice that in the context of the above discussion, where the variations of the capital stock growth rate are disregarded, the following two statements amount to the same: (a) low inflation rates, by affecting m, i, u and then $\hat{p}$, tend to be further reduced; (b) high ratios $m = M/pK$, by affecting i, u, $\hat{p}$ and then m, tend to be further increased (see also the loop in figure 3.7 below). The latter statement can be checked by differentiating the right-hand side of the differential equation (3.25) for real balances with respect to m – with the exception of the term $f_i(\ldots)$. The statement is true if a positive expression results. Using definition (3.36), the derivative is given by

$$\frac{\partial}{\partial m} - m\kappa \, h[u(m, \omega, \pi)] = -m\kappa \, (dh/du)(\partial u/\partial m) \tag{3.38}$$

Because of $\partial u/\partial m > 0$, (3.38) is positive precisely if dh/du is negative.

On the other hand, entry j_{11} in the Jacobian is equal to $\frac{\partial}{\partial m}\{-m\kappa[h(u(m, \omega, \pi)) - f_I(\dots)]\}$. It can be shown that $\partial f_I(\dots)/\partial m > 0$.[23] Thus, $j_{11} > 0$ entails a positive derivative (3.38), which implies $dh/du < 0$. It remains to reiterate that this inequality represents a negative output-inflation feedback, which has just been shown to bring about a destabilizing Keynes effect.

(3) The Mundell effect. Since investment was assumed to be responsive to the real rate of interest, changes in anticipated price inflation drive a wedge between the nominal interest rate, which clears the bond market, and the real interest rate, which determines the demand for goods. In the IS-LM framework, these effects are summarized by $\partial u/\partial \pi > 0$. Consequently, expectations about low inflation, $\pi < \pi^o$, induce subnormal utilization, which then, through the same channels as discussed above, affects the actual rate of inflation. Relying on the negative output-inflation nexus (3.36), (3.37), actual inflation will be rising. Via adaptive expectations insofar as $\kappa_\pi > 0$, this tendency will also drive up inflationary expectations. In contrast to the Sargent model, we have in sum a *negative* feedback loop in the expected rate of inflation, even if regressive expectations are totally absent!

Just as with the Keynes effect, the Mundell effect becomes 'perverse' if the output-inflation feedback is negative. Responsible for the latter is a sufficiently large coefficient $f'_{pv} > 0$ in the price Phillips curve, which was set this way in order to generate (nearly) procyclical real wage movements. Therefore, our findings about the direction of the Keynes and Mundell effects may not be perverse after all.

(4) The real wage effect. Regarding income distribution, let us begin with a real wage above its equilibrium value, $\omega > \omega^o$. The effect on output goes in the same direction as in the Sargent model with its marginal productivity principle. By virtue of Lemma 1, $\partial u/\partial \omega < 0$, the IS-LM level of utilization falls below normal. In the next step, the mechanism of the wage Phillips curve reduces the growth rate of nominal wages, $\hat{w}$. At the same time, due to the negative output-inflation nexus, the price inflation rate $\hat{p}$ increases.[24] The direction of change of the real wage rate $\omega = w/pz^o$ is thus definitely negative. On the whole, high real wages tend to be revised downward. In other words, the real wage effect proves to be stabilizing.

---

[23] Writing $u_\pi = \partial u/\partial \pi > 0$, $i_\pi = \partial i/\partial \pi < 1$, one computes in detail $\partial f_I(\dots)/\partial m = (if'_I/m\eta_{m,i})[y^n(1 - v + vf'_z)u_\pi + (1 - i_\pi)] > 0$.

[24] This description may be slightly qualified. If one refers to the reduced form of wage inflation in eq. (3.23) and κ_w is relatively large, then $\hat{w}$ might also increase as u falls (formally, $\partial \hat{w}/\partial u$ is proportional to $f'_w + \kappa_w(f'_{pu} - f'_z f'_{pv})$). Nevertheless, the effect from price inflation in the change of ω is still likely to be dominant, so that the statement in the text remains true.

It will be recalled that in the Sargent model, too, the real wage effect was a negative feedback loop. In addition, the first part of this chain was quite analogous. A crucial conceptual difference, however, is the way in which output impacts on prices or price inflation, respectively. In the Sargent model, output and prices are directly linked by the marginal productivity principle, whereas in the present model inflation reacts to changes in output, or utilization, via the price Phillips curve. The fact that the wage and price adjustments are closely connected makes it possible that, a priori, the total feedback loop might also be positive (especially if f'_{pv} is small). It should be emphasized that it is only the otherwise perhaps suspect negative output-inflation nexus that renders the real wage effect here unambiguously stabilizing.

The four feedback loops with their constituent components are summarized in figure 3.7.[25] The schema, in particular, elucidates the central role of the output-inflation nexus, from u to $\hat{p}$, for the respective loop to be negative (stabilizing) or positive (destabilizing). The positive sign of the last link in the real wage effect derives, of course, from the simple fact that the growth rate of w/p is equal to $\hat{w} - \hat{p}$ (reference to trend productivity z^o in the definition of ω has been omitted to ease the exposition).

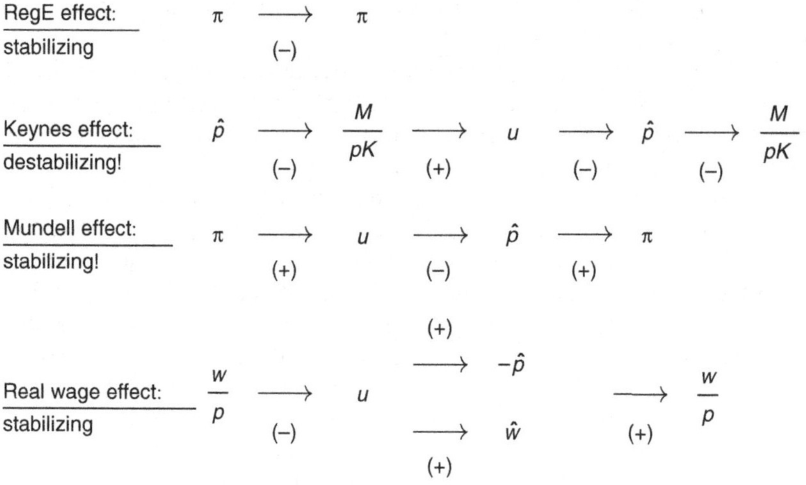

Figure 3.7: The model's basic feedback loops

[25] RegE stands for regressive expectations. An arrow signed $(+)$ (or $(-)$, respectively) indicates that an increase in the variable on the left-hand side causes the variable on the right-hand side to rise (or fall). The negative output-inflation nexus from u to $\hat{p}$ derives from (3.37).

Note also that the Keynes effect may be read as a loop from $\hat{p}$ to $\hat{p}$, or alternatively as a loop from $m = M/pK$ to $m = M/pK$.

The effects in figure 3.7 are encountered formally in the diagonal elements of the Jacobian matrix. The sense in which this applies to the Keynes effect, read from m to m, has just been mentioned in point 2. The regressive expectations effect is obtained as the derivative $\partial\hat{\pi}/\partial\pi$ in (3.27), with $\kappa_\pi = 0$. Its polar case, the Mundell effect, is given by $\partial\hat{\pi}/\partial\pi$ with $\kappa_\pi = 1$. The real wage effect is represented by the entry j_{22}, i.e. the derivative $\partial\hat{\omega}/\partial\omega$ in (3.26). To give a numerical example, consider the parameters in (3.34), (3.35) and set additionally

$$\kappa_\pi = 0.90 \quad \beta_\pi = 0.23 \tag{3.39}$$

This scenario gives rise to

$$\mathcal{J} = \begin{bmatrix} 0.40 & -0.62 & 0.14 \\ 2.74 & -2.94 & 1.92 \\ -0.63 & 0.94 & -0.46 \end{bmatrix} \tag{3.40}$$

The eigenvalues of $\mathcal{J}$ are $\lambda_1 = -3.022$ and $\lambda_{2,3} = 0.0066 \pm 0.193i$. Hence, despite the low adjustment speed β_π, the steady state is unstable; the pair (β_π, κ_π) of (3.39) is in fact near the stability frontier of figure 3.3, in the region of cyclical instability.

The actual value of j_{33} in (3.40) is a weighted average of the Mundell and regressive expectations effects. It is worth pointing out that the Mundell effect is more strongly stabilizing than the regressive expectations effect. With $\kappa_\pi = 1$, the first one is measured as $j_{33} = -0.49$; with $\kappa_\pi = 0$, the second results as $j_{33} = -0.23$. On the other hand, it is readily inferred from figure 3.3 that, given the other parameter values, the system is unstable at $\kappa_\pi = 1$, and stable at $\kappa_\pi = 0$ – not the other way round, as seems to be indicated by the relative strength of the two effects. How can this be?

Another aspect is that, once the Mundell effect is recognized as stabilizing, it seems reasonable to expect that reinforcing it will contribute to the stabilization of the economy. Obviously, the Mundell effect is reinforced by increasing the adjustment speed β_π. But, given that κ_π is not too small, we know that large values of β_π are certainly destabilizing. Again, how can this contradiction be resolved?

The answer is that the four effects in figure 3.7 focus on how the single-state variables feed back on themselves, by affecting just utilization and wage-price inflation. But this is only one aspect of the dynamic story. In a wider perspective, the cross-effects between the state variables themselves should also be taken into account. Additional destabilizing feedback loops can then be revealed, which, however, operate in a more roundabout way than discussed before. Using the information provided by the sign of the off-diagonal elements in $\mathcal{J}$, the following four examples may be presented (in obvious notation):

$$
\begin{array}{llllllll}
(a) & \pi\uparrow & \rightarrow & \omega\uparrow & \rightarrow & \pi\uparrow & & \\
(b) & \pi\uparrow & \rightarrow & m\uparrow & \rightarrow & \omega\uparrow & \rightarrow & \pi\uparrow \\
(c) & m\uparrow & \rightarrow & \omega\uparrow & \rightarrow & \pi\uparrow & \rightarrow & m\uparrow \\
(d) & \omega\uparrow & \rightarrow & m\downarrow & \rightarrow & \pi\uparrow & \rightarrow & \omega\uparrow
\end{array}
\tag{3.41}
$$

In feedback loop (a), the first effect springs from $j_{23} > 0$, the second from $j_{32} > 0$. Feedback loop (b) is generated by – in that order – $j_{13} > 0$, $j_{21} > 0, j_{32} > 0$; (c) by $j_{21} > 0, j_{32} > 0, j_{13} > 0$; and (d) by $j_{12} < 0, j_{31} < 0, j_{23} > 0$.

Notice that all four loops are cut off if $\kappa_{\pi} = 0$, because $j_{31} = j_{32} = 0$ in this case (see eq. (3.28)), while the Keynes and the real wage effect (and the first two rows of $\mathcal{J}$ altogether) are not modified by the variations of κ_{π}. It follows that local stability for $\kappa_{\pi} = 0$ can be attributed to the breaking down of the four destabilizing loops in (3.41).

Furthermore, the destabilizing effect of high values of β_{π} becomes more plausible when it is observed that increasing β_{π} not only decreases the negative entry j_{33}, and thus strengthens a stabilizing mechanism, it also decreases the negative entry j_{31} and raises the positive entry j_{32}, both of which appear in the feedback chains (3.41). Evidently, the destabilizing forces induced by the change in β_{π} (and represented by off-diagonal elements) dominate those of the stabilizing Mundell effect (which is represented by a diagonal element).

The discussion shows that the four elementary feedbacks in figure 3.7, although they are rather insightful and in some way or another referred to in the (older) literature, have only limited explanatory power with regard to the system's stability. The instability potential is better understood by, additionally, studying more circuitous feedback mechanisms like those in (3.41). Since the cross-effects here involved are themselves a concise summary of a number of more detailed, single components, the mechanisms in (3.41) can no longer be described so easily as those in figure 3.7. This is just a reflection of the fact that the interactions of the economic variables are already quite complex. It should also be considered that (3.41) still has to be weighed against similarly circuitous loops that are stabilizing. All these remarks point once more to the limitations of a purely verbal reasoning, however careful it might be. After all, a mathematical and numerical stability analysis is unavoidable. In the next stage, to which we now turn, this enquiry into the stabilizing and destabilizing forces may be supplemented by an investigation of the cycle-generating mechanisms, which also means that we proceed from the local to the global dynamics.

3.9   The cyclical pattern

In the preceding section various stabilizing and destabilizing feedback mechanisms have been singled out. Unfortunately, this discussion gives practically no hints as to whether convergence and divergence is monotonic or cyclical. On the other hand, we know from section 6 that the system typically exhibits oscillatory behaviour. The interaction of the stabilizing and destabilizing forces must, therefore, be quite involved. Rather than saying that one type generally prevails over the other, it seems more appropriate to view the evolution of (in the first instance) economic activity as a process where, in certain stages, one type dominates, whereas in certain other stages the other type does. Thus, we ask why it is that in a stage of deviation-amplifying dynamics the destabilizing forces are more and more weakened, such that divergence slows down and eventually a turning point comes about. To this end, we now study a concrete simulation of the economic system.

The functional forms of the labour productivity relationship $f_z(\cdot)$ and the wage-price reactions $f_w(\cdot)$, $f_{pu}(\cdot)$ and $f_{pv}(\cdot)$ have been specified in (3.29)–(3.32). The money demand function can be directly taken over from (2.42) and the investment function (2.41) has to be correspondingly adjusted. Both of them being linear, we have

$$f_I = f_I[r - (i - \pi)] = \beta_{Io} + \beta_{Iq}(r - i + \pi) \tag{3.42}$$

$$f_m = f_m(i) = \beta_{mo} - \beta_{mi}i \tag{3.43}$$

Of course, $\beta_{Iq}, \beta_{mi} > 0$. To be chosen exogenously here are the interest elasticity of money demand $\eta_{m,i}$ (evaluated at the steady state), the responsiveness of investment f_I', which equals β_{Iq}, and also the steady-state values of the real growth rate g^o, the wage share v^o, which equals ω^o, and the ratio of real balances m^o. The intercept of (3.42) is then obtained from solving the steady-state condition $f_I^o = g^o$ for β_{Io} (using $r^o = (1 - v^o)u^o y^n = (1 - \omega^o)y^n$). The two coefficients in (3.43) can be computed from the LM condition (3.22), $f_m(i^o) = m^o/y^n$, together with the definition of the interest elasticity, $\eta_{m,i} = +\beta_{mi}i^o/f_m(i^o)$.[26]

(3.42), (3.43) complete the functional specification of the system's behavioural equations. The simulations themselves are implemented by conceiving of the economy as a sequential, discrete-time economy with

---

[26] In explicit terms, the result is $\beta_{mi} = m^o \eta_{m,i}/y^n i^o$, $\beta_{mo} = (1 + \eta_{m,i})m^o/y^n$.

an adjustment period of length h. This device has already been described in chapter 2, section 8, for the Sargent model, so the details can be omitted here.[27] Regarding the length of the adjustment period we may choose a month, i.e. $h = 1/12$. The initial conditions, too, are borrowed from the previous chapter. Accordingly, the economy is initially supposed to grow on its long-run equilibrium path. At time $t = 1$ a shock increases the growth rate g_m of the money supply by three percentage points, from (approximately) 6 per cent to 9 per cent. This rate is maintained for one year, until $t = 2$, after which g_m returns to the original 6 per cent.

To produce the cyclical trajectories, we can adopt the parameter set of eqs. (3.34), (3.35) and (3.39) as our base scenario. From the eigenvalues computed for the corresponding Jacobian (3.40) it is clear that, locally, the oscillations have a slowly increasing amplitude. Figure 3.8[28] demonstrates that this property carries over to the global dynamics. Since we

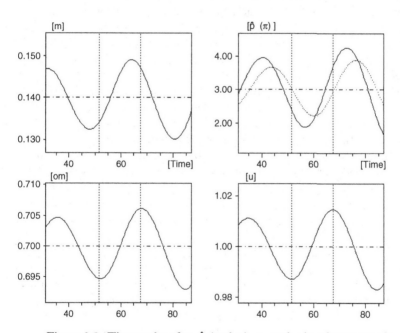

Figure 3.8: Time paths of m, $\hat{p}$ (and π), ω, and u in a base scenario

---

[27] Note that the procedure includes the specification of the growth rates such that, in the discrete-time framework, they are compatible with constant values of the composed variables. The steps to be taken here are analogous to the remarks made in connection with eq. (2.44).

[28] The solid line in the upper-right panel is $\hat{p}$, the dotted line π. The vertical dashed lines indicate the trough and peak of u.

are focusing at present on the cycle-generating mechanisms, the problem of the economy's global boundaries is left to one side. The unduly long cycle period is neglected as well (we return to these issues in the next section).

Over the time interval exhibited in figure 3.8, the transitional forces from the initial shocks have long disappeared and the system is operating in full swing. The evolution of capacity utilization shown in the lower-right panel can be explained by the effects that are exercised by the three state variables m, π and ω: real balances in intensive form, expected inflation and the deflated real wage rate (recall from Lemma 1 that $\partial u/\partial m > 0$, $\partial u/\partial \pi > 0$, $\partial u/\partial \omega < 0$). To ease the exposition, we discuss the motions of u at this level and leave the variables involved in the IS-LM adjustments in the background.

Looking at figure 3.8, it may be noted first that the cyclical pattern of the real wage rate is the same as in figure 3.2. Given the oscillatory time path of utilization, generated by whatever mechanism, this is just the outcome of the calibration discussed in section 6. As a result, the adjustments of ω (and of the wage share v) need not be detailed further.

Then, consider a stage of the dynamic process where the economy is recovering after utilization has reached a trough, at $t = 51.50$ (the first vertical dashed line in figure 3.8). ω begins to rise shortly after that point in time, while π is still falling. It can thus be concluded that, at the beginning, the expansion is driven by the rising ratio $m = M/pK$; this effect dominates the two opposite effects from π and ω.

As for the motion of m itself, it should be mentioned that the influence of the capital growth rate on m can be largely ignored; owing to the low responsiveness of investment $f_I' = \beta_{Iq}$, the growth rate $\hat{K}$ has only a small amplitude. Accordingly, the increase in m (via $\hat{m} = g_m - \hat{p} - \hat{K}$) can be attributed mainly to the rate of inflation, which is distinctly below its steady-state value at that time.

The rise in utilization is reinforced at a later stage when expected inflation, at $t = 60.17$, also starts rising. π follows the upward motion of $\hat{p}$, which sets in before, at $t = 56.83$. The actual rate of inflation, in turn, increases for two reasons: first, because of the ongoing improvement in utilization (the demand-pull component $f_{pu} = f_{pu}(u)$ in the price Phillips curve); second, because, as has been illustrated in figure 3.2, the wage share v also begins to increase (this concerns the target markup component $f_{pv} = f_{pv}(v)$ in the Phillips curve).

The positive influence of u on $\hat{p}$ has to be distinguished from the negative output-inflation feedback discussed in the preceding section. The latter was a *ceteris paribus* argument, where the negative feedback originates from the fact that v depends negatively on u, since $v = \omega/f_z(u)$.

In the present context, however, the real wage does not stay put but moves almost synchronously with u.

Higher inflation has an important implication for real balances. The ratio $m = M/pK$ reaches an upper turning point when the sum of inflation and the capital growth rate catches up with the growth rate of the money supply. $\hat{p}$ reaches its equilibrium value of 3 per cent at $t = 64.50$. Shortly before (since $\hat{K}$ exceeds g^o, but only slightly so), m peaks at $t = 64.25$.

Utilization continues to improve because m changes quite slowly near its peak value. At that stage the increase in u is brought about by the rising inflationary expectations, an effect that here dominates the two negative effects from m and ω. But soon, with actual inflation increasing further, the downward motion of m gains speed. The influence of m then becomes dominant again, such that it eventually causes u to turn around. This happens at $t = 67.42$ (the second dashed line in figure 3.8).

The fact that utilization starts to decline does not mean that inflation follows suit. Since the adjustments in the price Phillips curve are governed by the *levels* of utilization and the wage share, and both of them are still above normal, the inflation rate keeps on rising for a while. It does an about-turn roughly a quarter of a cycle later. At that time, utilization on its descent is about to pass the 100 per cent benchmark. Due to the adaptive expectations principle, the turning point of π occurs even later. From then on we have a mirror image of the expansion phase of the economy.

To cut this story short, the cyclical mechanism may be summarized as follows. As the expansion of the economy progresses, utilization impacts positively on inflation, in part directly and in part indirectly via the induced movements of real wages and the wage share. Rising inflation, in turn, has a negative influence on the changes of the real balances ratio $m = M/pK$, such that it eventually reverses the upward motion of m. Since, in the IS-LM temporary equilibrium framework, u is most strongly affected by the variations of m, the expansion falters and finally comes to an end. It takes considerable time, however, until the inflation rate too begins to fall.

3.10   Global stabilization through modified adaptive expectations

An unsatisfactory feature of the parameter set that was used to produce the illustrative simulation run is the unreasonably low speed of adjustment in the formation of inflationary expectations, $\beta_\pi = 0.23$. With respect to adaptive expectations this means that it would take $1/\beta_\pi = 4.34$ years until the gap between π and $\hat{p}$ is closed (if, for the sake of the argument, $\hat{p}$ remains unchanged in the meantime). It has been remarked before that medium or high values of β_π should be admissible as well. As this certainly implies local instability, which, because of the quasi-linear character of our functional specification of the system, carries over to the outer regions of the state space, we face up to the problem of how to contain the global dynamics within bounds. In other words, we have to design a global stabilization mechanism, which will set up an essential nonlinearity.

One candidate occasionally discussed in economic theory is the assumption of a downward rigidity in money wages. In empirical investigations this idea usually goes under the heading of a convex Phillips curve. In its simplest form, a kink may be introduced into the wage Phillips curve, such that $\hat{w}$ is equal to the maximum of zero and the right-hand side of eq. (3.18). However, while this mechanism has been successfully employed in Keynesian macrodynamic modelling,[29] in the present case the destabilizing forces are so strong that it fails to be effective (apart from their tendency to prolong the cycles). For example, in the base scenario (3.34), (3.35), (3.39), a moderate increase of β_π from 0.23 to 0.50 already gives rise to oscillations in which the variables grow or fall beyond any acceptable limits.

A more promising approach is to turn to a psychological variable and reassess the adaptive expectations component in the evolution of π. A first question to be posed here, which is hardly ever mentioned in the macroeconomic literature, concerns the time horizon underlying the inflationary expectations. Rather than viewing π as the prediction for the next (infinitesimally) short period, to which would correspond the limiting case $\beta_\pi \to \infty$, we judge it more appropriate to conceive of π as a point estimation of some average inflation over a medium range of time (where the near future might be weighted more heavily). After all, π is to enter the investment function. In view of the long lifetime of capital goods and the irreversibility of investment, the time horizon for π should therefore not be too short. Accordingly, large values of β_π should claim no priority in rationality. Nevertheless, the viability of the model should not depend on excessively small values of β_π either.[30]

These brief remarks can shed new light on the concept of the speed of adjustment, β_π, at which adaptive expectations are revised. It may no longer be a fixed magnitude since, at different stages of the business cycle, agents process the data of their most recent observations in different ways. To keep matters simple, consider a situation with $\hat{p} > \pi$ that

---

[29] An orderly study is Flaschel and Groh (1998). More concisely, a typical application may be found in Chiarella et al. (2000), pp. 17f. & 260ff.

[30] Arguments defending adaptive expectations against the widespread criticism that they violate the postulate of 'rationality' are collected in Flaschel et al. (1997, pp. 149–62) and Franke (1999).

is characterized by both $\hat{p}$ and π increasing. In addition, suppose that in the past agents have learned that the upward motion of $\hat{p}$ tends to be reversed; the higher $\hat{p}$, the more likely it seems that this event will occur in the near future. If π were still increased at the same speed as before, it would later be found to be above current inflation (or its time average), at a time when $\hat{p}$ is already on the downturn. With regard to the decisions about fixed investment, an overprediction would probably be more costly than a possible underestimation. It thus seems reasonable to assume that, in order to reduce the risk of overprediction, the adjustments of π are more sluggish in the – suspected – late phase of the upswing of $\hat{p}$, or in the early phase of its downturn. Later, with $\hat{p}$ and π coming down again to medium values, adjustments in π might gain momentum.[31]

The argument suggests a modification of adaptive expectations where, as long as inflation is within a normal range, agents adopt medium or even high values of β_π. As a consequence, the steady-state position is locally unstable. On the other hand, when inflation rates in the cyclically diverging process fall or increase too much, the adjustment speed is reduced. If β_π gets sufficiently small here, the stabilizing forces may become so strong that they are able to put a curb on the (otherwise increasing) amplitude of the oscillations. In sum, this elementary endogenization of β_π in the adaptive expectations mechanism would give rise to bounded, and persistent, cyclical behaviour.

Concretely, since the coefficient β_π has recourse to regressive expectations as well, we prefer a slightly different specification. It is, however, conceptually equivalent. Recall that, in order to determine the change in π, adaptive expectations compare π to the current rate of inflation. That is, the latter serves as a reference rate of inflation. Our idea is that, instead of β_π, we allow for some flexibility in such a reference rate. Introducing the notation π_{ref}, we conceive of it as a *function* of current inflation, $\pi_{ref} = \pi_{ref}(\hat{p})$. In this way, eq. (3.16) is generalized to

$$\dot{\pi} = \beta_\pi[\kappa_\pi(\pi_{ref}(\hat{p}) - \pi) + (1 - \kappa_\pi)(\pi^o - \pi)] \qquad (3.44)$$

Treating rising and falling inflation symmetrically, we postulate that over a medium range of inflation, defined as an interval $I_\pi := [\pi^o - d_\pi, \pi^o + d_\pi]$ with respect to a given number $d_\pi > 0$, π_{ref} coincides with $\hat{p}$. Here (3.16)

---

[31] This idea is supported by an experimental study undertaken by Schmalensee (1976), who presented human subjects with price observations from a nineteenth-century British wheat market. With respect to forecasts of five-year averages of the time series, an adaptive expectations model was found to outperform an extrapolative expectations model. Most remarkably, the response speed in the adaptive model tended to *fall* during turning points.

still prevails. Yet, when $\hat{p}$ leaves the interval, π_{ref} does not keep up with $\hat{p}$. The simplest assumption is that π_{ref} remains fixed then. This gives us the truncated linear function

$$\pi_{ref}(\hat{p}) = \begin{cases} \pi^o + d_\pi & \text{if } \hat{p} > \pi^o + d_\pi \\ \hat{p} & \text{if } |\hat{p} - \pi^o| \le d_\pi \\ \pi^o - d_\pi & \text{if } \hat{p} < \pi^o - d_\pi \end{cases} \qquad (3.45)$$

Obviously, if $\hat{p}$ is outside the interval I_π, adaptive expectations change more slowly in the direction of $\hat{p}$ than they would in (3.16). That is, eqs. (3.44), (3.45) have the same effect as a reduction of β_π in (3.16).

One can certainly devise smoother and more ambitious ways to introduce flexibility into adaptive expectations. At present, however, we do not strive for the greatest plausibility, and content ourselves with demonstrating that an unpretentious version of the idea already works. So, the specification (3.44) and (3.45) may do.

To test the stabilization mechanism, let us maintain the parameter scenario (3.34), (3.35), (3.39) and decrease the lag implied for adaptive expectations to half a year. Furthermore, let the interval of medium inflation be given by inflation rates 1.5 percentage points above or below the steady-state value. Accordingly,

$$\beta_\pi = 2.00 \quad d_\pi = 0.015 \qquad (3.46)$$

After the temporary shock sequence has disturbed the economy from its equilibrium growth path, the destabilising forces induced by $\beta_\pi = 2$ soon make inflation rates diverge more than 1.5 percentage points from π^o. On the other hand, by curtailing π, eqs. (3.44), (3.45) reliably prevent actual inflation as well from diverging too much. In fact, figure 3.9 shows that, after the initial shocks, it does not take long until the trajectories of $\hat{p}$ and the other variables enter a periodic motion.[32] We add that the strong stabilization effects are not confined to the moderate adjustment speed in (3.46); a similar cyclical pattern is obtained for much higher values of β_π.

The bottom panel of figure 3.9 illustrates the working of the adjustment mechanism for inflationary expectations. After $t = 40$, π quickly levels off as current inflation rises above $\pi^o + d_\pi = 4.5\%$. At that time, real balances $m = M/pK$ are already on the downturn. The main implication of the slowing down of π is that, concerning the impact on utilization, it is almost immediately the negative effect from m that then becomes

---

[32] The trajectories are periodic at least from a practical point of view. To be scrupulous, it might also be the case that (in the continuous-time system) they are 'quasi-periodic'. This problem is perhaps of some mathematical interest, but need not concern us here.

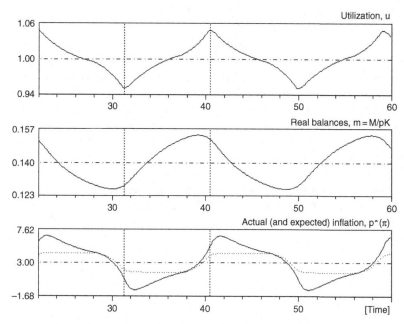

Figure 3.9: Time series of u, m, $\hat{p}$ and π (dotted line) resulting from
(3.44)–(3.46)

dominant. Consequently, u reaches an upper turning point. Suppose, by
contrast, π were to increase more strongly at that stage (because (3.44),
(3.45) failed to apply or d_π had a higher value). Then the positive effect
from π on u would still be predominant for a while. In this case the
turning point of u would occur later, and the value it attains at the peak
would be higher.

It is therefore seen that the modification of adaptive expectations has
two effects. First, the mechanism limits the amplitudes of the oscillations; or, equivalently, it succeeds in taming the centrifugal forces in the
outer regions of the state space. Second, the mechanism shortens the
duration of the cyclical motions; while, in the unrestricted case shown
in figure 3.8, the cycles extend over more than thirty years, the period
of the cycles in figure 3.9 is (slightly) less than twenty years. More precisely, the higher coefficient β_π in (3.46) speeds up the increase in π
and thus also in $\hat{p}$ (around $t = 40$, say). Hence, $m = M/pK$ peaks earlier.
On the other hand, as has just been remarked, if π soon levels off then
by virtue of (3.44), (3.45), the falling m regains its dominance over π
in the influence on u, so that utilization too peaks at an earlier date.

(This discussion has to be understood against the background of the comments on figure 3.8.)

It may now be imagined that rendering adaptive expectations flexible in a more skilful way could diminish the duration of the cycles even further (and improve upon the amplitudes). Note, in particular, the slow ascent and the slow descent of $\hat{p}$ after its turning points. This movement would be accelerated if inflationary expectations realized more early that the direction of the motion of $\hat{p}$ has already changed. On this basis, eqs. (3.44), (3.45) might be additionally refined. For example, π_{ref} could be conceived of as being influenced by the current state of economic activity, $\pi_{ref} = \pi_{ref}(\hat{p}, u)$.

It is interesting to point out that increasing the coefficients κ_w and κ_p does a similar job. To give an example, with $\kappa_w = \kappa_p = 0.75$, the period of the cycles comes down to slightly less than ten years. The price to be paid for this speeding up in the movement of $\hat{p}$ may not be concealed, namely a far higher amplitude of the rate of inflation (peak and trough values of around 11 per cent and -5 per cent, respectively).

There are two reasons why we do not pursue the approach of suitably setting the weight parameters κ_w and κ_p, or of refining the expectation formation mechanism. One is that such a procedure may appear somewhat artificial, or just too purposeful. The second reason refers to quite another source influencing the length of the cycles, which has not been mentioned yet. We think of the role of real balances $m = M/pK$, bearing in mind that we learned in the previous section that this is the most important variable determining the time path of utilization. The idea is that anything that accelerates the evolution of m, in the sense that it reverses the motion of m at an earlier time, can be expected to have a similar effect on u. Indeed, the considerations above aimed at more rapid movements of inflation, to the effect that it takes less time until $\hat{m} = g_m - \hat{p} - \hat{K}$ changes its sign from positive to negative, and vice versa. However, a higher variability in the capital growth rate would work in the same direction. Hence, greater realism apart, higher amplitudes of $\hat{K}$ are also desirable as a means to obtain shorter cycles.

So far, the possibility that the behaviour of the capital growth rate also contributes to the cyclical pattern has played no essential role. This was due to Assumption 1, which, at least in connection with the other steady-state values, seriously constrains the responsiveness of fixed investment f'_I and so implies rather limited variations of $\hat{K}$. We therefore face the following situation. To explore another determinant of the duration of the oscillations, a higher variability of the capital growth rate should be allowed for. This requires higher values of the coefficient f'_I, which in turn requires dropping Assumption 1. Since the latter cannot be done meaningfully within the IS framework, with respect to the representation of the goods market we arrive at the conclusion that it would be desirable to give up the familiar organizing device of temporary equilibrium.

3.11   Conclusion

The model in this chapter has emerged from Sargent's (1979, 1987) influential textbook model of a Keynesian economy. The main innovation was to discharge the 'ballast' of a central neoclassical building block. This does not imply the neoclassical production function as such but the marginal productivity principle for labour attached to it, the problematic features of which in a dynamic context have already been pointed out in chapter 2. Abandoning the principle, in particular, meant putting prices and wages on an equal footing – that is, both variables were treated equally as being predetermined in the short period. In finer detail, their adjustments were specified as two Philips curves, one – as in Sargent – for nominal wage inflation and the other for price inflation. While the Sargent model was basically supply-oriented, we thus obtained a model that is much more Keynesian in that it again placed greater emphasis on the demand-side.

Since the rest of Sargent's model formulation was essentially taken over without alterations, the model could again be reduced to an autonomous system of three differential equations in three dynamic-state variables. Regarding the local stability of its steady-state position, it is remarkable that the Sargent model's basic stability proposition also survived. The condition, which could be derived analytically, concentrates on the role of inflationary expectations, and (somewhat cut short) says that lower speeds at which they are revised are stabilizing, whereas fast adjustments are destabilizing. However, a stability analysis that seeks to go beyond this handsome result soon becomes quite complicated and necessitates resorting to numerical computations. This, in turn, required us to search for parameter values with an order of magnitude that could reasonably be justified.

To this end we followed a method, though still in a sketchy manner, that is known as calibration. Wherever the numerical coefficients may come from, from a straightforward grid search or a more informed reasoning, here one asks not so much for the values themselves but for their dynamic implications in the model under consideration. In this chapter we have focused on only one aspect, namely we controlled for the amplitude and the comovements of the model-generated real wage rate vis-à-vis the motions of capacity utilization as the measure of the business cycle. This helped us settle down on concrete parameters in the two Philips curves. A special result was that our slight extension of the price Philips curve proved significant. That is, we assigned the wage share an additional role to play in this relationship, and the coefficient that captures the influence of this extra variable had to be relatively high if, according to our postulate, the real wage was to move largely procyclically.

Taking up the discussion in the previous chapter, we again identified several theoretically significant feedback loops of the dynamic variables. Since, as just mentioned, the price level is a predetermined variable, it was now possible, unlike in the Sargent model, to single out a properly defined Keynes effect. The numerical parameters and especially the impact of the wage share on price inflation caused the Keynes effect to be destabilizing rather than stabilizing, as it is described in the textbooks. The Mundell effect, by contrast, was 'perverse' in the other way: it lost its destabilizing potential and turned out to be stabilizing. The real wage effect maintained its stabilizing momentum. Our main conclusion was nevertheless that, while they are insightful and a good basis for theoretical discussion, these 'own effects' were of limited value, because the cross-effects between different state variables have now become more important for the system's overall stability. In technical terms, referring to the Jacobian matrix, it might be said that in their entirety the off-diagonal entries dominate the entries on the diagonal.

Although the reduced form is only of dimension three, these results are also indicative of comparatively rich structural relationships already. Another manifestation of the model's richness is provided by the reswitching phenomena that we encountered in the numerical stability analysis. This, for example, means that medium values of a parameter bring about local stability, whereas low as well as high values render the steady unstable. Changes of such a parameter can no longer be unambiguously characterized as being favourable or unfavourable for stability.

Regarding the dynamic trajectories, we were particularly interested in the system's potential for producing cyclical dynamics. A universal feature the mathematical analysis could reveal was that, at least near the stability frontier, where small *ceteris paribus* changes let the system lose its stability, the two leading eigenvalues of the Jacobian are complex, so that oscillatory motions are generated. This is quite satisfactory for us as a basic property, but, within our deterministic framework, not quite sufficient insofar as we are striving for persistent cyclical behaviour.

In this respect the following procedure was employed. We chose a set of numerical parameters at which the steady state is unstable. Since with our specification of the functional relationships the model was (not linear but) quasi-linear, the cycles were (strongly) spiralling outward. We then introduced in one part of the model an essential nonlinearity that could put a curb on these explosive tendencies. Concretely, the mechanism was applied to inflationary expectations, where it plausibly assumed a flexibility according to which the adjustments take place at different speeds in different stages of the cycle. In fact, our device was so effective that the trajectories were contained in a compact region of the state space. In this way oscillations came about that did not die out, were globally bounded and thus persistent, and even turned out to converge to a unique periodic orbit – i.e. to a unique limit cycle.

The limit cycle could then conveniently serve as a reference to study the comovements of the model's main variables. Specifically, we could enquire into the reasons for an economic expansion or contraction to falter and eventually to reverse its motion. As a result, we were able to gain a better understanding of the economic mechanisms behind the turning points of a business cycle. In a qualitative sense the model could therefore be deemed to be successful.

A main quantitative shortcoming nevertheless remained, which was a much longer period than what we associate with a typical business cycle. Rather than look for alternative parameter combinations that are, however, quite likely to be artificial to a greater or lesser extent, one idea to improve on this feature is to let the model generate a higher (and more realistic) amplitude of the capital growth rate. We discussed the motive that this would be favourable for the cyclical pattern of the real balances ratio $m = M/pK$, which, in turn, was shown to be a key determinant of the motions of utilization.

The problem is that widening the narrow cyclical variations of the growth rate of fixed capital requires a higher reaction coefficient (derivative) f_I' of our investment function, but that, on the other hand, increase of f_I' are severely constrained by Assumption 1. The role of this assumption is to guarantee a downward-sloping IS curve, such that the reactions of the model's IS-LM equilibrium to the changes in the dynamic variables go in the usual direction. As this is a postulate that we agree should not be challenged, the analytically convenient temporary equilibrium concept for the good market reveals a dark side. It is one specific reason that actually led us to dispense with the IS equilibrium building block altogether – a task that is undertaken in the second part of the book.

Part II

Analytical Framework: Theory and Evidence

4   The Keynes–Metzler–Goodwin model

4.1   Introduction

The model that we are going to introduce in this chapter is the central model of the book. Analytically as well as numerically, it will therefore be investigated in great depth. Two variants are set up, which differ in the role of monetary policy, and they are dealt with in Parts II and III, respectively. In the first version we wish to study the private sector and its dynamic feedback mechanisms in a pure form. For this purpose a neutral monetary policy is hypothesized, which (as already in Part I of the book) takes the Friedmanian form of a constant growth rate of the money supply. The second version is concerned with an active monetary policy that treats the interest rate as a policy variable. Here an interest rate reaction function is postulated that is of the currently much discussed Taylor type.[1]

The model in Part II with the constant money growth rate can be conceived of as a direct extension of the three-dimensional model studied in chapter 3. Heuristically several motives were involved in its development over time, but in the context of this book we can depart from an observation that we made at the end of chapter 3, section 10. There a low responsiveness f_I' of fixed investment was identified as an obstacle to a more satisfactory cyclical growth pattern, the problem being that f_I' was severely bounded by the requirement to ensure a downward-sloping IS curve. The condition was made explicit in Assumption 1 in chapter 3, section 5. An analogous condition had to be formulated in Assumption 1 in chapter 2, section 4, for the Sargent model, and generally any model employing the organizing device of IS equilibrium has to adopt a similar restraint for the intensity with which its components of aggregate demand react (directly and indirectly) to changes in economic activity.[2]

---

[1] Taxes and government spending are neutral anyway. For them we continue to assume Sargent's fixed proportions, which have been underlying the previous two chapters.

[2] These conditions are well known to equivalently guarantee stable quantity adjustments, which, in a textbook-like manner, are supposed to take place within the short period.

While we had a specific reason why we wanted a higher responsiveness, other models with an IS curve will also, for different reasons, easily feel unduly constricted in their assumptions on aggregate demand if they become more ambitious. Hence, in elaborate macrodynamic modelling, the otherwise very convenient concept of temporary equilibrium on the goods market tends to become a straitjacket sooner or later. A major goal of our model is to get rid of it and provide a workable alternative.

Permitting production and demand to fall apart has, of course, a number of further conceptual implications. Since we consider rationing to be of secondary importance, we have to introduce inventories that can serve as a buffer for excess demand and supply. Production of firms will then also depend on their stocks piled up, so that the evolution of inventories is not only caused by goods market disequilibrium but also feeds back on this market.

These relationships were first profoundly investigated by L.A. Metzler in the 1940s (see Metzler, 1941, 1947). The goods market disequilibrium part of our model takes up his concepts and translates them into modern formal language, which takes growth into account and minimizes the number of additional dynamic variables. In fact, the model will thus be augmented by two state variables: one is the sales expectations that enter the production decisions of firms; the other keeps track of the inventories (both variables being specified as a ratio of the capital stock).

The other extensions of the chapter 3 model affect the general structure to a lesser extent. Basically, these are the following four.

(1) Besides the return differential, i.e. the excess of the rate of profit over the real interest rate, we allow utilization to play an extra role in the investment function. The idea is that the first magnitude captures the long-term aspect of investment in fixed capital, while the second is more oriented towards the medium term.

(2) We undo the simplifying assumption of chapter 3, where employment was proxied by capacity utilization in the wage Phillips curve. The reintroduction of the employment rate into this relationship gives us a third additional state variable (concretely; not the employment rate itself but the ratio of capital and labour supply), though its links with the rest of the economy are rather weak. Nevertheless, the whole model in its reduced form will thus comprise six state variables, the motions of which are governed by six differential equations.

(3) In addition to the standard arguments, the price Phillips curve in chapter 3 had already included a mechanism that referred to the wage share. We will now also augment the wage Phillips curve, in a way that will likewise, though with opposite sign, involve the wage share. The calibration later, in chapter 5, will then have to show if,

or to what extent, these wage share effects can be significant. To anticipate the main finding there, they will in fact be non-negligible.

(4) Regarding consumption demand, we distinguish between workers, who for simplicity consume their total wages, and 'capitalists', who save a constant fraction of their rentier income and consume the rest. This differentiation accentuates the role of real wages and the wage share, their impact on aggregate demand and, finally, capacity utilization. Together with the previous two points, the model, therefore, allows us to study the dynamic feedbacks between income distribution and economic activity. This topic is usually neglected in the Keynesian textbook models, but was Goodwin's (1967) major concern in his seminal, very nicely arranged growth cycle model. It can now be reconsidered in a wider framework.

Our model can thus be seen as a synthesis of well-known partial macro-dynamic systems into a coherent, integrated growth model. Admittedly, the determination of the interest rate on the money market (in the first version of the model) remains at an LM textbook level. On the other hand, the model emphasizes the disequilibria on the product and labour markets. Though we have sought to design the agents' reactions to these disequilibria in a parsimonious way, the model in its entirety exhibits a fairly rich structure already. Besides Keynes, of course, it has just been pointed out that we see this model as being, not exclusively but in particular, in the tradition of the work of Metzler and Goodwin. In this perspective it was natural to christen the framework a Keynes–Metzler–Goodwin model, or a KMG model for short.

The present chapter concentrates on a mathematical investigation of the KMG model, as far as it can go. Section 2 puts forward the model in its structural form. In particular, it discusses the innovations mentioned above and also carefully checks the implications of the stock and flow adjustments with respect to consistency in the accounting relationships across the economy as a whole. Section 3 reduces the model to its intensive form, which – as already indicated – gives us a six-dimensional differential equations system.

After establishing the existence of a unique steady-state position, we turn to the mathematical analysis of its local stability. Section 4 presents our general method by which we are still able, despite the model's high dimensionality, to obtain definite and reasonable stability conditions. The basic principle is to set a number of selected reaction coefficients to zero, in such a way that the eigenvalues of the Jacobian matrix can be read off from a suitable 3×3 submatrix (using the Routh–Hurwitz conditions). The zero assumptions are then successively dropped and replaced with sufficiently small coefficients. This allows us to infer from the stability of the 3×3 submatrix the stability of another suitable 4×4 submatrix that it comprises, and so on step by step until eventually we can assess the stability of the model's full 6×6 Jacobian. It is convenient here that we need only to compute the sign of the determinant of the $n \times n$ (sub-)matrices, where successively $n = 3, 4, 5, 6$. The precise stability propositions and the details of deriving this cascade of stable matrices are given in section 5. Section 6 concludes.

A mathematical appendix makes the method more explicit; in it we set up an economically meaningful discrete-time analogue of the continuous-time system. This is done in such a way that the computer simulations represent a sequential economy – a monthly economy, in fact – and are not just the outcome of some technical algorithm *à la* Runge–Kutta. The appendix also contains the core of the computer source code.

4.2   Formulation of the model

4.2.1   Households

Insofar as private households appear on the supply-side of a market, only worker households with their supply of labour are considered. We continue to assume that, in the light of imperfectly flexible wages, actual employment is always determined by firms' demand for labour. The details of the sluggish wage adjustments in response to labour market disequilibrium are given in subsection 4.2.4 below.

Demand on the part of households is formulated on the financial markets and on the goods market. Beginning with the financial sector, households own three assets: money, M; government fixed-price bonds, B (the price being normalized at unity); and equities issued by firms, $p_e E$, where E is the number of shares and p_e their price.[3] Their real wealth thus amounts to

$$W = (M + B + p_e E)/p \qquad (4.1)$$

(p is the price level). At each moment in time households allocate their existing wealth between these assets. To maintain the simple textbook LM equation to characterize equilibrium on the financial markets, bonds and equities are treated as perfect substitutes. The desired division of wealth between M and, on the other hand, $B + p_e E$ is described by a pair of stock demand functions,

$$M^d/p = \tilde{f}_m(i, Y, W)$$

$$(B^d + p_e E^d)/p = \tilde{f}_b(i, Y, W)$$

[3] The presentation of the financial sector follows Sargent (1987, chap. 1, sect. 2).

where i is the nominal interest rate on bonds, Y is production by firms (as a proxy for the rate of transacting in the economy, which concerns the transaction motive), d superscripts denote desired quantities, and the demand schedules obey the budget constraint

$$(M^d + B^d + p_e E^d)/p = \tilde{f}_m + \tilde{f}_b = W$$

As households are the only group in the economy owning the three assets, the market equilibrium conditions read

$$M^d = M/p, \quad (B^d + p_e E^d)/p = (B + p_e E)/p$$

Of course, by virtue of Walras' law (of stocks), either equation is sufficient for the financial sector to be in equilibrium. That is, eq. (4.1) and the budget identity imply that, if one condition is satisfied, the other is satisfied too.

It is moreover assumed that money demand is independent of wealth. This means that households desire to hold any *ceteris paribus* increase in real wealth entirely in the form of bonds and equities (since, with $\partial \tilde{f}_m / \partial W = 0$, Walras' law entails $\partial \tilde{f}_b / \partial W = 1$). Writing the demand function for real balances as $\tilde{f}_m(i, Y, W) = Y f_m(i)$, equilibrium on the asset markets is then represented by the familiar LM equation

$$M = p Y f_m(i), \quad f_m' < 0 \tag{4.2}$$

While eq. (4.2) determines the interest rate, the determination of the equity price p_e requires an additional mechanism. However, since equities, like bonds, will be assumed to play only a passive role in the economy and so do not feed back on the rest of the model, we need not be explicit about that.

Turning to the goods market, consumption demand C of the households has to be specified. In contrast to the previous two chapters we now differentiate between workers and asset owners, or, more precisely, between consumption financed out of wage income and consumption financed out of rental income. As for the former, it is assumed that disposable wage income is exclusively spent on consumption. With respect to a tax rate τ_w, the nominal wage rate w and hours worked L, this component of (nominal) consumption expenditures is given by $(1 - \tau_w)wL$.

The disposable income of asset owners consists of dividends plus interest payments iB less taxes pT^c. A fraction s_c of this income is saved; the remainder is consumed. Regarding dividends, firms are supposed to pay out all net earnings to the shareholders, where the earnings concept adopted by the firms is based on expected sales Y^e. K being the stock of fixed capital and δ its depreciation rate, we have

$$\text{dividends} = pY^e - wL - \delta pK \qquad (4.3)$$

so that consumption spending out of rental income is given by $(1 - s_c)$ $(pY^e - wL - \delta pK + iB - pT^c)$.

It should be mentioned that firms may alternatively base the concept of net earnings on realized sales, which are equal to goods demand Y^d (see subsection 4.2.2). Dividends would then be given by $pY^d - wL - \delta pK$, a rule that, conceptually, may perhaps even be reckoned preferable. The structure of the model, including the structure of the differential equations to be derived for the mathematical analysis, would not be affected by this modification; only a few coefficients in the terms referring to excess demand would be somewhat different. We nevertheless stick to eq. (4.3), since it has already been used in previous work[4] and we wish to maintain continuity in that specification feature. We do this in particular because, in this book, we are now clear about the many details of the mathematical proofs, whereas in the model versions treated in those earlier contributions the proofs were still rather sketchy.

The savings of asset owners as the complementary part of their consumption decisions are invested in newly issued bonds, equities and money. We make sure in subsection 4.2.5 that this is indeed compatible with the financial actions of the government and firm sectors.

In addition to consumption out of wage and rental income, we identify consumption by that part of the population that does not earn income from economic activities, such as people living on welfare or unemployment benefits, or retired people drawing on a pension. These expenditures are not too closely linked to the business cycle. For simplicity they are assumed to grow with the capital stock pK, with a proportionality coefficient $c_p \geq 0$. Formally, $c_p pK$ is financed by taxes; hence, this expression will also show up again in the government budget constraint.[5] The reason for introducing this type of consumption is that it takes better account of a countercyclical consumption ratio C/Y, which is a stylized empirical fact. We return to this matter later in the book, in chapter 6, section 3, subsection 3.

---

[4] See, for example, Chiarella and Flaschel (2000a) or Chiarella et al. (2000).
[5] In fact, $c_p pK$ has the same formal status as government expenditures. A part of the tax collections could be conceived of as payments into a pension fund, which are directly passed on to retired people. Admittedly, this interpretation neglects the fact that pension funds accumulate financial assets and actively operate on the financial markets, which might be an issue for a more elaborated financial sector.

Collecting together the terms of the three consumption components, total consumption expenditures sum to

$$pC = c_p pK + (1 - \tau_w)wL + (1 - s_c)(pY^e - wL - \delta pK + iB - pT^c) \quad (4.4)$$

4.2.2 Firms

As indicated, this chapter admits goods market disequilibrium. We abstain, however, from any rationing schemes, which we do not consider sufficiently relevant at the macro level, and assume that demand for finished goods is always realized. Demand is satisfied from current production and the existing stock of inventories; any excess of demand over sales replenishes inventories. Accordingly, the model has to keep track of the accumulation of inventories. In this setting, firms make three types of decisions: about fixed investment, inventory investment, and the level of production. Before discussing them it is useful to lay out the production technology.

Technology To represent the production technology of firms, the approach explained and motivated in chapter 3, section 2, is taken over unaltered. Given the stock of fixed capital K and y^n, the output–capital ratio that would prevail under normal conditions, productive capacity Y^n and its utilization u are defined by

$$Y^n = y^n K \quad (4.5)$$

$$u = Y/Y^n = y/y^n \quad (4.6)$$

Labour productivity with respect to hours is denoted by $z = Y/L$, while z^o is labour productivity when firms produce at their capacity level, $Y = Y^n$. The procyclicality of z is captured by linking it directly to utilization:

$$z = z^o f_z(u), \quad f_z(1) = 1, 0 \leq f'_z < 1 \quad (4.7)$$

Normal productivity itself is predetermined in the short period and grows at an exogenous rate g_z,

$$\hat{z}^o = g_z \quad (4.8)$$

If the state of technology is z^o and productive capacity is Y^n, employment (in hours) to produce output Y therefore assumes the form $L = L(Y) = Y/[z^o f_z(Y/Y^n)]$. L obviously rises less than proportionately with Y. The condition $f'_z < 1$ prevents L from falling when output increases – i.e. it ensures that $dL(Y^n)/dY > 0$.

Fixed investment In extending the investment function of chapters 2 and 3, two motives for investment in fixed capital are considered. Besides the previous positive reactions to the spread $q = r - (i - \pi)$ between profitability and the yields from holding bonds (r the profit rate, $i - \pi$ the real interest rate), we now also include the utilization of productive capacity. Here, for reasons not explicitly taken into account in the model formulation, firms in particular desire no permanent overutilization. Hence (net) investment increases with u. (That in the presence of underutilization, $u < 1$, the accumulation of capital tends to slow down is obvious anyhow.)

When the concept of a rate of profit r is invoked in the following, we continue to relate profits to the stock of fixed capital alone, rather than fixed capital plus inventories. This is done to rule out undue complications. The concept itself may be called an 'operative' rate of profit, $r = (pY - wL - \delta pK)/pK$, or, with the wage share $v = wL/pY$, $r = (1 - v)y - \delta$.

We again normalize real wages by trend productivity and define $\omega = (w/p)/z^o$. As in chapter 3, section 3, the wage share is decomposed as $v = (w/pz^o)z^o(L/Y) = \omega \cdot (z^o/z) = \omega/f_z(u)$ (the latter by (4.7)). Thus, on the whole, the investment schedule may be summarized as

$$I/K = f_I[r - (i - \pi), u], \quad f_{Iq} > 0, f_{Iu} \geq 0 \tag{4.9}$$

$$r = (1 - v)uy^n - \delta \tag{4.10}$$

$$v = \omega/f_z(u) \tag{4.11}$$

$$\omega = w/pz^o \tag{4.12}$$

$$\dot{K} = I \tag{4.13}$$

In the investment function, f_{Iu} abbreviates $\partial f/\partial u$ and f_{Iq} is the partial derivative with respect to the first argument, the differential in the two rates of return. Certainly, with $f_{Iu} = 0$, eq. (4.9) parallels the investment function (3.7) in chapter 3.

Since utilization u already affects the profit rate r, adding u itself as an extra argument in the investment function may perhaps appear as a double count. The uneasiness is comprehensible from the comparative statics of an IS-LM analysis. Here, however, we have dropped the IS temporary equilibrium assumption. Especially in a cyclical environment, which we will later seek to establish, this emphasizes the role of the dynamics of the two variables u and $q = r - (i - \pi)$. As the motions of q are composed of several influences besides u, we can expect (and this will indeed be confirmed in chapter 6, section 7, subsection 3) that q and

u behave sufficiently differently over the cycle. Hence, the two variables have their own justification in the determination of fixed investment, not only conceptually but also with respect to the dynamic feedbacks.[6]

To be complete, we make explicit the fact that the capital outlays are financed by equity issuance at the ruling price p_e and by windfall profits – i.e. the excess of actual sales (or demand) Y^d over expected sales Y^e (in nominal terms):

$$pI = p_e \dot{E} + p(Y^d - Y^e) \qquad (4.14)$$

If Y^d falls short of Y^e, the equation may be read as saying that the new shares also finance the corresponding windfall losses.

Inventory investment To model inventories and firms' production we follow the production-smoothing/buffer-stock approach, which was initiated by Metzler (1941). Although in recent times its economic significance has been questioned (see the survey article by Blinder and Maccini, 1991), it has been demonstrated in Franke (1996) that it can be made compatible with the main stylized facts of the inventory cycle.[7]

Our approach distinguishes between actual and desired changes in inventories. The actual change is just the difference between production Y and sales = demand Y^d,

$$\dot{N} = Y - Y^d \qquad (4.15)$$

Demand, of course, is given by the components

$$Y^d = C + I + \delta K + G \qquad (4.16)$$

(government demand is specified below). As for desired inventory changes, the stock management of firms is based on a desired ratio β_{ny} of inventories over expected sales. Correspondingly, the desired level N^d of inventories is given by

$$N^d = \beta_{ny} Y^e \qquad (4.17)$$

---

[6] Apart from this, more advanced modelling that attaches a greater weight to other expectations, or climate variables, than π could replace r with an 'expected' rate of profit r^e, adjustments to which would be determined in another part of the model. This extension can be assessed better if we compare the motions of r^e and their direct impact on investment with the motions of r and their effects.

[7] A conceptual alternative that has become quite popular is the (S,s) theory of inventory investment. Foote et al. (2000), however, conclude that the evidence for the importance of (S,s) adjustment is surprisingly weak. Moreover, the approach would not be very tractable within the present macrodynamic context.

β_{ny} may simply be called the inventory–sales ratio.[8] N^d generally differs from N, and firms seek to close this gap gradually with speed β_{nn}. That is, if everything else remained fixed, the stock of inventories would reach its target level in $1/\beta_{nn}$ years. In addition, firms have to account for the overall growth of the economy. To this end they employ a trend rate of growth. It is supposed for simplicity that it is fixed and coincides with the long-run equilibrium growth rate g^o, which is specified below.[9] The desired change in inventories, which we denote by I_N^d, thus reads

$$I_N^d = g^o N^d + \beta_{nn}(N^d - N) \tag{4.18}$$

Eq. (4.18) is the basis of the so-called 'production-smoothing' model; see, for example, Blinder and Maccini (1991, especially p. 81). The stock-adjustment speed β_{nn} is treated as a fixed parameter, although in Franke (1996) it is assumed to be flexible if firms experience larger disequilibrium fluctuations. We will return to this issue in the course of the stability analysis.

Production Firms decide on production before actual sales are known. As a consequence they produce to meet expected demand and their own desired change in inventories:

$$Y = Y^e + I_N^d \tag{4.19}$$

Eq. (4.19) represents the buffer-stock aspect. This is seen by inserting (4.19) into (4.15). The resulting equation $\dot{N} = I_N^d + (Y^e - Y^d)$ tells us directly that sales surprises are completely buffered by inventories.

It remains to specify the formation of sales expectations. A straightforward device is to assume adaptive expectations. Invoking growth in a similar manner to (4.18), they take the form

$$\dot{Y}^e = g^o Y^e + \beta_y(Y^d - Y^e) \tag{4.20}$$

As an alternative to the usual interpretation of partial adjustments of expected sales Y^e towards realized sales Y^d, (4.20) can also be viewed as an approximation to the results of extrapolative forecasts on the basis of a

---

[8] Metzler (1941, p.125) has called this magnitude the inventory accelerator.

[9] Especially if the steady state is never reached, firms will find it hard to come to know the exact value of g^o. A conceptually more satisfactory treatment is to posit an adaptive rule for such a perceived trend rate of growth. Since it is reasonable to assume that this mechanism should be quite slow, the dynamic feedback from this side of the model would be dominated by many other effects. So, we do not consider adopting the fixed growth rate g^o to be a serious simplification.

rolling sample period. If the latter has length T, the speed of adjustment β_y is related to T by $\beta_y = 4/T$ (Franke, 1992b). Such extrapolative predictions are in the same spirit as the simple extrapolative forecasts that Irvine (1981, p. 635) reports to be common practice in real-world retailer forecasting.

4.2.3 The government

As pointed out in the introduction, the government sector or the fiscal and monetary authorities, respectively, are supposed to play a neutral role. Accordingly, the specification of real government spending G and taxes T^c of asset owners is the same as in the preceding chapters,

$$G = \gamma K \tag{4.21}$$

$$T^c = \theta_c K + iB/p \tag{4.22}$$

(only indexation by 'c' is added, since we now additionally have taxes $\tau_w wL$ on wages). For reasons of consistency the government constraint should be stated, too. It says that the budget deficit is financed by issuing money and bonds. The deficit itself results from government demand G plus the transfers $c_p pK$ to the 'non-economic' households for consumption purposes in eq. (4.4) plus the interest payments on bonds, if these components are in excess over the government's tax receipts. Accordingly,

$$\dot{M} + \dot{B} = pG + c_p pK + iB - T^c - \tau_w wL \tag{4.23}$$

Monetary policy again keeps up a constant growth rate of the money supply,

$$\hat{M} = g_m \tag{4.24}$$

It follows that bond financing $\dot{B}$ of the deficit is residually determined from (4.23). As taxes T^c and the financial sector have been specified, these bonds have no repercussion effects on the economy and so, together with the equities, can remain in the background.

It should briefly be mentioned that another view of monetary policy has become popular over the last few years. Rather than the money supply, it conceives the (short-term) nominal rate of interest as the primary policy variable of the central bank. More specifically, the interest rate is seen to react, in a smooth way, to deviations of actual inflation from a target rate of inflation, and to deviations of real output from potential output.

This approach of a monetary policy rule reverses the causality in the government sector and the LM equation (4.2): first, the interest rate is determined from the reaction function (at the beginning of the short period, so to say), and then the central bank sets the money supply such as to support this interest rate via (4.2).[10]

There is strong empirical evidence for interest rate reaction functions (not only in the United States). We may nevertheless defend the autonomous constant growth rate of M in eq. (4.24). In our view it is useful to investigate first the dynamic stabilizing and destabilizing forces of the economy within the environment of a neutral monetary policy. Such a model may provide a benchmark against which, subsequently, the more active measure of an interest rate reaction function can be better evaluated. This analysis is initiated in Part III of the book.

4.2.4   The wage-price sector

Nominal wage and price inflation continue to be represented by Phillips curves. The expectational element entering them was captured by the variable π, which, following the literature, has so far been called the expected rate of inflation. We have already remarked, however, that it is not the inflation rate to be expected for the next month or quarter, but some sort of average over a medium period of time. Since our economy is populated by adaptive agents and not the so-called 'rational' agents with their model-consistent expectations, π will be a rough estimate of future inflation that, as we learn from psychology and the behavioural sciences, is considerably influenced by recent observations. Such a variable will therefore tend to express the general climate of the agents' beliefs about inflation. For this reason it appears more appropriate to us to call π from now on the *inflation climate*.

The revisions of π as well as the determination of $\hat{p}$ by way of a price Phillips curve are taken over unaltered from chapter 3, section 3. Therefore we simply reiterate, in that order, eqs. (3.19), (3.20), (3.16) and (3.17), though we now prefer to specify the core function f_{pu} of the Phillips curve directly in a linear manner. In addition, we make explicit the equilibrium rate of real growth g^o that determines equilibrium

---

[10] Note that, if (reasonably) wealth $W = (M + B + p_e E)/p$ were also to enter the LM equation, there would be a whole continuum of combinations of M and B to bring about a given interest rate. This would open up the possibility of different types of monetary policy; for example, M being endogenously determined within the short period, or B being endogenous, or the central bank could maintain a fixed policy mix M/B.

inflation and is also adopted by firms in (4.18) and (4.20) to capture the trend.

$$\hat{p} = \kappa_p(\hat{w} - g_z) + (1 - \kappa_p)\pi + f_p(u, v), \quad 0 \le \kappa_p \le 1 \tag{4.25}$$

$$f_p(u, v) = \beta_{pu}(u - 1) + \beta_{pv}[(1 + \mu)v - 1], \quad \beta_{pu} > 0, \beta_{pv} \ge 0 \tag{4.26}$$

$$\dot{\pi} = \beta_\pi[\kappa_\pi(\hat{p} - \pi) + (1 - \kappa_\pi)(\pi^o - \pi)], \quad 0 \le \kappa_\pi \le 1 \tag{4.27}$$

$$\pi^o = g_m - g^o \tag{4.28}$$

$$g^o = g_\ell + g_z \tag{4.29}$$

Regarding the adjustments of nominal wages, we put forward a more ambitious version of the wage Phillips curve than that used in chapter 3, section 3. To begin with a minor specification detail, recall that in the Phillips curve (3.18) the employment rate was proxied by capacity utilization. It is now time to undo this simplification and reintroduce the relevant labour market variable, the employment rate. To be exact, we refer to the employment rate e based on hours,

$$e = L/L^s \tag{4.30}$$

That is, L are the hours currently worked (converted into the annual flow magnitude) and L^s is the supply of working hours, which equals the number of workers in supply multiplied by the annual total of normal working hours per capita. This labour supply grows at an exogenous constant rate g_ℓ,

$$\hat{L}^s = g_\ell \tag{4.31}$$

While in empirical research the corresponding NAIRU rate of employment is usually implicitly determined in a regression approach, in a theoretical formulation it can appear directly in the Phillips curve. Without loss of generality, we may also posit that it is equal to unity.[11]

The major innovation in our wage Phillips curve, however, is that, in addition to the familiar positive effect of the employment rate on wage changes, we include the wage share as another variable that might possibly exert some influence. It is a straightforward idea that the parties

---

[11] In particular, $e = 1$ may prevail even though part of the workforce is unemployed when a fraction of the employed works overtime. Thus, our Phillips curve will implicitly assume an equal weight of outside and inside effects. For a wage Phillips curve, integrated in a small macrodynamic model of Goodwinian type, that differentiates between the influence of an outside and an inside employment rate and also allows for different weights of these effects; see Flaschel (2000).

in the wage-bargaining process also have an eye on the general distribution of total income. At relatively low values of the wage share, workers seek to catch up to what is considered a normal, or 'fair', level, and this is to some degree also taken up in the wage bargaining. By the same token, workers are somewhat restrained in their wage claims if v is currently above normal. Accordingly, if normal income distribution is (unanimously) characterized by its steady-state value v^o, the deviations of v from v^o may have a negative impact on $\hat{w}$. In a manner similar to that with the trend growth rate g^o above, v^o is assumed to be known for simplicity.

Reference to a benchmark term that takes current inflation and the inflation climate into account, both 'net' of productivity growth, is made in the same way as in the previous chapter. On the whole, our extended wage Phillips curve thus reads

$$\hat{w} = g_z + [\kappa_w \hat{p} + (1 - \kappa_w)\pi] + f_w(e, v), \quad 0 \leq \kappa_w \leq 1 \tag{4.32}$$

$$f_w(e, v) = \beta_{we}(e - 1) - \beta_{wv}(v - v^o)/v^o, \quad \beta_{we} > 0, \beta_{wv} \geq 0 \tag{4.33}$$

Eqs. (4.32),(4.33) can also be given another and somewhat richer theoretical underpinning. Blanchard and Katz (1999) specify a wage-setting model in which the tighter the labour market the higher the level (!) of the real wage, given the workers' reservation wage. They go on to interpret the latter as depending on labour productivity and lagged wages. If we rescale their unemployment rate U such that $U = 0$ in a steady state and $U = 1 - e$ with respect to the present employment rate, and write $\tilde{x} := \ln x$ for a dynamic variable x, then the central equation (6) in Blanchard and Katz (1999, p. 5) can be rearranged such that it becomes (maintaining their coefficients)

$$\tilde{w}_t - \tilde{w}_{t-1} = [\mu a - \mu\lambda\Delta\tilde{z}_t^o - (1 - \mu\lambda)\tilde{v}^o] + (1 - \mu\lambda)\Delta\tilde{z}_t + \mu\lambda\Delta\tilde{z}_t^o$$
$$+ (\tilde{p}_t^e - p_{t-1}) + \beta(e_t - 1) - (1 - \mu\lambda)(\tilde{w}_{t-1} - \tilde{p}_{t-1} - \tilde{z}_{t-1} - \tilde{v}^o)$$

The coefficients a and β are positive, $0 \leq \mu, \lambda \leq 1$, and the intercept in square brackets on the right-hand side can be shown to vanish. The term $(1 - \mu\lambda)\Delta\tilde{z}_t + \mu\lambda\Delta\tilde{z}_t^o$, which is a weighted average of the growth rates of actual and trend productivity, corresponds to g_z $(= \Delta\tilde{z}_t^o)$ in (4.32).[12] $\tilde{p}_t^e$ is

---

[12] Conceptually, g_z in (4.32) may well be generalized to such a weighted average. We abstain from this option since, by including $\hat{z}$ $(= \Delta\tilde{z}_t)$, the time derivative $\dot{u}$ of utilization would show up in the model via (4.7), which would lead to great complications in the stability analysis that do not seem worthwhile.

an expected price level to which the nominal wage rate is related in the original formulation of Blanchard and Katz's wage equation, or 'wage curve'. So, $\tilde{p}_t^e - p_{t-1}$ may be identified with our inflation climate π, and the full weight of this expectational variable corresponds to $\kappa_w = 0$. The relationship $\beta_{we} = \beta$ is obvious. Finally, note that $\tilde{w}_{t-1} - \tilde{p}_{t-1} - \tilde{z}_{t-1}$ equals $\tilde{v}_{t-1}$, the log of the wage share. If we neglect the difference in the timing of the wage share, then the last term $(1 - \mu\lambda)(\tilde{w}_{t-1} - \tilde{p}_{t-1} - \tilde{z}_{t-1} - \tilde{v}^o)$ corresponds to $\beta_{wv}(v - v^o)/v^o$ in (4.33).

Blanchard and Katz quote evidence from macroeconomic as well as from regional data that, for the United States, the coefficient $1 - \mu\lambda$ is close to zero. In most European countries, by contrast, $\tilde{w}_{t-1} - \tilde{p}_{t-1} - \tilde{z}_{t-1}$ (which in the regression equations is usually referred to as an error correction term) comes in with a significantly negative coefficient; on average, $1 - \mu\lambda$ is around 0.25.[13] We shall shed light on the magnitude of this coefficient from another angle in our chapter on calibration.

4.2.5   Checking on accounting consistency

The LM approach to the financial markets formulates demand and supply as stock magnitudes. For this treatment to be meaningful it must be compatible with the flow relationships in the financial sector. It should therefore be verified that the savings of private households, designated S_p (in real terms), do indeed match the increase in the financial assets issued by firms and the government.

To see this, we begin with expected sales. Solve the finance equation (4.14) of firms for $pY^e = p_e\dot{E} - pI + pY^d$, substitute eq. (4.16) for aggregate demand Y^d and then eq. (4.4) for consumption pC entering here. As a result, pY^e shows up on the left-hand side as well as on the right-hand side, while pI cancels out. Solving this equation for $s_c pY^e$, using $iB - pT^c = -\theta_c pK$ from (4.22), and collecting terms leads to

$$s_c pY^e = p_e\dot{E} + (s_c - \tau_w)wL + c_p pK + s_c \delta pK - (1 - s_c)\theta_c pK + pG$$

As remarked on the specification of dividends in eq. (4.3), nominal private savings are given by $pS_p = s_c[pY^e - wL - \delta pK + iB - pT^c]$.

[13] See also Plasmans et al. (1999, sect. 3). There may, however, be questions as to the sensitivity of these results with respect to the exact measure of 'expected inflation', $\tilde{p}_t^e - p_{t-1}$.

Substituting the expression we have just derived for $s_c p Y^e$ in this equation and again making use of (4.22) yields

$$pS_p = p_e \dot{E} - \theta_c pK - \tau_w wL + c_p pK + pG$$

$\theta_c pK$ being taxes T^c of asset owners, the last four terms on the right-hand side make up the government deficit in eq. (4.23), which is financed by issuing money and bonds, $\dot{M} + \dot{B}$. Hence, in the end, we obtain

$$S_p = [p_e \dot{E} + \dot{M} + \dot{B}]/p \qquad (4.34)$$

as required.

A second consistency check regards total savings in the economy, which should turn out to equal total investment – i.e. fixed investment plus inventory investment. Savings accrue in the household sector (S_p), in the firm sector (S_f) and in the government sector (S_g). In nominal terms they are given by

$$pS_f = pY - wL - \delta pK - \text{dividends}$$

$$pS_g = -[pG + c_p pK + iB - pT^c - \tau_w L]$$

$$pS_p = s_c[\text{dividends} + iB - pT^c]$$

As for the definition of S_f, we follow the usual practice of specifying current production by firms as their gross proceeds. Government saving is, of course, the budget deficit in (4.23) with a negative sign.

On the basis of the dividend rule (4.3), savings of firms are equal to unintended inventory changes, $S_f = Y - Y^e$. Using (4.23) and (4.34) gives $S = S_f + S_g + S_p = Y - Y^e + p_e \dot{E}/p$ in total. By virtue of the finance equation (4.14) of firms, the change in equities can be expressed as $p_e \dot{E}/p = I - (Y^d - Y^e)$, so that $S = I + Y - Y^d$. The excess of production over demand is just the change in inventories, as stated in (4.15). Thus, we do indeed arrive at

$$S = S_f + S_g + S_p = I + \dot{N} \qquad (4.35)$$

It is seen in the next section that, with the LM textbook version of the financial sector, not all equations of the model will actually enter the formal analysis. In this respect, eqs. (4.1), (4.3), (4.14) and (4.23) are dispensable at present. They have nevertheless been added in the exposition of the model in order to show that the model satisfies the basic accounting principles, and since these or similar equations would play an active role in the analysis of a more advanced version of the model, where our simplifying restrictions in the financial and government sector were to be relaxed.

4.3   The model in intensive form

Compared to chapter 3, the main extension of the model formulated in the preceding section is disequilibrium in the goods market. In this way inventories and expected sales are newly introduced as basic variables. In addition, the wage Phillips curve refers to the employment rate and no longer to capacity utilization. In its reduced form, the dimensions of the model will therefore increase from three to six. Specifically, we will derive a closed system of differential equations for the following variables:

$$
\begin{array}{lll}
m = M/pK & \text{real balances ratio} & \\
\omega = w/pz^{o} & \text{real wage rate} & \\
y^{e} = Y^{e}/K & \text{expected sales ratio} & \\
k^{s} = K/z^{o}L^{s} & \text{capital per head} & (4.36) \\
n = N/K & \text{inventory ratio} & \\
\pi & \text{inflation climate} &
\end{array}
$$

Clearly, the term 'ratio' refers to the stock of fixed capital. When speaking of the real wage rate, it is to be understood as being deflated by labour productivity. Capital per head is a shorthand expression for capital per hour of labour supplied, measured in efficiency units.

Other variables entering the differential equations will be utilization, u; the output–capital ratio, $y = Y/K$; the demand–capital ratio, $y^{d} = Y^{d}/K$; the employment rate, e; the wage share, $v = wL/pY$; the nominal interest rate, i; and the capital growth rate, g_{k}. They are functionally dependent on the above six state variables. In order to avoid clumsy notation, we retain these symbols when formulating the differential equations.

Let us begin with the output–capital ratio. Using (4.19), (4.18) and (4.17) we have $Y = Y^{e} + I_{N}^{d} = Y^{e} + (g^{o} + \beta_{nn})\beta_{ny}Y^{e} - \beta_{nn}N$. Division by K gives

$$
y = y(y^{e}, n) = [1 + (g^{o} + \beta_{nn})\beta_{ny}]y^{e} - \beta_{nn}n \qquad (4.37)
$$

Correspondingly, the utilization of productive capacity in eq. (4.6) reads

$$
u = u(y^{e}, n) = y(y^{e}, n)/y^{n} \qquad (4.38)
$$

Economic activity is thus seen to increase more than proportionately with expected sales. This is due to production also taking care of the induced growth (via g^o) and of the disequilibrium adjustments (via the coefficient β_{nn}) towards the desired level of inventories, which in turn depends on expected sales (via β_{ny}). On the other hand, economic activity decreases as inventories pile up, since a greater part of the current demand for goods can then be satisfied from stocks.

From the LM equation (4.2) and from (4.37), the interest rate is determined by the equation $f_m(i) - M/pY = f_m(i) - m/y = f_m(i) - m/y(y^e, n) = 0$, which is generally an implicit equation for i. As f_m is strictly decreasing and $y = y(y^e, n)$ is strictly monotonic in both of its arguments, the existence and uniqueness of a value of i fulfilling this equality with m, y^e, n given is no problem. Hence, i can be conceived as a function of the other three variables involved,

$$i = i(m, y^e, n) \tag{4.39}$$

The partial derivatives are easily calculated by means of the implicit function theorem. For later use they are stated in an extra proposition.

Proposition 1
The nominal interest rate i satisfying the LM equation (4.2) is a function (4.39) of the three state variables m, y^e, n. The partial derivatives are

$$\partial i / \partial m = -i/m\eta_{m,i} < 0$$

$$\partial i / \partial y^e = [1 + (g^o + \beta_{nn})\beta_{ny}]i/y\eta_{m,i} > 0$$

$$\partial i / \partial n = -\beta_{nn}i/y\eta_{m,i} < 0,$$

where $\eta_{m,i}$ is defined as the interest elasticity of money demand, $\eta_{m,i} = -if_m'/f_m > 0$, expressed as a positive magnitude.

It is obvious from (4.36) that, when being differentiated with respect to time, the growth rate of fixed capital $g_k = \hat{K} = I/K = f_I(\dots)$ will be invoked several times in the time rate of change of the state variables. Abbreviating

$$v = v(\omega, y^e, n) = \omega/f_z[u(y^e, n)] \tag{4.40}$$

by way of (4.11) and (4.38), and referring to (4.9), (4.10), (4.38) and (4.39), the capital growth may be written as

$$g_k = g_k(m, \omega, y^e, n, \pi)$$

$$= f_I\{[1 - v(\omega, y^e, n)]u(y^e, n)y^n - \delta - i(m, y^e, n) + \pi, u(y^e, n)\} \tag{4.41}$$

To derive the demand–capital ratio y^d, note first that $wL/pK = (wL/pY) \cdot (Y/K) = vy$. Dividing consumption spending pC in (4.4) by pK and using (4.22) gives $C/K = (1 - s_c)y^e + (s_c - \tau_w)vy + c_p - (1 - s_c)(\delta + \theta_c)$. Substituting this expression in total demand Y^d in (4.16) divided by pK, and taking (4.21) regarding government spending into account, leads to

$$y^d = y^d(m, \omega, y^e, n, \pi) = \gamma + c_p + s_c\delta - (1 - s_c)\theta_c + (1 - s_c)y^e$$

$$+(s_c - \tau_w)v(\omega, y^e, n)y(y^e, n) + g_k(m, \omega, y^e, n, \pi) \qquad (4.42)$$

Of course, the dependency of y^d on the variables m, y^e, n occurs through eqs. (4.37)–(4.41). Lastly, to represent the employment rate, make use of $L/Y = 1/z = 1/z^o f_z(u)$ from (4.7) to decompose it as $e = L/L^s = (L/Y) \cdot (Y/K) \cdot (K/L^s) = (1/z^o f_z)y(K/L^s) = (y/f_z) \cdot (K/z^o L^s)$. Thus,

$$e = e(y^e, k^s, n) = y(y^e, n)k^s/f_z[u(y^e, n)] \qquad (4.43)$$

Having established the functional relationships for the auxiliary variables, the motions of the six state variables are readily described. The differential equations for m, ω, π have already been determined in chapter 3, section 4, eqs. (3.25)–(3.27), except that now the slope term f_w in the wage Phillips curve has to be modified correspondingly: $f_w = f_w(e, v)$.

The time rate of change of the expected sales ratio $y^e = Y^e/K$ is obtained with the aid of (4.20), which yields $\hat{y}^e = \hat{Y}^e - \hat{K} = g^o + \beta_y[(Y^d - Y^e)/K] \cdot (K/Y^e) - g_k$. It remains to multiply this equation with y^e. Equations (4.8), (4.31) and (4.29) give $\hat{k}^s = \hat{K} - \hat{z}^o - \hat{L}^{hs} = g_k - g_z - g_\ell = g_k - g^o$ for the motions of capital per head. The variations in the inventory ratio $n = N/K$ are based on eq. (4.15), $\hat{n} = \hat{N} - \hat{K} = (\dot{N}/K) \cdot (K/N) - g_k = [(Y - Y^d)/K]/n - g_k$, and subsequent multiplication with n. On the whole, we end up with a system of six differential equations for the six state variables. With a view to the mathematical stability analysis, they are written in the following order:

$$\dot{\omega} = \omega\kappa[(1 - \kappa_p)f_w(e, v) - (1 - \kappa_w)f_p(u, v)], \quad \kappa := 1/(1 - \kappa_p\kappa_w)$$
$$(4.44)$$

$$\dot{m} = m\{g_m - \pi - \kappa[\kappa_p f_w(e, v) + f_p(u, v)] - g_k\} \qquad (4.45)$$

$$\dot{y}^e = (g^o - g_k)y^e + \beta_y(y^d - y^e) \qquad (4.46)$$

$$\dot{k}^s = k^s(g_k - g^o) \qquad (4.47)$$

$$\dot{n} = y - y^d - ng_k \qquad (4.48)$$

$$\dot{\pi} = \beta_\pi\{\kappa_\pi\kappa[\kappa_p f_w(e, v) + f_p(u, v)] + (1 - \kappa_\pi)(\pi^o - \pi)\} \qquad (4.49)$$

Naturally, regarding the definition of κ it is presupposed that κ_p and κ_w are not both unity; e, u, v, y, y^d and g_k are the auxiliary variables that depend on the state variables as determined in (4.37)–(4.43).

Before we begin the analysis of the differential equations system, this economy should be briefly compared with its predecessors in the literature. Closest to eqs. (4.44)–(4.49) are the formulations put forward in Chiarella and Flaschel (2000a, p. 299, eqs. (6.93)–(6.98)) and Chiarella et al. (2000, pp. 63–65, eqs. (3.1)–(3.7)). To make out the model genealogy, it may be noted that there the reciprocal of k^s is employed (designated as l). This is, however, only a matter of notation and, regarding the differential equation for this variable, the sign of the right-hand side.

The present model nevertheless differs from the cited literature in a number of ways. Three minor specification details are the following. (a) In the profit rate r entering the investment function, our output measure is current production Y. In contrast, in the other models expected sales Y^e are used at this place. (b) The forerunner models do not tax wages – i.e. $\tau_w = 0$. (c) In these models there is no consumption of 'non-economic' households – i.e. $c_p = 0$.

In addition, there are three much more important aspects in which the forerunner models are generalized. First, these models treat labour productivity z as a constant, while now not only is z growing over time but, with eq. (4.7), it also varies systematically with capacity utilization. The two other aspects are the enrichment of the price and wage Phillips curves by including a second variable in their core terms. Though in both cases this is the wage share, the underlying economic mechanisms are very different. The motive for all three of these innovations was that they may help the model's time series to match certain cyclical features that are observed in reality. These 'stylized facts' will be assessed later when it comes to a numerical calibration of the model. For comparison, the specification of the abovementioned predecessors could be regained by setting $f_z(u) = 1$ and $\beta_{pv} = \beta_{wv} = 0$.

System (4.44)–(4.49) may also be set against the economy of chapter 3. Eqs. (4.44), (4.45) and (4.49) for the motions of ω, m and π correspond directly to eqs. (3.26), (3.25) and (3.27), respectively. Equations (4.44)–(4.49) are obviously more general in that they comprise three more state variables. They come into being since the employment rate in the wage Philips curve is no longer proxied by utilization (this introduces k^s) and since utilization is no longer determined by a temporary IS equilibrium (this leads to the introduction of y^e and n). Apart from that, the wage Philips curve and the investment function have been extended by including, respectively, the wage share v and utilization u as additional arguments.

Let us now turn to the issue of the existence and uniqueness of a stationary point of (4.44)–(4.49), which of course constitutes the steady-state position of the economy. We may recall the remarks on the target markup when it was introduced in the price Phillips curve in chapter 3, section 3. To make our treatment perfectly clear, we posit the corresponding assumption explicitly. Note that here it is not needed for existence or uniqueness, but is employed to ensure that the steady state is economically meaningful.[14]

Assumption 1
The target markup rate μ in the price Phillips curve (4.25),(4.26) is compatible with income distribution in the steady-state position. That is, μ fulfils the equality $pY = (1 + \mu)wL$ in that state.

Evidently, the markup and the equilibrium wage share are linked by the equation $(1 + \mu)v^o = 1$. Proposition 2 makes explicit how μ must be related, in quite an involved way, to the other parameters of the model. As already indicated in chapter 3, section 3, a more extensive version of the model could make μ an endogenous variable responding to some perceived disequilibrium features. The consistency condition $pY = (1 + \mu)\,wL$, with respect to a state of normal utilization, would then have to be brought about by such an adjustment mechanism.

Proposition 2
Suppose Assumption 1 applies. Then system (4.44)–(4.49) has a unique long-run equilibrium. The following variables are determined in explicit terms:

$$u^o = 1, \quad y^o = y^n, \quad e^o = 1, \quad (k^s)^o = 1/y^n,$$

$$(y^d)^o = (y^e)^o = y^n/(1 + g^o \beta_{ny}), \quad n^o = \beta_{ny}y^n/(1 + g^o \beta_{ny}),$$

$$\omega^o = [s_c(y^d)^o - g^o - \gamma - c_p - s_c\delta + (1 - s_c)\,\theta_c]/(s_c - \tau_w)y^n,$$

$$v^o = \omega^o, \quad \mu = (1 - v^o)/v^o.$$

It will be observed that, even in the steady-state position, output systematically exceeds demand. This deviation is due to the fact that desired

---

[14] There would be no problems in the present model if the coefficient β_{pv} in f_p, which corresponds to the term f_{pv} in chapter 3, were zero. The reason is that here the employment rate is included in the wage Phillips curve and so provides an additional equilibrium condition, whereas in chapter 3 it was proxied by utilization to save one state variable.

inventories also grow as the economy expands, so that, in addition to satisfying final demand, a part of production has to be scheduled for this additional purpose.

Proof: The single components of the stationary point of the dynamic system can be successively derived in eleven steps. Each one is unambiguous, so that uniqueness is obvious. For better readability, the superscript 'o' for the state variables is omitted here.

(1) $\dot{k}^s = 0$ gives $g_k = g^o$.

(2) This step is the same as step 1 in proving existence in chapter 3, section 4. We reiterate: $\dot{m} = 0$ together with (4.28) implies $\kappa[\kappa_p f_w + f_p] = g_m - \pi - g^o = \pi^o - \pi$. Substituting this in $\dot{\pi} = 0$ gives $\kappa_\pi(\pi^o - \pi) + (1 - \kappa_\pi)(\pi^o - \pi) = 0$. Hence, expected inflation in the steady state is indeed equal to π^o as defined in (4.28).

(3) Step 3 is the same as the second step in chapter 3, section 4. Two equations determine f_w and f_p: $\kappa_p f_w + f_p = 0$ from $\dot{m} = 0$, and $(1 - \kappa_p)f_w - (1 - \kappa_w)f_p = 0$ from $\dot{\omega} = 0$. The two equations are independent since $1 - \kappa_p \kappa_w \neq 0$ was assumed. Consequently, $f_p = 0, f_w = 0$ is the only solution.

(4) Dividing the consistency condition of Assumption 1 by pY gives $1 = (1 + \mu)v$, so that $f_p = \beta_{pu}(u - 1)$ in (4.26). Hence, $u = 1$ from $f_p = 0$.

(5) $f_w = 0$ gives $e = 1$, by virtue of $v = v^o = 1/(1 + \mu)$ in (4.32).

(6) $y = y^n$ now follows from (4.38), and $k^s = 1/y^n$ from (4.43) and (4.7).

(7) Because of step 1, $\dot{y}^e = 0$ gives $y^d = y^e$. Then, with the aid of (4.37), $\dot{n} = 0$ gives $0 = y - y^d - ng_k = [1 + (g^o + \beta_{nn})\beta_{ny}]y^e - \beta_{nn}n - y^e - ng^o = (g^o + \beta_{nn})\beta_{ny}y^e - (g^o + \beta_{nn})n$. Hence, $n = \beta_{ny}y^e$.

(8) Using the previous result in (4.37) provides us with $y = (1 + \beta_{ny}g^o)y^e$. That is, $y^e = y^d = y^n/(1 + \beta_{ny}g^o)$ and $n = \beta_{ny}y^n/(1 + \beta_{ny}g^o)$.

(9) Substituting $y^e = y^d$ in eq. (4.42) and solving for ω leads to the expression for ω stated in the proposition. $v = \omega$ follows from (4.40) and (4.7)

(10) Step 1 and eq. (4.41) give $g^o = f_I[(1 - v)y^n - \delta - i + \pi, u]$. The equilibrium values for all variables except i are by now determined. Since $f_{Iq} > 0$, the equilibrium rate of interest i can be obtained as the unique (possibly implicit) solution of this equation.

(11) It remains to consider the LM equation in intensive form (see the derivation of (4.39)) and solve it for m, which yields $m = f_m(i)/y^n$.

QED

4.4   The general strategy of the stability proof

A local stability analysis of system (4.44)–(4.49) has to examine its Jacobian matrix $\mathcal{J}$, evaluated at the steady-state values. Omitting the superscript 'o', it may be written down as follows:

$$
\mathcal{J} =
\begin{bmatrix}
\omega(\hat{w}_\omega - \hat{p}_\omega) & 0 & \omega(\hat{w}_y - \hat{p}_y) \\
-m(\hat{p}_\omega + g_{k\omega}) & -mg_{km} & -m(\hat{p}_y + g_{ky}) \\
\tilde{\beta}_y g_{k\omega} + \beta_y \tilde{y}^d_\omega & \tilde{\beta}_y g_{km} & \tilde{\beta}_y g_{ky} + \beta_y \tilde{y}^d_y - \beta_y \\
k^s g_{k\omega} & k^s g_{km} & k^s g_{ky} \\
-\tilde{y}^d_\omega - (1+n)g_{k\omega} & -(1+n)g_{km} & y_y - \tilde{y}^d_y - (1+n)g_{ky} \\
\beta_\pi \kappa_\pi \hat{p}_\omega & 0 & \beta_\pi \kappa_\pi \hat{p}_y
\end{bmatrix}
$$

$$
\begin{bmatrix}
\omega(\hat{w}_k - \hat{p}_k) & \omega(\hat{w}_n - \hat{p}_n) & \omega(\hat{w}_\pi - \hat{p}_\pi) \\
-m\hat{p}_k & -m(\hat{p}_n + g_{kn}) & -m(\hat{p}_\pi + g_{k\pi}) \\
0 & \tilde{\beta}_y g_{kn} + \beta_y \tilde{y}^d_n & \tilde{\beta}_y g_{k\pi} \\
0 & k^s g_{kn} & k^s g_{k\pi} \\
0 & y_n - \tilde{y}^d_n - (1+n)g_{kn} - g^o & -(1+n)g_{k\pi} \\
\beta_\pi \kappa_\pi \hat{p}_k & \beta_\pi \kappa_\pi \hat{p}_n & \beta_\pi(\kappa_\pi \hat{p}_\pi - 1)
\end{bmatrix} \quad (4.50)
$$

Here the term a_x denotes the partial derivative of the functional expression a with respect to the state variable x. The single derivatives themselves will be computed in the course of the analysis, when they are needed. To avoid stacking of indices, a_y and a_k stand for $\partial a / \partial y^e$ and $\partial a / \partial k^s$, respectively. In the first row of $\mathcal{J}$, which contains the partial derivatives of the changes in the real wage $\dot{\omega} = \omega(\hat{w} - \hat{p} - g_z)$, it is notationally convenient to refer to the reduced-form expressions for wage and price inflation, as they have already been derived in eqs. (3.23), (3.24). In the present context they read

$$
\hat{w} = \hat{w}(\omega, y^e, k^s, n, \pi) = g_z + \pi + \kappa[f_w(e, v) + \kappa_w f_p(u, v)] \quad (4.51)
$$

$$
\hat{p} = \hat{p}(\omega, y^e, k^s, n, \pi) = \pi + \kappa[\kappa_p f_w(e, v) + f_p(u, v)] \quad (4.52)
$$

In addition, we have introduced the abbreviations

$$
\tilde{\beta}_y = \beta_y - y^e, \quad \tilde{y}^d = \tilde{y}^d(\omega, y^e, n) = y^d - g_k \quad (4.53)
$$

At first sight it may seem that a stability analysis is an almost hopeless undertaking. In fact, the Jacobian $\mathcal{J}$ does not exhibit an accommodating structure of zeros and the other entries are not too simple, either, so that the Routh–Hurwitz stability conditions for a matrix of that size are intractable. Closer inspection of the partial derivatives showing up in $\mathcal{J}$, however, reveals that certain reaction coefficients predominantly enter just one specific row or column. If these parameters attained zero values, a more convenient structure of zeros would come about. They are not actually allowed to become zero, but it can in the end be shown that the steady state is stable if these reaction intensities remain small enough. Nevertheless, a first important point to note here is that the proof of this statement does not directly check the stability conditions for a matrix of order 6. It is, rather, carried out in a more indirect way, employing some sort of inductive reasoning.

With respect to the simpler model versions discussed, the types of stability conditions indicated have been put forward in Chiarella et al. (2000, p. 66) and, treating a still slightly more simplified version, in Chiarella and Flaschel (2000a, p. 321). The proofs given there were, however, still rather cursory. A sufficiently rigorous mathematical proof was spelled out for the first time by Köper (2000).[15] Thus, our mathematical analysis will heavily draw on this contribution.

The basic idea of the proof is to decompose the stability problem into a number of successive steps, where we proceed from lower-order to higher-order matrices. The method rests on the following lemma.

Lemma 1
Given a natural number n, let $\mathcal{J}^{(n)}(\beta)$ be $n \times n$ matrices, $h(\beta) \in \mathbb{R}^n$ row vectors, and $h_{n+1}(\beta)$ real numbers, all three of them varying continuously with the parameter β over some interval $[0, \varepsilon]$. Put

$$\mathcal{J}^{(n+1)}(\beta) = \begin{bmatrix} \mathcal{J}^{(n)}(\beta) & z \\ h(\beta) & h_{n+1}(\beta) \end{bmatrix} \in \mathbb{R}^{(n+1) \times (n+1)},$$

where z is an arbitrary column vector, $z \in \mathbb{R}^n$. Assume $h(0) = 0$, $\det \mathcal{J}^{(n)}(0) \neq 0$, and let $\lambda_1, \ldots, \lambda_n$ be the eigenvalues of $\mathcal{J}^{(n)}(0)$. Furthermore, for $0 < \beta \leq \varepsilon$, $\det \mathcal{J}^{(n+1)}(\beta) \neq 0$ and of opposite sign to $\det \mathcal{J}^{(n)}(\beta)$. Then, for all positive β sufficiently small, n eigenvalues of $\mathcal{J}^{(n+1)}(\beta)$ are close to $\lambda_1, \ldots, \lambda_n$, while the $n + 1$st eigenvalue is a negative real number. In particular, if the matrix $\mathcal{J}^{(n)}(0)$ is asymptotically stable, so are the matrices $\mathcal{J}^{(n+1)}(\beta)$.

Of course, the statement of the Lemma equally holds true for the transpose of $\mathcal{J}^{(n+1)}(\beta)$ – that is, if the vector $h(\beta)$ appears in the $n + 1$st column. Likewise, if β does not enter matrix $\mathcal{J}^{(n)}$, $h(\beta)$ in the $n + 1$st row or column also may converge to zero as β itself tends to infinity.

---

[15] His model differs in one or two further specification details from the other models, but that does not affect the general working of his method of proof.

We use the Lemma to proceed with the Jacobian matrix (4.50) in the following manner. Suppose in the nth step, so to speak, a submatrix $\mathcal{J}^{(n)}$ made up of the first n rows and columns of $\mathcal{J}$, $n < 6$, has been established to be stable. Suppose, moreover, that there exists a parameter β (not affecting $\mathcal{J}^{(n)}$, to simplify the argument) such that all entries of the $n+1$st row, except perhaps for the diagonal entry $j_{n+1,n+1}$, converge to zero as $\beta \to 0$. If we are able to verify that the determinant of the augmented matrix $\mathcal{J}^{(n+1)} = \mathcal{J}^{(n+1)}(\beta)$ has the opposite sign to det $\mathcal{J}^{(n)}$, the Lemma applies and we conclude that $\mathcal{J}^{(n+1)}(\beta)$ is stable as well, provided β is chosen sufficiently small.

In this way a collection of parameter values are found that render the submatrix consisting of the first $n+1$ rows and columns of $\mathcal{J}$ stable. This result completes the $n+1$st step and we can go over to consider matrix $\mathcal{J}^{(n+2)}$, etc. Beginning with $n = 3$, we therefore strive to obtain a cascade of stable matrices $\mathcal{J}^{(3)}, \mathcal{J}^{(4)}, \mathcal{J}^{(5)}, \mathcal{J}^{(6)}$, until at $n = 6$ with $\mathcal{J}^{(6)} = \mathcal{J}$ stability of the original matrix $\mathcal{J}$ is verified, given that the parameters involved in the single steps are held sufficiently small.

Proof of the Lemma: With respect to $\beta = 0$, it is easily seen that $\mathcal{J}^{(n+1)}(0)$ has eigenvalues $\lambda_1, \ldots, \lambda_n, h_{n+1}(0)$. In fact, if λ is an eigenvalue of $\mathcal{J}^{(n)}$ with right-hand eigenvector $x \in \mathbb{R}^n$, the column vector $(x, 0) \in \mathbb{R}^{n+1}$ satisfies $\mathcal{J}^{(n+1)}(x, 0) = \lambda \cdot (x, 0)$ (omitting reference to the argument β for the moment). This shows that λ is an eigenvalue of $\mathcal{J}^{(n+1)}$, too. It is, furthermore, well known that the product of the eigenvalues of a matrix equals its determinant, which gives us det $\mathcal{J}^{(n)} = \lambda_1 \cdot \ldots \cdot \lambda_n$ and det $\mathcal{J}^{(n+1)} = \lambda_1 \cdot \ldots \cdot \lambda_n \cdot \lambda_{n+1}$. On the other hand, expanding det $\mathcal{J}^{(n+1)}$ by the last row yields det $\mathcal{J}^{(n+1)} = h_{n+1}(0) \cdot$ det $\mathcal{J}^{(n)} \neq 0$. Hence, $\lambda_{n+1} = h_{n+1}(0)$.

Then, consider the situation in the Lemma and denote the $n+1$ eigenvalues of $\mathcal{J}^{(n+1)}(\beta)$ by $\lambda_i(\beta)$. It has just been shown that $\lambda_i(0) = \lambda_i$ for $i = 1, \ldots, n$, while $\lambda_{n+1}(0)$ is a real number. Eigenvalues vary continuously with the entries of the matrix.[16] As det $\mathcal{J}^{(n)}(0) \neq 0$, this implies that sign$[\lambda_1(\beta) \cdot \ldots \cdot \lambda_n(\beta)] = $ sign$[\lambda_1 \cdot \ldots \cdot \lambda_n] = $ sign$[$det $\mathcal{J}^{(n)}(0)]$ also for small positive β. The relationship det $\mathcal{J}^{(n+1)}(\beta) = \lambda_1(\beta) \cdot \ldots \cdot \lambda_n(\beta) \cdot \lambda_{n+1}(\beta)$ entails sign$[$det $\mathcal{J}^{(n+1)}(\beta)] = $ sign$[$det $\mathcal{J}^{(n)}(0)] \cdot$ sign$[\lambda_{n+1}(\beta)] \neq 0$. Since det $\mathcal{J}^{(n+1)}(\beta)$ and det $\mathcal{J}^{(n)}(0)$ have opposite signs, $\lambda_{n+1}(\beta)$ is a negative real number for all β sufficiently small (but, of course, β still positive, should $h_{n+1}(0)$ happen to be zero).

---

[16] This proposition is so intuitive that it is usually taken for granted. Somewhat surprisingly, a compelling proof, which indeed is non-trivial, is not so easy to find in the literature. One reference is Sontag (1990, pp. 328ff.).

The final statement about the stability of det $\mathcal{J}^{(n+1)}(\beta)$ follows from the fact that, by hypothesis, the n eigenvalues of det $\mathcal{J}^{(n)}(0)$ all have strictly negative real parts. So, for small β, the same holds true for the $\lambda_i(\beta)$.

QED

4.5   Proving local stability with a cascade of stable matrices

The central result of chapter 4 is our theorem about the local stability of system (4.44)–(4.49). It is stated in Proposition 3. A side result of its proof is that the dynamics is liable to a Hopf bifurcation, which is subsequently formulated in Proposition 4. The remainder of the section is devoted to the mathematical proofs.

Proposition 3
Suppose that $\tau_w < s_c$, $\beta_y > y^n/(1+g^o\beta_{ny})$, $v^o < 1/(1+g^o\beta_{ny})$, $\kappa_w < 1$, and consider strictly positive reaction parameters $\beta_{nn}, \beta_{we}, \beta_{pu}, \beta_{\pi}, \eta_{m,i}, f_{Iq}$ only. Then the steady state of system (4.44)–(4.49) is locally asymptotically stable if the parameters $\beta_{nn}, \beta_{we}, \beta_{wv}, \beta_{pv}, \beta_{\pi}$ and $\eta_{m,i}$ are sufficiently small.

The first three inequalities in the proposition are sufficient conditions for stability; they are not necessary. Since they are in no way restrictive there is, however, no need to make an attempt at further refinements (which would be clumsier to formulate). Suffice it to note that, referring to annual flows, the desired Inventory–sales ratio β_{ny} has an order of magnitude of around 0.20. Hence, setting the growth rate g^o at 3 per cent, we have $v^o < 1/(1+g^o\beta_{ny}) \approx 1/1.006 \approx 0.994$.

In contrast, the fourth inequality, $\kappa_w < 1$, is somewhat peculiar. Recall that κ_w simply weights the influence of current inflation and the inflation climate on benchmark inflation in the wage Phillips curve. As a result, it does not appear to be a very focal parameter. Nevertheless, ruling out the polar case $\kappa_w = 1$ seems to be necessary for the stability conclusion to hold – at least if, in order to be compatible with previous work, we still want to admit zero values for β_{wv} and β_{pv} in the two Phillips curves.

The stability conditions of Proposition 3 are somewhat different from those put forward in Köper (2000). He invokes the following conditions. (a) $s_w < s_c$ for the savings propensities of workers (s_w) and asset holders (s_c): this corresponds to our inequality $\tau_w < s_c$.[17] (b) The government

---

[17] In the details of the proof's computations, the expressions involving s_w are, in fact, very similar to our expressions involving τ_w.

runs a deficit in the steady state: it can be shown that this is a sufficient (though not necessary) condition for $v^o < 1/(1 + g^o \beta_{ny})$; we verify this at the end of this section. (c) β_y sufficiently large: this corresponds to our explicit lower boundary $y^n/(1 + g^o \beta_{ny})$ for β_y. (d) β_{pu} (in our notation) sufficiently small: Proposition 3 is not dependent on this condition. (e) The condition $\kappa_w < 1$ is not explicitly mentioned in Köper's propositions and lemmata surrounding the final stability statement. However, in the proof of his Lemma 1, when he computes the determinant of a 3×3 submatrix of the Jacobian, he notes that this determinant is negative (as it has to be at this stage of the mathematical analysis) 'because $\kappa_w - 1 < 0$' (Köper, 2000, p. 16). In fact, $\kappa_w - 1 < 0$ is sufficient as well as necessary for a negative determinant.

The other conditions in Köper (2000) are the same as our positivity assumptions on the other parameters (except for β_{wv} and β_{pv}, which are not present in his model version). It can thus be said that the stability conditions stated in Proposition 3 are slightly less demanding. Given, however, that a qualitative statement such as 'sufficiently small' is not very concrete, this advance will not be overrated.

Proposition 4 provides us with information about what happens if the system loses its stability. An immediate consequence of the proof of Proposition 3 is that the transition from the stable to the unstable case occurs by way of a Hopf bifurcation (for the details of this concept see the appendix to chapter 2).

Proposition 4

Assume $\tau_w < s_c$, $v^o < 1/(1 + g^o \beta_{ny})$, *and let the steady state of system (4.44)–(4.49) be locally asymptotically stable. Consider a parameter of the model, which may generally be denoted by* α, *and suppose that under continuous ceteris paribus changes of* α *the steady state becomes unstable at some critical value* α^H. *Then, at* α^H, *the system undergoes a Hopf bifurcation.*

A Hopf bifurcation asserts that for some interval of parameter values close to α^H, above or below this critical mark, closed orbits of the dynamical system exist. They may be attracting or repelling; which case prevails might be numerically computed, but, unfortunately, it is practically impossible to derive economically meaningful conditions from a purely analytical investigation. These limits to a mathematical study are a sufficient reason here not to overstate this phenomenon of strictly periodic trajectories. Instead, we emphasize the more general feature associated with it, namely that the dynamics is basically determined by complex eigenvalues. They allow us to conclude that there is broad scope for the economy to exhibit cyclical behaviour, which, so far, without further and more specific nonlinearity assumptions pertaining to the outer regions of the state space, may be damped or undamped.

Proof of Proposition 3: The starting point of the stability proof is the submatrix $\mathcal{J}^{(3)}$ given by the first three rows and columns of the Jacobian $\mathcal{J}$ in (4.50). To enquire into its eigenvalues, we first compute a few selected partial derivatives of the functions $y = y(y^e, n)$, $g_k = g_k(\omega, m, y^e, n, \pi)$ and $\tilde{y}^d = \tilde{y}^d(\omega, y^e, n)$; see eqs. (4.37), (4.41) and (4.53). Note that, regarding $g_{ky} = \partial g_k / \partial y^e$ and $g_{km} = \partial g_k / \partial m$, use is made of the derivatives of the LM interest rate function in Proposition 1, and that the function $v = v(\omega, y^e, n)$ entering at various places is given by eq. (4.40). Also, the steady-state equality $\omega = v$ is repeatedly utilized. The superscript 'o' for the steady-state values is still omitted.

$$y_y = 1 + (g^o + \beta_{nn})\beta_{ny} > 0 \tag{4.54}$$

$$\tilde{y}_\omega^d = (s_c - \tau_w)y^n > 0 \tag{4.55}$$

$$\tilde{y}_y^d = 1 - s_c + (s_c - \tau_w)(1 - f_z')vy_y \tag{4.56}$$

$$g_{k\omega} = -y^n f_{Iq} < 0 \tag{4.57}$$

$$g_{km} = if_{Iq}/m\eta_{m,i} > 0 \tag{4.58}$$

$$g_{ky} = [f_{Iu}/y^n + f_{Iq}(vf_z' + 1 - v - i/y^n\eta_{m,i})]\, y_y \tag{4.59}$$

Let us call a square matrix stable if all its eigenvalues have negative real parts. Regarding $\mathcal{J}^{(3)}$, we claim that this matrix is stable if $\beta_{we} = \beta_{wv} = \beta_{pv} = \beta_{nn} = 0$ and, given the other parameters in that block of the Jacobian, if $\eta_{m,i}$ is sufficiently small. The demonstration of this property may be summarized as 'Steps 1 – 3'. The subsequent 'Steps 4 – 6' are concerned with the higher-order submatrices $\mathcal{J}^{(n)}$, $n = 4, 5, 6$.

Steps 1 – 3: The proof of the stability of matrix $\mathcal{J}^{(3)}$, under the conditions stated, employs the Routh–Hurwitz conditions. They read

$$a_1 = -\text{trace } \mathcal{J}^{(3)} > 0 \qquad a_2 = \mathcal{J}_1^{(3)} + \mathcal{J}_2^{(3)} + \mathcal{J}_3^{(3)} > 0$$

$$a_3 = -\det \mathcal{J}^{(3)} > 0 \qquad b = a_1 a_2 - a_3 > 0$$

($\mathcal{J}_i^{(3)}$ are the three second-order principal minors of $\mathcal{J}^{(3)}$ – i.e. the determinants of the 2×2 matrices when the i-th row and column of $\mathcal{J}^{(3)}$ are deleted.)

Note that the real wage ω enters $\hat{w}$ and $\hat{p}$ in (4.51) and (4.52) only through the wage share $v = v(\omega, y^e, n)$. Thus, $\beta_{wv} = \beta_{pv} = 0$ entails $\hat{w}_\omega = \hat{p}_\omega = 0$; see eqs. (4.26) and (4.33). In particular, the first diagonal element in $\mathcal{J}^{(3)}$ becomes zero, besides entry $j_{12}^{(3)}$, which is zero anyway. Furthermore, with $\beta_{we} = 0$ wage inflation $\hat{w}_y$ simplifies to $\hat{w}_y = (\kappa \kappa_w \beta_{pu}/y^n) y_y$ and $\hat{p}_y$ to $\hat{p}_y = (\kappa \beta_{pu}/y^n) y_y$. On this basis we compute

$$-\text{trace } \mathcal{J}^{(3)} = (m + \tilde{\beta}_y y_y) i f_{Iq}/m \eta_{m,i}$$
$$- \tilde{\beta}_y [f_{Iu}/y^n + f_{Iq}(1 - v + v f_z')] y_y - \beta_y (\tilde{y}_y^d - 1)$$

$$\mathcal{J}_1^{(3)} = (i f_{Iq}/\eta_{m,i} [(\kappa \tilde{\beta}_y \beta_{pu}/y^n) y_y - \beta_y (\tilde{y}_y^d - 1)] > 0$$

$$\mathcal{J}_2^{(3)} = \omega \kappa (1 - \kappa_w) \beta_{pu} [\tilde{\beta}_y (s_c - \tau_w) - \beta_y f_{Iq}] y_y$$

$$\mathcal{J}_3^{(3)} = 0$$

$$- \det \mathcal{J}^{(3)} = i \omega \kappa (1 - \kappa_w) \beta_{pu} \beta_y (s_c - \tau_w) y_y f_{Iq}/\eta_{m,i} > 0$$

$\mathcal{J}_1^{(3)}$ is positive since, $\tilde{\beta}_y = \beta_y - (y^d)^\circ = \beta_y - y^n/(1 + g^\circ \beta_{ny}) > 0$ by hypothesis, and since, with $\beta_{nn} = 0$ in eq. (4.54) for y_y, we also have $-(\tilde{y}_y^d - 1) = s_c - (s_c - \tau_w)(1 - f_z')v y_y = s_c - (s_c - \tau_w)(1 - f_z')v(1 + g^\circ \beta_{ny}) > 0$. To see the latter inequality, note that the expression increases in τ_w and f_z' and, at $\tau_w = f_z' = 0$, is equal to $s_c[1 - v(1 + g^\circ \beta_{ny})]$, which is positive by the assumption on the upper boundary on $v = v^\circ$.

Evaluating the Routh–Hurwitz terms, we first observe that sufficiently small values of $\eta_{m,i}$ ensure that $a_1 > 0$. $\mathcal{J}_2^{(3)}$ may have any sign, but being independent of $\eta_{m,i}$ it is eventually dominated by $\mathcal{J}_1^{(3)} > 0$ if $\eta_{m,i}$ is small enough. Hence, $a_2 > 0$ as well. The term a_3 is positive anyway. Lastly, as for the composite expression $a_1 a_2 - a_3$, we make use of the fact that all three terms a_1, a_2, a_3 are linearly increasing in $1/\eta_{m,i}$. It follows that $a_1 a_2$ will exceed a_3 if $\eta_{m,i}$ is made sufficiently small once again. This completes the proof of the stability of the submatrix $\mathcal{J}^{(3)}$.

Step 4: In this step the assumption $\beta_{we} = 0$ is dropped. Regarding submatrix $\mathcal{J}^{(4)}$ of the original Jacobian (4.50), we claim that this matrix is stable if β_{we} is positive but sufficiently small. The rest of the previous supposition, $\beta_{wv} = \beta_{pv} = \beta_{nn} = 0$ and $\eta_{m,i}$ small enough, is maintained.

Computing the partial derivatives with respect to k^s: $\hat{w}_k = \kappa f_{wk} = \kappa \partial e/\partial k^s = \kappa y^n \beta_{we}$ and $\hat{p}_k = \kappa \kappa_w f_{wk} = \kappa \kappa_w y^n \beta_{we}$ (see eqs. (4.51) and (4.52) and (4.43)), it is seen that the entries in the 4th column of $\mathcal{J}^{(4)}$ tend to zero as $\beta_{we} \to 0$. Since $\mathcal{J}^{(3)}$ is stable for $\beta_{we} = 0$ and thus $\det \mathcal{J}^{(3)} < 0$ in this case, all we have to do according to the Lemma in section 4.4 is to show that the determinant of $\mathcal{J}^{(4)}$ is positive for $\beta_{we} > 0$.

To compute det $\mathcal{J}^{(4)}$, factorize ω, $-m$ and k^s in the 1st, 2nd and 4th rows, respectively. Subtracting the 4th row from the 2nd row and $\tilde{\beta}_y \times$ the 4th row from the 3rd row, we get

$$\det \mathcal{J}^{(4)} = -\omega m k^s \begin{vmatrix} 0 & 0 & \hat{w}_y - \hat{p}_y & \hat{w}_k - \hat{p}_k \\ 0 & 0 & \hat{p}_y & \hat{p}_k \\ \beta_y \tilde{y}_\omega^d & 0 & \beta_y(\tilde{y}_y^d - 1) & 0 \\ g_{k\omega} & g_{km} & g_{ky} & 0 \end{vmatrix}$$

Add the 2nd row to the 1st row, expand this determinant by the 2nd column, factorize β_y in the 3rd row, use (4.51), (4.52) for the partial derivatives of $\hat{w}$ and $\hat{p}$, and factorize κ in the 1st and the 2nd rows. This leads to

$$\det \mathcal{J}^{(4)} = -\omega m k^s g_{km} \beta_y \kappa^2 \begin{vmatrix} 0 & \kappa_\omega f_{py} + f_{wy} & f_{wk} \\ 0 & f_{py} + \kappa_p f_{wy} & \kappa_p f_{wk} \\ \tilde{y}_\omega^d & \tilde{y}_y^d - 1 & 0 \end{vmatrix}$$

Here it remains to subtract $\kappa_p \times$ the 1st row from the 2nd row, so that entry (2,3) vanishes, too. In this way the determinant results as

$$\det \mathcal{J}^{(4)} = -\omega m k^s g_{km} \beta_y \kappa^2 \tilde{y}_\omega^d (-1)(1 - \kappa_p \kappa_w) f_{py} f_{wk}$$

$g_{km} > 0$ and $\tilde{y}_\omega^d > 0$ by (4.58) and (4.55). $f_{wk} = y^n \beta_{we}$ has already been remarked above. With $\beta_{pv} = 0$, we have $f_{py} = \beta_{pu} \partial u / \partial y^e = \beta_{pu} y_y / y^n$, which by (4.54) is likewise positive. Hence det $\mathcal{J}^{(4)} > 0$ for $\beta_{we} > 0$, as required.

Step 5: Maintaining, in particular, $\beta_{wv} = \beta_{pv} = 0$, in this step the assumption $\beta_{nn} = 0$ is dropped. Our claim is that matrix $\mathcal{J}^{(5)}$ is stable if β_{nn} is chosen sufficiently small. We verify in a moment that the first four entries in the 5th column of $\mathcal{J}^{(5)}$ tend to zero as $\beta_{nn} \to 0$. Thus, according to the Lemma, we have only to show that det $\mathcal{J}^{(5)}$ has the opposite sign of det $\mathcal{J}^{(4)}$, at least for β_{nn} small enough.

As for the derivatives in the 5th column, we first note that

$$\begin{aligned} y_n &= \partial y / \partial n = -\beta_{nn} \\ v_n &= \partial v / \partial n = -v f_z' y_n / y^n \\ e_n &= \partial e / \partial n = (1 - f_z') y_n / y^n \end{aligned} \tag{4.60}$$

(the latter two equations use $\omega^o = v^o$ and $(k^s)^o = 1/y^n$). On this basis one gets

$$f_{pn} = -\beta_{nn}\beta_{pu}/y^n$$
$$f_{wn} = -\beta_{nn}\beta_{we}(1 - f_z')/y^n$$
$$g_{kn} = -\beta_{nn}[f_{Iu}/y^n + f_{Iq}(1 - v + vf_z' - i/y^n\eta_{m,i})]$$
$$\tilde{y}_n^d = -\beta_{nn}(s_c - \tau_w)(1 - f_z')v$$

(4.61)

and matrix $\mathcal{J}^{(5)}$ can be written as

$$\mathcal{J}^{(5)}(\beta_{nn}) = \begin{bmatrix} \mathcal{J}^{(4)}(\beta_{nn}) & h(\beta_{nn}) \\ z & h_5(\beta_{nn}) \end{bmatrix}$$

where $h(\beta_{nn}) = 0$ and $h_5(\beta_{nn}) = -g^o$ for $\beta_{nn} = 0$. Hence $\det \mathcal{J}^{(5)}(\beta_{nn}) = -g^o \cdot \det \mathcal{J}^{(4)}(\beta_{nn})$ in this case, and approximately so for β_{nn} sufficiently small, which completes the proof of the stability of $\mathcal{J}^{(5)}$.

Step 6: In the last step the parameter β_π comes into play, which enters only the 6th row of the Jacobian. We exploit the fact that all the entries in the 6th row tend to zero as $\beta_\pi \to 0$. It follows from the Lemma that, if matrix $\mathcal{J} = \mathcal{J}(\beta_\pi) = \mathcal{J}^{(6)}(\beta_\pi)$ has a determinant opposite in sign to $\det \mathcal{J}^{(5)}$ (i.e. if $\det \mathcal{J}(\beta_\pi) > 0$ for $\beta_\pi > 0$), then $\mathcal{J}(\beta_\pi)$ is stable for β_π sufficiently small (but positive). Of course, the other assumptions previously employed are taken over. The final observation to make is that, so far, $\beta_{wv} = \beta_{pv} = 0$ has been underlying. However, the stability of $\mathcal{J}$ is preserved if these two parameters are increased slightly (though not too much).

So, the remainder of the proof is a demonstration of $\det \mathcal{J} > 0$. We add that this property holds for all positive values of the parameters β_{nn}, β_{we}, β_{wv}, β_{pu}, β_{pv}, β_π, $\eta_{m,i}$, f_{Iq}; they do not need to be small.

To begin with, take $\det \mathcal{J}$ in (4.50) and factorize ω, $-m$, k^s and β_π in the corresponding rows. Subtract the 4th row from the 2nd row, subtract $\tilde{\beta}_y \times$ the 4th row from the 3rd row, and add $(1 + n) \times$ the 4th row to the 5th row. Then add the (new) 2nd row to the 1st row. At this stage suppose for the time being that $\kappa_\pi > 0$. Subtracting $(1/\kappa_\pi) \times$ the 6th row from the 2nd row and adding $\beta_y \times$ the 5th row to the 3rd row, we obtain

$$\det \mathcal{J} = -\omega m k^s \beta_\pi \begin{vmatrix} \hat{w}_\omega & 0 & \hat{w}_y & \hat{w}_k & \hat{w}_n & \hat{w}_\pi \\ 0 & 0 & 0 & 0 & 0 & 1/\kappa_\pi \\ 0 & 0 & \beta_y(y_y - 1) & 0 & \beta_y(y_n - g^o) & 0 \\ g_{k\omega} & g_{km} & g_{ky} & 0 & g_{kn} & g_{k\pi} \\ -\tilde{y}_\omega^d & 0 & y_y - \tilde{y}_y^d & 0 & y_n - \tilde{y}_n^d - g^o & 0 \\ \kappa_\pi \hat{p}_\omega & 0 & \kappa_\pi \hat{p}_y & \kappa_\pi \hat{p}_k & \kappa_\pi \hat{p}_n & \kappa_\pi \hat{p}_\pi - 1 \end{vmatrix}$$

Expand the determinant by the 2nd column, and expand the determinant of the resulting 5×5 matrix by the 2nd row (here, observe the minus sign in the chessboard pattern for the only non-zero entry $(2,5)$, $1/\kappa_\pi$). Factorizing κ_π in the 4th row of the determinant of the resulting 4×4 matrix yields

$$\det \mathcal{J} = \omega m k^s \beta_\pi g_{km}(\kappa_\pi/\kappa_\pi) \begin{vmatrix} \hat{w}_\omega & \hat{w}_y & \hat{w}_k & \hat{w}_n \\ 0 & \beta_y(y_y-1) & 0 & \beta_y(y_n-g^o) \\ -\tilde{y}_\omega^d & y_y-\tilde{y}_y^d & 0 & y_n-\tilde{y}_n^d-g^o \\ \hat{p}_\omega & \hat{p}_y & \hat{p}_k & \hat{p}_n \end{vmatrix}$$

Since κ_π cancels out in this equation, we can undo the assumption $\kappa_\pi > 0$ and conclude that the equation, with (κ_π/κ_π) deleted, holds true for $\kappa_\pi = 0$ as well.[18]

We proceed by factorizing β_y in the 2nd row, using eqs. (4.51), (4.52) for $\hat{w}$ and $\hat{p}$ and then factorizing in the 1st and 2nd row the coefficient κ that newly arises here:

$$\det \mathcal{J} = \omega m k^s \beta_\pi g_{km} \beta_y \kappa^2 \begin{vmatrix} \kappa_w f_{p\omega}+f_{w\omega} & \kappa_w f_{py}+f_{wy} & f_{wk} & \kappa_w f_{pn}+f_{wn} \\ 0 & y_y-1 & 0 & y_n-g^o \\ -\tilde{y}_\omega^d & y_y-\tilde{y}_y^d & 0 & y_n-\tilde{y}_n^d-g^o \\ f_{p\omega}+\kappa_p f_{w\omega} & f_{py}+\kappa_p f_{wy} & \kappa_p f_{wk} & f_{pn}+\kappa_p f_{wn} \end{vmatrix}$$

Next, subtract $\kappa_p \times$ the 1st row from the 4th row. In this way the derivatives f_{wx} ($x = \omega, y, k, n$) in the 4th row disappear and entry $(4,3)$ becomes zero. The determinant of the resulting matrix is thus easily expanded by the 3rd column. Taking account of $1 - \kappa_p \kappa_w = 1/\kappa$, the coefficient of the terms f_{px} that is factorized in the 4th row, we get

$$\det \mathcal{J} = \omega m k^s \beta_\pi g_{km} \beta_y (\kappa^2/\kappa) f_{wk} \cdot D \tag{4.62}$$

$$\text{where} \quad D := \begin{vmatrix} 0 & y_y-1 & y_n-g^o \\ -\tilde{y}_\omega^d & y_y-\tilde{y}_y^d & y_n-\tilde{y}_n^d-g^o \\ f_{p\omega} & f_{py} & f_{pn} \end{vmatrix}$$

The derivatives in D that have not yet been computed are

$$f_{p\omega} = \beta_{pv}/v \qquad (= \beta_{pv}(1+\mu))$$

$$f_{py} = \beta_{puv} y_y/y^n, \quad \beta_{puv} := \beta_{pu} - f_z' \beta_{pv}$$

$$f_{pn} = \beta_{puv} y_n$$

---

[18] To spell out the argument in full detail, consider a sequence of positive $\kappa_\pi^{(n)}$ converging to zero as $n \to \infty$. Since the determinant is a continuous function of the entries of a matrix and since the equation holds for all $\kappa_\pi^{(n)} > 0$, it also holds in the limit, $\kappa_\pi = 0$.

Expanding D by the first column, taking account of (4.55), (4.56) and (4.61) for the derivatives of $\tilde{y}^d$, and abbreviating $\tilde{s} := (s_c - \tau_w)(1 - f'_z)v$, we have

$$D = (s_c - \tau_w)\beta_{puv}(g^o y_y - y_n) + f_{p\omega}[(-y_n)(s_c - \tilde{s}) + g^o(s_c - \tilde{s}y_y)]$$

Straightforward calculations yield

$$D = \beta_{pu}(s_c - \tau_w)(g^o y_y - y_n)$$
$$+\beta_{pv}\{(-y_n/v)[s_c - (s_c - \tau_w)v] + (g^o/v)[s_c - (s_c - \tau_w)vy_y]\}$$

With $-y_n = \beta_{nn}$ in (4.60), the terms on the right-hand side can be rearranged such that D reads

$$D = [\beta_{pu}(s_c - \tau_w) + \beta_{pv}\tau_w](g^o y_y + \beta_{nn})$$
$$+ (\beta_{pv}s_c/v)(\beta_{nn} + g^o)(1 - v - vg^o\beta_{ny})$$

We can thus turn back to eq. (4.62). Regarding the factors in front of D, substitute (4.58) for g_{km}, $y^n\beta_{we}$ for f_{wk} (see the second paragraph in step 4) and $1/y^n$ for k^s (the steady-state relationship). In this way we arrive at the following explicit expression for the determinant of $\mathcal{J}$:

$$\det \mathcal{J} = \omega i \kappa \beta_y \beta_\pi \beta_{we}(1/\eta_{m,i})f_{Iq} \cdot \{[\beta_{pu}(s_c - \tau_w) + \beta_{pv}\tau_w](g^o y_y + \beta_{nn})$$
$$+(\beta_{pv}s_c/v)(\beta_{nn} + g^o)(1 - v - vg^o\beta_{ny})\} \qquad (4.63)$$

It remains to note that $y_y = 1 + (g^o + \beta_{nn})\beta_{ny} > 0$ from (4.54) and $1 - v - vg^o\beta_{ny} > 0$ by virtue of the assumption on the upper boundary on v^o in the proposition. Hence, under the proposition's positivity assumptions on the reaction coefficients, $\det \mathcal{J}$ is unambiguously positive.

QED

Proof of Proposition 4: Step 6 in the proof of Proposition 3 has established that the Jacobian $\mathcal{J}$ set up in (4.50) is non-singular for all admissible values of the model's parameters. This implies that, if the eigenvalue $\lambda = \lambda(\alpha)$ with largest real part crosses the imaginary axis in the complex plane, at $\alpha = \alpha^H$, it cannot be zero. At $\alpha = \alpha^H$ we therefore have a pair of purely imaginary eigenvalues, $\lambda(\alpha^H) = \pm ib$ in obvious notation. This is the key condition for a Hopf bifurcation to occur.

The usual version of the Hopf theorem (see, for example, Seydel, 1988) demands that (a) $\lambda(\alpha^H)$ is a simple pair of eigenvalues, and (b) $d[\text{Re}\lambda(\alpha^H)]/d\alpha \neq 0$. Of course, these two conditions are generically satisfied. They can, furthermore, be largely avoided (in particular, the velocity condition) if one uses the version of *Theorem A* presented in Alexander and Yorke (1978, pp. 263–266). This is also the reason why we did not make reference to the technical assumptions (*a*) and (*b*) in the formulation of the proposition.

QED

Proof of remark (b) following Proposition 3:

In discussing the stability conditions of Proposition 3 it was mentioned that the inequality $v < 1/(1 + g^o \beta_{ny})$ follows from a positive deficit in the government budget constraint. To see this, note first that the constraint (4.23) in intensive form reads $(\dot{M} + \dot{B})/pK = \gamma + c_p - \theta_c - \tau_w vy$. By eq. (4.42) we have in the steady state $y^e = y^d = (1 - s_c)y^e + s_c vy - \tau_w vy + g_k + \gamma + c_p - s_c \delta - (1 - s_c)\theta_c$, or $s_c(y^e - vy) = [\gamma + c_p - \theta_c - \tau_w vy] + g_k + s_c(\delta + \theta_c)$. The right-hand side of this equation is positive since, by virtue of $(\dot{M} + \dot{B})/pK > 0$, the term in square brackets is positive. On the other hand, using the steady-state relationship $y^e = y/(1 + g^o \beta_{ny})$, the left-hand side of the equation can be written as $s_c[1 - v(1 + g^o \beta_{ny})]y^e$. The proof is completed by the observation that a positive square bracket is equivalent to $v < 1/(1 + g^o \beta_{ny})$.

QED

4.6   Conclusion

In this chapter a six-dimensional macrodynamic model has been advanced that, in the tradition of, in particular, Keynes, Metzler and Goodwin, has been set up as a compromise between richer feedback mechanisms and parsimony in the modelling design. Under the hypothesis of a neutral monetary policy, the central theorem has put forward conditions that ensure the stability of the long-run equilibrium position: roughly stated, local stability prevails if certain reaction parameters are sufficiently low. Though this proposition may conform quite well to economic intuition, it is not obvious that such a result can be analytically proven for a 6×6 Jacobian matrix. The theorem can therefore be considered a remarkable achievement, and the outcome may improve confidence in the general architecture of the model.

On the other hand, this is probably as far as one can go mathematically. More definite statements about the meaning of 'sufficiently small', or which parameters may in this respect be more important than others, are beyond the reach of mathematical arguments. Also, some of the parameters involved in the stability conditions will, typically, not be very small. Will other parameters 'compensate' for these – presumably destabilizing – effects? Again, these are questions that elude a purely mathematical approach. So, it may be concluded that our theorem gives a first insight, or perhaps confirmation, of which parameter variations are conducive to stability, but the picture thus emerging is still rather uncertain and can be regarded only as preliminary. For a more revealing study of the system's properties, the qualitative mathematical analysis has to be complemented by quantitative investigations, dealing with concrete numerical parameters. This is a task that we will tackle in the next chapters of the book.

4.7   Appendix: The discrete-time approximation

For a mathematical stability analysis in higher dimensions, it is often useful to have the model set up in continuous time. By contrast, when it comes to simulating the model on a computer it has to be discretized in some form. This can either be done in a more technical way, most prominently by applying a procedure of the Runge–Kutta variety, or in a way that seeks to preserve the economic content in the discretized equations. For macroeconomic feedback systems, we consider the second alternative more appropriate.

In the present case, this approach does not refer to the condensed final differential equations (4.44)–(4.49) but goes back to the formulation of the model in extensive form in section 2. The philosophy is to regard the adjustments there specified as taking place in a sequential economy with adjustment periods, or market periods, $[t, t+h)$, $[t+h, t+2h)$, $[t+2h, t+3h)$, etc., where the length h of the period may be any positive number. The translation into discrete time must, however, be compatible with the continuous-time system, in the sense that for $h \to 0$ the limit in the single equations is well defined (mostly after dividing them by h) and recovers the original differential or structural equations. Given that this condition is satisfied, it can reasonably be expected that, provided h is fixed at a sufficiently small value, the trajectories generated by the corresponding computer simulations will be close to the solutions of the differential equations; in particular, the qualitative features, such as stability, instability or periodic orbits, should be the same.[19]

Our underlying time unit will be a year. Accordingly, all flow variables – independently of the number h and also in continuous time – are expressed as annual magnitudes. To give a straightforward

---

[19] For an investigation of the precise relationships between differential equations systems and their one-step discretization, with respect to Lyapunov stable equilibrium points or sets, see Kloeden and Lorenz (1986). Though our discretization may not precisely be covered by their study, the essential arguments should carry over.

example of how this has to be interpreted in the sequential economy, consider $g_{k,t}$, the capital growth rate per year that prevails over the period $[t, t+h)$. This means that, while $g_{k,t}K_t$ would be the (hypothetical) volume of investment over the full year (if nothing changed in the meantime), investment over the short period of h years amounts to the fraction $hg_{k,t}K_t$. Correspondingly, with K_t being the capital stock at the beginning of $[t, t+h)$, the evolution of K is governed by the equation

$$K_{t+h} = K_t + hg_{k,t}K_t = [1 + hg_{k,t}]K_t$$

(since no implementation lag is assumed). Obviously, as it should be, the continuous-time counterpart obtained with an infinitesimally short adjustment period, $h \to 0$, is the familiar differential equation $\dot{K} = g_k K$. Other adjustment equations are treated similarly.

More care has to be taken, however, when composed variables are involved in growth rate equations. An example is the reduced-form of nominal wage inflation in eq. (3.24), which may be written as $\hat{w} = g_w^{ref} + \kappa(f_w + \kappa_w f_p)$. The extra notation g_w^{ref} emphasizes the role of the reference growth of wages. For $f_w = f_p = 0$ it would ensure that the productivity-deflated wage rate w/z^o grows at the rate given by the inflation climate (i.e. $\pi = \widehat{(w/z^o)} = \hat{w} - \hat{z}^o = g_w^{ref} - g_z$), so that $g_w^{ref} = \pi + g_z$, as it is directly stated in (3.24). In the sequential economy, the same relationship reads $1 + h\pi_t = (1 + h\hat{w}_t)/(1 + hg_z)$. Solving it for $\hat{w}_t = g_{w,t}^{ref}$ yields a slightly different expression for the reference growth rate. In the discrete-time setting, wage inflation is therefore determined by the equation

$$\hat{w}_t = \pi_t + g_z + h(\pi_t g_z) + \kappa(f_w + \kappa_w f_p)$$

By the same token, the equilibrium growth rate of real output, which in continuous time is given by $g^o = g_z + g_\ell$ (the sum of the growth rates of trend productivity and the labour force), changes to $g^o = g_z + g_\ell + h(g_z g_\ell)$. The continuous-time growth rate of the money supply, $g_m = \pi^o + g^o$, now becomes $g_m = \pi^o + g^o + h(\pi^o g^o)$. The two equations derive from the requirements that, in the long-run equilibrium, (1) Y and $z^o L = (Y/L) \cdot L$ and (2) M and pY must grow in step. Whether all such relationships are properly taken into account can be checked by letting the economy evolve from a steady-state position and seeing if it is accurately reproduced over time.

After sketching the general principles for the formulation of the discrete-time adjustments, we make things more concrete and present in table 4.1 the core of the computer program. It is written in Delphi (or what for this part of the program amounts to the same: in Pascal). The

Table 4.1: *The core of the Pascal source code*

```
1:   Procedure DetNewState( Var tt,  m, om, y_e, ks, n, pi,
2:                              LevYe, LevN, LevW, LevP,
3:                              LevM, LevLs, LevZo, LevK : Real );
4:   Var
5:      y, u, e, v, i, r, q, gK, y_d,           { needed only within procedure }
6:      gwRef, wHat, LevY, LevYd, tmp : Real;
7:
8:   Begin
9:      {  Dynamic variables (m, om, y^e, k^s, n, pi) are predetermined    }
10:     {  at the beginning of period [t,t+h), as well as the level        }
11:     {  variables LevW, LevP, etc. The following magnitudes are         }
12:     {  then determined within that period.                             }
13:     {  -------------------------------------------------------------   }
14:
15:     y     := y_From_eq37( y_e, n );                    { from eq.(37)  }
16:     u     := y / y_n;                            { eqs. (6),(38) }
17:     e     := EmploymentRate( u, ks );                  { from eq.(43)  }
18:     v     := WageShare( om, u );                  { eqs. (11),(40) }
19:     i     := i_LM( m, y );                   { linear version from (6.11) }
20:     r     := ProfitRate( u,om );                       { from eq.(10)  }
21:     q     := r - i + pi;
22:     gK    := gK_FuncNL( q, u );         { nonlinear version (6.30/31) }
23:     y_d   := yd_From_eq42( y_e, y, v, gK );              { from eq.(42)  }
24:
25:     gwRef := pi + g_z + StepSize*(pi*g_z);
26:                  { in discrete time, wages must grow at this rate     }
27:                  { in order to grow in step with (p*z^o), if price    }
28:                  { level p is (on average) expected to grow at rate pi. }
29:
30:     wHat  := gwRef + kappa * ( f_w(e,v) + kap_w*f_p(u,v) );
31:     pHat  := pi    + kappa * ( kap_p*f_w(e,v) + f_p(u,v) );
32:                      { f_p(u,v), f_w(e,v) from eqs. (26),(33);    }
33:                      { wHat, pHat are the reduced-form eqs.       }
34:                      { (3.24),(3.23), or (5.17),(5.18)            }
35:     LevY  := y   * LevK;
36:     LevYd := y_d * LevK;
37:
38:                  { Levels of dynamic variables at beginning of next period, }
39:                  { [t+h,t+2h); where StepSize = h                           }
40:                  { ------------------------------------------------------   }
41:
42:     LevYe := LevYe + StepSize * (g_o*LevYe + beta_y*(LevYd-LevYe));
43:     LevN  := LevN  + StepSize * (LevY - LevYd);
44:                                          { from eqs. (20) and (15) }
45:
46:     LevW  := ( 1 + StepSize * wHat ) * LevW;         { monthly       }
47:     LevP  := ( 1 + StepSize * pHat ) * LevP;         { changes from  }
48:     LevM  := ( 1 + StepSize * g_m )  * LevM;         { annualized    }
49:     LevLs := ( 1 + StepSize * g_ell) * LevLs;        { growth rates  }
50:     LevZo := ( 1 + StepSize * g_z )  * LevZo;
51:     LevK  := ( 1 + StepSize * gK )   * LevK;
52:
53:                      { State variables (in intensive form), at time t+h  }
54:                      { ------------------------------------------------  }
55:
56:     tmp   := kap_pi * pHat + (1-kap_pi) * pi_o - pi;
57:     pi    := pi + StepSize * beta_pi * tmp;
58:
59:     m     := LevM / (LevP * LevK);
60:     om    := LevW / (LevP * LevZo);
61:     y_e   := LevYe / LevK;
```

Table 4.1: (cont.)

```
62:     n      := LevN / LevK;
63:     ks     := LevK / (LevZo * LevLs);
64:
65:     tt     := tt + StepSize;                          { time next round }
66:  End;
```

code snippet in table 4.1 is the procedure DetNewState, which, given the dynamic variables at the beginning of period $[t, t+h)$, determines their values at the beginning of the next short period $[t+h, t+2h)$ (the procedure determines the new state of the economy).

The program's main variables are the time index t, the dynamic variables in intensive form $(m, \omega, y^e, k^s, n, \pi)$ and the level variables $(Y^e, N, w, p, M, L^s, z^o, K)$. They enter the procedure as inputs (lines 1 – 3), are transformed within the procedure, and at the end are returned to the main program.[20] The variables declared in lines 5 and 6 are local to the procedure; other parts of the program do not need to take notice of them. The rest of the program is concerned with processing the variables of lines 1 – 3: storing them, writing them to tables on the screen or in a text file, plotting them, and perhaps also computing several time series statistics from them. (Apart from that, the program must allow the user to reset the most important parameter values.)

Together with the comments in curly brackets, the names of the variables and the calculations from line 15 onwards should be self-explanatory. The procedure has recourse to a number of functions, such as y_From_eq37 in line 15, EmploymentRate in line 17, WageShare in line 18, etc., that are set up in the program beforehand. y_From_eq37, for example, is a short code segment that takes the current values of y^e and n and calculates the expression given by the right-hand side of eq. (4.37). gK_FuncNL in line 22 corresponds to the investment function $f_I = f_I(q, u)$ in eq. (4.9), where $q := r - (i - \pi)$ (see line 21). While (4.9) is only the general formulation, we will later, in chapter 6, introduce a specific nonlinear version of the investment function, in eqs. (6.30), (6.31) as indicated. The reference growth rate g_w^{ref} for nominal wage rises and the rate of wage inflation $\hat{w}$ itself (lines 25 and 30) have just, been discussed (the variable StepSize represents, of course, the length h of the adjustment period). To be exact, wHat $= \hat{w}_t$ is

---

[20] It would not be necessary to list these global variables as extra inputs to the procedure. This is done only for greater clarity, to enable us to see at a glance the variables that the procedure is acting on.

here the forward growth rate, $\hat{w}_t = (w_{t+h} - w_t)/hw_t$, which also becomes clear from line 46 of the code snippet.

Lines 35, 36 just define the levels of Y and Y^d induced by y, y^d, and the level of the capital stock, K. On the whole, lines 15 – 36 provide all the magnitudes that are necessary to determine the levels Y^e, N, etc. that describe the state of the economy in the next round, at the beginning of period $[t + h, t + 2h)$. The (elementary) formulae are stated in lines 42 – 51. Subsequently, in lines 56 – 63, the intensive forms of the dynamic variables are computed. Except for the inflation climate π in lines 56, 57, they are directly obtained from the level variables and the definitional relationships such as $m = M/pK$ (line 59), etc. It is thus clear that the simulations do not invoke (4.44)–(4.49) in any way; only the extensive formulation of the model is used.

The final assignment in line 65 is the updating of the time index. In all simulations of the KMG model reported in this book, the step size h is set at $h = 1/12$, so that we are always dealing with a monthly economy in which, we repeat, all flows are measured at annual rates. It turns out that this value of h is sufficiently small. The trajectories are smooth and, in particular, locally stable or unstable according to what the eigenvalues of the Jacobian of the continuous-time system predict (unless the parameter values are very close to a Hopf bifurcation).

5 Calibration of three wage-price modules

5.1 Introduction

Chapter 4 has put forward our Keynes–Metzler–Goodwin model, the framework with which we will be concerned in the rest of the book. Assuming a neutral monetary policy, it has also presented a stability theorem, saying essentially that local asymptotic stability is ensured by sufficiently low values of a number of reaction parameters. This kind of proposition is, nevertheless, still very general. At the end of the chapter it was therefore concluded that, in order to ascertain the scope of the stability statements, a quantitative analysis would be necessary. In the first instance this means that a base scenario of numerical parameter values has to be established; subsequently we can examine how local stability is affected when these parameters are varied. In addition, of course, we will have to study the global dynamics generated by the base scenario.

Hence, the major task before us, which will occupy the next two chapters, is to find numerical values for the model's parameters that can serve as a base scenario. At the beginning a few words should be said about the general method, since numerical parameter setting can be approached in two different ways. Probably the more obvious one is econometric estimation. Here one takes the single equations or certain subsystems of the model and runs more or less sophisticated regressions. In the present context, however, this approach is beset with two difficulties. In order to obtain regression statistics that fulfil the usual goodness-of-fit criteria, these estimates will have to involve several lags of the independent variables, which is a feature that (for reasons of parsimony and tractability) is totally absent in our model. It might be argued that such a regression could include several lags and we could take the sum of the coefficients as the parameter value that is associated with the single (contemporaneous) variable we are looking for. Unfortunately, the choice of the number of lags will not be obvious, and we also know little about the reliability of this rescue attempt.

196

The second problem is that, in regressions with two or more variables on the right-hand side, these time series often show a high degree of multicollinearity. Accordingly, while the standard error of the whole estimation can be satisfactory, the single coefficients themselves will be rather uncertain: with strong comovements of the independent variables it becomes difficult to separate out the precise effect that each of these variables has on the dependent variable.

Even if these two problems could be handled in some way, there is still another problem of overriding importance, namely whether the single model components thus estimated fit together and give a coherent whole. That is, when these components are 'patched together', will the resulting dynamics of the total system still be sufficiently realistic? As we cannot take this for granted, we may be ready to 'correct' some of the numerical coefficients found before, though not every econometrician might accept this as a legitimate procedure. Even if it is accepted, the questions then arising are which coefficients should be chosen for this purpose, why just these coefficients and not others, and by how much should they be corrected. All these problems might be manageable in the end, but can the whole procedure be sufficiently systematic and comprehensible?

Calling attention to possible difficulties need not mean discarding the method altogether. On the basis of US data and using single equation or subsystem estimations, the econometric approach was tried for a slightly different version of the present model in Flaschel et al. (2002). While this study contains fruitful aspects regarding the treatment of unobservable variables and also provides a number of valuable partial results, on the negative side it should not be concealed that in some respects it is still opaque, especially with regard to the dynamics of the integrated system. Moreover, not all reaction coefficients appear credible.[1] Apart from these criticisms, there is only a very cursory discussion of the implications for the various features of the system's cyclical behaviour.

The latter shortcoming brings us to a second approach to numerical parameter setting. This alternative to econometric estimation is called calibration. It is, in fact, the method that we choose to employ in the following. To appreciate what it is being done here, it is important to note that its methodological point of view is markedly different from the econometric mode of thinking.

In short, the aim of calibrating a model economy is to conduct (computer) experiments in which its properties are derived and compared

---

[1] One example is the stock adjustment speed, β_{nn} in our notation, which is implausibly low. Besides, this is a well-known fundamental problem, which, however, the study leaves to one side.

to those of an actual economy. In this respect calibration procedures can be understood as a more elaborate version of the standard back-of-the-envelope calculations that theorists perform to judge the validity of a model. The crucial point, which econometricians may acknowledge, is the underlying notion that *every model is known to be false*. A model is not a null hypothesis to be tested; it is, rather, an improper or simplified approximation of the true data-generating process of the actual data. A model is theoretically motivated, and, ideally, with respect to the purpose it is designed for, satisfies the famous KISS principle coined by Zellner (1992): 'Keep it sophisticatedly simple.'[2] Hence, a calibrator is not interested in verifying whether the model is true; the answer is already known from the outset. Instead, he or she is concerned with identifying those aspects of the data that a false model can replicate.[3]

Our investigation of how well the model-generated trajectories match the data follows the usual practice. We select a set of stylized facts of the business cycle, simulate the model on the computer and assess the corresponding cyclical properties of the resulting time series. Since a (false) model is chosen on the basis of the questions it allows to be asked, and not on its being realistic or being able to mimic the data best, we share the point of view that rough reproduction of simple statistics for comovements and variability is all that is needed to evaluate the implications of a model. As opposed to econometrics, the discussion is more or less informal here. This should not be considered a lack of precision; it is, rather, a way to discuss where parameters are easy or difficult to find, and to elucidate the kind of compromises that we have to make in the multi-purpose endeavour with which we are concerned. In all this, the theoretical model remains central, and is not just a point of departure for an econometrically suitable regression approach.[4] In sum, our philosophy of setting the numerical parameters is similar to that of the real business cycle school, though the methods will be quite different in detail.

Fortunately, it turns out that the model gives rise to a hierarchical structure in the calibration process. Some variables that are exogenous in one model building block are endogenous within another block at a higher level. Thus, the parameters need not all be chosen simultaneously,

---

[2] Occasionally, KISS is translated as 'Keep it simple, stupid', which is not quite appropriate, since there are models that are simple as well as stupid (Zellner, 2002, pp. 1f.).

[3] See also the introductory discussion in Canova and Ortega (2000, pp. 400–3).

[4] It is also interesting to refer to Summers (1991, p. 145), who has expressed his scepticism about decisive formal econometric tests of hypotheses: "the empirical facts of which we are most confident and which provide the most secure basis for theory are those that require the least sophisticated statistical analysis to perceive."

but fall into several subsets that can be successively determined. This handy feature makes the search for suitable parameters and the kind of compromises that we finally accept more intelligible.

The evaluation of the numerical parameters takes place in three main stages. The major part of the work is done at the first stage. Here we suppose exogenous motions of two variables that drive the rest of the model. These are capacity utilization and, synchronously with it, the capital growth rate. Since random shocks are neglected in our framework, the exogenous motions may well be of a regular and strictly periodic nature, most conveniently specified as sine waves. This perhaps somewhat unusual approach can be viewed as a heuristic device. It is more carefully defended later in this chapter, and, in any event, has to be judged in the end by the results.

Letting utilization and the capital growth rate oscillate in the sine wave manner, we study the thus induced motions of all the other variables of interest, which will likewise be cyclical. We compute the statistics measuring their variability and comovements and assess them with respect to the benchmark statistics that have already been set up as desirable cyclical features, by observing the time series of the corresponding variables in the real world. As has just been emphasized, all this is organized in a stepwise fashion that is determined by the hierarchy levels. At the end of stage one, a whole numerical scenario of the model's parameters will have been obtained, except for the investment function, which will be treated at the third stage.

Having established this set of parameter values, it is checked at stage two whether the previous results are seriously affected if the exogenous sine waves are replaced with the more noisy time paths of the empirical counterpart of the utilization variable and the (still fictitious) synchronous capital growth rate that is directly linked (by assumption) to utilization.

The decisive test to which the numerical parameters are put is, however, stage three. This is also the place where the model is completed, which requires the endogenization of capacity utilization and, now, the specification of the investment function. The parameters in this function will be set in such a way that the steady state becomes unstable.[5] On the other hand, a nonlinearity is introduced that in the outer regions of the state space should prevent the economy from totally diverging. Being locally unstable but globally bounded, the system will produce persistent, and undamped, cyclical behaviour. If this is achieved, we can finally study the properties of the resulting trajectorie. On the whole,

---

[5] To anticipate, this concerns the two partial derivatives f_{Iu} and f_{Iq} in the investment function (4.9).

the calibration will be judged to be successful if the model happens to generate time series with similar cyclical features as found before.

All this certainly means a lot of work. In the present chapter we concentrate on stages one and two, and on the first three hierarchy levels of the calibration procedure. Thus, we are basically concerned with the wage-price relationships. At the same time we wish to widen the perspective a little here; that is, in addition to the model components already laid out in chapter 4, two other variants of wage-price modelling are proposed and investigated. In greater detail, all three of these wage-price modules have the following three building blocks in common: our straightforward specification of procyclical labour productivity, the adjustment equation for the inflation climate, and the (extended) nominal wage Phillips curve.

On this basis three different ways to determine price inflation are considered. First, of course, the price Phillips curve of the previous two chapters has to be included. For ease of reference the acronym PPC may be used for this device. The second module postulates that the *changes* in the rate of inflation (and not inflation itself) are positively linked to utilization. This feedback, which is also called an accelerationist Phillips curve, directly brings about a countercyclical price level (CCP). The third approach takes up a Kaleckian idea of a variable markup (VMK) on unit labour costs, the adjustments of which exhibit a certain countercyclical element. All three cases will be calibrated, so that we can subsequently compare the cyclical features of the wage-price dynamics to which these numerical parameters give rise.

The remainder of the chapter treats the following issues. Before we can begin with the calibration, we first have to elucidate the stylized facts of the business cycle and make explicit the cyclical statistics that the global dynamics of the model should seek to match or come close to. This is done in section 5.2. The equations surrounding the wage Phillips curve, which are underlying all three model variants, are recapitulated in subsection 5.3.1. The three alternative inflation modules are subsequently formulated in subsections 5.3.2 to 5.3.4. These subsections also work out the different hierarchy levels at which the parameters are determined in the calibration procedure. Section 5.4 introduces the exogenous sine waves of utilization and the capital growth rate, and the motions of the employment rate that are thus generated.

Sections 5.5 to 5.7 provide an extensive discussion of the cyclical properties of the three wage-price modules and our strategy for arriving at a base scenario of parameter values for each module. Employing these scenarios, section 5.8 gives an evaluation of the three model variants. In particular, as an upshot it presents a synopsis of the coefficients in the three modules on which we eventually settle down, and a table of the main cyclical statistics that characterize the time series of the real wage, the wage share and the price level. Finally, in section 5.9, the stylized sine wave of capacity utilization is dropped and the numerical simulations are rerun with empirical values of that variable. Section 5.10 concludes. An appendix gives some details about the construction of the empirical data we use.

5.2   Stylized facts of wage-price dynamics

In the theoretical model, the business cycle is measured by capacity utilization. Assuming a given level y^n of the output–capital ratio at which normal utilization prevails, utilization u and the output–capital ratio y are linked by a fixed proportionality factor, $u = Y/Y^n = y/y^n$ (with $Y^n := y^n K$). Hence, the obvious empirical counterpart of our notion of u is given by the fluctuations of the output–capital ratio of the firm sector (i.e. nonfinancial corporate business).

While, in the model's production technology, y^n is a constant magnitude, in reality one observes some variations in y at lower than the business cycle frequencies. We therefore detrend the empirical series of y and, treating the 'normal' output–capital ratio as variable over time, set $y^n = y^n_t$ equal to the 'trend' value of y at time t. In this way the model's deviations from normal utilization, $u - 1$, can be identified with the empirical percentage trend deviations $(y_t - y^n_t)/y^n_t$.

To correct for the low frequency of y, let us first consider a detrending method that in modern time series analysis is regarded as overly naive, namely detrending by a segmented linear trend. The upper two panels in figure 5.1[6] display the output–capital ratio over the period 1960 to 1992. The dotted line in the top panel is the 'trend' line, with three breaks in the trough quarters 1970:4, 1975:1 and 1982:4. Despite its naivety, this appears to be an appropriate kind of detrending for the purpose at hand.

Although it does not go uncriticized, either, the detrending method probably most widely used in applied empirical work is the Hodrick–Prescott filter. For quarterly data, its smoothing parameter λ is almost exclusively set at $\lambda = 1600$. The outcome for the output–capital ratio is shown as the dotted line in the second panel of figure 5.1.[7] In comparison

---

[6] The dotted lines in the upper two panels are an segmented linear trend and an HP 1600 trend line of the output–capital ratio, respectively.

[7] The trend is computed over a longer period than shown in the diagram, so there are no end-of-period effects, where the HP trend line tends to approach the actual time series unduly. The total period underlying the HP computation is 1952:1 to 1998:2.

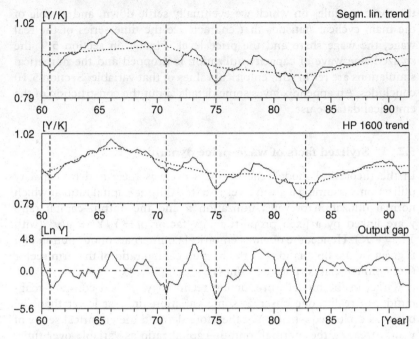

Figure 5.1: Measures of the business cycle

to the first panel, one may feel that this trend line nestles too closely against the actual time path of y. In fact, this phenomenon is not too surprising, since the HP 1600 filter amounts to defining the business cycle by those fluctuations in the time series that have a periodicity of less than eight years (see King and Rebelo, 1999, p. 934), whereas figure 5.1 demonstrates that the US economy experienced two trough-to-trough cycles exceeding this period.[8]

Judging from the visual impression, the segmented linear trend might therefore be preferred. On the other hand, there are other empirical time series that we will have to detrend, especially series that are systematically growing over time. Since its use is so widespread for these variables, we should then indeed work with the HP filter. It seems expedient, furthermore, to use a uniform detrending procedure. For these reasons we employ the HP filter for the output–capital ratio too.

---

[8] According to the National Bureau of Economic Research (NBER) reference data, one is from February 1961 to November 1970, the other from November 1982 to March 1991.

The percentage trend deviations thus constructed are shown in the top panel of figure 5.2.[9]

Besides, this choice is less dramatic than a comparison of the top two panels in figure 5.1 might suggest, because the most important cyclical feature for us – the timing of the peaks and troughs of y – remains practically unaffected by it. The crucial difference between the two detrended series is the amplitude, where detrending by HP 1600 evidently yields a lower standard deviation than the segmented linear trend.[10] Even if we think that the series with the higher variability is the more appropriate one, we can accept the HP 1600 method here because, as has just been said, the other empirical time series will be detrended by the same method and their variability will always be expressed in terms of the variability of the utilization series.

In passing, a word may also be said on the usual measure of the business cycle, which is the output gap. This concept does not invoke the capital stock but is specified directly as the percentage deviation of the output series from its trend (or the difference in logs, for that matter). However, since the capital stock grows significantly more smoothly than output, the general cyclical pattern of the output gap and our detrended output–capital ratio is very similar. Visual evidence of this is provided in the bottom panel of figure 5.1, where the output gap may be contrasted with the output–capital series in the middle panel of figure 5.1 or its trend deviations in the top panel of figure 5.2. Our empirical proxy for capacity utilization is very compatible with the more familiar concept of the output gap as the indicator of the business cycle.

Another remark should be added regarding the general acceptance of the Hodrick–Prescott filter. Beginning with Nelson and Plosser (1982), it has been argued that the trends in macroeconomic time series are stochastic, so that much of the variation that used to be considered as business cycles would actually be permanent shifts in trend. While this stochastic view of the world soon became predominant, the pendulum has, in the meantime, swung back from that consensus. In a succinct summary of recent research on this issue, it can be concluded that 'at the very least there is considerable uncertainty regarding the nature of the trend in many macroeconomic time series, and that, in particular, assuming a fairly stable trend growth path for real output – perhaps

---

[9] Trend deviations in per cent: $100 \cdot (\ln x - \ln x^o)$ for $x = y$ (in top panel), $z, L, w/p, p$; and $100 \cdot (x - x^o)$ for the wage share $x = v$, where superscript 'o' denotes the HP 1600 trend. The thin line is the utilization variable from the top panel. The vertical dashed lines indicate the NBER trough quarters.

[10] Over the period 1961:1 to 1991:4, the standard deviations of the two series $100 \cdot (y_t - y_t^n)/y_t^n$ are 2.05 per cent and 2.92 per cent, respectively; the correlation coefficient between the series is 0.88.

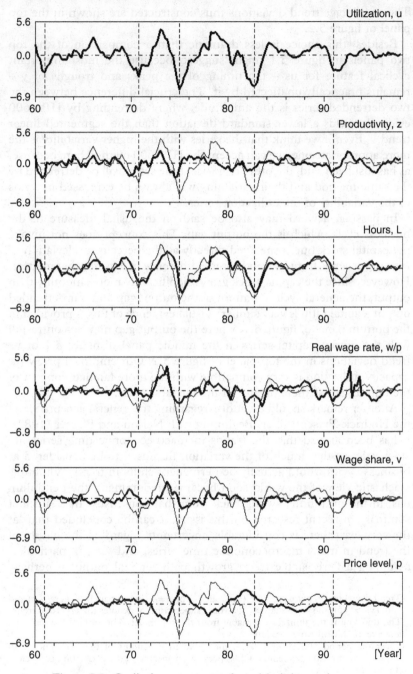

Figure 5.2: Cyclical components of empirical time series

even a linear deterministic trend – may not be a bad approximation' (Diebold and Rudebusch, 2001, p. 8).[11] Against this background, we feel legitimated to work with the notion of a deterministic trend, where Hodrick–Prescott provides a sufficient degree of flexibility and, for convenience, $\lambda = 1600$ is taken over as the standard smoothing parameter for quarterly data.[12]

After these preparations we can turn to the empirical variables characterizing the wage-price relationships. Some features have already been discussed in chapter 3, but in order to be self-contained we admit a little repetition. The main variables to be investigated are undoubtedly the real wage rate w/p per hour, the wage share $v = wL/pY$ and the rate of price inflation. As for the latter, it will be more useful to refer to the behaviour of the price level p. Two other variables that should be studied in addition are the rate of employment, since it enters the wage Phillips curve, and labour productivity $z = Y/L$, since it enters the determination of the wage share along with the employment rate. To exclude demographic factors and long-term changes in normal working hours, the rate of employment is here conveniently proxied by the percentage deviations of total working hours L from their trend L^o, where we directly interpret the trend line as labour supply – i.e. as the supply of normal working hours. Thus, $e_t - 1 = (L_t - L_t^o)/L_t^o \approx (\ln L_t - \ln L_t^o)$.

The fluctuations of the variables around their HP 1600 trend values are displayed in the last five panels in figure 5.2; the precise specification of these trend deviations is made explicit in the caption. The general visual impression is complemented by the cyclical statistics in table 5.1, which reports the standard deviation of the series in relation to the standard deviation of utilization u, and also to the cross-correlations of the variables with u. (Recall that the empirical values of u are given by $u_t - 1 = (y_t - y_t^n)/y_t^n$, with y_t^n being the HP 1600 trend of the output–capital ratio.) In the last row, table 5.1 additionally includes the growth rate of fixed capital g_k, the cyclical properties of which will be considered

---

[11] This short paper is a slightly revised version of the introductory chapter of their comprehensive book on business cycles (Diebold and Rudebusch, 1999).

[12] In recent times the band-pass (BP) filter developed by Baxter and King (1995) has gained in popularity. This procedure rests on spectral analysis and so is mathematically more precise about what constitutes a cyclical component. The BP(6, 32) filter preserves fluctuations with periodicities between six quarters and eight years while eliminating all other fluctuations, including the low-frequency fluctuations that are associated with trend growth and the high frequencies associated with, for instance, measurement error. More exactly, with finite data sets the BP(6, 32) filter approximates such an ideal filter. As it turns out, for the time series with relatively low noise (little high-frequency variation) the outcome of the HP 1600 and the BP(6, 32) filter is almost the same. For real national US output, this is exemplified in King and Rebelo (1999, p. 933, fig. 1).

Table 5.1: *Descriptive statistics for cyclical components of quarterly series,*
1961:1–1991:4

		Cross-correlations between u at time t and x at time						
Series x	σ_x/σ_u	$t-3$	$t-2$	$t-1$	t	$t+1$	$t+2$	$t+3$
u	–	0.48	0.70	0.89	1.00	0.89	0.70	0.48
z	0.44	0.56	0.58	0.53	0.46	0.17	−0.06	−0.27
L	0.83	0.03	0.30	0.57	0.79	0.88	0.86	0.77
w/p	0.51	0.31	0.48	0.57	0.61	0.56	0.48	0.34
v	0.38	−0.21	−0.05	0.09	0.21	0.42	0.53	0.57
p	0.51	−0.59	−0.70	−0.73	−0.70	−0.62	−0.49	−0.32
g_k	0.29	−0.06	0.20	0.48	0.72	0.84	0.86	0.80

NB: The cyclical components are measured by the percentage deviations from the HP
1600 trend, as they are specified in the note to figure 5.1; g_k is treated like v. σ denotes
the standard deviation.

further below. The sample period underlying the computations of the
table covers the four major trough-to-trough cycles from 1961 to 1991.

Let us begin by considering labour productivity $z = Y/L$, which has long
been counted a procyclical variable. May it suffice to mention that Okun
(1980, pp. 821f.) lists it among his stylized facts of the business cycle.
Procyclical variations of z can to some degree also be recognized in the
second panel in figure 5.1, perhaps with a slight lead before u. The cross-
correlation coefficients of z with u indicate a stronger relationship than
one might possibly infer from a visual inspection of the time series alone,
especially if a lead for z of between one and three quarters is reckoned in.[13]

The employment rate e_t, as specified above and depicted in the third
panel of figure 5.2, is a markedly procyclical variable. The juxtaposition with utilization is suggestive of a short lag for z. This is also fully
confirmed in the third row of table 5.1, where the lag relationship is
strongest for one or two quarters.

The controversy surrounding the comovements of the real wage rate
is usually summarized by saying that, if anything, it moves (weakly)

[13] Unfortunately, the statistics cannot be compared with the most recent comprehensive
compilation of stylized business cycle facts by Stock and Watson (1999), since they
employ real GDP as their output variable. Over the sample period 1953 to 1996 they
report a cross-correlation coefficient as large as $\rho(z_{t-k}, GDP_t) = 0.72$ for a lead of $k = 2$.
Curiously enough, we could not reproduce a similar number with the trend deviations
of the GDP series taken from Ray Fair's database (see the appendix), which is due to
the fact that (especially) over the subperiod 1975 to 1982 this series is quite different
from the Citibase GDP series used by Stock and Watson (statistically, it shows less
first-order autocorrelation).

procyclically, rather than countercyclically. Results about the cyclical properties of the real wage appear to be quite sensitive to precisely how it is constructed, depending on whether the numerator (w) includes various compensation items and on the index in the denominator (p). Since our modelling context is a one-good economy, we adopt the deflator of total output as our price level, so that w/p denotes the product real wage. On the other hand, we follow Ray Fair's procedure (see the appendix) and include a uniform 50 per cent wage premium as a rough measure for overtime payment.

On the basis of this specification, figure 5.1 (fourth panel) shows that the real wage rate is fairly closely connected to the motions of capacity utilization, while quantitative evidence for its (strict) procyclicality is given in table 5.1. Although this finding is in some contrast to what is reported in the literature, it should play an important role in the calibration later on.[14]

The distribution of income between workers and capital owners is described more directly by the wage share v. Its motions are, however, only rarely mentioned in the discussion of typical features of a business cycle. This might in part be due to the special difficulties that one encounters for this variable in separating the cyclical from some intermediate quasi-trend behaviour. The HP 1600 trend deviations depicted in the fifth panel in figure 5.1 might therefore be treated with some caution.

Accepting them as they are, we see another explanation for the infrequent reference to the wage share: it does not exhibit a distinctive and unique cyclical pattern. During the 1960s v looks rather countercyclical, whereas from 1970 to 1990 it appears to be more or less procyclical. In fact, over the 1960s the highest (in modulus) correlation coefficient is negative, as large as $\rho(u_t, v_{t-1}) = -0.71$. Over the period 1970 to 1991 the maximal coefficient is positive; at a lag of three quarters it amounts to $\rho(u_t, v_{t+3}) = 0.67$. For this reason, the cross-correlations given in table 5.1 over the full period 1961 to 1991 have to be interpreted cautiously. They do not summarize a general law of a systematic relationship between the business cycle and income distribution; instead, they reflect,

---

[14] For example, King and Rebelo (1999, p. 938) obtain a contemporaneous correlation of compensation per hour with output of $\rho = 0.12$, and the coefficient for the correlation with GDP that is presented by Stock and Watson (1999, table 2) is similarly low. As regards the present data, with no overtime payment in the wage rate the contemporaneous correlation is reduced to 0.34 (and no lagged coefficients are higher), even though the correlation between the trend deviations of the two real wage series themselves is as high as 0.93. On the other hand, considering the issue more carefully, Barsky et al. (1994) argue that real wage indices may fail to capture changes in the composition of employment over the cycle. They conclude that real wages are procyclical if the composition is held constant.

in attenuated form, the relationship over a limited span of time. As for the amplitude of the wage share, note that figure 5.2 and table 5.1 refer to the pure deviations $v_t - v_t^o$; unlike for the other variables, these differences are *not* divided by the trend value (since v is itself a percentage variable).

As indicated in the introductory section, we will discuss three modules for representing price inflation. Time series of inflation rates are, however, relatively noisy and so cannot be easily related to the motions of utilization with its high persistence.[15] It is therefore more convenient to study the variations of the price level directly. While prices were formerly regarded as procyclical, there seems now to be general consensus that they move in a countercyclical manner; see, for example, Cooley and Ohanian (1991), Backus and Kehoe (1992) and Fiorito and Kollintzas (1994). With respect to the price index for total output, this phenomenon is plainly visible in the bottom panel of figure 5.1. According to table 5.1, the inverse relationship between p and u is strongest at a lead of the price level by one quarter. Given the tightness of the relationship, countercyclical prices are a challenge for any theory of inflation within a business cycle context.[16]

The statistics in table 5.1 are the basis on which we now put forward the quantitative cyclical features that we wish our model, or the three wage-price modules, to fulfil – at least, insofar as they exhibit smooth and regular oscillations in a deterministic environment. These desirable features are listed in table 5.2. We leave some play in the numbers since a small model cannot reasonably be expected to match all the empirical statistics accurately. Moreover, when we state a zero lag for productivity z, then this is already due to our simplifying modelling assumption on the production technology, where z is directly linked to utilization u.

The motive for fixing the standard deviation of z somewhat lower than the coefficient 0.44 given in table 5.1 is the apparently lower amplitude of z in the recent past. In fact, over the sample period 1975 to 1991, the ratio σ_z/σ_u falls to 0.33 (and the relationship with utilization becomes weaker). The desired standard deviation of the real wage is slightly reduced for the same reason; its (relative) empirical standard deviation

---

[15] Quarterly inflation rates have first-order serial correlation in the region of 0.35, which may be compared to the AR(1) coefficients for the trend deviations of u and p, which are 0.89 and 0.92, respectively.

[16] A discussion of the issue of countercyclical prices should make clear what in (structural and descriptive) economic theory the trend line is supposed to reflect: (*a*) the evolution of prices on a deterministic, long-run equilibrium path around which the actual economy is continuously fluctuating, or (*b*) the time path of an expected price level. From the latter point of view, Smant (1998) argues that procedures other than HP detrending should be adopted, and, doing this, he concludes that the so specified (unexpected) price movements are clearly procyclical (p. 159). By contrast, our theoretical background is notion (*a*).

Table 5.2: *Desirable features of macrodynamic oscillations*

Variable x	σ_x/σ_u	Lag x
$(z - z^o)/z^o$	0.40	0.00
$e - 1$	0.80–0.85	0.00–0.75
$(\omega - \omega^o)/\omega^o$	0.45–0.50	−0.50–0.50
$v - v^o$	0.30–0.40	–
$-(p - p^o)/p^o$	0.47–0.53	−0.75–0.25

NB: σ_x means the standard deviation of the respective trend, or steady-state, deviations of variable x. ω is the productivity-deflated real wage rate, $\omega = (w/p)/z^o$. The lags (with respect to u) are measured in years.

over 1975 to 1991 is 0.46. Similarly, we should not be too definitive about the variation of the wage share, because the precise empirical construction of this variable and the outcome of the specific detrending mechanism may not be overly robust against alternative procedures. By the same token, it would not be appropriate to commit oneself to a particular phase shift of v. Both points are all the more true when the lead in labour productivity is neglected (as has already been seen in the previous chapters, v is equal to the ratio of ω over z/z^o). Given that $\sigma_v/\sigma_u = 0.31$ over the subperiod 1975 to 1991, we content ourselves with proposing the range 0.30–0.40 for that ratio and leave the issue of desirable lags of v open. Lastly, the variability of the price level is more stable over time than that of z, v and w/p; $\sigma_p/\sigma_u = 0.50$ over the subperiod 1975 to 1991. Hence, we centre the desired relative standard deviation of p around 0.50.

5.3 The three wage-price modules

5.3.1 *The common nominal wage dynamics*

We begin with the model components that are common to all three variants of the determination of price inflation. Regarding the procyclicality of labour productivity, we take over eq. (4.7) and linearize the function $f_z = f_z(u)$. Trend productivity z^o again grows at a constant rate g_z. However, in order to check whether the calibration results could be improved in this way, we now also allow for the variable growth rate of actual productivity. That is, although it would be analytically awkward since the time derivative of u would show up in the formulation of the model, we do not necessarily require $\hat{z}$ to cancel out.

The subsequent equations reiterate the definition of the state variables ω and k^s, the productivity-deflated real wage rate and the capital–labour ratio in efficiency units. They write down the wage share v and the employment rate e expressed in terms of these state variables, besides u, of course (in the latter relationship, recall that y^n is the normal output–capital ratio). Postulating a constant growth rate g_ℓ of (hourly) labour supply L^s as well as exogenous oscillations of the capital growth rate g_k (which are specified below), the motions of k^s can be described by a differential equation. In sum, we have the following block of equations, which – except for $\hat{z}$ in (5.3) – have already been put forward in the previous chapter as, in the corresponding order, (4.7), (4.8), (4.12), (4.11), (4.36), (4.43), (4.31) and (4.47):

$$z/z^o = f_z(u) := 1 + \beta_{zu}(u - 1) \tag{5.1}$$

$$\hat{z}^o = g_z \tag{5.2}$$

$$\hat{z} = g_z + \beta_{zu}\dot{u}/f_z(u) \tag{5.3}$$

$$\omega = w/pz^o \tag{5.4}$$

$$v = \omega/f_z(u) \tag{5.5}$$

$$k^s = K/z^o L^s \tag{5.6}$$

$$e = y^n u k^s/f_z(u) \tag{5.7}$$

$$\hat{L}^s = g_\ell \tag{5.8}$$

$$\dot{k}^s = k^s(g_k - g_z - g_\ell) \tag{5.9}$$

The wage Phillips curve will be slightly more general than (4.32), (4.33). As has just been indicated, the productivity growth term entering here may also include the actual growth rate $\hat{z}$; a priori, reference is made to a weighted average of $\hat{z}^o$ and $\hat{z}$, with weighting parameter κ_{wz} between 0 and 1. For a better distinction, the other weighting parameter for price inflation $\hat{p}$ and the inflation climate π is now designated κ_{wp} (rather than simply κ_w, as before). To ease the exposition later on, the core function f_w makes explicit reference to the reaction coefficients, too. Thus, the present wage Phillips curve reads

$$\hat{w} = [\kappa_{wz}\hat{z} + (1 - \kappa_{wz})\hat{z}^o] + [\kappa_{wp}\hat{p} + (1 - \kappa_{wp})\pi]$$
$$+ f_w(e, v; \beta_{we}, \beta_{wv}) \tag{5.10}$$

$$f_w = f_w(e, v; \beta_{we}, \beta_{wv}) := \beta_{we}(e - 1) - \beta_{wv}(v - v^o)/v^o \tag{5.11}$$

The law governing the variations of the inflation climate π entering (5.10) will also be the same across the three inflation modules. We again make it a mix of the two simple mechanisms of adaptive expectations, gradually adjusting towards current inflation $\hat{p}$, and regressive expectations, which tend to return to the equilibrium rate of inflation π^o. While the two rules are weighted by the parameter κ_π, the general speed of adjustment is β_π:

$$\dot{\pi} = \beta_\pi [\kappa_\pi (\hat{p} - \pi) + (1 - \kappa_\pi)(\pi^o - \pi)] \tag{5.12}$$

It has been mentioned in the introduction that, in the first stage of the calibration, utilization and the capital growth rate are supposed to undergo exogenous oscillations. Once the time paths $u = u(t)$ and $g_k = g_k(t)$ are thus given, the time path of the employment rate is determined as well, via (5.9) and (5.7) – independently of the rest of the economy. The only parameter involved here is β_{zu} from the hypothesis on labour productivity in eq. (5.1). This constitutes the first and highest level in the hierarchy of the single calibration steps:

Level 1: Employment rate e (parameter β_{zu})

$$\dot{k}^s = k^s(g_k - g_z - g_\ell) \tag{5.9}$$

$$e = y^n u k^s / [1 + \beta_{zu}(u - 1)] \tag{5.7}$$

The evolution of the real wage and the wage share is determined at lower hierarchy levels. These, however, will differ from each other, depending on the particular inflation module applied.

5.3.2   Inflation module CCP: countercyclical prices

In the first of the three submodels determining inflation and prices, we postulate countercyclical movements of the price level in an almost direct way. In macrodynamic models there is, of course, no scope for detrending procedures. A countercyclical price level (CCP) can, however, be brought about by referring to the rate of inflation. To this end, it is not $\hat{p}$ that is to be – positively – linked to utilization, but its time rate of change, $d\hat{p}/dt$ (the second derivative of the level, so to speak). This kind of relationship is therefore often called an accelerationist Phillips curve.

Since no other variable interferes, we thus have a second hierarchy level for determining inflation, or the price level, for that matter. Conveniently, only one reaction coefficient $\beta_p > 0$ enters:

CCP Level 2: Price level p (parameter β_p)

$$d\hat{p}/dt = \beta_p(u - 1) \qquad (5.13)$$

Incidentally, because (5.13) has the time path of utilization as its only input, it might also be considered a level-1 equation. We have assigned it the second level to be more in line with the discussion of the other two inflation modules, which make reference to the productivity function $f_z = f_z(u)$ and its parameter β_{zu}.

Equation (5.13) implies that the variations of $\hat{p}(\cdot)$ lag $u(\cdot)$ a quarter of a cycle, at least if the oscillations of utilization are sufficiently regular. From this pattern one easily infers that the (detrended) series of the induced price level does indeed move countercyclically. Owing to the simplicity of the adjustment equation there are no leads or lags., so (5.13) cannot account for the finer details of table 5.1 in the cross-correlations between u and p. On the other hand, we will have no difficulty in setting the coefficient β_p such that the resulting standard deviation of the percentage deviations of $p(\cdot)$ from an HP 1600 trend line matches the desired ratio from table 5.2.[17]

Theoretically, (5.13) may be regarded as a behavioural equation. Being aware that they live in an inflationary environment, firms see some room for adjusting their current rate of price inflation upward if utilization is above normal, while they feel some pressure to revise it downward if they have excess capacity. If this point of view does not appear convincing, the equation might be regarded as a reduced-form expression for the price adjustments of firms. The inflation module could then be given the status of a semi-structural model building block.

Making $\hat{p}$ itself a dynamic state variable, an equation such as (5.13) may well also be tractable in the analysis of a small macromodel. Franke and Asada (1994) is an example of a four-dimensional model with

---

[17] A discrete-time formulation of (5.13), by the way, has been empirically tested with success by Gittings (1989). At the textbook level, this relationship is presented as a good description of the facts in, for example, Blanchard (2000, especially p. 155, fig. 8.5) and Taylor (2001, especially p. 569, fig. 24.9).

Keynesian and Goodwinian elements and a pronounced expectations dynamics regarding a general business climate, where this specification of inflation adjustments proves very helpful. A wider field where the basic idea of (5.13) is utilized are the many low-dimensional macromodels that study the effects of monetary policy rules, although in discrete-time formulations the relationship is often augmented by several lags on the inflation rate and also a stochastic term. Such a pure or hybrid accelerationist Phillips curve is then combined with a dynamic (and stochastic) IS equation and an interest rate reaction function. We will study economies of this type in chapter 8.

Given the the inflation dynamics at hierarchy level 2, together, of course, with the oscillations of capacity utilization, one can next compute the time path of the inflation climate by solving the differential equation (5.12). Involved here are the two parameters β_π and κ_π:

CCP Level 3: Inflation climate π (parameters β_π, κ_π)

$$\dot{\pi} = \beta_\pi[\kappa_\pi(\hat{p} - \pi) + (1 - \kappa_\pi)(\pi^o - \pi)] \qquad (5.12)$$

Subsequently the time path of the real wage rate is obtained by differentiating (5.4) with respect to time, $\hat{\omega} = \hat{w} - \hat{p} - \hat{z}^o$, and using (5.10) together with (5.2), (5.3) and (5.5). Note that the motions of the employment rate $e(\cdot)$, which enter the wage Phillips curve, have already been determined at hierarchy level 1. All this gives us the fourth level:

CCP Level 4: Real wage ω, wage share v (parameters κ_{wz}, κ_{wp}, β_{we}, β_{wv})

$$\dot{\omega} = \omega[\kappa_{wz}(\hat{z} - g_z) - (1 - \kappa_{wp})(\hat{p} - \pi) + f_w(e, v; \beta_{we}, \beta_{wv})] \quad (5.14)$$

$$\hat{z} = g_z + \beta_{zu}\dot{u}/f_z(u) \qquad (5.3)$$

$$v = \omega/f_z(u) \qquad (5.5)$$

As hinted at before, small macromodels may hardly wish to include eq. (5.3) because the time derivative of u would cause too many complications. However, the calibration will still have to prove if $\kappa_{wz} = 0$ is possible without impairing the cyclical features of the trajectories. So, generally, we will also investigate the implications of $\kappa_{wz} > 0$ in (5.14).

5.3.3   Inflation module PPC: the extended price Phillips curve

Despite its – by construction – pleasant property of a countercyclical price level, eq. (5.13) may not be reckoned fully satisfactory from a theoretical point of view, since it somewhat lacks in structure. An obvious and immediate alternative with its long tradition in economic theory is a Phillips curve governing the rate of price inflation. And, of course, we have to test the extended price Phillips curve that has already been employed in the previous two chapters. Also, the concept of a price Phillips curve (PPC) may be particularly appealing in connection with the wage Phillips curve (5.10) above, because it puts nominal wage and price adjustments on an equal footing. Only a slight modification now has to be taken into account: the productivity growth term by which $\hat{w}$ in the specification of benchmark inflation is corrected should be the same as in the wage Phillips curve. We thus have

$$\hat{p} = \kappa_p\{\hat{w} - [\kappa_{wz}\hat{z} + (1 - \kappa_{wz})\hat{z}^o]\} + (1 - \kappa_p)\pi + f_p(u, v; \beta_{pu}, \beta_{pv}) \quad (5.15)$$

$$f_p = f_p(u, v; \beta_{pu}, \beta_{pv}) := \beta_{pu}(u - 1) + \beta_{pv}[(1 + \mu^o)v - 1] \quad (5.16)$$

It may be recalled that the first two terms in (5.15) represent what firms currently regard as benchmark inflation, a weighted average (with κ_p) of (productivity-corrected) current wage inflation and the inflation climate. $\beta_{pu}(u - 1)$ is the ordinary demand-pull term, and $\beta_{pv}[(1 + \mu^o)v - 1]$ with the influence of the wage share is interpreted as a cost-push term proper. μ^o in (5.16) is a fixed target markup rate that should be compatible with the equilibrium wage share v^o in (5.11), $(1 + \mu^o)v^o = 1$.

Since, in (5.10) and (5.16), $\hat{w}$ and $\hat{p}$ are mutually dependent on each other, the two equations have to be solved for $\hat{w}$ and $\hat{p}$. In the resulting reduced-form expressions for wage and price inflation it must again be presupposed that the weights κ_p and κ_{wp} are not both unity. We reiterate that wage inflation depends on the core terms in the price Phillips curve, and price inflation on the core terms in the wage Phillips curve:

$$\hat{w} = \kappa_{wz}\hat{z} + (1 - \kappa_{wz})\hat{z}^o + \pi + \kappa[\kappa_{wp}f_p(u, v) + f_w(e, v)] \quad (5.17)$$

$$\hat{p} = \pi + \kappa[f_p(u, v) + \kappa_p f_w(e, v)] \quad (5.18)$$

$$\kappa = 1/(1 - \kappa_p\kappa_{wp}) \quad (5.19)$$

The two Phillips curves preserve the property that in the growth rate of the real wage, $\hat{\omega} = \hat{w} - \hat{p} - \hat{z}^o$, the inflation climate π cancels out. The income distribution dynamics is therefore determined at a higher level than in the CCP module. While its independence from inflationary expectations may be considered another attractive feature of the PPC approach, there are, on the other hand, seven parameters that are entering at this level:

PPC Level 2: Real wage ω, wage share v (parameters κ_p, κ_{wp}, κ_{wz}, β_{pu}, β_{pv}, β_{we}, β_{wv})

$$\dot{\omega} = \omega\{\kappa_{wz}(\hat{z} - g_z) + \kappa[(1 - \kappa_p)f_w(e, v; \beta_{we}, \beta_{wv})$$

$$-(1 - \kappa_{wp})f_p(u, v; \beta_{pu}, \beta_{pv})]\} \qquad (5.20)$$

$$\hat{z} = g_z + \beta_{zu}\dot{u}/f_z(u) \qquad (5.3)$$

$$v = \omega/f_z(u) \qquad (5.5)$$

$$\kappa = 1/(1 - \kappa_p\kappa_{wp}) \qquad (5.19)$$

The relationship between $\hat{p}$ and π, too, is different from its treatment in the CCP module. In that module the computation of the time path of $\pi(\cdot)$ requires the computation of the time path of $\hat{p}(\cdot)$ here it is the other way round. The time paths of $\omega(\cdot)$ and $v(\cdot)$ being computed at level 2, eq. (5.18) can be plugged in the dynamic equation (5.12) for the adjustments of π. Subsequently, the solution of $\pi(\cdot)$ can be used in (5.18) to get the time path of the inflation rate. Apart from the two parameters β_π, κ_π, all parameters have already been set at level 2. We summarize these operations in one step:

PPC Level 3: Price inflation $\hat{p}$, inflation climate π (parameters β_π, κ_π)

$$\dot{\pi} = \beta_\pi[\kappa_\pi(\hat{p} - \pi) + (1 - \kappa_\pi)(\pi^o - \pi)] \qquad (5.12)$$

$$\hat{p} = \pi + \kappa[f_p(u, v) + \kappa_p f_w(e, v)] \qquad (5.18)$$

5.3.4   *Inflation module VMK: a variable markup*

The third approach seeks to translate a Kaleckian line of reasoning on a variable markup (VMK) into formal language, where the adjustments are basically of a countercyclical nature. The markup rate μ applies to unit labour costs and gives rise to the price level

$$p = (1 + \mu)wL/Y \tag{5.21}$$

μ is a dynamic variable that is assumed to respond negatively to its own level as well as to capacity utilization. It is convenient to use a growth rate formulation, so that we have

$$\dot{\mu} = (1 + \mu)f_\mu(u, \mu; \beta_{\mu u}, \beta_{\mu \mu}) := (1 + \mu)[-\beta_{\mu u}(u - 1) - \beta_{\mu \mu}(\mu - \mu^o)/\mu^o] \tag{5.22}$$

The gradual adjustment of μ towards μ^o expresses the notion of a target markup; the principle is similar to that in the price Phillips curve. The central issue, however, is the negative impact of utilization. Kalecki observes that, in a recession, overheads are increasing in relation to prime costs, and then goes on to argue that 'there will necessarily follow a "squeeze of profits", unless the ratio of proceeds to prime costs is permitted to rise. As a result, there may arise a tacit agreement among firms of an industry to "protect" profits and consequently to increase prices in relation to prime costs' (Kalecki, 1943, p. 50). Another reason for the reluctance of firms to reduce prices is their fear of unleashing cut-throat competition (Kalecki, 1939, p. 54), whereas the danger of new competitors will appear much lower in a recession. As for the opposite phase of the business cycle, Kalecki states that this 'tendency for the degree of monopoly [which corresponds to the present markup rate μ] to rise in a slump ... is reversed in the boom' (1943, p. 51). An argument here may be that this deters new entry into the industry.[18]

Eq. (5.21) connects the markup factor with the wage share. Solving it for v, and subsequently solving (5.5) (which relates the wage share to the real wage) for ω, it turns out that the income distribution dynamics is already fully determined by the markup variations in (5.22). Remarkably,

---

[18] See also the discussion in Steindl (1976, p. 17). Kalecki himself undertook an elementary empirical analysis, where the Polish and American time series he examined showed weak support for his theory (1939, p. 71; 1943, p. 57). Without the target markup, eq. (5.22) has been introduced in macroeconomic theory by Lance Taylor; see, for example, Taylor (1989, p. 7). For a small macrodynamic model of the business cycle that integrates (5.22), see also Flaschel et al. (1997, chap. 11).

the wage Phillips curve has no role to play at that stage. Taken together, level 2 of the VMK model variant is described by:

VMK Level 2: Real wage ω, wage share v (parameters $\beta_{\mu u}$, $\beta_{\mu \mu}$)

$$\dot{\mu} = (1 + \mu) f_{\mu}(u, \mu; \beta_{\mu u}, \beta_{\mu \mu}) \tag{5.22}$$

$$v = 1/(1 + \mu) \tag{5.23}$$

$$\omega = f_z(u)/(1 + \mu) \tag{5.24}$$

The wage Phillips curve contributes to the price inflation dynamics. As before, the target wage share v^o in (5.11) should be supposed to be consistent with the target markup μ^o in (5.22), $v^o = 1/(1 + \mu^o)$. Writing (5.21) as $p = (1 + \mu)w/z$, the rate of inflation is obtained from logarithmic differentiation: $\hat{p} = \dot{\mu}/(1 + \mu) + \hat{w} - \hat{z}$. Plugging in (5.22), (5.10) and (5.2), and ruling out a unit weight κ_{wp} for current inflation in the wage Phillips curve, the motions of $\hat{p}$ and π are computed at level 3 as follows:

VMK Level 3: Price inflation $\hat{p}$, inflation climate π (β_π, κ_π, κ_{wp}, κ_{wz}, β_{we}, β_{wv})

$$\dot{\pi} = \beta_\pi [\kappa_\pi (\hat{p} - \pi) + (1 - \kappa_\pi)(\pi^o - \pi)] \tag{5.12}$$

$$\hat{p} = \pi + \frac{1}{1 - \kappa_{wp}} \Big[-(1 - \kappa_{wz})(\hat{z} - g_z) + f_\mu(u, \mu)$$
$$+ f_w(e, v; \beta_{we}, \beta_{wv}) \Big] \tag{5.25}$$

$$\hat{z} = g_z + \beta_{zu} \dot{u}/f_z(u) \tag{5.3}$$

Notice that the resulting hierarchy is the same as in the PPC approach: ω and v are determined at level 2, π and $\hat{p}$ at level 3. However, the number of parameters entering at these levels is very different: in the PPC approach, there are seven (additional) coefficients at level 2 and two at level 3; in the present VMK approach, level 2 is based on just two parameters, while six are required at level 3.

It is also worth mentioning that, in a full macroeconomic model, $\kappa_{wz} = 1$ would certainly be desirable in VMK, in (5.25). In contrast, the polar case $\kappa_{wz} = 0$ would be preferred in the other two modules CCP and PPC; see eqs. (5.14) and (5.20), respectively.

5.4   Preparing the calibrations

5.4.1   The exogenous sine wave oscillations

As indicated by table 5.2, among the endogenous variables in the three model variants we are interested in the cyclical features of five variables: z, e, ω, v and p. Their time paths are fully determined by the variations of utilization u and the capital growth rate g_k. The influence of u is apparent at various places. By virtue of (5.9) g_k governs the evolution of k^s, which, in turn, only enters eq. (5.7) for e at level 1. For both u and g_k, regular oscillations will be assumed, which may take the convenient form of a sine wave.

Sine waves would be the outcome in a linear deterministic model, but such undamped and persistent oscillations will occur there only by a fluke. Self-sustained cyclical behaviour in a deterministic modelling framework will, accordingly, be typically nonlinear, so that even if the solution paths were quite regular they would still be more or less distinct from a sine wave motion. Unfortunately, we have no indication as to the form in which these nonlinearities may manifest themselves. Any proposal in this direction would have to introduce additional hypotheses, for which at present no solid indications exist. Note, however, that the detrended empirical time series in figure 5.2 do not seem to exhibit any systematic asymmetries – a visual impression that is largely confirmed by the literature.[19] At least the symmetry in the sine waves would therefore be no counter-argument.

It may, on the other hand, be argued that the exogenous variables are driven by a random process. An obvious problem with this device is that our modelling approach has not intended to mimic the random properties of the time series under study. As a consequence, the three model versions could not be evaluated statistically unless they were augmented by some random variables (see Gregory and Smith, 1993, p. 716). As with the nonlinearities just mentioned, however, there are no clear options for such stochastic extensions. Thus, a stochastic fluctuations

---

[19] A standard reference is DeLong and Summers (1986). For a more sophisticated approach, see Razzak (2001).

method would be no less arbitrary here than the deterministic sine wave method.[20]

The deterministic sine waves have an advantage over stochastic series of u and g_k in that they require less effort. First, for each set of given parameters one simulation run (over, say, thirty years) suffices to establish the cyclical features of the endogenous variables. This means that no averaging across a greater number of different realizations of the stochastic error terms is needed – for which the sampling properties will also be quite unknown, so that the analysis will first have to deal with the problem of reasonable confidence intervals for the cyclical statistics. Second, because of its smoothness, the cyclical pattern of an endogenous variable can be readily characterized by just one statistic, namely the time its turning points lead or lag the turning points of utilization. Instead, with random fluctuations, a description of the comovements with u would have to have recourse to several cross-correlation coefficients.

Another reason why random perturbations cannot be readily introduced into the present deterministic framework relates to the fact that the exogenous sine waves bring about (approximately) symmetrical oscillations of the endogenous variables around the steady-state values, provided the initial conditions are suitably chosen. This phenomenon is more important than it might seem at first sight, because it allows us to maintain π^o, v^o, μ^o and $e^o = 1$ as constant benchmark values in the adjustment functions (5.11), (5.12), (5.15) and (5.22). By contrast, in a stochastic setting there may easily arise asymmetric fluctuations in the medium term, especially if, realistically, the exogenous random process has a near-unit root. The asymmetry that over a longer time horizon u, for example, would be more above than below unity would lead to systematic distortions in the adjustment mechanisms. The distortions may even be so strong that they prompt the question: do the adjustment rules continue to make economic sense?[21]

---

[20] To underline the fact that stochastic simulations are no easy way out, we may quote from a short contribution to an econometric symposium: 'Most econometricians are so used to dealing with stochastic models that they are rarely aware of the limitations of this approach', a main point being that 'all stochastic assumptions, such as assumptions on the stochastic structure of the noise terms, are not innocent at all, in particular if there is no a priori reasoning for their justification' (Deistler, 2001, p. 72). More specifically, regarding a random shock term in a price Phillips curve, which (especially in the context of monetary policy) may possibly have grave consequences for the properties of a stochastic model, McCallum (2001, pp. 5f) emphasizes that its existence (and nature) is an unresolved issue, even when it is treated simply as white noise.

[21] To avoid dubious adjustments in these circumstances, the benchmark values might themselves be specified as (slowly) adjusting variables, similar to, for example, a time-varying NAIRU in empirical Phillips curve estimations. While this device may be appealing, it would add further components – and parameters – to the model.

Our methodological standpoint, therefore, is that, in the absence of a superior alternative, sine wave motions of the exogenous variables are a reasonable device to begin with, in the first stage of our investigations. Subsequently, however, we will also have a look at a special 'random' series of the exogenous variables: in selected parameter scenarios we will replace the sine wave of utilization with the empirical trend deviations over the sample period underlying the stylized facts of table 5.1.

After these methodological remarks, we can turn to the numerical details of the sine wave oscillations. As the US economy went through four cycles between 1961 and 1991, and another cycle seems to have run its course over the following ten years or so,[22] we base our investigations on a cycle period of eight years. For utilization, we furthermore assume an amplitude of $\pm\,4$ per cent, so that we have

$$u(t) = 1 + 0.04 \cdot \sin(\phi t), \quad \phi = 2\pi/8 \tag{5.26}$$

The amplitude amounts to a standard deviation of $u(\cdot)$ over a full cycle of 2.84 per cent, while the corresponding empirical value is 2.05 per cent. We opt for the higher amplitude because of our feeling (expressed in section 5.2) that the HP 1600 trend line of the empirical output–capital ratio absorbs too much medium-frequency variation. The choice of the amplitude is, however, only for concreteness and has no consequences for setting the parameters, since the amplitudes, or standard deviations, of the endogenous variables will always be related to that of utilization.

In contrast, it should be pointed out that the cycle period (i.e. the parameter ϕ) generally does matter. It obviously makes a difference to the amplitude of an endogenous variable whether, with respect to a fixed adjustment coefficient and thus similar rates of change per unit of time, it increases for twenty-four months or only for, say, eighteen months. Or, the other way round, a change in ϕ would require a change in (some of) the adjustment coefficients if the amplitude of the variable is to remain the same.

Regarding the motions of the capital growth rate, we see in table 5.1 that it lags utilization by one, two or even three quarters. In economic theory, this delay is usually ascribed to an implementation lag, according to which investment decisions respond quite directly to utilization or similarly fluctuating variables, but it takes some time until the investment projects are completely carried out and the plant and equipment has actually been built up. For simplicity, most macromodels neglect the implementation lag, so that utilization and the capital growth rate

---

[22] At the time of writing.

tend to move in line (though this will have to be an endogenous feature of any particular model). For this reason, we assume that g_k is perfectly synchronized with u. According to the ratio of the two standard deviations reported in table 5.1, the amplitude of g_k is a fraction of 0.29 of the 4 per cent in (5.26). Thus, denoting the level around which g_k oscillates by g^o,

$$g_k(t) = g^o + 0.29 \cdot [u(t) - 1] \tag{5.27}$$

g^o has the status of a long-run equilibrium growth rate. Of course, it is given by adding the (constant) growth rate of labour supply g_ℓ and the productivity trend rate of growth g_z. Numerically, we specify

$$g_z = 0.02, \quad g_\ell = 0.01, \quad g^o = g_z + g_\ell \tag{5.28}$$

5.4.2   Productivity and employment

The highest level of our calibration hierarchy, eqs. (5.9) and (5.7), determines the evolution of the employment rate. The only parameter entering here is β_{zu}, which indicates the percentage increase in labour productivity when capacity utilization rises by 1 per cent. Settling on β_{zu} is tantamount to settling on the ratio of the standard deviations σ_z and σ_u of the oscillations of the two variables. In laying out the desirable features of a model calibration in table 5.2 above, we have already decided on a definite value in this respect. We therefore set

$$\beta_{zu} = 0.40 \tag{5.29}$$

Corresponding to the long-run equilibrium values of utilization $u^o = 1$ and the employment rate $e^o = 1$, the equilibrium level of capital per head is $(k^s)^o = 1/y^n$; see eq. (5.7).[23] By virtue of $g^o - g_z - g_\ell = 0$ from (5.28), the variations of k^s resulting from (5.9) are stationary, so that a suitable choice of the initial value of k^s at $t = 0$ can make the oscillations symmetrical around $(k^s)^o$. Owing to the slight nonlinearity in (5.7), the induced oscillations of the employment rate are only approximately symmetrical around e^o; the precise value of the time average of $e(\cdot)$ over a cycle is 0.9998.

As it turns out, the amplitude of the employment rate is lower than desired. The relative standard deviation is $\sigma_e/\sigma_u = 0.69$, while in table 5.2

---

[23] The specific value for y^n does not affect the results in any way. Concretely, as argued in the next chapter, we use $y^n = 0.70$.

we aspired to a ratio of at least 0.80. Regarding the second cyclical characteristic, the motions of e exhibit a lag of three quarters behind utilization; this is just at the upper end of the range given in table 5.2. It is, however, remarkable that a lag does come about and that it is not too long, either.

There are two reasons why the statistics do not accurately match the target values put forward in table 5.2: the hypothesis that labour productivity is directly a function of utilization, which neglects a certain lead of z in this relationship; and the assumption that the variations of the capital growth rate are strictly synchronous with u. For a wider perspective, let us for a moment relax the two assumptions and introduce a lead τ_z for productivity in eq. (5.1) and a lag τ_k for the capital growth rate in eq. (5.27):

$$z(t)/z^o(t) = 1 + \beta_{zu}[u(t + \tau_z) - 1] \qquad (5.1a)$$

$$g_k(t) = g^o + 0.29 \cdot [u(t - \tau_k) - 1] \qquad (5.27a)$$

These relationships, especially (5.1a), are by no means supposed to be a theoretical contribution; they simply serve an exploratory purpose.

In the light of the empirical cross-correlations in table 5.1, consider $\tau_z = 0.62$ and $\tau_k = 0.37$. Table 5.3 summarizes the impact of these modifications on the cyclical properties of employment in eqs. (5.9) and (5.7).[24] It is thus seen that the lag τ_k in the capital growth rate reduces the amplitude in the oscillations of e, whereas the lead τ_z in productivity increases it appreciably, up to the desired variability even. On the other hand, however, the lag of e tends to become unduly long in this way. In sum, table 5.3 reveals the merits and demerits of the straightforward approach of eq. (5.1) to procyclical labour productivity.

Back to our original economy, $\tau_k = \tau_z = 0$, another way to increase the amplitude of the employment rate is a lower value of β_{zu}. The effect is clear from eqs. (5.7) and (5.1). Indeed, reducing the coefficient to $\beta_{zu} = 0.30$ increases the ratio σ_e/σ_u to 0.78 and also slightly shortens the lag to 0.67 years. While this procedure might be considered suspicious, since we correct our mis-specification of the laws governing the cyclical component of labour productivity by a second 'mis-specification' of the number that summarizes the relative variabilities of productivity and utilization, it could nevertheless be accepted if the cyclical features of the employment rate were all that counts. However, the function $f_z = f_z(u)$

---

[24] In the simulations the differential equations are approximated by their discrete-time analogues with an adjustment period of one month. Correspondingly, the lags reported from table 5.3 onwards are measured only on a monthly basis.

Table 5.3: *Cyclical properties of the employment rate*

τ_k	τ_z	σ_e/σ_u	lag e
0.00	0.00	0.69	0.75
0.37	0.00	0.60	0.83
0.00	0.62	0.84	0.92
0.37	0.62	0.75	1.08

NB: τ_k and τ_z are the time delays in eqs. (5.1a) and (5.27a). The lags are measured in years.

with its coefficient β_{zu} also enters the relationship (5.5) between the wage share and the real wage rate. Here we should not unduly intervene now, and so we had better shy away from this manipulation.

In the remainder of the book we again disregard the time delays τ_k and τ_z and proceed to work with eqs. (5.1) and (5.27) as convenient modelling simplifications. Moreover, we stick to the coefficient β_{zu} in (5.29), and so accept the three-quarter lag in employment and the standard deviation $\sigma_e/\sigma_u = 0.69$. We may emphasize that the low amplitude can be considered to be just a matter of scale, which does not seriously affect the calibration of the other model components. Notice to this end that e only enters the wage Phillips curve in eqs. (5.10), (5.11). Since its influence there is linear, a possible downward bias in the variability of $e(\cdot)$ can be immediately compensated for by a correspondingly higher value of the coefficient β_{we} in the function f_w.[25]

5.5   Wage-price dynamics with inflation module CCP

The CCP model variant, where the countercyclical motions of the price level are already established at hierarchy level 2, has the advantage that the amplitude of these oscillations is directly determined by one differential equation, eq. (5.13). By the same token, the parameter β_p in this adjustment equation for the rate of inflation provides us with full control over the standard deviation σ_p.

In detail, we solve (5.13) for the rate of inflation, which gives us a monthly series in the simulations (see footnote 24), reconstruct from

[25] More precisely, the issue is the following. Suppose, for the sake of the argument, the Phillips curve (5.10), (5.11) is a correct description of the nominal wage adjustments and the parameter β_{we} is correctly estimated. Then, within the present theoretical framework, we would increase this coefficient by a factor 0.83/0.69, say, to make good for the lower amplitude of the employment rate.

it the time path of the log of the price level, extract a quarterly series, detrend it by Hodrick–Prescott with $\lambda = 1600$, and interpolate these trend deviations to get the same number of monthly data points as we have available for $u(\cdot)$. It is the standard deviation of the resultant time series to which we refer and that we designate σ_p.[26] By virtue of the smoothness of the time paths, interpolation is here no problem. (Incidentally, differences between the standard deviations of the monthly and the quarterly series would be negligible, too.)

It should be remarked that the HP 1600 trend does not happen to be a straight line, so that these trend deviations are different from the theoretically appropriate expressions $\ln p(t) - \ln p^o(t)$, where $\ln p^o(t) = \pi^o t + \text{const.}$ are the steady-state equilibrium prices that would rise at the constant equilibrium rate of inflation π^o. While, with the utilization sine wave in (5.26), one can analytically work out that the ratio of the standard deviation of the time path $\ln p(t) - \ln p^o(t)$ to that of $u(t)$ is given by $\beta_p/\phi^2 = \beta_p \cdot 1.621$, the present ratio σ_p/σ_u, which is based on the HP 1600 filter, is smaller.[27] Numerically, the latter relationship comes out as $\sigma_p/\sigma_u \approx \beta_p \cdot 1.10$.

In calibrating the price level, we wish to obtain a ratio $\sigma_p/\sigma_u = 0.50$ as the middle value of the interval given in table 5.2. This feature is realized by setting

$$\beta_p = 0.45 \tag{5.30}$$

The resulting trend deviations are indeed strictly countercyclical – i.e. the lag of the series $-(p - p^o)/p^o$ with respect to u is exactly zero. This holds true not only for the just mentioned linear trend line (which is mathematically obvious from twice integrating the sine wave in (5.13)) but also for the HP 1600 trend.

In order to limit the number of free parameters in the other parts of the wage-price dynamics, we take an a priori decision about the adjustments of the inflation climate π at CCP level 3. Given this interpretation of π, which, we reiterate, is *not* just expected inflation for the next quarter, the adjustments towards current inflation should not be too fast. Likewise, agents will not expect inflation to return to normal too

---

[26] The notation σ_p and σ_ω, σ_v further below are in accordance with table 5.2. Thus, for $x = p, \omega, v$, the indexation σ_x denotes the standard deviation of the series $(p - p^o)/p^o$, $(\omega - \omega^o)/\omega^o$ and $(v - v^o)$, respectively.

[27] The simulated log series of the price level may be viewed as arising from a first-order integrated process. On the other hand, it is well known that the HP filter is an optimal signal extractor for univariate time series x_t in an uncorrelated components model, which implies that x_t would be an I(2) process. Hence, by construction, the HP filter removes too much as trend from the price series.

quickly. We therefore choose a moderate size of the adjustment speed β_π in eq. (5.12), and as for the role of adaptive and regressive expectations let us assume equal weights. Correspondingly, if not otherwise stated, for the following investigations we posit

$$\beta_\pi = 1.00 \quad \kappa_\pi = 0.50 \tag{5.31}$$

Similar motions of π, by the way, can also be generated by quite different combinations of β_π and κ_π. A more ambitious study could proxy π by empirical inflation forecasts – the Livingston survey of professional forecasters or the Survey Research Center survey of individuals from a random population sample, for example – and try to obtain estimates of β_π and κ_π on this basis. The ensuing calibration of the model components could then proceed along the same lines as in eq. (5.31).

Employing the numerical values put forward in (5.30) and (5.31), the problem now is whether the countercyclical motions of the price level are compatible with the cyclical properties of the real wage and the wage share that we aimed at in table 5.2. At CCP level 4 there are still four parameters to achieve this goal: κ_{wp}, κ_{wz}, β_{we} and β_{wv}. After some explorations, we take a first step and lay a grid of 6825 points over this parameter space, run a simulation for each quadruple, and after each simulation compute the statistics we are concerned with. For κ_{wp} and κ_{wz} the five values 0.00, 0.25, 0.50, 0.75 and 1.00 are considered; for β_{we}, twenty-one equally spaced values between 0.200 and 0.700 (stepsize 0.025); for β_{wv}, thirteen equally spaced values between 0.000 and 1.500 (step size 0.125). The most important result of this grid search is a negative one, namely that not all the desirable features of table 5.2 can be accomplished simultaneously.

The nature of the hindrance can be seen by assigning the highest priority to the amplitude of the real wage rate, demanding $0.45 \leq \sigma_w/\sigma_u \leq 0.50$. Our general finding is that, if this range is met, either the lag of the real wage is too long or the amplitude of the wage share is too low. A shorter lag of ω is accompanied by lower standard deviations σ_v, and higher values of σ_v are accompanied by longer lags of ω. To give a few examples, lag $\omega \leq 0.50$ admits no higher a ratio σ_v/σ_u than 0.142 (over the entire grid, there are just three parameter combinations with lag $\omega = 0.50$ and $\sigma_v/\sigma_u \geq 0.140$). Increasing the delay, lag $\omega = 0.75$, admits no higher a ratio σ_v/σ_u than 0.199 (there being just five parameter combinations with lag $\omega = 0.75$ and $\sigma_v/\sigma_u \geq 0.193$). Likewise, $\sigma_v/\sigma_u \geq 0.210$ requires lag $\omega \geq 0.83$ (with lag $\omega = 0.83$ there are three combinations, entailing $\sigma_v/\sigma_u = 0.210, 0.210, 0.213$, respectively), while $\sigma_v/\sigma_u \geq 0.245$ even requires the real wage rate to lag utilization by at least one year.

To get a better feeling for these numbers, we add that in the present sine wave context a standard deviation σ_v/σ_u around 0.18 is tantamount to an amplitude of the wage share of roughly $\pm$ 0.7 percentage points. This order of magnitude might sound a bit more pleasant than the very small standard deviations. At the end of this section we will also test the effects from a lead in productivity, when we will have decided on a particular parameter combination. Apart from that, it is remarkable that the wage share exhibits a phase shift of about a quarter of a cycle – i.e. the wage share lags utilization by about two years. After all, we have $v = \omega/f_z(u)$ from (5.5), where $1/f_z(u)$ is strictly countercyclical and ω is procyclical with a lag behind u of 0.50 or 0.75 years. This shows that the cyclical features of the wage share might respond quite sensitively to changes in the patterns, or the amplitudes, of ω and $f_z(u)$ (though, regarding the real wage, it has to be noted that this is a two-way interaction, since in (5.14) v also feeds back on ω).

It is worth pointing out that similar phase shifts of v are encountered for all other parameter combinations that may interest us (i.e. that we define as 'admissible'; see below). This type of comovement between a measure of economic activity and income distribution is equally obtained in Goodwin's (1967) seminal growth cycle model and its various extensions. Hence, the present framework is highly compatible with this approach and could, indeed, provide a richer structure for its wage-price dynamics.

Following the results of the coarse grid search, we have to lower our sights. To proceed with our work, we put up a set of 'second-best' criteria that the model should satisfy. They are collected in table 5.4, where with respect to the employment rate the discussion in the previous subsection is taken into account. Regarding the other endogenous variables, in comparison with the desired features in table 5.2 we here admit a slightly longer lag for the real wage, and a considerably lower standard deviation for the wage share. Parameter combinations giving rise to the features in table 5.4 may henceforth be called *admissible*.

Agreeing on the second-best criteria and knowing that such admissible parameter combinations exist, let us turn to some numerical details concerning the level-4 coefficients κ_{wp}, κ_{wz}, β_{we} and β_{wv}. Three questions are of particular interest: (1) Given that a positive weight κ_{wz} in eq. (5.14) would make the growth rate of actual labour productivity and, thus, the time derivative of utilization enter the model's reduced-form equations, which will certainly impede a mathematical analysis, do admissible combinations with $\kappa_{wz} = 0$ exist? (2) Since wage Phillips curves usually do not make reference to the wage share, do admissible combinations with $\beta_{wv} = 0$ exist? (3) Are the values of the core coefficient of the wage Phillips

Table 5.4: *Second-best criteria for the macrodynamic oscillations*

Variable x	σ_x/σ_u	Lag x
$(z - z^o)/z^o$	0.40	0.00
$e - 1$	0.69	0.75
$(\omega - \omega^o)/\omega^o$	0.45–0.50	−0.50–0.75
$v - v^o$	0.18–0.40	–
$-(p - p^o)/p^o$	0.45–0.50	−0.75–0.25

curve, β_{we}, within a familiar range – say $0.30 \le \beta_{we} \le 0.50$? Information about these points is illustrated in Figure 5.3.[28]

The '+' symbol in figure 5.3 records the (β_{we}, β_{wv}) component of admissible parameter combinations that are obtained from the grid search just mentioned. While the answer to question (3) is in the affirmative, the second coefficient β_{wv} may be low, but it is still bounded away from zero. Hence, for the condition $\beta_{wv} = 0$ to be fulfilled, we would have to try to choose the coefficients β_π and/or κ_π in a more skilful way. This issue is taken up shortly.

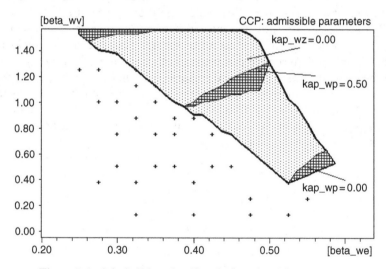

Figure 5.3: Admissible pairs (β_{we}, β_{wv}) under CCP

[28] Pairs (β_{we}, β_{wv}) in the dotted area match the second-best criteria of table 5.4 for eqs. (5.30) and (5.31), $\kappa_{wz} = 0$ and some suitable $\kappa_{wp} \in [0, 1]$; pairs in the hatched area, in addition, are associated with $\kappa_{wp} = 0$, $\kappa_{wp} = 0.50$ and $\kappa_{wp} \ge 0.95$ (as seen from below). '+' indicates (β_{we}, β_{wv}) meeting the criteria for some $\kappa_{wz} \in \{0.25, 0.50, 0.75, 1.00\}$ and $\kappa_{wp} \in \{0.00, 0.25, 0.50, 0.75, 1.00\}$ (coarse grid search).

To deal with point (1), we fix $\kappa_{wz} = 0$ and set up a finer grid of the other three coefficients κ_{wp}, β_{we} and β_{wv}. On the basis of this battery of simulation runs, it can be concluded that for all pairs (β_{we}, β_{wv}) in the dotted area in figure 5.3 there is a value between 0 and 1 of the coefficient κ_{wp} such that the corresponding parameter combination satisfies the second-best criteria.[29] The subsets of the hatched areas indicate admissible pairs (β_{we}, β_{wv}) that, besides $\kappa_{wz} = 0$, are combined with $\kappa_{wp} = 0$ (the lower region), $\kappa_{wp} = 0.50$ (the middle region) or $\kappa_{wp} \in [0.95, 1.00]$ (the small region in the upper left corner).

There is thus a certain tendency that, going along with a moderate decline in the coefficient β_{we}, higher values of κ_{wp} are associated with higher admissible values for β_{wv}. This can be explained by looking at eq. (5.14), which governs the motions of the real wage rate. Note that both series $\hat{p}$ and v, which here show up, lag utilization by about a quarter of a cycle, and $\hat{p}$ has a higher variability than π. Furthermore, both variables have a negative impact on the time derivative of ω and so make an essential contribution to the procyclicality of the level of the real wage. Now, as κ_{wp} increases from zero to unity, the influence of the term $\hat{p} - \pi$ diminishes. This adverse effect on the procyclicality as well as the standard deviation of ω can be made up by reinforcing the influence of v on $\dot{\omega}$ – that is, by increasing the coefficient β_{wv}.

Before we enquire into the existence of admissible parameter combinations with $\beta_{wv} = 0$, it is useful to set up a base scenario to which the outcomes of alternative parameters in this and the following sections can be compared. For theoretical reasons, we still want the employment rate to play a dominant role in the wage Phillips curve vis-à-vis the wage share. As will be more rigorously verified in a moment, this is achieved by pairs (β_{we}, β_{wv}) in the lower part of the dotted area in figure 5.3, where $\kappa_{wp} = 0$. We therefore choose:

Base scenario CCP:

$$\beta_{zu} = 0.40 \quad \beta_p = 0.45 \quad \beta_\pi = 1.00 \quad \kappa_\pi = 0.50$$

$$\kappa_{wp} = 0.00 \quad \kappa_{wz} = 0.00 \quad \beta_{we} = 0.55 \quad \beta_{wv} = 0.50$$

---

[29] There may nonetheless exist other values of κ_{wp} and $\kappa_{wz} > 0$ for which the same pair (β_{we}, β_{wv}) establishes an admissible parameter combination.

Table 5.5: *Parameter variations in base scenario CCP*

β_{wv}	β_{we}	κ_π	σ_ω/σ_u	Lag ω	σ_v/σ_u	Lag v
0.50	0.55	0.50	0.48	0.75	0.18	2.00
0.00	0.55	0.50	0.35	1.00	0.20	2.75
0.00	0.55	0.25	0.49	1.00	0.25	2.17
0.00	0.45	0.25	0.48	0.75	0.19	2.00
0.00	0.35	0.25	0.49	0.58	0.15	1.75

The first row in table 5.5 reports the precise statistics of ω and v that are generated by this reference set of coefficients. In order to compare the implied influence of the employment rate and the wage share in the wage Phillips curve, one has to take the amplitudes of these variables into account. Employing the standard deviations for this purpose, v can be said to be less influential than e if $\sigma_v\beta_{wv} < \sigma_e\beta_{we}$. Dividing the inequality through σ_u, the left-hand side is $0.18 \cdot 0.50 = 0.09$, the right-hand side amounts to $0.69 \cdot 0.55 = 0.38$ (rounded; see the first row in table 5.3 for σ_e/σ_u). Hence, the influence of the wage share is weaker than the influence of of the employment rate by a factor of almost four.[30]

The second row in table 5.5 shows the consequences of a *ceteris paribus* drop of β_{wv} to zero, which has two unpleasant effects for the real wage: a decrease in the standard deviation and a longer lag.[31] The decrease in σ_ω can be undone by giving regressive expectations in the adjustments of the inflation climate a greater weight – i.e. by reducing κ_π to 0.25. Subsequently, the lag of the real wage can be shortened by lowering the coefficient β_{we}. At the same time, this *ceteris paribus* change diminishes the (previously increasing) standard deviation of the wage share considerably, while under the given circumstances, perhaps somewhat surprisingly, the impact on σ_ω is very weak. At $\beta_{we} = 0.45$ all second-best criteria are met again. A further reduction of β_{we} would be desirable insofar as the real wage becomes more procyclical. Unfortunately, as we have observed above, this decreases σ_v too much.

There are other examples of admissible parameter combinations with a vanishing coefficient β_{wv}. As in the exercise of table 5.5, however, they always call for a specific conjunction of, in particular, β_π and κ_π. This is to say that the condition $\beta_{wv} = 0$, which relates to the wage Phillips

---

[30] Incidentally, this factor would be much smaller for a pair (β_{we}, β_{wv}) in the middle hatched region of figure 5.3.

[31] The adverse effects would be even more dramatic for admissible parameter combinations with a positive value of κ_{wp}.

curve, requires conditions to be met that have their place in another part of the model. In this sense, the assumption that $\beta_{wv} = 0$ rests on rather shaky grounds and might better be avoided.

Regarding the numerical specification of the core term of the wage Phillips curve, we therefore sum up that here, on the one hand, the wage share does have a non-negligible role to play, while, on the other hand, the rate of employment still exerts the dominant influence. We believe that the discussion has also made sufficiently clear the difference to an econometric estimation. It is not just the minimization of a loss function, possibly subject to some technical constraints, but, rather, that our decision-making process includes a substantial amount of additional theoretical judgement.

Lastly, we return to the problem of the low standard deviation of the wage share and ask whether we could improve on this feature by relaxing the assumption of the strictly procyclical labour productivity. Thus, let us employ eq. (5.1a) once again, $z(t)/z^o(t) = 1 + \beta_{zu}[u(t + \tau_z) - 1]$, with a lead $\tau_z = 0.62$. From section 5.4 we already know that, at the highest hierarchy level, this increases the standard deviation of the employment rate as well as its lag: $\sigma_e/\sigma_u = 0.84$ and lag $e = 0.92$. Regarding income distribution, it turns out that the cyclical statistics of the real wage are not affected by the phase shift in z. The motions of the wage share, however, do change: the lag is slightly reduced, lag $v = 1.92$, and not only does its variability rise but it is now even in the desired range of table 5.2, $\sigma_v/\sigma_u = 0.32$.

Therefore, recalling the relationship $v(t) = \omega(t)/f_z[u(t + \tau_z)]$, it is seen that the enhancement in the amplitude of the wage share is entirely attributable to the assumed lead in productivity. This is an important result, which might be taken into account in more ambitious versions of the model with a less rigid production technology. Nevertheless, in this book we have to keep this part of the model simple, and so we stick to the strictly synchronous motions of labour productivity.

5.6   Wage-price dynamics with inflation module PPC

As has been noted before, the inflation module with the price Phillips curve has the pleasant property that the real wage dynamics is determined independently of the inflation climate π, at PPC hierarchy level 2. On the other hand, this is achieved at the cost of seven parameters being involved. Macromodels working with two Phillips curves usually concentrate on the utilization measures on the goods and labour markets and ignore the possible influence of the wage share (or a related variable), which in the present setting amounts to $\beta_{wv} = \beta_{pv} = 0$. If technical progress is included, $\kappa_{wz} = 0$ is assumed as well. In this way, eq. (5.20) for the changes in the real wage becomes[32]

$$\dot{\omega} = \omega\kappa[(1 - \kappa_p)\beta_{we}(e - 1) - (1 - \kappa_{wp})\beta_{pu}(u - 1)] \qquad (5.20a)$$

The observation that is important for us here, especially for the model in chapter 4, has, in substance, already been made at the beginning of chapter 3, section 6; see eq. (3.33). Since the employment rate is a nearly procyclical variable, it is immediate that the oscillations of the real wage in (5.20a) will be shifted by about a quarter of a cycle; whether forward or backward depends on the relative magnitudes of $(1 - \kappa_p)\beta_{we}$ and $(1 - \kappa_{wp})\beta_{pu}$. It follows from this elementary argument that the approach of two standard Phillips curves is not compatible with the stylized fact of a procyclical real wage rate; either β_{wv} or β_{pv} must be nonzero, or both!

Taking it for granted that the two general Phillips curves (5.10), (5.11) and (5.15), (5.16) may not be prematurely simplified, we would nevertheless like to limit the variations of the seven parameters at PPC level 2. In addition, it should be possible to relate the investigations to our previous results. Therefore, in a way, we reverse the problem of the preceding section. There we had countercyclical motions of the price level and, on the basis of the given values for β_π and κ_π, asked whether we could find parameters for the wage Phillips curve that give us a satisfactory cyclical behaviour of the distribution variables ω and v. In contrast, we now take over the numerical values of κ_{wz}, κ_{wp}, β_{we} and β_{wv} in the wage Phillips curve, from which we know that they are compatible with the countercyclical price level, and ask whether we can find numerical values for κ_p, β_{pu} and β_{pv} in the price Phillips curve that generate such countercyclical prices, besides a suitable income distribution dynamics, of course. We hope that, with the proven values of β_π and κ_π, these three 'degrees of freedom' turn out to be sufficient for this task.

Figure 5.4[33] shows the outcome of a grid search across the parameters κ_p, β_{pu} and β_{pv}. The diagram shows the set of pairs (β_{pu}, β_{pv}) for which

---

[32] For example, equation (5.20a) is a constituting part of the models in Chiarella and Flaschel (2000a, pp. 182 & 298; 2000b, p. 937) or Chiarella et al. (2000, p. 63).

[33] Pairs (β_{pu}, β_{pv}) in the dotted area meet the second-best criteria of table 5.4 for some suitable value of $\kappa_p \in [0, 1]$. The pairs in the closely dotted area are associated with $\kappa_p = 0.00$ or $\kappa_p = 0.50$, respectively. The values of the other level-2 parameters are taken over from the CCP base scenario.

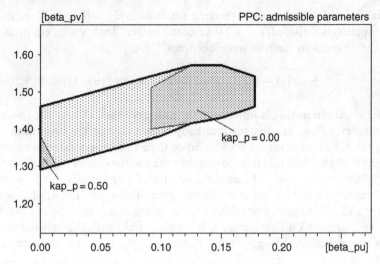

Figure 5.4: Admissible pairs (β_{pu}, β_{pv}) under PPC (level 2)

at least one value of κ_p exists such that these coefficients, together with the parameter values just mentioned, meet the six conditions for ω, v and p in the lower half of table 5.4. For each pair (β_{pu}, β_{pv}) in the dotted area there is a range of κ_p with that property (mostly a wider one). The diagram also indicates the sets where the accompanying κ_p can be 0.00 or 0.50, respectively. An insignificant subset of (β_{pu}, β_{pv}) has associated with it $\kappa_p = 0.55$, which is the maximum value of all admissible κ_p that we find.

The outstanding feature to note in figure 5.4 is that the coefficient β_{pu}, and not β_{pv} (!), may well vanish. Furthermore, even the highest admissible values of β_{pu} appear rather undersized. The influence of utilization in the price Phillips curve is, in fact, always markedly inferior to the wage share. That is, β_{pv} is always larger than $\beta_{pu}/(\sigma_v/\sigma_u) \approx \beta_{pu}/0.18 > 0.18/0.18 = 1$ (which means $\sigma_u \beta_{pu} < \sigma_v \beta_{pv}$). Arguably, a Phillips curve with such a strong influence of the wage share might even no longer be considered a Phillips curve proper!

While the parameter combinations illustrated in figure 5.4 meet the second-best criteria of table 5.4, they also do no better than that. Thus, the shortest lag of the real wage that we achieve is lag $\omega = 0.75$ years, and the maximum standard deviation of the wage share is $\sigma_v/\sigma_u \approx 0.20$. The oscillations of the price level are, without exception, strictly countercyclical – i.e. lag$[-(p - p^o)/p^o] = 0$.

In deciding on a base scenario, we may therefore go anywhere in the dotted area in figure 5.4. Let us choose a combination that still has a relatively high coefficient β_{pu}. Thus we arrive at:

Base scenario PPC:

$$\beta_\pi = 1.00 \quad \kappa_\pi = 0.50$$

$$\beta_{zu} = 0.40 \quad \kappa_p = 0.00 \quad \beta_{pu} = 0.15 \quad \beta_{pv} = 1.50$$

$$\kappa_{wp} = 0.00 \quad \kappa_{wz} = 0.00 \quad \beta_{we} = 0.55 \quad \beta_{wv} = 0.50$$

The cyclical features of this scenario resemble very much those of the CCP base scenario. In detail, $\sigma_\omega/\sigma_u = 0.47$, lag $\omega = 0.75$, $\sigma_v/\sigma_u = 0.18$, lag $v = 2.08$, $\sigma_p/\sigma_u = 0.48$ and $\text{lag}[-(p - p^o)/p^o] = 0.00$.

In concluding the discussion of the PPC module, again it may be asked whether parameter combinations with $\beta_{wv} = 0$ in the wage Phillips curve are possible. We investigated this question by abandoning the given values for β_π and κ_π. That is, we fixed $\beta_{wv} = 0$, $\kappa_{wz} = 0$ (besides $\beta_{zu} = 0.40$, of course) and laid a seven-dimensional grid over the parameters $\beta_{pu}, \beta_{pv}, \kappa_p, \beta_{we}, \kappa_{wp}, \beta_\pi$ and κ_π. Invoking a random mechanism, 50,000 of these grid points were checked, with the result that not one parameter combination satisfied the second-best criteria. For example, if all criteria are fulfilled except for lag ω, then the minimal lag of the real wage is 0.83 years, which is realized by no more than three combinations. If, instead, we relax the condition on the standard deviation of the wage share, there are only four combinations with $\sigma_v/\sigma_u \geq 0.14$, where three of them rest on very slow adjustments of the inflation climate, $\beta_\pi = 0.20$ or $\beta_\pi = 0.40$.[34] The evaluation of the assumption $\beta_{wv} = 0$ in the wage Phillips curve is therefore similar to, if not even more negative than, what it is for the wage-price dynamics under the CCP inflation module.

5.7   Wage-price dynamics with inflation module VMK

At its highest hierarchy level, the VMK model variant has only two parameters, $\beta_{\mu u}$ and $\beta_{\mu\mu}$, to regulate the three main statistics of the income distribution dynamics: σ_ω, lag ω and σ_v. It is thus a non-trivial

---

[34] The fourth combination exhibits $\beta_\pi = 1.00$. It also yields the 'best' combination, with $\sigma_v/\sigma_u = 0.17$. For completeness, the other coefficients are $\beta_{pu} = 0.05$, $\beta_{pv} = 1.80$, $\kappa_p = 0.20$, $\beta_{we} = 0.45$, $\kappa_{wp} = 0.00$ and $\kappa_\pi = 0.19$.

problem whether $\beta_{\mu u}$ and $\beta_{\mu\mu}$ are really capable of generating satisfactory cyclical properties in this respect. We repeat that the wage Phillips curve is not involved here.

After checking for an upper boundary of $\beta_{\mu u}$ and $\beta_{\mu\mu}$ beyond which there is no further scope for reasonable values of all three statistics, we set up a grid of twenty-one values of $\beta_{\mu u}$ that range from 0.050 to 0.350 (step size 0.015), and twenty-one values of $\beta_{\mu\mu}$ that range from 0.000 to 0.300 (likewise, step size 0.015). Among these 441 combinations, it turns out, there are four pairs that meet the second-best conditions. Three of them exhibit $\beta_{\mu u} = 0.200$, together with $\beta_{\mu\mu} = 0.000$, 0.015, 0.030; the fourth one is not very much different, with $\beta_{\mu u} = 0.215$ and $\beta_{\mu\mu} = 0.015$. The latter pair implies $\sigma_v/\sigma_u = 0.190$; for the remaining three the ratio σ_v/σ_u is between 0.177 and 0.181. One pair, $\beta_{\mu u} = 0.200$, $\beta_{\mu\mu} = 0.030$, entails a lag of the real wage of 0.67 years, while lag $\omega = 0.75$ characterizes the other cases. Since this is the shortest lag that we have encountered so far for admissible parameter combinations, we accept the slightly lower standard deviation of the wage share with which it goes along (i.e. $\sigma_v/\sigma_u = 0.178$) and base the following investigations on

$$\beta_{\mu u} = 0.20 \quad \beta_{\mu\mu} = 0.03 \quad\quad (5.32)$$

The phase shift of the wage share, by the way, is 1.92 years here, while the standard deviation of the real wage is $\sigma_\omega/\sigma_u = 0.49$. Shorter lags of ω are possible, but, as in the other modules, only at the price of higher values of σ_ω and lower values of σ_v.

It should also be pointed out that, apart from the precise numerical implications, another reason for choosing a strictly positive coefficient $\beta_{\mu\mu}$ may arise in the context of a full macroeconomic model. Here $\beta_{\mu\mu} > 0$ could help ensure uniqueness in a steady-state position, which is reflected by a regular Jacobian matrix. Otherwise, if utilization appears not only on the right-hand side of (5.22) but also in other reduced-form equations of the full dynamic system, the Jacobian might be singular.

As in the organization of the preceding simulations, we maintain the parameters β_π, κ_π as stated in (5.31). An obvious question, then, is for the integration of the wage Phillips curve from the CCP and PPC base scenarios: will VMK, at level 3, yield similar cyclical statistics for the price level? The answer is 'nearly so'. The standard deviation amounts to $\sigma_p/\sigma_u = 0.50$, but there is a short lag of $-\text{dev } p$ of one quarter, where we abbreviate $\text{dev}p := (p - p^o)/p^o$ (again with respect to the HP 1600 trend p^o, of course).

Even if this result is reckoned satisfactory, there are two coefficients in the Phillips curve that we would like to change. The first one is

κ_{wz}, which is set to zero in the CCP and PPC scenarios. Referring to eq. (5.25), we recall that, under VMK, $\kappa_{wz} = 1$ would be the preferred value in order to eliminate the growth rate $\hat{z}$ of actual productivity from the model. A direct *ceteris paribus* increase of κ_{wz} from zero to unity has, however, a drastic consequence for the price dynamics: while now $-\mathrm{dev}\,p$ leads utilization by three quarters, which might still be acceptable, the standard deviation falls to $\sigma_p/\sigma_u = 0.18$. This is another example of the strong influence that a weighting parameter may possibly have.

Much in line with the discussion of the CCP and PPC models, the second parameter in the wage Phillips curve that one would perhaps wish to determine a priori – i.e. fix at zero – is β_{wv}. Thus, set

$$\kappa_{wz} = 1.00 \quad \beta_{wv} = 0.00 \tag{5.33}$$

and let us see what the two remaining free parameters, β_{we} and κ_{wp}, can achieve. The outcome of a detailed grid search is shown in figure 5.5.[35] In the dotted area it depicts the pairs $(\beta_{we}, \kappa_{wp})$ that, given (5.29) and (5.31)–(5.33), imply $0.45 \le \sigma_p/\sigma_u \le 0.50$ and a lag of the price level (i.e. of $-\mathrm{dev}\,p$) between 0.25 and -0.50 years (the lags as indicated in the four subsets). The diagram, in particular, demonstrates that the admissible slope coefficients β_{we} in the Phillips curve continue to lie in a

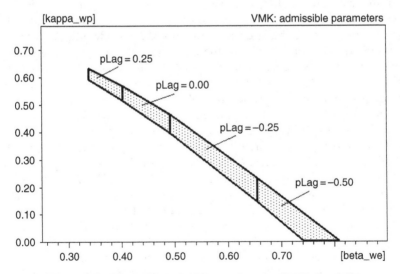

Figure 5.5: Admissible pairs $(\beta_{we}, \kappa_{wp})$ under VMK (level 3)

[35] Pairs $(\beta_{we}, \kappa_{wp})$ in the dotted area meet the second-best criteria of table 5.4, given (5.29) and (5.31)–(5.33). 'pLag' stands for lag $[-\mathrm{dev}\,p]$, in years.

familiar range. Associated with suitable values of the weight parameter κ_{wp}, the coefficient β_{we} may vary between 0.34 and 0.81. On the other hand, it is clear from (5.25) that κ_{wp} must be bounded away from unity. The precise upper bound in figure 5.5 is $\kappa_{wp} = 0.63$.

In the light of the stylized facts in table 5.1, we may, in setting up a base scenario, choose a pair $(\beta_{we}, \kappa_{wp})$ that entails a one-quarter lead of the countercyclical oscillations of the price level. In this way, we can even retain the previous slope coefficient β_{we}. In sum, we specify

---

Base scenario VMK:

$$\beta_{\pi} = 1.00 \quad \kappa_{\pi} = 0.50$$

$$\beta_{zu} = 0.40 \qquad \beta_{\mu u} = 0.20 \quad \beta_{\mu\mu} = 0.03$$

$$\kappa_{wp} = 0.35 \quad \kappa_{wz} = 1.00 \quad \beta_{we} = 0.55 \quad \beta_{wv} = 0.00$$

5.8   Evaluation of the calibration results

An important motive for undertaking the numerical simulations was to investigate whether the three wage-price submodels have sufficiently reasonable properties to be integrated into a broader modelling framework. It might even be asked which of the three versions would be best suited for this purpose. To ease the discussion of the topic, each model variant is represented by its base scenario. For convenience, the cyclical features produced by them are repeated in table 5.6.

The table summarizes that all three submodels satisfy the second-best criteria established in table 5.4, where, in particular, a certain lag of the real wage rate and a low variability of the wage share have to be accepted. Also, since no model can do any better than that, the three versions are, so far, on an equal footing. In finer detail, VMK might perhaps be said to have a slight edge over CCP and PPC, insofar as it admits a marginally shorter lag of ω and a slight lead in the countercyclical motions of the price level. But, given the still relatively simple structure of the modelling equations, this aspect should not be overrated.

Since the three submodels have the same functional specification of an underlying wage Phillips curve, one may ask for the compatibility of the inflation modules. That is, one may ask if one module can be exchanged for another while maintaining the numerical coefficients of the wage Phillips curve (and, of course, β_{zu}, β_{π}, κ_{π}). The synopsis of

Table 5.6: *Cyclical properties of the base scenarios*

	σ_ω/σ_u	Lag ω	σ_v/σ_u	Lag v	σ_p/σ_u	Lag $(-p)$
CCP	0.48	0.75	0.18	2.00	0.50	0.00
PPC	0.47	0.75	0.18	2.08	0.48	0.00
VMK	0.49	0.67	0.18	1.92	0.47	−0.25

NB: With respect to $x = p, \omega, v$, the indexation σ_x denotes the standard deviation of the series $(p - p^o)/p^o$, $(\omega - \omega^o)/\omega^o$ and $(v - v^o)$, respectively; lag $(-p)$ abbreviates lag $[-(p - p^o)/p^o]$. The statistics are computed over a full cycle of eight years.

Table 5.7: *A synopsis of the base scenario coefficients*

	β_{we}	β_{wv}	κ_{wp}	κ_{wz}	β_p	β_{pu}	β_{pv}	κ_{pw}	$\beta_{\mu u}$	$\beta_{\mu\mu}$	KC
CCP	0.55	0.50	0.00	0.00	0.45	–	–	–	–	–	4
PPC	0.55	0.50	0.00	0.00	–	0.15	1.50	0.00	–	–	6
VMK	0.55	0.00	0.35	1.00	–	–	–	–	0.20	0.03	4

NB: For all three model variants, the remaining parameters are given by eqs. (5.29) and (5.31). KC is the number of 'key coefficients' (see text).

the adjustment coefficients in table 5.7 points out that this is certainly true for the CCP and PPC base scenarios.

Thus, a decision between CCP and PPC would have to be made on other grounds. One argument supporting CCP is that this inflation module involves only one further parameter, against three for PPC. On the other hand, the approach of a price Phillips curve has theoretical content and is also widely applied in macroeconometric work, while one may tend to view the CCP equation as a reduced-form representation of a price adjustment process that is not made fully explicit.

Regarding the third inflation module, it has already been pointed out in section 5.7 that the wage Phillips curve with the CCP and PPC base scenario coefficients, when employed in the VMK model, leads to results that are only slightly inferior. Given suitably chosen numerical values of β_p, or $(\beta_{pu}, \beta_{pv}, \kappa_{pw})$ or $(\beta_{\mu u}, \beta_{\mu\mu})$, respectively, it can therefore be noted that the three inflation modules are indeed very compatible, in the sense that combining them with the same (suitably chosen) wage Phillips curve gives rise to very similar cyclical features. This is a remarkable conclusion, since theoretically, as well as formally, the three modules are quite distinct.

Two reasons have, however, been mentioned why incorporating the wage Phillips curve into the VMK model alternative would be preferable. The first reason concerns the weighting coefficient κ_{wz} and its consequences for the analytical tractability of the model. Under CCP and PPC, the growth rate of labour productivity, $\hat{z}$, would show up in the dynamic equations unless $\kappa_{wz} = 0$ (see eqs. (5.14) and (5.20)); under VMK, $\hat{z}$ would feed back on the dynamics unless $\kappa_{wz} = 1$ (see eq. (5.25)). Second, adopting this value $\kappa_{wz} = 1$ in the VMK model, it was found that a coefficient $\beta_{wv} = 0$ becomes admissible, whereas under CCP and PPC this is the case only for very special combinations of β_π and κ_π. Hence, if one wishes to work with a standard wage Philips curve in which possible effects from the wage share are excluded, the zero coefficient β_{wv} in the base scenario would favour VMK.

The VMK approach also fares well if, representing model parsimony, the mere number of coefficients were an argument. Table 5.7 records the number of 'key coefficients', by which we mean the number of coefficients here examined that cannot a priori be set equal to their desirable polar values, such as this is possible with $\kappa_{wz} = 0$ for CCP and PPC, or $\kappa_{wz} = 1$ and $\beta_{wv} = 0$ for VMK. Thus, there remain four key coefficients for CCP ($\beta_{we}, \beta_{wv}, \kappa_{wp}, \beta_p$), six for PPC ($\beta_{we}, \beta_{wv}, \kappa_{wp}, \beta_{pu}, \beta_{pv}, \kappa_{pw}$) for PPC and four for VMK ($\beta_{we}, \kappa_{wp}, \beta_{\mu u}, \beta_{\mu\mu}$). It might even be argued that VMK requires no more than three key coefficients, since putting $\beta_{\mu\mu} = 0$ would not violate the second-best criteria.[36]

Regarding a possible integration of CCP, PPC or VMK in a more encompassing macrodynamic model, the brief discussion can be summarized as follows. Either version may be employed if additional aspects come into play. A theoretical interest in the Kaleckian elements of oligopolistic price setting, for example, may be a powerful argument for VMK. On the other hand, this approach is not so familiar as a price Phillips curve, for which we opt in the other chapters of the book. The accelerationist CCP specification might be employed in low-dimensional models because of its reduced price side, while it might be discarded in more ambitious modelling work since it has less theoretical content than PPC and VMK.

5.9   The cyclical properties under the empirical utilization series

To conclude the calibration study of the wage-price dynamics, we return to the issue of the exogenous fluctuations of capacity utilization. Though one might be quite content with the above cyclical features, the base scenario parameters would generate more confidence if this outcome does not deteriorate too much when the regular sine waves of u are replaced with the empirical observations of this variable.

[36] Recall, however, the argument that $\beta_{\mu\mu} > 0$, apart from a conceptual desirability, might be needed in order to obtain a unique steady state within a full model.

Since the wage-price dynamics in the rest of the book are based on a price Phillips curve, let us in this investigation concentrate on the PPC model variant and its base scenario (incidentally, the results for CCP and VMK would make no great difference). In detail, we take as our exogenous fluctuations the quarterly data on the empirical utilization variable u, which is the series depicted in the top panel of figure 5.2, while eq. (5.27) for the capital growth rate is maintained. The sample period of u is the same as in table 5.1, 1961:1 to 1991:4. The simulation itself is again run for the monthly discrete-time analogues of the model, so a simple interpolation converts u to a monthly series. The outcome is shown in figure 5.6,[37] where the bold lines are the model-generated time paths of the real wage, the wage share and the price level. In the thin lines they are contrasted with their empirical counterparts, which have already been drawn in the lower three panels of figure 5.2 in section 5.2. More precisely, the artificial series are $(\omega - \omega^o)/\omega^o$, $(v - v^o)$ and $(p - p^o)/p^o$,

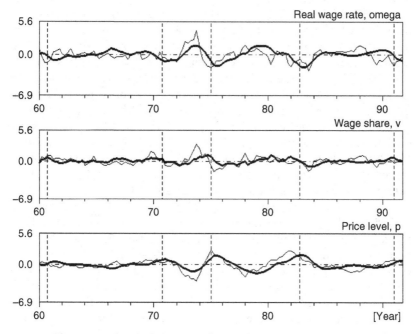

Figure 5.6: Model-generated time series under empirical fluctuations of utilization

[37] Bold (thin) lines are the simulated (empirical) data deviations from steady-state or trend values, respectively (see note to table 5.8). Underlying is PPC and its base scenario.

respectively, all three of them multiplied by 100 (ω^o and v^o being the steady-state values, p^o the HP 1600 trend).

The model-generated series are, of course, much smoother than the empirical series, as the only shocks considered here are those of utilization; the other relationships have upheld their deterministic character. The general visual impression is that the three model variables, including the wage share, are by and large successful in following the main movements of the empirical series, though perhaps with a certain delay. A striking feature is that the variables fail to trace out the high turning points in 1973. This should not be unexpected, however, since the empirical peaks of utilization in 1973 and at the end of the 1970s are about the same size, whereas for ω, v and p the first one of these turning points exhibits a markedly higher amplitude. In other words, the wage-price dynamics of the model does not allow for the apparently special forces that were operating, even after detrending, in the first half of the 1970s.

Regarding the variability of these model variables, table 5.8 reports their standard variations. As has just been pointed out, they are all lower than the empirical statistics given in table 5.1. Note, on the other hand, that the standard deviation of the rate of employment is not much different from that under the sine wave motions of u ($\sigma_e/\sigma_u = 0.66$ vs. 0.69 in table 5.3), and that the standard deviation of the wage share is actually a bit higher than in the sine wave experiments ($\sigma_v/\sigma_u = 0.21$ vs. 0.18 in table 5.7). That the standard deviation of the price level has fallen more than that of the real wage can be explained by the end-of-period effects of the HP detrending of the price level, for which we took the same time interval as the sample period underlying the whole simulation.

Table 5.8 also gives some insights concerning the comovements of the variables. First of all, it has to be taken into account that, because of the deterministic modelling framework, the relationship between utilization and the other variables is closer than observed in reality. In comparing table 5.8 with the empirical statistics in table 5.1 (section 5.2) and the admissible features collected in table 5.4 (section 5.5), we therefore have to look more at the profile of the cross-correlations. Here it is worth mentioning that the employment rate exhibits a shorter lag to utilization than in the sine wave simulations; and, with a one-quarter lag, the maximal cross-correlation coefficient is even at the same place as the empirical one in table 5.1, while the second-highest coefficient occurs at a zero lag vs. the two-quarter lag in table 5.1.

The fluctuations of the real wage, too, exhibit a shorter lag than in the sine wave setting; table 5.6 reports a lag of three quarters, while the maximal cross-correlation is now to be found at two quarters. This reduction is, however, not strong enough to match the empirical zero

Table 5.8: *Statistics obtained from the PPC base scenario under empirical utilization series*

Series x	σ_x/σ_u	Cross-correlations between u at time t and x at time						
		$t-3$	$t-2$	$t-1$	t	$t+1$	$t+2$	$t+3$
u	–	0.49	0.71	0.89	1.00	0.89	0.71	0.49
e	0.66	0.18	0.45	0.70	0.90	0.91	0.83	0.70
ω	0.41	−0.01	0.24	0.50	0.74	0.91	0.96	0.90
v	0.21	−0.66	−0.62	−0.51	−0.33	0.07	0.38	0.60
p	0.36	−0.36	−0.56	−0.74	−0.87	−0.94	−0.91	−0.78

NB: Statistics of the quarterly series, with the same sample period of u as in table 5.1. Regarding $x = \omega, p$, the deviation series is $(x - x^o)/x^o$; regarding $x = u, e, v$, the deviation series is $(x - x^o)$ (where $u^o = e^o = 1$).

lag indicated in table 5.1. On the other hand, the motions of the price level are slightly shifted backward; here the maximal (in modulus) cross-correlation is at a one-quarter lag, against a one-quarter lead in table 5.1 and the contemporaneous turning points under the sine wave of u. The cross-correlations of the wage share, lastly, are broadly compatible with those in table 5.1 insofar as they are positive for $t + \tau$ and negative for $t - \tau$ ($\tau = 2, 3$ quarters). Nevertheless, the simulated series in table 5.8 have a stronger countercyclical element.

While this discussion shows the merits and demerits of the PPC model and our numerical base scenario, one may ask if a suitable change of some of the parameters can bring about a better match with the empirical statistics of table 5.1, especially regarding the standard deviations. There are two sides to this question: a practical one and a fundamental one.

Beginning with a practical improvement of the standard deviations, an immediate candidate is a higher responsiveness of wage changes to the employment rate – i.e. a higher value of parameter β_{we}. A good choice is to raise β_{we} from 0.55 to 0.80. A few explorations with other parameters yield the result that a minor change of the weighting parameter κ_{wp} in the wage Phillips curve also serves our purpose; concretely, raising κ_{wp} from zero to 0.10 may do. Table 5.9 documents the success of this exercise. The standard deviations of both the real wage and the price level are almost the same as their empirical counterparts (considering the end-of-period effects in the latter series). Even the standard deviation of the wage share has considerably increased, at a level that had never been achieved in the sine wave experiments.

The cross-correlation coefficients, on the other hand, are not too seriously affected. There is, perhaps, a weak tendency for slightly longer lags

Table 5.9: *The same experiment as in table 5.8, with $\beta_{we} = 0.08$, $\kappa_{wp} = 0.10$*

		Cross-correlations between u at time t and x at time						
Series x	σ_x/σ_u	$t-3$	$t-2$	$t-1$	t	$t+1$	$t+2$	$t+3$
ω	0.49	−0.07	0.17	0.43	0.68	0.87	0.94	0.91
v	0.25	−0.63	−0.55	−0.40	−0.18	0.19	0.49	0.69
p	0.48	−0.42	−0.61	−0.77	−0.88	−0.93	−0.88	−0.75

of the real wage (stemming from the increase in κ_{wp}), while the profile of the wage share coefficients moves a bit closer to that of table 5.1. The modifications in the cross-correlations of the price level are almost negligible. This overall robustness of the pattern of the cross-correlations, despite the large and favourable changes in the standard deviations of the variables, is quite remarkable.

On this basis we could now try more parameter variations, to improve further on the detailed statistics. A higher value of κ_{wp}, for example, would lead to a further increase of σ_v. These attempts, however, bring us to a fundamental issue. The point is that the historical moments have sampling variability and so can differ from the model's population moments – even if, for the sake of argument, the model happened to be true. (Of course, as laid out in the introduction, there is no such thing as a true model, at least in macroeconomics.) As a matter of fact, the significance of a good match between the simulated and empirical sample moments is an unresolved problem. Given that a model cannot be expected to duplicate reality exactly, we can distinguish between a model variable (denoted by x_t^m, and its empirical counterpart by x_t^e) with error $\varepsilon_t = x_t^e - x_t^m$. To compare the standard deviations of x^m and x^e – i.e. their variances – the identity $\text{var}(x^e) = \text{var}(x^m) + 2\text{cov}(x^m, \varepsilon) + \text{var}(\varepsilon)$ has to be taken into account. As a consequence, if the difference between $\text{var}(x^m)$ and $\text{var}(x^e)$ is viewed as a statement about $\text{var}(\varepsilon)$, as indeed it mostly is, this would require $\text{cov}(x^m, \varepsilon) = 0$ to be fulfilled, which amounts to making an assumption that a priori is not really obvious. But, if one allows for potential correlation between x^m and ε, it might even be possible that $\text{var}(x^m) = \text{var}(x^e)$ despite large errors ε_t, or $\text{var}(x^m) < \text{var}(x^e)$ despite $\text{var}(\varepsilon) \approx 0$.[38]

[38] The problem is hinted at in Kim and Pagan (1995, p. 371). The authors conclude that 'the method of stylized facts really fails to come to grips with what is the fundamental problem in evaluating all small models, namely the assumptions that need to be made about the nature of the errors ζ_t' (ζ_t corresponds to ε_t in our notation). On pp. 378ff., Kim and Pagan elaborate more on the problems connected with the fact that, generally, the errors ζ_t cannot be recovered.

The interpretation of a comparison between, say, table 5.9 and table 5.1 is thus a deep methodological problem, which certainly goes beyond the scope of the book. Therefore, we cannot even say for sure that the results of table 5.9 are preferable to those of table 5.8, so that in the following we may just as well maintain the PPC base scenario. This applies all the more as, in the end, we want to integrate this module into a deterministic full model of the business cycle.

5.10   Conclusion

In this chapter we have examined three submodels of deterministic wage-price dynamics that may be integrated into a more encompassing macroeconomic framework. The models have in common a positive functional relationship between labour productivity and capacity utilization; a positive relationship between capacity utilization and the capital growth rate; an adjustment mechanism for a so-called inflation climate; and a nominal wage Phillips curve with, additionally, a non-standard negative influence of the wage share. Regarding the three alternative model components determining inflation and the price level, the first one postulates a positive relation between utilization and *changes* in the rate of inflation. This accelerationist specification almost directly implies a countercyclical price level (CCP). The second approach advances a price Phillips curve (PPC) augmented by the notion of a target markup, which here, too, brings the wage share into play. The third module formalizes adjustments of a variable markup rate (VMK) on unit labour costs that bear a certain countercyclical element.

This chapter has been concerned with the calibration of these models. The first stage of our numerical investigation was based on stylized sine wave oscillations for utilization as the only exogenous variable. The main goal has been to find plausible parameter values for each model variant such that the endogenous variables exhibit cyclical properties comparable to those that have been established previously as stylized facts for the corresponding (detrended) empirical time series.

The most important cyclical features we sought to reproduce are a procyclical employment rate, a procyclical real wage, a countercyclical price level and the order of magnitude of their standard deviations. Accounting for the latter two characteristics, it turned out that all three models generate a lag of the real wage that is somewhat larger than desired, as well as a fairly low variability of the wage share, unfortunately. The main reason for these shortcomings seems to be the simplified modelling of labour productivity (with no lags). However, once we are willing to pay the price for this and to accept the deficiencies in a set of 'second-best' criteria of the cyclical statistics, each model can be calibrated in a satisfactory way.

The models include several coefficients that weight the influence of certain benchmark terms, such as, for example, the influence of current inflation vs. the inflation climate in the wage Phillips curve. These parameters appear quite innocuous at the theoretical level. It is a side result of the numerical analysis that they nevertheless have a strong impact on the cyclical features of the endogenous variables, so that they, too, must be carefully considered in the calibration procedure. In addition, this finding suggests that the weighting coefficients may also have a non-negligible bearing on the stability properties of a full macrodynamic system.

Adopting suitable parameters, the three inflation modules are highly compatible. That is, given the numerical specification of the wage Phillips curve and the other common model components, one inflation module can be exchanged for another without affecting the cyclical properties too much. This is remarkable, because, theoretically and in their consequences for the structure of a full model, the three modules are quite disparate.

In finer detail we set up three base scenarios, one for each model variant, where the wage Phillips curve combined with VMK nonetheless has different parameters from the curve in the CCP and PPC contexts. One reason for this is different polar values that, ideally, a weighting parameter should attain in order to eliminate from the model the analytically rather inconvenient influence of the growth rate of actual productivity. Another reason concerns the core of the wage Phillips curve with its negative feedback for the wage share. Though somewhat weaker than the influence of the employment rate, this effect must be significant in both the CCP and PPC models, whereas it could be dispensed with in the VMK variant. If there are no other arguments, then, this theoretical and analytical simplification could be an attractive point for a model builder to choose the VMK inflation module. By contrast, in this book we have already made the decision to employ the price Phillips curve in a full model of the economy. In the PPC module, however, the above-mentioned (positive) feedback of the wage share on price inflation must be active and even dominate the influence of capacity utilization.

The base scenarios rely on parameters governing the adjustments of the inflation climate π, which, to limit the degrees of freedom, were fixed freehand at a priori plausible values. Comparing the implied time path of this unobservable variable with survey data, perhaps even proxying π with such data, one might find that alternative coefficients are more suitable in this respect. We suspect that the base scenarios need not be changed much, but, in any case, the calibration could be redone following the methods discussed in this chapter.

Finally, in the second stage of the analysis, we replaced the exogenous sine wave motions of capacity utilization with the corresponding empirical time series. It is an encouraging feature of the base scenarios, and of the modelling approach in general, that the qualitative cyclical behaviour of the endogenous variables was not seriously destroyed. We even obtained slight improvements concerning the lags of the employment rate. The main drawback was that the standard deviations of the real wage and the price level became too low, a phenomenon that could be explained by the apparently special forces operative in the 1970s. Concentrating on the PPC model variant, a moderate change of one or two parameter values was sufficient to raise the standard deviations to the desired level, without the other characteristics being essentially affected. It was, however, also pointed out that we have no firm basis on which to judge whether such a parameter combination really is 'better'. This is a fundamental methodological problem indeed, which is beyond the scope of the present book.

In contrast, let us emphasize the positive result that the whole modelling approach is rich enough, that it can indeed be calibrated to match a number of central cyclical statistics. In conclusion, all three wage-price submodels presented here can be useful workhorses in the (non-orthodox) modelling of small macrodynamic systems.

5.11   Appendix: The empirical time series

The time series examined in table 5.1 are constructed from the data that (at the time of writing this chapter) were made available by Ray Fair on his homepage (http://fairmodel.econ.yale.edu), with a description being given in appendix A of The US Model Workbook. Taking over Fair's abbreviations, the following time series of his database are involved. They all refer to the firm sector – i.e. non-financial corporate business.

HN	average number of non-overtime hours paid per job
HO	average number of overtime hours paid per job
JF	number of jobs
KK	real capital stock
PF	output price index
SIFG	employer social insurance contributions paid to US government
SIFS	employer social insurance contributions paid to state and local governments

WF   average hourly earnings excluding overtime of workers
      (but including supplements to wages and salaries, except
      for employer contributions for social insurance).
Y   real output

The variables in table 5.1 are then specified as follows. For Fair's
assumption of a 50 per cent wage premium for overtime hours, see, for
example, his specification of disposable income of households (YD in
eq. (115), table A.3, The Equations of the US Model).

$y = Y / KK$ (output–capital ratio)
$L = JF \times (HN+HO)$ (total hours)
$e = L/\text{trend-}L$ (employment rate)
$z = Y / [JF \times (HN+HO)]$ (labour productivity)
$w = WF \times (HN + 1.5 \times HO) / (HN+HO)$ (nominal wage rate)
$p = PF$ (price level)
$v = [WF \times (HN + 1.5 \times HO)$
$\quad \times JF + SIFG + SIFS] / [Y \times PF]$ (wage share)

6 Calibration of the full KMG model

6.1 Introduction

In this chapter we continue the calibration begun in chapter 5. Our aim is to provide a full set of numerical parameter values for the Keynes–Metzler–Goodwin model advanced in chapter 4, such that this six-dimensional system produces sustained (deterministic) growth cycles. In addition, the time series properties of the trajectories should be broadly compatible with stylized facts of the business cycle.

Regarding the wage-price dynamics of the KMG model, we can directly take over from chapter 5 the results for the so-called PPC module. This constitutes hierarchy levels 1 to 3 for the simulations in which we postulate exogenous sine wave motions for utilization and the capital growth rate. Moreover, the remainder of the KMG model can, in this respect, be decomposed into different hierarchy levels for the parameter search – levels 4 to 6, as it will turn out. All in all, we will have to determine fourteen behavioural parameters at this first stage of calibration, which does not include in the reckoning several other coefficients related to the steady-state relationships; these will be set on the basis of separate information.

In the second stage, we drop the sine waves for utilization u and instead consider the time series of its empirical counterpart, while the capital growth rate g_k is still presumed to move synchronously with u. It will then have to be seen how all the endogenous variables generated in this way compare to the empirical series. The numerical parameters previously found can be maintained if the cyclical features of the variables do not deteriorate too much in this experiment.

The model is fully endogenized in the third stage. Accordingly, u is treated here as an endogenous variable, determined by the model components that have already been specified before. For g_k, on the other hand, an investment function of the type described in chapter 4 is now introduced. This means that another four parameters have to be set, two of them governing an 'extrinsic' nonlinearity that is built in to prevent the system from totally diverging in the outer regions of the state space.

The other two parameters will be chosen such that the steady-state is (mildly) unstable. As a consequence, persistent cyclical behaviour will genuinely be obtained. The calibration can be deemed successful if this full model, which is a true KMG model of the kind discussed in chapter 4, gives rise to similar cyclical features, qualitatively and quantitatively, to those established at stages 1 and 2.

The chapter is organized into the following sections. The next section presents the stylized facts regarding the variables in the model beyond the wage-price dynamics. This involves the money and the goods market. Section 3 recapitulates calibration levels 1 to 3 of the PPC module from chapter 5 and then puts forward levels 4 to 6 for the rest of the model. Section 4 reports the numerical steady-state (and similar) ratios that we adopt. Subsequently, our search for the parameters at levels 4 to 6 is discussed. Sections 5 offers a synopsis of what has been achieved so far, which completes the analysis at stage 1. Section 6 is concerned with the time series that are generated by the empirical fluctuations of u, stage 2 of the calibration as we have just called it. The fully endogenous model with the nonlinear investment function is studied in section 7. The investigation includes the agreeably regular long-run properties of the model – a prerequisite before we can turn to the evaluation of the cyclical features themselves. Section 8 concludes. Appendix 1 contains information about the empirical data we have used, while appendix 2 discusses recent macroeconometric work, and its results, that can be related to our approach to choosing the investment parameters.

6.2   Stylized facts of the goods market

When evaluating the dynamics of our KMG model, we will be especially concerned with the cyclical behaviour of nine endogenous variables, besides utilization and investment. Five variables relate to the adjustments of wages and prices: labour productivity, z; the employment rate, e; the (productivity-deflated) real wage rate, ω; the wage share, v; and the price level, p. They have been studied in the previous chapter, the empirical time series as well as the model-generated trajectories. Not involved in these investigations were the goods and money markets. In this respect our interest now attaches to four additional variables: excess demand, ξ (in relative terms, $\xi = (Y^d - Y)/Y$, where Y^d are real sales); the consumption ratio, C/Y; the inventory ratio, $n = N/K$ (N the stock of inventories); and the bond rate of interest, i. The empirical counterparts of these variables are depicted as the

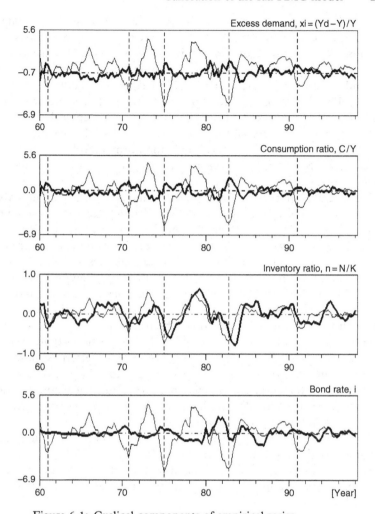

Figure 6.1: Cyclical components of empirical series

bold lines in figure 6.1.[1] For a first assessment of their cyclical properties and the size of their variation, the thin lines reproduce the reference series of capacity utilization u as the measure of the business
cycle.[2]

---

[1] With the exception of the top one, the panels show the differences between the variables
and their trend values (HP 1600), both measured in percentage points. The thin line is
the cyclical component of utilization (in the third panel it is scaled down by the standard
deviation of n).

[2] See chapter 5, section 2, for its construction from the output–capital ratio.

Note that these (quarterly) series x, which are expressed in percentage points, are just the differences $x_t - x_t^o$ between the original values and the trend values, where detrending is again by Hodrick–Prescott with smoothing parameter $\lambda = 1600$. The only exception is relative excess demand ξ, which is plotted directly. Here the reference line is not the zero level but is drawn at -0.657 per cent, which is the time average of the series. We already know from Proposition 2 in chapter 4, section 3, that even in long-run equilibrium excess demand will be negative (since $(y^d)^o = (Y^d/K)^o$ is less than $Y^n/K = y^n$, the normal level of the output–capital ratio). So this time average may be identified with the steady-state value ξ^o.

The crucial point for studying excess demand is the letter 'M' in KMG, for 'Metzler' – the feature that this type of model allows for disequilibrium on the goods market, which is buffered by inventories. It is well known that, in low-dimensional versions of the Metzlerian approach, inventory investment is capable of being strongly destabilizing through an accelerator mechanism. Because the motions of inventories and their feedbacks on the rest of the economy are determined by the variations of excess demand, it is important to have a representation of this latter variable with reliable cyclical properties. The top panel of figure 6.1 shows that relative excess demand $\xi = (Y^d - Y)/Y$ in fact behaves quite systematically: ξ displays a fairly consistent countercyclical pattern with respect to utilization, though at a much lower amplitude than u. The cross-correlations with u computed in table 6.1 give a numerical confirmation of this impression. According to them, the fluctuations of excess demand do not even display significant lags or leads.

Given that, in other model variants, some components of aggregate demand could be specified in a more flexible way than they are at present, consumption may also be considered on its own. Referring to the consumption ratio C/Y, it is seen that this series exhibits similar properties to ξ.

The state variable in the model that keeps track of the evolution of inventories is the inventory ratio $n = N/K$. The third panel in figure 6.1 indicates that the motions of the capital stock and excess demand give rise to markedly procyclical behaviour by this ratio, with a short lag of two or three quarters. The variation of n is, however, quite small (note the different scale of n in figure 6.1).

The final endogenous variable is the bond rate i in the bottom panel of figure 6.1. Since the modelling of the financial sector and monetary policy will remain at a very elementary level, we should be content with meeting only some crude qualitative features of this variable, mainly its long lags behind utilization.

Table 6.1: *Descriptive statistics for cyclical components of quarterly series, 1961:1–1991:4*

		Cross-correlations between u at time t and x at time						
Series x	σ_x/σ_u	$t-3$	$t-2$	$t-1$	t	$t+1$	$t+2$	$t+3$
ξ	0.32	−0.29	−0.39	−0.49	−0.62	−0.52	−0.35	−0.17
C/Y	0.35	0.07	−0.17	−0.43	−0.68	−0.69	−0.62	−0.51
n	0.13	0.01	0.17	0.36	0.59	0.74	0.81	0.79
i	0.36	−0.59	−0.59	−0.50	−0.37	−0.27	−0.18	−0.09

NB: Same series as in figure 6.1. σ designates the standard deviation.

Table 6.2: *Desirable features of macrodynamic oscillations*

Variable x	σ_x/σ_u	Lag x
$-\xi$	0.28−0.35	−0.50−0.50
$-C/Y$	0.30−0.40	−0.25−0.75
n	0.10−0.15	0.00−1.00
i	0.30−0.40	−

NB: Second set of variables. The lags are measured in years.

Just as we did in chapter 5, section 2, for the wage-price dynamics, we now take the statistics of the four variables in table 6.1 to summarize the cyclical features that we ideally wish the KMG model to generate – at least insofar as it exhibits smooth and regular oscillations. Leaving some small play in the numbers, the intervals given in table 6.2 are straightforward. Regarding the cyclical pattern of the bond rate, we cannot be very ambitious because of our theoretical benchmark assumption on monetary policy (a constant growth rate of the money supply) and the extremely simple financial sector (the LM equation). Hence, no particular desired lag for i is put forward.

6.3   The calibration levels

6.3.1   *Recapitulation of the wage-price dynamics*

The wage-price dynamics of the KMG model corresponds to the PPC module of chapter 5. We need not repeat all the detailed equations of this model building block; instead, it may suffice to summarize it directly by the three hierarchy levels of the calibration procedure. This will also put the calibration of our variables in table 6.2 into better perspective.

The first hierarchy level refers to the simplified hypothesis on procyclical labour productivity, $z/z^o = f_z(u) = 1 + \beta_{zu}(u-1)$. Given the exogenous oscillations of utilization u and the (synchronous) capital growth rate g_k, this level determines the motions of the employment rate e. Recall that $k^s = K/z^o L^s$ is capital per hour of labour supplied (in efficiency units), and g_z and g_ℓ are the constant growth rates of trend productivity z^o and labour supply L^s, respectively.

Level 1: Employment rate e (parameter β_{zu})

$$\dot{k}^s = k^s(g_k - g_z - g_\ell) \tag{6.1}$$

$$e = y''uk^s/[1 + \beta_{zu}(u-1)] \tag{6.2}$$

Hierarchy level 2 determines the trajectories of income distribution in the form of the real wage rate $\omega = (w/p)/z^o$ and the wage share $v = wL/pY$. Besides the labour productivity function $f_z = f_z(u)$, the mechanisms here operating are the two Phillips curves, the wage and the price Phillips curve. Regarding the weight coefficient of the growth rate of actual productivity (as opposed to trend productivity) in the wage adjustments, we already know that it can be set equal to zero; so we need no longer refer to κ_{wz}. Level 2 nevertheless still invokes six new parameters.

Level 2: Real wage ω, wage share v (κ_p, κ_{wp}, β_{pu}, β_{pv}, β_{we}, β_{wv})

$$\dot{\omega} = \omega\{\kappa[(1-\kappa_p)f_w(e, v; \beta_{we}, \beta_{wv}) - (1-\kappa_{wp})f_p(u, v; \beta_{pu}, \beta_{pv})]\} \tag{6.3}$$

$$v = \omega/[1 + \beta_{zu}(u-1)] \tag{6.4}$$

$$\kappa = 1/(1 - \kappa_p\kappa_{wp}) \tag{6.5}$$

$$f_w = \beta_{we}(e-1) - \beta_{wv}(v - v^o)/v^o \tag{6.6}$$

$$f_p = \beta_{pu}(u-1) + \beta_{pv}[(1+\mu^o)v - 1] \tag{6.7}$$

Naturally, the target markup rate μ^o and the equilibrium wage share v^o, which show up in the core terms f_w and f_p of the two Phillips curves, are supposed to satisfy the consistency condition $(1 + \mu^o)v^o = 1$.

The rate of price inflation $\hat{p}$, together with the inflation climate π, is treated at level 3. The two additional parameters entering this submodel pertain to the equation governing the ongoing revisions of the inflation climate. These are the general adjustment speed β_π and the parameter κ_π, which weighs the adaptive expectations against the regressive expectations. Incidentally, both coefficients were set freehand to simplify the analysis. In sum, hierarchy level 3 reads:

Level 3: Price inflation $\hat{p}$, inflation climate π (parameters β_π, κ_π)

$$\dot{\pi} = \beta_\pi[\kappa_\pi(\hat{p} - \pi) + (1 - \kappa_\pi)(\pi^o - \pi)] \qquad (6.8)$$

$$\hat{p} = \pi + \kappa[f_p(u, v) + \kappa_p f_w(e, v)] \qquad (6.9)$$

The numerical analysis in chapter 5 and the compromises that we made gave rise to the following values for the nine parameters so far involved:

$$\begin{array}{lll}
\beta_{zu} = 0.40 & \beta_\pi = 1.00 & \kappa_\pi = 0.50 \\
\beta_{pu} = 0.15 & \beta_{pv} = 1.50 & \kappa_p = 0.00 \\
\beta_{we} = 0.55 & \beta_{wv} = 0.50 & \kappa_{wp} = 0.00
\end{array} \qquad (6.10)$$

6.3.2   The money market

The bond rate of interest i is determined by the simple LM equation from chapter 4, section 2, subsection 1. With respect to the money supply M, it may be specified here in the following linear form (which is eq. (3.43) in chapter 3, section 9):

$$M = pY(\beta_{mo} - \beta_{mi}i) \qquad (6.11)$$

In intensive form with output–capital ratio $y = Y/K = (Y/Y^n)(Y^n/K)$ and real balances normalized by the capital stock, $m = M/pK$, eq. (6.11) is readily solved as

$$i = (\beta_{mo} - m/y)/\beta_{mi} \qquad (6.12)$$

$$y = uy^n \qquad (6.13)$$

The responsiveness of money demand is best measured by the interest elasticity $\eta_{m,i}$, which, as before, is conceived of as a positive number. Referring to an equilibrium position with output–capital ratio $y^o = y^n$, a real balances ratio m^o and bond rate i^o, the elasticity is defined as $\eta_{m,i} = (\partial M / \partial i) \cdot (i/M) = \beta_{mi} i^o / (\beta_{mo} - \beta_{mi} i^o) = \beta_{mi} i^o / (m^o / y^n)$. Hence, if for the calibration we choose a value of the interest elasticity, the two coefficients β_{mo} and β_{mi} are computed as

$$\beta_{mi} = \eta_{m,i} m^o / y^n i^o \tag{6.14}$$

$$\beta_{mo} = \beta_{mi} i^o + m^o / y^n \tag{6.15}$$

Using the constant growth rate g_m of the money supply from eq. (4.24), logarithmic differentiation of $m = M/pK$ yields the differential equation

$$\dot{m} = m(g_m - \hat{p} - g_k) \tag{6.16}$$

for the evolution of real balances. Since $g_k(\cdot)$ is exogenous and the time path of $\hat{p}(\cdot)$ is obtained at level 3 of the calibration, no further parameter is needed to determine the solution of (6.16). On this basis, we can then study the implications of different values of the interest elasticity $\eta_{m,i}$ for the motions of the interest rate i. To summarize:

Level 4: Interest rate i (parameter $\eta_{m,i}$)

$$\dot{m} = m(g_m - \hat{p} - g_k) \tag{6.16}$$

$$i = (\beta_{mo} - m/y)/\beta_{mi} \tag{6.12}$$

$$y = uy^n \tag{6.13}$$

$$\beta_{mi} = \eta_{m,i} m^o / y^n i^o \tag{6.14}$$

$$\beta_{mo} = \beta_{mi} i^o + m^o / y^n \tag{6.15}$$

6.3.3　Production and the goods market

The Metzlerian part of the KMG model allows for disequilibrium on the goods market. It is assumed that demand for final goods is always realized, where this demand is satisfied from current production and the existing stocks of inventories, while any excess of production over sales replenishes inventories. Real aggregate demand Y^d is made up of consumption C, net investment in fixed capital I, replacement investment δK (δ the constant rate of depreciation) and real government spending G – that is, $Y^d = C + I + \delta K + G$.

Consumption demand has been put forward as eq. (4.4) in chapter 4, section 2, subsection 1. Formulated in nominal terms it reads $pC = c_p pK + (1 - \tau_w)wL + (1 - s_c)[pY^e - wL - \delta pK + iB - pT^c]$. Here τ_w denotes the tax rate on total wages wL, and the term in square brackets sums up the dividends paid out to the firms' shareholders (profits on the basis of expected sales Y^e) plus the interest on government bonds minus taxes on non-wage income. s_c is the constant propensity to save out of this source of income, and the proportionality coefficient c_p represents the share of consumption expenditures by that part of the population that does not earn income from economic activities (c_p is related to the capital stock because it grows with lower fluctuations than total output Y).

Fiscal policy is supposed to be neutral, with minimal feedbacks on the private sector. This is achieved by regarding taxes as net of interest receipts, $pT^c - iB = \theta_c pK$ with a constant tax parameter θ_c. The second assumption is that government spending G also remains in a fixed proportion γ to the capital stock, $G = \gamma K$, so that aggregate demand is now fully determined. Defining the constant term

$$a_y := c_p + \gamma + s_c\delta - (1 - s_c)\theta_c \qquad (6.17)$$

and normalizing aggregate demand Y^d and expected sales Y^e by the capital stock, $y^e = Y^e/K$, $y^d = Y^d/K$, we obtain

$$y^d = a_y + (1 - s_c)y^e + (s_c - \tau_w)vy + g_k \qquad (6.18)$$

which is eq. (4.42) in chapter 4, section 3. We reiterate that g_k is treated at present as an exogenous variable.

The parameters entering (6.17) and (6.18), however, cannot all be freely chosen. The reason is that we reverse the causality in some of the steady-state relationships. By this we mean that in our calibration procedure we directly assign numerical values to some of the steady ratios that in the theoretical model, are endogenously determined. Hence, some of the previously exogenous parameters are now endogenous magnitudes.

In detail, we shall later directly set the equilibrium values g^o for the real growth rate, v^o for the wage share and $y^o = y^n$ for the output–capital ratio. Having recourse to Proposition 2 in chapter 4, we also have to take into account the fact that the equilibrium values of y^d and y^e in (6.18) derive from y^n, g^o and another parameter β_{ny} (which, as repeated in the next subsection, is related to inventories): $(y^d)^o = (y^e)^o = y^n/(1 + \beta_{ny}g^o)$. β_{ny} will equally be determined in advance, as will the parameters δ, γ and θ_c in (6.17). Considering (6.18) in the steady state and solving this equation with $(y^d)^o = (y^e)^o$ for a_y, we therefore have only two 'free' parameters left on which this magnitude depends, namely the tax rate on wages, τ_w, and the propensity, s_c, to save out of rental income. In explicit terms, a_y from (6.18) and, subsequently, c_p from (6.17) result as

$$a_y = a_y(s_c, \tau_w) = s_c y^n/(1 + \beta_{ny}g^o) - (s_c - \tau_w)v^o y^n - g^o \qquad (6.19)$$

$$c_p = c_p(s_c, \tau_w) = a_y(s_c, \tau_w) - \gamma - s_c\delta + (1 - s_c)\theta_c \qquad (6.20)$$

Being concerned with the motions of relative excess demand $\xi = (Y^d - Y)/Y$, it remains to put

$$\xi = y^d/y - 1 \qquad (6.21)$$

In addition, we are interested in the cyclical pattern of the consumption ratio C/Y. This dominant component of total demand may, for example, become more relevant in models where the rigid proportionality rule for government expenditures is relaxed. Using the above expression for consumption and the tax rule with parameter θ_c, C/Y is given by

$$C/Y = (s_c - \tau_w)v + [(1 - s_c)y^e + c_p - (1 - s_c)(\delta + \theta_c)]/y \qquad (6.22)$$

The variations of excess demand give rise to changes in inventories N, as actual inventory investment is just the difference between production Y and sales = demand Y^d – i.e. $\dot{N} = Y - Y^d$. For the inventory ratio $n = N/K$, logarithmic differentiation yields $\hat{n} = \hat{N} - \hat{K} = (\dot{N}/K) \cdot (K/N) - g_k = [(Y - Y^d)/K]/n - g_k$, or

$$\dot{n} = y - y^d - ng_k \qquad (6.23)$$

Entering the equations for excess demand and consumption are expected sales. In eq. (4.20), firms were assumed to entertain adaptive expectations, which, invoking a steady growth component $g^o Y^e$ and the speed of adjustment β_y, read $\dot{Y}^e = g^o Y^e + \beta_y(Y^d - Y^e)$. The time rate of change of the expected sales ratio $y^e = Y^e/K$ is then obtained from $\hat{y}^e = \hat{Y}^e - \hat{K} = g^o + \beta_y[(Y^d - Y^e)/K] \cdot (K/Y^e) - g_k$, or

$$\dot{y}^e = (g^o - g_k)y^e + \beta_y(y^d - y^e) \qquad (6.24)$$

The following box collects the equations that represent the goods market dynamics. Although the equations require no more input variables (computed previously at a higher level) than the motions of the rate of interest at level 4, we assign them the collective title level 5. Not only would other numbering conventions be more cumbersome, later extensions of the present model might also include the interest rate as another argument in private consumption. We recall that, in particular, the parameters y^n, δ, γ, θ_c and β_{ny} will be determined in advance of the cyclical calibration, so that at the present level we deal only with the savings propensity s_c, the tax rate on wages τ_w and the adjustment speed of the adaptive sales expectations β_y.

Level 5: Excess demand ξ, consumption ratio C/Y, inventory ratio n (parameters s_c, τ_w, β_y)

$$\xi = y^d/y - 1 \tag{6.21}$$

$$C/Y = (s_c - \tau_w)v + [(1 - s_c)y^e + c_p - (1 - s_c)(\delta + \theta_c)]/y \tag{6.22}$$

$$\dot{n} = y - y^d - ng_k \tag{6.23}$$

$$\dot{y}^e = (g^o - g_k)y^e + \beta_y(y^d - y^e) \tag{6.24}$$

$$y^d = a_y + (1 - s_c)y^e + (s_c - \tau_w)vy + g_k \tag{6.18}$$

$$a_y = a_y(s_c, \tau_w) = s_c y^n/(1 + \beta_{ny}g^o) - (s_c - \tau_w)v^o y^n - g^o \tag{6.19}$$

$$c_p = c_p(s_c, \tau_w) = a_y(s_c, \tau_w) - \gamma - s_c\delta + (1 - s_c)\theta_c \tag{6.20}$$

6.3.4   Endogenous utilization

It may have been noticed that, so far, not all the modelling equations from chapter 4 have been made use of. More precisely, the production decisions of firms put forward there have played no role, yet. The point with this building block is that, once we have the level of production determined within the model, the rate of capacity utilization becomes an endogenous variable. So we face the following situation: the exogenous variations of utilization u and the capital growth rate g_k give rise to variations in income distribution (and inflation), which in turn determine aggregate demand, which in turn determines sales expectations and the motions of inventories, from which firms then derive their output decisions and, thus, the utilization of their present productive capacity.

Denoting the endogenously determined value of utilization by u^{endo}, the crucial problem is how such an endogenous time path of $u^{endo}(\cdot)$ compares to the exogenous time path $u(\cdot)$ from which it has been ultimately generated. Ideally, we would like the two trajectories $u^{endo}(\cdot)$ and $u(\cdot)$ to coincide. That is, we are looking for a set of parameters that not only produce acceptable cyclical patterns for the variables already discussed but that also imply that the underlying motions of utilization exhibit a fixed-point property. It goes without saying that we will be content if the time paths of $u^{endo}(\cdot)$ and $u(\cdot)$ are close, while excessively large discrepancies between the two will clearly be discouraging.

The production of firms in the KMG model is given by the sum of expected sales Y^e and desired inventory investment I_N^d. The latter rests on the notion of a desired level of inventories N^d towards which actual inventories are planned to adjust gradually with stock adjustment speed β_{nn}. Again adding a steady growth component, planned inventory changes are $I_N^d = g^o N^d + \beta_{nn}(N^d - N)$. The desired level of inventories, in turn, is related to expected sales by the above-mentioned coefficient β_{ny}: $N^d = \beta_{ny} Y^e$.

The equations here sketched are eqs. (4.19), (4.18) and (4.17) from chapter 4, section 2, subsection 2. Combining them determines the level of production as $Y = Y^e + I_N^d = Y^e + (g^o + \beta_{nn})\beta_{ny} Y^e - \beta_{nn} N$. Division by K gives the endogenous output–capital ratio y^{endo} as a function of y^e and n:

$$y^{endo} = f_y(y^e, n) := [1 + (g^o + \beta_{nn})\beta_{ny}]y^e - \beta_{nn} n \qquad (6.25)$$

Of course, the corresponding rate of capacity utilization is $u^{endo} = y^{endo}/y^n$. As the parameter β_{ny} is set on the basis of other arguments, only the stock adjustment speed β_{nn} enters as an additional parameter influencing the time of endogenous utilization. This takes place at hierarchy level 6 of the calibration.

Level 6: Endogenous utilization u^{endo} (parameter β_{nn})

$$u^{endo} = f_y(y^e, n)/y^n \qquad (6.26)$$

$$f_y(y^e, n) = [1 + (g^o + \beta_{nn})\beta_{ny}]y^e - \beta_{nn} n \qquad (6.25)$$

6.4   Calibration under exogenous fluctuations of utilization

6.4.1   Steady-state values and other constant ratios

This section is concerned with the calibration of levels 4 to 6 of the KMG model. As before, in the first stage we treat utilization and the capital growth rate as exogenous variables that are oscillating in a sine wave manner. Before we can do this, however, a number of more 'technical' coefficients have to be set, namely the steady-state ratios and certain related coefficients. Most of them were not needed in the wage-price dynamics; they show up only in the formulation of supply and demand on the goods and money markets, from hierarchy level 4 onwards. Continuing to denote steady-state values by a superscript 'o', our numerical choice is as follows:

$$g_z = 2\% \qquad g_\ell = 1\% \qquad g^o = 3\% \qquad g_m = 6\%$$
$$y^n = 0.70 \qquad v^o = 70\% \qquad \mu^o = 0.429 \qquad \delta = 9.5\%$$
$$(k^s)^o = 1.429 \qquad \pi^o = 3\% \qquad i^o = 7\% \qquad m^o = 0.140 \tag{6.27}$$
$$\gamma = 0.077 \qquad \theta_c = 0.025 \qquad \beta_{ny} = 0.220 \qquad n^o = 0.153$$

The growth rates of trend productivity and labour supply in the first row and the corresponding equilibrium growth rate of the real variables $g^o = g_z + g_\ell$ are the same as in eq. (5.28). The constant growth rate of the money supply is then given by $g_m = g^o + \pi^o$, where for equilibrium inflation π^o we put 3 per cent.

To check the other data we use the package of empirical time series of the US economy that is provided by Ray Fair on his home page (see appendix 1), which is particularly helpful since it also contains a capital stock series of the non-financial firm sector. With regard to the output–capital ratio, the ratio of the empirical real magnitudes, Y/K, is in the region of 0.90. The price ratio p_y/p_k of the output and capital goods is, however, systematically different from unity. It varies around 0.75 until the early 1980s and then steadily increases up to around 1 at the end of the 1990s. Correspondingly, the nominal output–capital ratio, $p_y Y/p_k K$, first varies around 0.65 and then steadily increases up to 0.90. On the grounds that in a two- or multisectoral context the relevant ratio would be $p_y Y/p_k K$, we prefer to make reference to the nominal magnitudes and choose an equilibrium value $y^o = y^n = 0.70$, which is slightly higher than 0.65.

When employer social security contribution is included in the definition of the wage share, $v = wL/pY \approx 0.70$ results as the time average between 1952 and 1998. Insofar as wages are a cost on the part of firms, entering the definition of profits, this is an obvious convention. Insofar as, implicitly, these receipts from social insurances are included in the theoretical model, they are taxed at the same rate as wages and the rest is, likewise, fully spent on consumption. Taking v^o for granted, the target markup rate μ^o derives from the consistency condition $(1 + \mu^o)v^o = 1$.

The physical depreciation rate of the capital stock given by Fair is lower than the value of δ proposed here. However, what Fair calls (nominal) 'capital consumption' in his identity for profits in the firm sector yields a higher ratio when related to the nominal capital stock $p_k K$. In this way we decide on $\delta = 9.5\%$. Note that the implied equilibrium (gross) rate of return on real capital is $(1 - v^o)y^o - \delta = 11.5\%$, which does not appear too unreasonable.

In the third row of (6.27), the equilibrium value of k^s follows from Proposition 2 in chapter 4, section 3. Thus, $(k^s)^o = 1/y^n = 1.42857$.

Setting the equilibrium values of inflation and the bond rate takes into account the fact that, over the period 1960 to 1998, the real rate of interest is nearly 4 per cent on average. The real balances ratio m is based on a value of 0.20 for M/pY, which is roughly the time average of M1 to nominal output in the last twenty years, when this ratio was relatively stable (as compared to the steady decline until the end of the 1970s). It remains to calculate $m = M/pK = (M/pY)(pY/pK)$, i.e. $m^o = 0.20 \cdot y^n$. In a similar manner, the government spending coefficient γ is decomposed as $\gamma = G/K = (G/Y)(Y/K)$. Here we take for G/Y the average ratio of nominal government demand to nominal output between 1960 and 1998, which amounts to 0.11 (though the ratio varies considerably over different subperiods).

To get an idea of the order of magnitude of the tax parameter θ_c, view taxes on rental income net of interest receipts, $pT^c - iB = \theta_c pK$, as a fraction τ_c of the profit flow $pY - wL - \delta pK$. Dividing the equation $\tau_c(pY - wL - \delta pK) = \theta_c pK$ by pK allows us to express θ_c as $\theta_c = \tau_c[(1 - v^o)y^n - \delta]$. Setting $\tau_c = 0.20$ yields 0.023 for θ_c, and $\tau_c = 0.25$ increases this value to 0.02875. Against this background we settle for the value given in (6.27).

Regarding the ratio β_{ny} of desired inventories to expected sales, we can rewrite the steady state relationship $(y^d)^o = y^n/(1 + \beta_{ny}g^o)$ in Proposition 2 in chapter 4, section 3, as $Y/Y^d = 1 + \beta_{ny}g^o$. On the other hand, in commenting on figure 6.1 the time average of $\xi = (Y^d - Y)/Y$ was reported to be $\bar{\xi} = -0.657\%$. Rearranging these terms as $Y/Y^d = 1/(1 + \bar{\xi})$, we may equate $1 + \beta_{ny}g^o$ to $1/(1 + \bar{\xi})$, which solving for β_{ny} gives $\beta_{ny} = -\bar{\xi}/(1 + \bar{\xi})g^o = 0.220$. This number is also trustworthy since it is close to the empirical time average of the ratio of inventories over total sales.

Lastly, the steady-state value of the inventory ratio n^o is directly computed from the formula in Proposition 2.

6.4.2 Interest rate oscillations

The exogenous sine wave oscillations of utilization and the capital growth rate are, of course, the same as in chapter 5, eqs. (5.26), (5.27). We repeat

$$u(t) = 1 + 0.04 \cdot \sin(\phi t), \quad \phi = 2\pi/8 \tag{6.28}$$

$$g_k(t) = g^o + 0.29 \cdot [u(t) - 1] \tag{6.29}$$

We are thus ready to continue the calibration of the model with level 4 for the bond rate of interest. We take the parameters of levels 1 to 3 as set in eq. (6.10) and make the following investigations on the basis of the time series generated by this wage-price dynamics. Among these variables, at level 4 we need only the time path of the rate of inflation. The evolution of the real balances ratio $m = M/pK$ is then determined by eq. (6.16). With a suitable initial value of m, the ratio oscillates around the steady-state value m^o since, over time, the term $g_m - \hat{p} - g_k$ on the right-hand side of (6.16) (nearly) averages out to zero. Setting the parameters β_{mi} and β_{mo} of the money demand function as done in eqs. (6.14), (6.15) ensures that the bond rate, which is calculated in (6.12), likewise oscillates around its equilibrium value $i^o = 7\%$.[3]

Inspection of equation (6.12) shows that the cyclical pattern of the interest rate is independent of the interest elasticity, as $\eta_{m,i}$ affects only the coefficients β_{mo} and β_{mi} and not the time path of m/y. Since $m(\cdot)$ shortly leads $y(\cdot)$ and the sign of the time derivative of i is given by the expression $\dot{m}\dot{y} - y\dot{m}$, it follows that i still increases when y is already on the downturn (di/dt being still positive when $\dot{y}$ is already negative but so small that $|\dot{m}\dot{y}| < -y\dot{m}$). Numerically, it turns out that the bond rate peaks 1.17 years after u or y, respectively. In this way the bond rate and utilization display less negative correlation than the empirical coefficients in table 6.1, but at least the lag is sizeable. In fact, taking into account the extreme simplicity of the financial sector as well as the chosen specification of neutral monetary policy, this result may even be considered rather acceptable. That is, while a more elaborate financial sector is certainly an important task for future modelling, for the time

---

[3] To be precise, the time average of the inflation rate $\hat{p}$ over a cycle is (very) slightly less than π^o. There is hence a weak upward trend in the time path of m, and a weak downward trend in the time path of the bond rate. It takes more than thirty years, however, for this effect to become directly visible in the time series diagrams.

Table 6.3: *The standard deviation (σ_i) of the bond rate at calibration level 4*

$\eta_{m,i}$	0.08	0.10	0.12	0.14	0.16	0.20
σ_i/σ_u	0.38	0.30	0.25	0.21	0.19	0.15

being the LM specification, together with the constant money growth rate, does not do too much harm.

As the only effect of the interest elasticity is on the amplitude of the bond rate oscillations, $\eta_{m,i}$ may be set at any level desired. Table 6.3 reports the outcome in terms of the relative standard deviation σ_i/σ_u.

A familiar order of magnitude of the elasticity is perhaps $\eta_{m,i} = 0.20$. However, this brings about a fairly low variation of the bond rate. On the other hand, to achieve a standard deviation in the empirical range of $\sigma_i/\sigma_u = 0.36$ of table 6.1, $\eta_{m,i}$ has to be reduced as much as $\eta_{m,i} = 0.10$ or 0.08. The reason for this phenomenon is, of course, the relatively low variation in the real balances ratio M/pK, which is due to the constant growth rate of M. Incidentally, it may be noted that empirically in the pre-Volcker period the bond rate showed much less variation. For example, over the period 1961 to 1975 (which excludes the soaring levels in the second half of the 1970s, rising to more than 14 per cent at the beginning of the 1980s) we measure $\sigma_i/\sigma_u = 0.19$.

As $\eta_{m,i} = 0.10$ or 0.08 appears unusually small, a value between 0.10 and 0.20 may be chosen. Concretely, let us pick $\eta_{m,i} = 0.14$.

6.4.3   Goods market dynamics

Because of the limited compatibility that our still relatively simple modelling framework exhibits with empirical data on the income flows of groups such as 'workers' and 'rentiers', we have some freedom in choosing the numerical values for the latters' savings propensity, s_c, and the tax rate on wages, τ_w. In particular, the presence of the term $c_p pK$ in the consumption function (4.4) allows us to set these parameters somewhat higher than is perhaps usually suggested. The range of a priori admissible values is nevertheless bounded. So, we consider $s_c = 0.60, 0.80, 1.00$ for the savings propensity and $\tau_w = 0.30, 0.35$ for the tax rate. A finer subdivision is not necessary.

First, a quick check should be made as to how these values affect the coefficients a_y and c_p in (6.19) and (6.20). From this side, however, we get no problems. a_y and c_p remain within a reasonable range and do not vary too much with changes in s_c and τ_w. Thus, with $\tau_w = 0.35$, a_y increases from 0.265 to 0.347 as s_c rises from 0.60 to 1.00, while c_p

increases from 0.141 to 0.175. The effect is similar when $\tau_w = 0.30$ is underlying, only that the values are slightly lower.

Since the cyclical characteristics of the variables turn out to change in a monotonic and regular way, it also suffices to report the results for just two selected values of the adjustment speed β_y of sales expectations: $\beta_y = 4.0$ and 8.0. As discussed in subsection 6.3.3, the three parameters s_c, τ_w, β_y constitute level 5 in the calibration hierarchy and determine the time paths of excess demand ξ, the consumption ratio C/Y and the inventory ratio n.

Setting the stock adjustment speed β_{nn} subsequently at level 6 has some influence on the endogenous utilization variable u^{endo}. One may, however, be prepared that, once the time paths of $n(\cdot)$ and also $y^e(\cdot)$ have been determined at level 5, the chances of suitable and meaningful variations of β_{nn} controlling for the cyclical features of $u^{endo}(\cdot)$ are restricted. For this reason, we set a value of β_{nn} simultaneously with s_c, τ_w, β_y and also then have a look at the characteristics of $u^{endo}(\cdot)$. Concretely, β_{nn} is fixed at 3.0. After dealing with these simulation runs, β_{nn} is changed and we examine if the previous results can thus be improved.

Our final choice of the four parameters s_c, τ_w, β_y and β_{nn} can be discussed on the basis of the results given in table 6.4. With respect to $\tau_w = 0.35$, $\beta_y = 8$, $\beta_{nn} = 3$ underlying, it shows the consequences of variations of the savings propensity s_c. An increase in s_c raises the standard deviation of the consumption ratio C/Y and relative excess demand ξ. The increase is not sufficient, however, to reach the desired levels of table 6.2, the gap being larger for excess demand than for consumption. This deficiency cannot be essentially reduced with other values of τ_w and β_y. If we are to maintain the model's otherwise convenient specifications of aggregate demand, then the variability of C/Y and ξ has to be accepted as being confined to the order of magnitude of table 6.4.

Both the consumption ratio and excess demand display a certain tendency for countercyclical movements, though this feature is weaker for excess demand. It is a bit surprising that, despite the imperfections of excess demand, the cyclical features of the inventory ratio $n = N/K$ are within the desired range. This gives us some hope that, in the fully endogenous model later on, the implications of the simplifying assumptions on aggregate demand are not too injurious to the inventory dynamics and its repercussion effects.

Regarding the variations of the savings propensity, higher values of s_c are favourable for the countercyclicality of C/Y and ξ and, weakly so, for their amplitudes as well. s_c is, of course, bounded from above by unity. Since $s_c = 1$ appears too extreme, we may settle for $s_c = 0.80$. An additional argument for this value is that the associated oscillations, under $\beta_{nn} = 3$, of endogenous utilization u^{endo} are rather promising. The standard

Table 6.4: *Cyclical features of variables at calibration levels 5 and 6*

	C/Y		ξ		n		u^{endo}	
s_c	$\tilde{\sigma}$	Lag	$\tilde{\sigma}$	Lag	$\tilde{\sigma}$	Lag	$\tilde{\sigma}$	Lag
0.60	0.22	3.25	0.14	2.50	0.12	0.00	1.04	0.50
0.80	0.26	3.42	0.16	2.92	0.12	0.42	0.95	0.25
1.00	0.28	3.50	0.17	3.08	0.12	0.67	0.91	0.08

NB: Besides the parameters set at levels 1 to 3, $\tau_w = 0.35$, $\beta_y = 8$, $\beta_{nn} = 3$ are underlying. $\tilde{\sigma}$ is the standard deviation of the respective variable in relation to σ_u. The cycle period is eight years.

deviation of $u^{endo}(\cdot)$ is not too different from the standard deviation of the exogenous sine wave $u(\cdot)$, and the two series are almost synchronous. Note that the more desirable features of C/Y and ξ that can be brought about by increasing s_c go at the expense of a lower amplitude of $u^{endo}(\cdot)$.

As a preliminary conclusion it can thus be stated that, given $\tau_w = 0.35$, $\beta_y = 8$, $\beta_{nn} = 3$, setting $s_c = 0.80$ is a good compromise between the conflicting goals regarding C/Y and ξ on the one hand and u^{endo} on the other. The value for the savings propensity is also economically meaningful (within the present framework).

Taking this for granted, we can now ask as to the effects of changing the numerical values of the underlying three parameters. A lower value of the tax rate, $\tau_w = 0.30$, slightly reduces the standard deviation of C/Y and ξ as well as their lags. The latter carries over to lag n. The amplitude of $u^{endo}(\cdot)$ is higher, a little above 1, but the lag is longer, lag $u^{endo} = 0.50$. On the whole, $\tau_w = 0.30$ may be reckoned slightly inferior to $\tau_w = 0.35$, whereas $\tau_w = 0.40$ not only seems too high a value to us but also reduces the standard deviation of $u^{endo}(\cdot)$ by too much.

A slower adjustment speed of expected sales, $\beta_y = 4$, results in a small increase in the amplitudes of C/Y, ξ and n and affects the lags of these variables only marginally. These improvements are, however, more than outweighed by the strong decrease in the standard deviation of $u^{endo}(\cdot)$, the ratio of which to σ_u falls to 0.77 (the lag becomes half a year). It is therefore better if the original value $\beta_y = 8$ is maintained.

As pointed out before, changes in the stock adjustment speed β_{nn} have a bearing on $u^{endo}(\cdot)$ alone. While the impact on the lags of endogenous utilization turn out to be negligible, a reduction of β_{nn} lowers the standard deviation of $u^{endo}(\cdot)$, a phenomenon that could also be analytically inferred from the function $f_y = f_y(y^e, n)$ in (6.25). Numerically, $\tilde{\sigma}$, the ratio to σ_u, decreases to 0.90 if $\beta_{nn} = 1$. On the other hand, $\beta_{nn} = 5$ raises it to 1. For the time being we may, nevertheless, keep to $\beta_{nn} = 3$ for two reasons. This adjustment speed amounts to 1/3 years = 4 months, within which firms in (4.18) seek to close the gap between actual and desired inventories. By contrast, a lag of 1/5 years = 2.4 months might already appear a bit short. Second, at least in low-dimensional models of the inventory cycle, β_{nn} proves to be destabilizing; see Franke (1996). There is a danger for the endogenous model that the centrifugal forces evoked by $\beta_{nn} = 5$ might prove unpleasantly strong.

6.5   Synopsis of the calibration results

For a better overview of what our calibration has done and achieved so far under the exogenous sine wave motions of utilization and the capital growth rate, the numerical parameter values, which amount to fourteen in total, are collected in an extra box.

Table 6.5 lists the cyclical features to which the sine wave simulations give rise. The cyclical statistics of the first five rows have already been reported in chapter 5; see especially tables 5.3 and 5.6, in chapter 5, section 4, subsection 2, and chapter 5, section 8, respectively. Regarding this wage-price dynamics we recall that the statistics may be compared with the previous chapter's desirable cyclical features in table 5.2 (chapter 5, section 2), or the so-called second-best criteria in table 5.4 (chapter 5, section 5). Regarding the cyclical measures of the next four variables in table 5.5, the reference is table 6.2 in chapter 6, section 2. It has just been discussed in what way, and why, these features fail to meet our aspirations expressed these. Lastly, the characteristics of u^{endo} in the final row show that the exogenous and the model-generated time paths of utilization are broadly compatible.

Synopsis of numerical parameters

Level 1:	$\beta_{zu} = 0.40$		
Level 2:	$\beta_{pu} = 0.15$	$\beta_{pv} = 1.50$	$\kappa_p = 0.00$
	$\beta_{we} = 0.55$	$\beta_{wv} = 0.50$	$\kappa_{wp} = 0.00$
Level 3:	$\beta_{\pi} = 1.00$	$\kappa_{\pi} = 0.50$	(6.30)
Level 4:	$\eta_{m,i} = 0.14$		
Level 5:	$s_c = 0.80$	$\tau_w = 0.35$	$\beta_y = 8.00$
Level 6:	$\beta_{nn} = 3.00$		

Table 6.5: *Cyclical statistics of variables under exogenous sine wave oscillations of utilization*

Variable x	σ_x/σ_u	Lag x
$(z - z^o)/z^o$	0.40	0.00
$e - 1$	0.69	0.75
$(\omega - \omega^o)/\omega^o$	0.47	0.75
$v - v^o$	0.18	2.08
$-(p - p^o)/p^o$	0.48	0.00
$i - i^o$	0.21	1.17
$\xi - \xi^o$	0.16	2.92
$C/Y - (C/Y)^o$	0.26	3.42
$n - n^o$	0.12	0.42
$u^{endo} - 1$	0.95	0.25

We reiterate that it could not have been our goal to obtain a perfect match of the cyclical statistics of the empirical series. Moreover, even if we came close to full success in this respect, we would not yet know what it would be worth, as it has to be conceded that the exogenous sine wave motions of utilization u that characterize the first stage of our calibration study are very stylized indeed. It has been said before that the results, which are summarized here in table 6.5, and the way we arrived at them are more heuristic in nature. Nevertheless, it is now time to see how the present set of numerical parameters performs under different conditions, which brings us to stage 2 of the analysis.

6.6   Empirical fluctuations of utilization

To subject the numerical parameters in (6.30) to a second test, we follow the procedure of chapter 5, section 9, and replace the regular sine waves of u with the empirical observations of this variable over the sample period 1960:1 to 1991:4; the motions of the capital growth rate are still synchronous with u, according to eq. (6.29). As before, the simulation itself is run for the monthly discrete-time analogues of the model, after the quarterly series of u has been correspondingly interpolated. The resulting time paths of real wages, the wage share and the price level have already been presented in chapter 5, section 9, figure 5.6. Continuing this check, figure 6.2[4] now displays the three variables that are related to the goods market and contrasts them with the empirical data (the same

---

[4] Bold lines are simulated time series, thin lines are the empirical counterparts. Regarding C/Y and n, they are deviations from steady-state values or trend, respectively.

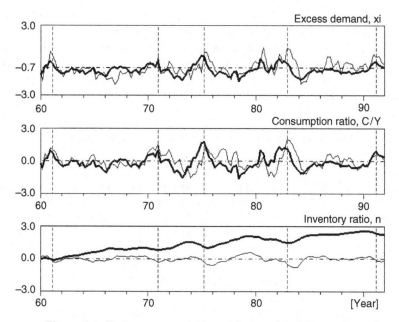

Figure 6.2: Endogenous variables under empirical fluctuations of u

time series as in figure 6.1 above, where, however, the different scale may be taken into account).

In comparing the model-generated variables with their empirical counterparts, the immediate observation in the wage-price dynamics of chapter 5, section 9, was that the former showed a lower amplitude than in reality (a phenomenon that was attributed to the particular forces that took effect in the first half of the 1970s in particular). Remarkably, this bias does not apply to the two demand variables ξ and C/Y. Over the whole sample period of figure 6.2, their standard deviation is also somewhat higher than in table 6.5; for ξ the ratio to σ_u increases to 0.20, for C/Y it increases to 0.30. Hence, the assumptions on the components of aggregate demand are not too bad a simplification. Finally, the slight upward trend in the inventory series, which to be precise is depicted as $100 \cdot (n - n^o)$, is due to the fact that the capital growth rate from (6.29) is not perfectly tuned to the other growth components that make themselves felt in the ratio N/K.[5]

Even without computing further statistics just as the cross-correlations with utilization, we may conclude that the model generates time series

---

[5] This distorting effect is even stronger in the real balances ratio $m = M/pK$, and thus in the simulated time series of the rate of interest.

on the goods market with characteristics, given the relatively simple and deterministic model, that come strikingly close to the empirical features. Interestingly, the degree of noise in the model variables is not much lower, either – at least until the mid-1980s. On the whole, the picture that we obtain here is quite encouraging. It certainly supports the numerical parameters as we have set them in (6.30) at stage 1 of the calibration.

6.7   The fully endogenous model and its dynamics

6.7.1   A nonlinear investment function

The modelling equations provided so far can already be viewed as constituting a fully endogenous macrodynamic model if the exogenous motions of utilization are dropped and $u = u^{endo}$ is obtained from (6.26). Eq. (6.29) for the capital growth rate g_k would then have the status of an investment function. In fact, this equation could be conceived of as the investment function (4.9) in chapter 4, section 2, subsection 2, $g_k = I/K = f_I[r - (i - \pi)]$, with a vanishing partial derivative f_{Iq} (the derivative with respect to the first term).

However, we do not wish to consider the capacity argument alone, $f_{Iu} > 0$, but also the profitability argument, $f_{Iq} > 0$, which we have been using all along in chapter 4 as well as in the precursor models in chapters 2 and 3. This argument refers to the differential returns $q := r - (i - \pi)$, or, spelling out the profit rate as $r = (1 - v)uy^n - \delta$ from (4.10),

$$q = (1 - v)uy^n - \delta - (i - \pi) \qquad (6.31)$$

The investment function is the only component of the model where we specify an extrinsic nonlinearity (as opposed to the intrinsic nonlinearities such as $v = \omega/f_z(u)$, $r = (1 - v)uy^n - \delta$ or similar terms). The need to invoke an extrinsic nonlinearity arises from our methodological approach to persistent cyclical behaviour, which is a deterministic one. In this respect, we should not rely on a Hopf bifurcation, which is so prominent in analytical work. A sufficient reason is that, a priori, we can by no means be sure that the periodic orbits of the Hopf bifurcation are attractive. But, even if they were, we would not know why, because the corresponding conditions are so complicated that only in very special cases can an economic meaning be found in them. Apart from that, we would still have the problem that meaningful cyclical trajectories will exist only over a very small range of parameter values.

Ruling out local asymptotic stability, since the cycles (if they exist at all) would die out otherwise, we are facing the situation that within the vicinity of the steady-state position the trajectories are diverging (almost all of them, to be exact). Moreover, although there are a number of intrinsic nonlinearities in the model, they are only weak, and they are 'dominated' by the many linear specifications in the behavioural functions. It thus turns out that the destabilizing forces are also globally operative. This is precisely the problem that can be treated by building in some additional, extrinsic nonlinearities, such that they take effect in the outer regions of the state space and so prevent the dynamics from totally diverging. Being locally unstable and globally stable, to express it in short, the resulting trajectories must be permanently fluctuating. For our present purpose, we can content ourselves with one extrinsic nonlinearity, which we introduce into the investment function. Besides, this choice appears to be in quite Keynesian in spirit.[6]

A simple idea will prove satisfactory. Suppose that utilization is steadily rising in an expansionary phase. The corresponding positive influence on the flow of investment may be reinforced or curbed by the differential returns q. If, however, utilization has become relatively high, firms will not expect the economy to grow at the same speed for too long. If additionally q is relatively low in that stage, so that this influence on investment is already negative, then the positive utilization motive may be further weakened. That is, we assume that under these circumstances the negative effect from q is stronger than it otherwise is at lower levels of capacity utilization. With signs reversed, the same type of mechanism applies when the economy is on the downturn. Introducing two positive reaction coefficients β_{Iu} and β_{Iq} and referring for simplicity directly to the growth rate g^o and the differential returns q^o in a long-run equilibrium, we specify this concept for g_k, the capital growth rate, as follows:

$$g_k = g_k(u, q) = g^o + \beta_{Iu}(u - 1) + \phi(u, q)\beta_{Iq}(q - q^o) \qquad (6.32)$$

where with respect to given values d_1 and d_2, $0 < d_1 < d_2$, the flexibility function $\phi = \phi(u, q)$ is defined as

$$\phi = \phi(u, q) = \begin{cases} 1 + [u - (1 + d_1)]/(d_2 - d_1) & \text{if } u \geq 1 + d_1 \text{ and } q \leq q^o \\ 1 + [(1 - d_1) - u]/(d_2 - d_1) & \text{if } u \leq 1 - d_1 \text{ and } q \geq q^o \\ 1 & \text{else} \end{cases}$$

$$(6.33)$$

The coefficients d_1, d_2 measure the responsiveness to u. Their order of magnitude can be assessed by the two benchmark cases $\phi = 1$ for

---

[6] Looking back to chapter 3, section 10, an immediate candidate for the introduction of a globally stabilizing nonlinearity is the adjustments of the inflation climate, just as has been done in eqs. (3.44) and (3.45). We will argue in the next chapter that the mechanism employed there is no longer reliable here.

$u = 1 \pm d_1$ and $\phi = 2$ for $u = 1 \pm d_2$. It may also be noted that, though the function $\phi(\cdot, \cdot)$ is not continuous in q, the multiplicative term $\phi \cdot (q - q^o)$ in eq. (6.32) is.

Evidently, for this mechanism to work out it is required that the q series peaks considerably before utilization – a property we have already checked in the sine wave experiments. Being essentially dependent on the relative amplitude of the bond rate and the rate of inflation, the mechanism cannot necessarily be expected to be effective under different circumstances. In this sense, (6.33) represents only a minimal nonlinearity to tame the centrifugal forces in the economy.

On the whole, we now have the differential equations system of chapter 4, with a more detailed investment function, that is. The six state variables, we repeat, are $k^s = K/z^o L^s$, capital per head (measured in efficiency units); $\omega = w/pz^o$, the real wage rate (deflated by trend labour productivity); π, the inflation climate; $m = M/pK$, the real balances ratio; $y^e = Y^e/K$, the expected sales ratio; and $n = N/K$, the inventory ratio (where, clearly, the term 'ratio' refers to the stock of fixed capital). Collecting the equations of the laws of motions in the order as they were presented at calibration levels 1 to 6, the system reads:

$$\dot{k}^s = k^s(g_k - g_z - g_\ell) \tag{6.1}$$

$$\dot{\omega} = \omega \kappa [(1 - \kappa_{pw}) f_w(e, v)$$
$$- (1 - \kappa_{wp}) f_p(u, v)], \quad \kappa := (1 - \kappa_p \kappa_{wp}) \tag{6.3}$$

$$\dot{\pi} = \beta_\pi [\kappa_{\pi p}(\hat{p} - \pi) + (1 - \kappa_{\pi p})(\pi^o - \pi)] \tag{6.8}$$

$$\dot{m} = m(g_m - \hat{p} - g_k) \tag{6.16}$$

$$\dot{n} = y - y^d - n g_k \tag{6.23}$$

$$\dot{y}^e = (g^o - g_k) y^e + \beta_y (y^d - y^e) \tag{6.24}$$

$$u = f_y(y^e, n)/y^n \tag{6.26}$$

$$g_k = g^o + \beta_{Iu}(u - 1) + \phi(u, q) \beta_{Iq}(q - q^o) \tag{6.32}$$

The last two equations for utilization u and the capital growth rate g_k have been added in order to emphasize the difference from stages 1 and 2 of the calibration, where these variables are exogenous. The functions f_w, f_p, f_y and ϕ are specified in eqs. (6.6), (6.7), (6.25) and (6.33), while the auxiliary variables are determined as depending on the state variables as follows: $q = q(u, v, i, \pi)$ in (6.31), $v = v(u, \omega)$ in (6.4), $e = e(u, k^s)$ in (6.2), $\hat{p} = \hat{p}(u, e, v, \pi)$ in (6.9), $i = i(m, y)$ in (6.12), $y = uy^n$ in (6.13) and $y^d = y^d(y^e, v, y, g_k)$ in (6.18).

For easier reference, let us in the remainder of the chapter call the dynamic system in the box (together with the notes just given) 'system KMG'.

6.7.2   Calibrating investment and the long-run dynamics

To simulate system KMG on the computer, it remains to find suitable values for the four investment parameters in (6.32) and (6.33). As has been pointed out in the previous subsection, in order to generate persistent oscillatory behaviour in our deterministic setting the steady-state position needs to be unstable. Responsible for this, given the other parameters as in the synopsis of section 6.5, are the two coefficients β_{Iu} and β_{Iq}. Figure 6.3[7] shows that such combinations exist; we have only to look for them outside the dotted region the pairs (β_{Iu}, β_{Iq}) of which induce local asymptotic stability. According to this parameter diagram it can be said that a stronger impact of capacity utilization on investment

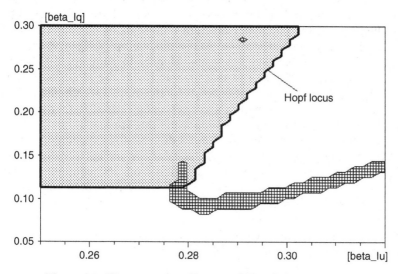

Figure 6.3: The parameter diagram of (β_{Iu}, β_{Iq})

---

[7] The dotted area indicates cyclical stability, and points in the hatched area induce eigen-values with a period between 7.5 and 8.5 years.

(a higher coefficient β_{Iu}) tends to destabilize the equilibrium, whereas a stronger impact of the return differential $q = r - (i - \pi)$ (a higher coefficient β_{Iq}) tends to stabilize it.[8]

From Proposition 4 in chapter 4, section 5, we know that for (β_{Iu}, β_{Iq}) on the stability frontier (the bold line dividing the stability from the instability region) the system undergoes a Hopf bifurcation. The relevant consequence for us is that all combinations (β_{Iu}, β_{Iq}) near the Hopf locus give rise to conjugate complex eigen-values as the leading eigen-values of the Jacobian matrix (i.e. those with maximal real parts), implying that, as required, the system is characterized by cyclical behaviour. It even holds that leading complex eigen-values prevail for all pairs (β_{Iu}, β_{Iq}) in the rectangle shown in figure 6.3, except for a small triangle in the lower right corner, where divergence becomes monotonic (β_{Iu} must then exceed 0.31 and β_{Iq} must be less than 0.07).

While the values for β_{Iu} and β_{Iq} have to be sought in the instability region, we should not move too far away from the stability frontier. A few explorations are sufficient to learn that the destabilizing tendencies soon become very strong, so that the nonlinearity (6.33) in the investment function has difficulty taming the centrifugal forces, or the cycles thus arising look somewhat artificial.

Furthermore, we have to pay attention to the period of the oscillations we obtain, which must not deviate too much from the eight-year period that was already underlying the exogenous utilization sine waves. The hatched area in the parameter diagram represents those pairs (β_{Iu}, β_{Iq}) for which the associated Jacobian has leading complex eigenvalues with a period between 7.5 and 8.5 years. Hence, to sum up, we should try a combination (β_{Iu}, β_{Iq}) in that area and near the Hopf locus (but outside the stability region, of course). In appendix 2 we discuss recent macroeconometric work within a conceptually related framework, the results of which can be taken as supporting this approach.

Since the computer simulations use a discrete-time version of system KMG (a monthly economy, in fact, as has been indicated before), the simulation results may be slightly different from the continuous-time system. We nevertheless soon find that choosing $\beta_{Iu} = 0.280$ and $\beta_{Iq} = 0.115$ gives rise to cycles with a period in the desired range. Setting the nonlinearity parameters d_1 and d_2 at 0.020 and 0.070, respectively, keeps the system within reasonable bounds and produces fairly regular oscillations of the economic variables. So we settle down on

$$\beta_{Iu} = 0.260 \quad \beta_{Iq} = 0.115 \quad d_1 = 0.020 \quad d_2 = 0.070 \qquad (6.34)$$

[8] A deeper numerical analysis will, however, reveal that there are exceptions to this clear-cut characterization. We reconsider this issue in the next chapter.

In detail, the simulations set the system in motion by starting out from a steady-state growth path and disturbing it by a strong temporary shock, at $t = 1$. Concretely, we do this by raising the growth rate of the money supply over the next year from 6 per cent to 8 per cent. Afterwards it is set back to its original level, from when on the economy is left to its own.

Figure 6.4 sketches the shock and its consequences. The positive monetary impulse is shown in the middle panel, which depicts the real balances ratio $m = M/pK$. Though, as seen in the bottom panel, the induced fall in the bond rate is quantitatively rather limited, and has even reverted already within the shock period (after eight months), it is nevertheless sufficient to initiate a distinct expansion. Initially, the increase in capacity utilization is hardly observable in the top panel, but after a while the propagation forces get so strong that u rises to 105.13 per cent. This peak value is reached roughly two years after the money growth rate has first been changed, at time $t = 3.25$. Subsequently, however, the economy steers into a severe recession. Four years after the suspension of the shock, the negative deviation of u from normal is almost twice as large as the previous positive deviation; the trough value $u = 91.33\%$ is reached at $t = 6.08$.

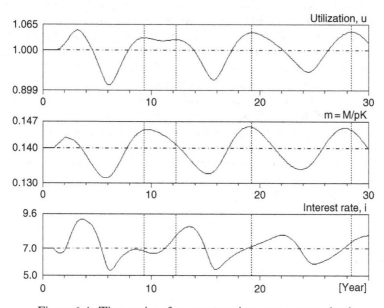

Figure 6.4: Time series after an expansionary monetary shock

With the recovery then setting in, the economy experiences a prolonged expansion. The pattern with the two peaks at $t = 9.33$ and $t = 12.25$ is actually reminiscent of the empirical utilization time series in the 1980s; see figure 5.2 in chapter 5, section 2. Some fifteen years after the shock, the oscillations become more and more regular, and the peak and trough values of the variables tend to level off. Eventually, the trajectories are even almost periodic; that is, the system approaches a limit cycle.

Intuitively, with the steady state being locally unstable and only one essential (global) nonlinearity in the system, the limit cycle should be unique, which means that – starting from different initial conditions – the trajectories of system KMG should always converge to the same periodic orbit. We have checked this conjecture by varying the strength of the initial monetary shock as well as the time interval over which the shock prevails. In all cases it was found that the trajectories converge to the same periodic orbit, though it may take more than a hundred years for the trajectories to come so close to the periodic orbit that they begin to melt into it on the computer screen. At least if the investigation is restricted to this type of initial conditions (starting from the steady state and subjecting the money growth rate to a temporary shock of different intensity and duration), we can thus say that the limit cycle is unique.

The phenomenon of the limit cycle is illustrated by the four phase diagrams in figure 6.5.[9] The limit cycle itself is represented by the bold closed orbits. The solid line exemplifies the convergence of the trajectory described above. Its projections on a plane clearly spiral inwards, but at the time that is shown here, between $t = 40$ and $t = 50$, the distance between the single cycles is already very reduced.

The first panel in figure 6.5 plots the wage share against utilization as the measure of economic activity (the '+' symbol indicates the steady-state values of the variables). The anticlockwise closed orbit of u and v conveys very much the same information as the diagram of the income distribution dynamics in a Goodwin (1967) growth cycle framework (apart from the infinitely many closed orbits in the Goodwin prototype model itself). The upper right panel of figure 6.5 displays the pairs of inflation and utilization as they evolve over time. What results is not a functional Phillips curve relationship but so-called Phillips loops, the anticlockwise orientation of which is indicative of a countercyclical price level. The real wage rate, too, forms no firm relationship with utilization. Instead we observe a similar looping behaviour, though the narrower shape of the loop is evidently different from the previous two variables.

---

[9] The bold line is the unique limit cycle. The arrows are drawn at identical points in time.

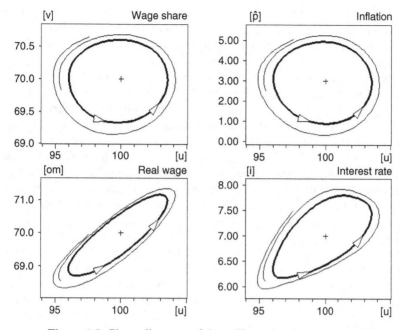

Figure 6.5: Phase diagrams of the calibrated endogenous model

While the loops in these first three panels are fairly symmetric, the panel in the lower right corner shows an example of a variable, namely the rate of interest, with less regularity. It indicates that the lag of the bond rate with respect to u is larger in the upper than in the lower turning point. This pattern had already begun to develop in figure 6.4.

6.7.3   Evaluation of the cyclical features

Having established the basically cyclical behaviour of the economy, we may turn to the time series characteristics of the trajectories. An introductory visual impression is given in figure 6.6,[10] at a time, between seventy-five and one hundred years, where the motions are already periodic for the naked eye. Note first of all the period of the oscillations, which is precisely 8.25 years and so only slightly longer than in our sine wave experiments.

The top panel of figure 6.6 shows utilization u as the central time series of the business cycle. It is contrasted with a sine wave motion – the dotted line – that has the same period and amplitude. The middle panel

---

[10] The two dotted lines are synchronous sine wave motions fitted in.

displays the capital growth rate g_k in a like fashion. It is therefore clear that the endogenous dynamics lets u and g_k move almost synchronously. Moreover, at least at first sight, both series do not differ very much from a sine wave. Hence, we may point out, the approach of specifying the exogenous variables as sine waves in the calibration procedure at stage 1 has not been too inappropriate after all. Besides, the amplitude of u is also of the same order of magnitude as in the calibration experiments.

At a closer look, the differences between u and the sine wave are greater in the expansion than in the contraction, and similarly so for g_k. The reason is that a contraction takes a bit longer: the time from peak to trough is 4.25 years, while the trough-to-peak period is 4.00 years. More consequential for the dynamic properties of the system is the fact that the peak and trough values are not exactly symmetric. Figure 6.6 demonstrates, and table 6.6 makes it numerically precise, that, for u as well as for g_k, the lower turning points deviate slightly more from the steady-state values than the upper turning points. Given the linear specification of the behavioural functions and the strictly symmetric nonlinearity in the investment function, this asymmetry is somewhat surprising. In the end, it must originate with the intrinsic nonlinearities in the model, however weak they are. More directly, it can be seen as

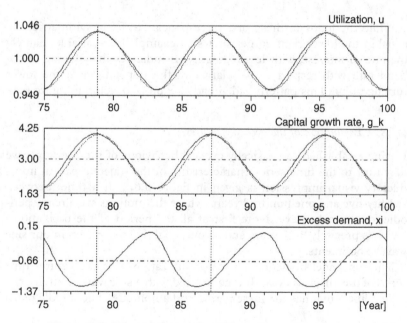

Figure 6.6: Selected time series of the calibrated endogenous model

Table 6.6: *Cyclical statistics of the calibrated endogenous model*

Variable x	x^o	In peak	In trough	σ_x/σ_u	Lag (peak)	Lag (trough)
u	100.00	+3.73	−4.32	−	−	−
g_k	3.00	+1.02	−1.16	0.27	−0.08	−0.08
e	100.00	+2.59	−2.97	0.70	0.75	0.42
ω	70.00	+1.23	−1.40	0.47	0.75	0.58
v	70.00	+0.64	−0.73	0.18	2.25	1.75
$-\text{dev}p$	0.00	+1.90	−2.04	0.50	0.08	0.08
$\hat{p}$	3.00	+2.08	−2.28	0.56	2.25	1.92
π	3.00	+0.87	−0.91	0.23	3.08	2.75
m	14.00	+0.44	−0.46	0.82	−0.58	−0.58
i	7.00	+0.85	−0.88	0.22	1.67	0.58
q	7.50	+0.51	−0.52	0.13	−3.17	−2.33
ξ	−0.66	+0.68	−0.58	0.16	3.83	2.92
C/Y	70.48	+1.12	−0.92	0.25	3.83	3.33
n	15.30	+0.40	−0.47	0.11	0.83	0.83

NB: Underlying is the peak-to-peak cycle from $t = 87.17$ to $t = 95.42$ (i.e. the period is 8.25 years). All variables multiplied by 100. x^o denotes the steady-state value of variable x, dev p is the deviation of the price level from its HP 1600 trend in per cent. The standard deviations of ω and m are divided by the respective steady-state values.

being brought about by the asymmetric timing of the turning points of the q series documented in table 6.6 (which can be traced back to the interest rate; see below) and its impact on investment.

   The table states in addition that the capital growth rate has a short lead of one month with respect to utilization. Admittedly, a lag would have been 'preferable', but with $g_k = g_k(u, q)$ this is impossible when q leads u. Comparing the peak and trough values of u with the coefficients d_1 and d_2 in (6.34), and observing the long lead of q in table 6.6, makes it clear that the nonlinearity in (6.32), (6.33) does indeed take effect. The particular choice of the two parameters accomplishes the desired feature that the standard deviation of g_k relative to that of u is about the same as for the empirical series in table 5.1 in chapter 5, section 2.

   In a similar manner to what the phase diagram in figure 6.5 has already indicated for the bond rate, excess demand ξ is a second variable the upper and lower turning points of which have different lags with respect to u. The bottom panel in figure 6.6 demonstrates that the peak in ξ moves quite close to the trough in u, whereas more time elapses from the trough in ξ until u reaches its peak. The numerical lags given in table 6.6 can also be read as saying that $-\xi$ leads utilization by 0.42 years in the trough and by 1.08 years in the peak. Excess demand has thus become more countercyclical than in the sine wave simulations (see table 6.5), where ξ also showed no apparent differences in its behaviour around the upper and lower turning points.

If we take the sine waves of u and g_k as a reference scenario then the high sensitivity of the cyclical features of the excess demand variable to the relatively minor changes in the time series of u and g_k can be explained by the very definition of ξ, which involves a *ratio* of two variables, y^d and y. Thus, $\xi = y^d/y - 1$ can be quite 'self-willed', although y is practically the same as u itself and y^d lags y by only one month in the peak as well as in the trough (the peaks and troughs are, however, 0.023 and 0.026 above and below $(y^d)^o = 0.695$). On the other hand, the implications of excess demand for the inventory ratio n, via the *difference* between y^d and y in (6.23) for $\dot{n}$, are confined to asymmetric peak and trough values of n. Their timing is again symmetric, with the lags being a little longer than in table 6.5 but within the desired range given in table 6.2.

A similar result to that for ξ holds for the consumption ratio C/Y (which likewise has somewhat improved in its countercyclicality) and for the rate of interest, where the differences in the lags at peak and trough times are even greater. The latter effect is just as remarkable as it was for ξ, since i depends on the ratio m/y according to (6.12), but m displays no asymmetry at all in the timing of its turning points. The irregularity in the cyclical pattern of the bond rate is also mainly responsible for a similar phenomenon in the abovementioned differential returns $q = r - (i - \pi)$, though it is shifted in time. Interestingly, the mean value of the lags 1.67 and 0.58 of the bond rate is nearly the same as its lag of 1.17 years in the sine wave scenario, which generated fairly symmetrical motions of i.

The inflation rate, too, exhibits different lags of its turning points. They are, however, completely washed out in the integrated series of the price level, which is almost perfectly countercyclical. Besides, the difference in the peak and trough lags of $\hat{p}$ is the same as for the inflation climate π, even though, as eq. (6.9) and the standard deviations of $\hat{p}$ and π show, the inflation rate is predominantly influenced by the price Phillips curve term $f_p = f_p(u, v)$ (the term $f_w = f_w(e, v)$ does not feed back on $\hat{p}$ because of $\kappa_p = 0$).

All the asymmetries that have been pointed out have no effect on the amplitude of the variables. The standard deviations in table 6.6 are therefore practically the same as those resulting from the sine wave calibration in table 6.5. We take this as another aspect corroborating our heuristic stage 1 approach to calibration.

Finally, in complementing the synopsis (6.30), it will be convenient to summarize the numerical parameter values of the scenario on which we have finally decided in an extra box.

The final parameter scenario

Level 1: $\beta_{zu} = 0.40$

Level 2: $\beta_{pu} = 0.15$ $\beta_{pv} = 1.50$ $\kappa_p = 0.00$
$\beta_{we} = 0.55$ $\beta_{wv} = 0.50$ $\kappa_{wp} = 0.00$

Level 3: $\beta_\pi = 1.00$ $\kappa_\pi = 0.50$

Level 4: $\eta_{m,i} = 0.14$ (6.35)

Level 5: $s_c = 0.80$ $\tau_w = 0.35$ $\beta_y = 8.00$

Level 6: $\beta_{nn} = 3.00$

Closing $\beta_{Iu} = 0.280$ $\beta_{Iq} = 0.115$
the model: $d_1 = 0.020$ $d_2 = 0.070$

6.8   Conclusion

The last three chapters have been concerned with a complete deterministic macromodel of the business cycle that takes up elements that may be connected with, in particular, the names of Keynes, Metzler and Goodwin. While chapter 4 introduced the model and provided a mathematical stability analysis, chapters 5 and 6 have aimed at a calibration of the model's parameters for the global dynamics. This procedure was organized in a hierarchical structure, so that the numerical coefficients did not all need to be determined simultaneously but could be chosen step by step. Given stylized sine wave oscillations of two exogenous variables, capacity utilization and the capital growth rate, each step gave rise to motions of some endogenous variables. Their cyclical pattern could then be compared to the behaviour of their empirical counterparts. These investigations constituted stage 1 of the calibration.

The analysis at that stage has ended up with numerical values of, in total, fourteen parameters. At stage 2 the exogenous sine waves of utilization were replaced with the corresponding empirical time series. In this way it was checked that the cyclical features found at the first stage did not change too much, which gave us more confidence in the parameter values.

Subsequently, in the third stage, the hitherto exogenous variables were endogenized. This meant that, as the last component of the model, an investment function had to be specified, which added another four numerical parameters. They were set such that the steady-state position of the fully endogenous model became unstable, while a suitable non-linearity in the investment function prevented the system from totally diverging. Hence, the model produces persistent cyclical behaviour. In the long run it actually takes the form of a limit cycle, which is seemingly unique.

The main characteristics of the model's time series, their variability and comovements, may be judged to be by and large satisfactory. Specifically, this concerns the more or less procyclical movements of the capital growth rate, the employment rate, the (productivity-deflated) real wage and the inventory ratio (relative to the capital stock), as well as countercyclicality in the price level, relative excess demand and the consumption ratio (the latter two variables in terms of total output). Given the still limited scope of the modelling framework, a number of compromises had to be made and not all of the cyclical statistics could be perfect. The discussion made clear, however, that calibration is a multi-objective problem, and that in the end we exploited the model's potential to the extent that a single statistic could hardly be improved any further without seriously affecting another one.

To sum up, it may be claimed that the results we arrived at can stand comparison with the properties generated by the competitive equilibrium models of the real business cycle school. Thus, not only at the purely theoretical but also at the quantitative level, we now have available a viable alternative to this ruling paradigm in the analysis of business cycles.

6.9   Appendix 1: The empirical time series

The empirical time series studied in this chapter are constructed from the same data base by Ray Fair, as documented in the appendix to chapter 5. In addition to the variables described there, we have made use of the following raw data.

CD   real consumption expenditures for durable goods
CN   real consumption expenditures for nondurable goods
CS   real consumption expenditures for services
RB   bond rate (percentage points)
V   real stock of inventories
X   real sales

The four variables examined in figure 6.1 and table 6.1 are specified as follows.

$$\xi = 100 \times (X - Y)/Y \qquad \text{(relative excess demand)}$$
$$C/Y = 100 \times (CD + CN + CS)/Y \qquad \text{(consumption ratio)}$$
$$n = V/KK \qquad \text{(inventory–capital ratio)}$$
$$i = RB \qquad \text{(nominal interest rate)}$$

6.10   Appendix 2: A semi-structural econometric model and its eigenvalues

In this appendix we indicate that our methodological approach of a locally unstable steady-state position is not necessarily in contradiction to the results of advanced econometric research. To this end, we refer to a macroeconometric modelling framework that has been developed over the years by A. R. Bergstrom and others, and estimated with data on the British economy. A prototype version dates back to Bergstrom and Wymer (1976), while a fairly elaborated model to work with is Bergstrom et al. (1992). The latter has been recently improved by Bergstrom and Nowman (1999), the improvement consisting in replacing the deterministic trends with unobservable stochastic trends (assuming a Brownian motion) and the formulation as a system of mixed first- and second-order differential equations (the 1992 model was a system of second-order equations only).

The 1999 model is a system of eighteen nonlinear differential equations of first and second order that contains sixty-three structural parameters. These are three trend or drift parameters, thirty-three long-run parameters related to steady-state relationships and twenty-seven speeds of adjustment. The estimation of this type of continuous-time model requires more than standard procedures and has become possible through recent progress in econometrics, where Bergstrom (1997) has provided a suitable algorithm. Very sketchily, the algorithm applies to the linearized model with white noise added, and the parameter estimates are obtained by maximizing the Gaussian likelihood function, which is derived from a so-called VARMAX model satisfied by the discrete observations generated by the continuous-time system (Bergstrom and Nowman, 1999, p. 21).

The model is also specified in such a way that its deterministic version gives rise to an explicit long-run equilibrium growth path, the stability or instability of which can then be assessed. One unifying construction principle prevails, namely that nearly every equation has the form of a partial adjustment equation, or error-correction equation in more econometric terms. Accordingly, the dependent variable is continuously adjusting in response to the deviation of its current level from a partial equilibrium level, which is a function of other variables in the model and so generally varies over time. In this respect – reference to a steady state, allowing for disequilibrium phenomena and seeking to close the disequilibrium gaps in a gradual manner – the model is at a similar conceptual level to ours.

On the other hand, the Bergstrom model has less structure than the KMG model. In particular, expectations or a 'climate' perceived by the agents are not made explicit, and budget relationships, on the consistency of which across the economy we put so much emphasis in chapter 4, section 2, subsection 5, are disregarded. Apart from the adjustment principle as such, economic theory enters the specification of the partial equilibrium levels, which allows the model builders to obtain a parsimonious parameterization and cross-equation restrictions. For these reasons we have called the Bergstrom model a semi-structural model in the title of the appendix.

The core of the model are eight error-correction equations for the following domestic macroeconomic variables: consumption, employment, residential fixed capital, private non-residential fixed capital, output, the price level, the nominal wage rate and the bond rate of interest.[11] The other adjustment equations cover the foreign relationships of the economy. Apart from the foreign sector, the scope of the Bergstrom model is therefore also much the same as ours.

To illustrate the nature of the Bergstrom model, its affinity with the KMG model and the conceptual differences to it, we can give three examples of adjustment equations: eqs. (4), (5) and (1) from Bergstrom and Nowman (1999). Regarding the notation, we change the symbols for the variables to ours but maintain their parameter symbols. The first adjustment equation is for fixed (non-residential) investment,

$$\dot{g}_k = \gamma_6(g^o - g_k) + \gamma_7 \ln\left[\frac{\beta_5 y^{1+\beta_6}}{i - \hat{p} + (1 - \beta_{10})\hat{p} + \beta_{11}}\right] \quad \text{(A1)}$$

The equation comprises two elements. First, there is always a tendency of the current capital growth rate g_k to return to the equilibrium value g^o. Second, the term in square brackets captures a disequilibrium of returns to the firms. It represents the ratio of the marginal product of capital to the real interest rate plus a risk premium. With respect to the former, a CES production function is underlying with $1/(1 + \beta_6)$ as the

---

[11] The equations are complemented by an identity for the change in inventories.

elasticity of substitution between labour and capital. With respect to the risk premium, it is constant if $\beta_{10} = 1$, but generally the risk premium is permitted to be related to the inflation rate (the estimate is indeed $\beta_{10} = 0.1535$). β_5 is essentially a scaling parameter taking care that the fraction is unity in long-run equilibrium.

If we go back to the Sargent model in chapter 2, then (A1) can be viewed as a slightly extended accelerated version of eq. (2.41), which reads

$$g_k = \beta_{Io} + \beta_{Iq}[\alpha_y y - \delta - (i - \pi)]$$
$$= g^o + \beta_{Iq}[\alpha_y y - \delta - (i - \pi) + (\beta_{Io} - g^o)/\beta_{Iq}] \qquad \text{(A2)}$$

Neglecting the rate of depreciation, the only difference to (A1) is that here a Cobb–Douglas function is supposed and the risk premium is constant.[12] For the behaviour of a dynamic system it may, of course, be a great difference whether it is the level of a variable (g_k) or its rate of change $(\dot{g}_k)$ that reacts to some disequilibrium gap. In a general verbal discussion of the theoretical content of a model, however, this aspect appears to be more technical and of secondary importance. In this sense it can be said that the investment functions (A1) and (A2) are on the same theoretical footing.

The second adjustment equation is the error-correction mechanism for total output,

$$\hat{Y} = g^o + \gamma_8 \ln[\tilde{\beta}(1 + \beta_{14}g^o)Y^d/Y] + \gamma_9 \ln[\beta_{14}Y^d/N]$$

$\tilde{\beta}$ is the proportion of total supply met from domestic output, as opposed to imports, which in particular varies with the exchange rate. For a comparison with our closed economy, we may simplify to $\tilde{\beta} = 1$.

Bergstrom and Nowman (1999, p. 9) read the two terms in square brackets as the ratio of the partial equilibrium level of output to the current level of output, and the ratio of the partial equilibrium level of inventories to their current level. The expression $1 + \beta_{14}g^o$ 'ensures that, in the state of partial equilibrium, total supply, from output ..., is sufficient to meet current sales and keeps stock growing at the rate $\lambda_1 + \lambda_2$ [$= g^o$], maintaining a constant ratio β_{14} of stocks to sales'. β_{14} can thus be identified with our inventory–sales ratio β_{ny}.

---

[12] Abbreviating the term in square brackets in (A1) as A/B, observe that $\gamma_7 \ln(A/B) \approx \gamma_7(A/B - 1) = (\gamma_7/B)(A - B)$. That is, the two rates of return A and B in (A1) can also be related to each other as a difference, rather than a ratio (if in the theoretical discussion we ignore the variations of the modified coefficient γ_7/B).

To relate this adjustment equation to the concept of determining total output in the KMG model, use the same argument as in the previous footnote and let us approximate the equation as

$$\hat{Y} = g^o + \gamma_8[(1 + \beta_{ny}g^o)(Y^d/Y) - 1] + \tilde{\gamma}_9[\beta_{ny}Y^d - N] \qquad (A3)$$

(with $\tilde{\gamma}_9 = \gamma_9/N$). Both square brackets in (A3) play a role in the KMG model, too. As for the first one, with eqs. (4.19), (4.18) and (4.17) from chapter 4 we get

$$Y = (1 + \beta_{ny}g^o)Y^e + \beta_{nn}[\beta_{ny}Y^e - N]$$

and assuming myopic perfect foresight, $Y^e = Y^d$ (since expectations do not show up in the Bergstrom model), the final expression in (A3) and this equation are seen to coincide. Second, consider our adaptive expectations for sales (4.20) and approximate the ratio Y/Y^e by its long-run equilibrium value $1 + \beta_{ny}g^o$. Then

$$\hat{Y} = (\hat{Y} - \hat{Y}^e) + \hat{Y}^e$$
$$= (\hat{Y} - \hat{Y}^e) + g^o + \beta_y[(Y^d/Y)(Y/Y^e) - 1]$$
$$= (\hat{Y} - \hat{Y}^e) + g^o + \beta_y[(1 + \beta_{ny}g^o)(Y^d/Y) - 1]$$

and the final term coincides with the first term in square brackets in (A3). On the whole, the relationship of the production decisions of firms in the KMG model to the output adjustment equation in the Bergstrom model is looser than was the case with investment, but certain common features can still be recognized.

The third example from Bergstrom and Nowman (1999) is the determination of private consumption. The changes in this variable are governed by an error-correction mechanism as well,

$$\hat{C} = g^o + \gamma_1 \ln[C^*(Y^D, i - \hat{p})/C] \qquad (A4)$$

where C^*, the partial equilibrium level of consumption, depends (positively) on real disposable income Y^D (correctly 'netted out' by current inflation) and (negatively) on the real interest rate $i - \hat{p}$. Here we have a greater conceptual difference from our consumption function in eq. (4.4), beyond the mere fact that, for simplicity, possible interest rate effects are disregarded there. Recall that our approach distinguishes different groups of income receivers in the economy. It takes their flows of disposable income as a basis and splits it up into savings and consumption, where the proportion is given by a constant propensity to save.[13] We chose this approach not only because it has a long tradition in small-scale structural Keynesian models but also as an element that allows us to keep track of the accounting in the economy.

These three adjustment equations from the Bergstrom model may be representative enough to point out its philosophy: it is a mixture of standard economic theory and somewhat mechanistic adjustment equations, which seem to spring more from econometric convenience than from arguments about the agents' actual, reasonable behaviour in disequilibrium. On the other hand, at a general theoretical level the model still shows a number of common elements with the Sargent model or our more elaborated KMG model, even if the precise specifications differ. Therefore, the dynamic properties of the Bergstrom model as they result from its econometric estimation may also be of some interest to us.

Bergstrom and Nowman (1999) evaluate the outcome of their estimation of the model on the basis of several criteria. First, they note that all sixty-three structural parameters have plausible values. Only one of them attains a boundary value that has been imposed on the estimation in advance.[14]

The second criterion, which is the most relevant for us, is provided by the stability analysis of the steady-state solution. To this end, three of the estimated structural parameters are changed to – it is argued – more realistic values. One of them implies that inflation is zero in the steady state (which looks a bit peculiar, though it will be expected that the main characteristics of the model are only marginally affected). Accepting these modifications, the authors then compute the eigen-values of the Jacobian matrix. The leading eigen-value that generically determines the local out-of-equilibrium dynamics comes out as $\lambda = a \pm bi = 0.162 \pm 0.155i$, where the underlying unit of time is one quarter. The authors stress the realism of this result: not only is the system's behaviour cyclical in nature but the period to which the imaginary part gives rise is roughly ten years.[15]

Equally remarkable is the instability of the steady state. This suggests that the situation in the parameter space is similar to figure 7.3 in chapter 7, section 2, for our KMG model. The stability and instability region are divided by a manifold of parameter values at which

---

[13] If we were to make consumption more flexible then it would be most natural to conceive of such a savings propensity as an endogenous variable (being dependent, for example, on the real interest rate).

[14] This is a markup parameter, the consequence being that the benchmark case of perfect competition prevails.

[15] The period T is calculated as $T = 2\pi/b = 2\pi/0.155 \approx 40.5$ quarters ≈ 10.13 years.

a Hopf bifurcation occurs, and the parameter combination on which the authors settle lies in the instability region.[16] We can therefore say that our approach of selecting the parameter values outside the stability region, but such that the leading eigen-value generates cyclical behaviour with a realistic business cycle frequency, is supported by econometric work within a qualitatively related modelling framework, where the same features result from a sophisticated estimation procedure.

In concluding our discussion of the Bergstrom model, we may criticize the fact that, in another respect, the leading eigen-value obtained there is not so realistic. This concerns the speed at which the system diverges from the steady state, which is represented by the term e^{at} that is associated with the above $\lambda = a \pm bi$. As an example, consider the time t it takes according to this eigen-value until a given distance from the steady state is doubled. Solving the equation $e^{at} = 2$ for t yields $t = \ln 2/a = 0.693/0.162 \approx 4.3$ quarters. This indicates that the centrifugal forces are very strong.

At least in Bergstrom and Nowman (1999) the authors are not interested in this kind of information from the eigen-value analysis. After noting that their estimation produces an explosive cycle, they just mention that 'the cycle can be prevented from exploding by taking account of constraints, such as a "full employment" ceiling, as proposed by Hicks (1950)' (Bergstrom and Nowman, 1999, pp. 23f.). This remark is somewhat gratuitous since, in particular, it is unclear how such a nonlinearity should be built in given the limited structure of the model. Because of the strong destabilization it would, moreover, be extremely hard for every nonlinear mechanism to work out, or the resulting cyclical pattern would look too unrealistic when it crawls along an explicit or implicit ceiling for an excessively long time.

To return to the KMG model, however, these are difficulties that we have avoided by construction, in that the investment coefficients β_{Iu} and β_{Iq} have been chosen not too far away from the Hopf bifurcation locus.[17] But, even for eigenvalues at a greater distance from the stability frontier, the richer structure of the KMG model would probably give us more options to tame the centrifugal forces by a suitable nonlinearity.

---

[16] If not on the whole parameter space, the statement on the Hopf bifurcation may at least apply in a wider neighbourhood of the final parameter scenario. Besides, for Bergstrom's 1992 model the existence of a Hopf locus has been verified by Barnett and He (1998).

[17] Interestingly, the estimation of Bergstrom's 1992 model yields a parameter combination that is practically just on the borderline between stability and instability, where, however, the character of the bifurcation is unclear. Concretely, the leading eigen-values are $\lambda_1 = 0.0033$ and $\lambda_{2,3} = 0.0090 \pm 0.0453i$. Note that here the period implied by the complex eigen-value is almost thirty-five years.

7 Subsystems and sensitivity analysis of the KMG model

7.1 Introduction

The main result of chapter 4 was the mathematical proposition that the steady state of the six-dimensional KMG model is locally asymptotically stable if certain reaction parameters are sufficiently small. The statement may suggest that these coefficients are destabilizing, in the sense that higher values cause the system to lose its stability. It is almost hopeless, however, to extend the mathematical analysis such that it can verify or falsify this conjecture. Therefore, if we want to gain deeper insights into the stabilizing or destabilizing role of the parameters, we have to turn to a different approach. Generally, we may choose between the following two options: either the mathematical treatment is restricted to a suitable low-dimensional submodel of the full system, or the KMG model is maintained as it stands and a numerical investigation is conducted.

Sections 7.2 to 7.4 are mainly, though not exclusively, devoted to the first alternative. Three two- or three-dimensional subdynamics are considered in turn. In short, these are the inventory dynamics (section 7.2), the real wage dynamics (section 7.3) and the monetary dynamics (section 7.4). These models, or at least the feedback mechanisms portrayed by them, are rather well known in the literature on Keynesian macrodynamics. The submodels will thus make more precise how the whole KMG model is rooted in the Keynesian tradition. Referring to the most prominent representatives, the first submodel can be said to isolate the Metzlerian part of KMG, the second one is basically influenced by the work of Goodwin and Rose, while the third one, in particular, has some Tobinian elements in it.

After identifying the basic feedback loops in the submodels, which, of course, are also a constituent part of the full model, our interest attaches to the key parameters in these model components and how their stabilizing or destabilizing effects relate to those in the full KMG model. In each of the submodels it will be possible to derive analytical stability conditions. As this kind of analysis, in our case as well as in macroeconomic theory in general, has always been undertaken in the expectation that the results from the partial models will find some reflection in a more encompassing model, and since we now have available a numerical basis for the latter, we should examine whether, or to what extent, these hopes are warranted in our setting. In fact, to anticipate a general finding, the low-dimensional models are not always a reliable guide to the parameters' stability properties in the full model.

From section 7.5 on the analysis again focuses exclusively on the six-dimensional KMG model. Section 7.5 itself is still concerned with local stability, and performs a thorough and extensive numerical investigation. In essence, it addresses thirteen central adjustment parameters. Taking the calibrated values as a point of reference, it aims at classifying these coefficients as (by and large) stabilizing, destabilizing or ambiguous. This evaluation is based on several sorts of parameter diagrams, where we can study the shape of the stability regions (i.e. the set of parameter combinations that give rise to local stability). Broadly speaking, in this way we arrive at a map of parameter stability effects, or – better, perhaps – at different maps on different scales. Table 7.3 in subsection 7.5.3 constitutes a concise message to take home.

Section 7.6 turns to the global dynamics of the model. Three themes are dealt with. First, we know from chapter 4 that, if in varying a parameter the steady state loses stability, a Hopf bifurcation occurs. This means that for certain parameter configurations periodic orbits exist, even in the absence of the stabilizing extrinsic nonlinearity in the investment function. In this respect we are looking for periodic orbits that are not only known to exist but that also turn out to attract other trajectories that do not start out on them.

Back to the normal case, where periodic orbits arising from a Hopf bifurcation are no longer effective, we consider the time series characteristics of the trajectories. As discussed in chapter 6 section 7, the base scenario yields a unique and globally attracting limit cycle, which is also quite regular. This feature was very convenient for a study of the variability and the comovements of the variables. What we now ask is whether a suitable change of a few parameter values can also lead to richer fluctuations. Specifically, the single cycles might have a varying amplitude, though they do not tend to die out, or there might even exist no limit cycle with strictly periodic behaviour (at least, not in a practical sense).

The third theme in section 7.6 is fiscal policy as an obvious candidate to stabilize an otherwise unstable economy. To this end, we relax our assumption on neutral government expenditures and add a countercyclical element to them. In a thus modified KMG model we study the impact of varying degrees of countercyclicality on local stability.

Regarding the global dynamics, we additionally examine if the amplitude of the oscillations in the base scenario is damped by a countercyclical policy. Section 7.7 concludes.

7.2   The Metzlerian subdynamics

7.2.1   *Mathematical two-dimensional stability analysis*

The Metzlerian part of the KMG model is concerned with the dynamic implications of goods market disequilibrium and the firms' decisions to buffer it by inventory investment. Focusing on these aspects in a suitable submodel, we therefore abstract from the monetary aggregates as well as from inflation and the real wage movements. Referring directly to the model in intensive form, this means we freeze the real balances ratio m, the inflation climate π and the real wage rate ω at their steady-state values, thus eliminating three dynamic equations from the KMG model formulation (4.44)–(4.49) in chapter 4, section 3. Capital per head k^s can then be ignored as a fourth variable, since it enters the determination only of the employment rate, which in turn has a bearing only on the wage-price dynamics. Therefore we are left with just two state variables: the expected sales ratio $y^e = Y^e/K$ and the inventory ratio $n = N/K$.

To prepare the ground for an unambiguous reading of the two differential equations for y^e and n, we recall that eqs. (4.37) and (4.38) have represented the output–capital ratio y and utilization u as functions of y^e and n. Given the constant steady-state values of ω and π, it follows that the wage share v, the return differential q, the capital growth rate g_k and the ratio of total aggregate demand y^d can all be expressed in terms of y, u and the bond rate i; see eqs. (4.40)–(4.42). Given, furthermore, the constant steady-state value of m, so that $i = i(m^o, y^e, n)$ from the LM solution (4.39), all the variables entering the Metzlerian subsystem are consequently functions of y^e and n alone:

$$y = y(y^e, n) = [1 + (g^o + \beta_{nn})\beta_{ny}]y^e - \beta_{nn}n$$

$$u = u(y^e, n) = y(y^e, n)/y^n$$

$$v = v(y^e, n) = \omega^o/f_z[u(y^e, n)]$$

$$q = q(y^e, n) = [1 - v(y^e, n)]y(y^e, n) - \delta - [i(m^o, y^e, n) - \pi^o]$$

$$g_k = g_k(y^e, n) = f_I[q(y^e, n), u(y^e, n)]$$

$$y^d = y^d(y^e, n) = (1 - s_c)y^e + (s_c - \tau_w)v(y^e, n)y(y^e, n) + g_k(y^e, n) + \text{const}$$

Having made explicit this functional dependency, eqs. (4.46) and (4.48) for the motions of y^e and n can now be written as a closed two-dimensional system:

$$\dot{y}^e = [g^o - g_k(y^e, n)]y^e + \beta_y[y^d(y^e, n) - y^e)] \qquad (7.1)$$

$$\dot{n} = y(y^e, n) - y^d(y^e, n) - ng_k(y^e, n) \qquad (7.2)$$

Building on the original work by Metzler (1941, 1947) on inventory cycles and adjusting, in particular, his framework to a growth context, a dynamic system of this kind was first advanced by Franke (1996). His formulation differs from eqs. (7.1) and (7.2) in that, for simplicity, it still has lent less structure to the demand side. Thus, both the investment function g_k and excess demand as a whole, $\xi = (Y^d - Y)/Y$, were exclusively dependent on the output–capital ratio (or utilization, for that matter).

Another example of a similar system can be found in Chiarella and Flaschel (2000a, pp. 309–313), where it is constructed as a subsystem from the KMG model put forward in that book. The specification details in which that KMG model version differs from the present one have already been identified in chapter 4, section 3, in a comment on eqs. (4.44)–(4.49). As the more important points relate to the wage and price Phillips curves and so do not apply to the inventory dynamics, there are only three minor elements that distinguish Chiarella and Flaschel's submodel from (7.1), (7.2): their rate of profit in the investment function is based on expected sales Y^e rather than current output Y; they also freeze the interest rate in the investment function; and they do not allow for procyclical labour productivity – i.e. $\beta_{zu} = 0$ in our notation.

We should note that the differences of eqs. (7.1), (7.2) from Franke (1996) and Chiarella and Flaschel (2000a) do not concern the basic structure of the submodel and that, moreover, all three systems lead to the same kind of results in the mathematical stability analysis. Deviations may occur at a quantitative level, such that the corresponding (composed) terms in the Jacobian matrix may come out quite differently.

One common feature of a general stability analysis of these systems is that, despite their low dimensionality, the expressions in the Jacobian are already so involved that, a priori, a greater number of cases have to be distinguished. To limit the analysis to the more relevant cases, we introduce the following assumption for (7.1), (7.2). It may in the first instance be viewed as a condition on the partial derivatives f_{Iu} and f_{Iq} of the investment function $f_I = f_I(q, u)$.

Assumption 1

Referring to the steady-state value $n = n^o$, the two terms α_I and α_v are so small relative to the savings propensity s_c that

$$(1 + g^o\beta_{ny})(\alpha_I + \alpha_v) + s_c n\alpha_I < s_c,$$

where with respect to, especially, $v = v^o$, $i = i^o$ and an interest elasticity $\eta_{m,i}$ of money demand which is not too small,

$$\alpha_I := f_{Iu}/y^n + f_{Iq}[vf_z' + (1-v) - i/\eta_{m,i}y^n] > 0$$

$$\alpha_v := (s_c - \tau_w)(1 - f_z')v > 0.$$

Assumption 1 is indeed satisfied by the coefficients that we have obtained in the calibration of the KMG model. These values also provide some additional play. Rounding to three digits, the numerical details are

$$\alpha_I = 0.280/0.70 + 0.115 \cdot [0.70 \cdot 0.40 + 0.30$$

$$-0.07/(0.14 \cdot 0.70)] = 0.385$$

$$\alpha_v = (0.80 - 0.35) \cdot (1 - 0.40) \cdot 0.70 = 0.189$$

so that the left-hand side of the assumption's basic inequality is given by

$$(1 + 0.03 \cdot 0.22) \cdot (0.385 + 0.189) + 0.80 \cdot 0.153 \cdot 0.385 = 0.624$$

which clearly falls short of $s_c = 0.80$. As the proof of the stability proposition will show, the significance of Assumption 1 lies in the fact that it rules out saddle-point dynamics. Hence, the steady state of system (7.1), (7.2) is either attractive or repelling (if we neglect the behaviour induced by parameters on the stability frontier itself). The formulation of the stability proposition focuses on the two central parameters of the inventory subdynamics, the stock adjustment speed β_{nn} and the speed of adjustment β_y of the adaptive sales expectations.

Proposition 1

Suppose that Assumption 1 is satisfied and define the critical value

$$\tilde{\beta}_{nn} := [(s_c - (1 + g^o\beta_{ny})(\alpha_I + \alpha_v))]/\beta_{ny}(\alpha_I + \alpha_v),$$

which thereby is positive. Then the steady state of the subsystem (7.1), (7.2) is locally asymptotically stable for all $\beta_y > 0$ if $\beta_{nn} \leq \tilde{\beta}_{nn}$. On the other hand, for all $\beta_{nn} > \tilde{\beta}_{nn}$ there exists a positive number β_y^H such that this equilibrium *is locally asymptotically stable if $\beta_y < \beta_y^H$, whereas it is repelling if $\beta_y > \beta_y^H$. The critical value β_y^H gives rise to a Hopf bifurcation, and it is a decreasing function of β_{nn}.*

Proof: In order to show the analogy to the system studied in Franke (1996), the presentation of the proof follows as closely as possible the proof given there (p. 260). To this end we define

$$D := y_y = 1 + (g^o + \beta_{nn})\beta_{ny} > 0$$

$$E := \alpha_I + \alpha_v > 0$$

$$H := 1 - (1+n)\alpha_I - \alpha_v > 0$$

Note that $H > 0$ is equivalent to $(\alpha_I + \alpha_v) + s_c n \alpha_I < 1 - (1 - s_c)n\alpha_I$. This inequality holds by virtue of Assumption 1 if the right-hand side exceeds s_c. The latter is true since $n\alpha_I < 1$, again by virtue of Assumption 1.

The Jacobian $\mathcal{J}_M$ of process (7.1), (7.2) is a 2×2 submatrix of the Jacobian $\mathcal{J}$ of the full KMG model, as expressed in (4.50) in chapter 4, section 4 (index 'M' alludes to Metzler as the patron saint of this subsystem). $\mathcal{J}_M$ is made up of the latter's entries j_{33}, j_{35} in the first row, and j_{53}, j_{55} in the second. With the terms just defined, this matrix can be written as

$$\mathcal{J}_M = \begin{bmatrix} \beta_y(DE - s_c) - y^e\alpha_I D & -\beta_{nn}(\beta_y E - y^e\alpha_I) \\ DH - (1 - s_c) & -(g^o + \beta_{nn}H) \end{bmatrix}$$

A comparison with Franke (1996) shows that, although the terms D, E and H are specified differently, they have the same signs. Also, if $s_c = 1$, the Jacobian $\mathcal{J}_M$ into which they enter reads the same as the matrix M that is obtained there. A savings propensity $s_c < 1$ yields a slight distortion in this respect, but this in no way affects the type of the stability result.

The determinant of $\mathcal{J}_M$ is given by

$$\det \mathcal{J}_M = \beta_y\{-g^o(DE - s_c) + \beta_{nn}[s_c - (1 + s_c n)\alpha_I - \alpha_v]\}$$
$$+ y^e\alpha_I[g^o D + \beta_{nn}(1 - s_c)]$$

The last square bracket is obviously positive. Taking account of $DE - s_c = \beta_{nn}\beta_{ny}E + (1 + g^o\beta_{ny})E - s_c$, the term in curly brackets is spelled out as

$$g^o[s_c - (1 + g^o\beta_{ny})(\alpha_I + \alpha_v)] + \beta_{nn}[s_c - (1 + g^o\beta_{ny})(\alpha_I + \alpha_v) - s_c n\alpha_I]$$

Assumption 1 implies that the square brackets showing up here are both positive, too. Hence $\det \mathcal{J}_M$ is unambiguously positive, so that it is the sign of the trace of the matrix that is decisive for stability.

Given that $H > 0$, trace $\mathcal{J}_M$ is clearly negative for all $\beta_y \geq 0$ if the term $DE - s_c$ is non-positive. $DE - s_c = 0$ is brought about by $\beta_{nn} = \tilde{\beta}_{nn}$ as defined in the proposition, and $DE - s_c \leq 0$ if $\beta_{nn} \leq \tilde{\beta}_{nn}$. On the other hand, $\beta_{nn} > \tilde{\beta}_{nn}$ being tantamount to $DE - s_c > 0$, trace $\mathcal{J}_M < 0$ results if

$$\beta_y < \beta_y^H := (y^e \alpha_I D + g^o + \beta_{nn} H)/(DE - s_c)$$

while the trace is positive if the inequality is reversed ($\beta_y^H > 0$ is obvious). Since $\det \mathcal{J}_M \neq 0$ in any case, β_y^H gives rise to a Hopf bifurcation.

Finally, express β_y^H as a function of β_{nn} (which enters D) and differentiate it. A little calculation yields that the sign of $d\beta_y^H/\beta_{nn}$ is given by the expression

$$-s_c y^e \alpha_I \beta_{ny} - [s_c - (1 + g^o \beta_{ny})(\alpha_I + \alpha_v)]H - g^o \beta_{ny}(\alpha_I + \alpha_v)$$

Assumption 1 ensures that the term in square brackets in positive, hence $d\beta_y^H/\beta_{nn} < 0$.

QED

7.2.2   The Metzlerian feedback mechanisms

Before considering the role of the adjustment parameters β_y and β_{nn} in greater detail, we should try to see what is behind the mathematics of Proposition 1. To this end we identify three feedback loops, which are schematically drawn out in figure 7.1.[1] For better reference when explaining the single links, the underlying equations (4.15) and (4.17)–(4.20) are repeated from chapter 4:

$$\dot{N} = Y - Y^d$$

$$N^d = \beta_{ny} Y^e$$

$$I_N^d = g^o N^d + \beta_{nn}(N^d - N)$$

$$Y = Y^e + I_N^d$$

$$\dot{Y}^e = g^o Y^e + \beta_y(Y^d - Y^e)$$

The first loop (A) in figure 7.1 represents a positive feedback effect for expected sales. Expectations of higher sales directly increase the

---

[1] Loop A disregards feedbacks from inventory changes, while loop B disregards the effects of expected sales. Loop A supposes that Y^d rises more than Y^e (which is tantamount to $\beta_{nn} > \tilde{\beta}_{nn}$), and bracketed up and down arrows indicate comparatively weak reactions; see text for details.

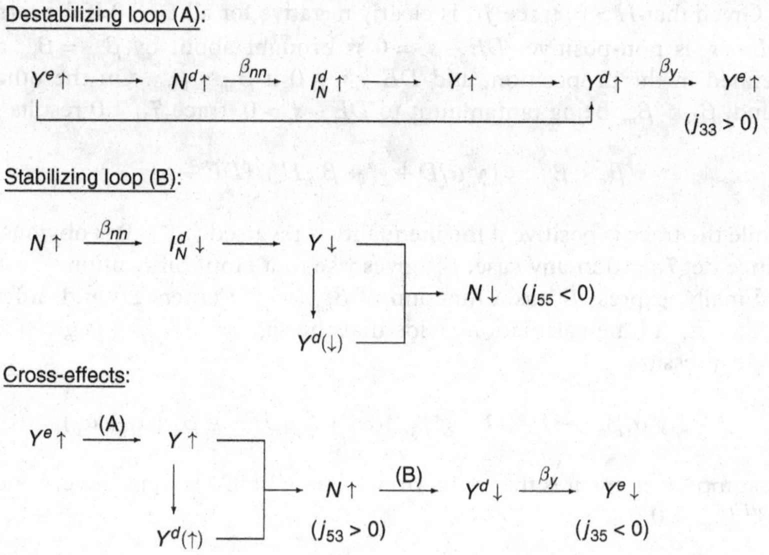

Destabilizing loop (A):

$$Y^e \uparrow \longrightarrow N^d \uparrow \xrightarrow{\beta_{nn}} I^d_N \uparrow \longrightarrow Y \uparrow \longrightarrow Y^d \uparrow \xrightarrow{\beta_y} Y^e \uparrow$$

$$(j_{33} > 0)$$

Stabilizing loop (B):

$$N \uparrow \xrightarrow{\beta_{nn}} I^d_N \downarrow \longrightarrow Y \downarrow$$

$$Y^d(\downarrow) \longrightarrow N \downarrow \quad (j_{55} < 0)$$

Cross-effects:

$$Y^e \uparrow \xrightarrow{(A)} Y \uparrow$$

$$Y^d(\uparrow) \longrightarrow N \uparrow \xrightarrow{(B)} Y^d \downarrow \xrightarrow{\beta_y} Y^e \downarrow$$

$$(j_{53} > 0) \qquad (j_{35} < 0)$$

Figure 7.1: Metzlerian feedback mechanisms

desired level of inventories N^d, desired inventory investment I^d_N, and thus production Y. Aggregate demand in turn rises, basically for three reasons: the increase in total wages (because of higher employment), which raises consumption expenditures; the increase in dividend payments to the shareholders (because according to (4.3) dividends are based on expected sales), which likewise raises consumption; and the increase in fixed investment, by virtue of the utilization argument in the investment function.[2] Note that the second channel is indicated by the lower long array in the loop that goes directly from Y^e to Y^d.

The key assumption in feedback loop A is that these combined effects make Y^d rise more than Y^e, which then leads firms to expect further increases in sales. In intensive form, $\Delta Y^d > \Delta Y^e$ corresponds to the condition $\partial y^d / \partial y^e > 1$. As we have

$$\partial y^d / \partial y^e = 1 - s_c + (\alpha_I + \alpha_v) \partial y / \partial y^e$$

$$\partial y / \partial y^e = 1 + (g^o + \beta_{nn}) \beta_{ny}$$

---

[2] The return differential $q = r - (i - \pi)$ in the investment function will somewhat fall as the LM interest rate rises with utilization. Formally, this effect shows up in the term α_I in Assumption 1, where, however, it was supposed that the interest rate effect would not become dominant (so as to render the whole term α_I negative).

it is easily checked that $\partial y^d / \partial y^e > 1$ is equivalent to $\beta_{nn} > \tilde{\beta}_{nn}$; that is, the stock adjustment speed exceeds the critical value given in Proposition 1. Otherwise, $\partial y^d / \partial y^e < 1$ results and the entire feedback in loop A would be a negative one, where the proposition asserts that this is a sufficient condition for the steady state to be locally stable.

Regarding the formal dynamic system, the first feedback loop in figure 7.1 captures the effect $\partial \dot{y}^e / \partial y^e$ in eq. (7.1) (apart from the minor growth effects in the exact formulae). This partial derivative is the upper diagonal entry in matrix $\mathcal{J}_M$ in the proof of Proposition 1, or, referring to the Jacobian $\mathcal{J}$ in eq. (4.50) of the full KMG model, it is entry j_{33}. The supposition $\beta_{nn} > \tilde{\beta}_{nn}$ makes it positive, $j_{33} > 0$, as indicated in the loop.

While the first loop leaves aside the reactions of firms to the resulting changes in inventories, the second feedback loop in figure 7.1 concentrates on inventories and neglects expected sales. Here it is sketched that a *ceteris paribus* rise in inventories reduces desired inventory investment and thus output. Aggregate demand decreases as well, but by less than output. This will be intuitively clear, and it is analytically confirmed by differentiating y^d with respect to n, which yields $\partial y^d / \partial n = (\alpha_I + \alpha_v) \partial y / \partial n$ (the inequality $\alpha_I + \alpha_v < 1$ follows immediately from Assumption 1). In the loop itself, the relationship $\Delta Y < \Delta Y^d < 0$ means that more is taken from the stock of inventories than is added to it. On the whole, we thus have a negative feedback loop in inventories. Its mathematical counterpart is the derivative $\partial \dot{n} / \partial n$ of eq. (7.2), the lower diagonal element in matrix $\mathcal{J}_M$ in the proof of Proposition 1, which was unambiguously negative. Referring again to the original Jacobian $\mathcal{J}$ in (4.50), we have $j_{55} < 0$.

The cross-effects forming the third feedback loop in figure 7.1 correspond to the off-diagonal entries in matrix $\mathcal{J}_M$. Starting out from a rise in expected sales, we already know from loop A that production as well as aggregate sales increase. Here, too, the increase in Y^d is weaker than that in Y. In fact, using the explicit computation of the partial derivatives above, it suffices to rewrite the condition $\partial y^d / \partial y^e < \partial y / \partial y^e$ as $[\alpha_I + \alpha_v - s_c] + [\alpha_I + \alpha_v - 1](g^o + \beta_{nn})\beta_{ny} < 0$ and to notice that the two square brackets are negative by virtue of Assumption 1. The immediate consequence of the relative changes of Y and Y^d is that inventories pile up. In a growth context, this point in the reaction chain is mathematically represented by $j_{53} = \partial \dot{n} / \partial y^e > 0$.

Next, as seen in loop B, the rise in inventories as such has a negative impact on aggregate demand, which in turn induces firms to revise their sales expectations downwards. The mathematical counterpart of this effect is $j_{35} = \partial \dot{y}^e / \partial n < 0$. Considering the entire chain from $Y^e \uparrow$ to $Y^e \downarrow$, another stabilizing feedback loop is identified.

Though what is going on economically in the single feedback relationships is quite comprehensible, the outcome for the system's stability when they are interacting is far from obvious. Apart from the effort in the computations that proved necessary to derive a mathematical stability result, a feeling for the difficulties involved here can be gained by looking at the ambiguous role of the two adjustment parameters β_y and β_{nn} in figure 7.1. In the third feedback loop, rapid adjustments of sales expectations (β_y high) appear to be conducive to stability, whereas in the first loop they tend to shore up the destabilizing forces. As for the stock adjustment speed β_{nn}, the second loop indicates that strong reactions of desired inventory investment are stabilizing, whereas in the first loop they are destabilizing.

It will thus be no surprise to find that combining the qualitative information of figure 7.1 in the Jacobian matrix of the two-dimensional subdynamics (7.1), (7.2) allows no definite conclusion. In fact, we have

$$\mathcal{J}_M = \begin{bmatrix} j_{33} & j_{35} \\ j_{53} & j_{55} \end{bmatrix} = \begin{bmatrix} + & - \\ + & - \end{bmatrix}$$

and neither the sign of the trace nor of the determinant of $\mathcal{J}_M$ can be inferred from the sign pattern alone. Quantitatively, however, things are straightforward if we adopt the numerical parameter values from the calibration (6.35) in the previous chapter, as far as they apply in the submodel. We then compute

$$\mathcal{J}_M = \begin{bmatrix} 0.80 & -12.96 \\ 0.92 & -1.65 \end{bmatrix}$$

showing that the trace is clearly negative and the determinant is clearly positive. Hence, under these circumstances there is broad scope for local stability–in contrast to the full six-dimensional KMG model, where an unstable steady-state position was obtained.

To discuss the impact of β_y and β_{nn} on stability, let us for the moment nevertheless remain within the two-dimensional Metzlerian subsystem. The intricate role of the two parameters is mathematically reflected in the fact that β_{nn} appears in all four entries of matrix $\mathcal{J}_M$ and β_y is still in three entries. As a consequence one has to go through all the details in the single computations to work out the systematic effects of β_y and β_{nn}. In the end, Proposition 1 and, in particular, the statement that the Hopf bifurcation value β_y^H is a decreasing function of β_{nn} enable us to conclude that both parameters β_y and β_{nn} tend to be destabilizing. Local stability of the equilibrium prevails if the two are sufficiently small; instability comes about if they are sufficiently high.

More precisely, stability is maintained for all β_y arbitrarily large as long as β_{nn} does not exceed a benchmark value $\tilde{\beta}_{nn}$, but sufficiently high values of β_y lead to instability when $\beta_{nn} > \tilde{\beta}_{nn}$. In the latter case, the width of the stability interval $(0, \beta_y^H)$ of the adjustment speed of adaptive sales expectations β_y varies with β_{nn}-that is, the interval becomes smaller as β_{nn} rises. In this sense the stock adjustment speed β_{nn} has a destabilizing influence.

Similarly the other way round, one easily infers that for all β_y that are not too small there exists a Hopf bifurcation value β_{nn}^H of the stock adjustment speed, such that the equilibrium is stable for $\beta_{nn} < \beta_{nn}^H$ and unstable for $\beta_{nn} > \beta_{nn}^H$. The adjustment speed of expected sales β_y is then destabilizing in the sense that higher values of β_y diminish the stability interval $(0, \beta_{nn}^H)$.

These stability properties of system (7.1), (7.2) are numerically illustrated in the parameter diagram for β_y and β_{nn} in figure 7.2.[3] The other coefficients are, of course, again fixed at the values of the final parameter scenario (6.35). Formulating the Hopf bifurcation value of the stock adjustment speed as a function of β_y, i.e. $\beta_{nn}^H = \beta_{nn}^H(\beta_y)$, the diagram indicates that it asymptotically decreases towards $\tilde{\beta}_{nn}$ as β_y gets large. The diagram also shows that this fall of β_{nn}^H is rather slow, since one computes $\tilde{\beta}_{nn} = 1.76$ for the expression in Proposition 1.

The findings of Proposition 1 are also the basis for the global analysis in the abovementioned two-dimensional Metzlerian model in Franke

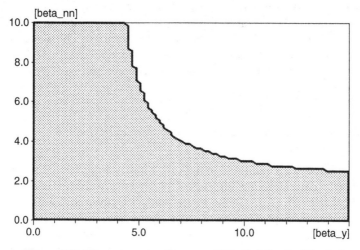

Figure 7.2: The parameter diagram of (β_y, β_{nn}) for the Metzlerian two-dimensional subdynamics

[3] Pairs in the dotted area induce local stability, instability prevails outside.

(1996), which differs from (7.1), (7.2) only in its simpler demand side. Just as in the calibration of the KMG model in chapter 6, section 7, the general approach to persistent cyclical behaviour is the assumption of an unstable steady-state position, while a suitable extrinsic nonlinearity takes care of keeping the system bounded in the outer state space. In Franke (1996), the nonlinearity was introduced into the stock adjustment speed β_{nn}, which is made a function of the expected sales ratio y^e. Given a (sufficiently high) value of β_y, the coefficient β_{nn} is supposed to be constant over a medium range of y^e, such that the steady state is unstable. On the other hand, β_{nn} falls below $\beta_{nn}^H(\beta_y)$ when y^e gets large as well as when y^e gets small. An economic argument for a similar flexibility in the stock management of firms and the observation that it has stabilizing effects can, by the way, be found as early as in Whitin (1957); see Franke (1996, p. 248) for a brief discussion.

Because this model is a planar system, its global dynamics can be mathematically analyzed with the help of the Poincaré–Bendixson theorem. In this way it was established that there exists a subregion R in the state space containing the steady state in its interior such that a trajectory starting from any point $(y^e, n) \in R$ either is, or converges to, a closed orbit. Unless the economy is not already in the steady state, such a closed orbit is non-degenerate (Franke, 1996, p. 253). Intuitively, the flexibility in the stock adjustment speed can be said to work, to the effect that, while the equilibrium is locally repelling, it proves to be attractive when the state variables are further away. Thus, it is the interplay between the locally destabilizing and the globally stabilizing forces that gives rise to bounded and non-damped fluctuations. The same type of global analysis could be undertaken for the present system (7.1), (7.2). This, however, is just a matter of technical details and would provide no additional insights.

7.2.3   The Metzlerian adjustment parameters in the full KMG model

The feedback loops exhibited in figure 7.1 have demonstrated the diverse and partly counteracting effects in the inventory dynamics. While in the subsystem (7.1), (7.2) the mathematical analysis still allowed us to characterize both parameters β_y and β_{nn} as destabilizing (over a certain range), it is easily conceivable that some additional effects from other variables in figure 7.1, which vary in strength in the single links where they enter, could considerably modify the stability results of Proposition 1. This is what we now investigate by means of numerical calculations in the full six-dimensional KMG model, eqs. (4.44)–(4.49).

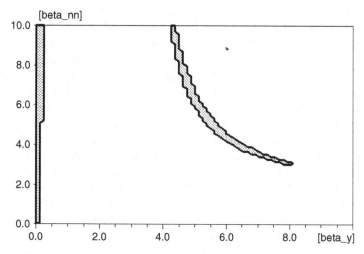

Figure 7.3: The parameter diagram of (β_y, β_{nn}) for the full KMG model

To begin with, for this economy the same kind of parameter diagram (β_y, β_{nn}) should be computed as was done for the subdynamics. The outcome is presented in figure 7.3.[4]

Evidently, the stability properties of the submodel and the KMG model arising from β_y and β_{nn} are very different. The only common feature is that local stability obtains for slow adjustments in sales expectations. These values of β_y have, however, to be exceptionally low. On the other hand, even extremely low values of the stock adjustment speed β_{nn} are no longer sufficient to ensure stability.

Already for values of β_y as low as $\beta_y = 0.5$ or $\beta_y = 2.0$, say, there is no value of β_{nn} that could bring about stability – neither low values of β_{nn}, as in figure 7.2, nor higher values that are reasonably bounded. We must therefore note that the stabilizing mechanism of a flexible stock adjustment speed, which proved so powerful in the Metzlerian two-dimensional submodel, fails to work out in the full model. That is, one of our hopes of taming the centrifugal forces by introducing a second extrinsic nonlinearity into the model is disappointed.[5] The general message

---

[4] Dotted areas are stability regions.

[5] It might be objected that, while the effects just described apply in the vicinity of the steady state, things could be different further away. Here, however, we recall the quasi-linear character of the model (if we cancel the extrinsic nonlinearity in the investment function), which makes the local and global dynamics look very much alike. This notwithstanding, we tried the flexible stock adjustment speed $\beta_{nn} = \beta_{nn}(y^e)$ from Franke (1996) in the dynamic simulations of the model, but came to understand that this device is no longer successful.

one can take home from a comparison of figures 7.2 and 7.3 is that the stability conclusions from too small a macromodel, however meaningful they may have been within that framework, can be quite misleading.

Coming to terms with the strong disposition to instability regarding the parameters β_y and β_{nn} (given the numerical values of the other parameters), there is yet another remarkable feature in figure 7.3, in that it exhibits a 'reswitching' phenomenon. So, fix a value of β_{nn} – such as $\beta_{nn} = 4$ – and let β_y increase from zero. Then we first have stability, then instability, and then stability again (for β_y around 6.5). A further increase leads to instability once again. We thus have a reswitching of stability, as well as a reswitching of instability. This makes it hard to speak of β_y as a destabilizing parameter, as was possible in the two-dimensional submodel; the impact of this coefficient on stability is, in fact, ambiguous.

Carrying out the same exercise for β_{nn} by fixing β_y at $\beta_y = 6$, for example, a reswitching of instability is also observed for this parameter. Hence the stock adjustment speed, too, has ambiguous stability effects.

Mathematically it is, of course, clear that the (complex) eigenvalues of a 2×2 matrix $\mathcal{J}_M = \mathcal{J}_M^{(2)}$ and the leading eigenvalues of a 6×6 matrix $\mathcal{J}$ that is 'built around it' will be generally quite different.[6] The fact that, besides four zero eigenvalues, $\mathcal{J}$ would have the same eigenvalues as $\mathcal{J}_M^{(2)}$ if all of its other entries were put to zero lets us ask how the leading eigenvalues of $\mathcal{J}$ emerge from the eigenvalues of $\mathcal{J}_M^{(2)}$. More specifically, we refer to the stability region in the (β_y, β_{nn}) parameter diagram and look for a single other parameter that we can vary and that for certain values produces a similar stability region to that in figure 7.2. β_{we} turns out to be one such parameter, the slope coefficient with respect to the employment rate in the wage Phillips curve.

The effects of the variations of β_{we} can be seen in figure 7.4, which displays four parameter diagrams of β_y and β_{nn} arising from different values of β_{we}. In the upper left panel a low value of β_{we} ($\beta_{we} = 0.05$) indeed produces a connected stability region that not only qualitatively but also quantitatively looks very much the same as figure 7.2. The other three panels in figure 7.4 exemplify how this area is progressively reduced as β_{we} increases from this value.

The effect of raising β_{we} from 0.05 to 0.15 is that instability eats a hole into the stability region, in the lower left corner of the diagram. This instability hole is extended as β_{we} continues to increase, with instability eating upwards as well as to the right, so to speak. Eventually, at

---

[6] Remember that the Jacobian $\mathcal{J}_M = \mathcal{J}_M^{(2)}$ of the Metzlerian two-dimensional submodel is made up of the entries j_{33}, j_{35} and j_{53}, j_{55} of the Jacobian $\mathcal{J}$ of the KMG model. The expression 'leading' eigenvalue of a matrix is, again, used for the eigenvalue with maximum real part.

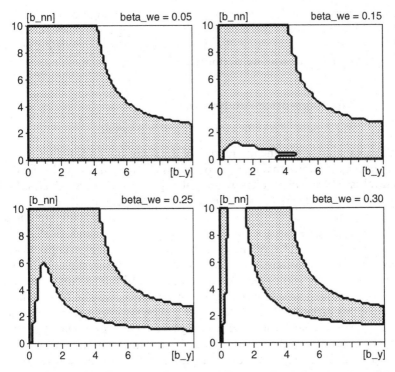

Figure 7.4: Parameter diagrams of (β_y, β_{nn}) for different values of β_{we}

$\beta_{we} = 0.25$, the stability region has lost its contact with the β_y axis, at least in the range of β_y shown here.[7] Setting $\beta_{we} = 0.30$, a further upward penetration into the stability area is observed. It is so strong that in the parameter range shown here the stability region is torn apart. The two dotted areas in the lower right panel of figure 7.4 are still connected, but only at values of the stock adjustment speed as high as $\beta_{nn} \geq 38$ (roughly), which are evidently meaningless. So, at this value of β_{we} we practically have two separate stability areas – qualitatively the same feature as in figure 7.3, where $\beta_{we} = 0.55$ from our final parameter setting is underlying. In this scenario, then, there is no more connection at all between the two stability areas, neither inside nor outside figure 7.3 – not even for β_{nn} higher than 500 and more.

In sum, the four diagrams in figure 7.4 illustrate how the ambiguous stability effects of β_y and β_{nn} can be viewed as emerging from the more familiar stability properties that would prevail at a weaker influence of the

---

[7] Stability still comes about when $\beta_y > 11.4$ and β_{nn} is sufficiently small.

wage Phillips curve. The metaphor of instability eating upwards and to the right into the stability region is all the more suggestive as, remarkably, the outer stability frontier to the north-east is only marginally affected by all the variations that we performed.

7.3   The wage-price subdynamics

7.3.1   *Mathematical two-dimensional stability analysis*

In this subsection it is the interaction of the wage-price adjustments with the output dynamics that is isolated from the rest of the system. The two central variables to be studied are the real wage rate and expected sales. The real wage rate, determined by wages and prices, impacts positively through the consumption of workers and negatively through the investment of firms on aggregate demand, and thus on expected sales and, finally, output. Changes in output, on the other hand, mean changes in capacity utilization and employment, which are the core variables in the two Phillips curves for wages and prices. As our augmented Phillips curves include the wage share as an additional factor of influence, we also have to keep track of this variable. Due to the procyclical behaviour of labour productivity, the wage share is affected not only by the changes in real wages but also by utilization (see. eq. (7.3) below). Its intervention can therefore complicate the mechanisms just alluded to. Despite the already relatively rich effects thus coming about, the partial model that is set up by these mechanisms may, for simplicity, be called the wage-price subdynamics.

The analysis of the wage-price submodel neglects the following four features: the feedback of the accumulation or de-accumulation of inventories on production; the (weak) influence of the evolution of the capital stock (i.e. capital per head of labour supply) on the employment rate (see eq. (7.3) below); the variations of the nominal rate of interest as far as they derive from the changes in the real balances ratio; and the variations of the real rate of interest as far as they derive from changes in the inflation climate (the latter two components would have a bearing on output via changes in fixed investment).[8] Accordingly, the inventory ratio, capital per head, the real balances ratio and the inflation climate are fixed at their steady-state values: $n = n^o$, $k^s = (k^s)^o$, $m = m^o$ and $\pi = \pi^o$.

In this way we can concentrate on two differential equations for the real wage rate ω and the expected sales ratio y^e. Owing to the simplifying assumptions, all the variables entering them are functions of ω and

---

[8] Freezing the real interest rate channel is the only essential limitation on the inflation climate π in the present setting, because, as has been repeatedly remarked, π cancels out in the equation determining the motions of the real wage rate.

y^e alone. Explicitly, eqs. (4.25), (4.26), (4.33), and (4.37)–(4.42) are involved here, which for convenience we repeat as

$$y = y(y^e) = [1 + (g^o + \beta_{nn})\beta_{ny}]y^e - \beta_{nn}n^o$$

$$u = u(y^e) = y(y^e)/y^n$$

$$e = e(y^e) = y(y^e)(k^s)^o/f_z[u(y^e)]$$

$$v = v(\omega, y^e) = \omega/f_z[u(y^e)]$$

$$f_p(u, v) = \beta_{pu}(u - 1) + \beta_{pv}[(1 + \mu)v - 1] \qquad (7.3)$$

$$f_w(e, v) = \beta_{we}(e - 1) - \beta_{wv}(v - v^o)/v^o$$

$$q = q(\omega, y^e) = [1 - v(\omega, y^e)]y(y^e) - \delta - [i(m^o, y^e, n^o) - \pi^o]$$

$$g_k = g_k(\omega, y^e) = f_I[q(\omega, y^e), u(y^e)]$$

$$y^d = y^d(\omega, y^e) = (1 - s_c)y^e + (s_c - \tau_w)v(\omega, y^e)y(y^e) + g_k(\omega, y^e) + \text{const}$$

The differential equations for ω and y^e have been stated in eqs. (4.44) and (4.46). Taking the expressions in (7.3) into account, the two-dimensional wage-price subdynamics is thus given by

$$\dot{\omega} = \omega\kappa[(1 - \kappa_p)f_w(e, v) - (1 - \kappa_w)f_p(u, v)], \quad \kappa := 1/(1 - \kappa_p\kappa_w) \quad (7.4)$$

$$\dot{y}^e = (g^o - g_k)y^e + \beta_y(y^d - y^e) \qquad (7.5)$$

The opposite effects of real wages on aggregate demand have already been mentioned: an increase in the real wage rate raises the consumption of workers, while it lowers profits and so reduces the fixed investment of firms. We confine our interest to situations where the positive expenditure effect dominates, which is made precise by Assumption 2.

Assumption 2
The responsiveness of fixed investment to changes in the return differential $q = r - (i - \pi)$ is bounded, such that, evaluated at the steady state, $f_{Iq} < s_c - \tau_w$.

That the inequality in Assumption 2 is indeed equivalent to a positive real wage effect is readily seen by computing the partial derivative of aggregate demand y^d in (7.3),

$$\partial y^d/\partial\omega = (s_c - \tau_w - f_{Iq})y^n > 0$$

Assumption 2 or its implication, respectively, may not only conform to economic intuition but is also satisfied without any problems by our calibration. Just recall $f_{Iq} = 0.115$ and $s_c - \tau_w = 0.80 - 0.35 = 0.45$.

The stability analysis of the wage-price submodel (7.4), (7.5) is divided into two parts. In the first step we investigate what may be called the plain real wage effects. By this we mean dropping our innovation of the wage share terms in the two Phillips curves, so that besides benchmark inflation only the employment rate e enters the wage Phillips curve, and only capacity utilization u enters the price Phillips curve. This is formally captured by $\beta_{wv} = \beta_{pv} = 0$. The stabilizing or destabilizing effects of higher wage and price flexibility in these circumstances are summarized in Proposition 2, where because of (7.5) and the relationship $y = y(y^e)$ we must be prepared for the Metzlerian coefficients β_{nn} and β_y to play a certain role as well.

Before stating the stability proposition, the following terms should be specified for easier reference, where $\alpha_I > 0$ and $\alpha_v > 0$ have been introduced in Assumption 1 in subsection 7.2.1 above:

$$y_y := 1 + (g^o + \beta_{nn})\beta_{ny} > 0$$

$$\alpha_y := (\alpha_I + \alpha_v)y_y - s_c \qquad (7.6)$$

$$\tilde{\beta}_{y,1} := y^e \alpha_I y_y / \alpha_y \quad (\text{if } \alpha_y > 0)$$

It goes without saying that, here and in all the formal expressions to follow, the state variables are always evaluated at their steady-state values.

Proposition 2 (Plain real wage effects)

Suppose that Assumptions 1 and 2 are satisfied and that $\beta_{wv} = \beta_{pv} = 0$. Let $\tilde{\beta}_{nn} > 0$ be the critical value of the stock adjustment speed specified in Proposition 1 and define

$$\tilde{\beta}_{we} := (1 - \kappa_w)\beta_{pu} / (1 - \kappa_p)(1 - f'_z)$$

(which may also attain the value infinity in the polar case $\kappa_p = 1$). Then the following statements hold true.

(a) *The steady state of subsystem (7.4), (7.5) is unstable if $\beta_{we} > \tilde{\beta}_{we}$.*
(b) *Given $\beta_{we} < \tilde{\beta}_{we}$, the steady is locally asymptotically stable if $\beta_{nn} < \tilde{\beta}_{nn}$.*
(c) *Suppose that $\beta_{nn} > \tilde{\beta}_{nn}$. Then $\alpha_y > 0$ in (7.6) and the steady state is locally asymptotically stable if $\beta_{we} < \tilde{\beta}_{we}$ and $\beta_y < \tilde{\beta}_{y,1}$, whereas it is unstable if $\beta_y > \tilde{\beta}_{y,1}$.*

Proof: Denote the Jacobian of the wage-price dynamics (7.4), (7.5) as $\mathcal{J}_{wp}$. Abbreviating

$$a_\omega := s_c - \tau_w - f_{Iq} > 0$$

$$\beta_{wp,eu} := (1 - \kappa_p)(1 - f'_z)\beta_{we} - (1 - \kappa_w)\beta_{pu}$$

$$\beta_{wp,v} := (1 - \kappa_p)\beta_{wv} + (1 - \kappa_w)\beta_{pv} \geq 0$$

$\mathcal{J}_{wp}$ and its determinant can be written as

$$\mathcal{J}_{wp} = \begin{bmatrix} -\kappa\beta_{wp,v} & \omega\kappa y_y(\beta_{wp,eu}+f_z'\beta_{wp,v})/y^n \\ y^n(\beta_y a_\omega+f_{Iq}y^e) & \beta_y\alpha_y-y^e\alpha_I y_y \end{bmatrix}$$

$$\det \mathcal{J}_{wp} = -\kappa[\beta_{wp,v}(\beta_y\alpha_y-y^e\alpha_I y_y)+\omega y_y(\beta_{wp,eu}+f_z'\beta_{wp,v})(\beta_y a_\omega+f_{Iq}y^e)]$$

In checking the necessary and sufficient conditions for local stability, trace $\mathcal{J}_{wp} < 0$ and det $\mathcal{J}_{wp} > 0$ under $\beta_{wp,v} = 0$, statement (a) of the proposition follows from det $\mathcal{J}_{wp} < 0 \iff \beta_{wp,eu} > 0$, which, in turn, is equivalent to $\beta_{we} > \tilde{\beta}_{we}$. Regarding statement (b) note that $\alpha_y < 0$ is equivalent to $\beta_{nn} < \tilde{\beta}_{nn}$. Hence det $\mathcal{J}_{wp} > 0$ and trace $\mathcal{J}_{wp}$, which equals the lower diagonal entry, is negative. The same holds true in statement (c) if, with $\alpha_y > 0$ now since β_{nn} exceeds the threshold value, $\beta_y < \tilde{\beta}_{y,1}$. Conversely, the lower diagonal entry is positive and the steady state unstable if $\beta_y > \tilde{\beta}_{y,1}$.

QED

As long as $\beta_{wv} = \beta_{pv} = 0$, wage and price flexibility can be identified with the Phillips curve slope coefficients β_{we} and β_{pu}, respectively. The proposition then says that in the wage-price submodel it is high wage flexibility and low price flexibility that prove to be destabilizing. Remarkably, these features alone are even sufficient for instability. On the other hand, for low wage flexibility and high price flexibility to be stabilizing, the stock adjustment speed β_{nn} or the adjustment speed β_y of expected sales must not be too high in addition.

Apart from that, it should not be neglected that the two weighting parameters κ_w and κ_p for the specification of benchmark inflation in the Phillips curves, which look rather innocent conceptually, have an important bearing on whether a given degree of flexibility β_{we} or β_{pu} induces local stability or instability. In particular, the critical condition $\beta_{we} < \tilde{\beta}_{we}$ is always fulfilled if $\kappa_p = 1$, and it is always violated if $\kappa_w = 1$.[9]

If reference is made to the calibration of the wage-price module, it is seen immediately that, with $\beta_{we} = 0.55$ and $\tilde{\beta}_{we} = (1-0) \cdot 0.15/[(1-0) \cdot (1-0.4)] = 0.25$, the steady state of (7.4), (7.5) is unstable regardless of β_{nn} and β_y. To check whether local stability could be achieved by suitable changes of $\beta_{we}, \beta_{pu}, \kappa_w, \kappa_p$, we also remark that (as reported in

---

[9] A two-dimensional real wage submodel was also set up in Chiarella and Flaschel (2000a, pp. 304–7). Their version, however, differs considerably from system (7.4), (7.5), the most important point being that their output is determined in an IS manner. The stabilizing and destabilizing effects of the Phillips curve slope coefficients are the same as in our Proposition 2, if (and only if) it is assumed that the IS solution of output responds positively to an increase in the real wage rate. Nevertheless, the condition for the latter reaction to come about finds no appropriate correspondence in our framework here, so the analogy should not be pursued too far.

subsection 7.2.2) the threshold value of the stock adjustment speed is $\tilde{\beta}_{nn} = 1.76$, which falls short of the calibrated coefficient $\beta_{nn} = 3.00$. So statement (b) of Proposition 2 fails to apply and we have to turn to the numerical value of $\tilde{\beta}_{y,1}$. With $\beta_{nn} = 3.00$ (which enters the term y_y in (7.6)), $\tilde{\beta}_{y,1} = 2.82$ results. Since the calibrated value of the adjustment speed $\beta_y = 8.00$ is almost three times as large, the steady state would still be unstable. It may, however, be noted that $\tilde{\beta}_{y,1}$ is rather sensitive with respect to changes in β_{nn}. For example, reducing the stock adjustment speed to $\beta_{nn} = 2.00 > \tilde{\beta}_{nn}$ increases $\tilde{\beta}_{y,1}$ to $\tilde{\beta}_{y,1} = 12.76$, so that local stability could then be obtained by virtue of statement (c) of the proposition.

After assessing the plain real wage effects, we can take the second step in the stability analysis of system (7.4), (7.5) and reintroduce the wage share into the Phillips curves. The mostly unfavourable stability results established so for prompt the question as to whether sufficiently high values of β_{wv} or β_{pv} could eventually stabilize the dynamics. Conversely, they might add to the already destabilizing forces. To avoid too much repetition in this kind of discussion, we retrieve the non-negative term $\beta_{wp,v}$ from the proof of Proposition 2,

$$\beta_{wp,v} := (1 - \kappa_p)\beta_{wv} + (1 - \kappa_w)\beta_{pv} \qquad (7.7)$$

and inaugurate the following mode of expression. In short, 'Statement S' makes precise in what sense both β_{wv} and β_{pv} may be stabilizing, 'Statement D' in what sense they may both be destabilizing.

Statement S: A steady state that is locally asymptotically stable in the situation of Proposition 2 remains stable for arbitrary positive values of $\beta_{wp,v}$; a steady state that is unstable in Proposition 2 becomes locally asymptotically stable if $\beta_{wp,v}$ is sufficiently high.
Statement D: A steady state that is locally asymptotically stable in Proposition 2 becomes unstable if $\beta_{wp,v}$ is high enough; an unstable steady state in Proposition 2 cannot be stabilized through any positive values of $\beta_{wp,v}$.

The proposition investigating these possibilities is not particularly handsome, but in some respects it is still instructive. It has to distinguish a number of different parameter combinations, for which we define

$$\tilde{\alpha}_I := f_{Iu}/y^n + f_{Iq}[1 - v - i/\eta_{m,i}y^n]$$
$$\tilde{\alpha}_v := (s_c - \tau_w)v \qquad (7.8)$$
$$\tilde{\beta}_{y,2} := |y^e \tilde{\alpha}_I y_y|/|(\tilde{\alpha}_I + \tilde{\alpha}_v)y_y - s_c|$$

Proposition 3 (**Augmented real wage effects**)
Let Assumptions 1 and 2 apply. Then the following statements hold true.

(a) Suppose that $\tilde{\alpha}_I < 0$ and $\tilde{\alpha}_I < s_c/y_y - \tilde{\alpha}_v$ in (7.8) (i.e. $(\tilde{\alpha}_I + \tilde{\alpha}_v)y_y - s_c < 0$). Then Statement S holds if $\beta_y > \tilde{\beta}_{y,2}$, and Statement D holds if $\beta_y < \tilde{\beta}_{y,2}$.

(b) If $s_c/y_y - \tilde{\alpha}_v < \tilde{\alpha}_I < 0$, Statement D holds for all $\beta_y > 0$.

(c) If $0 < \tilde{\alpha}_I < s_c/y_y - \tilde{\alpha}_v$, Statement S holds for all $\beta_y > 0$.

(d) Suppose that $\tilde{\alpha}_I > 0$ and $\tilde{\alpha}_I > s_c/y_y - \tilde{\alpha}_v$ (i.e. $(\tilde{\alpha}_I + \tilde{\alpha}_v)y_y - s_c > 0$). Then Statement S holds if $\beta_y < \tilde{\beta}_{y,2}$, while Statement D holds if $\beta_y > \tilde{\beta}_{y,2}$. If in addition $(\tilde{\alpha}_I + \tilde{\alpha}_v)y_y - s_c > (s_c - \tau_w - f_{Iq})vf'_z y_y$ (the latter expression being positive by Assumption 2), the critical value $\tilde{\beta}_{y,2}$ is less than the (likewise positive) critical value $\tilde{\beta}_{y,1}$ in Proposition 2.

The first point to be noted is that the stability effects of the wage share coefficient β_{wv} are indeed always in the same direction as those of the other coefficient β_{pv} (if $\kappa_w, \kappa_p < 1$). The effects themselves, however, are dependent, in complicated ways, on the relative magnitude of other parameters in the model. In particular, in some cases β_{wv} and β_{pv} are stabilizing if the adjustment speed β_y is high enough, whereas in other cases β_y must be sufficiently low to bring about this effect (which again stresses the ambiguous role of this parameter).

Regarding the impact of β_{wv} and β_{pv} on stability, it is, moreover, intriguing to relate Proposition 2(c) to Proposition 3(d). According to Proposition 2(c), where besides $\beta_{wv} = \beta_{pv} = 0$ the inequality $\beta_{nn} > \tilde{\beta}_{nn}$ is assumed, the steady state is stable if β_{we} as well as β_y are small enough; specified as $\beta_{we} < \tilde{\beta}_{we}$ and $\beta_y < \tilde{\beta}_{y,1}$. With positive values of β_{wv} and β_{pv}, however, this stability may get lost, namely if in the situation of the second part of Proposition 3(d) the adjustment speed β_y still exceeds $\tilde{\beta}_{y,2}$ – i.e. $\tilde{\beta}_{y,2} < \beta_y < \tilde{\beta}_{y,1}$. On the other hand, if instability prevails in Proposition 2(c) because of $\beta_{we} > \tilde{\beta}_{we}$, but β_y is so small that that $\beta_y < \tilde{\beta}_{y,2} < \tilde{\beta}_{y,1}$, then sufficiently high values of β_{wv} and/or β_{pv} can stabilize the subdynamics.

Though only one of the four cases in Proposition 3 is numerically important for us, the other three cases have been included as a first indication that, in the full KMG model, the effects of β_{wv} and β_{pv} may be severely influenced by the other parameters. Thus, their impact on the system's stability could possibly be rather ambiguous (which has to be investigated in detail later on).

A numerical check makes sure that it is actually item (d) in Proposition that has to be regarded as the relevant case. Rounding to three digits, we have

$$\tilde{\alpha}_I = 0.280/0.70 + 0.115 \cdot [0.30 - 0.07/(0.14 \cdot 0.70)] = 0.352$$

$$\tilde{\alpha}_v = (0.80 - 0.35) \cdot 0.70 = 0.315$$

Solving the inequality $\tilde{\alpha}_I > s_c/y_y - \tilde{\alpha}_v$ in (d) for y_y, it is seen that the premises stated there are fulfilled if $y_y > s_c/(\tilde{\alpha}_I + \tilde{\alpha}_v) = 0.80/(0.352 + 0.315) = 1.199$. A look at the definition of y_y in (7.6), $y_y = 1 + (g^\circ + \beta_{nn})\beta_{ny}$, shows that already low values of β_{nn}, such as $\beta_{nn} = 1$ or somewhat less, are sufficient to bring this inequality about (we recall that $\beta_{ny} = 0.22$).

On the basis of the calibration, we can then gather from Proposition $3(d)$ that there is no scope for β_{wv} and β_{pv} to stabilize the steady state of (7.4), (7.5), since $\beta_y = 8$ and $\tilde{\beta}_{y,2} < \tilde{\beta}_{y,1} = 2.82$.[10] Also, reducing the stock adjustment speed to $\beta_{nn} = 2.00$, which as mentioned above raises $\tilde{\beta}_{y,1}$ to 12.76, does not help very much. Even in this case the critical value $\tilde{\beta}_{y,2}$ still turns out to be as low as $\tilde{\beta}_{y,2} = 2.14$.

Proof of Proposition 3: Regarding the impact of β_{wv} and β_{pv} on stability, it is clear from the Jacobian $\mathcal{J}_{wp}$ in the proof of Proposition 2 that only the composite term $\beta_{wp,v}$ matters. Since a suitable increase of $\beta_{wp,v}$ can always render the trace of $\mathcal{J}_{wp}$ negative, only the determinant of the matrix has to be examined. Differentiating $(1/\kappa) \det \mathcal{J}_{wp}$ with respect to $\beta_{wp,v}$ gives $-[\beta_y a_y - y^e \alpha_I y_y + \omega y_y f_z'(\beta_y a_\omega + f_{Iq} y^e)]$. With respect to a_y it has to be taken into account that $\alpha_I = \tilde{\alpha}_I + v f_{Iq} f_z'$ and $\alpha_v = \tilde{\alpha}_v - (s_c - \tau_w) v f_z'$. Remarkably, f_z' thus cancels out in the derivative and we arrive at

$$(1/\kappa)\, \partial \mathcal{J}_{wp}/\partial \beta_{wp,v} = -\beta_y[(\tilde{\alpha}_I + \tilde{\alpha}_v)y_y - s_c] + y^e \tilde{\alpha}_I y_y$$

Statements (a) to (d) in the proposition enumerate the cases in which this derivative is positive, which gives rise to Statement S, and the cases in which the derivative is negative, which gives rise to Statement D.

To verify the additional statement in point (d) regarding $\tilde{\beta}_{y,2}$, note that $\tilde{\beta}_{y,1} = y^e \alpha_I y_y/\alpha_y$, that $\tilde{\alpha}_I > 0$ implies $\alpha_I > 0$, and that $\alpha_y = (\alpha_I + \alpha_v)y_y - s_c = (\tilde{\alpha}_I + \tilde{\alpha}_v)y_y - s_c - a_\omega v f_z' y_y$ is positive if (and only if) the additional condition in (d) is satisfied ($a_\omega = s_c - \tau_w - f_{Iq} > 0$ by Assumption 2). To prove that then also $\tilde{\beta}_{y,2} < \tilde{\beta}_{y,1}$, let ϕ_I, ϕ_v be two strictly monotonic functions of some variable x such that $\phi_I(0) = \alpha_I$, $\phi_v(0) = \alpha_v$ and $\phi_I(1) = \tilde{\alpha}_I$, $\phi_v(1) = \tilde{\alpha}_v$. Obviously, $\phi_I' < 0$, $\phi_v' > 0$. Substituting ϕ_I, ϕ_v in the expression for $\tilde{\beta}_{y,1}$, formulating it as a function of x called $\phi = \phi(x)$ and differentiating it, one gets the result that the sign of $d\phi/dx$ is given by the sign of $\phi_v \phi_I' - \phi_I \phi_v'$, which is unambiguously negative. Hence $\tilde{\beta}_{y,1} = \phi(0) > \phi(1) = \tilde{\beta}_{y,2}$.

QED

---

[10] Given that $\alpha_I > 0$, $\tilde{\beta}_{y,1}$ is positive if and only if $a_y > 0$ in (7.6). The latter inequality, in turn, is equivalent to the proposition's additional assumption in (d), $(\tilde{\alpha}_I + \tilde{\alpha}_v)y_y - s_c > (s_c - \tau_w - f_{Iq})v f_z' y_y$. Hence, without computing $\tilde{\beta}_{y,2}$ explicitly, it can directly be concluded from point (d) and the result $\tilde{\beta}_{y,1} = 2.82 > 0$ that $\tilde{\beta}_{y,2}$ falls short of $\tilde{\beta}_{y,1}$.

7.3.2   The real wage feedback mechanisms

As in the Metzlerian subsystem, the feedback loops that can be identified with respect to real wages correspond closely to the entries of the Jacobian matrix $\mathcal{J}_{wp}$ of process (7.4), (7.5), which have already been explicitly computed in the proof of Proposition 2. Referring to the Jacobian $\mathcal{J}$ in (4.50) of the full model, $\mathcal{J}_{wp}$ may for our present purpose be sketched as

$$\mathcal{J}_{wp} = \begin{bmatrix} j_{11} & j_{13} \\ j_{31} & j_{33} \end{bmatrix} = \begin{bmatrix} 0 \text{ or } -\{\beta_{wp,v}\} & ?\{\beta_{wv}, \beta_{pv}\} \\ + & ?\{\beta_y, \beta_{nn}\} \end{bmatrix}$$

The parameters in curly brackets after the question marks indicate that the sign of the corresponding entries is crucially contingent on the relative magnitude of these coefficients. Entry $j_{11} = \partial\dot\omega/\partial\omega$ is negative precisely when $\beta_{wp,v}$ in (7.7) is positive.

Let us begin with the plain real wage effects where $\beta_{wv} = \beta_{pv} = 0$, which is the subject of Proposition 2. The feedback mechanisms involved here are depicted in figure 7.5a. As discussed in connection with Assumption 2, an increase in real wages increases aggregate demand y^d. From the Metzlerian part we know that, subsequently, sales expectations y^e also rise. The mathematical counterpart of this short chain of reaction is $j_{31} = \partial\dot y^e/\partial\omega$, which is unambiguously positive.

The higher sales expectations induce firms to raise production. The resulting higher capacity utilization u and employment rate e, formally supported by (7.3), lead to a (relative) increase of price as well as wage inflation. The effect on the real wage rate depends on which of the two rates of inflation increases more. With the wage share currently playing no role, this is exclusively governed by the relative size of the slope coefficients β_{we} and β_{pu} in the two Phillips curves. The upper loop in figure 7.5a shows a situation where $\hat p > \hat w + \hat z^o$, because β_{pu} in the

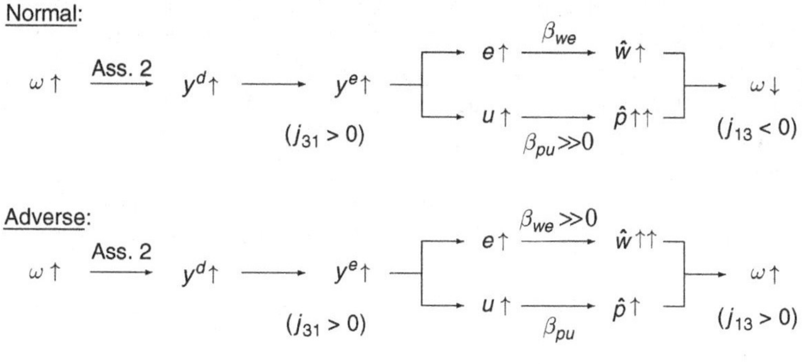

Figure 7.5a: Plain real wage effects ($\beta_{wv} = \beta_{pv} = 0$)

price Phillips curve dominates β_{we} in the wage Phillips curve. Hence, the (productivity-deflated) real wage rate $\omega = (w/p)/z^o$ decreases.

In total, a negative feedback loop for real wages is obtained here, which in economic theory is often thought to be the 'normal' case. Mathematically, the chain from $y^e \uparrow$ to $\omega \downarrow$ is captured by $j_{13} = \partial\dot\omega/\partial y^e$. It was easy to see in the proof of Proposition 2 that (under $\beta_{wv} = \beta_{pv} = 0$) $j_{13} < 0$ is equivalent to $\beta_{we} < \tilde\beta_{we} = (1 - \kappa_w)\beta_{pu}/(1 - \kappa_p)(1 - f'_z)$.

The lower loop in figure 7.5a describes the opposite effects, which come about if the coefficient β_{we} dominates the coefficient β_{pu}: $\beta_{we} > \tilde\beta_{we}$, so that $\hat p < \hat w + \hat z^o$. In this case $j_{13} = \partial\dot\omega/\partial y^e > 0$ and the real wage rate increases at the end of the loop. As a consequence, the feedback loop in its entirety is destabilizing. Proposition 2 reveals in addition that these effects are also sufficient to render the steady state unstable, irrespective of the feedback of the second state variable y^e onto itself. The fact that entry j_{33} in $\mathcal{J}_{wp}$ does not matter in this respect is mathematically immediate, since, with $j_{11} = 0$, $\det\mathcal{J}_{wp} = 0 - j_{13}\cdot j_{31} < 0$ and (at least) one of the two Routh–Hurwitz stability conditions is violated.

In the former case of 'normal' real wage effects, where $j_{13} < 0$ and thus $\det\mathcal{J}_{wp} = -j_{13}\cdot j_{31} > 0$, the stability of the steady state is determined by the nature of the feedback loop of expected sales – i.e. by the sign of $j_{33} = \partial\dot y^e/\partial y^e$. Points (b) and (c) of Proposition 2 spell out when it happens to be negative, $j_{33} < 0$, which then ensures local stability.

Figure 7.5b[11] completes the argument of figure 7.5a by including the wage share effects in the Phillips curves, $\beta_{wp,v} = (1 - \kappa_p)\beta_{wv} + (1 - \kappa_w)\beta_{pv} > 0$. The upper part of the diagram recapitulates the real wage effects of figure 7.5a, which, as reflected by a positive or negative element j_{13}, are generally ambiguous.

In addition, the increase in utilization u diminishes the wage share owing to the procyclical labour productivity, $v = \omega/f_z(u)$ and $f'_z > 0$. Since v enters the core term $f_w(e, v)$ of the wage Phillips curve in a negative way and the core term $f_p(u, v)$ of the price Phillips curve in a positive way, the reduction of the wage share has a positive effect on wage inflation and a negative effect on price inflation. Taken together, we have a positive effect on the real wage rate; that is, this channel from y^e to ω contributes to a destabilization.

On the other hand, the rise in ω with which the feedback chain starts has a direct effect on v, which likewise rises. The Phillips curve

---

[11] Different slope coefficients f'_z have virtually no impact on the the stability of process (7.4), (7.5), since in the determinant $j_{11}j_{33} - j_{13}j_{31}$ of the Jacobian matrix the (destabilizing) effects of f'_z that may increase j_{13} in the diagram just cancel against the (stabilizing) effects that may increase $j_{33} = \partial\dot y^e/\partial y^e$ (not shown in the diagram).

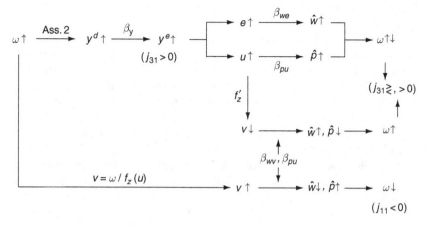

Figure 7.5b: Augmented real wage effects $(\beta_{wv}, \beta_{pv} > 0)$

mechanisms just discussed now work in the opposite direction. In the end we have here a negative effect on the real wage, which is sketched in the lower part of figure 7.5b. It corresponds to a negative diagonal entry in $\mathcal{J}_{wp}$, $j_{11} = \partial\dot{\omega}/\partial\omega < 0$.

The arrow from $u \uparrow$ to $v \downarrow$ might suggest that, with a weak procyclicality of productivity (i.e. f_z' low or even zero), the destabilizing channel from $u \uparrow$ to $\omega \uparrow$ can be 'dominated' by the stabilizing loop $\omega \uparrow \to v \uparrow \to \omega \downarrow$. However, Proposition 3(d), which covers the numerically relevant case for us, shows that this conjecture is false: low or even zero values of f_z' do not improve the stability prospects. The reason is that this feedback argument neglects the fact that the slope f_z' also enters the feedback loop from y^e to y^e, i.e. the element $j_{33} = \partial\dot{y}^e/\partial y^e$, which is not included in figure 7.5b. The two effects are 'confronted' in the determinant of the Jacobian $\mathcal{J}_{wp}$, where they happen to cancel out; the positive effect of higher values of f_z' on entry j_{13} is just offset by the positive effect on j_{33}. More exactly, if we differentiate $\det \mathcal{J}_{wp} = j_{11} \cdot j_{33} - j_{13} \cdot j_{31}$ with respect to $\beta_{wp,v}$, in order to see whether an increase of $\beta_{wp,v}$ could render the determinant positive, then the resulting expression is completely independent of f_z' (see the proof of Proposition 3 for the explicit formulae).

Another aspect is the adjustment speed β_y regarding expected sales. Suppose, for example, that β_{we} is so small (or β_{pu} so large) that $\omega \downarrow$ comes about in the upper part of figure 7.5b. Suppose, furthermore, that this also dominates the counteracting effect from $u \uparrow$ to $\omega \uparrow$, such that on the whole $j_{13} < 0$. Then, as indicated in the diagram, one might conjecture that high values of β_y are favourable for stability, since they reinforce this negative type of feedback. By contrast, Proposition 3 shows that this conjecture is false, too.[12]

These arguments are clear examples of the limits of feedback diagrams, if the interactions between the variables become too complex. Figure 7.5b may nevertheless be a useful tool that can provide at least some economic reasoning behind the pure mathematics. Moreover, it gives an impression of the conflicting effects in the real wage dynamics.

The general lesson to be learned from figure 7.5b and the surrounding discussion may be the following one. Supplementary information is already required in the two-dimensional submodel (7.4), (7.5) to resolve the stability question, and we have seen that the dominance of some effects over others is heavily dependent on further parameters in the model, which are not alluded to in the diagram itself. Thus, even if by accepting selected conditions on these other parameters it was possible in the two-dimensional case to derive a definite statement on the stability of the steady state, or on the impact of β_{wv} and β_{pv} upon its stability, it is easily conceivable that in the full KMG model additional factors may come into play that influence the single links shown in figure 7.5b in ways that can decisively perturb the relative strength of the stabilizing and destabilizing loops. As a consequence, the stability effects of certain parameter variations may be different in different regions of the parameter space, even when the parameter combinations are not so exotic as in the first three points of Proposition 3.

7.3.3   Parameter diagrams for the two-dimensional and six-dimensional dynamics

Given the Metzlerian adjustments with, in particular, the two reaction coefficients β_{nn} and β_y, the key parameters in the real wage dynamics are the ordinary slope coefficients β_{we} and β_{pu} in the wage and price Phillips curves, respectively. In addition, it has been asked whether the augmented part of the Phillips curve regarding the influence of the wage share is potentially stabilizing, which concerns the coefficients β_{wv} and β_{pv}. In this subsection we compare the stability effects of these four coefficients in the two-dimensional submodel (7.4), (7.5) with the effects coming about when they are embedded in the complete KMG dynamics.

---

[12] Note that, while fast adjustments of sales expectations would also reinforce a destabilizing feedback loop $y^e \uparrow \rightarrow y^e \uparrow$, this in turn could be neutralized by sufficiently high values of β_{wv} and β_{pv}, such that the negative entry j_{11} would dominate the positive entry j_{33} and the trace of $\mathcal{J}_{wp}$ gets negative. The condition that requires $\beta_y < \tilde{\beta}_{y,2}$ for stability in Proposition 3(d) is therefore quite involved.

Since, under the calibrated values $\beta_{nn} = 3.00 > 1.76 = \tilde{\beta}_{nn}$ and $\beta_y = 8.00 > 2.82 = \tilde{\beta}_{y,1} > \tilde{\beta}_{y,2}$, Propositions 2(c) and 3(d) provide no scope for a stable steady-state position of the subdynamics, we also consider a second pair of these parameters that offer better stability prospects. So we choose $\beta_{nn} = 2.00$ and $\beta_y = 2.00 < 2.14 = \tilde{\beta}_{y,2} < \tilde{\beta}_{y,1}$. For easier reference the two combinations are called Scenario S1 and S2.

Scenario S1: $\beta_{nn} = 3.00$, $\beta_y = 8.00$ (the baseline scenario)
Scenario S2: $\beta_{nn} = 2.00$, $\beta_y = 2.00$

We begin the investigation with the plain real wage effects. Accordingly, we put $\beta_{wv} = \beta_{pv} = 0$ and plot parameter diagrams for the 'genuine' slope coefficients β_{we} and β_{pu}, which is done in figure 7.6.[13] The upper two panels are parameter planes for the submodel (7.4), (7.5) under Scenarios S1 and S2, respectively. They illustrate Proposition 2(c): in S1 (the upper right panel) instability prevails for all values of β_{we} and

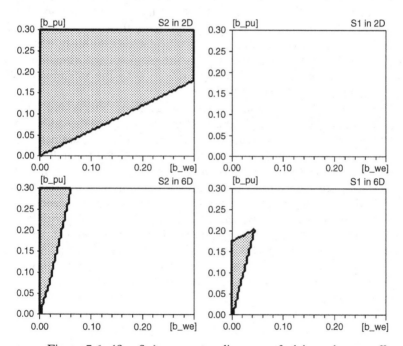

Figure 7.6: (β_{we}, β_{pu}) parameter diagrams of plain real wage effects $(\beta_{wv} = \beta_{pv} = 0)$

[13] Dotted areas are the stability regions. '2D' refers to the two-dimensional subdynamics (7.4), (7.5); '6D' refers to the full six-dimensional KMG model.

β_{pu}, since $\beta_{nn} > \tilde{\beta}_{nn} = 1.76$ as well as $\beta_y > \tilde{\beta}_{y,1} = 2.82$; in S2 (the upper left panel) stability is possible, since here $\beta_y < \tilde{\beta}_{y,1}$. The stability frontier in the latter case is given by the straight line $\beta_{we} = (1 - \kappa_w)\beta_{pu}/(1 - \kappa_p)(1 - f_z')$, or $\beta_{pu} = 0.60 \cdot \beta_{we}$. As remarked before, a higher (lower) slope coefficient β_{we} in the wage Phillips curve is always destabilizing (stabilizing), and a higher (lower) coefficient β_{pu} in the price Phillips curve is always stabilizing (destabilizing).

The lower two panels in figure 7.6 demonstrate that there is no clear answer to the question as to whether the real wage dynamics in the full KMG model are more or less stable than in the submodel. With respect to Scenario S2 it could be said that the full model is 'less stable', since the stability region of the pairs (β_{we}, β_{pu}) in the lower left is considerably smaller than its counterpart above. Under the S1 parameter values of β_{nn} and β_y, however, we have the opposite effect: while there is no stability at all in the submodel, the stability region is non-empty for KMG.

Note, moreover, that in Scenario S1 in the lower right corner neither is the parameter β_{we} unambiguously destabilizing any more, nor is the parameter β_{pu} unambiguously stabilizing. In both cases a reswitching of instability is observed when the coefficient continuously increases from zero (as for the variations of β_{we}, the phenomenon results over a small range of given values of β_{pu}; for $\beta_{pu} \leq 0.18$ the unambiguously destabilizing effect of a rising β_{we} remains).

In the next step we reintroduce the wage share effects and let the coefficients β_{wv} and β_{pv} attain their original values from the calibration: $\beta_{wv} = 0.50$, $\beta_{pv} = 1.50$. These values are underlying the parameter diagrams in figure 7.7, which are otherwise of the same kind as in figure 7.6 (except for the wider subset of the parameter plane shown here). As far as Scenario S2 in the submodel is concerned, we know from Proposition 3(d) and the above-mentioned figure $\tilde{\beta}_{y,2} = 2.14$, which exceeds $\beta_y = 2.00$, that higher values of β_{wv} and β_{pv} are stabilizing. In line with Statement S in the proposition, the stability region in the upper left panel of figure 7.7 embraces that of figure 7.6 as a subset. A comparison of the lower left panels of figures 7.6 and 7.7 demonstrates that this property carries over to the six-dimensional dynamics.

Regarding the calibrated values $\beta_{nn} = 3$, $\beta_y = 8$ in Scenario S1, the instability part of Proposition 3(d) for the submodel applies, so that the empty stability region in the upper right panel of figure 7.6 is maintained. As before with this scenario, stability becomes possible in the full model. Comparing the lower right panels of figures 7.6 and 7.7, it is seen that the positive values of β_{wv} and β_{pv} have considerably enlarged the stability region. Hence, under the circumstances considered in these two figures, the discussion strongly points into the direction that the wage share

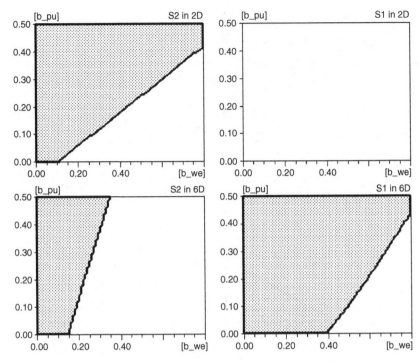

Figure 7.7: (β_{we}, β_{pu}) parameter diagrams of augmented real wage effects $(\beta_{wv} = 0.50, \beta_{pv} = 1.50)$

effects in each of the two Phillips curves, in the form of the coefficients β_{wv} and β_{pv}, are stabilizing.

This pleasing picture has to be modified when we look directly at the parameter diagrams constituted by the two parameters β_{wv} and β_{pv} themselves, which are presented in figure 7.8. A first point to be noted with respect to Scenario 2 is the different shapes of the (β_{wv}, β_{pv}) stability region in the submodel and in the full model. Given the calibrated slope coefficients $\beta_{we} = 0.55$ and $\beta_{pv} = 0.15$, for which $\beta_{we} > \tilde{\beta}_{we} = (1 - \kappa_w)\beta_{pu}/(1 - \kappa_p)(1 - f_z')$ holds, the steady state in the submodel can be stabilized by large values of β_{wv} and β_{pv}. Again, this is exactly what Proposition 3(d) predicts (one might even compute the stability frontier in explicit terms). It is perhaps remarkable that numerically very high values of β_{wv} and/or β_{pv} are required for a stable steady state; see the upper left panel in figure 7.8.

In the full KMG model, on the other hand, much lower values of β_{wv} and β_{pv} are already capable of bringing about stability, which is shown in the lower left panel. Also, β_{wv} presents itself as a stabilizing parameter,

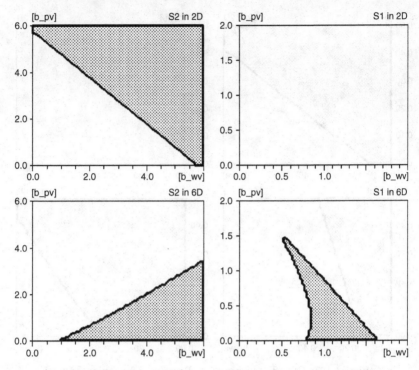

Figure 7.8: (β_{wv}, β_{pv}) parameter diagrams (given, in particular, $\beta_{we} = 0.55$, $\beta_{pu} = 0.15$)

since it entails stability if, and only if, it is sufficiently large. The role of β_{pv}, however, is now reversed in this respect. It cannot stabilize the steady state when β_{wv} is relatively small, $\beta_{wv} < 1$ roughly. For $\beta_{wv} \geq 1$, the steady state is stable for zero or low values of β_{pv}, but it becomes unstable as β_{pv} increases too much. In this parameter diagram, therefore, β_{pv} can be characterized as a destabilizing parameter.

Things become even more puzzling in the baseline scenario for β_{nn} and β_y, Scenario S1. In the submodel nothing new happens, since here, as we know well enough by now, β_{wv} and β_{pv} cannot possibly stabilize the steady state. The (β_{wv}, β_{pv}) stability region is accordingly empty, which for completeness is exemplified in the upper right corner of figure 7.8. In contrast, stability can come about in the six-dimensional model – though in no clear way. Rather, we obtain a reswitching of instability in the lower right panel, not only for β_{pv} but also for β_{wv}. For either coefficient there are situations where the steady state is unstable at low values, becomes stable as the coefficient increases sufficiently and becomes unstable again as it rises further.

On the basis of these results it may be said that the impact on local stability of the wage share in the two Phillips curves is ambiguous, both in a wider sense and in a narrower sense. By ambiguity in a wider sense we mean that high coefficients β_{wv} and β_{pv} are stabilizing under certain combinations of the other parameters in the model (such as β_{nn} and β_y, for instance), and they are destabilizing in different circumstances. In the real wage subdynamics, this phenomenon has even been established analytically, in Proposition 3.

In the complete KMG model, ambiguity in a narrower sense is observed. Here all other parameters are considered fixed and we refer only to a single (β_{wv}, β_{pv}) parameter diagram. Then, in some regions of this parameter plane an increase of β_{wv} or β_{pv} is stabilizing, whereas in other regions of the same plane an increase has the opposite effect. It was indicated in the discussion of the feedback diagram in figure 7.5 that we should be prepared to find that the relative strength of the single feedbacks in the chain of reaction can be sensitively affected by additional factors if this schema is embedded in a wider framework. The finding of, in particular, the lower right panel of figure 7.8 for the KMG model is a good example to substantiate this suspicion.

7.4   The monetary subdynamics

7.4.1   A necessary condition for stability in the three-dimensional system

The previous two sections were concerned with selected aspects of the disequilibrium adjustments within the real sector. In the present section we now turn to the monetary feedbacks in the KMG model, which arise from the movements of real balances and the real rate of interest (under constant growth of the money supply). The central variable is, therefore, the rate of inflation. On the one hand, changes in inflation affect the real money supply and, thus, the nominal bond rate of interest. On the other hand, the same changes have a bearing on the general inflation climate. The resulting real rate of interest influences aggregate demand and, in the next step, expected sales and output, the variations of which in turn feed back on the rate of inflation.

Involved in these feedbacks are the Keynes effect and the Mundell effect. In the numerical analysis of the compact model of chapter 3, section 8, they were both found to act in the 'wrong' direction, which was due to a negative output–inflation nexus. Given the present framework and our calibration of, in particular, the wage-price dynamics, we will have to see if these effects will likewise happen to be 'perverse', and what the implications will be for the system's stability. Apart from this, we will be interested in how local stability is affected by the parameters that govern the adjustments of the inflation climate.

To isolate the monetary dynamics from the rest of the economy, the real wage rate is frozen at its equilibrium value, $\omega = \omega^o$. Note that this does not apply to the wage share, which, because of the procyclical labour productivity, will still vary with capacity utilization. These reactions will, in fact, be a salient feedback channel. In addition, the capital–labour ratio and the inventory ratio are put to rest, $k^s = (k^s)^o$ and $n = n^o$. What must be retained as state variables are, of course, the real balances ratio $m = M/pK$ and the inflation climate π. Since, in comparison with chapter 3, the KMG model has abandoned the IS device on the goods market, for output to be variable we also have to include the expected sales ratio y^e among the dynamic variables. In this way a three-dimensional subsystem is obtained. The composite terms entering it are formulated as functions of these three state variables m, y^e and π:

$$y = y(y^e) = [1 + (g^o + \beta_{nn})\beta_{ny}]y^e - \beta_{nn}n^o$$

$$u = u(y^e) = y(y^e)/y^n$$

$$e = e(y^e) = y(y^e)(k^s)^o/f_z[u(y^e)]$$

$$v = v(y^e) = \omega^o/f_z[u(y^e)]$$

$$f_p(u, v) = \beta_{pu}(u - 1) + \beta_{pv}[(1 + \mu)v - 1]$$

$$f_w(e, v) = \beta_{we}(e - 1) - \beta_{wv}(v - v^o)/v^o \tag{7.9}$$

$$\hat{p} = \hat{p}(y^e, \pi) = \pi + \kappa[f_p(u, v) + \kappa_p f_w(e, v)], \quad \kappa := 1/(1 - \kappa_p \kappa_w)$$

$$q = q(m, y^e, \pi) = [1 - v(y^e)]y(y^e) - \delta - [i(m, y^e, n^o) - \pi]$$

$$g_k = g_k(m, y^e, \pi) = f_I[q(m, y^e, \pi), u(y^e)]$$

$$y^d = y^d(m, y^e, \pi) = (1 - s_c)y^e + (s_c - \tau_w)v(y^e)y(y^e) + g_k(m, y^e, \pi) + \text{const}$$

Except for the variables that are here considered to be fixed, and for the rate of inflation $\hat{p}$, the reduced form of which has last been stated as eq. (6.9) in chapter 6, these expressions have already been collected in (7.3).

The differential equations for m, y^e and π themselves are those stated in eqs. (4.45), (4.46) and (4.49). On the basis of (7.9), the monetary subdynamics is thus described by the three differential equations

$$\dot{m} = m[g_m - \hat{p} - g_k]$$

$$\dot{y}^e = (g^o - g_k)y^e + \beta_y(y^d - y^e) \tag{7.10}$$

$$\dot{\pi} = \beta_\pi[\kappa_\pi(\hat{p} - \pi) + (1 - \kappa_\pi)(\pi^o - \pi)]$$

The numerical investigations further below will be sufficiently indicative of the fact that a complete stability analysis of system (7.10) is extremely complicated (even more so than before). For this reason we limit the mathematical treatment to a necessary stability condition. It is formulated in a way that emphasizes the role of the wage share parameter β_{pv} in the price Phillips curve.[14]

Proposition 4
With respect to the steady-state values, suppose that $\beta_y > y^e$ and define

$$\alpha_v := (s_c - \tau_w)(1 - f_z')v$$

$$y_y := 1 + (g^o + \beta_{nn})\beta_{ny}$$

$$\alpha_{vy} := \beta_y(s_c - \alpha_v y_y)y^n/y_y(\beta_y - y^e)$$

$$\tilde{\beta}_{pw} := \beta_{pu} + \kappa_p[(1 - f_z')\beta_{we} + f_z'\beta_{wv}]$$

$$\beta_{pv}^c := [\tilde{\beta}_{pw} + (1 - \kappa_\pi)(1 - \kappa_w\kappa_p)\alpha_{vy}]/f_z'.$$

Then a necessary condition for the equilibrium of the subdynamics (7.10) to be locally asymptotically stable is the inequality

$$\beta_{pv} < \beta_{pv}^c.$$

The message of Proposition 4 is clear: the influence of the wage share in the price Phillips curve must not be too strong if stability is to prevail in the monetary subsystem. Because $f_z' < 1$ and there is also a huge range of parameter values that still entail $\alpha_{vy} > 0$ (in particular, $s_c - \alpha_y y_y = 0.485 > 0$ in the base scenario), β_{pv} may well exceed the 'main' coefficient β_{pu} in the Phillips curve to some extent without violating the stability condition. Nevertheless, β_{pv} is not permitted to be as high as it results from our calibration, where $\beta_{pv} = 1.50$ vis-à-vis $\beta_{pu} = 0.15$, since, given the other numerical parameters, the critical value of β_{pv} is computed as

$$\beta_{pv}^c = 0.654$$

Proof of Proposition 4: Denote the Jacobian of the monetary subsystem by $\mathcal{J}_m$. Using the same notation as in the mathematical analysis in chapter 4, section 4, and, in particular, abbreviating $\tilde{\beta}_y := \beta_y - y^e$ and

---

[14] The corresponding parameter β_{wv} in the wage Phillips curve could be of some concern, too. In our calibration, however, it will take no effect at all, since $\kappa_p = 0$ in the formula for $\hat{p}$. Note also that the terms α_v and y_y in the following proposition are taken over from the definitions in Assumption 1 and eq. (7.6), respectively.

$\tilde{y}^d := y^d - g_k$ as in (4.53), it derives from the Jacobian $\mathcal{J}$, eq. (4.50), of the full KMG model as

$$\mathcal{J}_m = \begin{bmatrix} j_{22} & j_{23} & j_{26} \\ j_{32} & j_{33} & j_{36} \\ j_{62} & j_{63} & j_{66} \end{bmatrix} = \begin{bmatrix} -mg_{km} & -m(\hat{p}_y + g_{ky}) & -m(\hat{p}_\pi + g_{k\pi}) \\ \tilde{\beta}_y g_{km} & \tilde{\beta}_y g_{ky} + \beta_y(\tilde{y}^d_y - 1) & \tilde{\beta}_y g_{k\pi} \\ 0 & \beta_\pi \kappa_\pi \hat{p}_y & \beta_\pi(\kappa_\pi \hat{p}_\pi - 1) \end{bmatrix}$$

$$(7.11)$$

One of the conditions necessary for local stability is a negative determinant. To compute det $\mathcal{J}_m$ for $\kappa_\pi > 0$, factorize $-m$, β_π, g_{km} and subtract $(1/\kappa_\pi) \times$ 3rd row from the 1st row, which does not change the value of det $\mathcal{J}_m$. The resulting matrix is then easily seen to give rise to

$$\det \mathcal{J}_m = +mg_{km}\beta_\pi[(1 - \kappa_\pi)\beta_y(\tilde{y}^d_y - 1) - \tilde{\beta}_y\hat{p}_y] \qquad (7.12)$$

Obviously, (7.12) is equally true if $\kappa_\pi = 0$. For the terms involved here, we have $g_{km} = if_{Iq}/m\eta_{m,i}$, $\tilde{y}^d_y - 1 = -s_c + \alpha_v y_y$ and $\hat{p}_y = (\kappa y_y/y^n)(\tilde{\beta}_{pw} - f'_z\beta_{pv})$. As g_{km} is positive, det $\mathcal{J}_m < 0$ if the square bracket is negative, which when solved for β_{pv} is just the condition stated in the proposition if we finally recall that $1/\kappa = 1 - \kappa_w\kappa_p$.

QED

7.4.2   The role of the output–inflation nexus

The stability condition of Proposition 4 is tantamount to a negative determinant of the subsystem's 3×3 Jacobian matrix $\mathcal{J}_m$. The proof of the proposition also reveals a main economic factor that may be responsible for instability. This is the reaction of the inflation rate to variations in economic activity, which is formally captured by the partial derivative of $\hat{p}$ with respect to expected sales y^e. Indeed, eq. (7.12) demonstrates that a positive derivative, $\hat{p}_y = \partial\hat{p}/\partial y^e > 0$, ensures a negative determinant, since $g_{km} > 0$ and $\tilde{y}^d_y - 1 = -s_c + \alpha_v y_y$, which – as remarked above – can safely be assumed to be negative. Even a moderately negative derivative $\hat{p}_y$ would still admit det $\mathcal{J}_m < 0$, as long as

$$-\hat{p}_y < (1 - \kappa_\pi)\beta_y|\tilde{y}^d_y - 1|/\tilde{\beta}_y$$

The condition $\beta_{pv} < \beta^c_{pv}$ then spells out how much the parameter β_{pv} is allowed to increase above zero without reversing this inequality. It has, however, also been pointed out that the calibrated value for β_{pv} markedly exceeds the upper boundary β^c_{pv}.

If we identify changes in expected sales with the induced changes in production, the derivative $\hat{p}_y$ can be said to represent the output–inflation nexus. The general notion of this feedback has already been introduced in chapter 3, section 8. In the numerical example that was studied there a negative output–inflation nexus was obtained; see eq. (3.37). We now see that the same holds true for the calibration of the more detailed KMG economy, and that, again, the negative reaction of the inflation rate is due to a dominating wage share parameter in the price Phillips curve. Beyond the mere mathematical expressions, the single effects contributing to this outcome can be illustrated in a feedback diagram; see figure 7.9.[15] The double downward arrows associated with the Phillips curve term f_p in the upper loop are meant to indicate that the indirect effect of utilization, which first lowers the wage share, prevails over the direct positive impact of utilization on f_p in the lower loop.

The determinant of the Jacobian $\mathcal{J}_m$ of process (7.10) summarizes a greater number of interactions between the variables, and states that a certain combination of the interactions gives rise to either a 'negative' or 'positive' effect. For the 3×3 matrix in (7.11) with only one zero entry, the economic meaning behind this overall effect is hard to grasp in detail. It is thus perhaps somewhat surprising that the outcome of all the mathematical calculations is a plain economic proposition: whether the interactions, as they are combined, go in the direction required for stability boils down to a single condition on the sign or, if it is negative, on the strength of the output–inflation nexus.

Proposition 4 is nevertheless only one necessary condition for stability, and there are other effects that have to be taken into account on this matter. A most obvious effect, which we already know very well, starts

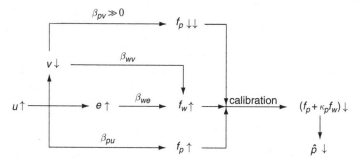

Figure 7.9: The negative output–inflation nexus (*ceteris paribus*)

---

[15] Regarding the model equations, the increase in utilization u is identified with an increase in expected sales y^e. In reduced form, the inflation rate is determined by $\hat{p} = \pi + \kappa(f_p + \kappa_p f_w)$; see (7.9)

out from expected sales and in a large variety of circumstances generates a positive feedback loop. Sufficiently fast adjustments of expected sales, i.e. β_y sufficiently high, could thus completely destabilize the steady state. At present, however, we should concentrate on effects that are more closely connected to the monetary sector, and that have already been studied within the IS-LM framework of chapter 3, section 8. These are the feedback loops constituted by the Keynes effect and the Mundell effect.[16]

While the literature discusses the Keynes effect as a stabilizing element and the Mundell effect as a destabilizing one, chapter 3, section 8, has pointed out that with the augmented price Phillips curve both effects can become 'perverse', namely if the output–inflation nexus happens to be negative. The basic mechanisms are not essentially modified when the IS-LM temporary equilibrium assumption is replaced with the KMG model's disequilibrium adjustments on the goods market. This is demonstrated in figure 7.10.[17]

As indicated in the diagram, the positive feedback loop of real balances, which is produced by the Keynes effect, involves the two entries j_{32} and j_{23} of the Jacobian $\mathcal{J}_m$ in (7.11). Regarding the mathematical Routh–Hurwitz stability conditions they, most directly, play a role in the principal minors, the sum of which $\mathcal{J}_{m,1} + \mathcal{J}_{m,2} + \mathcal{J}_{m,3}$ is required to be positive for stability.[18] That the signs $j_{32} > 0$ and $j_{23} > 0$ are unfavourable for stability is reflected in the expression $\mathcal{J}_{m,3} = j_{22}j_{33} - j_{32}j_{23}$, on which they have a negative impact. The mathematical counterpart of the entries

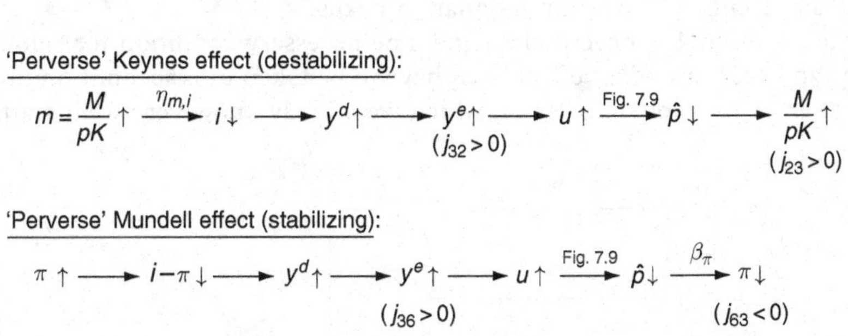

'Perverse' Keynes effect (destabilizing):

$$m = \frac{M}{pK} \uparrow \xrightarrow{\eta_{m,i}} i \downarrow \longrightarrow y^d \uparrow \longrightarrow y^e \uparrow \longrightarrow u \uparrow \xrightarrow{\text{Fig. 7.9}} \hat{p} \downarrow \longrightarrow \frac{M}{pK} \uparrow$$
$$\phantom{m = \frac{M}{pK}} (j_{32} > 0) (j_{23} > 0)$$

'Perverse' Mundell effect (stabilizing):

$$\pi \uparrow \longrightarrow i - \pi \downarrow \longrightarrow y^d \uparrow \longrightarrow y^e \uparrow \longrightarrow u \uparrow \xrightarrow{\text{Fig. 7.9}} \hat{p} \downarrow \xrightarrow{\beta_\pi} \pi \downarrow$$
$$ (j_{36} > 0) (j_{63} < 0)$$

Figure 7.10: The basic feedback loops of the monetary subdynamics

[16] In addition, with respect to the revisions of the inflation climate π the regressive expectations effect was mentioned in chapter 3, section 8, the strength of which is represented by the weighting parameter $(1 - \kappa_\pi)$. Since by leading π back to normal it is trivially stabilizing, the following discussion may not refer to it especially.

[17] $\eta_{m,i}$ is the interest elasticity of money demand, which determines the responsiveness of the bond rate as $\partial i / \partial m = -i/m\eta_{m,i}$. Inequalities $j_{32} > 0$ etc. refer to the Jacobian $\mathcal{J}_m$ in (7.11), or $\mathcal{J}$ in (4.50).

[18] $\mathcal{J}_{m,k}$ ($k = 1, 2, 3$) is the determinant of the submatrix of $\mathcal{J}_m$ that results from deleting the k-th row and column.

$j_{36} > 0$ and $j_{63} < 0$ in the negative Mundell feedback loop is similar; they show up in the minor $\mathcal{J}_{m,1} = j_{33}j_{66} - j_{36}j_{63}$ and, with their positive impact on $\mathcal{J}_{m,1}$, are favourable for stability. On the other hand, this examination also makes clear that the Keynes and Mundell effects are just two factors among many others, even within the principal minors alone or within their sum $\mathcal{J}_{m,1} + \mathcal{J}_{m,2} + \mathcal{J}_{m,3}$, let alone the mixed terms in the Routh–Hurwitz conditions.

The upper chain in figure 7.10 suggests that a lower interest elasticity of money demand contributes to a destabilization, since in the first link it increases the responsiveness of the bond rate to changes in the real money supply, $\partial i/\partial m = -i/m\eta_{m,i}$, and thus reinforces the subsequent reactions in this positive feedback loop. Attention, however, should also be called to the fact that a reduction of $\eta_{m,i}$ would affect aggregate demand in such a way that, mathematically, entry j_{33} decreases in the trace of $\mathcal{J}_m$ – which would favour stability.

Likewise, higher values of β_π, by speeding up the adjustments of the inflation climate in the negative feedback loop of the Mundell effect, seem to be beneficial to stability at first sight. The previous example of $\eta_{m,i}$ nonetheless warns us that here, too, there might be other effects in the opposite direction. On the whole, therefore, we have to resort to a complete stability analysis to reach definite conclusions about the stabilizing or destabilizing potential of the parameters. Before dealing with this issue in subsection 7.4.4, we have one more look at the output–inflation nexus.

7.4.3 Can a negative output–inflation nexus be detected in the data?

A negative output–inflation nexus might, perhaps, still appear somewhat puzzling – both the effect itself (in figure 7.9) and its implications for the Keynes and Mundell effects (in figure 7.10). Even if it is accepted as it stands, the discussion so far has been concerned exclusively with the *ceteris paribus* reactions. Therefore, it is legitimate to ask: what will happen after the impact effects – i.e. what will become of these reactions in a dynamic setting? Leaving the monetary subdynamics and returning to the full KMG model within this subsection, let us to this end compute the corresponding impulse–response functions of the system, two examples of which are displayed in figure 7.11.[19]

On the basis of the parameter calibration with, specifically, $\beta_{pv} = 1.50$ in the price Phillips curve, the economy is started in the steady-state

---

[19] The diagrams display the impulse–response functions of u and $\hat{p}$ that (in the full KMG model) arise from a positive 2 per cent one-time shock to expected sales at $t = 1$. The two panels to the left have the base scenario underlying with, in particular, $\beta_{pv} = 1.50$; in the other two panels this parameter is set at zero.

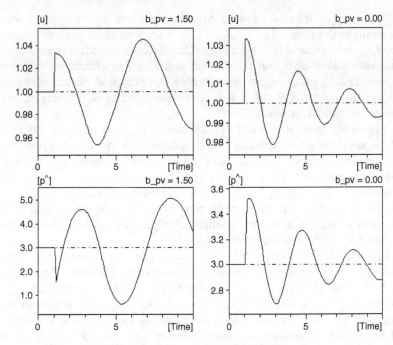

Figure 7.11: The dynamic output–inflation nexus

position. At time $t = 1$, a strong one-time shock of 2 per cent is imposed on expected sales, which instantly drives up utilization by more than these 2 per cent to $u = 1.033$. The impact on the rate of inflation is a drop to $\hat{p} = 1.54\%$. These are the numerical magnitudes of the *ceteris paribus* reactions considered above.[20] From then on, the system is left to itself and we can study how output and inflation are related dynamically.

The two panels to the left in figure 7.11 show that both variables immediately seek to 'undo' the shock event, moving back to their equilibrium values but then overshooting them. In this way, a negative relationship between output and inflation continues to exist, until $t = 2.75$, when inflation reaches a peak while utilization is still falling. Utilization attains its trough value one year later, at $t = 3.83$, after which u and $\hat{p}$ again proceed in opposite directions. It is thus seen that the negative output–inflation nexus is not just the construction of a *ceteris paribus* exercise but persists over a considerable span of time after the shock.

After several years the time series generated by the shock impulse find the cyclical pattern of the limit cycle, to which they eventually converge.

---

[20] To be exact, in the discrete-time approximation of the differential equations the inflation rate reacts one month after the initial change in utilization.

We know from figure 6.5 in chapter 6, section 7, subsection 2, that fairly regular Phillips loops in the $(u, \hat{p})$ phase plane then come about. Here half the time u and $\hat{p}$ move in the same direction, and half the time they move in the opposite direction (as it must be if they are to produce a countercyclical price level). In this long-run behaviour it finally becomes meaningless to speak of a positive or negative output–inflation nexus. That is, this notion may be reserved for the *ceteris paribus* reactions and the transitional dynamics.

As a contrast to the adjustments in the base scenario, we conduct a second experiment and reduce the coefficient β_{pv} to zero. Hence, according to figure 7.9, a positive output–inflation nexus is created. The two right-hand panels in figure 7.11 illustrate that, in these circumstances, the positive relationship between u and $\hat{p}$ survives the impact reactions and also largely applies to the subsequent cyclical adjustments.

Incidentally, the impression that the oscillations tend to die out is deceptive. After some fifteen years the system initiates oscillations with a period of more than thirty years (where only the nonlinearities (6.32), (6.33) in the investment function prevent them from exploding). Nevertheless, even then the motions of u and $\hat{p}$ are almost synchronous, so that in this parameter scenario the positive output–inflation nexus is a generally valid phenomenon. On the other hand, this pattern is clearly incompatible with the stylized fact of a countercyclical price level.

In the above discussion we ventured into speaking of impulse–response functions. Since they are a central concept in vector autoregressions (VARs), which themselves are a widespread tool in time series analysis, this mode of expression prompts the question: would it be possible to extract a similar reaction pattern from empirical data? Most conveniently, a two-variable VAR in utilization and inflation should be tried.

Our proxy for u is the quarterly series of the percentage deviations of the output–capital ratio from its HP 'trend', which has already been used in chapters 5 and 6. Since quarterly inflation is much noisier than output, a moderate smoothing is appropriate for this variable. However, we do not apply it directly to the quarterly inflation rates but, rather, to the price series from which they derive. That is, the trend deviations of the price level from chapter 5 are taken and slightly smoothed by a centred five-quarter moving (arithmetic) average. Subsequently, quarterly inflation rates are computed from this series (and multiplied by four to annualize them). Besides, in this way there are no further problems with inflation detrending, either. The VAR estimation is then performed on these two quarterly series of u and $\hat{p}$, where four lags on each variable are fully adequate and the sample period, 1961 to 1991, is the same as in the calibration chapters.

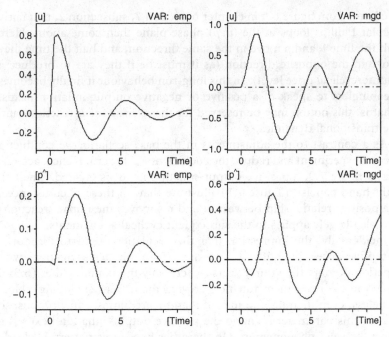

Figure 7.12: Impulse–response functions of u and $\hat{p}$ from VARs

The two panels to the left in figure 7.12[21] display the impulse–response functions of u and $\hat{p}$ (which, of course, start in equilibrium) that result from a shock to u in quarter 1.[22] Afterwards, the innovations are reset to zero in the VAR equations. Comparing these time paths to the two left-hand panels in figure 7.11, at first the differences leap to the eye. Although in figure 7.12 the positive shock to u induces a negative change in $\hat{p}$, it is only negligibly small. A second point is that, while also being cyclical, the trajectories soon converge back to equilibrium. This is of no great significance, however, since it is a necessary implication of the linear econometric approach as such.

At a second look, figures 7.11 and 7.12 reveal an important feature in common. In both diagrams, utilization after the shock falls back

[21] Vertical axes show deviations from trend in percentage points, and time is measured in years. Underlying the functions in the two left-hand panels are empirical ('emp') estimates; the two other panels are based on the VAR estimation of the model-generated dynamics ('mgd').

[22] The ordering of the perturbation terms (or 'innovations', as they are often called) ranks u before $\hat{p}$, so that the initial shock to u also affects $\hat{p}$ in the same quarter, where the sign and the size is given by the covariance of u and $\hat{p}$. By contrast, a shock to $\hat{p}$ (which we do not consider) would leave u unaffected in the first quarter.

to normal and then overshoots this level, whereas the inflation rate increases. Hence, the empirical VAR as well gives rise to a transition dynamics that is characterized by a negative output–inflation relationship. In this sense the question formulated in the title of this subsection can be answered in the affirmative.

After the transition phase, let us say after quarter 7, figure 7.12 displays a phase shifting of inflation similar to the way it starts to evolve a little later in figure 7.11. On the whole, we can certainly conclude that the results from the (almost completely) atheoretical VAR does not contradict the results from the model economy with its very explicit theoretical structure concerning the shock to utilization and the induced reactions of the rate of inflation.

To see what can reasonably be expected from the impulse–response functions of an empirical VAR, we consider this issue from a different angle. Let us assume briefly that the KMG model is a correct representation of the real world, where, however, the structural equations are unknown and only the time paths of the variables are available. Ideally, suppose that the economy is already on the limit cycle and the trajectories remain purely deterministic. The two panels to the right in figure 7.12 show the impulse–response functions of u and $\hat{p}$ that are generated by the VAR estimation of this model-generated dynamics. The shock to u is scaled such that the first peak of utilization is about as high as in the left-hand panel.

A difference from the empirical as well as from the theoretical (in the left-hand panels of figure 7.11) impulse–response functions is that the reactions of u and $\hat{p}$ after the shock are a bit more persistent; u does not immediately decline and $\hat{p}$ does not immediately increase after the shock. On the other hand, the initial fall of the rate of inflation is more pronounced than in the empirical VAR. The negative reaction is, however, much weaker than in the stylized experiment in figure 7.11. An empirical VAR can therefore hardly be expected to yield such a clear-cut negative output–inflation nexus as was obtained theoretically in figure 7.11. Again, we conclude that the empirical impulse–response functions are at least not in contradiction to what is implied by the model economy and the calibration of, in particular, its adjustments of the rate of inflation.

7.4.4 *Parameter diagrams for the three-dimensional and six-dimensional dynamics*

We now return to the three-dimensional monetary subsystem (7.10) and investigate the stabilizing or destabilizing tendencies of selected parameters, where the numerical results are also to be contrasted with what prevails in the full six-dimensional KMG model. An overall finding of these computations will be the unambiguously stabilizing effects of lower interest elasticities $\eta_{m,i}$ of money demand – that is, of stronger reactions of the bond rate.[23] This can be gathered from the following parameter diagrams, in all of which the stability region for two other parameters contracts when $\eta_{m,i}$ is increased. The regularity is so apparent that we will no longer need to direct special attention to it. Note, however, that the phenomenon is exactly right the opposite of what the destabilizing feedback loop of the Keynes effect would predict; see the remark on figure 7.10 above.

Proposition 4 has provided a critical value β_{pv}^c for the wage share parameter β_{pv} in the price Phillips curve, beyond which the subdynamics (7.10) is necessarily unstable. Certainly, $\beta_{pv} < \beta_{pv}^c$ alone does not ensure local stability. Just recall that in many circumstances a high adjustment speed β_y can make the auto-feedback of y^e on itself so strong (i.e. the corresponding positive entry in the trace of the Jacobian $\mathcal{J}_m$ so dominant) that the steady state becomes unstable.[24] But, even in situations where stability is possible, the proposition, because it utilizes only one of the Routh–Hurwitz conditions, does not tell us whether the effective upper bound on β_{pv} for stability is equal to or less than β_{pv}^c; nor do we know if (also) small or zero values of β_{pv} would stabilize the steady state. This issue is studied in figures 7.13a and 7.13b, which include β_π as a second parameter and draw the regions of stability in the (β_π, β_{pv}) parameter plane as they emerge under variations of the interest elasticity.

In figure 7.13a[25] it is first of all seen that stability is possible if $\eta_{m,i}$ is sufficiently reduced from the baseline value $\eta_{m,i} = 0.14$. The upper left corner shows that, at $\eta_{m,i} = 0.065$, the inequality $\beta_{pv} < \beta_{pv}^c = 0.654$ is a necessary as well as a sufficient condition for stability. This strong stability result gets lost, however, if $\eta_{m,i}$ is increased a bit. In particular, it then also depends on the parameter β_π whether a particular value of β_{pv} entails stability.

In all cases that have been examined it is found that, if stability is possible for a given value of β_π, then β_{pv}^c is still the relevant upper bound, in the sense that stability then obtains for slightly smaller values of β_{pv}. On the other hand, a further reduction of β_{pv} may well result in instability. In figure 7.13a this possibility opens up in the second panel under $\eta_{m,i} = 0.081$, where $\beta_{pv} \in [0, \beta_{pv}^c) = [0, 0.654)$ brings about

---

[23] The derivatives $\partial i / \partial x$, with $x = m$, y^e and n, are reciprocal to $\eta_{m,i}$; see Proposition 1 in chapter 4, section 3.

[24] The trace of $\mathcal{J}_m$ is independent of β_{pv}.

[25] Under variations of the interest elasticity $\eta_{m,i}$ of money demand. Dotted areas are the stability regions.

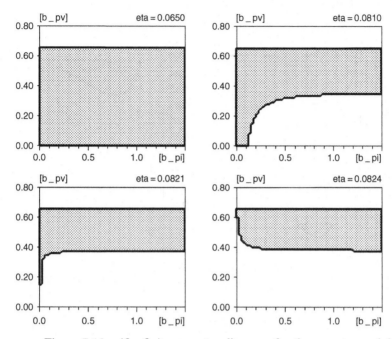

Figure 7.13a: (β_π, β_{pv}) parameter diagrams for the monetary subdynamics (I)

stability if β_π is small; but already, when β_π exceeds 0.13, zero is no longer contained in the stability interval of β_{pv}. In other words, we again have a reswitching of instability: the steady state is unstable if β_{pv} is zero or small, it becomes stable at medium values of β_{pv} and it is unstable if $\beta_{pv} > 0.654$. Precisely the same applies in all the other examples depicted.

The panel in the lower left corner of figure 7.13a demonstrates that, when $\eta_{m,i}$ increases to 0.0821, the stability region loses its contact with the β_π axis. Here the reswitching phenomenon for β_{pv} occurs even at arbitrarily small values of β_π. Nevertheless, the latter adjustment speed for the revisions of the inflation climate is still a plainly destabilizing parameter, since the stability intervals of β_{pv} to which the parameter β_π gives rise become smaller (or remain as they are) as β_π increases.

The destabilizing property of β_π is, however, not very robust. A marginal change of $\eta_{m,i}$ from 0.0821 to 0.0824 destroys and, in fact, reverses it. As evidenced in the lower right panel, the β_{pv} stability intervals are widening as β_π increases from zero. Accordingly, β_π would now be classified as a stabilizing parameter.

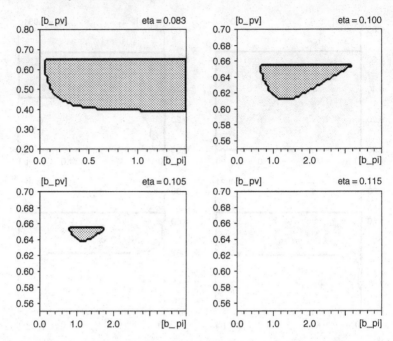

Figure 7.13b: (β_π, β_{pv}) parameter diagrams for the monetary subdynamics (II)

The feature that high, rather than low, values of β_π are stabilizing is also observed in the upper left panel of figure 7.13b. In addition, the panel points out that, under $\eta_{m,i} = 0.083$, the stability region is separated from both the β_π axis as well as the β_{pv} axis. It has been checked that the region continues to be unbounded to the right, as is the case in all panels of figure 7.13a. But unboundedness is not general, either. With $\eta_{m,i} = 0.100$, the panel in the upper right corner of figure 7.13b demonstrates that the region has become an island in the parameter plane. Here instability reswitching occurs for β_{pv} as well as β_π.

The island shrinks as $\eta_{m,i}$ is further increased, so steadily that at $\eta_{m,i} = 0.115$ it has finally disappeared. For this and higher interest elasticities no pair (β_π, β_{pv}) exists that could possibly render the monetary subdynamics locally stable.

The examples collected in figure 7.13 make sufficiently clear that there is no straightforward characterization of the circumstances that ensure, and exclude, stability. It would thus only be cumbersome to distinguish the different situations and enumerate the intricate conditions that could be derived from a mathematical treatment. In any case, the general message so far is that both parameters β_π and β_{pv} can be rather ambiguous in their stability effects.

The next parameter diagrams in figure 7.14[26] may first be seen in correspondence to similar results obtained in the more compact model of chapter 3. These diagrams combine the effects of the two parameters β_π and κ_π, which are important for the monetary dynamics insofar as they determine the adjustments of the inflation climate π. In figures 3.3 and 3.4 in Chapter 3, section 7, the stability region of (β_π, κ_π) was found to have a nice and regular shape. A higher responsiveness β_π was unambiguously destabilizing and lower values of κ_π, which in favour of regressive expectations attach a smaller weight to the 'adaptive expectations' component in the revisions of π, were unambiguously stabilizing.

The same holds true for the present submodel. Presupposing that β_{pv} is not too large ($\beta_{pv} < \beta_{pv}^c$), figure 7.14 demonstrates how higher interest elasticities $\eta_{m,i}$ shift the stability frontier steadily toward the origin, while the north-west–south-east trade-off of β_π vs κ_π and also the smooth shape of this geometric locus are maintained. The trade-off, by the way,

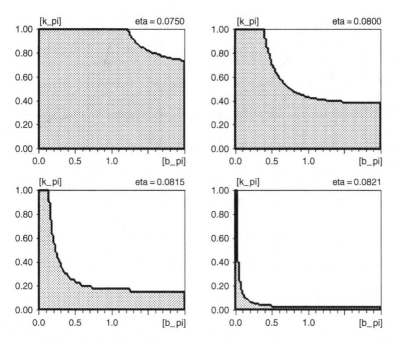

Figure 7.14: (β_π, κ_π) parameter diagrams for the monetary subdynamics

[26] The values of $\eta_{m,i}$ vary as indicated. In addition, all panels are based on $\beta_{pv} = 0.30$.

is always strict: for every (large) value of β_π there exists a (small) value of κ_π such that the pair (β_π, κ_π) entails stability. In comparison to the previous phenomena, this sequence of stability regions is not particularly spectacular. On the other hand, it can be taken as an indication that in the submodel the more 'exciting' stability effects of β_π are connected to the Phillips curve parameter β_{pv}. Our main motive for presenting figure 7.14 is, however, a comparison with the complete KMG model.

Let us take the KMG model and conduct the same type of experiment as in figure 7.13 in the (β_π, β_{pv}) parameter plane. Figures 7.15a and 7.15b illustrate the changes in the shape of the – again shrinking – stability region as $\eta_{m,i}$ increases from small values to the calibrated value and a little higher.

Already, at the beginning of the sequence, at such a low interest elasticity as $\eta_{m,i} = 0.050$ a difference from the first panels in figure 7.13a can be noted. There the steady state soon gets unstable at zero and low values of β_{pv}, which is not the case in the upper left panel in figure 7.15a. Here, as well as in the second panel, for $\eta_{m,i} = 0.075$, β_{pv} is a perfectly

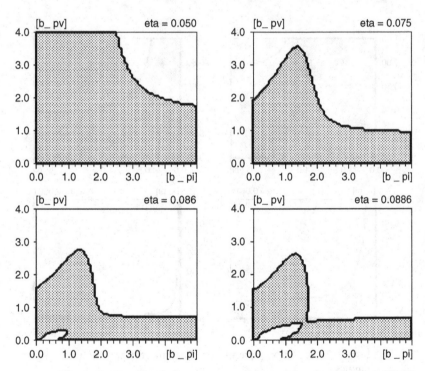

Figure 7.15a: (β_π, β_{pv}) parameter diagrams for the complete KMG model (I)

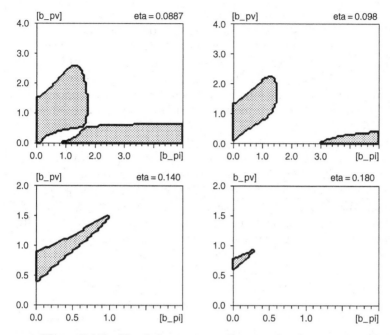

Figure 7.15b: (β_π, β_{pv}) parameter diagrams for the complete KMG model (II)

destabilizing parameter. On the other hand, while at $\eta_{m,i} = 0.050$ the adjustment speed β_π is destabilizing, too (at least within the area shown, which is relatively large), instability reswitching occurs at slightly higher elasticities and is clearly visible at $\eta_{m,i} = 0.075$. Of course, reswitching will by now not come unexpectedly, but here, in the course of $\eta_{m,i}$ rising, β_π reswitches before β_{pv} – not the other way round, as in figure 7.13b.

When the instability reswitching of β_{pv} is first observed in the lower left panel in figure 7.15a at $\eta_{m,i} = 0.086$, it is only a rather limited phenomenon. Geometrically, it manifests itself in the form of instability nibbling at the stability region from below. The bites that instability takes out of the stability region become larger when $\eta_{m,i}$ increases further. In the lower right corner it is then also better apparent that, over a small range of given values of β_π, we have reswitching of instability as well as of stability for β_{pv}.

The metaphor that instability bites into a stability region is also natural because the rest of the region in the two lower panels in figure 7.15a is only marginally affected. The panel for $\eta_{m,i} = 0.0886$ in the lower right corner suggests that instability is just about to tear through the stability region; and this is indeed what has happened at $\eta_{m,i} = 0.0887$, the first panel in figure 7.15b. Obtaining two separate stability regions in this way, the parameter β_π now exhibits stability reswitching as well.

As the interest elasticity continues to rise, the two stability regions drift apart. More precisely, as demonstrated by the upper right panel, for $\eta_{m,i} = 0.098$, it is mainly the region to the right that appears to float away; the other region to the left is only moderately reduced. Besides, the latter is by then completely disconnected from the β_π axis.

At still higher values of $\eta_{m,i}$, the right-hand stability region eventually moves so far (and also becomes so small) that it ceases to play a significant role. Meanwhile, the region to the left is further diminished. The lower left panel shows what remains at the calibrated value $\eta_{m,i} = 0.14$ (notice the different scale in the axes of this diagram). The rest of the story is indicated in the figure's last panel, for $\eta_{m,i} = 0.18$. Finally, at about $\eta_{m,i} = 0.218$, the stability region completely dissolves.

A second eight-picture sequence, which is presented in figure 7.16, has its plot in the (β_π, κ_π) plane. At smaller values of the interest elasticity, up to $\eta_{m,i} = 0.088$ roughly, there is no essential difference from the stability effects of the parameters in the subdynamics; see figure 7.14. In particular, the upper left panel in figure 7.16 is to indicate that the stability region is unbounded in the β_π direction (if not mathematically, perhaps, certainly practically). This is no longer the case at $\eta_{m,i} = 0.089$, in the upper right panel.

Another remarkable property also begins to unfold here, concerning the parameter κ_π. So far, in chapter 3 as well as in the monetary sub-model above, one will have been inclined to think that attaching a greater weight to the simple negative feedback loop of regressive expectations (a smaller value of κ_π) would be favourable for stability. What we now see for the first time is that stability may prevail over a certain range of positive weights κ_π, but not at small – not even at zero – values of κ_π. In other words, κ_π begins to display instability reswitching too.

The next three pictures in figure 7.16 demonstrate how the stability region breaks away from the axes: first from the β_π axis at $\eta_{m,i} = 0.090$, then from the κ_π axis at $\eta_{m,i} = 0.095$ and finally from the third axis, the boundary $\kappa_\pi = 1$, at $\eta_{m,i} = 0.115$. In the course of these changes the area is gradually reduced. Indeed, this continues after the stability region has become an island. Its further shrinking is exemplified for $\eta_{m,i}$ increasing to 0.12 and then for the calibrated elasticity $\eta_{m,i} = 0.14$, when the region, at least at the scale chosen here, is really tiny (note that the scale has, in any case, changed in the last four panels). The panel in the lower right corner announces the disappearance of stability, which occurs shortly afterwards at $\eta_{m,i} = 0.15$.

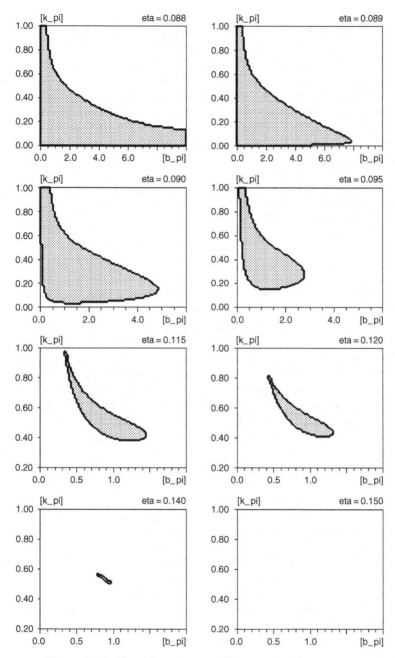

Figure 7.16: (β_π, κ_π) parameter diagrams for the complete KMG model

Even more strongly than in the previous sections, we can conclude from this section about the monetary side of the economy that, for certain parameters, the reswitching of instability – and even of stability – may no longer be regarded as a special and somewhat exotic case. This is true for the monetary subsystem, and all the more so for the complete KMG model. The details of the metamorphosis of the stability regions that we have studied help us understand that, nevertheless, their somewhat peculiar shape does not come out of the blue but that, under suitable variations of an underlying parameter, gradually emerges from more familiar and regular stability regions.

7.5   Towards a landscape of the parameter stability effects

7.5.1   Reference to the (β_{Iu}, β_{Iq}) parameter plane

In the previous sections we have gained some experience with the stabilizing or destabilizing effects of several adjustment coefficients, within the subsystems where they play a central role and subsequently in the complete six-dimensional KMG model. In this section, which is now exclusively concerned with the full model, we examine more systematically how local stability is affected by variations of the calibrated parameters. The main aim is to classify the parameters broadly as stabilizing, destabilizing or ambiguous. In several instances the system's responsiveness to such parameter changes will also be discussed in finer detail.

The basic tool of our numerical sensitivity analysis will, again, be parameter diagrams in the plane. For a first battery of experiments, we choose as a reference the stability region in the (β_{Iu}, β_{Iq}) parameter diagram as it was obtained in chapter 6, section 7, subsection 2, figure 6.3. We then take another parameter (β_{we}, for example), subject it to a *ceteris paribus* change and study its impact on the (β_{Iu}, β_{Iq}) stability region – seeing whether it is enlarged or reduced, or whether no definite effects are observed. The varying parameter (i.e. β_{we}) may in this context be called an *exogenous* parameter. This means that it is not just exogenous to the model dynamics (which is trivial) but that it is exogenously varying in the framework of the present stability discussion. Likewise, we may speak of β_{Iu} and β_{Iq} as *endogenous* parameters. Of course, β_{Iu} and β_{Iq} are still exogenous to the model, and what is endogenous is the stability region of these coefficients if the exogenous parameter varies, but for ease of reference β_{Iu} and β_{Iq} themselves may also be called endogenous.

Apart from β_{Iu} and β_{Iq} (and the nonlinearity coefficients in the investment function), fourteen parameters have been determined in the calibration. Table 7.1 summarizes the changes that the (β_{Iu}, β_{Iq}) stability

Table 7.1: *The impact of parameter variations on the stability region in the (β_{Iu}, β_{Iq}) plane*

'Exogenous' parameter	Impact on stability region	Local distance if param.↑	param.↓
β_{zu} (= 0.40)	a	↑	↑
β_{pu} (= 0.15)	+	↓	↑
β_{pv} (= 1.50)	a	↑	↑
κ_p (= 0.00)	+	↓	--
β_{we} (= 0.55)	−	↑	↓
β_{wv} (= 0.50)	a	↑	↑
κ_w (= 0.00)	a	↑	--
β_{π} (= 1.00)	a	↑	↑
κ_{π} (= 0.50)	a	↑	↑
$\eta_{m,i}$ (= 0.14)	−	↑	↓
s_c (= 0.80)	a	↑	↑
τ_w (= 0.35)	+	↓	↑
β_y (= 8.00)	a	↑	↑
β_{nn} (= 3.00)	a	↑	↑

NB: Numbers in parentheses are the calibrated values.
The symbols are explained in the main text.

region is undergoing as they are modified. To describe these effects, the following symbols are used.

Symbols for the effects of *ceteris paribus* parameter variations in the (β_{Iu}, β_{Iq}) plane (Table 7.1)

+ : An increase of the exogenous parameter (β_{pu}, for example) generally enlarges the stability region in the (β_{Iu}, β_{Iq}) plane (except perhaps for small subsets), such that it contains the original stability region for the base scenario as a subset. And also the other way round: a decrease reduces the stability region such that it becomes a subset of the original one. In this respect the exogenous parameter is *stabilizing*.

− : An increase (decrease) of the exogenous parameter (β_{we}, for example) reduces (enlarges) the stability region in the sense just described. Accordingly, the exogenous parameter is characterized as *destabilizing*.

a : This letter denotes *ambiguous* effects. An increase of the parameter noticeably enlarges the stability region in some parts of the (β_{Iu}, β_{Iq}) plane and reduces it in others, so that neither the new stability region nor the original one tends to be a subset of the other; and the same holds true if the exogenous parameter decreases.

Local distance: This refers to the distance of the calibrated pair of the investment coefficients $(\beta_{Iu}, \beta_{Iq}) = (0.280, 0.115)$ to the stability region, after the exogenous parameter has changed upwards ($\uparrow$) or downwards ($\downarrow$), respectively. The reaction is denoted by an upward arrow ($\uparrow$, in the main body of table 7.1) if the distance thus widens, and by a downward arrow ($\downarrow$) if the distance narrows. Because (β_{Iu}, β_{Iq}) is originally close to the stability frontier, the latter means that a minor change of the exogenous parameter already causes $(\beta_{Iu}, \beta_{Iq}) = (0.280, 0.115)$ to be contained in the new stability region (the distance becomes negative, so to speak).

Figure 7.17[27] illustrates the different cases that may arise. On the basis of the calibrated values of the parameters, the upper left panel has a *ceteris paribus* increase of β_{we} from 0.55 to 0.70 underlying (the slope coefficient of the employment rate in the wage Phillips curve). The

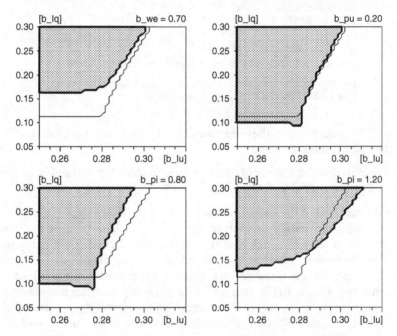

Figure 7.17: The impact of selected parameter variations on the (β_{Iu}, β_{Iq}) stability region

---

[27] The dotted areas are the stability regions in the new situation, with *ceteris paribus* $\beta_{we} = 0.70$, etc. The thin lines are the stability frontiers in the base scenario. There, the calibration has set the two investment coefficients at $(\beta_{Iu}, \beta_{Iq}) = (0.280, 0.115)$.

new stability frontier – i.e. the frontier of the stability region represented by the dotted area – has 'withdrawn' from the original frontier of the base scenario, where the latter is indicated by the thin line (which is reproduced from figure 6.3 in chapter 6, section 7, subsection 2). In other words, the new stability region is a (strict) subset of the original stability region. Since the region is also enlarged by lower values of β_{we}, the parameter is clearly destabilizing. The effect is expressed by the minus sign in the β_{we} row of table 7.1.

A consequence of the shrinking stability region is that its distance to the baseline investment parameters $(\beta_{Iu}, \beta_{Iq}) = (0.280, 0.115)$ increases (see the upward arrow in the same row of table 7.1). The panel does not show that the phenomena are reversed if β_{we} is diminished (by a certain amount). Then the new stability region includes the original one (as well as the point $(\beta_{Iu}, \beta_{Iq}) = (0.280, 0.115)$); the 'negative distance' of this pair from the stability set motivates the downward arrow in the β_{we} row of table 7.1).

The upper right panel in figure 7.17 for a higher value of β_{pu} (the slope coefficient of utilization in the price Phillips curve) is an example of a (mainly) stabilizing parameter. While in the lower part in the plane the original stability region is a subset of the new one, this is not exactly true at somewhat higher values of β_{Iq}, where the new stability frontier has moved to the left of the original frontier. In table 7.1 β_{pu} is nevertheless characterized as a stabilizing parameter, because the latter effect is seen to be of minor importance.

The lower two panels of figure 7.17, which consider variations of the adjustment speed β_{π} of the inflation climate, are typical for ambiguous stability effects. A decrease of β_{π} from 1.00 to 0.80 enlarges the region in the lower part and reduces it (now in a noticeable way) in the upper right part. Things are exactly the other way round if β_{π} is increased to 1.20. Note that in both cases the stability frontier moves away from the point $(\beta_{Iu}, \beta_{Iq}) = (0.280, 0.115)$. This is, in particular, due to the fact that this point is close to the 'vertex' of the original stability region.

In the preceding three sections, several parameters have been found to have ambiguous effects on stability. Table 7.1 shows that these cases are by no means exceptional. Indeed, the overview classifies nine out of the fourteen parameters as ambiguous. Among the remaining five, two are significantly destabilizing, namely the slope of the employment rate in the price Phillips curve, β_{we}, and the interest elasticity of money demand, $\eta_{m,i}$. In contrast to β_{we}, its counterpart in the price Phillips curve with respect to utilization, β_{pu}, is stabilizing. This is also true for the weighting parameter, κ_p, of current inflation in this Phillips curve and the tax rate on wages, τ_w. Note that the counterpart of κ_p in the wage

Phillips curve, κ_w, does not fit into the pattern that the corresponding coefficients in the two Phillips curves have opposite stability effects; κ_w is neither clearly destabilizing nor stabilizing.

Table 7.1 also confirms the stability effects that have been observed in the sections on the subdynamics, when at the end of each single investigation we returned to the complete model. In the Metzlerian section, β_y and β_{nn} showed ambiguous effects (see figures 7.3 and 7.4); in the section on the wage-price submodel, both β_{pv} and β_{wv} were ambiguous, β_{pu} was stabilizing and β_{we} destabilizing (see figure 7.8); in the section on the monetary aspects of the model, an increase of $\eta_{m,i}$ was consistently destabilizing, while the effects from β_π and κ_π were ambiguous. Apart from that, the shape of the stability regions in figure 7.17 suggests that the two investment coefficients have an opposite impact on stability: β_{Iq} is largely stabilizing, while β_{Iu} tends to be destabilizing.

7.5.2   Reference to different stability intervals

The compatibility of table 7.1 with the previous results certainly gives us additional confidence in this classification scheme. The characterization of the table and our evaluation of β_{Iu} and β_{Iq} are, nevertheless, checked by an extensive second round of experiments. Here we take the crucial behavioural parameters of the model, thirteen in total, and ask how variations of them affect the stability interval of five specific parameters that are selected from them. In this way we get more information about the consistency of the stabilizing or destabilizing effects of a parameter, which should protect us against premature conclusions. The results are collected in table 7.2. The symbols entering it are analogous to those in table 7.1 but here are more differentiated. So we first indicate how they are to be interpreted.

Symbols for the effects of *ceteris paribus* parameter variations on the stability intervals of selected other parameters (table 7.2):

+ : Given the values of the base scenario for all other parameters, an increase of the exogenous parameter (β_{Iq}, for example) widens the interval of the values of the (single) endogenous parameter under consideration ($\eta_{m,i}$, for example) that induce local stability. A decrease of the exogenous parameter, on the other hand, diminishes the stability interval of the endogenous parameter. As before, an exogenous parameter giving rise to these effects is called *stabilizing*.

(+) : The effects just described are rather weak.

− : An increase of the exogenous parameter (β_{Iu}) reduces the stability interval of the endogenous parameter (β_π), while a decrease

Table 7.2: *The impact of parameter variations on the stability intervals of five selected ('endogenous') parameters*

Exogenous parameter	Impact on stability interval of				
	$\eta_{m,i}$	β_{Iu}	β_{Iq}	β_{we}	β_{π}
β_{Iu}	$-[\sim]$	$\times$	$-[\sim]$	$-[\sim]$	$-$
β_{Iq}	$+$	$+$	$\times$	$+$	$+$
β_{pu}	$+[\sim]$	$+[\sim]$	$+$	$+$	$+$
β_{pv}	a	$+[a]$	a	a	$(-)$
κ_p	$(+)$	$\sim$	$+$	$+$	$+$
β_{we}	$-[a]$	$-[\sim]$	$-[a]$	$\times$	$-$
β_{wv}	a	$+[a]$	a	a	$(-)$
κ_w	$-$	$-$	$-$	$-$	$-$
β_{π}	a	a	a	a	$\times$
κ_{π}	a	$-[a]$	a	a	$(+)[a]$
$\eta_{m,i}$	$\times$	$-[\sim]$	$-$	$-$	$-$
β_y	a	$+[a]$	a	a	$(-)$
β_{nn}	a	$+[a]$	a	a	$\sim[a]$

NB: The symbols are explained in the main text.

broadens it. The exogenous parameter is accordingly characterized as *destabilizing*.

$(-)$: The effects just described are rather weak.

  a: This again stands for *ambiguous* effects. For example, significant subsets of higher values as well as of lower values of the exogenous parameter widen the stability interval of the endogenous parameter.

  $\sim$: Variations of the exogenous parameter have only marginal effects on the stability interval. Alternatively, the effects, which are not too strong either, are induced only at values of the exogenous parameter that deviate appreciably from its calibrated value.

$+[a]$: The $+$ effect described above is clearly visible over a certain range of the exogenous parameter around its calibrated value, but there are also non-negligible subsets where the effects on the stability region of the endogenous parameter are ambiguous. Other combinations of a symbol and a bracketed symbol are to be read correspondingly.

The classification of the stability effects in table 7.2 was carried out on the basis of parameter diagrams in the plane, established where the row and column of the respective parameters intersect in the table. Figure 7.18 gives a few typical examples of how we arrive at the evaluation in such a cell. The first panel in the upper left corner serves to

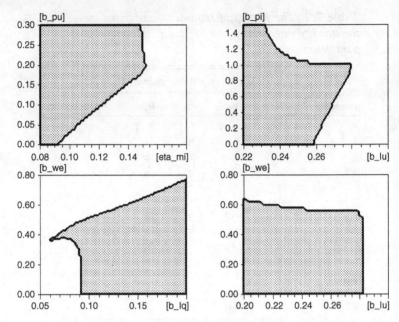

Figure 7.18: Examples of parameter diagrams underlying the classification in table 7.2

obtain the impact of β_{pu} on the stability intervals for $\eta_{m,i}$. A decrease of β_{pu} from its calibrated value $\beta_{pu} = 0.15$ reduces the range of values of $\eta_{m,i}$ that induce stability, while an increase widens this interval. Accordingly, β_{pu} has a stabilizing effect, which is indicated by the plus sign in the $(\beta_{pu}, \eta_{m,i})$ cell in table 7.2. However, as β_{pu} rises beyond 0.20, the broadening of the stability interval of $\eta_{m,i}$ comes to an end and the interval gets even smaller, though only marginally so. This phenomenon is assigned the symbol $\sim$. Since it occurs only well above the calibrated value of β_{pu}, this symbol is added in brackets to the abovementioned plus sign.

The upper right panel provides us with information about how β_{Iu} affects the stability interval of β_{π} as well as the other way round: how β_{π} modifies the stability interval of β_{Iu}. To begin with the variations of β_{Iu}, rising values of this coefficient strictly reduce the length of the (vertical) stability interval for β_{π}, until it eventually disappears slightly before β_{Iu} reaches the calibrated value $\beta_{Iu} = 0.280$ (which was a constituent part of the instability scenario constructed in chapter 6, section 7, subsection 2). Hence the minus sign in the $(\beta_{Iu}, \beta_{\pi})$ cell. By contrast, increasing values of β_{π} have ambiguous effects on the (horizontal) stability interval for β_{Iu}; first it widens until $\beta_{\pi} \approx 1.0$, from when on it changes in the other direction. These changes give rise to the a symbol in the $(\beta_{\pi}, \beta_{Iu})$ cell.

The lower left panel, too, covers two parameters in table 7.2 that are both acting on each other. As β_{Iq} increases, more and more values of β_{we} are able to stabilize the steady state, which is noted by the plus sign in the corresponding cell. On the other hand, if we refer to the calibrated value of $\beta_{we} = 0.55$, the changes of this parameter are clearly destabilizing with respect to β_{Iq}. This is the main effect, indicated by the minus sign in the (β_{we}, β_{Iq}) cell. Additional effects come into play for β_{we} around 0.40; here we observe a certain ambiguity, which explains the bracketed a symbol in the same cell.

With these illustrations, we need no further comment on the fourth panel in figure 7.18 and the $-[\sim]$ characterization we derive from it in both the (β_{we}, β_{Iu}) and the (β_{Iu}, β_{we}) cell.

7.5.3   A succinct characterization of the parameters

Apart from the stability effects of the single parameters in detail, the results of table 7.2 are important in a general way. We were prepared to find that a parameter has different effects on the stability intervals or regions of different other parameters; so it may have a stabilizing impact on one parameter and an ambiguous effect on another. There are, indeed, examples of this phenomenon in table 7.2, concerning β_{pv}, β_{wv}, κ_π, β_y and β_{nn}. On the other hand, in all cases (if we leave the less notable symbols in the square brackets to one side) the stabilizing impact is on just one parameter, which, interestingly, is always the same: β_{Iu}. In addition, their impact on the stability intervals of each of the other parameters is ambiguous in the great majority of the cells in table 7.2. Hence, the exceptional effects on β_{Iu} might also be viewed as expressing the fundamental ambiguity of β_{pv}, β_{wv}, etc. at a different level.

What we hoped for at the beginning of our stability investigations was to put each parameter into one of the broad categories 'stabilizing', 'destabilizing' and 'ambiguous'. On the basis of the preceding discussion and, in particular, table 7.2, we are now in a position to do this. In a number of cases the assignment is not without qualification, but in order to generate a short and definite message the procedure is justifiable. Thus, we present table 7.3 as a concise summary of the entire sensitivity analysis regarding local stability.

In its two top rows, table 7.3 confirms from a different angle that investment is still a central variable for stability in this Keynesian model. It also conforms to the general intuition that faster reactions to the fluctuations of current economic activity (a rise in the coefficient β_{Iu}) reinforce the positive feedback effects and so tend to be destabilizing. By contrast, a greater responsiveness to returns, here in the form of the

Table 7.3: *A succinct characterization of the parameter stability effects*

Parameter	Theoretical context	General effect
β_{Iu}	Utilization in fixed investment	Destabilizing
β_{Iq}	Return differential in investment	Stabilizing
β_{pu}	Utilization in price Phillips curve	Stabilizing
β_{pv}	Wage share in price Phillips curve	Ambiguous
κ_p	Weight of current inflation in price Phillips curve	Stabilizing
β_{we}	Employment rate in wage Phillips curve	Destabilizing
β_{wv}	Wage share in wage Phillips curve	Ambiguous
κ_w	Weight of current inflation in wage Phillips curve	Destabilizing
β_π	Adjustment speed for inflation climate π	Ambiguous
κ_π	Weight of 'adaptive erpectations' in revisions of π	Ambiguous
$\eta_{m,i}$	Interest elasticity of money demand	Destabilizing
β_y	Adjustment speed for expected sales	Ambiguous
β_{nn}	Stock adjustment speed	Ambiguous

differential of the profit rate and the real rate of interest (a higher β_{Iq}), reinforces the system's corrective actions and so tends to stabilize the steady state. Such a higher responsiveness is likewise brought about by a lower interest elasticity in the demand for money, since this induces larger variations of the bond rate of interest. As this is the only channel where the interest rate takes effect, $\eta_{m,i}$ is clearly a destabilizing parameter.

By the same token, the inflation climate π as a determinant of the real interest rate may be expected to be crucial for stability. Accordingly, the general adjustment speed β_π for the revisions of the inflation climate would have a definite impact on local stability, and equally so the weight of the 'adaptive expectations' component in the rule that governs the revisions of π. It has to be taken into account, however, that the same inflation climate additionally enters the two Phillips curves. Indeed, it turns out that the combination of these mechanisms impairs the definite stability effects; both β_π and κ_π have to be classified as ambiguous parameters.

This result is fairly remarkable, for there are a great variety of Keynesian-oriented models, usually with adaptive expectations for the – as it is called – expected rate of inflation, where fast adjustments are destabilizing (and sluggish adjustments are favourable for stability). As a matter of fact, we know of no relevant counter-example in the literature. Our faith in the generality of this property is so great that in the present book, in the precursory model in chapter 3, we used it to introduce an extrinsic nonlinearity that was able to prevent the trajectories from total divergence; see eqs. (3.44), (3.45) and their motivation in chapter 3, section 10, as well as the regular (β_π, κ_π) parameter diagrams of figures 3.3 and 3.4 in chapter 3, section 7, on which the argument was based.

Although the model in chapter 3 already includes a rather rich array of feedback mechanisms, table 7.3 now tells us that the definite stability properties that originate with the adjustments of the inflation climate do not carry over to the full Keynes–Metzler–Goodwin modelling framework, where, in particular, the IS temporary equilibrium hypothesis is dropped and replaced by the Metzlerian inventory dynamics. Hence, the theoretical significance of the two rows for β_π and κ_π in table 7.3 lies in the consequence thus suggested, namely to downplay the role of inflation as an expectations variable. Since the overwhelming majority of macrodynamic models, 'backward-looking' and 'forward-looking' models alike, concentrate on expected inflation as the one and only expectations variable, which is absolutely critical to the dynamic properties of the model, we do not wish to undervalue our finding of the limited role for the – as we prefer to call it – inflation climate.

All other parameters that have a definite impact on local stability belong to the field of the wage-price dynamics. This does not mean that the converse holds true: there are two parameters in the wage and price Phillips curves that are still ambiguous, both of them measuring the influence of the wage share (β_{wv} and β_{pv}). However, the theoretical core coefficients in the Phillips curves, β_{we} for the employment rate in the wage Phillips curve and β_{pu} for utilization in the price Phillips curve, can be classified as having unambiguous effects. Provided that such general terms as wage flexibility and price flexibility are restricted to the responsiveness to employment and utilization, respectively, a concise conclusion emerging from table 7.3 is that higher wage flexibility is destabilizing, whereas higher price flexibility is stabilizing.

As for the statement on flexible wages, it seems that only a minority of contemporary economists would subscribe to it. On the other hand, we see it in a tradition that goes back to Keynes and the famous chapter 19 in his *General Theory*. In a formalized and more elaborate setting, we have here confirmed some of his basic arguments pointing to negative implications from high wage flexibility.

Regarding the beneficial role of price flexibility, even when restricted to a narrow theoretical framework, this property is not obvious. For example, in an elementary IS-LM model of wage-price dynamics by Flaschel and Franke (2000), which extends Tobin's (1975) often cited macromodel on 'recession and depression' to two structural Phillips curves, just the opposite is found to apply. One reason might be that there the inflation rate is specified as moving with marginal wage cost, though it is also shown that this principle comes very close to an ordinary

Phillips curve, where prices respond to utilization, if this notion involves a neoclassical Cobb–Douglas production function and productive capacity is constituted by the output level that would maximize short-run profits (Flaschel and Franke, 2000, p. 277).

Certainly, we have greater confidence in the present 'positive' price flexibility result of table 7.3, which is also in line with what was obtained within the compact dynamic IS-LM model in chapter 3, section 7. But the alternative outcome just mentioned should induce us to check the robustness of the conclusion on wage and price flexibility anew when putting forward a variant or generalization of the KMG model. In addition, we recall that the results on the coefficients β_{we} and β_{pu} have the augmented Phillips curves underlying with a considerable or even dominating influence for the wage share. At least, this shows that the key words 'wage' and 'price flexibility' have to be used with great care when discussing the stability matter.

The two remaining parameters with definite stability effects are the weights κ_w and κ_p in the Phillips curves that, in the specification of benchmark inflation, are attached to current inflation vis-à-vis the general inflation climate π. In the calibration, both weights are zero and the benchmark is directly given by π. The analysis has now revealed that more emphasis on current wage inflation (less normal productivity growth) in the price Phillips curve – i.e. an increase in κ_p – is stabilizing, and that more emphasis on current price inflation in the wage Phillips curve (a higher κ_w) is destabilizing. Since, conceptually, these weights are of secondary importance and would scarcely be referred to in a verbal discussion of the Phillips curves, it is perhaps somewhat surprising that they have such a significant bearing on stability.

This fact is also pertinent to the wage and price flexibility issue, though to our knowledge it has never been put up in the literature. For example, the stabilizing effect of a higher slope coefficient β_{pu} could be undone by a simultaneous rise in the weight κ_w, the possible consequences of which for stability might not even be seriously considered.

For the last two parameters, β_y and β_{nn}, in table 7.3, which are central to the model's inventory dynamics, it has already been observed in subsection 7.2.3 that they are another good example of the possible pitfalls of low-dimensional models. Understanding the basic feedback mechanisms within this framework, one is tempted to assume that the stability properties of their key parameters will essentially carry over to more differentiated models. Thus β_y and β_{nn} are markedly destabilizing in a two-dimensional Metzlerian (sub)model, but these effects get lost in the full KMG model, where both parameters are found to affect local stability in ambiguous ways.

The 'map' of the parameter stability effects as they are summarized in table 7.3 is certainly important on its own, and allows us to learn about the model as it currently stands. In the perspective of a model builder, however, it can also give us some ideas where to introduce an alternative or additional extrinsic nonlinearity, which is supposed to exert a stabilizing influence on the trajectories in the outer state space. The slope parameters in the Phillips curves suggest two concepts. Thus, the reactions of the nominal wage rate may be limited in times of high over- as well as underutilization of the existing labour force. This can be schematically modelled by a strict floor and ceiling for the wage increases, which amounts to a sudden jump of β_{we} to zero or even a negative value (depending on the value of benchmark inflation in that situation); or one may prefer a smoother reduction of the slope coefficient by making β_{we} a continuous, hump-shaped function of the employment rate (and possibly other state variables as well).

On the other hand, though theoretically perhaps less familiar, we could turn to the price adjustments and assume that, in a phase of high overutilization of productive capacity, price competition among firms becomes so fierce that, the coefficient β_{pu} increases. In this manner another negative feedback effect in the boom might be generated. It would, however, work out in a much more roundabout way than verbal explanations could probably indicate.

Conversely, the 'map' of table 7.3 can give us an important hint where such attempts are likely to fail. As has been mentioned before, the stock adjustment speed β_{nn} in the inventory dynamics and the adjustment speed β_{π} for the changes of the inflation climate are theoretically meaningful candidates for introducing an extrinsic nonlinearity. The corresponding modifications have indeed succeeded in the low-dimensional models where these coefficients play a crucial rule. Unfortunately, the same coefficients change their properties and become ambiguous when these models are generalized to the six-dimensional dynamic system. This outcome leads us to expect that these (and other ambiguous) parameters are unsuitable for setting up a nonlinear stabilization mechanism.

It has to be admitted, nevertheless, that this is no more than an initial suspicion. It is not completely compelling since convergence and divergence are cyclical and, in the dynamics itself, the stabilizing/destabilizing forces may act differently in different phases of the cycle. We have checked that the ambiguous parameter β_{nn} provides no scope for simple and meaningful endogenous changes that could possibly stabilize the dynamics (see footnote 5), but this does not necessarily mean that attempts at other parameters are not more successful – even if we guess that, generally, the probability will be rather low.

7.5.4   Stability regions in the plane: the six elementary contours

In the two-dimensional parameter diagrams that have been computed in the previous sections, the stability regions show a great variety of shapes. If we abstract from the individual particularities of the diagrams, we should, however, be able to discriminate between six basic types of stability regions. They emerge from combining two parameters each of which is classified as either stabilizing, destabilizing or ambiguous. Denoting the categories as S, D and A, respectively, and disregarding the order of these symbols, the following six cases are obtained: SS, DS, AS, DA, AA, DD. We conclude the numerical stability analysis by drawing a final example for each case and compile them in one illustration. The outcome is presented in figure 7.19.[28]

To represent the three categories S, D and A, we choose coefficients that have not been in the centre of the discussion and, except for one, have not been depicted before. These are the three weight parameters κ_p, κ_w, and κ_π, where κ_p was found to be stabilizing, κ_w destabilizing and κ_π ambiguous. An additional parameter is employed only when we are to combine two parameters of the same category.

We begin with two stabilizing parameters in a diagram, one of them being κ_p, the weight coefficient in the price Phillips curve. It is most natural to combine it with the equally stabilizing slope coefficient β_{pu} of the same curve. The two give rise to the parameter diagram in the upper left corner of figure 7.19, where it is seen that an increase of κ_p widens the stability interval of β_{pu}, and vice versa. The diagram may be compared to the lower right panel for the two destabilizing parameters that are taken from the wage Phillips curve, the weight κ_w and the the slope β_{we}. The two diagrams are complementary in the sense that, topologically, the stability region in one diagram corresponds to the instability region in the other.

The two stabilizing and destabilizing weights themselves, κ_p and κ_w, are combined in the upper right panel. Confining the range of κ_p to $\kappa_p \le 0.87$, the stability interval of κ_p is reduced and eventually disappears as κ_w rises from zero, whereas a rising κ_p gradually enlarges the stability interval of κ_w. To be exact, the diagram is not fully representative of a DS combination when values of κ_p higher than 0.87 are taken into account and an ambiguity occurs. These values, however, which are far above the calibrated zero value of κ_p, are here exhibited only for completeness.

The remaining three panels include the ambiguous parameter κ_π. In all three cases, the reswitching of instability prevails. This even holds

---

[28] Letters S, D and A indicate parameters that are classified as stabilizing, destabilizing and ambiguous, respectively. The (κ_w, κ_π) diagram has $\eta_{m,i} = 0.10$ underlying.

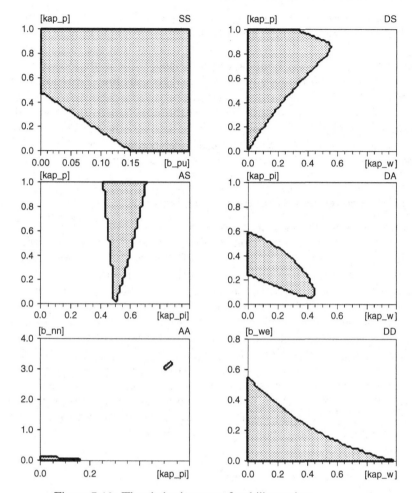

Figure 7.19: The six basic types of stability region

true for both parameters when κ_π is combined with another ambiguous parameter, such as β_{nn}, in the lower left panel. What actually comes about is a stability island, which is also rather small. The second stability area in the lower left corner of the diagram is again drawn only for completeness, since such low values of the stock adjustment speed β_{nn} are, in practical terms, out of consideration.

The two panels in the middle of figure 7.19 combine κ_π with the stabilizing κ_p and the destabilizing κ_w.[29] In both cases a finger stretches

[29] The (κ_w, κ_p) stability region is empty if all other parameters attain their calibrated values. Therefore, $\eta_{m,i}$ is lowered to $\eta_{m,i} = 0.10$ in this parameter diagram.

out from the boundary into the parameter plane. In the AS combination the finger extends from the upper boundary (or from the right boundary if the axes are interchanged). In an AD combination the finger would extend from the lower boundary of the plane, while in the present DA combination, with the axes being interchanged, the finger extends from the left boundary of the (κ_w, κ_π) plane.

Apart from the slight ambiguities in the upper right and lower left panels, which for purity could easily be cut off, the six diagrams of figure 7.19 give a short summary of the effects that the parameters of a model can have on the local stability of its equilibrium point.

7.6   Properties of the dynamic trajectories

After the detailed eigenvalue analysis in the previous sections, we finally turn to the dynamic simulations of the KMG model and study trajectories different from the base scenario. To recap, the latter was characterized by one extrinsic nonlinearity imposed upon an otherwise, as we said, quasi-linear differential equations system, which served to contain the oscillations within reasonable bounds. In the present section, we are concerned with three issues. First, we undo the extrinsic nonlinearity in the investment function and look for the existence of stable periodic orbits arising from a Hopf bifurcation. Second, retaining the nonlinearity, we look for more complicated patterns in the time series than the regular limit cycle, with its period of around eight years in the base scenario. Third, we allow for more flexible government expenditures and ask the obvious question of whether a countercyclical policy can contribute to a further stabilization of the dynamics.

7.6.1   Stable limit cycles from a Hopf bifurcation

It has already been established in chapter 4, section 5, Proposition 4, that when the system loses stability under *ceteris paribus* variations of a selected parameter α then this occurs by way of a Hopf bifurcation at some value α^H. In terms of eigenvalues, the eigenvalue with maximal real part is non-zero and purely imaginary then (its real part is zero), and for $\alpha < \alpha^H$ it has a negative real part, for $\alpha > \alpha^H$ a positive real part (or vice versa).

A Hopf bifurcation signals the existence of periodic orbits. More precisely, it means the following. There is a non-degenerate interval $I = [0, \varepsilon_{max})$ of real numbers, an interval A of parameters α with $\alpha^H \in A$, a subset S of the system's state space, and a continuous mapping $f: I \longrightarrow A \times S$, $\varepsilon \mapsto (\alpha, x^o)$ with the property: for $\varepsilon = 0$, $\alpha(\varepsilon)$ equals a^H and $x^o(\varepsilon)$ is the system's equilibrium point; while, for $\varepsilon > 0$, $x^o(\varepsilon)$ is the starting point of a non-degenerate periodic orbit under the dynamics constituted by the parameter value $\alpha(\varepsilon)$.

Mostly, the parameter interval A is closed on (at least) one side and α^H is the corresponding end point. In a 'degenerate' Hopf bifurcation, the interval may even be a singleton, $A = \{\alpha^H\}$, which happens especially if the system is linear or of so-called Lotka–Volterra type; in this case the state space is 'filled' with periodic orbits – that is, with respect to the parameter value $\alpha = \alpha^H$, every point in the state space has a periodic orbit running through it (see, for example, Hirsch and Smale, 1974, p. 262). For 'sufficiently' nonlinear and 'well-behaved' systems, however, $\alpha_1 = \alpha(\varepsilon_1) \neq \alpha(\varepsilon_2) = \alpha_2$ if $\varepsilon_1 \neq \varepsilon_2$, and the periodic orbits parameterized by the initial conditions $x^o(\varepsilon_1)$ and $x^o(\varepsilon_2)$ are locally unique in the respective dynamics under parameters α_1 and α_2.

A periodic orbit that is locally unique is a limit cycle. Just as with a point of equilibrium (with a non-singular Jacobian), it is essentially either locally attracting or unstable.[30] Accordingly, the two cases of sub- and supercriticality can be distinguished. Suppose the equilibrium point is unstable for $\alpha > \alpha^H$ (otherwise the following relationships are reversed). If α^H is the lower boundary of the parameter interval A, then for $\alpha \in A$ (and $\alpha \neq \alpha^H$) the trajectories of the system will move away from the equilibrium point and converge to the corresponding periodic Hopf orbit.[31] This case is called the supercritical case. By contrast, if α^H is the upper boundary of A, then for $\alpha \in A$ the trajectories will all converge to the equilibrium point and the corresponding Hopf orbit is repelling. This is the so-called subcritical case. (Standard diagrams illustrating the two cases can, for example, be found in Gabisch and Lorenz, 1989, pp. 164f.)

Which case prevails can be determined by an analytical condition. Involving the coefficients of a third-order Taylor expansion, it is, however, rather complicated (see Guckenheimer and Holmes, 1983, pp. 144–52) and usually devoid of any economic content. More directly, the supercritical case would easily be detected by simulating the dynamical system on the computer, whereas, in order to identify a subcritical case, the dynamics could be run backwards in time.

In the following we give an example of a supercritical Hopf bifurcation. A few explorations are sufficient to find it. In order to emphasize

---

[30] 'Essentially' means apart from some mixed cases, which we may disregard in this general discussion. For example, in the plane a limit cycle may be attracting from the outside and repelling in its interior.

[31] Except for those trajectories, in higher dimensions than two, that start on the stable manifold. This set, however, has measure zero; that is, the (unconditional) probability of finding by chance an initial condition from which the system converges to the equilibrium point is, mathematically, zero.

that the limit cycles we observe do indeed emerge from a Hopf bifurcation, which is still a basically local phenomenon, we temporarily remove
the nonlinearity from the investment function, which was introduced to
contain the global dynamics. On the other hand, regarding the compatibility with the local stability results, it has to be taken into account
that the simulations are discrete-time approximations of the differential
equations system. In particular, it turns out that the two systems have
slightly different Hopf bifurcation values.[32]

Let us take β_{pu} as the parameter to be varied. For its calibrated value
$\beta_{pu} = 0.15$, we know that in the simulations the steady state is unstable. This is also compatible with the eigenvalues of the Jacobian of
the continuous-time system, the maximal real part $(\text{Re}\lambda_1)$ being slightly
above zero there $(\text{Re}\lambda_1 = 0.0168)$. β_{pu} has, furthermore, been identified as a stabilizing parameter. The property is brought out here by
figure 7.20, which depicts the maximal real part of the eigenvalues as
a function of β_{pu} and so shows that stability prevails for all β_{pu} slightly
higher than 0.15 (at least for all β_{pu} in a medium range). The exact
bifurcation value of the continuous-time system can be computed as
$\beta_{pu}^H = 0.15257$.

The stabilization by β_{pu} was already apparent from the upper left
panel of figure 7.18. The function displayed in figure 7.20, however,
helps us understand what comes about in the discrete-time simulations.
There, not only is the steady state still unstable when β_{pu} is marginally
increased above the value β_{pu}^H, which had to be expected from the remark
about the approximate nature of the simulations, but we also encounter
local instability for considerably higher values of β_{pu}. This fact can be
explained by the short dashed line in figure 7.20: to β_{pu} rendering the
steady state stable in the discrete-time system corresponds a situation in
the continuous-time system where the maximal real part of the eigenvalues must be below this line. Accordingly, as opposed to what results
from the continuous-time analysis, the discrete-time system has two
bifurcation values of β_{pu} (the two points of intersection of the solid and
the dashed line), and it is locally stable for β_{pu} only around 0.16.[33]

---

[32] We recall that our approximation is not mathematically oriented, by employing some
Runge–Kutta procedure, for example, but it preserves the economic content in the
discretized equations, such that they represent adjustments in a sequential economy with
monthly market periods. The details were documented in the appendix to chapter 4. In
principle, the monthly economy could be formulated as an ordinary difference equations
system, though this would be quite involved. We therefore abstain from a numerical
stability analysis of the sequential economy, which would allow us to determine the
exact differences in the Hopf bifurcation values, and content ourselves with observing
the trajectories in the discrete-time simulations.

[33] Since these values of β_{pu} are very close to the stability frontier, the simulated trajectories
converge extremely slowly then.

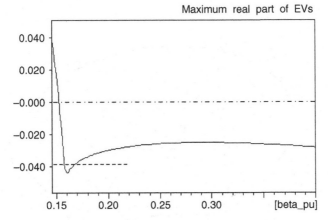

Figure 7.20: The maximal real part of the eigenvalues under variations of β_{pu}

We report this finding not so much for the instability reswitching in the discrete-time economy but for what we observe when β_{pu} is raised beyond the second bifurcation value; here, a supercritical Hopf bifurcation prevails. Thus, while the steady state is unstable again for these higher values of β_{pu}, attracting limit cycles come into being.

Figure 7.21[34] illustrates the phenomenon in the $(u, \hat{p})$ phase plane for $\beta_{pu} = 0.17$, where we obtain the anticlockwise utilization–inflation Phillips loops. The bold trajectories represent three closed orbits.[35] To indicate that the closed orbits are not dense in the state space but are indeed limit cycles, the two solid lines are drawn. They are trajectories that eventually converge to the outer and the medium cycles, respectively.

The fact that different periodic orbits exist at the same value $\beta_{pu} = 0.17$ of the varying parameter suggests that, in the notation above, now applied to the discrete-time system, the parameter interval A of the mapping $f = f(\varepsilon)$ is a singleton, so that $\beta_{pu}^H = 0.17$ and $A = \{\beta_{pu}^H\}$, corresponding to $\alpha(\varepsilon) = \alpha^H$ for all $\varepsilon \in I$ (identifying the symbol α with β_{pu}, of course). As has been mentioned, this is what occurs in a linear system. It would not be surprising in the present case, either, since our system has several times been described as quasi-linear.

On the other hand, attracting limit cycles are also obtained at other values of β_{pu}, at $\beta_{pu} = 0.18, 0.19, 0.20$, for example. This either means

---

[34] Underlying is $\beta_{pu} = 0.17$. Simulated is the discrete-time system with a monthly adjustment period.

[35] To make sure that they are also closed in the other dimensions, three additional phase planes were checked.

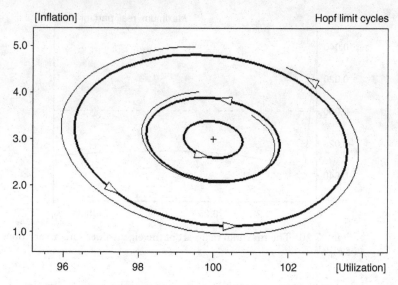

Figure 7.21: Stable limit cycles emerging from a Hopf bifurcation of β_{pu}

that the component $\varepsilon \mapsto \alpha(\varepsilon)$ of the mapping $f : I \longrightarrow A \times S$ is more intricate, or that some of the trajectories that we perceive as closed orbits on the computer screen are not exactly closed. However, we regard them as closed for all practical reasons: they are closed with respect to the time horizon of 500 years that we considered and with respect to the resolution of the plots on the screen. More detailed investigations to find out the exact function $\varepsilon \mapsto \alpha(\varepsilon) = \beta_{pu}(\varepsilon)$ would be of purely mathematical importance.

We do not want to push the analysis too far, and content ourselves with just pointing out the system's potential for a supercritical Hopf bifurcation. In our view, it is not very worthwhile to check this for all the other parameters. After all, the range of the parameter values and the initial conditions that give rise to periodic orbits with reasonable amplitudes would still be very narrow. In figure 7.20, for example, only the outer cycle exhibits acceptable amplitudes of the state variables, but it requires a relatively strong perturbation from the steady-state growth path if the economy is to converge to it; otherwise the amplitudes would be too small.

7.6.2   Is there scope for complex cyclical behaviour?

The limit cycle and its global stability in the base scenario can be understood as arising from two elementary principles. When all the behavioural functions, including the investment function, are specified in a linear way, the intrinsic nonlinearities that still originate with the multiplication or division of some of the dynamic variables turn out to be rather weak. It was on that account appropriate to characterize this system as quasi-linear (our first principle). As a consequence, the global dynamics are very much like the local dynamics. If, as we have chosen them, the parameters entail an unstable equilibrium and the leading eigenvalue is complex, this means the trajectories are cycling around with ever-increasing amplitudes.

The nonlinearity in the investment function was then introduced to counteract this tendency (the second principle). Since the mechanism takes effect in the outer regions of the state space, local instability is preserved, while the global trajectories are smoothly prevented from further spiralling outwards. As the nonlinearity was laid out, it would in a planar system almost be compelling that only one periodic orbit comes about, which would be attracting, of course. Although it might not be generally compelling in higher dimensions, the nonlinearity is sufficiently effective to generate the same phenomenon in our six-dimensional, calibrated system. Thus, a unique and, moreover, globally attracting limit cycle is obtained, which was also seen to be fairly regular – for some variables not even very different from a sine wave.

This notwithstanding, the question arises whether the cyclical dynamics must always be that 'unexciting'. In previous work, though in a five-dimensional simplification of the model and with different extrinsic nonlinearities, more intricate behaviour was revealed (see the sketches given in Chiarella and Flaschel, 2000a, pp. 323–34). The simulations there were still of an exploratory nature and the time series exhibited various unrealistic features. The experiments nevertheless showed a certain potential for complex cyclical trajectories, which induces us to ask if similar behaviour can also be found in the present KMG model and under more acceptable parameter values.

Our investigation will not be an in-depth search for 'chaos' or 'a route to chaos'. A few examples are, however, sufficient to point out three types of cyclical motions that go beyond the regular limit cycles of the base scenario. They may be called long-period dynamics (scenario LP), almost period dynamics (scenario AP) and complex dynamics (scenario CD). We are aware that the latter two expressions have a definite mathematical meaning, but here we use them in an informal sense only.

Four behavioural parameters are changed to generate these scenarios, namely the stock adjustment speed, β_{nn}, the slope and the wage share coefficients in the wage Phillips curve, β_{we} and β_{wv}, and the investment coefficient, β_{Iq}. The combinations of the alternative values assigned to them are recorded in the upper part of table 7.4.

Table 7.4: *Parameters and eigenvalues constituting scenarios LP, AP and CD*

	Scenario			
	Base	LP	AP	CD
β_{we}	0.550	0.500	0.500	0.500
β_{wv}	0.500	0.350	0.350	0.350
β_{nn}	3.000	3.400	3.400	3.500
β_{Iq}	0.115	0.115	0.125	0.090
$\mathrm{Re}\lambda_{1,2}$	0.0168	−0.0047	−0.0204	0.0541
$T_{1,2}$	7.25	9.13	9.20	9.03
$\mathrm{Re}\lambda_{3,4}$	−0.1042	−0.0346	−0.0373	−0.0235
$T_{3,4}$	7.02	5.10	4.84	5.82

NB: Acronyms LP, AP, CD stand for long periodicity, almost periodic dynamics, and complex dynamics. T is the period associated with the respective complex eigenvalue.

The type of long periodicity obtained in scenario LP is illustrated by the utilization time series in the first panel of figure 7.22. It is extracted from the limit cycle to which the economy has (practically) converged after some 300 years (the trajectories have already come close to it much earlier). The motions of a single cycle take a similar span of time to that in the base scenario: on average, slightly more than 9.5 years. There are, however, small differences from one such cycle to another. What eventually repeats itself is not the cycles with a business cycle frequency but a sequence of several of them. On the whole, six single cycles form one, as it is mathematically called, periodic orbit with a period of about 57.5 years. Two time intervals of this length are marked by the dashed lines.[36]

In the neighbourhood of the reported parameter values there are many other examples of long periodic oscillations with, perhaps, even more attractive features. To mention two of them, more variation in the single cycles is obtained by raising β_{nn} from 3.40 to 3.42, though the (long) period is somewhat shorter then. On the other hand, the period can be increased to seventy-five years by raising the investment coefficient to $\beta_{Iq} = 0.120$ (β_{nn} reset to 3.40). While the latter example is more spectacular than in figure 7.22, we have not shown it since a periodicity in that range would be harder to recognize by purely visual inspection.

What, then, contributes to the slight differences between subsequent single cycles? We seek an explanation in the eigenvalues. The idea is

---

[36] The accurate closedness of these long periodic orbits has been checked in different phase planes – up to the resolution of the computer screen, which is sufficient for the present, somewhat informal analysis.

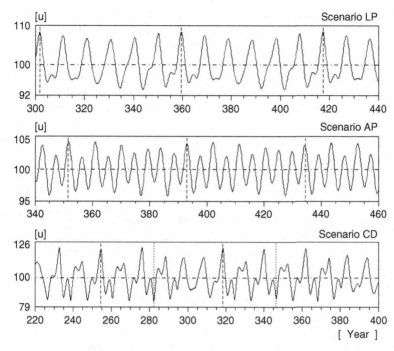

Figure 7.22: Time series of utilization in the three scenarios LP, AP and CD

that there is some scope for less regular limit cycles if the system has two pairs of complex eigenvalues with similar real parts and dissimilar associated periods. Clearly, one of the eigenvalues dominates the other, but if the real parts are close then, in certain stages of an oscillatory motion, the second eigenvalue may have a non-negligible influence on the dynamics and so distort the cyclical pattern that is generated by the first eigenvalue. The influence of the inferior complex eigenvalue may become stronger in particular when the nonlinearity takes effect and the trajectories are already somewhat perturbed from the time path determined by the first eigenvalue.

To check this hypothesis, the lower part of table 7.4 gives the real part of the two leading pairs of complex eigenvalues $\lambda_{1,2}$ and $\lambda_{3,4}$ (in all cases, the remaining two eigenvalues are real and a lot more negative). In the base scenario the real part of eigenvalue $\lambda_{3,4}$ is quite distinct from $\text{Re}\lambda_{1,2}$, whereas in the LP scenario the two real parts are much closer.[37]

---

[37] It has already been pointed out that, as also applies to the LP scenario, as well as the AP scenario further below, the steady state can be unstable in the simulations even though all eigenvalues of the continuous-time system have negative real parts.

By contrast, in the LP scenario there is a considerable difference in the periods $T_{1,2}$ and $T_{3,4}$ of the two complex eigenvalues. These features cannot 'prove' the hypothesis of the eigenvalue effects, but we see them as meaningful.

According to the hypothesis, the fluctuations should become richer if the real parts of the complex eigenvalues are closer still. As shown in table 7.4, this happens in the AP scenario. For the utilization time series coming about after more than 300 years, the middle panel of figure 7.22 indicates two time intervals of forty-one years with a self-repeating sequence of business cycle oscillations. So it seems at first sight, but a closer look reveals subtle differences in the sequences. For example, the second trough after the dashed line at $t = 352$ is deeper than the second trough after $t = 393$; or the sixth peak after $t = 352$ is not higher than the subsequent two peaks, whereas the sixth peak after $t = 393$ is. We did not check what becomes of these differences after, say, 3000 years. For our present purpose we consider it appropriate to characterize this type of dynamics as almost periodic.

That the phenomenon is essentially due to the influence of the second pair of complex eigenvalues is also supported by the fact that, owing to the stabilizing influence of the higher coefficient β_{Iq}, utilization has a lower amplitude, so that the nonlinearity effect in the investment function is weaker here. In addition, the average period of the single cycles is 4.55 years, which is just the order of magnitude given by the period $T_{3,4} = 4.84$ that is associated with eigenvalue $\lambda_{3,4}$.

In the third scenario, the distance between the real parts of the two leading eigenvalues has again widened, though not as much as in the base scenario. The last column in table 7.4 also shows that $\lambda_{1,2}$ is more destabilizing than before. Accordingly, the fluctuations of utilization in the bottom panel of figure 7.22 exhibit a higher amplitude. This seems to be favourable for the occurrence of several 'mini'-cycles of short duration, and with peaks and troughs that would be graded as inessential. Actually, the mini-cycles may be thought of as being brought about by the combined influence of eigenvalues $\lambda_{1,2}$ and $\lambda_{3,4}$ and the investment nonlinearity, which because of the higher amplitude of u is stronger here than in the other examples.[38] Note also that, with respect to the discrete-time simulations, the time path that can be conceived as being generated by eigenvalue $\lambda_{3,4}$ is practically unstable, too.

The occurrence of the mini-cycles is remarkable. Observing them in a time series from an unknown data-generating process, we would be

---

[38] The amplitude of u is probably unrealistically high. Responsible for the large deviations of utilization from normal is the relatively weak extrinsic nonlinearity. Stronger nonlinearity effects would also reduce the amplitude of u.

inclined to ascribe them to transitory shocks (especially if the discussion explicitly or implicitly refers to a linear framework). The present case demonstrates that this interpretation is not conclusive and that they can also be caused by purely deterministic mechanisms.

The main reason for presenting the third panel in figure 7.22 is the following phenomenon. There are indications that, after some time, a sequence of single cycles again starts to repeat itself; for example, after the dashed lines at $t = 254$ and $t = 318$. Over thirty years the motions resemble each other closely (compare the troughs at $t = 282$ and $t = 346$), but then they become more and more different. This does not appear to be a transient feature, and, later in time, no recurrent or almost recurrent patterns of cyclical motions are found. The fluctuations for which the third panel give an example may therefore, informally, be called complex dynamics. In order to decide whether this system can legitimately be termed 'chaotic', we would have to take a much longer time series and compute the maximal Lyapunov exponent. While this might be of some mathematical interest, we feel we would thus push the model and its interpretation too far.

As has been said before, the purpose of this subsection is to reveal that the model may give rise to richer dynamical behaviour than the regular limit cycle in the base scenario suggests. Deterministic simulations are an easy and straightforward way to examine the basic tendencies inherent in a dynamic system, whereas, realistically, an economy is prone to frequent exogenous shocks. The present deterministic simulations can show us that, in a long-term perspective, the seemingly more or less irregular phenomena we observe, like a changing amplitude or the mini-cycles just mentioned, need not be exclusively due to a possibly singular series of shocks but may have originated with the deterministic macroeconomic relationships (even under non-varying reaction coefficients).

7.6.3   Are countercyclical government expenditures stabilizing?

The extrinsic nonlinearity that was designed to tame the diverging oscillations in the base scenario takes effect on the demand side of the economy. When introducing it, we did not mention another mechanism that may readily come to mind in this respect, if we turn from the private sector to the government sector. Thus, the question we ask here is whether countercyclical government spending could also be stabilizing.

The stabilizing forces of a nonlinear softening of investment demand at higher levels of utilization appear to suggest an answer in the affirmative. On the other hand, the problem has a long tradition, and from the beginnings of systematic investigations in formal models it will be remembered that the effects are not so obvious as they may seem in a verbal discussion. An important contribution was by Phillips (1957), who ran computer simulations (already at that time!) of a linear, but sophisticated multiplier–accelerator model with several lag relationships, enhanced by inventory adjustments. As a first warning against overestimating the stabilizing potential of government expenditures, we may quote one of his results (p. 274):

If the proportional correction only is applied, the fluctuations in the response [to the initial shock] are slightly reduced when the value of the proportional correction factor is very low, but if it is raised above 0.1 the fluctuations become worse again and the system becomes unstable when the proportional correction factor is raised above 0.28.[39]

Regarding government spending G in the present KMG model, it has to be noted that the neutrality assumption of linking it with a constant factor γ to the capital stock, $G = \gamma K$ in eq. (4.21), already implies a certain element of countercyclicality. At least, as the simple identity $G = \gamma(K/Y^n)(Y^n/Y)Y = (\gamma/y^n)(1/u)Y$ shows, G does not move strictly proportionally with Y but this relationship is somewhat dampened. Nevertheless, in order to allow for variations in the degree of countercyclicality in this subsection, we generalize (4.21) to

$$G = \gamma_k K - \gamma_y (Y - Y^n), \quad \gamma_k, \gamma_y = \text{const}, \quad Y^n = y^n K$$

Dividing through the capital stock, it is seen that the formerly constant ratio γ becomes a function of the output–capital ratio y,

$$\gamma = \gamma(y) = \gamma_k - \gamma_y (y - y^n) \tag{7.13}$$

Evidently, putting $\gamma_y = 0$ re-establishes the original model, and raising γ_y above zero makes government spending more countercyclical.

Eq. (7.13) is a minor structural extension of the model. The only place where the variability of γ makes itself felt is aggregate demand y^d in (4.42). With a view to the final representation and recalling that eq. (4.37) treats y as a function of y^e and n, γ has to be replaced here by the expression $\gamma = \gamma[y(y^e, n)]$. The demand ratio y^d itself shows up in the differential equations (4.46) and (4.48). The Jacobian matrix $\mathcal{J}$ in (4.50) can therefore remain as it is, except for the entries 3 and 5 in rows

---

[39] As in our specification below, a 'proportional correction' means that government spending is negatively proportionally related to economic activity – i.e. its deviation from a target level. In addition, Phillips examines the effects of derivative and integral corrections, which refer to the time derivative and the integral of aggregate production (1957, p. 267). These aspects seem to have been largely forgotten in the literature since then.

3 and 5. Denoting the Jacobian of the KMG model with generalization (7.13) as $\mathcal{J}_\gamma$ and taking (4.37) into account, these entries change to

$$j_{\gamma,33} = j_{33} + \beta_y \partial\gamma/\partial y^e \qquad j_{\gamma,35} = j_{35} + \beta_y \partial\gamma/\partial n$$

$$j_{\gamma,53} = j_{53} - \partial\gamma/\partial y^e \qquad j_{\gamma,55} = j_{55} - \partial\gamma/\partial n \qquad (7.14)$$

$$\partial\gamma/\partial y^e = -\gamma_y[1 + (g^o + \beta_{nn})\beta_{ny}] \quad \partial\gamma/\partial n = \gamma_y\beta_{nn}$$

Figure 7.23[40] illustrates the main results of a numerical eigenvalue analysis of $\mathcal{J}_\gamma$ as far as the impact of positive or rising values of γ_y on local stability are concerned. The dotted area in the upper left panel shows the change of the stability region in the (β_{Iu}, β_{Iq}) parameter plane if in the base scenario γ_y is increased to $\gamma_y = 0.10$. To compare, the solid line is the stability frontier in the original model under $\gamma_y = 0$. Since there is a large area of previously unstable pairs (β_{Iu}, β_{Iq}) that have become

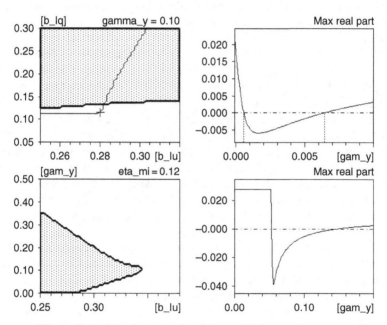

Figure 7.23: The impact of countercyclical government spending on local stability

<hr/>

[40] Panels to the left: the stability region (dotted area) in parameter diagrams in the (β_{Iu}, β_{Iq}) plane (with $\gamma_y = 0.10$ underlying in upper left) and in the (β_{Iu}, γ_y) plane (with $\eta_{m,i} = 0.12$ underlying in lower left). Panels to the right: the maximum real part of eigenvalues under variations of γ_y in the base scenario (upper right) and with $\eta_{m,i} = 0.12, \beta_{Iu} = 0.32$ (lower right, truncated at 0.028).

stable under $\gamma_y = 0.10$, and only a small area of previously stable pairs that have now become unstable, the diagram gives the impression that the rise in γ_y is mostly stabilizing. The calibrated values of (β_{Iu}, β_{Iq}) themselves, however, which are indicated by the cross, exhibit a greater distance to the stability frontier than under $\gamma_y = 0$.

Nevertheless, a certain stabilizing effect of γ_y can still be observed even if β_{Iu} and β_{Iq} are fixed at their calibrated values, although it is rather weak. The upper right panel draws the maximum real part of the eigenvalues in this situation as γ_y varies from 0.000 to 0.010. We see that there is a narrow range of values of γ_y that can render the steady state stable; the two Hopf bifurcation values are $\gamma_y^{H1} = 0.00055$ and $\gamma_y^{H2} = 0.00643$. It will be noted that over this range the negative real part does not drop very far, so in the discrete-time simulations the dynamics would remain unstable (see the remark on figure 7.20 above). As a counterpart of this observation, we should add that, when the maximum real part, $\mathrm{Re}\lambda_{1,2}$, becomes positive again after γ_y^{H2}, it does not rise very high, either. In fact, $\mathrm{Re}\lambda_{1,2}$ asymptotically approaches the value 0.01206 from below.

Since with respect to the base scenario the stability interval of γ_y is almost negligibly small, we look for other configurations where the properties of γ_y may come out more clearly. To this end we first improve the general stability prospects of the model, which can be conveniently achieved by reducing the interest elasticity of money demand to $\eta_{m,i} = 0.12$. The stability region in the (β_{Iu}, γ_y) parameter plane, shown in the lower left panel of figure 7.23, represents a typical case for the effects of the coefficient γ_y (qualitatively similar pictures are obtained in many other circumstances). As was intended, the steady state is locally stable under $\beta_{Iu} = 0.280$ and $\gamma_y = 0$. Stability is here maintained over a relatively wide interval of positive values of γ_y; it gets lost only as γ_y increases above $\gamma_y^H = 0.26449$.

The original model (with $\gamma_y = 0$ and $\eta_{m,i} = 0.12$) becomes unstable at higher values of β_{Iu} – at $\beta_{Iu} = 0.320$, for instance. Countercyclical government spending can then stabilize the economy if it is suitably administered, whereas too high a dosage will again destabilize it. The precise stability interval in this case is $(\gamma_y^{H1}, \gamma_y^{H2}) = (0.05378, 0.14483)$; the lower right panel of figure 7.23 provides a sketch of it.

The maximum real part of the eigenvalues in this panel also indicates the degree of stability and instability, respectively. Instability is strong or extremely strong for $\gamma_y < \gamma_y^{H1}$ (for the rest of the function $\gamma_y \mapsto \mathrm{Re}\lambda_{1,2}$ still to be clearly visible, it is truncated at 0.028; as γ_y decreases from γ_y^{H1} to zero, $\mathrm{Re}\lambda_{1,2}$ rises to about 0.80). In contrast, the stabilizing forces are very weak; between γ_y^{H1} and γ_y^{H2} the real part does not even reach -0.040 (which, referring to figure 7.20 once more, would not be sufficient for stability in the discrete-time simulations). It is equally remarkable that the instability setting in for $\gamma_y > \gamma_y^{H2}$ is excessively weak, too. The asymptotic value to which $\mathrm{Re}\lambda_{1,2}$ then converges from below is as low as 0.01118.

Despite the first impression from the upper left panel in figure 7.23 we can thus conclude that γ_y is an ambiguous parameter. In certain circumstances a countercyclical policy is able to stabilize the steady state, provided γ_y is skilfully chosen. This result is of the same kind as in the above quotation from Phillips (1957). A difference with respect to his multiplier–accelerator model, however, is the degree of instability. While Phillips found strong instability if his 'proportional correction factor' was raised too much, in the KMG model the (positive) maximum real part of the eigenvalues stays close to zero. The latter property does not just hold in the examples reported here, but it seems to be an almost universal phenomenon (at least, in our explorations we did not come across one counter-example). Moreover, even in situations where γ_y does not succeed in rendering the steady state locally stable, a sufficient increase of γ_y brings the maximum real part fairly close to zero.

Local stability is not the only criterion to evaluate the effectiveness of countercyclical government spending. We would also count it a success if it were able to dampen the amplitude of business cycles, a topic that requires an investigation of the global dynamics. A very natural experiment in this respect is to take the limit cycle of the non-modified KMG model and, in an upward motion of utilization, switch from $\gamma_y = 0$ to $\gamma_y = 0.10$, say. The outcome is presented as the bold lines in figure 7.24,[41] where the switch occurs when utilization passes its normal level at $t = 51.67$. The solid lines, which depict the time series of the base scenario under $\gamma_y = 0$, serve as a reference.

The immediate effect of the change in γ_y is exactly what it is supposed to be. The increase in aggregate demand and, thus, production and utilization immediately slows down, so strongly that utilization in the top panel reaches a low peak of $u = 101.12\%$ only nine months later (at that time, around $t = 52.42$, y^d is still rising, but at a rate hardly worth mentioning). This event however, initiates no downturn motion. Over the next eleven months utilization falls by an insignificant 0.27 per cent and then, at $t = 53.33$, starts to rise again, two months after y^d has begun to increase.

It appears that, in the medium term, the policy switch has a more complicated impact on the economy than the direct changes in demand

[41] The solid line is the limit cycle of the KMG model with $\gamma_y = 0$, the bold line arises from a switch to $\gamma_y = 0.10$ shortly before $t = 52$.

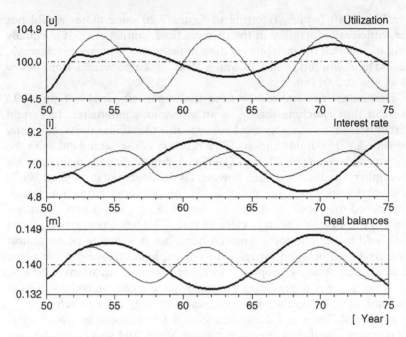

Figure 7.24: Time series resulting from $\gamma_y = 0$ and $\gamma_y = 0.10$

suggest. The second panel in figure 7.24 shows what is responsible for the unexpected demand effect. As utilization eases off, the rate of interest declines by an appreciable amount. This revitalizes investment at a stage when the capital growth rate should normally keep on falling. The opposite motion in this demand component becomes temporarily dominant, such that it undoes the contraction that is beginning.

The next task of course, is to find out what generates the decrease in the interest rate, as opposed to the evolution on the reference cycle, where it is markedly rising. Here it is useful to have a look at the explicit formula (6.11) for the interest rate, $i = (\beta_{mo} - m/y)/\beta_{mi}$. Hence, the lower values of u or y, respectively, as compared to their values on the reference cycle, are the first reason for the falling interest rate. A second reason is that this motion is reinforced, furthermore, by the relative increase of the real balances ratio $m = M/pK$. Referring to the growth rate formula $\hat{m} = g_m - \hat{p} - g_k$, this in turn can be explained by the relatively low level of the capital growth rate g_k in the first few years after $t = 52$ (and perhaps also by some modifications in the time path of the inflation rate, though for brevity we neglect this aspect here).

The renewed increase in utilization is not for long and comes to an end around $t = 56$. From then on, with $\gamma_y = 0.10$ maintained, the economy settles onto a new set of economic fluctuations. For these, the following features bear attention. First, for some thirty years after the switch in γ_y, the fluctuations in utilization are still below those of the reference cycle. In this respect the stabilization policy might be said to serve its purpose. At the same time, however, it has to be noted in the middle panel that the lower variability of utilization is associated with an increase in the amplitude of the interest rate. Incidentally, this phenomenon is mainly due to the higher amplitude of the real balances ratio m; see panels 2 and 3 in figure 7.24. Other variables may possibly be subjected to similar changes, but the present observation can suffice. What we learn from it is that 'stabilization' is not necessarily a one-dimensional problem; a stabilization of one variable may go along with a destabilization of another variable.

A second aspect brought out by figure 7.24 is that the countercyclical policy measures increase the period of the oscillations. This is not limited to the present example but is a general property. The period of about fifteen years that comes about in the time series diagrams corresponds closely to the results of the local dynamics. With $\gamma_y = 0.10$, the Jacobian $\mathcal{J}_\gamma$ yields a leading eigenvalue of $\lambda_{1,2} = \alpha \pm \beta i = 0.0104 \pm 0.419i$, which implies a period of $T = 2\pi/\beta = 15.0$ years.

As a third point, figure 7.24 also shows the first signs of the most important feature of the alternative dynamics, namely that the amplitude of the oscillations is steadily increasing over time. Remarkably, such has the extrinsic nonlinearity in the investment function been calibrated that it is no longer capable of containing the diverging oscillations within bounds. In other words, the nonlinear mechanism is dominated by the destabilizing forces that originate with the countercyclical government spending pattern, however weak they are in terms of the real part of the leading eigenvalue, with $\text{Re}\lambda_{1,2} = 0.0104$ (in the base scenario with $\gamma_y = 0$, $\text{Re}\lambda_{1,2} = 0.0168$ was obtained).

The magnitude of the maximum real part of the eigenvalues explains the speed at which the oscillations diverge, which is very low indeed. Seventy years after the switch in γ_y, for example, utilization is still within a range of ± 6 per cent around its normal level. Moreover, while stronger countercyclical expenditures (i.e. higher values of γ_y) prolong the period of the cycles, the rise in the amplitude of utilization is further slowed down (even if the timescale is not just years but the number of cycles). On the other hand, as has been indicated before, the interest rate is more seriously affected. A first disturbing consequence is that, if the dynamic laws remained unaltered, the interest rate would turn negative at a time when utilization is still within reasonable bounds.

With this remark we conclude our short digression on countercyclical government expenditures. It shows once more the positive and adverse effects of this kind of policy, and it will also be clear that we have no more than touched upon the problems of designing a straightforward (and robust) stabilization rule. A complementary task would be to ascertain whether such a rule could be supported by an active monetary policy that avoids the undesired interest rate effects we have encountered here – which leads us to the topic of the next chapter, where not the money supply but the interest rate is treated as the central bank's policy variable.

7.7   Conclusion

On the basis of the calibration of the KMG model in chapters 5 and 6, the present chapter has undertaken a numerical sensitivity analysis. We may distinguish between using the term in a narrower and in a wider sense. A sensitivity analysis in a wider sense starts out from a lower-dimensional submodel. In fact, three two- or three-dimensional submodels of the KMG model have been set up, where even analytical stability conditions could be derived. Such small systems are, of course, constructed because with them it is easier to identify the salient dynamic feedback loops, and because one expects that the stabilizing or destabilizing effects established there carry over to a more encompassing model. However, the most important result that we have obtained in a comparison of our submodels with the full KMG model is that the reaction coefficients regulating the strength of the feedback mechanisms may have different stability effects in the two types of models. Hence, apart from a number of properties that are of some interest on their own (especially the subject of wage and price flexibility), a general lesson to be learned from our investigation is that the insights gained in highly stylized low-dimensional models may occasionally be rather misleading.

This negative finding underlines the necessity of studying the parameter effects within the full model, which according to the wording above is a sensitivity analysis in a narrower sense, in the way that the term is usually adopted. In this respect we were concerned with local stability as well as with some features of the global dynamics. Regarding the thirteen central adjustment parameters and their impact on local stability, our final aim was to assign each of them to one of the following three broad categories: stabilizing, destabilizing or ambiguous. The properties of these coefficients were evaluated by studying the shape of the stability regions in a great variety of parameter diagrams. Based on the material thus collected we eventually arrived at the parameter characterization in subsection 7.5.3, table 7.3, which is the upshot of this sensitivity analysis.

The chapter concluded with a few themes concerning the global dynamics. First, we examined the scope for globally attracting limit cycles that are generated by a Hopf bifurcation. Second, we demonstrated the model's potential for richer dynamics than the regular and stable limit cycle that was conveniently obtained in the calibration of the base scenario. Finally, the model was extended to allow, in additional, for countercyclical government expenditures in varying degrees. In short, it was found here that their stability properties, in the local as well as in the global case, are ambiguous.

The numerical analysis in this chapter has sought to reveal the basic properties of a dynamic economy designed from a Keynesian theoretical point of view. For such a task it is meaningful that, in the economy itself, policy issues are dealt with in a neutral way. For this reason, and not just for simplification, taxes and government spending have been linked to the trend as it is represented by the relatively smoothly growing capital stock. More importantly, the additional postulate of a constant growth rate of the money supply amounts to a purely passive monetary policy. In the light of frequent discussions about the central bank's interest rate adjustments to changing economic conditions, we believe that alternative and more active monetary policy rules are the most urgent feature that should be taken into account in contemporary Keynesian modelling. The third part of the book is a first step in this direction.

Nevertheless, we consider the model and the analysis conducted so far to be useful. Whatever an active monetary policy will be able to achieve can be better assessed, or appreciated, if we have a profound knowledge of the fundamental stabilizing and destabilizing forces in the economy, such as they would prevail in stylized circumstances under a number of neutrality assumptions on the part of the government and the central bank.

Part III

Monetary Policy

8 The Taylor rule in small macromodels

8.1 Introduction

The Keynes–Metzler–Goodwin model that has been extensively studied in chapters 4 to 7 has its roots in the IS-LM modelling framework. It has, however, extended the IS-LM textbook version in several ways; in particular, it drops IS as a temporary equilibrium relationship and admits goods market disequilibrium with the correspondingly induced changes of inventories, and it introduces nominal price and wage adjustment together with its consequences for income distribution and aggregate demand.

In contrast, the LM curve is taken over unaltered. The main criticism in this respect is not so much that LM is too simple as a representation of the financial markets as that this device in which the money supply features as an exogenous variable ignores an important change in central banking. That is, most central banks, including the US Federal Reserve, nowadays pay little attention to monetary aggregates in conducting policy. Over the last decade a general consensus has instead been reached that the central bank follows a (real) interest rate rule. In the fields of Keynesian modelling (whether 'Old' or 'New', whether purely backward-looking or also forward-looking with rational expectations), the consensus has grown so strong that it actually could be said to form a new paradigm.

It thus follows that the KMG model with its LM curve and the assumption of a constantly growing money supply cannot be considered to be a fully descriptive model of the economy. Instead, we may regard the KMG model as creating some kind of vacuum, which allows us to study the disequilibrium adjustments of the private sector and their stabilizing and destabilizing effects in an environment where the government and the central bank are present but keep completely neutral. In this part of the book it is now time to abandon this point of view and give monetary policy a more descriptive flavour, which means that we take the new paradigm seriously and integrate it into the KMG model. Accordingly, the determination of the interest rate through the LM curve has to be replaced by an interest rate rule set up by the central bank. Most naturally, the interest rate rule that we will work with is a variant of the famous Taylor rule, which has attracted increased attention not only from theorists but also from analysts, policymakers and the financial press.

The new KMG model resulting from this transformation, which will equally be of dimension six, is analyzed in chapter 9. In the present chapter we prepare the ground for a better evaluation of its properties. To this end, we first discuss the concept of the Taylor rule (in a narrow and a broad sense) and some problems surrounding it. The functioning of the Taylor rule as a stabilizing device is then worked out in the framework of four small macromodels formulated in continuous time, which constitute a set of theoretical prototype models. Subsequently, we take an estimated discrete-time model from the literature, which against this background can be viewed as a slight extension of prototype model 4. In some form or another it has been so widely used in recent research as to be a workhorse, so its dynamic properties that we will have to reveal in a numerical investigation are an obvious reference for our own modified KMG model in the next chapter.

8.2   The concept of the Taylor rule

8.2.1   The interest rate as a policy variable

Before turning to the rule determining the adjustments of the interest rate, a few words are in order as to how the central bank influences the nominal rate of interest (and thus, with inflation or the inflation climate being given, the real interest rate). After all, it cannot do this by decree or by direct control. In this respect, two leading advocates of teaching the new paradigm already at the undergraduate level, Romer (2000) and Taylor (2001), indicate that the 'central banks acts by injecting or draining high-powered money from financial markets' (the quote is from Romer 2000, p. 20). More specifically, Taylor (2001, p. 559) mentions the federal funds rate as the interest rate that is relevant in the first instance here, the rate of return on the overnight loan market for commercial banks in the United States: 'When the Fed wants to lower this interest rate, it supplies more reserves to this market. When it wants to raise the interest rate, it reduces reserves.' The amount of reserves can be changed through open market operations, i.e. by buying and selling government bonds.

The concept of the LM relationship could, nevertheless, be retained. As Romer (2000, pp. 20f.) emphasizes, it should then employ high-powered money as the correct measure of money. What changes, however, is the causation. This is readily seen by referring to the LM equation (4.2) specified in chapter 4,

$$M/pY = f_m(i) \tag{8.1}$$

where M now may be interpreted as high-powered money and i as the federal funds rate. The traditional view on (8.1) is that the central bank sets M (increases or decreases it from the previous period's level) and temporary equilibrium on the money market brings about a new value for i. In short, the direction of cause and effect is $M \longrightarrow i$. The new paradigm exactly reverses the causation. Here the central bank sets a new level of i (or maintains its level of the previous short period) and then adjusts M in such a way that eq. (8.1) is fulfilled. This procedure can be denoted as $i \longrightarrow M$. If M or i, respectively, are set according to some rule, the two alternative views can be summarized as:

traditional view: money supply rule $\longrightarrow$ M $\longrightarrow$ i
new view: interest rate rule $\longrightarrow$ i $\longrightarrow$ M

For simple models, where neither money nor bonds enter one of the behavioural functions, an important difference thus becomes apparent. In the traditional mode, M (or $m = M/pK$, for that matter) is one of the state variables since it is needed to (co)determine the interest rate, which in turn determines investment and so aggregate demand. In contrast, if M does not feed back on the rest of the model, it may be altogether dismissed from it. More precisely, while an LM-like relationship may still be present conceptually, it is no longer an integral part of the model formulation but only an appendix.

The title of Romer's (2000) article, 'Keynesian macroeconomics without the LM curve', has to be understood in that sense. This becomes particularly clear when, regarding the details of open-market operations, Romer writes: 'Describing exactly how it [the central bank] must adjust the quantity of high-powered money in response to various disturbances to follow a particular rule is of no great interest. When I teach this material, I tell my students that, having shown that it is possible for the central bank to affect the real interest rate, we can leave the specifics of how it needs to adjust the money supply to follow its real rate rule to the professionals at its open-market desk' (2000, pp. 23f.).[1]

Since, with respect to money and bonds, the KMG model is also a simple model, we can apply Romer's comment to it as well. Correspondingly, a money variable such as $m = M/pK$ will completely disappear from the scene. If, then, the Taylor rule were to determine the interest rate in a statically endogenous way (i.e. directly as a function of the other variables of the model), we would save one state variable. In fact, however, in our specification of the Taylor rule the interest rate will be governed by a differential equation. It can thus be said that the

---

[1] Stiglitz and Walsh (2000) is another principles textbook into which the concept of a monetary policy rule without money is creeping.

dynamic variable money supply (in intensive form) will be exchanged for the dynamic variable interest rate, so that we will still end up with a six-dimensional differential equations system.

Incidentally, the neglect of money in connection with the interest rate may not be justified solely by model simplicity. In recent times attention has been directed to the possibility that changes in the federal funds rate are associated with far weaker changes in the monetary aggregates than an ordinary LM relationship (or a more elaborated portfolio approach to the financial sector) would conceive. With respect to the United States, to which our interest will be confined at present, this reduced role for money is based on the fact that, since 1994, the Federal Reserve has provided explicit information about its federal funds rate target. At that time the Federal Open Market Committee (FOMC) began to issue a public statement whenever it increased or decreased this intended level for the federal funds rate.[2]

The concept of the federal funds rate is important, since it has been observed that, once the FOMC makes such a change in its target publicly known, market reaction moves the federal funds rate from trading around the old target to trading around the new one, 'most often without any action beyond the announcement, at least not right away' (Orphanides, 2001, p. 49). An explanation for the immediate response is that the mere announcement of the target for the funds rate already poses a credible threat to the federal funds rate market. It seems to have been so effective that Meulendyke (1998, p. 142) concludes that 'the [federal funds] rate has tended to move to the new, preferred level as soon as the banks knew the intended rate'. This phenomenon is now described as the *announcement effect*, as opposed to the classical liquidity effect.[3] A pithier keyword is that open-market operations have to some extent been replaced by *open-mouth operations*.[4]

Regarding cause and effect, however, the issue requires a closer look. Thus, in an empirical investigation of the close relationship between the federal funds rate and the federal funds rate target, Thornton (2000) finds little evidence to support the view that it is due to either

[2] Also, in earlier years the FOMC decisions were made in terms of a federal funds rate target, but these decisions were communicated to the market in a less explicit way than they are now. Thornton (2000, p. 26), for example, mentions that, over the period 1974 to 1979, the funds rate target was adjusted ninety-nine times. However, the communications were misinterpreted on a number of occasions.

[3] See Demiralp and Jorda (2001). This paper provides evidence on how the Fed uses the liquidity effect in conjunction with the announcement effect to execute monetary policy. In addition, it investigates the implications of the announcement effect in term structure behaviour and the rational expectations hypothesis.

[4] The term 'open-mouth operations' was coined by Guthrie and Wright (2000) for the central bank of New Zealand.

open-market or open-mouth operations. He then goes on to propose looking at the relationship the other way around (p. 21), for which he quotes Goodfriend (1991, p. 10) with an argument put forward more than ten years earlier:

It should not be said that a Federal funds rate target change causes a change in market rates since the Fed is merely reacting to events in much the same way as the private sector does. More generally, to the extent that we believe the Fed reacts purposefully to economic events, we should not say that funds rate target changes are ever the fundamental cause of market rate changes, since both are driven by more fundamental shocks. Of course, such shocks may originate either in the private sector or the Fed, the latter as policy mistakes or shifts in political pressure on the Fed.

Money will have no essential role to play under these circumstances. Thornton (2000, p. 26) therefore points out that 'if there are large shocks to the natural rate or inflation, the Fed might adjust its funds rate target rather quickly rather than generate large changes in the supply of money [i.e. reserves]'.[5]

These sketchy remarks may be an indication of the challenges for a more detailed modelling of monetary policy and its transmission mechanisms in the financial sector. In the context of the present discussion, the specification of monetary policy will then be required to include assumptions about both the federal funds rate and the federal funds rate target. Schematically, the two rates may respond in two different ways to changes in the central bank's environment. On the one hand, the central bank may be supposed to maintain the funds rate at its present level, although an exogenous shock or an event in another part of the model puts pressure on the actual rate. In this case, the central bank must operate by appropriately changing reserves. For example, in response to an increase in loan demand, commercial banks will bid up the interest rates on the model's sources of loanable funds, including funds acquired on the federal funds rate market. To prevent the funds rate from rising, the central bank would have to increase the supply of reserves until all the increase in loan demand is satisfied at the existing funds rate. Alternatively, on the other hand, it may be assumed that the central bank does not accommodate the loan demand but is willing to permit an increase in the federal funds rate, which it could signal to the market by raising the funds rate target. In this case, the money supply need not be affected. Naturally, an ambitious modelling that seeks to take these issues into account would also have to assign a central role to expectations, which should not merely concern inflation.

[5] This might account for the rapid adjustments of the funds rate target over the 1974 to 1979 period, which was mentioned in footnote 2.

In this book we still leave these problems to one side. We do not distinguish between the federal funds rate and its target, nor do we concern ourselves with the motions of money or reserves implied by them. We just speak of the federal funds rate or, even shorter, the rate of interest as the central bank's policy variable, and denote it by the same letter i as the bond rate in the preceding chapters. (Further below it will be made explicit that in our setting the adjustments of the bond rate are, in a certain sense, identified with the variations of the federal funds rate.)

8.2.2   Specification of the Taylor rule

After the general remarks on the role of the interest rate as a policy variable, we now consider the specific rule that it will be supposed to follow. Though interest rate rules have been proposed and investigated before, Taylor's is 1993 article (1993a) is usually regarded as the seminal paper that started a lively and still ongoing discussion revolving around interest rate reaction functions. The interest rate rule put forward by Taylor (1993a, p. 202) reads

$$i = 2 + \hat{p}^{(4)} + 0.50 \cdot \tilde{y} + 0.50 \cdot (\hat{p}^{(4)} - 2) \qquad (8.2)$$

where i is the federal funds rate, $\hat{p}^{(4)}$ the rate of inflation over the previous four quarters, and $\tilde{y}$ the output gap, all measured in percentage points. The output gap is the deviation of real GDP from a trend line or an estimate of potential GDP.

Rule (8.2) has the feature that the federal funds rate rises if inflation increases above a target of 2 per cent or if real GDP rises above trend GDP. The responsiveness is equally strong to both types of deviations, and the reactions are symmetric to positive and negative deviations. If inflation and output are on target, the nominal federal funds rate would equal $2 + \hat{p}^{(4)} = 2 + 2 = 4$ per cent. Accordingly, the first number 2 on the right-hand side of (8.2) represents a long-run equilibrium real rate of interest.

Taylor introduces the rule as a normative prescription as well as an approximate description of actual behaviour (Taylor, 1993a, pp. 200ff.). Regarding the first aspect he discusses the (then) recent compilation by Bryant et al. (1993), which compares nine different multi-country econometric models and the performance of different monetary policy rules in them. Experience from his own work is also added (Taylor, 1993b). He concludes from this research that central banks are well advised to set interest rates based on conditions in their own country (neglecting exchange rates), and that placing a positive weight on both the price level and real output in the interest rate rule is preferable in most countries.[6] The reaction coefficients in (8.2) are chosen as rounded numbers to make for easy discussion.

After noting the excellent stabilization properties and their robustness across different models, Taylor points out that 'what is perhaps surprising is that this rule fits the actual policy performance during the last few years remarkably well' (1993a, p. 202). He illustrates this by plotting a time series diagram over the six-year period 1987 to 1992 displaying the empirical federal funds rate and the path implied by the policy rule (8.2).[7]

Even if it is admitted that (8.2) is a good description of the adjustments of the federal funds rate, this does not necessarily mean that the Fed's policy has actually been guided by this or a similar rule. Taylor is thus precise in summarizing the good fit in his time series diagram by saying that

the Fed policy has been conducted *as if* the Fed had been following a policy rule much like the one called for by recent research on policy rules (emphasis added).

Moreover, even if the Fed were basically following a rule like (8.2), there will have been many occasions on which the monetary policy decisions were influenced by economic events beyond the scope of the rule. Examples for such motives are the exchange value of the dollar in 1985; ensuring adequate liquidity in the financial system after the stock market crash of 1987, which Taylor (1993a, p. 202) himself mentions; discretionary responses to the financial strains between 1989 and 1993; and the response to the dramatic financial market turbulence in 1998.[8]

Therefore, when discussing a central bank in the real world following a particular policy rule, the rule is certainly not supposed to be adopted as a mechanical formula. To quote Taylor (1993a, p. 198): 'A policy rule can be implemented and operated more informally by policymakers who recognize the general instrument responses that underlie the policy rule, but who also recognize that operating the rule requires judgment and cannot be done by computer.' In contrast, when the properties of

---

[6] Other model simulation studies have later reinforced this conclusion; see, for example, Levin et al. (1998), or the contributions to Taylor (1999).

[7] The series of his output gap is based on a log-linear trend of real GDP (with a 2.2 per cent growth rate) over the period 1984 to 1992.

[8] Goodfriend (2002) gives a compact account of the interaction between interest rate policy and the economy since 1987. He emphasizes that the situations that confronted the Fed were remarkably varied. See also the two short 'case studies' discussed by Taylor (1993a, pp. 210ff.).

one or several policy rules are examined within a model, we are allowed
to abstract from the special and, by hypothesis, exogenous events that
have just been alluded to. In a theoretical model, possible discretionary
measures by the central bank need not be considered.[9]

Of course, a systematic analysis of the Taylor rule will not confine itself
to the original coefficients in (8.2). Furthermore, when incorporating
the interest rate rule into our modelling framework, it also appropriate
to modify slightly the variables specified there. First, we replace the
four-quarter inflation rate $\hat{p}^{(4)}$ in (8.2) by the corresponding outcome in
a continuous-time setting, which is the instantaneous rate of inflation $\hat{p}$.
The benchmark to which it is compared – i.e. the central bank's target
rate of inflation – is denoted by $\hat{p}^\star$. The second point concerns the output
gap. As its role in our model is performed by over- and underutilization,
it is natural to substitute $u - 1$ for $\tilde{y}$. Third, instead of referring directly to
2 per cent as the equilibrium real interest rate, we write $i^o - \hat{p}$ (i^o being the
nominal rate of interest in the steady state). The policy coefficients that
generally measure the responsiveness of the interest rate to the deviations
of inflation and utilization are designated α_p and α_u, respectively. The
resultant interest rate i is marked by a star symbol. Accentuating that it
is a functional expression of inflation $\hat{p}$ and utilization u, we have

$$i^\star = i^\star(\hat{p}, u) = (i^o - \hat{p}^\star) + \hat{p} + \alpha_p(\hat{p} - \hat{p}^\star) + \alpha_u(u - 1) \qquad (8.3)$$

$i^\star$ is the obvious counterpart of (8.2) with general coefficients, and, for
short, may therefore be called the *Taylor rate of interest*. Non-negativity
of the coefficients α_p and α_u will be understood.

A still more general view is that $i^\star$ represents only what the central
bank considers to be the appropriate level of the interest rate (which
is not to be confused with the federal funds rate target discussed in
the previous subsection). Especially, however, when the inflation rate
is subjected to a greater shock, the central bank may not decide to
increase or decrease the interest rate immediately as predicted by (8.3),
which would change the rate by more than one to one. Such large and
abrupt adjustments may be viewed as undesirable because they increase
interest rate volatility. The central bank may, rather, prefer to smooth
the interest rate by moving gradually over several quarters, say, to bring
the current level of the rate in line with the appropriate level $i^\star$. For a

---

[9] Nevertheless, after the policy rule has ben established in a model one may still want to
study the consequences of selected temporary deviations from the rule. Usually, however,
one will also assume that this will not affect the central bank's credibility; that is, the
model's reaction coefficients will remain constant.

formulation in continuous time, we introduce a speed of adjustment α_i for the interest rate, and translate the concept as

$$di/dt = \alpha_i[i^*(\hat{p}, u) - i] \tag{8.4}$$

α_i measures the degree of, as it is called, *interest rate smoothing*; the lower α_i is, the higher the degree of smoothing. On the other hand, (8.3) is recovered by letting the adjustment speed tend to infinity, $\alpha_i \to \infty$. In this sense, (8.3) is a special case of (8.4).

The interest rate reaction function (8.4) is the monetary policy rule that we will work with. As the common practice is in the literature, we too continue to classify this version as a 'Taylor rule'. More specifically, three different cases of increasing generality can be distinguished in (8.4), to which we occasionally refer as follows:[10]

Original Taylor rule: $\alpha_i = \infty$ $\alpha_p = 0.50$ $\alpha_u = 0.50$

Taylor rule in a narrow sense: $\alpha_i = \infty$ $\alpha_p > 0$ $\alpha_u \geq 0$

Taylor rule in a broad sense: $\alpha_i > 0$ $\alpha_p > 0$ $\alpha_u \geq 0$

8.2.3   Estimation of the Taylor rule

Taylor's (1993a) claim of the descriptive value of his simple rule has proved very stimulating for empirical research. A first straightforward test is to extend the sample period over which the interest rate determined by (8.2) is contrasted with the actual federal funds rate. Beginning their study with this check, Judd and Rudebusch (1998, pp. 5f.) report a reasonably good fit beyond Taylor's end-year 1992. Over the period 1987 to 1997 the original Taylor rule succeeds in capturing the major swings in the funds rate, though with less amplitude. Numerically, the R^2 for this period is as high as 87 per cent for quarterly levels of the nominal funds rate, and 52 per cent for quarterly changes.

On the other hand, Judd and Rudebusch also present a time series diagram plotting the two rates prior to 1987 (back to 1970). Here such large differences leap to the eye that any further statistical measures are redundant. In detail, during the period when Paul Volcker was chairman of the Fed (1979:Q3 to 1987:Q2: a time when the Fed significantly reduced inflation), the funds rate was consistently higher than what the

---

[10] To avoid the technical details of an additional remark, we neglect the fact that the amplitudes of utilization u in (8.4) will differ somewhat from the amplitudes of the output gap $\tilde{y}$ in (8.2), which implies that α_u would have to be slightly scaled up or down to correspond exactly to the weight 0.50 placed on $\tilde{y}$ in (8.2).

rule recommended; with regard to the period of Arthur Burns' chairmanship (1970:Q1 to 1978:Q1), the funds rate fell consistently short of the rule's recommended rate. The obvious lesson to be learned from these observations is that the coefficients of this or other versions of the Taylor rule may not be stable over a longer time span.

Since Taylor did not estimate his equation econometrically, the idea of running regressions on different specifications of the rule suggests itself. This is not the place to discuss the ample literature on this subject (where, in particular, different purposes underlying the studies have to be taken into account). Rather, we present directly a representative example of such an econometric result, which is taken from the already mentioned paper by Judd and Rudebusch (1998; JR in the following). We limit ourselves to the main result, which will also be utilized in the model simulations later on. The sample period of this estimation is Alan Greenspan's chairmanship between 1987:Q3 and 1997:Q4; the time unit is a quarter.

The Taylor rate of interest i^* entering the estimation refers to the output gap $\tilde{y}$ and to four-quarter inflation $\hat{p}^{(4)}$. Adjusting the notation to the present context, it reads

$$i_t^* = (i^o - \hat{p}^*) + \hat{p}_t^{(4)} + \tilde{\alpha}_p(\hat{p}_t^{(4)} - \hat{p}^*) + \tilde{\alpha}_y\tilde{y}_t \tag{8.5}$$

The policy coefficients are distinguished by a tilde from those in (8.3) since the variables are slightly different. $\hat{p}^{(4)}$ is precisely average inflation over the contemporaneous and prior three quarters (GDP deflator).

The dynamics of adjustment of the actual level of the federal funds rate to i_t^* are specified as

$$i_t - i_{t-1} = \tilde{\alpha}_i(i_t^* - i_{t-1}) + \tilde{\alpha}_\Delta \Delta i_{t-1} \tag{8.6}$$

The last term on the right-hand side serves to maintain some of the 'momentum' from last period's funds rate change ($\Delta i_{t-1} = i_{t-1} - i_{t-2}$). Without it, $\tilde{\alpha}_\Delta = 0$, eq. (8.6) is clearly the discrete-time counterpart of (8.4).

JR estimated (8.5), (8.6) by running a regression on the first differences of the funds rate. This equation is readily obtained by substituting (8.5) into (8.6). It has to be noted however, that this approach is not capable of identifying separately the target rate of inflation $\hat{p}^*$ and the equilibrium rate of interest i^o. The constant $\tilde{\alpha}_o$ that thus appears on the right-hand side of the regression equation is given by $\tilde{\alpha}_o = \tilde{\alpha}_i(i^o - (1 + \tilde{\alpha}_p)\hat{p}^*)$, so i^o can be determined only once a particular value for $\hat{p}^*$ is assumed, and vice versa. The estimated value of $\tilde{\alpha}_o$ nevertheless inspires confidence since the average long sample (1961 to 1997) and Greenspan sample real funds rates and the end-of-sample inflation rate are consistent with a fairly narrow range of trade-offs. The implied values for both the inflation target $\hat{p}^*$ and the real equilibrium funds rate $i^o - \hat{p}^*$ all lie in a range between 1.8 and 2.8 per cent, which is not far from the 2 per cent rates that Taylor has postulated (JR, p. 8).

The outcome of the regression depends somewhat on the particular measure for the output gap $\tilde{y}$. The authors themselves believe that a structural approach is conceptually more appropriate than an atheoretical procedure that fits a trend to the data. They also argue that the structural approach is the one typically used by policymakers, at the Fed and elsewhere. Concretely, JR (p. 8) use a structural definition Y^* of potential GDP that was developed at the Congressional Budget Office, which estimates it in terms of a relationship with future inflation similar to the way a time-varying NAIRU is estimated within the context of a Phillips curve.[11]

It will be helpful for us that, in examining the robustness of their results, JR also report the estimates obtained on the basis of additional specifications of the output gap, since one of these measures can easily be constructed by ourselves and so related to our model's capacity utilization concept u. This alternative defines the output gap more technically as deviations from a quadratic trend (over 1961 to 1997). Though, with a coefficient of 0.99, the structural output gap on the basis of Y^* is almost perfectly correlated with the quadratic-trend deviations (JR, p. 13), the corresponding point estimates of the policy coefficients differ to some extent. Hence, we refer directly to the results from the latter output gap concept. For the Greenspan period, the policy coefficients come out as follows (JR, p. 14):

$$\tilde{\alpha}_p = 0.37 \quad \tilde{\alpha}_y = 0.82 \quad \tilde{\alpha}_i = 0.28 \quad \tilde{\alpha}_\Delta = 0.52 \qquad (8.7)$$

All coefficients have the expected sign and are statistically significant. The two estimates for $\tilde{\alpha}_i$ and $\tilde{\alpha}_\Delta$, however, require a second thought. While $\tilde{\alpha}_\Delta > 0$ is rather an issue of convenient specification, to which we return further below, a value of $\tilde{\alpha}_i$ less than one is conceptually a more fundamental issue (note that $\tilde{\alpha}_i = 1$ would yield the Taylor rule in a narrow sense, $i_t = i_t^*$).

It may first be noted that, in a regression equation, the coefficient $\tilde{\alpha}_i$ itself measures only the persistence in the adjustments of the federal funds rate, which may be present for several reasons. The outcome

---

[11] JR mention that this potential output series is conceptually similar to and highly correlated with the Q^* series, which is widely used in other work on monetary policy rules.

$0 < \tilde{\alpha}_i < 1$ (in our notation) is a typical result that is found in many econometric investigations, not only for the United States but internationally as well.[12]

The problem is how to interpret this persistence. The conventional wisdom is that the central bank adjusts the actual funds rate gradually in several steps towards the (as we call it) Taylor rate of interest i^* (or, generally, a similar concept of a recommended interest rate). This is the interpretation of interest rate smoothing, which has already been mentioned when eq. (8.4) was introduced. The literature points out three main motives of the central bank for such partial adjustments.[13] (1) To ensure the existence of well-functioning capital markets, as volatile interest rates may result in capital losses, which would be disruptive for the financial sector. (2) Inertial behaviour is (in some sense) optimal in a forward-looking environment (a topic that has, in particular, been investigated in small New-Keynesian rational expectations models). (3) Inertial behaviour is also optimal in the presence of uncertainty regarding central structural parameters of the economy (or the model, respectively).

On the other hand, in addition to inflation and output, the central bank may react more or less systematically to other economic conditions. Accordingly, a positive coefficient $\tilde{\alpha}_i$ would capture effects that are not included in the formulation of the Taylor rule. As Brüggemann and Thornton (2003) sum up their econometric results (in the abstract), the strong persistence in estimated Taylor rules reflects the degree to which the central bank does *not* follow the Taylor rule. This summary is, nevertheless, controversial. Castelnuovo (2003) reaches the diametrically opposite conclusion from his econometric tests for the presence of interest rate smoothing: that the smoothing degree is not due to an omitted variable bias.

---

[12] See, for example, Srour (2001), who considers twelve countries. Here we may remark in passing that even the behaviour of the German Bundesbank, which, officially, was heavily oriented towards the money supply, could well be described by some versions of the Taylor rule. Examples of such discussions are those by Bernanke and Mihov (1997), Clarida and Gertler (1997) and Issing (1997).

[13] Regarding some of these (and other) explanations, Sack and Wieland (2000) present empirical results from several recent papers. Another interesting approach is that of Ozlale (2003), who seeks to estimate directly the relative strength of the motive for interest rate smoothing. To this end the central bank is assumed to minimize the expected value of an intertemporal quadratic loss function, where the private sector is represented by a Phillips curve and a dynamic IS equation (in fact, such as they are specified in eqs. (8.19) and (8.20) below). Estimating the parameters of the loss function, Ozlale finds significant values of the weight attached to $(i_t - i_{t-1})^2$ (over different subperiods), which are not negligible relative to the other two weights of the terms $(\hat{p}_t^{(4)} - \hat{p}^*)^2$ and $(\hat{y}_t)^2$.

Rudebusch (2001) takes into consideration the fact that direct evidence against the partial adjustment rule, in the form of non-rejection of the $\tilde{\alpha}_i = 0$ hypothesis, is difficult to develop. Instead, he uses indirect evidence regarding the term structure, since partial adjustments would imply predictable future changes in the policy rate over horizons of several quarters. The alternative interpretation of the positive estimations of $\tilde{\alpha}_i$ he then proposes is that it reflects serially correlated or persistent special factors or shocks that cause the central bank to deviate from the policy rule.

An important contribution in this respect, also because it is not another econometric study, is that by Cobham (2003), who refers to the Bank of England. Using the remarkably detailed evidence available from the minutes of the Monetary Policy Committee to evaluate the relevance of the various explanations of smoothing for the United Kingdom, he concludes that the explanation of interest rate smoothing should be sought primarily in the serial correlations of shocks, together with some minor and short-term influences from uncertainty. Other explanations along the lines is of the ones alluded to above turn out to be not relevant.

A special example of serially correlated shocks, which has received great interest in the empirical and theoretical literature, are so-called measurement errors. This means that, at the time when the central bank has to decide on the interest rate, its information about inflation and, in particular, the output gap is only provisional. As later revisions of the data show, these 'real-time' data may differ from the 'true' gaps by non-negligible amounts. That these effects may indeed have a bearing on the coefficient $\tilde{\alpha}_i$ is nicely demonstrated by Lansing (2002), who simulates a small model where, in each period, the Fed constructs a real-time estimate of trend output by running a regression on past output data. Here, efforts to identify the Fed's policy rule using final data can create the illusion of interest rate smoothing when, in fact, none exists. The lagged funds rate enters into regressions spuriously because it helps pick up the Fed's serially correlated measurement errors, which are not taken into account by the standard estimation procedure. Lansing finds that this mis-specification problem can explain as much as one half of the apparent degree of 'inertia' or 'partial adjustment' in the funds rate.

A better understanding of all these problems around $\tilde{\alpha}_i > 0$ is important for predictions of the actual federal funds rate and also for the design of optimal monetary policy. On the other hand, the problems can be largely neglected if $\tilde{\alpha}_i > 0$ is used as part ofa compact description of interest rate adjustments. The previous brief discussion shows that a positive coefficient may have a broader scope for interpretation than the straightforward argument of interest rate smoothing. In a rough way, $\tilde{\alpha}_i$ might also capture the influence of factors that are not explicitly mentioned in our still relatively small macroeconomic model. What, in particular, the model does not account for are the central bank's problems with imprecise real-time data.[14]

Regarding the fourth coefficient in (8.7), a positive value of $\tilde{\alpha}_\Delta$ is for us a matter of specification. The problem is that the coefficient has no counterpart in the continuous-time version (8.3), (8.4) of the Taylor rule. However, including the 'momentum' effect that $\tilde{\alpha}_\Delta$ represents in these equations would certainly lead to greater complications. To maintain the parsimonious approach to the policy rule we therefore decide to ignore this effect, which amounts to postulating $\tilde{\alpha}_\Delta = 0$. Although JR's estimate of $\tilde{\alpha}_\Delta$ is significantly positive, there are, besides simplification, two other reasons why $\tilde{\alpha}_\Delta = 0$ can be accepted. First, in contrast to $\tilde{\alpha}_i > 0$, this result does not appear to be very robust. JR (p. 9, fn. 17) remark that, when they respecified the regression using end-of-quarter funds rate data, the lagged change in the funds rate became statistically insignificant, while the remaining coefficients were close to the results in the original specification.[15] The second reason is that the impulse–response functions, which we will discuss in the discrete-time model of subsection 8.4.3 below, are only marginally affected whether $\tilde{\alpha}_\Delta = 0.52$ or $\tilde{\alpha}_\Delta = 0$ is assumed.

After this background discussion, we can return to the Taylor rule formulation (8.3), (8.4) for the KMG model (which, as has been remarked, makes it a KMGT model). The first three coefficients $\tilde{\alpha}_p$, $\tilde{\alpha}_y$, $\tilde{\alpha}_i$ in (8.7) can now be used to obtain numerical values for α_p, α_u, α_i. The value of the coefficient $\tilde{\alpha}_p$, which measures the responsiveness to the inflation gap, need not be altered, except that we round it up to $\alpha_p = 0.40$. As regards the responsiveness to utilization, α_u, we recall that the empirical counterpart of this variable was the output–capital ratio, in the form of percentage deviations from a Hodrick–Prescott 'trend' (see chapter 5, section 2). Although this series is closely correlated with the GDP quadratic-trend deviations, it has to be taken into account that the two series differ in amplitude. Over JR's sample period 1961 to 1997

---

[14] Because of the uncertainty that exists in measuring the current levels of output and potential output, policy rules have been proposed in which the funds rate responds to the growth rate of the output gap instead of its level. Mehra (2002) shows that, empirically, such a growth rate version of the interest rate rule predicts actual policy almost as well as the level version (where it has to be noted that his estimation includes the bond rate as a third explanatory variable). To our knowledge, however, possible effects on the stability properties of a model have as yet not been investigated in the literature.

[15] The motive for the respecification was, as indicated by the Q statistic, signs of autocorrelation in the original estimation with time-aggregated data; they disappeared with the end-of-quarter data. Underlying here was the Y^* output gap concept; results for the quadratic-trend output gap are not reported.

for detrending, we compute a standard deviation of 2.74 for the GDP deviations, while the standard deviation of the utilization series is 1.89. Thus, to compensate for the smaller amplitude of utilization, the coefficient $\tilde{\alpha}_y$ should be multiplied by the ratio $2.71/1.89 = 1.45$. Rounding up gives us $\alpha_u = 1.20$.

JR's estimated adjustment speed $\tilde{\alpha}_i = 0.28$ says that, within one quarter, 28 per cent of the difference between the lagged actual and the Taylor rate of interest is eliminated. Over one year the elimination would be $4.28 = 112$ per cent. Since the time unit underlying the differential equation (8.4) is one year, we set the coefficient α_i equal to 1.10.[16]

Summing up, in the numerical analysis of the KMGT model we will work with the following policy coefficients for eqs. (8.3), (8.4):

$$\alpha_p = 0.40 \quad \alpha_u = 1.20 \quad \alpha_i = 1.10 \qquad (8.8)$$

8.3   Four prototype models

Monetary policy rules are designed for stabilization. In macroeconomic theory, the notion of stabilization is usually made explicit within stochastic (discrete-time and mostly linear) models, where it means that a suitable rule, or suitable coefficients for a given specification of a rule, are able to reduce the variability of output and inflation; or they might even minimize a weighted average of the variances of output and inflation (or a loss function), in which case the rule is optimal (a concrete model from the literature where this holds is presented in the appendix). Investigating this issue, of course, requires that the deterministic versions of such models have a stable equilibrium point. Hence, the Taylor rule should achieve the (local) stability of a model over a reasonable range of its policy coefficients. Less demandingly, stability should at least be ensured in models with relatively simple feedback mechanisms determining output and inflation.

There is by now a standard modelling framework in the literature within which the performance of Taylor rules and the problems surrounding them are studied. It outlines 'a distinctive modern form of macroeconomics that is now being used widely in practice' (Taylor, 2000, p. 93). The single models differ in a number of specification details; in particular, they may be forward-looking (the New-Keynesian variants), which means myopic perfect foresight of next quarter's output or/and inflation rate, or they may be purely backward-looking. Nevertheless, all these models share two constituent features: inflation is

---

[16] More formally, eq. (8.4) approximates the changes $i_t - i_{t-h} = h\alpha_i(i^* - i_{t-h})$, for short adjustment periods h. With $\tilde{\alpha}_\Delta = 0$ and referring to a one-year time unit, eq. (8.6) reads $i_t - i_{t-h} = \tilde{\alpha}_i(i^* - i_{t-h})$, $h = 1/4$. Hence, $\alpha_i = \tilde{\alpha}_i/h = 4 \cdot \tilde{\alpha}_i$.

determined by some kind of Phillips curve, and output is determined by some (mostly dynamic) IS relationship. According to this characterization they might handily be called *Keynes–Phillips–Taylor* models, though no one seems to have done this, yet.[17]

To understand the basic stabilization effects in this framework it is easier to translate the concepts into continuous time. To this end, we here put forward four slightly varying models that are so elementary that we can view them as prototype models. In all four versions the Phillips curve will be the same. What varies is (1) the specification of the Taylor rule: it may, or may not, include interest rate smoothing; and (2) the IS relationship, which may be static or dynamic. The models formalize and extend what, at a principles textbook level, Romer (1999, 2000) and Taylor (2001, chaps. 24 & 25) discuss in a more colloquial way and analyse by means of curve shifting in graphical illustrations. Romer uses the acronyms IS-MP-IA to christen the approach, where MP and IA stand for monetary policy and inflation adjustments, respectively.

8.3.1   Model 1: Taylor interest rate and static IS

We begin the presentation of the first prototype model with the Phillips curve, which will also be common to the other three versions. Corresponding to Romer (2000, p. 16) and Taylor (2001, pp. 566ff.), it assumes an accelerationist relationship, which is to say that the rate of inflation is given at any point in time and shifts up (down) when utilization is above (below) normal. The formulation is precisely the one of eq. (5.13) in chapter 5, section 3, subsection 2, where in the calibration of stylized price dynamics its implication of countercyclical prices was emphasized. Hence, with a positive coefficient $\beta_p > 0$,

$$d\hat{p}/dt = \beta_p(u - 1) \qquad (8.9)$$

In a static IS relationship, economic activity and the real rate of interest are inversely related. For simplicity, the nominal interest rate that is relevant here and the short-term interest rate set by the central bank are identified.[18] Solving IS for the rate of utilization u, we get

$$u = f_u(i - \hat{p}), \quad f_u' < 0 \qquad (8.10)$$

---

[17] A representative, estimated model of the backward-looking variety will be examined in section 8.5.

[18] This equally holds true for the vast majority of the more advanced investigations using one of the above-mentioned Keynes–Phillips–Taylor models (except that expectations of next quarter's real interest rate may enter; see the appendix for such a term structure equation and its treatment by assuming rational expectations).

(technically, f_u is supposed to be twice differentiable). Regarding the central bank's policy rule, Model 1 neglects persistence in the interest rate and lets i be directly given by the Taylor rate of interest i^*. For teaching purposes, Romer (2000, p. 13) and Taylor (2001, p. 559) in this respect limit themselves to reactions of the interest rate to inflation, but we may just as well add the influence of capacity utilization. Eq. (8.3) then gives us

$$i = i^*(\hat{p}, u) = (i^o - \hat{p}^*) + \hat{p} + \alpha_p(\hat{p} - \hat{p}^*) + \alpha_u(u - 1) \qquad (8.11)$$

Model 1 is thus specified by the three equations (8.9), (8.10), (8.11). Despite its simplicity it can already teach an important lesson: the existence of a steady-state solution is not obvious; to have it consistent with the inflation target, the central bank must, rather, set the benchmark i^o for the nominal interest rate at a suitable level. In all variants of the Keynes–Phillips–Taylor model family the central bank is assumed to do so, mostly without discussion. In the present model, the suitable level for i^o is easily seen to be characterized by the compatibility of i^o with the IS curve at normal utilization $u = u^o = 1$. Formally, i^o must attain the value that satisfies the equation $f_u(i^o - \hat{p}^*) = u^o = 1$, which by virtue of $f'_u < 0$ is clearly unique.[19]

A second elementary observation is no less important. It is concerned with the first point in an evaluation of the Taylor rule, which is the question whether it is really needed to stabilize the economy. Specifically, we ask whether, for the system's stability, the central bank is to put the Taylor rule to rest and hold the nominal rate of interest constant at $i = i^o$. It is immediately seen that the steady state would then be unstable. In fact, suppose that current inflation has risen above the target rate of inflation. Since this diminishes the real interest rate $i^o - \hat{p}$ below the equilibrium real rate of interest $i^o - \hat{p}^*$, utilization in (8.10) rises above normal and (8.9), in turn, drives inflation further upwards. The positive feedback effect is reflected in the formal argument that, under these circumstances, system (8.9)–(8.11) reduces to the differential equation $d\hat{p}/dt = \beta_p[f_u(i^o - \hat{p})]$, and that its right-hand side has a positive derivative with respect to $\hat{p}$.

We therefore conclude that, in a framework with an accelerationist Phillips curve and a negatively sloped IS curve (an inverse relationship between utilization and the real interest rate), the central bank is

---

[19] Model 1 still has an equilibrium with normal utilization if this condition is violated. However, the nominal interest would differ from i^o and inflation would be different from the target $\hat{p}^*$. Hypothetically, in such an ideal situation, the central bank might then adjust its value for i^o.

required to pursue an active policy regarding the nominal rate of interest; otherwise, the economy would diverge.

We can carry the argument a step further and ask about the effect of the policy rule with zero coefficients α_p and α_u. This amounts to the supposition that the central bank fixes the real rate of interest at its equilibrium value. Here utilization in (8.10) will always be at its normal level, $u = 1$, regardless of current inflation $\hat{p}$, and the right-hand side of (8.9) will always vanish. This means that an exogenous shock to inflation so that $\hat{p} \neq \hat{p}^*$, would be permanent. While this kind of policy would not contribute to a further divergence of inflation, it would not be sufficient to bring it back to the target rate of inflation either. Note also that the argument remains the same if $\alpha_u > 0$. It can thus be stated that a positive responsiveness α_p to inflation in the Taylor rule (8.11) is a necessary condition for the central bank to stabilize utilization as well as inflation.

Taking $\alpha_p > 0$ for granted now, it is readily established that utilization, obtained by substituting the Taylor rule (8.11) in the IS curve (8.10), is negatively related to inflation. That is, there exists a differentiable function $u = u(\hat{p})$ with negative derivative $du/d\hat{p} < 0$. The existence of the function is trivial if $\alpha_u = 0$. The general case $\alpha_u > 0$ introduces a simultaneity, which can be dealt with by, first, defining the function $F = F(\hat{p}, u)$ by $F(\hat{p}, u) := f_u[i^*(\hat{p}, u)] - u$. An IS equilibrium with the Taylor rate of interest inserted is then represented by the pairs $(\hat{p}, u)$ satisfying $F(\hat{p}, u) = 0$. The partial derivatives of F are both negative, $\partial F/\partial \hat{p} = f'_u \alpha_p < 0$, $\partial F/\partial u = f'_u \alpha_u - 1 < 0$. Second, applying the implicit function theorem to the equation $F(\hat{p}, u) = 0$, where $\hat{p}$ is treated as the exogenous variable, u can be conceived as a function of $\hat{p}$ with derivative $du/d\hat{p} = -(\partial F/\partial \hat{p})/(\partial F/\partial u) < 0$.

Based on the function $u = u(\hat{p})$, system (8.9)–(8.11) can be condensed to a scalar differential equation in the rate of inflation:

$$d\hat{p}/dt = \beta_p[u(\hat{p}) - 1] \tag{8.12}$$

Evidently, the derivative of the right-hand side of (8.12) with respect to $\hat{p}$ is negative. Combining this property with the above discussion on $\alpha_p = 0$, we get the following stability proposition, which, for simplicity, refers to local stability only. With a minor additional technical remark added, global stability could also be established.

Proposition 1
A positive responsiveness to inflation, $\alpha_p > 0$, is a necessary and sufficient condition for the equilibrium of Model 1, eqs. (8.9)–(8.11), to be locally asymptotically stable.

The economic mechanism behind the formal stability result is easily explained. If a supply shock raises the inflation rate above the target $\hat{p}^*$, the central bank increases the nominal rate by more than one to one (since $\alpha_p > 0$), so that the real interest rate rises above its equilibrium value. This depresses capacity utilization below its normal level, an effect that is somewhat weakened in the IS relationship if $\alpha_u > 0$.[20] There is thus a downward pressure on prices, or, more precisely, their rate of change. In the present context, the right-hand side of the Phillips curve (8.9) turns negative and the inflation rate starts a gradual downward adjustment. Without a further shock, $\hat{p}$ will fall until it reaches the target rate of inflation, when the economy will be back in equilibrium.

In praising the merits of the, as he calls it, IS-MP-IA approach, Romer (2000, p. 18) summarizes this kind of mechanism as 'Advantage 6. The model's dynamics are straightforward and reasonable.'

8.3.2   Model 2: Taylor interest rate and dynamic IS

In almost all models of the Keynes–Phillips–Taylor approach, the output gap is determined by a reduced-form equation of what is viewed as a dynamic IS relationship. This means that the output equation has an element of persistence built in. Formally, these equations could be rewritten such that they determine the *change* in the output gap. The main factor on the right-hand side is the real interest rate, whereas the lagged values of the output gap, which are also showing up, are of minor conceptual importance. To set up a similar but simple model in continuous time the latter may therefore be neglected, so that the time rate of change of, in our setting, utilization is exclusively governed by the real interest rate. Thus, our second prototype model emerges from the first by replacing the static IS relationship (8.10) with the following dynamic counterpart:

$$\dot{u} = \phi_u(i - \hat{p}), \quad \phi_u' < 0 \qquad (8.13)$$

Maintaining the Phillips curve and the Taylor rate of interest, Model 2 is described by eqs. (8.9), (8.11), (8.13).

What has been said for Model 1 on the existence of a steady-state position carries over correspondingly. An equilibrium requires the central bank to set i^o such that it fulfils the equation $\phi_u(i^o - \hat{p}^*) = 0$. This will, of course, be presumed.

---

[20] Checking this, however, requires something of a formal argument.

To investigate the stability of Model 2, we substitute (8.11) in (8.13) to obtain the following two-dimensional differential equations system in the variables $\hat{p}$ and u:

$$d\hat{p}/dt = \beta_p(u-1)$$
$$\dot{u} = \phi_u[i^*(\hat{p}, u) - \hat{p}]$$

Its Jacobian evaluated at $\hat{p} = \hat{p}^*$ and $u = 1$ is

$$\mathcal{J} = \begin{bmatrix} 0 & \beta_p \\ \phi'_u \alpha_p & \phi'_u \alpha_u \end{bmatrix}$$

with trace $\mathcal{J} = -|\phi'_u|\alpha_u$ and $\det \mathcal{J} = \beta_p |\phi'_u| \alpha_p$. The trace is negative if $\alpha_u > 0$, the determinant is positive if $\alpha_p > 0$. Under these circumstances, the system is unambiguously locally asymptotically stable.

Turning to the special cases of zero policy coefficients, consider first $\alpha_p = 0$. The system then has a continuum $\mathcal{E}$ of equilibria with $u = 1$ and $\hat{p}$ arbitrary. One eigenvalue of $\mathcal{J}$ is zero and the other negative (if $\alpha_u > 0$). What is attracting here is not the single point $(\hat{p}, u) = (\hat{p}^*, 1)$ but the whole equilibrium set $\mathcal{E}$. That is, after a shock has perturbed the economy from $(\hat{p}^*, 1)$, it returns to a point on the set $\mathcal{E}$, but not necessarily to the same point $(\hat{p}^*, 1)$.[21] Accordingly, the equilibrium point $(\hat{p}^*, 1)$ is locally stable, but not asymptotically stable.[22] In economic terms, shocks to the system have permanent effects on the rate of inflation.

The uniqueness of the equilibrium is, on the other hand, not affected if $\alpha_u = 0$ (and $\alpha_p > 0$). In this case the Jacobian has two purely imaginary eigenvalues. If the function $\phi_u(\cdot)$ is linear, so that the whole system is linear, this implies persistent cyclical motions around the equilibrium (closed orbits). Again, the equilibrium would be locally stable, but not asymptotically stable. In the phase plane, the trajectories may spiral inwards or outwards if $\phi_u(\cdot)$ exhibits a suitable nonlinearity. Proposition 2 summarizes these results.

Proposition 2

In Model 2, which is given by eqs. (8.9), (8.11), (8.13), a positive policy coefficient $\alpha_p > 0$ is a necessary condition for the equilibrium point $(\hat{p}, u) = (\hat{p}^*, 1)$ to be locally asymptotically stable. If $\alpha_u > 0$, then $\alpha_p > 0$ is also sufficient for this. If $\alpha_p > 0$ and $\alpha_u = 0$, the equilibrium may be locally asymptotically stable, locally stable or repelling, depending on the kind of nonlinearity in the function $\phi_u(\cdot)$.

---

[21] While this may be intuitively clear, the mathematics are rather unwieldy. A rigorous proof can be found in Franke (1987, pp. 77–92).

[22] A stable equilibrium is mathematically defined by the property that, once perturbed from it, the state variables remain close to it, without necessarily converging to it (in which case stability is also asymptotic).

8.3.3   Model 3: Interest rate smoothing and static IS

Presupposing positive policy coefficients, the analysis of Models 1 and 2 has demonstrated the powerful stabilization potential of the Taylor rule in a narrow sense. In the next two models we introduce persistence in the interest rate, as formulated in eqs. (8.3), (8.4), and ask whether this might affect stability. It was pointed out in subsection 8.2.3 that the estimated persistence (corresponding to $\alpha_i > 0$ but finite in the continuous-time framework) can have several sources. For short, and in order to be less technical, we may exclusively attribute it here to interest rate smoothing, as done in the title above.

Regarding IS, Model 3 assumes the static relationship. All the equations of the model have thus already been put forward: (8.9) for the accelerationist Phillips curve, (8.10) for the IS curve and (8.3), (8.4) for the adjustments of the interest rate. Substituting the functional expression $f_u(i - \hat{p})$ for utilization u, two differential equations in the inflation rate $\hat{p}$ and the interest rate i are obtained:

$$d\hat{p}/dt = \beta_p[f_u(i - \hat{p}) - 1] \tag{8.14}$$

$$di/dt = \alpha_i[i^*(\hat{p}, f_u(i - \hat{p})) - i] \tag{8.15}$$

Exactly as in Model 1, an equilibrium position $(\hat{p}, i) = (\hat{p}^*, i^o)$ consistent with the intentions of the central bank exists if the benchmark for the nominal interest rate i^o is set such that it satisfies the equation $f_u(i^o - \hat{p}^*) = u^o = 1$. Evaluating the Jacobian of (8.14), (8.15) at this point gives

$$\mathcal{J} = \begin{bmatrix} -\beta_p f_u' & \beta_p f_u' \\ \alpha_i(1 + \alpha_p - \alpha_u f_u') & \alpha_i(\alpha_u f_u' - 1) \end{bmatrix}$$

Having discussed the effects of zero policy coefficients, let us now take it directly for granted that α_i and α_p are both positive. Then, the Jacobian has an unambiguously positive determinant, $\det \mathcal{J} = \alpha_p \alpha_i \beta_p |f_u'| > 0$. The trace, in contrast, can become positive, since combining the Phillips curve with IS yields a positive auto-feedback of inflation in the first diagonal entry, which may dominate the negative auto-feedback of the interest rate in the other diagonal entry (recall that $f_u' < 0$). Local stability, therefore, requires sufficiently fast adjustments of the interest rate towards the Taylor rate of interest. Observe that this fits in with Model 1, which would be obtained in the limit by letting α_i approach infinity. Furthermore, because of the non-zero determinant, the transition from instability to stability as α_i increases is associated with a Hopf bifurcation. In sum, we have

Proposition 3
Define $\alpha_i^H := \beta_p |f_u'|/(1 + \alpha_u |f_u'|)$. Then the equilibrium $(\hat{p}^*, i^o)$ of Model 3, which is given by system (8.14), (8.15), is locally asymptotically stable if $\alpha_i > \alpha_i^H$, whereas it is repelling if the inequality is reversed. A Hopf bifurcation occurs at $\alpha_i = \alpha_i^H$.

8.3.4   Model 4: Interest rate smoothing and dynamic IS

Model 4 modifies Model 3 by replacing the static IS relationship (8.10) with the dynamic version (8.13). This adds utilization as another dynamic variable and so leads to a three-dimensional differential equations system in $\hat{p}$, u, and i:

$$d\hat{p}/dt = \beta_p(u - 1) \tag{8.16}$$

$$\dot{u} = \phi_u(i - \hat{p}) \tag{8.17}$$

$$di/dt = \alpha_i[i^*(\hat{p}, u) - i] \tag{8.18}$$

Concerning the equilibrium, it is again, as for Model 2, assumed that the equation $\phi_u(i^o - \hat{p}) = 0$ holds true. The Jacobian of (8.16)–(8.18) at this point reads

$$\mathcal{J} = \begin{bmatrix} 0 & \beta_p & 0 \\ -\phi_u' & 0 & \phi_u' \\ \alpha_i(1 + \alpha_p) & \alpha_i \alpha_u & -\alpha_i \end{bmatrix}$$

Though $\mathcal{J}$ is a 3×3 matrix, the Routh–Hurwitz terms for the local stability analysis are easily obtained as follows:

$$a_1 = -\text{trace } \mathcal{J} = \alpha_i$$

$$a_2 = \mathcal{J}_1 + \mathcal{J}_2 + \mathcal{J}_3 = |\phi_u'|(\alpha_i \alpha_u - \beta_p)$$

$$a_3 = -\det \mathcal{J} = |\phi_u'|\alpha_i \alpha_p \beta_p$$

$$b = a_1 a_2 - a_3 = |\phi_u'|\alpha_i[\alpha_i \alpha_u - (1 + \alpha_p)\beta_p]$$

($\mathcal{J}_k$, $k = 1, 2, 3$, are the principal minors, i.e. the determinants of the 2×2 submatrices of $\mathcal{J}$ that arise from deleting the k-th column and row).

All eigenvalues of $\mathcal{J}$ have negative real parts if, and only if, the four terms are positive. For a_1 and a_3 this is always the case, whereas a_2 and b

can be negative. Decisive for the latter is the term b, since $b > 0$ implies that $a_2 > 0$. Thus we end up with one single stability condition. It is made explicit in Proposition 4, together with the Hopf bifurcation result that immediately follows from $\det \mathcal{J} \neq 0$.

Proposition 4
Define $\alpha_i^H := (1 + \alpha_p)\beta_p/\alpha_u$. *Then the equilibrium* $(\hat{p}, u, i) = (\hat{p}^*, 1, i^o)$ *of Model 4, system (8.16)–(8.18), is locally asymptotically stable if* $\alpha_i > \alpha_i^H$, *and unstable if* $\alpha_i < \alpha_i^H$. *The value* $\alpha_i = \alpha_i^H$ *gives rise to a Hopf bifurcation.*

It is remarkable that stability is not affected by the speed ϕ'_u with which, in the dynamic IS equation, utilization reacts to the real interest rate. Model 4 shares with Model 3 the property that it is stable if (and only if) the adjustment speed α_i of the interest rate is sufficiently large. In other words, stability requires that the degree of interest rate smoothing is not too strong. A difference from Model 3 is that stability now also depends on the other two policy coefficients α_u and α_p in the Taylor rate of interest. Given α_i, the central bank must be sufficiently responsive to utilization (α_u must not be too small). While this result seems normal, the influence of the coefficient α_p is perhaps surprising. One might expect at first sight that strong reactions of the central bank to the deviations of the inflation rate from its target will accelerate the return of the economy back to this equilibrium rate. As a matter of fact, however, just the opposite is true: too strong a responsiveness α_p to inflation is destabilizing.

Although the possibility of instability is theoretically interesting since it warns against overestimating the stabilization potential of the Taylor rule, we should also ask whether it would be numerically reasonable. The question can be immediately answered, as values for the policy coefficients have been obtained in eq. (8.8) and a numerical value for the Phillips curve coefficient β_p has already been derived in the calibration of the wage-price dynamics in chapter 5, section 5, eq. (5.30), which was $\beta_p = 0.45$. On this basis, the critical value for α_i is computed as $\alpha_i^H = (1 + \alpha_p)\beta_p/\alpha_u = (1 + 0.40) \cdot 0.45/1.20 = 0.525$. As this is clearly less than $\alpha_i = 1.10$ in (8.8), the equilibrium of Model 4 can safely be regarded as stable.

The great scope for stability can also be underlined by calculating the critical value of α_p above which instability would prevail. Solving the instability inequality $\alpha_i < \alpha_i^H$ for α_p leads to the condition $\alpha_p > \alpha_i \alpha_u/\beta_p - 1 = 2.93 - 1 = 1.93$, which yields a value far above the empirical coefficient $\alpha_p = 0.40$.

8.4   An estimated Keynes–Phillips–Taylor model from the literature

The model discussed in this section is a next natural step in studying the effects of an interest rate policy. On the one hand, it can be viewed as a discrete-time counterpart of the last prototype model, Model 4, with only minor conceptual extensions. On the other hand, it is a standard model that, in this or similar versions, is widely used or referred to in the literature. Since besides the Taylor rule (in the broad sense) its dynamic IS equation and the accelerated Phillips curve have also been estimated, the stability properties and the dynamics of this model provide a useful benchmark against which the behaviour of our own model with the Taylor rule can be evaluated later.

8.4.1   Formulation and estimation of the Rudebusch–Svensson model

This model has been advanced by Rudebusch and Svensson (1999). They employ different versions of a Taylor rule on the basis of two empirical equations determining quarterly output and inflation. The choice of the latter was motivated by three considerations (see pp. 205–11). (1) The equations are linear, so that the analysis is tractable and the results are transparent. (2) The equations capture the spirit of many practical policy-oriented macroeconometric models. (3) Applying several criteria, the fit to the data and the implications of the estimates are reasonable. It may be interesting to note that Judd and Rudebusch (1998), who were so important for us in subsection 8.2.3, themselves made use of this model (in its stochastic form). After presenting their estimates of the interest rate reaction functions over the subperiods of three different chairmanships of the Federal Reserve, out of which we adopted the results for the Greenspan period in eqs. (8.3), (8.6) and (8.7), they inserted the different policy functions in the model and measured their performance by the standard deviations of the output gap and the inflation rate that the policy rules generated in the long run. This is the kind of exercise that Rudebusch and Svensson (1999), and many others, have also conducted in order to examine a much wider range of a priori possible policy functions.

In the following, the estimated output and inflation equations of Rudebusch and Svensson are combined with the above estimate of the Taylor rule by Judd and Rudebusch (1998) for the Greenspan period. Let us call this (stochastic) model the Rudebusch–Svensson model, or the RS model for short. To situate it in the literature, it should be pointed out that it is a so-called backward-looking model. This means that in the structural equations the state variables in period t are determined by the values ruling in the preceding period(s). In contrast, in the forward-looking models of a more or less New-Keynesian tenor, the state variables are additionally determined by their expected values for the next quarter (or perhaps the next four quarters), where the expectations are assumed to be rational (and are then called, sloppily, 'forward-looking expectations').

Rudebusch and Svensson (1999, p. 206) contend that the neglect of this type of expectations can be justified. One argument concerns the estimation of the Phillips curve and states that the New-Keynesian estimates are at least not superior. A standard reference in this respect is that by Fuhrer (1997). He tests an autoregressive Phillips curve like the one used by RS against a forward-looking version and finds that it cannot be rejected.[23] Another argument is that backward-looking models are taken more seriously by policymakers than models that rely on forward-looking expectations. This, as RS point out, includes Federal Reserve governor L.H. Meyer (1997) and former vice-chairman A.S. Blinder (1998). In a subsequent comment on these opinions, Mishkin (1999, p. 251) supports this point of view.

In the present context, however, the differences between backward-looking and forward-looking models are not overly dramatic. Mostly in the forward-looking models, possibly if some of the variables are purposefully dated, a closed-form solution can be derived analytically that looks exactly like a purely backward-looking model. What differs is the meaning of the coefficients attached to the lagged variables; they no longer directly measure a responsiveness but are a combination of several other coefficients of the structural form. Of course, this may also affect the dynamic properties of the model. An example of such a New-Keynesian model and its reduced form is given in the appendix. Incidentally, this model introduces a term structure equation, according to which the real interest rate entering the dynamic IS equation is a weighted average of the current and expected federal funds rate, minus the average of the current and expected rate of inflation (i.e. expected for the next quarter).

It is, furthermore, worth mentioning that the structure of the RS model is typical of many central bank policy models (Rudebusch and

---

[23] An investigation by Rudd and Whelan (2001) buttresses this result at a more elaborate level. Using instrumental variables techniques to estimate 'hybrid' specifications for inflation that allow for the effects of both lagged and future inflation, the study shows that these tests of forward-looking behaviour have very low power against backward-looking specifications. It furthermore demonstrates that results previously interpreted as evidence for the New-Keynesian model are also consistent with a backward-looking Phillips curve. Alternative and more powerful tests that the authors develop also yield a very limited scope for forward-looking expectations.

Svensson, 1999, p. 206). In particular, it is within the same spirit as the eleven models described in the central bank model comparison project for the Bank for International Settlements (1995).

After thus establishing the relevance of the RS model, we can now present the model equations themselves. The adjustment period is a quarter. Since we wish to maintain one year as our time unit, we put $h = 1/4$ and consider the periods $t = 0, h, 2h, 3h, \ldots$. All three state variables are measured in percentage points. Besides the federal funds rate, i_t, these are the output gap, $\tilde{y}_t$, and the quarterly rate of inflation, $\hat{p}_t$, expressed as an annual rate, $\hat{p}_t = (100/h)(p_t - p_{t-h})/p_{t-h}$. Continuing with the notation already used in eqs. (8.5) and (8.6), we write the equations of the RS model as follows:

$$\hat{p}_{t+h} = \sum_{k=0}^{3} \beta_{pk}\hat{p}_{t-kh} + \beta_{py}\tilde{y}_t + \varepsilon_{p,t} \quad (h = 1/4, \sum_{k=0}^{3}\beta_{pk} = 1) \quad (8.19)$$

$$\tilde{y}_{t+h} = \beta_{y0}\tilde{y}_t + \beta_{y1}\tilde{y}_{t-h} - \beta_{yi}\left[\frac{1}{4}\sum_{k=0}^{3}(i_{t-kh} - \hat{p}_{t-kh}) - (i^o - \hat{p}^\star)\right] + \varepsilon_{y,t} \quad (8.20)$$

$$i_{t+h} = i_t + \tilde{\alpha}_i(i^\star_{t+h} - i_t) \quad (8.21)$$

$$i^\star_t = (i^o - \hat{p}^\star) + \frac{1}{4}\sum_{k=0}^{3}\hat{p}_{t-kh} + \tilde{\alpha}_p\left(\frac{1}{4}\sum_{k=0}^{3}\hat{p}_{t-kh} - \hat{p}^\star\right) + \tilde{\alpha}_y\tilde{y}_t \quad (8.22)$$

Eqs. (8.21) and (8.22) for the interest rate adjustments and the Taylor rate of interest, respectively, reiterate eqs. (8.6) and (8.5), where the four-quarter inflation rate $\hat{p}_t^{(4)}$ in (8.5) is given by the average of the last four quarter-to-quarter rates of inflation (Rudebusch and Svensson, 1999, p. 207). As discussed above, $\tilde{\alpha}_\Delta$ in (8.6) is set at zero.

The lags of inflation in the Phillips curve (8.19) are said to be an autoregressive or adaptive representation of inflation expectations. Since the β_{pk} are supposed to sum up to unity (which is not rejected by an OLS regression), it nevertheless has an accelerationist form. (8.20) is the dynamic IS equation that in its core relates the output gap to the difference between the average funds rate and average inflation over the contemporaneous and prior three quarters, which is to approximate an *ex post* real rate. The term in square brackets is considered to be a simple representation of the monetary transmission mechanism, 'which, in the view of many central banks, likely involves nominal interest rates (e.g. mortgage rates), ex ante real short and long rates, exchange rates, and possibly direct credit quantities as well. Equation (2) [i.e. eq. (8.20) in our numbering] appears to be a workable approximation of these various intermediate transmission mechanisms' (Rudebusch and Svensson, 1999, p. 207).

In addition, the lagged output terms introduce some persistence in the output adjustments. A theoretical justification for their presence might be found in the habit persistence model developed by Fuhrer (2000).[24]

The full formulation of the RS model includes the two terms $\varepsilon_{p,t}$ and $\varepsilon_{y,t}$ in (8.19) and (8.20). They are random perturbations that are supposed to be identically and normally distributed around zero (the non-existence of autocorrelation is supported by a Durbin–Watson coefficient close to two in the regressions). The terms are usually referred to as supply and demand shocks, respectively.

Rudebusch and Svensson estimate the Phillips curve and the IS equation over the period 1961:Q1 to 1996:Q2. They stress (p. 208) that the estimated equations easily pass a number of econometric tests for subsample stability. We refer here to the parameter values reported in Judd and Rudebusch (1998, p. 11), which are based on a slightly longer sample period and differ only marginally. Together with the numerical policy coefficients from eq. (8.7) above, we have:

Estimated parameters of the Rudebusch–Svensson model:

$$\beta_{p0} = 0.68 \quad \beta_{p1} = -0.09 \quad \beta_{p2} = 0.29 \quad \beta_{p3} = 0.12$$

$$\beta_{y0} = 1.17 \quad \beta_{y1} = -0.27 \quad \beta_{yi} = 0.09 \quad \beta_{py} = 0.15 \qquad (8.23)$$

$$\tilde{\alpha}_i = 0.28 \quad \tilde{\alpha}_p = 0.37 \quad \tilde{\alpha}_y = 0.82$$

8.4.2   Stability analysis

System (8.19)–(8.22), which is a linear stochastic process, is meaningful only if its deterministic part is asymptotically stable. Since the Phillips curve, the IS equation and the interest rate rule have been estimated independently of each other, it is not obvious that the numerical coefficients in (8.23) ensure this. Though stability may be expected, it has to checked by a rigorous analysis.

To this end the system is transformed into its ten-dimensional state space representation. The high dimension arises from the fact that, besides $\hat{p}_t$, $\tilde{y}_t$ and i_t in period t, the equations include three lags of inflation and the interest rate and one lag of the output gap. All these magnitudes are now collected in a state vector $x_t \in \mathbb{R}^{10}$. Defining another,

---

[24] A simpler version of (8.19) and (8.20) assumes $\beta_{y1} = 0$ and substitutes the quarterly magnitudes for the four-quarter averages of inflation and the interest rate. It exhibits less persistence but is easier to treat analytically – for example, to compute an optimal interest rate policy. Often cited references here are those by Ball (1997) and Svensson (1997).

fixed vector $b \in \mathbb{R}^{10}$ and a square matrix A of the same format, we wish to write the deterministic part of (8.19)–(8.22) equivalently as

$$x_{t+h} = Ax_t + b \qquad (8.24)$$

Straightforward though somewhat tedious calculations show that this is achieved by setting x_t, b, A as follows:

$$x_t = \begin{bmatrix} \hat{p}_t \\ \hat{p}_{t-h} \\ \hat{p}_{t-2h} \\ \hat{p}_{t-3h} \\ \tilde{y}_t \\ \tilde{y}_{t-h} \\ i_t \\ i_{t-h} \\ i_{t-2h} \\ i_{t-3h} \end{bmatrix} \qquad b = \begin{bmatrix} 0 \\ 0 \\ 0 \\ 0 \\ \beta_{yi}(i^o - \hat{p}^*) \\ 0 \\ b_7 \\ 0 \\ 0 \\ 0 \end{bmatrix} \qquad (8.25)$$

$$b_7 = \tilde{\alpha}_i[(1 + \tilde{\alpha}_y \beta_{yi})(i^o - \hat{p}^*) - \tilde{\alpha}_p \hat{p}^*]$$

$$A = \begin{bmatrix} \beta_{p0} & \beta_{p1} & \beta_{p2} & \beta_{p3} & \beta_{py} & 0 & 0 & 0 & 0 & 0 \\ 1 & 0 & 0 & 0 & 0 & 0 & 0 & 0 & 0 & 0 \\ 0 & 1 & 0 & 0 & 0 & 0 & 0 & 0 & 0 & 0 \\ 0 & 0 & 1 & 0 & 0 & 0 & 0 & 0 & 0 & 0 \\ \bar{\beta}_{yi} & \bar{\beta}_{yi} & \bar{\beta}_{yi} & \bar{\beta}_{yi} & \beta_{y0} & \beta_{y1} & -\bar{\beta}_{yi} & -\bar{\beta}_{yi} & -\bar{\beta}_{yi} & -\bar{\beta}_{yi} \\ 0 & 0 & 0 & 0 & 1 & 0 & 0 & 0 & 0 & 0 \\ a_{71} & a_{72} & a_{73} & a_{74} & a_{75} & a_{76} & a_{77} & a_{78} & a_{79} & a_{7,10} \\ 0 & 0 & 0 & 0 & 0 & 0 & 1 & 0 & 0 & 0 \\ 0 & 0 & 0 & 0 & 0 & 0 & 0 & 1 & 0 & 0 \\ 0 & 0 & 0 & 0 & 0 & 0 & 0 & 0 & 1 & 0 \end{bmatrix} \qquad (8.26)$$

$$\bar{\beta}_{yi} = \beta_{yi}/4$$

$$a_{7k} = \tilde{\alpha}_i[(1 + \tilde{\alpha}_p)(\beta_{p,k-1} + 1) + \tilde{\alpha}_y \beta_{yi}]/4, \qquad k = 1, 2, 3$$

$$a_{74} = \tilde{\alpha}_i[(1 + \tilde{\alpha}_p)\beta_{p3} + \tilde{\alpha}_y \beta_{yi}]/4$$

$$a_{75} = \tilde{\alpha}_i[(1 + \tilde{\alpha}_p)\beta_{py}/4 + \tilde{\alpha}_y \beta_{y0}]$$

$$a_{76} = \tilde{\alpha}_i \tilde{\alpha}_y \beta_{y1}$$

$$a_{77} = 1 - \tilde{\alpha}_i(1 + \tilde{\alpha}_y \beta_{yi}/4)$$

$$a_{7k} = -\tilde{\alpha}_i \tilde{\alpha}_y \beta_{yi}/4, \qquad k = 8, 9, 10$$

It is clear that $\hat{p} = \hat{p}^*$, $\tilde{y} = 0$, $i = i^o$ constitute an equilibrium point of (8.19)–(8.22). Of course, $x = x^o$ correspondingly defined is an equilibrium of (8.24). Note, furthermore, that the equilibrium is not unique if $\tilde{\alpha}_p = 0$. From (8.20) one immediately derives that, together with $\tilde{y} = 0$, all pairs $(i, \hat{p})$ satisfying $i - \hat{p} = i^o - \hat{p}^*$ would then form a whole continuum of equilibria. As a consequence, the matrix A cannot be asymptotically stable but has a unit root.[25] This phenomenon is completely analogous to the multiple equilibria in the second and fourth prototype model of section 8.3, where in continuous time the Jacobian $\mathcal{J}$ has a zero eigenvalue.

Regarding the conditions for the (asymptotic) stability of the matrix A when $\tilde{\alpha}_p$ is strictly positive, we resort to a numerical analysis. The initial question was whether the estimated parameters summarized in (8.23) entail stability. It can now be answered in the affirmative. Asymptotic stability requires all ten eigenvalues of A to be less than one in modulus. The eigenvalue λ^* with largest modulus, which may be called the dominant eigenvalue, is computed as

$$\lambda^* = 0.9770 \qquad (8.27)$$

Since λ^* is a real eigenvalue, we also know that, as far as the deterministic basis is concerned, system (8.19)–(8.22) has no great scope for cyclical dynamics; in the absence of stochastic shocks, convergence towards the equilibrium will eventually be monotonic. Nevertheless, it is well known that even in a deterministically monotonic system random forces are generally capable of generating cyclical elements. Whether this is a relevant perspective in the present case will be seen in the next subsection.

The fact that λ^* in (8.27) is so close to unity implies that the equilibrium is approached rather slowly. In a quick argument, $(\lambda^*)^t$ may be directly adopted as a rough indicator of a trajectory's distance from the equilibrium point at time t, when the initial perturbation at $t = 0$ is normalized at one. Then, the equation

$$(\lambda^*)^T = 0.10$$

says that at time T the system has reduced the distance to 10 per cent of its original size (time is here measured in quarters). Taking logarithms on both sides of the equation and solving for T yields

$$T = \ln 0.10 / \ln \lambda^* = 99.04 \text{ quarters} \qquad (8.28)$$

---

[25] Let $x^o = Ax^o + b$ and $x^1 = Ax^1 + b$ be two distinct equilibria. Subtracting the two equations yields $A(x^1 - x^o) = x^1 - x^o$; that is, $x^1 - x^o$ is a (non-zero) eigenvector associated with the eigenvalue $\lambda = 1$.

It therefore takes the system almost twenty-five years to bridge 90 per cent of an initial gap to the equilibrium position. We should repeat, however, that the argument is a strong oversimplification, just to get a first impression of the speed of convergence. In particular, the dynamic simulations in the next subsection will show that some variables approach their equilibrium values much more rapidly than indicated by the convergence time in (8.28).

Returning to the stability issue, we take the numerical coefficients in (8.23) as our reference scenario and ask what parameter variations, and to what extent, would eventually destabilize the model. In the light of Model 4 as the simple continuous-time counterpart of the RS model and the corresponding stability condition in Proposition 4, we are in the first instance interested in the effects of the policy coefficients $\tilde{\alpha}_i$, $\tilde{\alpha}_p$, $\tilde{\alpha}_y$.

Let us begin with the consequences of interest rate smoothing, which in the said proposition was found to be destabilizing. We recall that increasing values of $\tilde{\alpha}_i$ represent a weaker degree of interest rate smoothing, where in the limiting case $\tilde{\alpha}_i = 1$ the interest rate is always set at the level of the Taylor rate of interest without delay, $i_t = i_t^*$ for all t. If we take Proposition 4 as a prediction for the RS model and adapt the stability statement to the present discrete-time framework, then there should be a critical value of the adjustment speed $\tilde{\alpha}_i^c$ such that the equilibrium is unstable if $0 \leq \tilde{\alpha}_i < \tilde{\alpha}_i^c$, and (asymptotically) stable if $\tilde{\alpha}_i^c < \tilde{\alpha}_i \leq 1$. To check this, figure 8.1[26] plots the modulus of the dominant eigenvalue λ^* of matrix A as a function of $\tilde{\alpha}_i$. At least with respect to the given numerical values of the other coefficients, we see that the prediction is fully confirmed.

In addition, over the rest of the interval, until $\tilde{\alpha}_i = 1.00$, the function remains flat, as in the diagram. The system's asymptotic behaviour under the empirical interest rate adjustment speed $\tilde{\alpha}_i = 0.28$ is therefore not very different from what it would be under a Taylor rule in a narrow sense, when $\tilde{\alpha}_i = 1.00$. Concretely, we compute $\lambda^* = 0.9814$ for $\tilde{\alpha}_i = 1.00$, while at $\tilde{\alpha}_i = 0.28$ we had $\lambda^* = 0.9770$ in (8.27).

The bold (solid) line in figure 8.1 indicates that the dominant eigenvalue is complex (real). Hence, as $\tilde{\alpha}_i$ rises from zero and the system changes from instability to stability at $\tilde{\alpha}_i = \tilde{\alpha}_i^c$, a Hopf bifurcation occurs, which is a second result that tallies with Proposition 4.[27] The proposition

---

[26] The bold line indicates that λ^* is complex, the solid line that it is real. The Hopf bifurcation occurs at $\tilde{\alpha}_i = 0.04870$.

[27] The discrete-time case, when a pair of (non-degenerate) conjugate complex eigenvalues crosses the unit circle, is completely analogous to the continuous-time case, when it crosses the imaginary axis. In line with the previous notation, the critical value could also be designated $\tilde{\alpha}_i^H$; but we did not know in advance that it would give rise to a Hopf bifurcation.

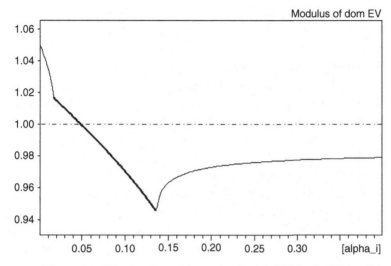

Figure 8.1: The dominant eigenvalue $\lambda^* = \lambda^*(\tilde{\alpha}_i)$ in the RS model

also says that the critical value $\tilde{\alpha}_i^c$ increases as the central bank responds more aggressively to inflation or its responsiveness to output weakens. This feature, too, carries over. In fact, the whole function $\lambda^* = \lambda^*(\tilde{\alpha}_i)$ shifts upwards as $\tilde{\alpha}_p$ rises and downwards as $\tilde{\alpha}_y$ rises. The shift in the relevant range is, however, rather limited, so that, given the steep slope of the function at its points of intersection with the line $\lambda = 1$, the same holds true for the bifurcation value $\tilde{\alpha}_i^c$.

In the reference scenario in figure 8.1 the exact numerical value of $\tilde{\alpha}_i^c$ results as $\tilde{\alpha}_i^c = 0.04870$, which is much lower than the empirical adjustment speed $\tilde{\alpha}_i = 0.28$. Together with the other observations it can therefore be concluded that the stability of the estimated RS model is preserved under a (very) wide range of parameter variations.[28]

For another comparison with Model 4, and also with a view to the Keynes–Metzler–Goodwin–Taylor model later on, we wish to have a more direct look at the stability effects of the other two policy coefficients, $\tilde{\alpha}_p$ and $\tilde{\alpha}_y$, when the speed of adjustment for the interest rate is fixed. Solving the stability condition $\alpha_i > \alpha_i^H$ of Proposition 4 for α_u yields the stability frontier $\alpha_u = (\beta_p + \beta_p \alpha_p)/\alpha_i$ in the (α_p, α_u) parameter plane, and the equilibrium of Model 4 is stable if α_u lies above this linear function. Note that the function has a positive intercept $\beta_p/\alpha_i > 0$.

---

[28] This claim was checked more carefully by subjecting the other reaction coefficients to greater changes as well.

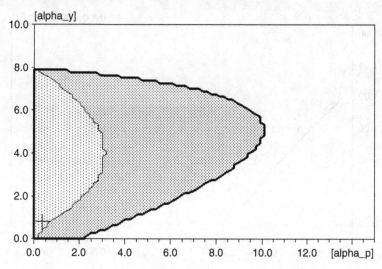

Figure 8.2: $(\tilde{\alpha}_p, \tilde{\alpha}_y)$ parameter diagram of the RS model

Thus, as has been remarked, large values of α_p and low values of α_u are destabilizing.

For the RS model, the stability region in the $(\tilde{\alpha}_p, \tilde{\alpha}_y)$ plane is given by the dotted area in figure 8.2.[29] Again, stability is seen to require that $\tilde{\alpha}_p$ must not be too large.[30] In contrast, the role of the output responsiveness $\tilde{\alpha}_y$ is more differentiated. On the one hand, large values of this responsiveness now also turn out to be destabilizing. On the other hand, as long as $\tilde{\alpha}_p$ remains moderately bounded, ignoring output in the policy rule ($\tilde{\alpha}_y = 0$) would no longer destroy stability.

Pairs $(\tilde{\alpha}_p, \tilde{\alpha}_y)$ in the subregion with the wider dots, which, as indicated by the cross, also contains the estimated values $(\tilde{\alpha}_p, \tilde{\alpha}_y) = (0.37, 0.82)$, give rise to monotonic dynamics (in the deterministic model), since the corresponding dominant eigenvalue is a real number then. Conversely, coefficients outside this area generate cyclical dynamics. This, in particular, holds true on the stability frontier. Any loss of stability occurring through variations of the responsiveness $\tilde{\alpha}_p$ or $\tilde{\alpha}_y$ is, therefore, associated with a Hopf bifurcation. This scope for persistent cyclical behaviour is nevertheless rather deceptive, because it would call for unrealistically large policy coefficients.

---

[29] The dotted area is the stability region. Wide dots (lighter shade) indicate that the dominant eigenvalue is real, while it is complex otherwise. The cross represents the estimated values of $\tilde{\alpha}_p$ and $\tilde{\alpha}_y$ in (8.23).

[30] It may be added that, unlike in Proposition 4, negative values of $\tilde{\alpha}_p$ would also render the equilibrium unstable.

Furthermore, even though the estimated coefficients are not too far from the subregion with complex eigenvalues, (dampened) cyclical motions with a reasonable period T require a much stronger change in the coefficients than just crossing this borderline. To illustrate this point, hold the output coefficient constant at $\tilde{\alpha}_y = 0.82$. Then values of $\tilde{\alpha}_p \geq 0.78$ induce a complex dominant eigenvalue, but over a wider interval the corresponding cycle period T is considerably longer than the time of a typical business cycle. For example, we compute $T = 160$ years for $\tilde{\alpha}_p = 0.78$, $T = 22.5$ years for $\tilde{\alpha}_p = 1.00$, and still $T = 12.6$ years for $\tilde{\alpha}_p = 2.00$.

The eigenvalue analysis can thus be summarized in two short conclusions. First, the stability of the model is endangered only by obviously extreme parameter values. And second, while the Rudebusch–Svensson model has a certain tendency for complex eigenvalues, meaningful (deterministic) cyclical behaviour presupposes numerical coefficients that are also quite different from the estimated values.

8.4.3   Dynamic properties

Computation of the dominant eigenvalue in (8.27) has already revealed that convergence in the estimated RS model towards the equilibrium may be fairly slow. The rough-and-ready measure of the convergence time T in eq. (8.28) has quantified a period of almost twenty-five years to undo 90 per cent of an initial perturbation from the equilibrium. As a warning against a premature overinterpretation it has also been remarked, however, that the three variables $\hat{p}_t$, $\tilde{y}_t$, i_t need not converge uniformly. It is now time to reconsider these dynamic properties.

An appropriate tool for studying adjustment processes in finer detail is the impulse–response function. Let us here employ the impulse–response function resulting from an adverse demand shock. Accordingly, the deterministic part of system (8.19)–(8.22) is started in the equilibrium point $(\hat{p}, \tilde{y}, i) = (\hat{p}_t^*, 0, i^o)$, a weak negative shock $\varepsilon_{y,t} = -0.20\%$ is introduced at time $t = 0$, and the system is left to itself without any further noise afterwards. The time paths of the three variables over the next twenty years are plotted in figure 8.3[31] (the solid lines). For concreteness, we follow Rudebusch and Svensson (1999, p. 238) and set the target rate of inflation at $\hat{p}^* = 2\%$ and the nominal equilibrium rate of interest at $i^o = 4.50\%$ (which, of course, is only a matter of scale).

---

[31] The Solid line is generated by the estimated parameters (8.23), the dotted line by the corresponding Taylor rule in a narrow sense, with $\tilde{\alpha}_i = 1$. All variables are measured in percentage points; $\hat{p}$ and i are annualized.

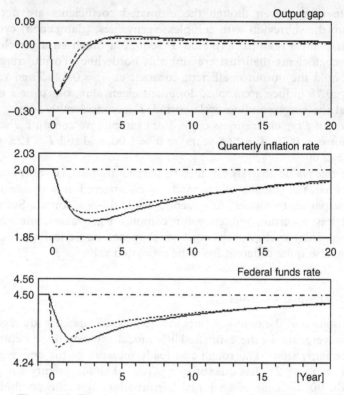

Figure 8.3: The impulse–response function of the RS model (adverse demand shock)

The central bank begins to combat the sudden drop in output in the same quarter $t = 0$. The immediate cure of lowering the interest rate is, however, not the full dose of the Taylor rate of interest in (8.22), which would be $i^* = 4.336\%$ (see the dotted line in the bottom panel of figure 8.3). According to the smoothing principle in (8.21) the central bank reduces i by only $\tilde{\alpha}_i = 28\%$ of the total difference from 4.50 per cent. This gives $0.28 \cdot (4.500 - 4.336) = 0.046\%$, and so $i_t = 4.454\%$ in $t = 0$ results.

Owing to the one-quarter lag in the impact of the output gap in (8.19), inflation does not change in $t = 0$, so the real interest falls too. Output is positively affected by this in the next quarter, in $t = 0.25$. However, since the real interest rate effect is attenuated by the averaging procedure over the preceding quarters in (8.20), the persistence from the two lagged output terms in this equation is still dominant (note that $\beta_{y0} = 1.17 > 1$

in (8.20)). Hence the output gap declines further, though much less vigorously now ($\tilde{y}_t = -0.233\%$ at $t = 0.25$).

Economic activity starts to recover one quarter later, from $t = 0.50$ on. Since not only the nominal but also the real rate of interest remains below its equilibrium value for a longer time, output then steadily increases. It nevertheless takes up to three years before it reaches its potential level: $\tilde{y}_t = 0.004\%$ at $t = 3.00$. The top panel shows a minor overshooting of the output gap at that time and, successively, a monotonic return to zero. For practical reasons it can thus be said that output has a convergence time of three years.

It appears that convergence is much slower for the other two variables in figure 8.3. The rate of inflation falls in the wake of the demand shock, which is caused by the negative output gap in the Phillips curve. Due to the strong persistence in form of the lagged inflation rates in (8.19), inflation continues to fall long after the output gap has begun to rise again. On the whole it takes $t = 2.75$ years until $\hat{p}_t$ has reached the trough. Even worse, however, the ensuing quarterly increments in inflation happen to be minute. Responsible for this is the output gap, which in the meantime is close to zero, and the moderate responsiveness $\beta_{py} = 0.15$ in the Phillips curve. What we therefore observe is that, unlike the output variable, the rate of inflation approaches its target at a very low speed.

If the inflation gap $|\hat{p} - \hat{p}^*| = |1.976 - 2.000| = 0.024\%$ at $t = 20$ is compared with the maximum gap $|1.888 - 2.000| = 0.112\%$ at $t = 2.75$, then the gap remaining in our closing quarter is still more than 20 per cent. By virtue of the system's linearity, this ratio remains the same if the initial shock is larger and so the induced gaps are also larger. Hence, these figures underline the significance of the auxiliary measure of the convergence time in (8.28).

Convergence of the interest rate takes just as long as inflation. The parallel development is easily explained, first, by the fact that after three years the Taylor rate of interest i^* is mainly determined by the inflation gap and, second, by the additional delay of the partial adjustments of i towards i^*.[32]

We can thus conclude that in the estimated Rudebusch–Svensson model the policy of the central bank succeeds in bringing actual output

---

[32] At the end of subsection 8.2.3 on the estimation of the Taylor rule, where we reported Judd and Rudebusch's (1998) original estimate of the 'momentum' effect $\tilde{\alpha}_\Delta = 0.52$ in (8.6) and then decided to ignore it, we mentioned that the impulse–response functions for $\tilde{\alpha}_\Delta = 0.52$ and $\tilde{\alpha}_\Delta = 0.00$ do not differ very much. Here we can be more precise. Eventually, the functions for all three variables are almost identical, at least for $t \geq 10$. The initial reduction of the interest rate under $\tilde{\alpha}_\Delta = 0.52$ is somewhat stronger in the first two years, while its readjustments towards the equilibrium value is a bit faster over $2 \leq t \leq 7$. On the other hand, the consequences on the output gap and inflation, vis-à-vis the time paths of figure 8.3, are so trifling as to be unworthy of closer attention.

back to its potential level about three years after a demand shock. In contrast, the interest rate rule is much less effective in undoing the induced changes in inflation. The return of the rate of inflation to its target would actually take more than two decades. This means that, in practice, these adjustments will in the meantime be dominated by completely different events; in particular, by the many supply shocks $\varepsilon_{p,t}$ occurring over such a long period.

Above, we have reported the Taylor rate of interest $i_t^* = 4.336\%$ that is immediately brought about by the demand shock in $t = 0$, a value that is considerably lower than the initial reaction of the actual interest rate and still lower than i_t over the entire convergence process. The observation might suggest that convergence could be improved by getting rid of the interest rate smoothing. To check the conjecture, we conduct the same experiment of the impulse shock with a Taylor rule in a narrow sense. Accordingly, all parameter values of (8.23) are maintained, except for the adjustment speed of the interest rate in (8.21), which is set at $\tilde{\alpha}_i = 1.00$. The resulting time paths are shown as the dotted lines in figure 8.3. The obvious short summary is that the hope of thus speeding up convergence is largely disappointed. Despite noticeable deviations of the interest rate from that in the reference scenario (the solid line in the bottom panel), the output gap reaches the zero level just one quarter earlier, and the fall of the rate of inflation in the first two years is somewhat smoothed. Twelve years after the shock, however, the trajectories of the two cases are no longer distinguishable.

In search for an improvement to, in particular, the adjustments of the rate of inflation, another idea is that, after its trough, inflation may increase more rapidly if the overshooting of the output gap is more sustained. This, in turn, would be possible if lower values of the interest rate prevailed over a longer time. It may therefore be asked whether a higher responsiveness in the Taylor rule to output or inflation could directly accelerate convergence. The answer is a qualified 'yes', if the inflation coefficient $\tilde{\alpha}_p$ is increased, and if it is increased to a sufficient extent. The mechanism is exemplified in figure 8.4[33] (by the solid lines), where $\tilde{\alpha}_p$ is almost tripled from 0.37 to $\tilde{\alpha}_p = 1.00$. For comparison, the dotted lines reproduce the adjustments shown in figure 8.3. Although the positive output gap between $t = 2$ and $t = 8$ is not much higher than in the reference scenario, this small difference is already sufficient to let inflation return to its target after ten years. Note, however, that the numerical value of the policy coefficient that can achieve this is certainly outside the confidence interval of the parameter estimation.

---

[33] The dotted lines are the time paths in the reference scenario, where $\tilde{\alpha}_p = 0.37$ (the solid lines in figure 8.3).

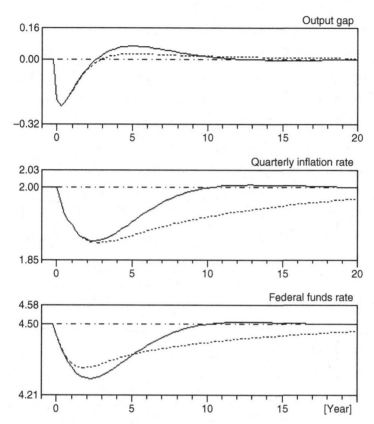

Figure 8.4: The impulse–response function of the RS model with $\tilde{\alpha}_p = 1.00$

An increase of the second policy coefficient, the responsiveness to output $\tilde{\alpha}_y$, cannot fulfil the same purpose. Figure 8.5[34] demonstrates this with a similar strong change in the coefficient as before, $\tilde{\alpha}_y = 2.00$ (instead of $\tilde{\alpha}_y = 0.82$). Here, after the overshooting of the output gap, the return of the interest rate to i^o is so fast, and correspondingly the output gap is so close to zero, that the adjustments of the inflation rate slow down considerably after $t = 4$. The middle panel in figure 8.5 indicates that the final convergence of $\hat{p}$ back to the target takes even longer than in the reference scenario.[35]

---

[34] The dotted lines are the time paths in the reference scenario, where $\tilde{\alpha}_y = 0.82$ (the solid lines in figure 8.3).

[35] The convergence time T specified in eq. (8.28), which was $T = 24.8$ years in the reference scenario, is here computed as $T = 50.0$ years.

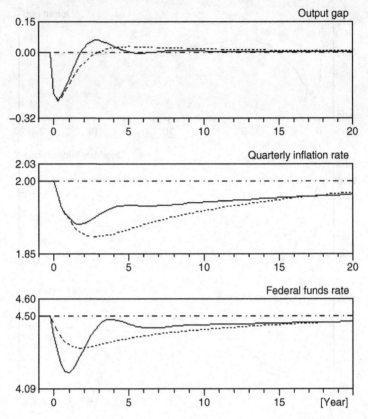

Figure 8.5: The impulse–response function of the RS model with $\tilde{\alpha}_p = 2.00$

Despite certain improvements in the convergence behaviour or the transitory dynamics shortly after the demand shock, the basic phenomenon of figure 8.3 persists: while output is brought back to its potential level in the relatively short time of two or three years, the adjustments of inflation take much longer, if they are (approximately) completed at all within a reasonable span of time.

After examining model (8.19)–(8.22) in the laboratory vacuum of the impulse–response functions, we should also look at the time series that are generated by the stochastic system when the so-called innovations $\varepsilon_{y,t}$ and $\varepsilon_{p,t}$ arrive every quarter. Simple visual inspection can then give a first indication of whether the dynamics of the RS model are sufficiently credible.

The perturbations $\varepsilon_{y,t}$ and $\varepsilon_{p,t}$ were already said to have identical (over time) normal probability distributions with zero mean. To simulate the system, we still need information about their standard deviations σ_y and σ_p, respectively. To this end we refer to the estimations of (8.19) and (8.20) by Rudebusch and Svensson (1999, p. 208), whose results differ only marginally from (8.23). The authors make the explicit point that the error terms in the two regression equations exhibit no significant serial correlation and also that their cross-correlation is essentially zero. σ_y and σ_p can thus be identified with the standard errors of the equations, which are reported, too. On this basis we adopt

$$\sigma_p = 1.009 \quad \sigma_y = 0.819 \tag{8.29}$$

The sample run in figure 8.6 illustrates the dynamic outcome over a period of 200 years. A remark on the possibly negative interest rates is postponed until the next subsection. Regarding the cyclical features of the time series, the output gap fluctuates most realistically. This, however, is not so much a merit of the model as a whole. To see this, note that, if the feedback of the real interest rate is neglected in the dynamic IS equation (8.20), a second-order autoregressive process in $\tilde{y}_t$ will be obtained. These processes are well known to be, in their simplicity, a fairly good approximation to describe the cyclical behaviour of the output gap. Since the two coefficients β_{y0} and β_{y1} in (8.23) are the usual order of magnitude and the responsiveness β_{yi} of output to the real interest rate is not very strong in comparison, the main properties of the AR(2) processes carry over to the present model's output dynamics.

The second panel in figure 8.6 shows inflation, where for greater clarity the quarterly noise is smoothed and the four-quarter rate of inflation is plotted. The basic cyclical pattern of this series is distinctly different from the output gap. There might be a weak tendency for small-scale fluctuations at a similar frequency as the output gap, but they are clearly dominated by cycles with a larger amplitude and longer period. As a matter of fact, this behaviour is not very typical of business cycles.

Moreover, inflation does not fluctuate too regularly around the target $\hat{p}^*$. In particular, after $t = 100$ there is a period of some seventy years when the rate of inflation persistently exceeds the target rate. Under these circumstances, monetary policy would certainly no longer be called successful.

The phenomenon is connected to the long convergence time for inflation that we observed in the impulse–response function. There it was noted that, if the readjustments back to $\hat{p}^*$ take too much time, inflation will in the meantime be dominated by the supply shocks $\varepsilon_{p,t}$. As a consequence, now and again the shocks will reinforce the existing inflation gaps, which is, essentially, what happens after $t = 100$. More technically,

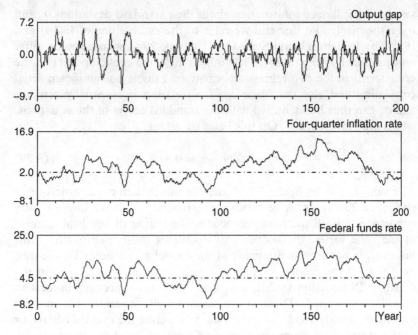

Figure 8.6: A sample run of the stochastic RS model

this could be a short description of a random walk, and in fact the Phillips curve specification (8.19) would be a (slightly elaborated) random walk if the coefficient β_{py} were zero. Since the estimated value of β_{py} is rather low and the output gap to which it relates remains within a moderately bounded interval, the central mechanism of a random walk continues to be effective. Although the medium-term deviations of inflation from target in figure 8.6 are less extreme than in a pure random walk, its basic features are still visible.

The interest rate in the bottom panel of figure 8.6 is seen to move in similar ways to the rate of inflation. Despite the higher output coefficient in the two policy parameters of the Taylor rate of interest, inflation is the main determining force. Nevertheless, the interest rate is unable to avert the long positive deviations of the inflation rate.

In addition to an assessment of the qualitative features of the stochastic dynamics, a more detailed investigation of the RS model computes some quantitative statistics and asks how they are influenced by changes in the policy coefficients. The central statistics are the standard deviations of the time series of inflation and the output gap, $\sigma(\hat{p}_t)$ and $\sigma(\tilde{y}_t)$, which are said to measure the variability of these variables. While in this book the expression 'stabilization' has referred to the local stability of the equilibrium of a deterministic dynamic system, in the present context 'stabilization' means a reduction in these standard deviations.

A parameter change will not always affect $\sigma(\hat{p}_t)$ and $\sigma(\tilde{y}_t)$ in the same direction. Often there will, rather, be a trade-off: one standard deviation is lowered at the cost of the other. The two magnitudes can be made comparable by endowing the central bank with a loss function L. A convenient version defines L as a weighted average of the variances of $\hat{p}_t$ and $\tilde{y}_t$ (i.e. of the squares of the standard deviations). This or similar quadratic loss functions are particularly well suited to determine an optimal interest rate rule, which minimizes the expected loss. The search for a characterization of optimal monetary policy rules has been an intensively studied field of research in the last decade. An extensive discussion of such optimal rules in the framework of system (8.19)–(8.22) can be found in Rudebusch and Svensson (1999). Most interesting, and challenging, is the result that the optimal policy coefficients are generally considerably larger than the estimated values.

Here it suffices for us to illustrate the effects of the same *ceteris paribus* parameter changes that we have carried out in the examination of the impulse–response functions. The latter can also serve as a guideline of what impact we may expect on $\sigma(\hat{p}_t)$ and $\sigma(\tilde{y}_t)$, where the readjustments over the first few years are probably more important than the final convergence behaviour. If we dare a conjecture from the time paths of figures 8.3 to 8.5, the following effects can be predicted. The Taylor rule in a narrow sense, $\tilde{\alpha}_i = 1$, lowers both standard deviations since inflation falls less strongly and the output gap recovers a bit earlier in figure 8.3. The rise in the inflation coefficient, $\tilde{\alpha}_p = 1.00$, diminishes $\sigma(\hat{p}_t)$ and, because of the slightly stronger overshooting in figure 8.4, increases $\sigma(\tilde{y}_t)$. The rise in the output coefficient, $\tilde{\alpha}_y = 2.00$, diminishes $\sigma(\hat{p}_t)$, while the impact on $\sigma(\tilde{y}_t)$ is unclear: on the one hand, the return of $\tilde{y}_t$ to zero is faster; on the other hand, the overshooting is stronger.

To obtain the standard deviations of inflation and the output gap in the stochastic system (8.19)–(8.22), 100 sample runs over a period of 500 years were performed. In each run the first ten years were discarded to control for the (minor) transitory effects of the initial conditions, and the standard deviations were computed over the remaining time interval $[10, 500]$. Then the mean of these hundred standard deviations was computed, which yields the statistics collected in table 8.1. Since for each set of parameters the same seed in the (pseudo) random number generator was also adopted, the differences between the scenarios can be considered to be 'significant', though we abstain from establishing this in more technical terms.

Table 8.1: *Output and inflation variability in the stochastic RS model*

Scenario	$\sigma(\tilde{y}_t)$	$\sigma(\hat{p}_t)$
Reference	2.21	4.33
$\tilde{\alpha}_i = 1.00$	1.98	3.97
$\tilde{\alpha}_p = 1.00$	2.60	3.07
$\tilde{\alpha}_y = 2.00$	2.00	4.45

NB: σ denotes the standard deviation of the time series $\tilde{y}_t$ and $\hat{p}_t$, respectively. For each of the four parameter sets, the numbers are the mean of the standard deviations of 100 simulation runs over 500 years.

Evaluating our conjecture, the second row in table 8.1 confirms that without interest rate smoothing ($\tilde{\alpha}_i = 1.00$) there would be lower variability in both output and inflation. The reduction in the standard deviations is, however, quite moderate. The greatest effect is brought about by the higher responsiveness of the central bank to inflation, $\tilde{\alpha}_p = 1.00$. The higher coefficient diminishes the variability of inflation by almost one-third, while the output variability increases to a lesser extent. The last row in table 8.1 falsifies the above conjecture regarding the higher output coefficient, $\tilde{\alpha}_y = 2.00$. Here it is not $\sigma(\hat{p}_t)$ but $\sigma(\tilde{y}_t)$ that is reduced; $\sigma(\hat{p}_t)$ increases by roughly the same amount as $\sigma(\tilde{y}_t)$ decreases. Both changes are, nevertheless, not very pronounced.

Although we present no diagrams of the time series of the inflation rate in the alternative scenarios, the standard deviations of $\hat{p}_t$ in table 8.1 still indicate that the problem of the unsatisfactory inflation dynamics does not disappear easily. That is, in the other scenarios as well we will occasionally encounter periods of several decades with lasting positive or negative deviations of the inflation rate from the central bank's target, which does not seem credible. Since we have identified the strong persistence in the Phillips curve as the main source of this shortcoming, eq. (8.19) would be the first place to look for a respecification that could improve upon this phenomenon.

One alternative could be the introduction of so-called forward-looking inflation expectations in the Phillips curve, similar to those put forward in the appendix. Since the coefficients in the reduced-form equations of these systems combine the parameters of the structural equations in complicated ways, it is a priori unclear whether this would give rise to more realistic cyclical patterns in the inflation time series. Although

New-Keynesian model variants are widely used in the literature, this topic is apparently not discussed. The investigations are, instead, directly concerned with the summary statistics of the variances or standard deviations, or the related loss functions. Even for illustrative purposes, we have found no time series diagram like figure 8.6 in the literature.

In an effort to speed up the convergence of the inflation rate in the impulse–response functions and thus reduce the random walk elements in the stochastic dynamics, another modelling device is to refer to an expectational variable of its own in the Phillips curve. That is, the benchmark of the lagged inflation rates in (8.19), which are said to represent expected inflation in a backward-looking manner, may be replaced by something like an 'inflation climate', the changes in which also, in a backward-looking manner, are to be determined in another part of the model. The RS model would not be much extended in this way, but, again, we know of no discussion of this or a similar alternative approach in the literature. Of course, the proposal of the concept of the inflation climate, together with the simple adjustment mechanisms of adaptive or regressive expectations, is exactly what we have been using throughout the book. And we will meet this device again when we take the private sector of the KMG model, which can be viewed as a more elaborate private sector of the RS model, and apply the Taylor-type interest rate reaction function to it.

8.4.4 A note on low rates of interest

At the end of this discussion of the RS model we should return to the initial observation in figure 8.6 that, occasionally, the rate of interest becomes negative. This is, of course, counter-factual. As an immediate idea to avoid this, one can directly impose a non-negativity constraint on the interest rate in the adjustment equation (8.21). The central bank may actually realize the same idea in a more flexible way, but the specification of a simple zero bound can better clarify the basic problem of low rates of interest. So, eq. (8.21) may be extended to read

$$i_{t+h} = \max\{0, i_t + \tilde{\alpha}_i(i^*_{t+h} - i_t)\} \tag{8.30}$$

The modification is not so technical and innocent as it might seem. The first point to note is that it gives rise to a second state of equilibrium for system (8.19), (8.20), (8.30), (8.22). Distinguishing the state by the superscript 'z' (for zero bound), we get

$$\tilde{y}^z = 0, \quad \hat{p}^z = -(i^o - \hat{p}^*), \quad i^z = 0 \tag{8.31}$$

Clearly, $\tilde{y}^z = 0$ satisfies (8.19) for any stationary inflation rate, and $\hat{p}^z = -(i^o - \hat{p}^\star)$ then satisfies (8.20) with $i = i^z = 0$. Inserting these values in (8.22) for the Taylor rate of interest gives $i^\star = (i^o - \hat{p}^\star) - (i^o - \hat{p}^\star) + \tilde{\alpha}_p(-i^o + \hat{p}^\star - \hat{p}^\star) + 0 = -\tilde{\alpha}_p i^o < 0$, so the zero constraint in (8.30) is indeed binding.

The second point is the crucial one, namely that the second equilibrium is unstable. This is easily seen without invoking any mathematics. Consider the deterministic part of (8.19), (8.20), (8.30), (8.22), suppose that the system is in $(\tilde{y}^z, \hat{p}^z, i^z)$, and a negative demand shocks occurs. In the same period nothing else happens because $i^\star$ is further diminished, so the constraint in (8.30) remains binding. In the next quarter $\hat{p}$ is lowered in the Phillips curve (8.19) and $\tilde{y}$ through the 'accelerator' coefficient β_{y0} in the IS equation (8.20). One quarter later both of these changes have a negative impact on the Phillips curve as well as on the IS equation (since $1.17 = \beta_{y0} \gg -\beta_{y1} = 0.27$). In addition, the downward pressure on $i^\star$ is reinforced, which leaves the actual interest rate i_t at the zero level. The adjustments repeat themselves in the following periods: the output gap decreases and inflation falls even more. It follows that the economy is caught in a deflationary trap. Sometimes it is also said that the famous liquidity trap has been resurrected.

The implications for the full stochastic system are obvious. As also illustrated in figure 8.6, almost surely the economy will eventually enter a situation where the negative deviations of the output gap and the inflation rate are so strong that, in the absence of the constraint, the interest rate would fall below zero. Then the mechanism just described begins to work and reinforces the downward tendencies. If not, very soon strong positive demand and/or supply shocks arrive; inflation and output will attain such extreme values that the economy could no longer be considered to be viable.

It has to be added that the problem of a deflationary trap is more or less directly encountered in all elementary models that combine an interest rate rule with a Phillips curve and IS relationship. On the other hand, the kind of destabilizing feedbacks that have been outlined cannot be viewed as plausible. This class of models is therefore not suited to deal with the effects of low rates of interest. It is thus only consistent when, in their examination of interest rate reaction functions, they usually disregard the zero bound altogether.

To stimulate the economy when short-term interest rates are near zero, the central bank must rely on other mechanisms beyond the Phillips curve and the simple specification of IS. The first and most important thing one can learn from the literature concerned with the additional transmission mechanisms is that, whatever actions the central bank may take, they will remain ineffective if they do not change expectations about the future conduct of monetary policy (see, for example, Eggertsson and Woodford, 2003).

More specifically, we conclude with the recommendations of one of the proponents of the Rudebusch–Svensson model. Referring to an open economy, Svensson (2003) suggests a 'foolproof' way of escaping from a liquidity trap, which consists of a price-level target path, a devaluation of the currency and a temporary exchange rate peg. In particular, in the wake of this policy mix, inflation expectations may rise again. As regards the Taylor rule itself, Reifschneider and Williams (2000) propose modifying it by incorporating a response to past constraints on policy, which is similar to price level targeting. (They study the effects of their generalization within the large-scale open-economy model with rational expectations that is used by the Federal Reserve.)

8.5   Appendix: The reduced form of forward-looking models

Monetary policy models in a New-Keynesian vein and Keynesian backward-looking models, just as the Rudebusch–Svensson model in section 8.4, are in accord on focusing on output and inflation and characterizing the private sector by a Phillips curve and a dynamic IS equation. The difference is that, where the RS and similar models use lagged values of the state variables, New-Keynesian-oriented models introduce a weighted average of lagged and expected values and assume that these expectations are rational. Regarding the exact dating of the variables, two variants have, however, to be distinguished. Let us begin with the standard specification of a New-Keynesian equation determining a dynamic variable x_t on which another variable (or vector) z_t feeds back, which reads

$$x_t = a_x[\mu_x E_t x_{t+1} + (1 - \mu_x)x_{t-1}] + a_z z_t + \varepsilon_{x,t} \qquad (8.32)$$

Here $\varepsilon_{x,t}$ is a random perturbation, E_t is the expectation operator conditional on information available at time t, and the New-Keynesian element is represented by the weight μ_x, $0 \le \mu_x \le 1$, which governs the extent to which behaviour looks backwards and forwards. More generally, expectations $E_t z_{t+1}$ of the other variable(s) might also be involved (see, for example, Leeper and Zha, 2001), or expectations look more than one period ahead into the future (as in subsection 8.5.2 below). In the present context, x_t is either the rate of inflation in the Phillips curve or the output gap in the IS relationship. In explicit derivations of (8.32) from microeconomic principles, the weight μ_x often equals unity.[36]

The analysis of models employing equations like (8.32) reveals that their variables fall into two categories: at starting time $t = 0$, say, one set of variables is predetermined (by an empirical or assumed history), while the other variables (usually expected variables) are so-called jump variables, which jump, as it were, at that time onto a stable manifold, irrespective of their previous history. This property tends to make the reduced forms of these models, and even the computation of the corresponding matrices, a highly complicated task.

Another strand of the literature avoids these intricacies and all the effort they require by changing the dating on the left-hand side of (8.32) from x_t to x_{t+1}:

$$x_{t+1} = a_x[\mu_x E_t x_{t+1} + (1 - \mu_x)x_{t-1}] + a_z z_t + \varepsilon_{x,t} \qquad (8.33)$$

As it turns out, the great advantage of this modification is that it allows us to treat all variables as predetermined, which makes these models far more tractable than the models incorporating (8.32). If the latter relationship has a theoretically more fashionable story behind it, specification (8.33) can be sold as a simplifying approximation to it. (8.33) might also have some theoretical appeal of its own. Thus, with respect to a unit weight $\mu_x = 1$ and $x = \hat{p} =$ inflation, so that (8.33) represents a Phillips curve, Lansing and Trehan (2001, p. 4, fn. 9) make it explicit that this version can be viewed (not as a New-Keynesian but) as a 'Neoclassical'-style Phillips curve.[37]

In the following we sketch how these two types of models can be transformed into a recursive law of motion – that is, into an ordinary stochastic difference equation. We start with specification (8.33), which we briefly call the neoclassical specification.

8.5.1   A neoclassical specification

The model that serves as an example in this section is borrowed from Lansing and Trehan (2001, 2003). In a first step, we temporarily simplify

---

[36] An expectational IS curve may be a linear approximation to the representative household's Euler condition for optimal consumption, and a Phillips curve may result from monopolistic competition where individual firms adjust prices in a staggered, overlapping fashion; this is, for example, worked out by Walsh (2003, sects. 5.4 & 5.7.3). Note that $a_x = \beta < 1$ in his and many other New-Keynesian Phillips curves, which presupposes a zero equilibrium rate of inflation (Walsh, 2003, p. 263).

[37] For further details on this issue they refer to Roberts (1995) and Kiley (1998).

the paper's output–inflation dynamics in that the forward-looking principle applies to the inflation rate in the Phillips curve and to the output gap in the IS equation, but not yet to the real interest rate that enters the IS equation. With $\tilde{y}$ again denoting the output gap, the following three equations are considered:

$$\hat{p}_{t+1} = \mu_p E_t \hat{p}_{t+1} + (1 - \mu_p)\hat{p}_t + \beta_{py}\tilde{y}_t + \varepsilon_{p,t+1} \qquad (8.34)$$

$$\tilde{y}_{t+1} = \beta_{yy}[\mu_y E_t \tilde{y}_{t+1} + (1 - \mu_y)\tilde{y}_t] - \beta_{yp}(\rho_t - \rho^o) + \varepsilon_{y,t+1} \qquad (8.35)$$

$$\rho_t = i_t - \hat{p}_t \qquad (8.36)$$

Obviously, in the polar case of weights $\mu_p = \mu_y = 0$, eqs. (8.34)–(8.36) are a simplified version of the first two equations (8.19) and (8.20) of the RS model (with $\beta_{y1} = 0$ and the four-quarter averages of inflation and the interest rate replaced by the quarterly magnitudes).[38]

ρ_t in the IS equation (8.35) is generally conceived of as the long-term real interest rate. For simplicity, ρ_t is here still identical to the current *ex post* real rate of interest – a restriction that will be relaxed below. The stochastic perturbations $\varepsilon_{p,t+1}$ and $\varepsilon_{p,t+1}$ play the same role as in the RS model. They are the supply and demand shocks, respectively, which are supposed to be normally and identically distributed around zero.

Eqs. (8.34)–(8.36) can be readily transformed into two purely backward-looking difference equations. The procedure is based on the elementary rule that under rational expectations the reduced form of a structural equation such as $z_{t+1} = \alpha E_t z_{t+1} + \beta x_t + \varepsilon_{t+1}$ (with $E_t \varepsilon_{t+1} = 0$) is given by $z_{t+1} = \beta x_t/(1 - \alpha) + \varepsilon_{t+1}$. ($\beta$ and x_t may well be row and column vectors, respectively.) To see this, take the expectations of both sides of the structural equation, solve it for $E_t z_{t+1}$, which yields $E_t z_{t+1} = \beta x_t/(1 - \alpha)$, and substitute these expectations back into the original equation.

Incidentally, the neoclassical specification (8.33) can be directly solved for $E_t x_{t+1}$, the only difference being that here more lags may be involved. While things will become more complicated if a second expectation term shows up in (8.33), the mathematical treatment would be similar to that below, where we will even have two additional expected values in eq. (8.36). System (8.34)–(8.36) and the extended version below are thus not unduly restrictive.

---

[38] Such a simple backward-looking model is employed in a number of other studies; see, for example, Ball (1997) and Svensson (1997, sect. 6).

In the present model, the rule that has just been spelled out can be applied to eqs. (8.34) and (8.35). Plugging in (8.36), we then obtain

$$\hat{p}_{t+1} = \hat{p}_t + \frac{\beta_{py}}{1 - \mu_p}\tilde{y}_t + \varepsilon_{p,t+1} \tag{8.37}$$

$$\tilde{y}_{t+1} = \frac{\beta_{yy}(1 - \mu_y)}{1 - \beta_{yy}\mu_y}\tilde{y}_t - \frac{\beta_{yp}}{1 - \beta_{yy}\mu_y}(i_t - \hat{p}_t - \rho^o) + \varepsilon_{y,t+1} \tag{8.38}$$

Formally, eqs. (8.37), (8.38) cannot be distinguished from the simplified RS model just mentioned. It can, however, be said that the forward-looking element increases the speeds of reaction. If the structural responsiveness of inflation to the output gap, β_{py} in (8.34), is compared with the responsiveness of $\hat{p}_{t+1}$ to the output gap in the reduced-form equation (8.37), we see that the latter (compound) coefficient rises with the weight μ_p of the forward-looking expectations in the structural Phillips curve. A similar statement holds true for the IS equation and the weight μ_y. The economic interpretation of the stronger reactions is that (an increasing) part of the later adjustments are already anticipated by the agents in the current period.

In a next step we drop eq. (8.36) and employ a slightly more ambitious specification of the long-term real interest rate ρ_t. A convenient formulation of a term structure equation is given in Lansing and Trehan (2003, p. 250), where only the agents' one-period-ahead expectations enter. The degree to which these forward-looking expectations matter is measured by a weight μ_r, so that the equation reads[39]

$$\rho_t = (1 - \mu_r)(i_t - \hat{p}_t) + \mu_r E_t(i_{t+1} - \hat{p}_{t+1}) \tag{8.39}$$

Eqs. (8.34), (8.35), (8.39) constitute the private sector of the model studied by Lansing and Trehan (2001, 2003). So far, its reduced form will still contain the expectations of the future rate of interest. Before considering an interest rate policy, we first spell out the 'standard techniques' (Lansing and Trehan, 2003, p. 250) that allow us to eliminate the other forward-looking variables in (8.34), (8.35), (8.39).

Write (8.39) as $\rho_t - \rho^o = (1 - \mu_r)(i_t - \rho^o - \hat{p}^*) - (1 - \mu_r)\hat{p}_t + \hat{p}^* + \mu_r E_t(i_{t+1} - \rho^o - \hat{p}^*) - \mu_r E_t \hat{p}_{t+1}$. Taking the expectations in (8.37), which gives $E_t \hat{p}_{t+1} = \hat{p}_t + [\beta_{py}/(1 - \mu_p)]\tilde{y}_t$, and abbreviating

---

[39] Denoting the weight as μ_p would be more consistent, but the index ρ is not easily distinguished from the index p already used.

$A_i := (1 - \mu_r)(i_t - \rho^o - \hat{p}^\star) + \mu_r E_t(i_{t+1} - \rho^o - \hat{p}^\star) - (\hat{p}_t - \hat{p}^\star)$, we have $\rho_t - \rho^o = -[\mu_r \beta_{py}/(1 - \mu_p)]\tilde{y}_t + A_i$. If we take a step back in eq. (8.38) and resubstitute ρ_t for $i_t - \hat{p}_t$, we can plug in this expression and obtain $\tilde{y}_{t+1} = \tilde{y}_t[\beta_{yy}(1 - \mu_y) + \beta_{yp}\mu_r\beta_{py}/(1 - \mu_p)]/(1 - \beta_{yy}\mu_y) - \beta_{yp}A_i/(1 - \beta_{yy}\mu_y) + \varepsilon_{y,t+1}$. On the whole, system (8.34), (8.35), (8.39) can thus be transformed into

$$\hat{p}_{t+1} = \hat{p}_t + \frac{\beta_{py}}{1 - \mu_p}\tilde{y}_t + \varepsilon_{p,t+1} \qquad (8.40)$$

$$\tilde{y}_{t+1} = \frac{1}{1 - \beta_{yy}\mu_y}\Big\{[\beta_{yy}(1 - \mu_y) + \mu_r\beta_{yp}\beta_{py}/(1 - \mu_p)]\tilde{y}_t + \beta_{yp}(\hat{p}_t - \hat{p}^\star)$$
$$- \beta_{yp}[(1 - \mu_r)(i_t - \rho^o - \hat{p}^\star) + \mu_r E_t(i_{t+1} - \rho^o - \hat{p}^\star)]\Big\} + \varepsilon_{y,t+1} \qquad (8.41)$$

(The two equations coincide with eqs. (4), (5) in Lansing and Trehan, 2003, p. 250, except for a minor misprint in the latter.) Comparing (8.41) and (8.38), it is seen that the forward-looking real interest rate (8.39) in the term structure equation reinforces the positive feedback of the output gap on itself.

Regarding the role of the interest rate, (8.40) shows that $\hat{p}_{t+1}$ cannot be influenced by policy at time t because $\hat{p}_t$ and $\tilde{y}_t$ are predetermined state variables. In contrast, the other constraint (8.41) shows that the output gap $\tilde{y}_{t+1}$ can be influenced through changes in i_t or $E_t i_{t+1}$. Through this channel, in turn, inflation two periods ahead can be affected. Hence, eqs. (8.40) and (8.41) imply that the central bank exerts control over the output gap with a one-period lag and the inflation rate with a two-period lag. This results holds for practically all discrete-time models of the private sector with a Phillips curve and a dynamic IS equation, backward-looking and forward-looking versions alike.

Eqs. (8.37), (8.38), as well as (8.40), (8.41), are still open systems since both of them include the nominal interest rate i, the latter also as an expected value, which has not yet been determined. Limiting our interest now to (8.40), (8.41), the following connection between an optimal monetary policy and the Taylor rule is a striking result.[40] Assume that the central bank has no genuine interest rate smoothing motive. Referring to an initial period $t = 0$, its preferences are, rather, represented by an intertemporal quadratic loss function L of the form $L = \sum_{t=0}^{\infty} \delta^t [(\hat{p}_t - \hat{p}^\star)^2 + \lambda \tilde{y}_t^2]$. Here $\delta < 1$ is the central bank's subjective discount

---

[40] It has, however, a wider field of application than this specific version.

factor and $\lambda \geq 0$ is the subjective weight it assigns to stabilizing output fluctuations relative to stabilizing inflation fluctuations.[41] Then a time path of the nominal interest rate that minimizes the expected value of L subject to (8.40), (8.41) is given by the following prescription: $i_t = \rho^o + \hat{p}^* + \gamma_p(\hat{p}_t - \hat{p}^*) + \gamma_y \tilde{y}_t$, where γ_p and γ_y are suitable coefficients (Lansing and Trehan, 2003, p. 251; the theorem given there also provides the explicit formula for γ_p and γ_y, which are extremely complicated functions of the other parameters in the model). In other words, the Taylor rule (in a narrow sense and with suitable policy coefficients) describes an optimal monetary policy.[42]

Against this background, let us then combine eqs. (8.34), (8.35), (8.39) with the Taylor rate of interest. Collecting the equations in one block, the following system is considered:

$$\hat{p}_{t+1} = (1 - \mu_p)\hat{p}_t + \mu_p E_t \hat{p}_{t+1} + \beta_{py}\tilde{y}_t + \varepsilon_{p,t+1} \qquad (8.42)$$

$$\tilde{y}_{t+1} = \beta_{yy}[(1 - \mu_y)\tilde{y}_t + \mu_y E_t \tilde{y}_{t+1}] - \beta_{yp}(\rho_t - \rho^o) + \varepsilon_{y,t+1} \qquad (8.43)$$

$$\rho_t = (1 - \mu_r)(i_t - \hat{p}_t) + \mu_r E_t(i_{t+1} - \hat{p}_{t+1}) \qquad (8.44)$$

$$i_t = \rho^o + \hat{p}^* + \gamma_p(\hat{p}_t - \hat{p}^*) + \gamma_y \tilde{y}_t \qquad (8.45)$$

Again, our task is to transform these equations into a purely backward-looking version. We begin by noting that the rational expectations of the private-sector agents now include the central bank's policy rule. So they use their knowledge of (8.45) to compute $E_t i_{t+1} = \rho^o + \hat{p}^* + \gamma_p(E_t \hat{p}_{t+1} - \hat{p}^*) + \gamma_y E_t \tilde{y}_{t+1}$. Using the inflation expectations, (8.37) without the random term, this becomes $E_t i_{t+1} = \rho^o + \hat{p}^* + \gamma_p(\hat{p}_t - \hat{p}^*) + [\gamma_p \beta_{py}/(1 - \mu_p)]\tilde{y}_t + \gamma_y E_t \tilde{y}_{t+1}$.

In a similar way to the above, the term structure equation (8.44) then gives us $\rho_t - \rho^o = \mu_r \gamma_y E_t \tilde{y}_{t+1} + [\mu_r \beta_{py}(\gamma_p - 1)/(1 - \mu_p)]\tilde{y}_t + A_t$, with $A_t := (1 - \mu_r)(i_t - \rho^o - \hat{p}^*) - (1 - \mu_r \gamma_p)(\hat{p}_t - \hat{p}^*)$. Substituting this into

---

[41] As Rudebusch and Svensson (1999, p. 215) remark, when going to the limit, $\delta \to 1$, the intertemporal loss function (suitably rescaled) can be interpreted as the unconditional mean of the period loss function. It thus equals the weighted sum of the unconditional variances of the goal variables – that is, $L = \text{Var}(\hat{p}_t) + \lambda \text{Var}(\tilde{y}_t)$.

[42] Observe that the expression of the optimal rule corresponds exactly to i^* in (8.5) or (8.11) if γ_p is identified with $1 + \tilde{\alpha}_p$. Incidentally, the optimal coefficients remain well defined in the limit, as $\delta \to 1$. It may, furthermore, be mentioned that, as the quantitative analysis by Lansing and Trehan (2001, 2003) demonstrates, the optimal coefficients are typically (considerably) larger than the values proposed by Taylor or estimated in empirical investigations.

(8.42) and collecting terms, we have $\tilde{y}_{t+1} = (\beta_{yy}\mu_y - \beta_{yp}\mu_r\gamma_y)E_t\tilde{y}_{t+1} + [\beta_{yy}(1 - \mu_y) - \beta_{yp}\mu_r\beta_{py}(\gamma_p - 1)/(1 - \mu_p)]\tilde{y}_t - \beta_{yp}A_t + \varepsilon_{y,t+1}$. Here it only remains to apply the rule mentioned above. Together with (8.37), the reduced-form version of (8.42)–(8.45) is therefore obtained as follows:

$$\hat{p}_{t+1} = \hat{p}_t + \frac{\beta_{py}}{1 - \mu_p}\tilde{y}_t + \varepsilon_{p,t+1} \tag{8.46}$$

$$\begin{aligned}
\tilde{y}_{t+1} = \frac{1}{1 - \beta_{yy}\mu_y + \beta_{yp}\mu_r\gamma_y}&\left\{\left[\beta_{yy}(1 - \mu_y) - \frac{\mu_r\beta_{yp}\beta_{py}(\gamma_p - 1)}{(1 - \mu_p)}\right]\tilde{y}_t\right.\\
&+\beta_{yp}(1 - \mu_r\gamma_p)(\hat{p}_t - \hat{p}^\star)\\
&\left.-\beta_{yp}(1 - \mu_r)(i_t - \rho^o - \hat{p}^\star)\right\} + \varepsilon_{y,t+1}
\end{aligned} \tag{8.47}$$

$$i_t = \rho^o + \hat{p}^\star + \gamma_p(\hat{p}_t - \hat{p}^\star) + \gamma_y\tilde{y}_t \tag{8.48}$$

Formally, system (8.46)–(8.48) is a set of ordinary difference equations with some additive noise. At this level, there is no fundamental difference between forward-looking and backward-looking models. On the other hand, the conceptual differences manifest themselves in the compound coefficients. They capture the agents' expectations of the next-period variables, which are formed on the basis of their perfect knowledge of the economic relationships. It is, however, quite another matter as to which dynamic properties of the model the compound coefficients give rise, how well they are supported by empirical evidence, and what becomes of the coefficients if the structural equations are only slightly modified.

8.5.2   A New-Keynesian specification

This subsection sketches the mathematical treatment of New-Keynesian models in a fairly general manner. For concreteness, however, we begin with the formulation of a specific model that can be regarded as a New-Keynesian version of the Rudebusch–Svensson equations (8.19)–(8.22). It also generalizes our New-Keynesian reference equation (8.32), in that agents look not just one but three periods (quarters) ahead into the future. Such IS and Phillips curve relationships are taken over from Ellingsen and Söderström (2004, p. 3). While these authors are concerned with optimal monetary policy, we here combine the two equations with a Taylor rule that, in the spirit of the rest of model, is now forward-looking in inflation. If we let the time unit be a quarter (in this section only) and define $\bar{\pi}_t = (1/4) \sum_{j=0}^{3} \hat{p}_{t-j}$ as the average four-quarter inflation rate, the model reads

$$\hat{p}_t = \mu_p E_{t-1} \bar{\pi}_{t+3} + (1 - \mu_p) \sum_{j=1}^{4} \beta_{pj} \hat{p}_{t-j} + \beta_{py} \tilde{y}_{t-1} + \eta_{p,t} \tag{8.49}$$

$$\tilde{y}_t = \mu_y E_{t-1} \tilde{y}_{t+1} + (1 - \mu_y) \sum_{j=1}^{2} \beta_{yj} \tilde{y}_{t-j} - \beta_{yi} [i_{t-1} - E_{t-1} \bar{\pi}_{t+3}] + \eta_{y,t} \tag{8.50}$$

$$i_t = i_{t-1} + \tilde{\alpha}_i (i_t^* - i_{t-1}) \tag{8.51}$$

$$i_t^* = (i^o - \hat{p}^*) + E_{t-1} \bar{\pi}_{t+3} + \tilde{\alpha}_p [E_{t-1} \bar{\pi}_{t+3} - \hat{p}^*] + \tilde{\alpha}_y \tilde{y}_{t-1} \tag{8.52}$$

Of course, the coefficients β_{pj} sum to unity again. The random perturbations η are allowed to be first-order autoregression processes (compactly specified in a moment).

In the first step, the analysis of (8.49)–(8.52) has to separate the jump variables from the predetermined variables. In allusion to the usual notation in the Ramsey infinite horizon optimizing model of consumption and capital accumulation, where k is the predetermined capital stock and c the consumption variable that at time $t = 0$ jumps onto the stable manifold of the model's saddle-point,[43] we denote the (column) vector of predetermined variables by $k \in \mathbb{R}^n$ and the (column) vector of jump variables by $c \in \mathbb{R}^m$. In detail, $m = 4$, $n = 8$ and the vectors are

$$k_t = (\hat{p}_t, \hat{p}_{t-1}, \hat{p}_{t-2}, \hat{p}_{t-3}, \tilde{y}_t, \tilde{y}_{t-1}, i_t, i_{t-1})' \tag{8.53}$$

$$c_t = (E_t \hat{p}_{t+3}, E_t \hat{p}_{t+2}, E_t \hat{p}_{t+1}, E_t \tilde{y}_{t+1})' \tag{8.54}$$

Suitably filled up with zeros (conforming to the matrix notation in (8.57) below), the perturbation terms are collected in another (column) vector v_t, partitioned into $v_t = (v_{1t}, v_{2t})' \in \mathbb{R}^m \times \mathbb{R}^n$. With suitably formatted matrices A_{11}, B_{11}, etc., it is easily shown that the equations (8.49)–(8.52) can be rewritten as

$$A_{11} E_t c_{t+1} = B_{11} c_t + B_{12} k_t + D_1 v_{1,t+1} \tag{8.55}$$

$$k_{t+1} = B_{21} c_t + B_{22} k_t + D_2 v_{2,t+1} \tag{8.56}$$

$$v_{t+1} = N v_t + \varepsilon_t; \quad E_t \varepsilon_t = 0 \tag{8.57}$$

(see Ellingsen and Söderström, 2004, p. 15, for the basic argument; incidentally, the pattern of zero entries in the matrix B made up of

---

[43] See chapter 2 in Blanchard and Fischer (1989), for example.

$B_{11}, \ldots, B_{22}$ looks similar to that in the matrix A of the Rudebusch–Svensson model in (8.26)). Although in the present model D_1 and D_2 are identity matrices, further analysis does not depend on this. The square matrix N in (8.57) contains on its diagonal the autocorrelation coefficients of the supply and demand shocks $\eta_{p,t}$ and $\eta_{y,t}$, but non-zero (off-diagonal) cross-correlations are generally admitted, too. The non-zero components of the random vector ε_t are i.i.d. with mean zero and constant standard deviations.

Eqs. (8.55)–(8.57) are the basis of the derivation of the model's recursive law of motion. The solution approach is, of course, linear, so that for suitably formatted matrices P, Q, R, S the reduced form of the model should take the form

$$k_{t+1} = Pk_t + Qv_{t+1} \tag{8.58}$$

$$c_t = Rk_t + Sv_{t+1} \tag{8.59}$$

The rest of the analysis has to verify this approach and indicate a procedure that allows us to determine the four solution matrices P, Q, R, S.

The logic of (8.58), (8.59) is that at starting time $t = 0$ the expectational variables jump onto a stable manifold. As described by (8.59), the precise point is determined by the initial conditions k_o that are given by the recent history of inflation, output and the interest rate, $k_o = (\hat{p}_o, \hat{p}_{-1}, \ldots, i_{-1})'$, together with the realization of the random shocks in vector v (here dated as $t + 1 = 0 + 1 = 1$). These expectations serve to determine inflation, output and the interest rate in the next period $t = 1$. For this we can refer to (8.56), or directly to (8.58), where the relationships are already reduced to a dependency on the predetermined variables alone. Generally, only the ordinary stochastic difference equations system (8.58) needs to be iterated forward; the expected values c_t are a mere appendix to these equations, which, if desired, can be computed from (8.59).

No further problems arise if the matrix $P \in \mathbb{R}^{n \times n}$ in (8.58) turns out to be stable – i.e. if all its eigenvalues lie within the unit circle. Otherwise the dynamics might explode or indeterminacy might prevail, which is an extra topic in New-Keynesian models beyond the present discussion.

The next stage in the analysis is to gather information about the (prospective) solution matrices P, Q, R, S. An elementary procedure for this is the so-called method of undetermined coefficients (McCallum, 1999). Doing some straightforward manipulations on (8.55)–(8.57) and substituting suitable expressions from this in the reduced-form approach

(8.58), (8.59), the solution matrices can thus be related to the structural matrices of the model.

To this end, expectations $E_t c_{t+1}$ are first expressed in terms of the predetermined variables. Thus, lead (8.59) by one period, take expectations and use (8.57), (8.58) to obtain $E_t c_{t+1} = RE_t k_{t+1} + SE_t v_{t+2} = R(Pk_t + Qv_{t+1}) + SNv_{t+1}$. Substituting this and (8.58), (8.59) into (8.55), (8.56) yields

$$A_{11}[R(Pk_t + Qv_{t+1}) + SNv_{t+1}] = B_{11}(Rk_t + Sv_{t+1}) + B_{12}k_t + D_1 v_{t+1}$$

$$Pk_t + Qv_{t+1} = B_{21}(Rk_t + Sv_{t+1}) + B_{22}k_t + D_2 v_{t+1}$$

These equations have to hold for arbitrary k_t and v_{t+1}. Hence one can collect the matrices that are multiplied by k_t on either side of the equality sign and equate them. Writing the result in compact form we get

$$\begin{bmatrix} A_{11} & 0 \\ 0 & I \end{bmatrix} \begin{bmatrix} RP \\ P \end{bmatrix} = \begin{bmatrix} B_{11} & B_{12} \\ B_{21} & B_{22} \end{bmatrix} \begin{bmatrix} R \\ I \end{bmatrix} \qquad (8.60)$$

The terms in v_{t+1}, on the other hand, imply that

$$A_{11}RQ + A_{11}SN = B_{11}S + D_1 \qquad (8.61)$$

$$Q = B_{21}S + D_2 \qquad (8.62)$$

Eqs. (8.60)–(8.62) are the relationships between the solution matrices and the structural matrices that we have been looking for. Solving them for P, Q, R, S, however, goes beyond the basics of linear algebra. In the following we briefly report two approaches that are taken from McCallum (1999) and Uhlig (1999), respectively. In both procedures, the four solution matrices are sequentially computed one after the other, where in each case the first matrix poses the most difficult task.

McCallum (1999) determines matrix R in the first step, for which he uses the generalized Schur decomposition theorem. Letting A and B denote the two square matrices in (8.60), this theorem guarantees the existence of (unitary and therefore invertible) matrices F and G such that $U := FAG$ and $V := FBG$ are both triangular.[44] The ratios $\lambda_i = v_{ii}/u_{ii}$ are, furthermore, generalized eigenvalues of B with respect to A; that is, together with eigenvectors s_i they satisfy the equations $\lambda_i As_i = Bs_i$. Without loss of generality, the matrices F and G can be

---

[44] The theorem presupposes that $\det(B - \lambda A) \neq 0$ for some complex number λ. Unless the model is poorly formulated (i.e. fails to place any restriction on some endogenous variable), the requirement will be met even with singular A_{11} and (if $m = n$) B_{21}, B_{22}.

determined such that these ratios are arranged in order of decreasing modulus. Partitioning F, G, U, V in submatrices of the same format as the matrices B_{ij} in (8.60), it can then be shown that R and subsequently P are given by

$$R = G_{12}G_{22}^{-1}, \quad P = G_{22}U_{22}^{-1}V_{22}G_{22}^{-1} \quad (8.63)$$

The relatively straightforward formulae for the remaining two matrices Q and S may be looked up in McCallum (1999, sect. 3), where the derivation of (8.63) can also be found. The matrix P is stable if the number of generalized eigenvalues λ_i with modulus less than one equals the number of predetermined variables (i.e. $n = 8$ in the present model).

The second approach to solve (8.60)–(8.62) for P, Q, R, S, which is discussed in Uhlig (1999), section 6.2), determines the matrix P in the first step. It turns out that this amounts to solving a quadratic matrix equation in P, which is no less involved than the procedure just described. Before turning to the operations themselves, we announce that they make use of the concept of the pseudo-inverse of matrix B_{21} (Uhlig also gives further hints to this and other advanced mathematics that he uses). Generally, the pseudo-inverse of a matrix $C \in \mathbb{R}^{n \times m}$ is the matrix $C^+ \in \mathbb{R}^{m \times n}$ satisfying $C^+CC^+ = C^+$ and $CC^+C = C$. If C has full rank, C^+ is given by $C^+ = (C'C)^{-1}C'$, so that $C^+C = (C'C)^{-1}C'C = I$.

As before, the analysis starts out from (8.60). Assuming that B_{21} has full rank, we can rewrite the second block in this equation as $B_{21}R = P - B_{22}$, premultiply it by B_{21}^+ and so get

$$R = B_{21}^+(P - B_{22}) \quad (8.64)$$

Substitution in the first block of (8.60) and rearranging terms leads to

$$A_{11}^+B_{21}P^2 - [A_{11}^+B_{21}B_{22} + B_{11}B_{21}^+]P - B_{11}B_{21}^+B_{22} - B_{12} = 0 \quad (8.65)$$

(8.65) is complemented by another equation in P. It involves a matrix B_{21}^0, the rows of which form a basis of the null space of B_{21}, such that $B_{21}^0B_{21} = 0$ (for a matrix $C \in \mathbb{R}^{n \times m}$ with $n > m$, C^0 has $n - m$ rows and n columns). As a consequence, premultiplication of the second block in (8.60) by B_{21}^0 gives us

$$B_{21}^0P - B_{21}^0B_{22} = 0 \quad (8.66)$$

To combine the conditions (8.65) and (8.66) in a compact form, define

$$H_0 = \begin{bmatrix} B_{11}B_{21}^+B_{22} + B_{12} \\ B_{21}^0B_{22} \end{bmatrix}, \quad H_1 = \begin{bmatrix} A_{11}^+B_{21}B_{22} + B_{11}B_{21}^+ \\ -B_{21}^0 \end{bmatrix}, \quad H_2 = \begin{bmatrix} A_{11}^+B_{21} \\ 0 \end{bmatrix}$$

In this way we finally end up with the quadratic matrix equation in P,

$$H_2 P^2 - H_1 P - H_o = 0 \tag{8.67}$$

Uhlig (1999, sect. 6.3) gives the additional hint that eq. (8.67) can be solved by turning it into a generalized eigenvalue problem (for which most mathematical packages have preprogrammed routines). This problem differs, however, from the eigenvalue problem appearing in McCallum's analysis. Once a meaningful solution for P is found (which should render P stable), matrix R is directly obtained from (8.64). Subsequently, as mentioned above, Q and S can be computed.

To conclude, there exist several procedures in the literature that allow one to determine all four matrices P, Q, R, S in the reduced-form equations (8.58), (8.59) from the model's structural matrices A, B, D, N. It has become clear, however, that the coefficients of the latter are transformed in highly complicated ways. Despite the fascinating mathematical and computational challenges, of which we have gained a first impression, it seems to us that the effort to deal with these complications and the repercussion effects to which they give rise are quite disproportional in comparison to the originally formulated structural relationships, which are still of a fairly elementary nature. Are such models really useful to policymakers given that all the important dynamics feedback effects are contained in a huge black box, and that nearly every economic effect that is non-trivial has to be attributed to the agents' perfect forward-looking capabilities? The remark made in subsection 8.4.1, that policymakers tend to take backward-looking models more seriously than models that rely on forward-looking expectations, is now understandable. Thus, it may at least be asked why the New-Keynesian methodology (in the sense of the introductory equation (8.32)) should be considered better, more profound or more insightful than the approach of, as they are called, purely backward-looking models, in which (in principle in more or less sophisticated econometric ways) expectations are formed on the basis of past observations only.

9 Incorporating the Taylor rule into KMG

9.1 Introduction

After studying the Taylor rule in the setting of small macrodynamic models in chapter 8, we now take the obvious step and integrate these interest rate adjustments into the KMG model. It has already been made clear that the Taylor rule is here substituted for the LM part of the model, while all the other components of KMG are maintained. We can emphasize this conception by calling the resulting model a *Keynes–Metzler–Goodwin–Taylor model*. Referring to the full label is somewhat cumbersome, but the simple acronym KMGT is more fluid. Since it also has the advantage of squarely pointing to the distinction between employing, or not employing, the Taylor rule in our KMG framework, we hereby formally introduce the term KMGT. It will be used in particular when we compare the properties of this new model to those of the original KMG model.

In setting up the reduced form of the KMGT model, it turns out that the KMG model's equation for the motion of real balances $m = M/pK$ is replaced by a differential equation for the rate of interest i. The equations governing the other five dynamic variables are preserved, except that now the interest rate enters directly as a state variable in the investment function instead of the LM schedule $i = i_{LM}(m, y^e, n)$. Already this moderate change, however, makes a serious difference, in that the attractive properties that have been found in the KMG model do not generally carry over to KMGT. As a consequence, a stability condition of the kind that sufficiently low reaction intensities in a few selected behavioural relationships guarantee local stability, which we were previously able to prove analytically and which we feel should similarly hold true in KMGT, can now be addressed only in numerical ways. All this – the mathematical stability analysis, its limitations, and a numerical Monte Carlo simulation of stability conditions – is treated in section 9.2.

Subsequently, in section 9.3, we turn to the global dynamics, for the numerical analysis of which we adopt the estimated Taylor rule coefficients from chapter 8, section 2, subsection 3. Maintaining the numerical parameters from the calibration of the KMG model (except for one), we look for suitable values of the four coefficients in the linear and nonlinear part of the investment function that render the equilibrium unstable and generate a unique and stable limit cycle, which should, moreover, exhibit similar cyclical features to KMG.

In addition, however, we want to relate the KMGT model to the Rudebusch–Svensson model discussed in chapter 8, section 4. To this end a second scenario of the investment coefficients is considered that stabilizes the steady-state position (where we also require that, just as in RS, the leading eigenvalue of the Jacobian is real). Besides comparing the impulse–response functions of the two models, we introduce quarterly random shocks on a supply and a demand component into KMGT and then compare the time paths of a sample run to that of the stochastic (quarterly) RS model. It will be seen that the richer structure of the KMGT model pays off, in the sense that (even with a real leading eigenvalue) it behaves more satisfactorily than RS. On the whole, we thus establish that both the deterministic and the stochastic versions of KMGT are workable numerical macroeconomic models of medium size.[1]

Sections 9.4 and 9.5 are devoted to the effects from *ceteris paribus* parameter changes. Section 9.4 concentrates on the policy coefficients. Here it is examined whether they stabilize or destabilize the steady state, and also how they affect the time paths of, in particular, utilization, inflation and the interest rate. These investigations are carried out for both the deterministic and stochastic versions mentioned above. Section 9.5 is concerned with the other behavioural parameters, where for simplicity we content ourselves with their impact on local stability. Our goal is to categorize them succinctly as stabilizing, destabilizing or ambiguous in the KMGT model. Finally, this list is contrasted with the parameter characterization at which we have arrived with the KMG model, so that we can conclude with a neat summary of the basic properties of the two models.

9.2   The Keynes–Metzler–Goodwin–Taylor model

After studying the effects of the Taylor-type interest rate reaction function in small macrodynamic models, it is time to return to the central modelling framework of the book, the Keynes–Metzler–Goodwin model,

---

[1] Regarding calibration, the stochastic version may still be improved upon by a more suitable choice of the investment coefficients, which would reinforce the model's cyclical potential, but we will not pursue this issue any further.

and to investigate how the Taylor rule acts on it. Thus, we proceed from KMG to KMGT: the Keynes–Metzler–Goodwin–Taylor model. Although the accumulation of patron saints is somewhat cumbersome, it is expressive of the model's key elements. The acronym is more fluid and mainly a matter of habit.

9.2.1   Formulation of the model

Most of the relationships of the KMG model remain unaffected by the introduction of an interest rate rule. Basically, there is only one major change. As indicated in chapter 8, section 2, subsection 1, real balances $m = M/pK$ disappear from the model and are replaced by the nominal interest rate i as a dynamic variable of its own. That is, i no longer derives from LM and is statically endogenously determined by the functional relationship $i = i(m, y^e, n)$ of eq. (4.39), but it is also governed by the same differential equation (8.4) that has already been specified for the two prototype models with interest rate smoothing in chapter 8, section 3, subsections 3 and 4. Correspondingly, eq. (8.4) is substituted for KMG's differential equation (4.45) that determined the changes in m. The only place where, in turn, the interest rate enters in other parts of the model is the investment function f_I; here the LM function $i = i(m, y^e, n)$ has to be replaced merely by the variable i, which has become a state variable.

It has been mentioned above that the interest rate i in a Taylor rule is a short-term rate of interest. Concretely, it may be identified with the federal funds rate in the United States. On the other hand, the interest rate in an investment function should relate to a longer time horizon. When we nevertheless use i as an argument in f_I, we implicitly assume that long-term und short-term rates move in step – which is a simplification. We are, however, in good company in this respect. Almost all the models of which the Rudebusch–Svensson model in chapter 8, section 4 was a representative example employ the short cut as well (without making reference to a rate of profit as the alternative rate of return to which it is compared, as we do). We may thus follow Rudebusch and Svensson in that we touch upon several monetary transmission mechanisms (only symbolically now) and then conclude that the use of the short-term real rate of interest as a determinant of aggregate demand 'appears to be a workable approximation of these various intermediate transmission mechanisms' (Rudebusch and Svensson, 1999, p. 207).

In its reduced form, the KMGT model is again of dimension six. The six state variables are:

ω the real wage rate (deflated by trend productivity), $\omega = (w/p)/z^o$;
i the short-term rate of interest;
y^e expected demand as a ratio of the capital stock, $y^e = Y^e/K$;
k^s the capital–labour ratio (in efficiency units), $k^s = K/z^oL^s$;
n the inventory–capital ratio, $n = N/K$; and
π the inflation climate.
       (9.1)

In a statically endogenous manner, they determine the Taylor rate of interest i^*, the output–capital ratio y, capacity utilization u, the wage share v, the employment rate e, the rate of price inflation $\hat{p}$, the return differential q (the difference between profit rate and real interest rate), the growth rate of the capital stock g_k, and aggregate demand in intensive form $y^d = Y^d/K$. Except for i^*, which is taken over from eq. (8.3), the functional expressions have been derived in chapter 4, section 3. Taking account of the change in the role of the interest rate, we now have:

$$i^* = i^*(\hat{p}, u) = (i^o - \hat{p}^*) + \hat{p} + \alpha_p(\hat{p} - \hat{p}^*) + \alpha_u(u - 1) \qquad (9.2)$$

$$y = y(y^e, n) = [1 + (g^o + \beta_{nn})\beta_{ny}]y^e - \beta_{nn}n \qquad (9.3)$$

$$u = u(y^e, n) = y/y^n \qquad (9.4)$$

$$v = v(\omega, y^e, n) = \omega/f_z(u) \qquad (9.5)$$

$$e = e(y^e, k^s, n) = yk^s/f_z(u) \qquad (9.6)$$

$$f_p = f_p(\omega, y^e, n) = \beta_{pu}(u - 1) + \beta_{pv}[(1 + \mu)v - 1] \qquad (9.7)$$

$$f_w = f_w(\omega, y^e, k^s, n) = \beta_{we}(e - 1) - \beta_{wv}(v - v^o)/v^o \qquad (9.8)$$

$$\hat{p} = \hat{p}(\omega, y^e, k^s, n, \pi) = \pi + \kappa(f_p + \kappa_p f_w), \quad \kappa := 1/(1 - \kappa_p\kappa_w) \qquad (9.9)$$

$$q = q(\omega, i, y^e, n, \pi) = (1 - v)y - \delta - (i - \pi) \qquad (9.10)$$

$$g_k = g_k(\omega, i, y^e, n, \pi) = f_I(u, q) \qquad (9.11)$$

$$y^d = y^d(\omega, i, y^e, n, \pi) = (1 - s_c)y^e + (s_c - \tau_w)vy + g_k$$
$$+ \gamma + c_p + s_c\delta - (1 - s_c)\theta_c \qquad (9.12)$$

As for the constant parameters involved, we, in particular, recall that $\hat{p}^*$ is the central bank's target rate of inflation and $(i^o - \hat{p}^*)$ the real rate of interest in the steady state;[2] g^o is the equilibrium growth rate (exogenously given by technical progress and the growth of the labour force); y^n is the output–capital ratio under 'normal' conditions; $f_z(\cdot)$ represents the procyclical element in labour productivity; f_p and f_w are the core terms in the price and wage Phillips curve, respectively; μ is the target markup over labour unit costs; v^o is the equilibrium wage share, which satisfies $(1 + \mu)v^o = 1$; δ is the capital depreciation rate, and $(1 - v)y - \delta$ the expression for the operative rate of profit of firms; the investment function $f_I(\cdot, \cdot)$ increases in both utilization and the return differential; s_c is the propensity to save out of rental income; τ_w is the tax rate on wages; γ is the ratio of government spending; c_p is a parameter in the consumption function (4.4);[3] and θ_c is the tax parameter for rental income.

The six differential equations into which the KMGT model can be transformed are given by the equations (4.44)–(4.49) from chapter 4, section 3, where, first, eq. (8.4) governing the adjustments of the nominal interest rate replaces eq. (4.45) for the real balances $m = M/pK$ and, second, possible changes in the role of the arguments in the functional expressions have to be taken into account. The various terms showing up in the equations are now specified in (9.2)–(9.12). The way in which they are written down makes clear that it is indeed only the six variables listed in (8.32) that enter the six laws of motions. On this basis, our Keynes–Metzler–Goodwin–Taylor model is fully described by the following differential equations system, which is well defined:

$$\dot{\omega} = \omega\kappa[(1 - \kappa_p)f_w - (1 - \kappa_w)f_p], \quad \kappa := 1/(1 - \kappa_p\kappa_w) \tag{9.13}$$

$$di/dt = \alpha_i(i^* - i) \tag{9.14}$$

$$\dot{y}^e = (g^o - g_k)y^e + \beta_y(y^d - y^e) \tag{9.15}$$

$$\dot{k}^s = k^s(g_k - g^o) \tag{9.16}$$

$$\dot{n} = y - y^d - ng_k \tag{9.17}$$

$$\dot{\pi} = \beta_\pi[\kappa_\pi\kappa(\kappa_p f_w + f_p) + (1 - \kappa_\pi)(\pi^o - \pi)], \quad \pi^o = \hat{p}^\star \tag{9.18}$$

---

[2] Listing $\hat{p}$ and u as the direct entries of i^* in (9.2) is in line with eq. (8.3) but is not strictly consistent with the use of the arguments in the other expressions of the equations block, which is to point out that each term is a function of no more than the six state variables in (9.1). It is clear that, through (9.3) and (9.8), i^* is on the whole dependent on $(\omega, y^e, k^s, n, \pi)$.

[3] It captures the consumption of that part of the population who do not earn income from economic activities.

It goes without saying that, again, the two weights κ_p and κ_w are not both unity. Regarding the regressive expectations in (9.18) for the changes of the inflation climate, it is directly assumed that their pivot is consistent with the central bank's inflation target $\hat{p}^*$.

Given the parameters of the model it will, of course, be expected that a set of variables that constitutes a steady-state position in the KMG model performs the same function in the KMGT model just as well. Besides the compatibility of the target markup μ (in the core term f_p (9.7) of the price Phillips curve) with equilibrium income distribution, this now also requires the central bank to know the equilibrium real rate of interest. The reason for grounding the Taylor rate of interest i^* in (9.2) on a correct value of the real interest rate is that it takes effect in the investment function, which in equilibrium has to support the exogenously given equilibrium growth rate g^o. Since the profit rate is another determinant of investment, the central bank must also know the equilibrium wage share and how changes in the return differential q affect fixed investment. We make these consistency postulates explicit as an extra assumption.

Assumption 1

1. *The central bank sets i^o in the Taylor rate of interest (9.2) so that it satisfies the equation*

$$f_I[u^o, (1-v^o)y^n - \delta - (i^o - \hat{p}^*)] = g^o,$$

where $g^o = g_z + g_\ell$ is the exogenous equilibrium growth rate (the sum of the growth rates of productivity and labour supply), $u^o = 1$ is normal utilization and, given the parameters of the model, v^o is determined as

$$v^o = \frac{s_c y^n/(1+g^o\beta_{ny}) - g^o - \gamma - c_p - s_c\delta + (1-s_c)\theta_c}{(s_c - \tau_w)y^n}.$$

2. *The target markup rate μ entering the core term f_p of the price Phillips curve, which here shows up in (9.7), is compatible with the wage share v^o. Correspondingly, μ satisfies the equation $(1+\mu)v^o = 1$.*

Within the strict context of the model, Assumption 1.1 demands a considerable amount of information from the central bank about the structure of the economy. In reality, this may be less dramatic. On the one hand, the central bank will have a certain idea of what range of the real interest rate is (or would be) compatible with normal utilization and equilibrium (or trend) growth. At least in a wider distance from the steady state, on the other hand, errors in this respect may be viewed as being dominated by the response of i^* to the output and inflation gap. Hence, even if the central bank bases its calculation of i^* on a wrong value of i^o, the interest rate i^* would still exceed the true value of i^o when, because of $\alpha_p(\hat{p} - \hat{p}^*) + \alpha_u(u - 1) > 0$, it should do so. In this case only the implied coefficients α_p or α_u (if the true value of i^o were underlying) would deviate from the intended responsiveness. In the simulations we will nevertheless return to this issue and ask how robust the dynamics are to changes in the value of i^o.

Just like the corresponding (perhaps implicit) assumptions in the Rudebusch–Svensson model and the many other models in this vein, Assumption 1 serves mainly to ease the exposition and concentrate on the essential effects. Taking it for granted, the steady-state position of the KMG model carries over.

Proposition 1
If Assumption 1 holds true, system (9.13)–(9.19) has an equilibrium position that, denoting it by superscript 'o', is given as follows:

$$u^o = e^o = 1, \quad y^o = y^n, \quad \hat{p}^o = \pi^o = \hat{p}^*, \quad i^*(\hat{p}^*, u^o) = i^o,$$

$$\omega^o = v^o = \frac{s_c y^n/(1 + g^o\beta_{ny}) - g^o - \gamma - c_p - s_c\delta + (1 - s_c)\theta_c}{(s_c - \tau_w)y^n},$$

$$(k^s)^o = 1/y^n,$$

$$(y^d)^o = (y^e)^o = y^n/(1 + g^o\beta_{ny}), \quad n^o = \beta_{ny}y^n/(1 + g^o\beta_{ny}).$$

Proof: $\dot{k}^s = 0$ and then $\dot{y}^e = 0$ imply $(g_k)^o = g^o$ and $(y^d)^o = (y^e)^o$. Inserting (9.3) in $\dot{n} = 0$ gives $0 = y - y^d - ng_k = y - y^e - ng^o = [1 + (g^o + \beta_{nm})\beta_{ny}]y^e - \beta_{nm}n - y^e - ng^o = (g^o + \beta_{nm})\beta_{ny}y^e - (\beta_{nm} + g^o)n$. Hence $n^o = \beta_{ny}(y^e)^o$. Substituting this back in (9.3) and solving for y^e, we have $(y^e)^o = y^o/(1 + g^o\beta_{ny})$ and $n^o = \beta_{ny}y^o/(1 + g^o\beta_{ny})$. Incidentally, these relationships must hold in any stationary point of (9.15)–(9.17).

Using $g_k = g^o$ and the just derived expression for $(y^e)^o$ in (9.12), equating this expression for $y^d = (y^d)^o$ to $y^e = (y^e)^o$ and solving it for v yields the proposition's formula for v^o. It is then obvious that $u = u^o = 1$ $e = e^o = 1$ and $v = v^o$, together with Assumption 1.2, give $f_p = f_w = 0$ and, thus, $\dot{\omega} = 0$.

$\pi = \pi^o = \hat{p}^*$, furthermore, ensures that $\dot{\pi} = 0$ and also $\hat{p}^o = \hat{p}^*$ in (9.9). The nominal interest rate in the equilibrium is $i = i^*(\hat{p}^o, u^o) = i^o$, just as the latter rate is set by the central bank. By virtue of Assumption 1.1, the interest rate now entails that the predetermined equilibrium growth rate g^o is supported by the investment function (9.11), $g^o = (g_k)^o = f_I(u^o, q^o)$. Finally, it remains to note that $y^o = y^n$ by (9.4), $(k^s)^o = 1/y^n$ by (9.6) and $\omega^o = v^o$ by (9.5); as for the latter two equalities, recall the specification $f_z(u^o) = f_z(1) = 1$.

QED

9.2.2 *Possible non-uniqueness of the equilibrium*

In the KMG model, not only the existence but also the uniqueness of the steady-state position was taken as a matter of course. A rigorous proof was in fact straightforward and could proceed step by step; see Proposition 2 and its proof in chapter 4, section 3. In the present model, however, this kind of argument breaks down. The main reason is that step 3 of the proof no longer goes through, by which it was ascertained that the core terms f_p and f_w in the two Phillips curves must both be zero.[4] Once $f_p = f_w = 0$ is no longer ensured right from the beginning, equating the right-hand sides of (9.13)–(9.18) to zero gives several equations that determine the equilibrium values of two or even three variables, while there are no other equations that would allow us to express one of them in terms of the others.

Moreover, this is not only a problem of a difficult mathematical proof. We find that a second and third stationary point of (9.13)–(9.14) may indeed exist. To enquire into this possibility, it proves convenient to consider a special class of economies where two coefficients are put equal to zero. Within this setting, we can reveal that uniqueness is ensured if the investment function (9.11) is linear (which, nevertheless, requires some effort). In contrast, its nonlinearity can give rise to additional equilibrium points. Since this result is remarkable enough, and, of course, we still focus on the normal steady state of Proposition 1 with, in particular, 'normal' utilization, we will leave it at that and refrain from searching for possible further causes for non-uniqueness.

The analytical part of these findings is formulated in Proposition 2. The occurrence of multiple equilibria under a nonlinear investment function is subsequently demonstrated by means of a numerical example. Here we also present dynamic trajectories starting out from the (perturbed) normal steady state, which are of interest on their own.

---

[4] This step involved the differential equation for the real balances $m = M/pK$, which, as has been pointed out, is now replaced by the adjustments of the rate of interest.

Proposition 2

Besides Assumption 1, suppose that $\kappa_p = 0$ and $\beta_{pv} = 0$. Then the following holds true for system (9.13)–(9.18).

1. *The steady-state position of Proposition 1 is locally unique.*
2. *This equilibrium is unique over the range of variables where the investment function $g_k = f_I(u, q)$ of (9.11) is linear in its two entries; that is, where it is of the form*

$$f_I(u, q) = g^o + \beta_{Iu}(u - u^o) + \beta_{Iq}(q - q^o)$$

(β_{Iu} and β_{Iq} being non-negative and positive constant parameters, respectively).
3. *Additional equilibria may exist in regions of the state space where $f_I(\cdot, \cdot)$ is nonlinear.*

If not the second part of the proposition, we would have liked to extend at least the weaker result of the first part to the general case when the supposition $\kappa_p = \beta_{pv} = 0$ is dropped. Although the property seems very obvious, a mathematical proof turns out to be extremely complicated. We therefore content ourselves with the hint that a zero determinant of the Jacobian matrix is a necessary (but not sufficient) condition for a continuum of equilibria, and that in the numerical stability analysis below we observe this for special parameter combinations only.[5] In this sense, local uniqueness can still be taken for granted.

Proof: The core of the proof of Proposition 2.2 is establishing an equation that determines the steady-state value of utilization u in a unique way. Working back in the model's equations it is, subsequently, seen readily that the equilibrium values of the other variables are also unique. The whole procedure is subdivided into seven steps, where the superscript 'o' or another indication of the equilibrium situation is omitted.

1. $\dot{\pi} = 0$, together with $\kappa_p = 0$ and $\beta_{pv} = 0$, gives $\kappa_\pi \kappa \beta_{pu}(u - 1) + (1 - \kappa_\pi)(\pi^o - \pi) = 0$. The equilibrium value of π can thus be expressed as a linear function of the equilibrium value of u, with slope $A_{\pi u}$ and constant term $A_{\pi c}$: $\pi = A_{\pi c} + A_{\pi u} u$.
2. Substituting this in (9.9) for the rate of inflation, it is seen that, by virtue of $\kappa_p = 0$ and $\beta_{pv} = 0$, $\hat{p}$ is a linear function u, $\hat{p} = A_{pc} + A_{pu} u$.

---

[5] Mathematically speaking, the set of these parameters has measure zero. Or, less technically, the unconditional probability that arbitrary parameter values will entail $\det \mathcal{J} = 0$ for the system's Jacobian $\mathcal{J}$ is zero.

3. Substituting the expression for $\hat{p}$ in (9.2) for $i = i^*$, the difference $i - i^o$ can be written in the form $i - i^o = A_{ic} + A_{iu}u$.

4. From the first part of the proof of Proposition 1 and $y = y^n u$ from (9.4), we know that $y^e = y^n u/(1 + g^o \beta_{ny})$ and $n = \beta_{ny} y^n u/(1 + g^o \beta_{ny})$. Plugging this into $0 = \dot{n} = y - y^d - n g_k$, using the condition $g^k = g^o$ and eqs. (9.4), (9.12) for y and y^d, and solving the resulting equation for vy, we obtain an equation of the form $vy = A_{vc} + A_{vu}u$.

5. On the basis of the steps above, $q = (1 - v)y - \delta - (i - \pi) = y^n u - vy - \delta - (i - i^o) - i^o + \pi$ can be written as $q = A_{qc} + A_{qu}u$.

6. Over the range where the investment function is linear, any equilibrium point must satisfy the equation $g^o = g_k = f_I(u, q) = \phi(u) := g^o + \beta_{Iu}(u - 1) + \beta_{Iq}(q - q^o)$. Taking account of step 5, this equation has the form $g^o = A_{Ic} + A_{Iu}u$. Since it is linear in u, the equilibrium value of u is uniquely determined.

7. The uniqueness of the equilibrium values of $\pi = A_{\pi c} + A_{\pi u}u$ and, likewise, of i, y^e, n and v is then obvious from the previous steps. Subsequently, the uniqueness of e follows from $\dot{\omega} = 0$. Eqs. (9.6) and (9.7) finally allow us to compute the unique equilibrium values of k^s and ω as the last two state variables.

As regards the first part of the proposition, it suffices to note that steps 1 to 5 can be the same and that, locally around u^o, the function $\phi = \phi(u)$ in step 6, in which β_{Iu} and β_{Iq} may now no longer be constant, is strictly increasing or decreasing (since, in the linear approximation $\beta_{Iq} = f_{Iq} = \partial f_I/\partial q > 0$, $\beta_{Iu} = f_{Iu} = \partial f_I/\partial u \geq 0$). Hence, locally, $u = u^o$ is the only value satisfying $g^o = \phi(u)$. Step 7 then completes the proof of the local uniqueness of the entire equilibrium position of Proposition 1.

QED

In the remainder of this subsection on possible multiple equilibria, the third statement of Proposition 2 is proved by means of a numerical example. We begin by collecting the variables' steady-state values of Proposition 1 and the structural parameters that give rise to them. This is essentially a reiteration of eq. (6.27) in the calibration of chapter 6, section 4, subsection 1. Exceptions are the following three points. (1) The real balances ratio m^o and the money growth rate g_m are dropped. (2) Since the interest rate is now a short-term rate, we diminish the previous 7 per cent; let us work with an equilibrium value of 4.5 per cent. (3) We also slightly reduce equilibrium inflation, which is given by the central bank's target rate $\hat{p}^*$ and for which we now adopt a rate of 2.5 per cent.

Naturally, both choices are not crucial; they are only a matter of scale. We thus have (numbers occasionally rounded)

$$\hat{p}^* = 2.5\% \qquad \pi^o = 2.5\% \qquad i^o = 4.5\% \qquad g^o = 3\%$$

$$\omega = 0.70 \qquad v^o = 70\% \qquad \mu = 0.429$$

$$y^n = 0.70 \qquad (k^s)^o = 1.429 \qquad (y^e)^o = 0.695 \qquad n^o = 0.153 \qquad (9.19)$$

$$\delta = 9.5\% \qquad \gamma = 0.077 \qquad \theta_c = 0.025 \qquad \beta_{ny} = 0.220$$

Besides the particular kind of nonlinearity in the investment function, the additional equilibrium or equilibria depend on a number of reaction coefficients, though not on all. Those that are not relevant in this respect may nevertheless have a bearing on the system's stability properties. Since we also present a sample dynamics, we report the numerical values of all parameters.

As regards the policy coefficients, eq. (8.8) is taken over, except that here we temporarily set the output gap coefficient to zero. Apart from the investment function, the other parameters are mostly borrowed from the calibration procedure. The only changes we make in the corresponding eq. (6.30), where the parameters are summarized, are that zero values are assigned to β_{pv} as well as κ_π, and that the interest rate elasticity $\eta_{m,i}$ of the money demand function is discarded since it no longer matters. On the whole, the parameters read as follows:[6]

$$\beta_{zu} = 0.40$$

$$\alpha_i = 1.10 \qquad \alpha_p = 0.40 \qquad \alpha_u = 0.00$$

$$\beta_{pu} = 0.15 \qquad \beta_{pv} = 0.00 \qquad \kappa_p = 0.00$$

$$\beta_{we} = 0.55 \qquad \beta_{wv} = 0.50 \qquad \kappa_w = 0.00 \qquad (9.20)$$

$$\beta_\pi = 1.00 \qquad \kappa_\pi = 0.00$$

$$s_c = 0.80 \qquad \tau_w = 0.35 \qquad \beta_y = 8.00$$

$$\beta_{nn} = 3.00$$

Departing from the linear specification of the investment function as it was formulated in Proposition 2.2, the nonlinear modification of chapter 6, section 7, subsection 1 is close at hand for us. To capture a precautionary motive in the more extreme stages of the business cycle,

---

[6] As for β_{zu}, we recall the linear specification of the labour productivity function $z/z^o = f_z(u) = 1 + \beta_{zu}(u-1)$ from eq. (5.1), chapter 5, section 3, subsection 1.

it addresses the responsiveness β_{Iq} to the return differential q and makes it a flexible function of u and q. So, we need only introduce two positive parameters d_1, d_2, with $0 < d_1 < d_2$, and reiterate eqs. (6.32) and (6.33):

$$g_k = g_k(u, q) = g^o + \beta_{Iu}(u - 1) + \phi(u, q)\beta_{Iq}(q - q^o) \qquad (9.21)$$

$$\phi = \phi(u, q) = \begin{cases} 1 + [u - (1 + d_1)]/(d_2 - d_1) & \text{if } u \geq 1 + d_1 \text{ and } q \leq q^o \\ 1 + [(1 - d_1) - u]/(d_2 - d_1) & \text{if } u \leq 1 - d_1 \text{ and } q \geq q^o \\ 1 & \text{else} \end{cases}$$

$$(9.22)$$

The four coefficients in (9.21), (9.22) are assigned the following values:

$$\beta_{Iu} = 0.100 \quad \beta_{Iq} = 0.050 \quad d_1 = 0.020 \quad d_2 = 0.035 \qquad (9.23)$$

If the nonlinearity is able to bring a second stationary point of system (9.13)–(9.18) into being then, because of its symmetric character, a third one should also exist with values lying on the other side of the normal equilibrium values of eq. (9.19). This is indeed what we compute. Designating the two new equilibria by superscripts 1 and 2 and limiting ourselves to the three central variables utilization, inflation and the interest rate, we get

$$u^{1,2} = u^o \pm \Delta u \quad \hat{p}^{1,2} = \hat{p}^* \pm \Delta\hat{p} \quad i^{1,2} = i^o \pm \Delta i$$

$$\Delta u = 0.04520 \quad \Delta\hat{p} = 0.67799\% \quad \Delta i = 0.94919\%$$

$$(9.24)$$

In particular, the alternative lower rates of interest and inflation are both still positive (incidentally, satisfying this requirement is facilitated by putting $\alpha_u = 0$).

Additional equilibria can be neglected if they are unstable and the trajectories of the system are otherwise meaningful. To check this, we let the economy start in the normal steady state and then subject it to an adverse demand shock. However, if it is specified as a one-time perturbation of aggregate demand y^d in eq. (9.12), the effect on utilization u will be rather weak, since it is channelled through expected sales y^e via (9.3), (9.4), and these adjust only partially to the observed change in demand. Hence, soon after the shock, in the next short period, so to speak, y^d will return close to its original level $(y^d)^o$, so that y^e as well as u will have hardly moved in response to the shock.

To produce a stronger and less temporary output effect, similar to that in the impulse–response function for the Rudebusch–Svensson model in figure 8.3 (chapter 8, section 4, subsection 3), we assume a sudden drop in sales expectations directly, at time $t = 0$. The postulated fall in y^e decreases y and, therefore, utilization u and, the employment rate e (see eqs. (9.4) and (9.6)), which in turn impacts on inflation: now explicitly price and wage inflation in the two Phillips curves. Income distribution reacts, too; immediately by eq. (9.5) and through the change in real wages in (9.13). Beginning with these effects, all the variables of (9.13)–(9.18) are affected by the initial shock and the whole dynamic system is set into motion. Focusing on the same three variables as in the Rudebusch–Svensson model (utilization u (the counterpart of the output gap), the rate of price inflation $\hat{p}$, and the nominal short-term rate of interest i), the adjustments over the first ten years after the shock are shown in figure 9.1.

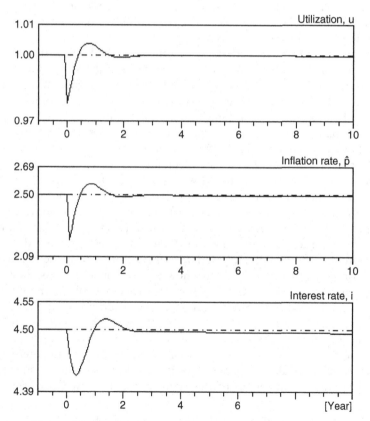

Figure 9.1: The trajectory of the KMGT model after an adverse demand shock

It is interesting to compare the time paths with those in figure 8.3. Common to both diagrams are three features: the fall in output decreases inflation; in response the central bank reduces the interest rate; and the fact that this measure is capable of bringing output and inflation back towards normal. A difference is the overshooting not only of output but also of inflation. More importantly, in figure 9.1[7] there is not the least indication of the strong persistence in the rate of inflation that prevailed in the RS model. In fact, it now takes only six months for $\hat{p}$ to reach its target again. Since, in addition, the ensuing overshooting is moderate, it seems that the economy has essentially returned to the original steady-state position within two years. This is in sharp contrast to the convergence time of twenty years and more in the RS model, which we considered a weakness of its dynamic properties. Thus, the present model with the parameters from (9.19), (9.20), (9.23) appears to provide more favourable conditions for the working of the Taylor interest rate rule. Note also that, so far, the nonlinearity in the investment function has not become effective.

However, one might perhaps be a little disturbed about the further evolution of the interest rate, where it looks as if the slight downward deviation from $i^o = 4.50\%$ would widen over the years (though we would have failed to become aware of this phenomenon if the economy were exposed to only minor random influences). Figure 9.2, which extends the time paths of figure 9.1 beyond $t = 10$, reveals that the widening gap, tiny though it remained in the first ten years, has to be taken seriously. In fact, it was a first clue to the instability of the equilibrium (9.19), which, again, has nothing to do with nonlinear investment. What we observe in the long run is a very slow but unbroken, monotonic divergence from u^o, $\hat{p}^*$, i^o, respectively. After a long period of some eighty years, the time paths eventually swing in towards new equilibrium values, which are the lower values given in (9.24). Obviously, since u deviates by more than $d_1 = 0.020$ and even $d_2 = 0.035$ from $u^o = 1$, the nonlinear function $\phi = \phi(u, q)$ in (9.22) has now become operative. As stated in Proposition 2.3, figure 9.2 thus gives evidences that suitable nonlinearities in the investment function can give rise to additional equilibria.

The adjustment paths shown in figures 9.1 and 9.2 are not dependent on the special way in which the steady state (9.19) was perturbed. The same equilibrium u^1, $\hat{p}^1$, i^1, etc. is approached in a similar manner if the initial shock is weaker or stronger, or if the other variables are shocked, too. Over a certain region of the state space, the new equilibrium is

---

[7] System (9.13)–(9.18) with steady-state parameters (9.19) and reaction coefficients (9.20), (9.23). The nonlinearity (9.21), (9.22) – i.e. the flexibility function ϕ – does not take effect.

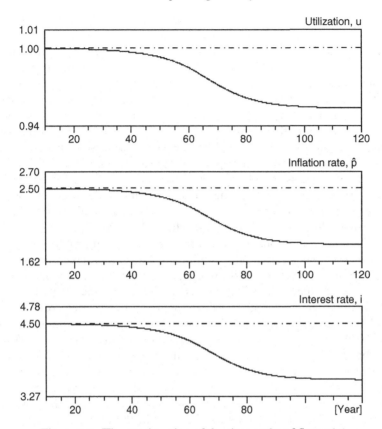

Figure 9.2: The continuation of the time paths of figure 9.1

therefore attracting. Furthermore, a mirror image of the trajectories in figures 9.1 and 9.2 is obtained if the system is set in motion by a positive demand shock. In this case, the economy converges to the other equilibrium u^2, $\hat{p}^2$, i^2 specified in (9.24). It is likewise stable, and its basin of attraction is symmetric to that of u^1, $\hat{p}^1$, i^1 (with u^o, $\hat{p}^\star$, i^o as pivot).

Although the alternative equilibrium values (9.24) are within an economically meaningful range, this does not imply that the equilibrium positions themselves are reasonable. Indeed, such a state of the economy would hardly be reproduced by the agents. What, for example, is the meaning of the central bank's target rate of inflation and its interest rate reaction function if the target is constantly missed? What is the meaning of 'normal' utilization u^o as a benchmark in the disequilibrium adjustment mechanisms when it is never observed and, instead, another level of utilization incessantly prevails – or another output–capital ratio $y \neq y^n$, for that matter? If we refer to the convergence path of figure 9.2, it will be argued that, long before the second equilibrium is reached, the agents will realize that the economy is going astray (or the variables pertinent to them) and, consequently, change their behaviour. This means that the model equations as they have been formulated above would no longer apply; the economic agents would be in a different model, we may say.

This argument may suggest looking for a better specification of some parts of the model that would rule out multiple equilibria. On the one hand, however, this is not very desirable, since the present specifications are quite convenient in other respects. On the other hand, a respecification is not strictly necessary. The reason is that additional unstable equilibria are, is practice, irrelevant for the model's dynamics, and that additional stable equilibria do not raise a new problem but simply make us more conscious of an already existing problem – the problem of viability.

If the steady-state position on which we focus is unstable, and if in addition the trajectories are not confined to a meaningful region in which they persistently cycle around (in a regular or complex manner), then it does not really matter if divergence is complete and some of the variables eventually attain meaningless values, or if the trajectories converge to another stationary point in which the agents' behaviour would have to be considered meaningless. In either case, the system is not viable. And, in either case, if we wish to maintain the modelling framework, we will have to search for other, justifiable parameter values that render the 'good' equilibrium stable or generate sustained cyclical dynamics.

In conclusion, three findings are noteworthy. First, with the possible occurrence of multiple equilibria that are, furthermore, attracting, we have become aware of a phenomenon that did not exist in the KMG model and that we had no reason to expect when we incorporated the Taylor rule into KMG. Second, while stable additional equilibria are here devoid of economic meaning, they do not create a new problem. What we are facing, then, is just another facet of the basic problem of viability.

The third point is that, although in our numerical example the deterministic model is not viable in the long run, it nevertheless does not need to be discarded because in the short and medium run the Taylor rule has proved to be so effective. The impulse–response function in figure 9.1 showed a rapid return to the equilibrium values u^o, $\hat{p}^\star$, i^o with which any central bank would have been fairly satisfied, and which over the first ten or twenty years after the shock was much superior to the adjustments in the estimated RS model.

We have also remarked that, for decades, the slow divergence would hardly be noticed if the dynamics were subjected to some stochastic noise. In this respect we may now go one step further and ask if the initially stabilizing properties of the interest rate come out even more forcefully when repeated shocks arrive. The intuition is that, if immediately after such a shock the system shows a strong tendency back to u^o, $\hat{p}^*$, i^o rather than one of the other equilibria, and if the next shock arrives long before divergence can take over, then the stabilizing properties of the Taylor rule can be dominant. The shocks, so to speak, do not leave the system sufficient time to diverge.

Figure 9.3 illustrates the idea by assuming some infrequent, selected demand shocks. Adopting the same numerical parameters as above, negative shocks are imposed on y^e not only at $t = 0$ but also at time $t = 4$ and $t = 7.25$, and two positive shocks close on one another at $t = 6$ and $t = 6.33$. Their occurrence is clearly visible as the five spikes in the utilization series and, equally, in the rate of inflation. The main impression from

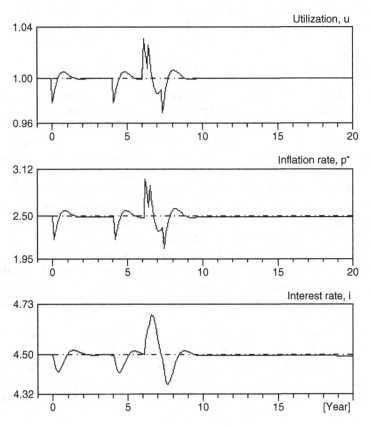

Figure 9.3: Five demand shocks in the unstable case of Figures 9.1 and 9.2

this little experiment is undoubtedly the excellent working of the Taylor rule. From a visual inspection of figure 9.3 alone we would have no reason to suspect that the equilibrium u^o, $\hat{p}^*$, i^o is unstable, especially if we imagine that the shocks do not die out after $t = 7.25$.

Figure 9.3 points to the possibility that, while an equilibrium position is unstable in a deterministic model, it is in a practical sense 'stable' in a stochastic environment.[8] Of course, the diagram is no proof, not so much because of the infrequent arrival of the shocks (in the monthly discrete-time analogue of the differential equations) but because of their special nature. Reasonably, other kinds of the shocks than those to y^e should also be investigated. Although it may be mathematically interesting to pursue this issue in greater detail, we abstain from it here since we do not consider the numerical parameters fully convincing (in particular, the limitation to a constant inflation climate $\pi = \pi^o$ owing to $\kappa_\pi = 0$, and the central bank's zero responsiveness to changes in utilization, $\alpha_u = 0$). We will, however, touch on this subject again in chapter 9, section 4, subsection 2.

9.2.3   Mathematical stability analysis and its limitations

Although the KMG model is of dimension six, it was still possible to undertake a mathematical stability analysis. The central result we obtained was that local asymptotic stability prevails if a number of reaction coefficients are sufficiently low (given that a few additional, but unproblematic inequalities are satisfied); see Proposition 3 in chapter 4, section 5. The proof of the proposition proceeded in several steps, in each of which the sign of the determinant of a submatrix of the system's Jacobian $\mathcal{J}$ had to be computed. The final step established that the determinant of $\mathcal{J}$ itself is unambiguously positive. This property immediately implies (Proposition 4 in chapter 4, section 5) that, if the steady state loses its stability upon the continuous variation of a parameter, a Hopf bifurcation occurs. What was important for us was not so much the existence of periodic orbits, because the circumstances under which they emerge can be rather special, but a certain tendency for cyclical behaviour in general.

In the KMGT model that we are currently dealing with, an analogous result holds true and the proof can run along similar lines if the following restrictions are accepted: (a) labour productivity is not procyclical but grows at a constant rate, i.e. $f_z' = 0$ in (9.5) and (9.6); (b) the wage share effect is absent in the two Phillips curves, i.e. $\beta_{pv} = \beta_{wv} = 0$ in

---

[8] In technical terms, it may be stable in the sense that the variance of the stochastic process is bounded.

(9.7) and (9.8); (c) the changes in the inflation climate are exclusively governed by the adaptive expectations mechanism, i.e. $\kappa_\pi = 1$ in (9.18). For a slightly differently specified KMGT model with conditions (a) to (c), the mathematical stability proposition is stated, but not really proved, by Asada et al. (2003, p. 268). The problem that we are now facing is that, at least if the assumption $\kappa_\pi = 1$ is relaxed, the Hopf bifurcation part of the stability result breaks down. Even worse, this also undermines the entire strategy of proving stability that we used in chapter 4, section 5. Since we know of no promising alternative approach, either, our general KMGT model comes up against the limitations of a mathematical analysis.

Our plan in this section is therefore as follows. First we deliver a rigorous proof that, under the restrictions just listed, the determinant of the Jacobian $\mathcal{J}$ is ensured to be positive. In contrast, one counter-example suffices to demonstrate that, generally, det $\mathcal{J} > 0$ does not survive if $\kappa_\pi < 1$ is admitted. After these preparations we leave the special case of assumptions (a) to (c) to one side. Rather than take the trouble to derive a mathematical stability proposition in this restricted setting, we consider the general economy directly and resort to a Monte Carlo simulation of the eigenvalues of $\mathcal{J}$. It will enable us to establish conditions on some of the model's parameters that are in practice sufficient to guarantee local stability.

As a basis for the mathematical as well as the numerical analysis, we begin by writing down the Jacobian $\mathcal{J}$ of system (9.13)–(9.18). $\mathcal{J}$ is, of course, evaluated at the steady-state position of Proposition 1 (the superscript 'o' in $y^e = (y^e)^o$ and $n = n^o$ is omitted).

$$
\mathcal{J} = \begin{bmatrix}
\omega(\hat{w}_\omega - \hat{p}_\omega) & 0 & \omega(\hat{w}_y - \hat{p}_y) \\
\alpha_i(1 + \alpha_p)\hat{p}_\omega & -\alpha_i & \alpha_i[(1 + \alpha_p)\hat{p}_y + \alpha_u u_y] \\
-y^e g_{k\omega} + \beta_y y^d_\omega & -y^e g_{ki} + \beta_y y^d_i & -y^e g_{ky} + \beta_y(y^d_y - 1) \\
k^s g_{k\omega} & k^s g_{ki} & k^s g_{ky} \\
-y^d_\omega - n g_{k\omega} & -y^d_i - n g_{ki} & y_y - y^d_y - n g_{ky} \\
\beta_\pi \kappa_\pi \hat{p}_\omega & 0 & \beta_\pi \kappa_\pi \hat{p}_y
\end{bmatrix}
$$

$$
\begin{bmatrix}
\omega(\hat{w}_k - \hat{p}_k) & \omega(\hat{w}_n - \hat{p}_n) & 0 \\
\alpha_i(1 + \alpha_p)\hat{p}_k & \alpha_i[(1 + \alpha_p)\hat{p}_n + \alpha_u u_n] & \alpha_i(1 + \alpha_p) \\
0 & -y^e g_{kn} + \beta_y y^d_n & -y^e g_{k\pi} + \beta_y y^d_\pi \\
0 & k^s g_{kn} & k^s g_{k\pi} \\
0 & y_n - y^d_n - n g_{kn} - g^o & -y^d_\pi - n g_{k\pi} \\
\beta_\pi \kappa_\pi \hat{p}_k & \beta_\pi \kappa_\pi \hat{p}_n & \beta_\pi(\kappa_\pi - 1)
\end{bmatrix} \quad (9.25)
$$

The term a_x or a_{bx} stands for the partial derivative of the functional expression a or a_b with respect to the state variable x. To avoid the stacking of indices, we also adopt the notation $a_{by} = \partial a_b / \partial y^e$ in the third column. In the mathematical analysis, not all these terms have to be computed, but we certainly need them for the numerical eigenvalue analysis. The entries of $\mathcal{J}$ are, therefore, fully spelled out in the appendix to this chapter.

In comparison to the Jacobian of the KMG model in eq. (4.50), it may be noted that all the expressions remain unaffected in which the interest rate does not enter. That is, the expressions (9.3) to (9.9) for y, u, v, e, f_p, f_w and $\hat{p}$ are the same as before, while (9.11) and (9.12) for g_k and y^d are now different. This means that $\mathcal{J}$ in (9.25) differs from $\mathcal{J}$ in (4.50) not only in the second row and column. Since, besides m, the LM rate of interest was a function of y^e and n, these two partial derivatives for $q = (1-v)y - \delta - (i - \pi)$ in (9.10) and, thus, g_k and y^d are different. Hence, the entries containing the derivatives g_{ky}, g_{kn} and y_y^d, y_n^d also do not coincide with those in (4.50), though for the most part the differences are not very pronounced. On the other hand, the entries that remain identical in the two matrices are the first and sixth rows, and, if the entries in the second row are left out of account, the first, fourth and sixth columns.[9]

It has already been indicated that, provided several coefficients attain their polar values, the Jacobian of (9.25) still shares with that of (4.50) the property of an unambiguously positive determinant. The next proposition combines this statement with a note that this no longer applies if the assumptions (or only one of them) are relaxed.

Proposition 3

1. Suppose that in the KMGT model $f_z' = \beta_{pv} = \beta_{wv} = 0$ as well as $\kappa_\pi = 1$. Then the determinant of the Jacobian $\mathcal{J}$ in (9.25), which is evaluated at the equilibrium of Proposition 1, is given by

$$\det \mathcal{J} = \alpha_i \alpha_p \beta_{pu} \beta_{we} \beta_\pi \beta_y f_{Iq} \kappa (s_c - \tau_w) v^o A > 0,$$

   where $A := \beta_{nn} + g^o[1 + (g^o + \beta_{nn})\beta_{ny}]$.

2. The determinant can be negative if $\kappa_\pi < 1$. Moreover, a continuous parameter variation may change the determinant from positive to negative, so that the transition from stability to instability is not associated with a Hopf bifurcation.

---

[9] Entries j_{31}, j_{34}, j_{36} are indeed identical in (4.50) and (9.25), except that in (4.50) the terms have been split up in a different way since this was convenient for the ensuing mathematical treatment.

Writing the determinant in this full detail also shows which reaction coefficients should be strictly positive. Note that this, in particular, holds true for the responsiveness α_p to the inflation gap in the Taylor rule.

Proof of Part I: The first steps in computing $\det \mathcal{J}$ are exclusively concerned with operations on the three rows 1, 2 and 6, which, except for factorizing, leave the value of $\det \mathcal{J}$ unaffected. To begin with, factorize ω in the 1st row, α_i in the 2nd and β_π in the 6th, and then add the 6th row to the 1st and subtract $(1 + \alpha_p) \times$ the 6th row from the 2nd. Taking account of $\kappa_\pi = 1$, the three rows thus become

$$
\begin{vmatrix}
\hat{w}_\omega & 0 & \hat{w}_y & \hat{w}_k & \hat{w}_n & 0 \\
0 & -1 & \alpha_u u_y & 0 & \alpha_u u_n & 1 + \alpha_p \\
\hat{p}_\omega & 0 & \hat{p}_y & \hat{p}_k & \hat{p}_n & 0
\end{vmatrix}
$$

Because of $\hat{w} = \pi + g_z + \kappa(\kappa_w f_p + f_w)$ from (4.51) and $\hat{p} = \pi + \kappa(f_p + \kappa_p f_w)$ from (4.52) or (9.9), we have here, after factorizing κ one time in the 1st row and another time in the 6th row,

$$
\begin{vmatrix}
\kappa_w f_{p\omega} + f_{w\omega} & 0 & \kappa_w f_{py} + f_{wy} & f_{wk} & \kappa_w f_{pn} + f_{wn} & 0 \\
0 & -1 & \alpha_u u_y & 0 & \alpha_u u_n & 1 + \alpha_p \\
f_{p\omega} + \kappa_p f_{w\omega} & 0 & f_{py} + \kappa_p f_{wy} & \kappa_p f_{wk} & f_{pn} + \kappa_p f_{wn} & 0
\end{vmatrix}
$$

After subtracting $\kappa_p \times$ the 1st row from the 6th row, the terms in the latter are of the form $(1 - \kappa_p \kappa_w) f_{px}$, $x = \omega, y, k, n$ (where $f_{pk} = 0$). Then factorizing $1 - \kappa_p \kappa_w$ in the 6th row and subtracting $\kappa_w \times$ the resulting 6th row from the 1st, we get

$$
\begin{vmatrix}
f_{w\omega} & 0 & f_{wy} & f_{wk} & f_{wn} & 0 \\
0 & -1 & \alpha_u u_y & 0 & \alpha_u u_n & 1 + \alpha_p \\
f_{p\omega} & 0 & f_{py} & 0 & f_{pn} & 0
\end{vmatrix}
$$

If we now make use of the assumption $f_z' = \beta_{pv} = \beta_{wv} = 0$, then, with $u_x = y_x / y^n$ for $x = y, n$, this is equal to

$$
\begin{vmatrix}
0 & 0 & \beta_{we} y_y / y^n & y^n \beta_{we} & \beta_{we} y_n / y^n & 0 \\
0 & -1 & \alpha_u y_y / y^n & 0 & \alpha_u y_n / y^n & 1 + \alpha_p \\
0 & 0 & \beta_{pu} y_y / y^n & 0 & \beta_{pu} y_n / y^n & 0
\end{vmatrix}
$$

Factorize β_{pu}/y^n in the 6th row, subtract $y^n/\beta_{we} \times$ the new 6th row from the 1st row, and subtract $y^n/\alpha_u \times$ the new 6th row from the 2nd row. Lastly, factorize $y^n\beta_{we}$ in the resulting 1st row. If we denote by $\det_{\{1,2,6\}}\mathcal{J}$ the rows 1, 2, 6 in $\det\mathcal{J}$, if we take stock of the eight factorized terms $\omega\alpha_i\beta_\pi\kappa\kappa(1-\kappa_p\kappa_w)(\beta_{pu}/y^n)(y^n\beta_{we})$, and here take account of $\kappa(1-\kappa_p\kappa_w)=1$, we can summarize:

$$\det_{\{1,2,6\}}\mathcal{J} = A_1 \cdot \begin{vmatrix} 0 & 0 & 0 & 1 & 0 & 0 \\ 0 & -1 & 0 & 0 & 0 & 1+\alpha_p \\ 0 & 0 & y_y & 0 & y_n & 0 \end{vmatrix} \tag{9.26}$$

$$A_1 = \omega\alpha_i\beta_\pi\kappa\beta_{pu}\beta_{we}$$

A second set of operations concentrates on the other rows 3, 4, 5, for which we define, as in (4.53), $\tilde{y}^d = y^d - g_k$ and $\tilde{\beta}_y = \beta_y - y^e$. After factorizing k^s in the 4th row, these rows read

$$\begin{vmatrix} \tilde{\beta}_y g_{k\omega} + \beta_y\tilde{y}^d_\omega & \tilde{\beta}_y g_{ki} & \tilde{\beta}_y g_{ky} + \beta_y\tilde{y}^d_y - \tilde{\beta}_y & 0 & \tilde{\beta}_y g_{kn} + \beta_y\tilde{y}^d_n & \tilde{\beta}_y g_{k\pi} \\ g_{k\omega} & g_{ki} & g_{ky} & 0 & g_{kn} & g_{k\pi} \\ -\tilde{y}^d_\omega - (1+n)g_{k\omega} & -(1+n)g_{ki} & y_y - \tilde{y}^d_y - (1+n)g_{ky} & 0 & y_n - \tilde{y}^d_n - (1+n)g_{kn} - g^o & -(1+n)g_{k\pi} \end{vmatrix}$$

Subtract $\tilde{\beta}_y \times$ the 4th row from the 3rd row, add $(1+n) \times$ 4th row to the 5th row, factorize β_y in the new 3rd row and add the new 5th row to the thus resulting 3rd row. Subsequently, subtract the 6th row in (9.26) from the 5th row as well as from the 3rd row. This simplifies the previous three rows to

$$\begin{vmatrix} 0 & 0 & -1 & 0 & -g^o & 0 \\ g_{k\omega} & g_{ki} & g_{ky} & 0 & g_{kn} & g_{k\pi} \\ -\tilde{y}^d_\omega & 0 & -\tilde{y}^d_y & 0 & -\tilde{y}^d_n - g^o & 0 \end{vmatrix}$$

To proceed with this part of the determinant the explicit calculations of the partial derivatives are needed. To this end we abbreviate[10]

$$A_2 := f_{Iu}/y^n + f_{Iq}(vf'_z + 1 - v)$$

$$\tilde{s} := (s_c - \tau_w)(1 - f'_z)v$$

---

[10] At this point the assumption $f'_z = 0$ is not very disturbing. So we include f'_z in the following expression for better reference to the appendix.

Besides $g_{k\omega} = -y^n f_{Iq}$, $g_{ki} = -f_{Iq}$, $g_{k\pi} = f_{Iq}$, $\tilde{y}^d_\omega = (s_c - \tau_w)y^n$, the more complicated derivatives can then be written as (see the appendix)

$$g_{ky} = A_2 y_y \qquad g_{kn} = A_2 y_n$$
$$\tilde{y}^d_y = 1 - s_c + \tilde{s} y_y \qquad \tilde{y}^d_n = \tilde{s} y_n$$

so that the three rows become

$$
\begin{vmatrix}
0 & 0 & -1 & 0 & -g^o & 0 \\
-y^n f_{Iq} & -f_{Iq} & A_2 y_y & 0 & A_2 y_n & f_{Iq} \\
-(s_c - \tau_w)y^n & 0 & -(1 - s_c) - \tilde{s} y_y & 0 & -\tilde{s} y_n - g^o & 0
\end{vmatrix}
$$

A final simplification is easily done: subtract $A_2 \times$ the 6th row in (9.26) from the 4th row and add $\tilde{s} \times$ the 6th row to the 5th row. Using the notation introduced in (9.26) and recalling the factorization of k^s and β_y, we arrive at

$$
\det{}_{\{3,4,5\}} \mathcal{J} = \beta_y k^s \cdot
\begin{vmatrix}
0 & 0 & -1 & 0 & -g^o & 0 \\
-y^n f_{Iq} & -f_{Iq} & 0 & 0 & 0 & f_{Iq} \\
-(s_c - \tau_w)y^n & 0 & -(1 - s_c) & 0 & -g^o & 0
\end{vmatrix} \quad (9.27)
$$

Combining (9.26) and (9.27) yields

$$
\det \mathcal{J} = A_1 \beta_y k^s \cdot
\begin{vmatrix}
0 & 0 & 0 & 1 & 0 & 0 \\
0 & -1 & 0 & 0 & 0 & 1 + \alpha_p \\
0 & 0 & -1 & 0 & -g^o & 0 \\
-y^n f_{Iq} & -f_{Iq} & 0 & 0 & 0 & f_{Iq} \\
-(s_c - \tau_w)y^n & 0 & -(1 - s_c) & 0 & -g^o & 0 \\
0 & 0 & y_y & 0 & y_n & 0
\end{vmatrix}
$$

In the determinant on the right-hand side we take the following steps, where each step operates on the previously created determinant: (1) the 2nd column is added to the 6th column; (2) the determinant is expanded by the 4th column; (3) the resulting 5×5 determinant is expanded by the 5th column, where the factorized α_p from entry 1,5 attains a negative sign; (4) the resulting 4×4 determinant is expanded by the 2nd column, with no change in the sign of $-f_{Iq}$ as the factorized entry 2,2. This gives us

$$\alpha_p f_{Iq} \cdot \begin{vmatrix} 0 & -1 & -g^o \\ -(s_c - \tau_w)y^n & -(1-s_c) & -g^o \\ 0 & y_y & y_n \end{vmatrix}$$

and expansion of the 1st column leads to

$$+(s_c - \tau_w)y^n \alpha_p f_{Iq}[-y_n + g^o y_y]$$

Computation of y_y and y_n shows that the expression in square brackets is equal to the definition of the term A in the proposition. On the other hand, collecting the factorized terms and writing A_1 out gives

$$\omega \alpha_i \beta_\pi \kappa \beta_{pu} \beta_{we} \beta_y k^s (s_c - \tau_w) y^n \alpha_p f_{Iq}$$

It remains to note that $\omega = v$ and $y^n k^s = 1$ by Proposition 1 to obtain the proposition's full expression for det $\mathcal{J}$.

QED

The second part of the proposition is demonstrated by means of a numerical example. The parameters relating to the steady-state position are those of (9.19). Regarding the other coefficients we start out from the calibrated values of chapter 6, section 5 – eq. (6.30) – and the policy coefficients (8.8). In sum, they read

$$\begin{aligned} f'_z &= 0.40 & s_c &= 0.80 & \tau_w &= 0.35 \\ \beta_{pu} &= 0.15 & \beta_{pv} &= 1.50 & \kappa_p &= 0.00 \\ \beta_{we} &= 0.55 & \beta_{wv} &= 0.50 & \kappa_w &= 0.00 \\ \beta_\pi &= 1.00 & \kappa_\pi &= 0.50 \\ \beta_{nn} &= 3.00 & \beta_y &= 8.00 \\ \alpha_i &= 1.10 & \alpha_p &= 0.40 & \alpha_u &= 1.20 \end{aligned} \qquad (9.28)$$

The statement of Proposition 3.2 is most clearly shown by letting one parameter vary over a certain range. We choose the responsiveness of investment to changes in utilization, f_{Iu}, for this role. The other investment coefficient f_{Iq} is set at 0.05. In order to point out that a transition from a positive to a negative determinant of $\mathcal{J}$ can be exclusively due to $\kappa_\pi < 1$, we let f'_z, β_{pv}, β_{wv} vanish. Furthermore, the slope β_{we} in the wage Phillips curve is reduced to a value of 0.10. The numerical parameters underlying our example are thus given by numerical parameters from (9.28) except:

$$f'_z = 0.00 \quad \beta_{pv} = 0.00 \quad \beta_{wv} = 0.00$$
$$\beta_{we} = 0.10 \quad f_{Iq} = 0.05 \tag{9.29}$$

Given these data, we present a diagram where the selected coefficient f_{Iu} rises from zero to 0.12. Rather than plot $\det \mathcal{J}$ as a function of f_{Iu}, we directly compute the eigenvalue $\lambda^* = \lambda^*(f_{Iu})$ with maximum real part, which we call the dominant eigenvalue. Figure 9.4[11] displays the graph of the function $\text{Re}\lambda^* = \text{Re}\lambda^*(f_{Iu})$. The real part is seen to be negative, and hence the steady state is locally asymptotically stable, if f_{Iu} is sufficiently small, while increasing values of f_{Iu} render $\text{Re}\lambda^*$ eventually positive. So we can note in passing that, at least on the basis of the present set of parameters, the responsiveness f_{Iu} happens to be comparably destabilizing to how it acts in the KMG model.

However, at the critical value $f^c_{Iu} = 0.10032$, where the real part of λ^* becomes zero, this eigenvalue is no longer complex (as it was in the KMG model). Figure 9.4 provides this information by plotting $\text{Re}\lambda^*$ as a bold line if λ^* is a complex eigenvalue and as a solid line if λ^*

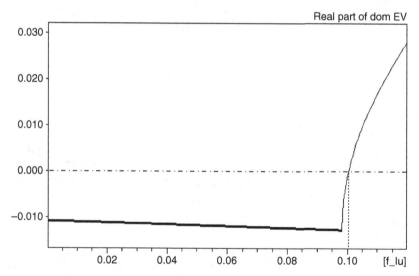

Figure 9.4: Dominant eigenvalue $\lambda^* = \lambda^*(f_{Iu})$ in the KMGT model (real part)

---

[11] The bold line indicates that λ^* is complex, the solid line that it is real. Underlying are the numerical parameters (9.19), (9.28), (9.29).

is a real eigenvalue. We therefore know that, in contrast to the KMG model, the change from a stable to an unstable equilibrium at the critical value $f_{lu} = f_{lu}^c$ does *not* give rise to a Hopf bifurcation. This observation completes the proof of Proposition 3.

According to Proposition 3.1 the phenomenon of figure 9.4 must disappear if $\kappa_\pi = 1$. We conclude the numerical example with a sketch of how a Hopf bifurcation comes into being as κ_π is increased. Figure 9.5[12] indicates that the qualitative feature of the two branches of the function $\mathrm{Re}\lambda^* = \mathrm{Re}\lambda^*(f_{lu})$ is maintained: one branch where λ^* is complex and the other where λ^* is real. What happens as κ_π rises is that the first branch of the function shifts upwards and, furthermore, rotates anticlockwise, such that its slope changes from negative to positive. The effect is that, finally, roughly from $\kappa_\pi = 0.90$ onwards, it is the branch with the complex eigenvalue that intersects the zero line. Figure 9.5 exemplifies this for $\kappa_\pi = 0.92$, showing that a Hopf bifurcation then occurs at $f_{lu} = f_{lu}^H = 0.09425$.

Incidentally, at $\kappa_\pi = 1$ the function $\mathrm{Re}\lambda^*(f_{lu})$ has already shifted so far upwards that it lies entirely above the zero line; that is, the steady state has become unstable for all values of f_u.

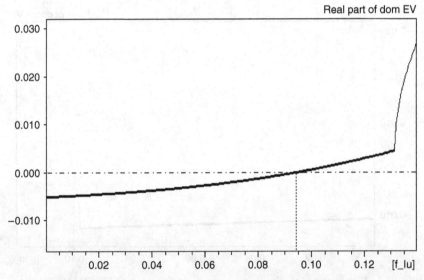

Figure 9.5: $\lambda^* = \lambda^*(f_{lu})$ in the KMGT model at a higher value of κ_π (real part)

[12] The same situation as in figure 9.4, except that κ_π has been increased from 0.50 to 0.92.

9.2.4   Numerical support for sufficient stability conditions

Having seen the limited prospects for a mathematical stability analysis, we resort to a numerical investigation. Our background consists of Proposition 3 in chapter 4, section 5 for the KMG model and a similar theorem in Asada et al. (2003, p. 268) for a more special version of the KMGT model, in which it could be mathematically established that the equilibrium is locally asymptotically stable if only certain reaction coefficients are sufficiently small. The general numerical approach, therefore, is to take these parameters or select a subset of them, choose zero or very small values for them and compute the eigenvalues of a great number of examples where the other parameters may have arbitrary values. Rather than lay a grid over the space of free parameters, which would be either too coarse or require the computation of too many grid points, we employ a random mechanism to assign the numerical values to them. Nevertheless, if in a large sample no case of instability is found, we can have great confidence that sufficiently small values of the selected parameters do indeed guarantee local stability, at least under the specified and economically meaningful circumstances.

For practical as well as economic reasons, the variations of the parameters will have to be subjected to certain limitations. Thus, the numerical parameters (9.19) that constitute the steady-state position will all remain fixed. Let us furthermore count the tax rate τ_w on wages and the propensity s_c to save out of rental income as steady-state parameters, which in like manner we will fix at the values $\tau_w = 0.35$ and $s_c = 0.80$ given in (9.28). The other fourteen parameters in (9.28), however, together with the two investment coefficients f_{Iu} and f_{Iq}, are either free to vary or are set at or close to zero. With regard to the free parameters, they, too, cannot be allowed to take on completely arbitrary values, but their variations are to be confined to meaningful and bounded intervals.

By the very concept of an active policy rule, which the KMGT model incorporates, the most prominent parameters in the – presumed – stabilizing properties of which one will be interested are the three policy coefficients α_i, α_p and α_u in the Taylor rule. It takes no more than a few explorations, however, to see that low values of α_p and α_u and larger values of α_i alone are not capable of ensuring stability. While the role of the policy coefficients will be studied in greater detail later on, we treat them here on an equal footing with the parameters relating to the private sector. Our starting point is thus the aforementioned proposition in Asada et al. (2003, p. 268), which in our notation supposes that $f'_z = \beta_{pv} = \beta_{wv} = 0$ and $\kappa_\pi = 1$ (and specifies one or two relationships in a slightly different way). The proposition states that local stability prevails if, on the one hand, β_y is large enough and, on the other hand, β_{we}, β_{pu}, β_π, β_{nn}, α_p and α_u are sufficiently small.

The relatively large number of coefficients involved here is dictated by the method of proof. The stability argument begins with a condition for a 3×3 submatrix $\mathcal{J}^{(3)}$ of the Jacobian $\mathcal{J}$. Using the Lemma in chapter 4, section 4, the proof then adds a row and a column of $\mathcal{J}$ and demonstrates that the thus augmented matrix $\mathcal{J}^{(4)}$ is stable if a parameter in that row or column is sufficiently small. Having achieved this, a further row and column of $\mathcal{J}$ is added to $\mathcal{J}^{(4)}$, and so on, until the newly created matrix $\mathcal{J}^{(6)}$ is identical to $\mathcal{J}$. Although in this way coefficients can be found that entail stability if they are small enough, this does not necessarily mean that all of them are essential for stability. As a matter of fact, another set of numerical explorations readily indicates that, at least if we have recourse to the investment coefficient f_{Iu} and assume that it is close to zero, the conditions just stated may be relaxed not only in the model of Asada et al. but also in the present, more general version of the KMGT model.

Besides f_{Iu}, a second parameter that should be sufficiently small is the core coefficient in the wage Phillips curve, β_{we}. In the calculations, the investment coefficient f_{Iu} can be directly set to zero, whereas β_{we} must remain strictly positive if, in order to make asymptotic stability possible, $\det \mathcal{J} > 0$ is to come about (see the formula in Proposition 3.1). Together with s_c and τ_w mentioned before, we therefore work with

$$f_{Iu} = 0.00 \quad \beta_{we} = 0.001 \quad s_c = 0.80 \quad \tau_w = 0.35 \qquad (9.30)$$

All the other parameters are basically free to vary within certain boundaries. These are f_z', β_{pu}, β_{pv}, κ_p, β_{wv}, κ_w, β_π, κ_π, β_y, β_{nn}, f_{Iq}, and α_i, α_p, α_u. A single simulation run is constituted by eqs. (9.19), (9.30) and by randomly assigning numerical values to these free parameters within the given limits. Then the corresponding Jacobian matrix is set up, its eigenvalues are computed, and we check whether all eigenvalues have negative real parts (or not), in which case this economy is locally asymptotically stable (or not). A larger set of such simulation runs that confine the parameters to the same limits forms a simulation experiment.

For a representative parameter ϕ in the set of the fourteen free parameters, we postulate a lower bound ϕ_1 and an upper bound ϕ_2. In each simulation run the random value assigned to ϕ is drawn from a uniform probability distribution over the interval $[\phi_1, \phi_2]$, so that (loosely speaking) every value in this interval is chosen with equal probability. For a few selected parameters we may also assume the degenerate case $\phi_1 = \phi_2$, to fix the parameter at a deterministic value. On the other hand, in order to take account of the assumption made in Proposition 3.1 we will wish that some parameters ϕ are generally positive but also attain the zero value with a certain probability. This feature is easily accomplished by letting ϕ_1 be negative and, having drawn a random number $\phi^r \in [\phi_1, \phi_2]$ in a simulation run, set $\phi = \max\{0, \phi^r\}$. For example, with $\phi_1 = -0.50$ and $\phi_2 = 0.50$, the parameter ϕ will be zero with probability $1/2$.

We began the investigation by imposing only minor constraints on the free parameters, and noted down the numerical values of all fourteen parameters if they gave rise to an unstable Jacobian. Combining this with information from parameter diagrams that plot the stability region in the two-parameter plane, we gained an impression of what range of which parameters may be unfavourable for stability. These conjectures were subsequently scrutinized by further simulation runs that narrowed the parameter intervals correspondingly. In this way we arrived at the following conditions:

(1) the interest rate should show a minimum degree of reactions – i.e. α_i in (9.14) should be bounded away from zero;
(2) the responsiveness of investment to changes in the return differential should be rather limited – i.e. f_{Iq} in (9.11) should not be very large; and
(3) utilization should have a minimum impact on price inflation – i.e. β_{pu} in the price Phillips curve (9.7) should be bounded away from zero.

On this basis, we first fixed κ_π at unity, so that the changes of the inflation climate are exclusively governed by the adaptive expectations mechanism, and looked for further parameters that, suitably constrained, would guarantee stability. It turned out that only the adjustment speed β_π is needed for this purpose, which is required to be sufficiently small. Regarding the other parameters we took the numerical values (9.28) and specified more or less wide intervals around them. On the whole, the first simulation experiment assumes the following parameter intervals:[13]

$$0.05 \leq \alpha_i \leq 3.00$$

$$0.05 \leq \beta_{pu} \leq 0.50 \qquad 0.00 \leq f_{Iq} \leq 0.05$$

$$0.00 \leq \beta_\pi \leq 0.05 \qquad 1.00 \leq \kappa_\pi \leq 1.00$$

$$-0.50 \leq \beta_{pv} \leq 2.00 \qquad 0.00 \leq \kappa_p \leq 0.75$$

$$-0.50 \leq \beta_{wv} \leq 1.00 \qquad 0.00 \leq \kappa_w \leq 0.75 \tag{9.31}$$

$$-0.50 \leq f_z' \leq 0.50$$

$$4.00 \leq \beta_y \leq 12.00 \qquad 0.00 \leq \beta_{nn} \leq 4.00$$

$$0.00 \leq \alpha_p \leq 3.00 \qquad 0.00 \leq \alpha_u \leq 3.00$$

---

[13] The negative lower bounds for β_{pv}, β_{wv}, f_z' have to be interpreted as described above, to allow for a positive probability of $\beta_{pv} = 0$, etc.

Using these data we set up 1,000,000 Jacobian matrices and computed their eigenvalues, with the result that not one single case of instability was detected. We thus feel entitled to summarize this finding (or non-finding) as a 'numerical proposition'.

Numerical Result 1

Suppose that $\kappa_\pi = 1$ and that α_i and β_{pu} are bounded away from zero, while f_{Iq} does not exceed a relatively small upper limit. All parameters, furthermore, remain within finite bounds. Then the normal equilibrium of Proposition 1 is locally asymptotically stable if f_{Iu}, β_{we} and β_π are sufficiently small (but β_{we}, β_π still positive).

The statement is supported by 1,000,000 simulation runs specified according to (9.19), (9.30), (9.31), which produced no case of instability.

Given the stabilizing forces of small values of f_{Iu} and β_{we}, it may be asked whether the role of β_π can in this respect be taken over by one or two other parameters. In fact, we easily find cases where at high values of β_π a small coefficient f_{Iq} or, alternatively, α_p can stabilize the steady state. However, other cases are found just as easily where the two variables, neither alone nor jointly, do not succeed in this task. Explorations with other variables revealed no better prospects. We thus conjecture that, for a sufficient stability condition in the presence of $\kappa_\pi = 1$, the small values of β_π cannot generally be dispensed with.

Having identified the destabilizing potential of the adaptive expectations component in the adjustments of the inflation climate (when $\kappa_\pi = 1$), which at least in the general case is to be tamed by low adjustment speeds β_π, our intuition was that when the adaptive expectations are combined with the regressive expectations, represented by $\kappa_\pi < 1$, it may be possible to relax the strong condition on β_π, or to substitute it for a moderate condition on another variable. The intuition was corroborated by extensive explorations in which κ_π was bounded away from unity. Inspecting the parameters of the unstable cases then arising and studying the corresponding stability regions in the parameter diagrams, we learned that, basically, three features are favourable for instability: if κ_π is still too close to unity, or β_π is too large (which could be both suspected) or if the policy coefficient α_p is too large. In addition, in all unstable cases the two Phillips curve weights κ_p and κ_w were fairly high (κ_p, $\kappa_w > 0.50$ as a rule), and β_{wv} was mostly zero.

These findings suggest examining if imposing a suitable restriction on one of these parameters would be capable of ensuring stability. While we continued to admit higher values of κ_p and κ_w and zero values of β_{wv}, we checked this hypothesis for the parameters κ_π, β_π and α_p. The result is informally summarized in a second 'numerical proposition'. Further details of the three simulation experiments, as well as of another experiment concerning β_{wv}, are reported subsequently.

Numerical Result 2
Suppose that α_i and β_{pu} are bounded away from zero, f_{I_q} is relatively small and all parameters remain within finite bounds. Then the normal equilibrium of Proposition 1 is locally asymptotically stable if f_{I_u} and β_{we} are sufficiently small (but β_{we} still positive) and, in addition, one of the following conditions is satisfied:

1. κ_π is not too large ($\kappa_\pi \leq 0.55$);
2. κ_π is distinctly bounded away from unity ($\kappa_\pi \leq 0.80$) and β_π is moderately bounded ($\beta_\pi \leq 1.75$);
3. κ_π is distinctly bounded away from unity ($\kappa_\pi \leq 0.80$) and α_p is moderately bounded ($\alpha_p \leq 1.75$).

The background of these statements consists of extensive simulation experiments using (9.19), (9.30) and tightened versions of (9.31).

The numerical upper bounds are, in the overwhelming majority of cases, unnecessarily low. Take the first statement, to begin with. Here we strongly favoured the occurrence of unstable cases by fixing β_π at such a high value as $\beta_\pi = 12$,[14] and by moreover confining α_p to larger values between two and three. The other parameter intervals for the random mechanism were those of (9.31). In 1,000,000 simulation runs we then only found four cases where $\kappa_\pi \leq 0.65$ did not bring about stability, and only one case where $\kappa_\pi \leq 0.60$ was not sufficient for this and κ_π had to be lowered a little further.

For the other statements of Numerical Result 2 instability was similarly favoured. For the second statement, α_p was again chosen between two and three while κ_π was fixed at 0.80 and β_π at 1.75. 1,000,000 simulation runs detected no instability under these circumstances. To support the third statement, β_π was reset at $\beta_\pi = 12$ and α_p was fixed at 1.75. Again, 1,000,000 simulation runs generated no unstable case, either.

We also investigated whether bounding β_{wv} moderately away from zero would entail stability. Apart from extremely rare exceptions, this was confirmed if κ_π is distinctly bounded away from unity ($\kappa_\pi \leq 0.70$) and β_{wv} does not fall below 0.20. More precisely, we first favoured instability by fixing $\beta_\pi = 12$, $\kappa_\pi = 0.70$ and confining α_p to the interval [2, 3]. No unstable case in a sample of 1,000,000 simulation runs could then be detected if β_{wv} was randomly chosen from the interval [0.20, 1.00]. If, however, the β_{wv} interval was narrowed to the degenerate case $\beta_{wv} = 0.20$,

---

[14] All parameter diagrams we explored showed that, if a set of parameters generates a stable Jacobian for, say, $\beta_\pi = 10$, then the matrix is also stable for $\beta_\pi \geq 12$.

then six unstable cases were obtained. In five of them stability could be 'restored' by slightly changing another suitable variable – for example, by reducing the upper limit of f_{I_q} to 0.04 (instead of 0.05). Lowering the upper limits of κ_p and κ_w to 0.50 ensured stability in all six cases.

The last observation was included for two reasons, First, it suggests that less restrictive, and more impressive, stability conditions could be established if we presume lower upper bounds for κ_p and κ_w. Second, and more importantly, the experiment demonstrates that the conditions in the Numerical Results 1 and 2 have no mathematical relevance but a 'practical' one. It might be that, if we search for additional parameters that are at least occasionally destabilizing, then in an interactive and skilful dialogue with the computer we would be able to construct a counter-example; this, nevertheless, remains to be seen. However, the great effort required here makes it clear that such an unstable case would be rather special.[15] The main message of the numerical results would be affected only inessentially.

We can therefore briefly sum up what has been achieved in this section. It has been shown that, when a mathematical analysis of sufficient stability conditions becomes intractable, it can be replaced by a numerical investigation. This can even yield more parsimonious conditions, which involve fewer parameters. Also, the conditions can be more specific than would be mathematically possible, in that they allow for statements that a parameter is distinctly or moderately bounded away from some benchmark value, which is then made numerically precise.

The risk that even large samples may fail to detect unstable cases could be further reduced by more careful experimental designs. In particular, a cluster analysis may help identify more clearly the circumstances favouring instability, which could be ruled out subsequently by assumption. We did not pursue this issue any further in order not to overrate the results and since, of course, we can never be absolutely sure of the stability conditions. On the whole, we feel fairly comfortable with the results as they are stated; for 'practical', rather than mathematical, purposes they may be quite sufficient.

In fact, we are content with pointing out here that, taking some accompanying and more or less precise conditions for granted, mainly low values of the two reaction coefficients f_{I_u} and β_{we} alone are capable of ensuring stability. This is a first useful piece of background information about some basic stabilizing forces in our model. On the other hand, we need

---

[15] In this respect it is interesting to mention the unstable cases that we found in the explorations when the conditions were not restrictive enough: these cases often had a similar 'structure', in the sense that the parameters were not too different relative to each other, and in the sense that they produced similar parameter diagrams. This indicates that, after tightening the conditions in the way we did, it may genuinely be difficult to disclose yet another case of instability.

not try to sharpen this kind of result much further, since we already know that the assumption as such is not very reasonable. We should, rather, turn to more realistic parameters, which for the private sector can be derived from our calibration study, while, regarding the coefficients of the central bank's Taylor rule, we can make use of the estimated values.

9.3   Global dynamics of the KMGT model

9.3.1   Setting up a stable and an unstable scenario

In this section we intend to show that the KMGT model can be used equally in two different methodological frameworks. On the one hand, we follow the same approach as for the KMG model and find a parameter scenario that generates self-sustaining cyclical behaviour in a deterministic setting. To this end, we render the equilibrium unstable and again introduce a suitable extrinsic nonlinearity in the investment function that is able to keep the dynamics within reasonable bounds.

On the other hand, having discussed at some length in chapter 8, section 4 the Rudebusch–Svensson model as a representative example of how monetary policy is studied in contemporary macroeconomic theory, we should also relate the KMGT model to a model of this type, which employs the so-called Frisch paradigm. These are stochastic and mostly linear models with a deterministically stable equilibrium the non-fading fluctuations of which are generated by exogenous random disturbances. Accordingly, we set up a second parameter scenario for the KMGT model that yields a stable steady-state position and impose stochastic supply and demand shocks on this system.

The numerical parameters for the two scenarios are obtained in a similar manner to those in chapter 6, where we had to simulate the dynamics of the KMG model. Besides the steady-state values (9.19), both sets of parameters are based on the parameter values (6.30) from our stepwise calibration procedure and the estimated policy coefficients (8.8). These parameters, which have been collected in (9.28) above, are all taken over except for one, which, for a reason that will shortly be explained, we decide to reset at another value. The two scenarios are distinguished by the remaining coefficients that characterize the nonlinear investment function (9.21), (9.22). Local stability is then governed (a) by the responsiveness to changes in utilization, $\beta_{Iu} = f_{Iu}$, and (b) by the responsiveness to changes in the return differential, $\beta_{Iq} = f_{Iq}$. Here we choose one pair (β_{Iu}, β_{Iq}) that, together with the already given parameters, causes the steady state to be stable, and a second pair (β_{Iu}, β_{Iq}) at which the steady state becomes unstable. The value of the – as it again turns out – destabilizing coefficient β_{Iu} is, in fact, the only coefficient in which the two scenarios will differ, since we also assume identical values for β_{Iq} and the two other coefficients d_1, d_2, which regulate the nonlinearity in the investment function (and do not enter the stability issue).

In chapter 6, section 7, subsection 2 suitable values for β_{Iu} and β_{Iq} in the KMG model were found by plotting the Jacobian's parameter diagram in the (β_{Iu}, β_{Iq}) plane, where we looked for a pair outside the stability region with dominant eigenvalues that not only are complex but also induce (slowly widening) oscillations with a period of about eight years; see figure 6.3. In the present case we compute the (β_{Iu}, β_{Iq}) parameter diagram of the Jacobian (9.25) on the basis of the numerical parameters (9.28). While the resulting stability region poses no problems, an unpleasant difference from the just mentioned diagram for the KMG model is that the pairs (β_{Iu}, β_{Iq}) that give rise to complex eigenvalues with the required period are now far off the stability frontier.[16] As a consequence, the diverging forces are rather strong and would be hard to tame by the relatively weak nonlinearity in the investment function on which we concentrate.

To overcome the problem we can change some of the other parameters and check if this moves the region of (β_{Iu}, β_{Iq}) with suitable complex eigenvalues closer to the stability frontier. The best parameter for this task would be β_{nn}, since, as has been pointed out in chapter 6, section 4, subsection 3, this coefficient has a limited bearing on the cyclical features of the state variables – at least if the oscillations of utilization are given. Fortunately, a little experimentation shows that a reduction of β_{nn} does indeed have the desired effect, and furthermore it proves to be sufficiently strong. We therefore cancel the original value $\beta_{nn} = 3$ in (9.28) and settle down on $\beta_{nn} = 1.25$. Thus, we will work with the following set of parameters:[17]

$$\beta_{zu} = 0.40 \qquad s_c = 0.80 \qquad \tau_w = 0.35$$

$$\beta_{pu} = 0.15 \qquad \beta_{pv} = 1.50 \qquad \kappa_p = 0.00$$

$$\beta_{we} = 0.55 \qquad \beta_{wv} = 0.50 \qquad \kappa_w = 0.00$$

$$\beta_\pi = 1.00 \qquad \kappa_\pi = 0.50 \tag{9.32}$$

$$\beta_{nn} = 1.25 \qquad \beta_y = 8.00$$

$$\alpha_i = 1.10 \qquad \alpha_p = 0.40 \qquad \alpha_u = 1.20$$

Employing (9.32), we obtain figure 9.6 as the part of the (β_{Iu}, β_{Iq}) parameter diagram that is relevant for us. The dotted area is the stability

---

[16] If here and in the following we refer to eigenvalues, it is, of course, understood that these are the dominant eigenvalues of the Jacobian (9.25) – i.e. the eigenvalues with maximum real part.

[17] As for the coefficient β_{zu}, we repeat footnote 6 and recall $\beta_{zu} = f_z'$ in the function $z/z^o = f_z(u) = 1 + \beta_{zu}(u-1)$.

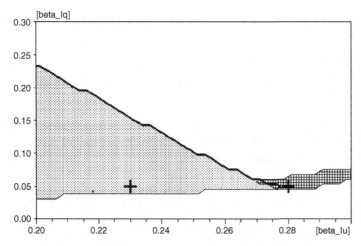

Figure 9.6: The parameter diagram of (β_{Iu}, β_{Iq}) for the KMGT model

region (i.e. the set of (β_{Iu}, β_{Iq}) that entails local asymptotic stability of the steady state), whereas instability prevails outside this set. The pairs in the hatched area imply that the dominant eigenvalues have a period of between seven and nine years.

The two crosses in figure 9.6 indicate the pairs (β_{Iu}, β_{Iq}) that we choose for the stable and unstable scenarios, respectively. In both cases β_{Iq} is set at 0.05, while $\beta_{Iu} = 0.23$ is adopted to induce stability and $\beta_{Iu} = 0.28$ specifies the unstable case. The nonlinearity coefficients d_1, d_2 of the investment function are taken over from (9.33). The choice of these special values for the four investment coefficients is vindicated by the results of the dynamic simulations in the next two subsections. In sum, our two scenarios for the KMGT model are calibrated as follows:

Calibration of the KMGT model

Dynamic equations (9.13)–(9.18),
which refer to (9.2)–(9.12), (9.21), (9.22).
Common numerical parameters (9.19) and (9.32).

Stable scenario:
  $\beta_{Iu} = 0.230$ $\beta_{Iq} = 0.050$ $d_1 = 0.020$ $d_2 = 0.035$

Unstable scenario:
  $\beta_{Iu} = 0.280$ $\beta_{Iq} = 0.050$ $d_1 = 0.020$ $d_2 = 0.035$

Inserting these coefficients in the Jacobian (9.25) and computing the dominant eigenvalues λ^* for the two scenarios, we obtain, as desired,

$$\text{Stable scenario: } \lambda^* = -0.039 \tag{9.33}$$

$$\text{Unstable scenario: } \lambda^* = 0.018 \pm 0.785i \quad (\text{period } T = 8.01 \text{ years}) \tag{9.34}$$

According to the real eigenvalue in (9.33), the stable scenario shares the additional property with the Rudebusch–Svensson model that the equilibrium is approached in a monotonic manner. The necessity of choosing β_{Iq} relatively small for this purpose can be inferred from figure 9.6, if it is noted that on the north-east stability frontier, which is drawn as the bold line, the dominant eigenvalue is complex (so that a Hopf bifurcation occurs there) and that on the lower stability frontier, and certainly sufficiently close to it, the eigenvalues are real. In detail, the switching from a real eigenvalue, as β_{Iq} increases from zero, to a complex eigenvalue is illustrated in figure 9.7,[18] where β_{Iu} is fixed at the value 0.230 from the stable scenario. It is thus seen that the real part of the complex eigenvalue becomes dominant precisely at $\beta_{Iq} = 0.10445$. On the other hand, the first bifurcation takes place at $\beta_{Iq} = 0.03759$ and the second at

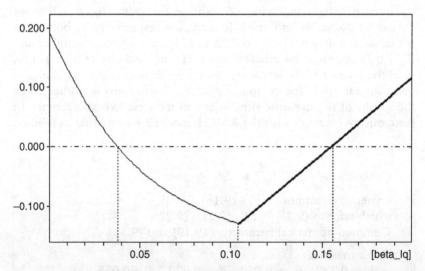

Figure 9.7: The real part of dominant eigenvalue $\lambda^* = \lambda^*(\beta_{Iq})$ in the KMGT model

[18] The bold line indicates that λ^* is complex, the solid line that it is real. Underlying are the numerical parameters (9.19), (9.32), and $\beta_{Iu} = 0.230$ from the stable scenario.

$\beta_{Iq} = 0.15509$. The eigenvalue diagrams of $\lambda^* = \lambda^*(\beta_{Iq})$ are (qualitatively) very similar if β_{Iu} is fixed at other values (less than 0.28).

9.3.2   Dynamics in the stable case: the Frisch paradigm

The first point when we set the dynamics generated by the stable scenario against the trajectories of the Rudebusch–Svensson model is the speed of convergence in an impulse–response function. To set the system in motion from the steady-state position, we again concentrate on an adverse demand shock. In the Rudebusch–Svensson model it was directly imposed on the dynamic IS equation that determines the output gap. Regarding the KMGT model it has been argued in subsection 9.2.2 that, for a better comparability, it is more appropriate here to assume a drop in sales expectations. Scaling the shock at 1.2 per cent, figure 9.8[19]

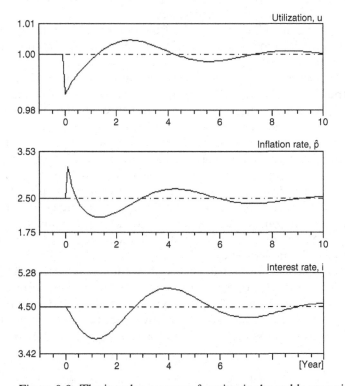

Figure 9.8: The impulse–response function in the stable scenario

[19] The steady state is disturbed at $t = 0$ by an adverse (one-time) shock to sales expectations.

results for the three central variables utilization u, price inflation $\hat{p}$ and the nominal interest rate i. For all three time series it can be said that convergence is effectively completed after ten years.

The same statement can be made for the output gap in the impulse–response function of the RS model, which was plotted in figure 8.3 (chapter 8, section 4, subsection 3). In this respect the time series of the output gap and utilization in the two models are roughly comparable. A slight difference is that in the KMGT model utilization appears to converge in a weakly cyclical manner, although the dominant eigenvalue in (9.33) was real.[20]

More important is another difference from figure 8.3. In figure 9.8 the three time series exhibit a fairly similar pattern (apart from the lags), whereas in the discussion of figure 8.3 the high persistence in inflation and, thus, the rate of interest as well was emphasized, which delayed convergence considerably. In this respect the behaviour in the KMGT model can be deemed more satisfactory.

Comparing the adjustment path of the rate of inflation in figure 9.8 to that in the RS model in figure 8.3 and even to the explorations of the KMGT model in figure 9.1 with its special parameter values, the initial reaction of $\hat{p}$ leaps to the eye. While conventional wisdom has it that a fall in output leads to lower inflation, and this also comes out in figures 8.3 and 9.1, we observe the opposite effect in figure 9.8. The phenomenon is, nevertheless, not new to us, since a negative output–inflation nexus has already been disclosed in the KMG model; see chapter 7, section 4, subsection 2. As the main cause for the counter-intuitive effect $u \uparrow \longrightarrow \hat{p} \downarrow$ or $u \downarrow \longrightarrow \hat{p} \uparrow$, respectively, the feedback diagram of figure 7.9 in that section identified the influence of the wage share v in the price Phillips curve and the relatively high value of the corresponding coefficient β_{pv}. In this limited context, the exogenous money supply and the KMG model's LM curve had no role to play, so the same mechanism applies to the KMGT model just as well.

Furthermore, figure 7.11 in chapter 7, section 4, subsection 3 for the whole KMG model showed a very similar impulse–response function to the in the present figure 9.8, apart from the fact that the dynamics were started by a positive, rather than a negative, shock on sales expectations. There it was also argued that a value such as $\beta_{pv} = 1.50$ should not be

---

[20] The next eigenvalue of the Jacobian is a pair of conjugate complex eigenvalues, $\lambda_{2,3} = -0.279 \pm 1.015i$, with a period of $T = 6.19$ years. The latter fits in nicely with the duration of a cycle in figure 9.8, even though $\mathrm{Re}\lambda_{2,3}$ is much lower than $\mathrm{Re}\lambda^*$. So, at least part of the phenomenon should probably be ascribed to the special initial conditions.

evaluated with regard to the immediate response of inflation to a change in utilization but with regard to the lags of $\hat{p}$ behind u, which, in accordance with the stylized facts of a cyclical economy, are required to give rise to a countercyclical price level. More on the empirical question 'can a negative output–inflation nexus be detected in the data?' may be found in chapter 7, section 4, subsection 3, with just that title. Despite the different roles of money and the interest rate in the KMG and KMGT models, the main arguments will carry over to the present framework.[21]

We can thus turn to our main motive for considering a stable scenario of the KMGT model, namely to use it for stochastic simulations that can subsequently be compared to a sample run like that of figure 8.6 from the Rudebusch–Svensson model. To be as close as possible to this model, we content ourselves with the same two types of random shocks: a supply and a demand shock that arrive every quarter. The supply shock ε_p, to begin with, is treated in exactly the same way; it is directly imposed on the deterministic equation for the rate of price inflation. Eq. (9.9) is thus modified as

$$\hat{p}_t = \pi_t + \kappa(f_{p,t} + \kappa_p f_{w,t}) + \varepsilon_{p,t} \tag{9.9a}$$

in obvious notation. We should add that, in the monthly discretization of the differential equations (9.13)–(9.18), the determination of π and ω does not use the right-hand sides of (9.18) and (9.13), respectively, but goes back to the original specification of these variables or their adjustments. This means that, having computed $\hat{p}_t$ by (9.9a) for period t, the inflation climate next month $t + h$ ($h = 1/12$)) is given by

$$\pi_{t+h} = \pi_t + h\beta_\pi[\kappa_\pi(\hat{p}_t - \pi_t) + (1 - \kappa_\pi)(\pi^o - \pi_t)]$$

As for the deflated real wage ω, we keep track of the level of prices p and wages w as well as trend productivity z^o, updating them as $p_{t+h} = (1 + h\hat{p}_t)p_t$, $w_{t+h} = (1 + h\hat{w}_t)w_t$ and $z_{t+h}^o = (1 + hg_z)z_t^o$, and then put[22]

$$\omega_{t+h} = w_{t+h}/p_{t+h}z_{t+h}^o$$

---

[21] The literature discusses the phenomenon of the so-called price puzzle, which means that prices increase, rather than decrease, in response to a monetary policy contraction. This is not quite the situation in figure 9.8, since the impulse is not a policy shock but an adverse demand shock and since the initial reaction in the interest rate is dominated by the fall in utilization. Our impulse–response function may nevertheless be related to this literature insofar as a fall in economic activity causes the rate of inflation to rise; see Gordon and Leeper (1994), Leeper et al. (1996) and Christiano et al. (1998).

[22] The rate of nominal wage inflation $\hat{w}_t$ derives from the reduced-form equation (3.24), or (5.17) with $\kappa_{wz} = 0$, for that matter. In discrete time we have, however, to take the remarks on eq. (2.44) in chapter 2, section 8 into account. That is, in $\hat{w}_t = g_{w,t} + \kappa(f_{w,t} + \kappa_w f_{p,t})$ we have to set $g_{w,t} = \pi_t + g_z + h(\pi_t g_z)$.

Because the demand shock ε_y now occurs on a regular basis and not just at one time to set the system in motion, we find it more appropriate to take it literally and apply it to aggregate demand y^d. Applying it to expected sales as before tends to produce a relatively ragged utilization series. Eq. (9.12) is accordingly modified as

$$y_t^d = y^d(\omega_t, i_t, y_t^e, n_t, \pi_t) + \varepsilon_{y,t} \qquad (9.12a)$$

To be in line with the quarterly model of Rudebusch and Svensson, the random terms $\varepsilon_{p,t}$, $\varepsilon_{y,t}$ in our monthly discrete-time version are assumed to be active only every three months. Of course, in those months they are identically, independently and normally distributed around zero with standard deviations σ_p and σ_y, respectively:

$$\varepsilon_{x,t} = \begin{cases} \mathcal{N}(0, \sigma_x) & \text{if } 4t \text{ is an integer number} \\ 0 & \text{else} \end{cases} \qquad x = p, y \qquad (9.35)$$

Regarding the size of the standard deviation for the rate of inflation, we take over Rudebusch and Svensson's value in (8.29), though their estimated price Phillips curve differs from our specification. In contrast, the value σ_y in (8.29) from their output gap regression cannot be compared meaningfully to the standard deviation of $\varepsilon_{y,t}$ in (9.12a). Instead, we 'calibrate' σ_y in the following way. We simulate our stochastic economy with alternative values of σ_y and compute the standard deviation σ_u of the time series of utilization thus obtained. The empirical standard deviation that we used to scale the policy coefficient α_u at the end of chapter 8, section 2, subsection 3 can serve as a benchmark that we thereby should seek to reach, which is $\sigma_u = 1.89$. Since we need only a reasonable order of magnitude, a few sample runs suffice to find a value of σ_y that roughly fulfils this purpose. So we decide to work with

$$\sigma_p = 0.01 \cdot 1.009 \quad \sigma_y = 0.01 \cdot 0.770 \qquad (9.36)$$

Figure 9.9[23] presents the time series of a sample run of this economy over a period of 100 years. Since in the middle panel the model's output of the monthly rate of inflation has been smoothed by taking the rate over the past twelve months, the diagram is directly comparable to figure 8.6 of the Rudebusch–Svensson model (apart from the longer sample period in figure 8.6). The most important result for the stochastic KMGT model is that both its inflation rate and its rate of interest exhibit far less persistence than in the RS model. Mere visual inspection allows us to conclude

---

[23] The random shocks are specified by eqs. (9.9a), (9.12a), (9.35), (9.36). The numerical parameters are those of the stable scenario in subsection 9.3.1.

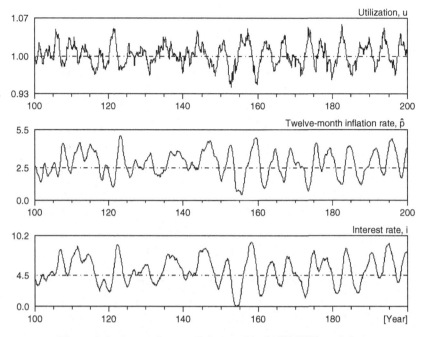

Figure 9.9: A sample run of the stochastic KMGT model

that our model is superior in this respect. As the discussion at the end of chapter 8, section 4, subsection 3 shows, this is mainly due to cancelling the accelerationist 'random walk' element in Rudebusch and Svensson's Phillips curve and substituting the concept of the inflation climate for it.

Not only are the fluctuations of the inflation rate now more strongly centred around the target $\hat{p}^* = 2.50\%$ but inflation is also nicely bounded from above and below, and the general cyclical pattern is more akin to that of utilization than in figure 8.6. Over a wide range of the chosen sample period the cycles of both variables look fairly reasonable, which is remarkable since, we repeat, the dominant eigenvalue was not complex. The average length of these cycles is perhaps a bit too short, but we abstain from searching for a better pair β_{Iu}, β_{Iq} that might improve upon this feature. We content ourselves here with pointing out that inflation suitably lags behind utilization. This is more clearly brought out by computing the implied price level and its Hodrick–Prescott trend. The trend deviations are drawn in the middle panel of figure 9.10[24] over the

[24] 'devP' are the deviations of the price level from a Hodrick–Prescott trend line (in percentage terms).

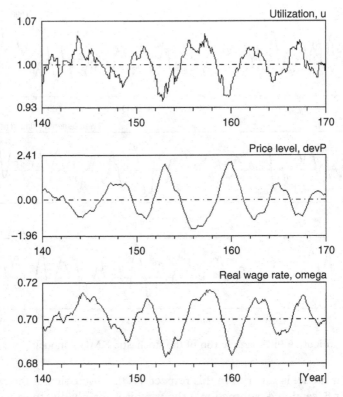

Figure 9.10: An extract from the sample run in figure 9.9

shorter time interval between $t = 140$ and $t = 170$. What we see is that, as desired, the price level is markedly countercyclical.

The bottom panel of figure 9.10 plots the real wage rate ω. This series also displays a very satisfactory cyclical pattern, and is certainly consistent with the stylized fact of procyclical real wages.

A consequence of the smaller amplitude in the fluctuations of the inflation rate is that there are considerably fewer problems with the zero bound of the rate of interest. In fact, in the sample shown in figure 9.9 the interest rate is always positive, the lowest value being $i = 0.03\%$ at time $t = 154.75$. Of course, i can become negative in other samples, but the effect is not nearly as serious as in figure 8.6. Moreover, it can plausibly be expected that a stronger nonlinearity in the investment function would reduce the probability of $i < 0$ to, practically, zero.[25]

---

[25] Incidentally, turning off the nonlinearity in (9.21), (9.22) by putting $d_1 = 1$, say (and $d_2 > d_1$), increases the standard deviation of the utilization series mildly from 1.87 to 1.96.

The few explorations that we have carried out in this section are sufficient to demonstrate that the KMGT is not open only to the mainstream methodology of the Frisch paradigm, which imposes random shocks on a stable deterministic model. They also indicate that its richer structure, when we compare it to models of the Rudebusch–Svensson variety, pays off. In particular, the KMGT model solves the problem of the high persistence in those models with an accelerationist price Phillips curve. Figure 9.10 illustrates that, additionally, the cyclical comovements of income distribution, which are not included in Rudebusch and Svensson, come out fairly well. It may thus be worthwhile to take up some of the issues studied in the literature on monetary policy and examine them anew in our (perhaps somewhat simplified) model. A first enquiry may be into the size of the – in some sense – optimal policy coefficients on output and inflation, which in the models by Rudebusch and Svensson and others are, typically, unreasonably large. In this book, however, we do not pursue this kind of research any further.

9.3.3   Dynamics in the unstable case: endogenous cycles

We now return to our standard methodology in this book to generate persistent cyclical behaviour in a deterministic model, which assumes a complex dominant eigenvalue, an unstable equilibrium and an extrinsic nonlinearity in the investment function to keep the oscillations within acceptable bounds. The numerical parameters that are supposed to achieve this goal for the KMGT model have already been introduced as the 'unstable scenario' in subsection 9.3.1. As a consequence, we can directly run simulations of this economy and see what happens.

As before, the system is activated by a shock on expected sales. The first two or three years after the impulse are not very different from the reactions in figure 9.8 for the stable scenario. Owing to the built-in instability, however, the cyclical motions do not die out. On the other hand, the nonlinearity proves to be sufficiently strong to prevent the oscillations from exploding. Moreover, soon after the start the oscillations become fairly regular, their amplitude steadily increases (if the initial shock was weak) or decreases (if it was strong), and eventually the trajectories are (practically) periodic. At least if the starting conditions are limited to a shock on y^e, the periodic orbit to which the trajectories converge is always the same, independently of the size of the initial shock. In this sense it can be said that the system has a unique limit cycle.

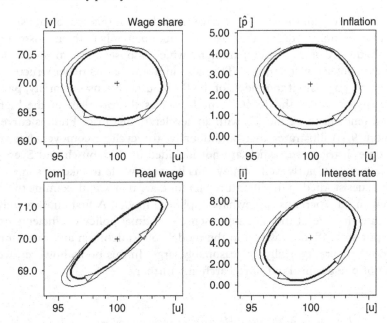

Figure 9.11: Phase diagrams of the KMGT model with endogenous cycles

Figure 9.11[26] illustrates the limit cycle in four phase diagrams, where utilization u is plotted, in turn, against the wage share v, the rate of inflation $\hat{p}$ (now the monthly rate again, annualized, of course), the real wage rate ω and the interest rate i. The limit cycle is depicted as the bold line, with the arrows indicating the anticlockwise orientation in all four cases. The solid line suggests the convergence of the trajectories after a strong shock, the projections of which on a plane spiral inwards. Conversely, after a weak shock, which is not shown here, they spiral outwards towards the closed orbit. The diagram is the counterpart of the limit cycle in figure 6.5 for the KMG model (chapter 6, section 7, subsection 2). There it was also mentioned that the existence as well as the uniqueness of the limit cycle is intuitively plausible, given that the steady state is locally unstable and that the system has only one essential (global) nonlinearity.

In three of the four panels the closed orbits in figure 9.11 are very similar to those in figure 6.5; in shape as well as size (regarding inflation, note that its steady-state value in figure 9.11 is 2.50 per cent, instead of the previous 3 per cent). By contrast, the interest rate is different,

---

[26] The bold lines are the unique limit cycles, where the arrows are drawn at identical points in time. The '+' symbols indicate the steady-state values. The interest rate is assumed to have a lower bound at zero.

as its motions are now just as symmetrical as those of the other variables. In addition, its amplitude is much larger. With a strong shock, the interest rate would actually become negative. We have ruled this out by introducing the zero value as a strict lower bound for i (similar to eq. (8.30)), an effect that is faintly visible in the lower right panel. It is remarkable that, other than discussed in chapter 8, section 4, subsection 4 for the Rudebusch–Svensson model, the economy does not enter a deflationary trap here. Even after still stronger shocks the system eventually converges to the limit cycle. However, this process may take considerably longer then, so the mere reflection of the deflationary trap is already serious enough.

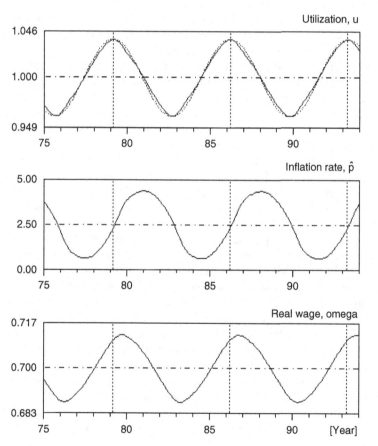

Figure 9.12: Selected time series of the limit cycle in the KMGT model

Figure 9.12[27] gives a visual impression of the time series characteristics of the limit cycle. First of all, the period is seen to be about seven years (seven years and one month, to be precise). This is shorter than the 8.25 years obtained for the KMG model in chapter 6, section 7, subsection 3, and the nonlinearity in investment works to the effect that it is also shorter than the 8.01 years resulting from the complex dominant eigenvalue in (9.34). A skilful variation of the investment coefficients could prolong the period, but this might seem like a case of carrying things too far.

The motions of all three variables selected for the time series diagram are very regular. The utilization series is not even very different from a sine wave, which is fitted in as the dotted line in the top panel. The resemblance is just as good as, if better than, in the calibration of the KMG model; see figure 6.6 in chapter 6, section 7, subsection 3. A comparison of the two figures also shows that both models give rise to about the same amplitude for utilization. We can therefore be confident that the KMGT model will reproduce the most important stylized facts of the business cycle just as well as the KMG model.

As far as can be inferred from visual inspection, these expectations are confirmed for inflation and income distribution by the other two panels in figure 9.12. The real wage rate ω is procyclical with a short lag, while the rate of inflation $\hat{p}$ exhibits an almost perfect phase shift with respect to u of a quarter of a cycle. As desired, the latter phenomenon will imply a nearly countercyclical price level.

A quantitative evaluation of the time series characteristics is given in table 9.1, which is the direct counterpart of table 6.6 for the KMG model in chapter 6, section 7, subsection 3. Comparing the two tables, the main observation is that many of the statistics are quite close to each other. This also holds true for the phase shifts of v, $\hat{p}$ and π, if the KMG model's longer cycle period of 8.25 years is taken into account.

Four differences between table 9.1 and table 6.6 are worth pointing out. (1) In the KMG model, the downswings of several variables were more pronounced than the upswings. For example, utilization had a trough value of $100\% - 4.32\%$, while the peak value was only $100\% + 3.73\%$. This asymmetry is still present in table 9.1, but it is decidedly weaker, so that without the experience in the KMG model it might have even been neglected. A similar reduction in the asymmetry of peak and trough values comes about for the capital growth rate g_k the employment rate e, the real wage rate ω, the wage share v, the trend deviations of the price level dev$p$, the inflation rate $\hat{p}$ and the inventory–capital ratio n.

(2) The behaviour of the interest rate is markedly different in the two models. For the KMGT model, the symmetrical timing of the turning

[27] The dotted line in the first panel is a synchronous sine wave fitted in.

Table 9.1: *Cyclical statistics of the KMGT model with endogenous cycles*

Variable x	x^o	In peak	In trough	σ_x/σ_u	Lag (peak)	Lag (trough)
u	100.00	+3.85	−3.93	−	−	−
g_k	3.00	+1.02	−1.04	0.26	−0.25	−0.25
e	100.00	+2.66	−2.71	0.71	0.25	0.25
ω	70.00	+1.23	−1.25	0.47	0.50	0.50
v	70.00	+0.61	−0.62	0.18	1.75	1.67
$-$ dev p	0.00	+1.77	−1.78	0.48	−0.08	−0.08
$\hat{p}$	2.50	+1.88	−1.88	0.53	1.83	1.75
π	2.50	+0.74	−0.72	0.20	2.58	2.58
i	4.50	+4.02	−4.04	1.11	1.33	1.33
q	7.50	+3.85	−3.82	1.06	−2.17	−2.17
$-\xi$	+0.66	+0.63	−0.70	0.16	0.08	0.08
$-C/Y$	−70.48	+0.93	−1.02	0.26	−0.25	−0.25
n	15.30	+0.30	−0.31	0.09	1.50	1.50

NB: Underlying is a peak-to-peak time interval of the limit cycle over 7.083 years. All variables are multiplied by 100. x^o denotes the steady-state value of variable x, dev p is the deviation of the price level from its HP 1600 trend in per cent. The standard deviation of ω is divided by its steady-state value.

points relative to utilization has already been noticed in the phase diagram, whereas in the KMG model the two lags were 1.67 vs. 0.58 years. Even more remarkable, however, is the much larger amplitude of ±4 per cent, as opposed to the less than 1 per cent in the KMG model. Of course, responsible for this are the estimated policy coefficients in the Taylor rule that we adopted.[28] The consequences of the interest rate characteristics for the return differential $q = r - (i - \pi)$ are obvious, since the amplitudes and the comovements of utilization, the wage share (and thus the profit rate r) and the inflation climate are fairly similar in the KMG and KMGT models.

The other two features relate to the Metzlerian part of the model and are of secondary importance. (3) While the KMGT model is unable to raise the amplitude of excess demand ξ and the consumption ratio C/Y (and could not have been expected to do so), its countercyclicality comes out better now and is within the desired range that we have made explicit at the beginning in table 6.2, chapter 6, section 2. (4) In contrast, the effect of the improvement of excess demand on the inventory–capital ratio n is less desirable. It slightly reduces the amplitude of n and increases the lag of inventories behind utilization so

---

[28] Variations of them and their effect on the cyclical dynamics will be studied in the next section.

much that we could even speak of a phase shift – which, however, is logical for this stock variable only if its constituting flow variable excess demand is strictly countercyclical.

In summing up the statistics collected in table 9.1, we can say that the calibration of the KMGT model also yields cyclical characteristics that are largely compatible with the stylized facts; they are similar to, or even a bit better than, what we obtained for the KMG model. The conclusion from chapter 6, section 8 thus carries over: with the KMGT model and its calibration we have put forward a (deterministic) macromodel the cyclical properties of which can stand comparison with the competitive equilibrium models of the real business cycle school.

9.4   The role of the policy coefficients in the Taylor rule

9.4.1   Stability effects

This section studies the stabilizing and, perhaps, destabilizing effects of the three policy parameters in the Taylor rule, α_i, α_p and α_u. As far as this is possible, they are contrasted with the stability effects in the most elaborated prototype model 4 from chapter 8, section 2, subsection 4, on the one hand, and the Rudebusch–Svensson model from chapter 8, section 4, on the other hand. Regarding the parameters pertaining to the private sector, we will distinguish between the stable and the unstable scenarios as they are defined in subsection 9.3.1. That is, besides $\beta_{Iq} = 0.05$ the numerical parameters (9.19), (9.32) are underlying, and $\beta_{Iu} = 0.23$ for the stable scenario, $\beta_{Iu} = 0.28$ for the unstable one.[29] The verbal descriptions below that a policy coefficient is stabilizing or destabilizing are, of course, to be understood on this basis; these properties may or may not carry over to other (more distant) parameter scenarios.

Let us begin with the role of interest rate smoothing. It is represented by the adjustment speed α_i; we recall that low values of α_i indicate a high degree of smoothing, while at high values the interest rate is always close to the Taylor rate of interest $i^* = i^*(\hat{p}, u)$. In the prototype model 4 (see Proposition 4 in chapter 8, section 3, subsection 4) as well as in the RS model (see figure 8.1 in chapter 8, section 4, subsection 2),

---

[29] To be precise, the expressions 'stable' and 'unstable' scenario presuppose the numerical values for the policy coefficients that are given in (9.32). When the latter are free to vary, instability may also prevail in the so-called stable scenario and vice versa. The expressions are, nevertheless, maintained for convenience. The 'stable scenario' may thus in the first instance be identified with $\beta_{Iu} = 0.23$, and the 'unstable scenario' with $\beta_{Iu} = 0.28$.

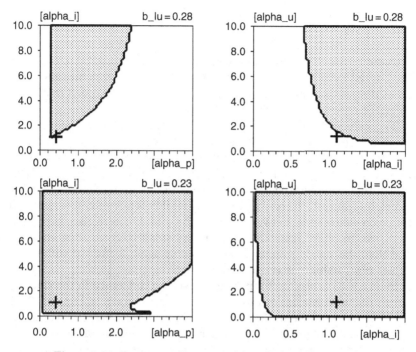

Figure 9.13: Parameter diagrams with policy coefficient α_i

low values of α_i were found to induce instability. Figure 9.13,[30] which for both scenarios computes the parameter diagrams in the (α_p, α_i) and the (α_i, α_u) planes, illustrates that this property survives in the KMGT model, since in all four panels the stability region is bounded away from the α_p and α_u axis, respectively (which is not very evident in the lower two panels, but it was checked there with a higher magnification). Hence, the conclusion continues to apply that a high degree of interest rate smoothing, or a high rigidity of the interest rate in its reactions to changes in utilization and inflation, is destabilizing.

In the prototype model 4 and in the RS model the converse was also true, so that sufficiently high values of α_i could guarantee (local) stability. In the KMGT model things are different in two respects. First, fast adjustments α_i are no longer able to restore stability if α_p is large. To take the upper left panel of figure 9.13 for the unstable scenario ($\beta_{lu} = 0.28$),

---

[30] The dotted areas are the stability regions, the crosses indicate the estimated policy coefficients. The numerical parameters underlying are those of the unstable scenario ($\beta_{lu} = 0.28$) and the stable scenario ($\beta_{lu} = 0.23$), respectively (see subsection 9.3.1 for the full specification).

if $\alpha_p = 2.6$, say, then extremely high values of α_i can still stabilize the steady state ($\alpha_i = 0.50$ and higher). At values $\alpha_p \geq 3.1$, however, α_i becomes ineffective in this regard. That the lower left panel for the stable scenario ($\beta_{Iu} = 0.23$) does not point to this kind of instability is due to the limited range of α_p shown here. Actually, instability comes about for all α_i if α_p is fixed at 6.2 or higher (though it may be argued that these values of α_p would be unreasonably high).

The reduced range of α_p in the lower left panel has the advantage that a second phenomenon can be recognized more clearly. Note first that the stability regions in the other three panels are convex, which implies in particular that, if stability prevails for some value α_i^s of the adjustment speed, then the steady state is also stable for all $\alpha_i \geq \alpha_i^s$. In the lower left panel, by contrast, the reswitching of instability is possible. It is observed for given values of α_p between roughly 2.4 and 2.9; as α_i rises here from zero, we first have instability over a very small interval, then stability, and then the steady state becomes unstable again, before at still higher values of α_i stability is eventually ensured.

Figure 9.13 is also useful in that it reveals a difference in the stability effects of the coefficient α_p from our two reference models. Figure 8.2 for the RS model in chapter 8, section 4, subsection 2 suggests that, if the system is stable at some value α_p^s, then it is also stable at all non-negative values $\alpha_p \leq \alpha_p^s$. The same holds true for the prototype model 4, which can easily be verified by solving the stability condition in Proposition 4, chapter 8, section 3, subsection 4, for α_p (see also the last paragraph in that section). The two panels to the left in figure 9.13 show that this stability property may be missing in the KMGT model. In both scenarios $\beta_{Iu} = 0.23$ and $\beta_{Iu} = 0.28$, low values of α_p render the steady state unstable even if stability prevails at higher values of this coefficient.

Interestingly, the lower bound of α_p below which the system is unstable is independent of α_i. In other words, in both panels to the left, the left boundary of the stability region is a vertical straight line (which we have checked in detail with a much higher resolution in this part of the parameter diagrams). It is furthermore remarkable that at the left boundary the leading eigenvalue of the Jacobian is real, whereas on the rest of the stability frontier (except for a very small part around the lower left corner in the lower left parameter diagram) the eigenvalue is complex, so that here – but only here – a Hopf bifurcation occurs.

After emphasizing the differences, a salient common property of α_p with the two reference models should be pointed out. In fact, what remains is that too high a responsiveness of the interest rate to the inflation gap overdoes it and destabilizes the economy (in the lower left panel of figure 9.13 this would be seen over the whole range of α_i if the α_p axis were suitably extended). It will also be seen below that the effect is independent of special values of the other policy coefficient α_u. Because of the accumulated evidence, the destabilizing potential of the inflation gap coefficient is an insight of principal importance for the central bank. On the other hand, how relevant it might become in the real world – i.e. whether the destabilizing values of α_p would be still within a plausible range – is an empirical question beyond the scope of the present model.

While the effects of especially low adjustment speeds α_i should not be neglected, the central parameters characterizing the stance of monetary policy are certainly the coefficients α_p and α_u in the Taylor rule. In this respect the stability effects of monetary policy are most conveniently studied by means of parameter diagrams in the (α_p, α_u) plane, just as has already been done in figure 8.2 for the RS model. Five properties of that diagram, which in parts have already been discussed, are notable (for easier reference the symbols $\tilde{\alpha}_p$, $\tilde{\alpha}_y$ used in the RS model may be identified with the present coefficients α_p and α_u, respectively):

(a) low values of α_p and α_u jointly ensure stability;
(b) stability for some $\alpha_p^s > 0$ implies stability for all $0 < \alpha_p \le \alpha_p^s$;
(c) large values of α_p are destabilizing;
(d) if α_p is large, then low values of α_u generate instability; and
(e) moreover, at higher (but not too high) values of α_p, the reswitching of instability may occur for α_u, such that instability prevails for low values of α_u, stability over a range of medium (or large) values of α_u, and instability again if α_u gets (very) large.

To see what becomes of these properties in the KMGT model, figure 9.14 plots four (α_p, α_u) parameter diagrams for four different values of the investment coefficient β_{Iu}; besides our two reference values $\beta_{Iu} = 0.23$ and $\beta_{Iu} = 0.28$, a still higher reaction intensity $\beta_{Iu} = 0.30$ and a much lower value $\beta_{Iu} = 0.15$ are considered.

At a glance it is immediately that property (a) is violated in three of the four cases. This means that, under what in our setting can be deemed to be 'normal' circumstances, at least one of the two policy coefficients must be sufficiently high for the steady state to be locally asymptotically stable. On the other hand, properties (c) and (d) continue to be observed in all four diagrams: in the two top panels (d) even holds for all values of α_p; in the two bottom panels (c) becomes more obvious if the α_p axis is extended.

The reswitching property (e) of α_u, however, is now ruled out, since all the stability regions are unbounded from above (this statement, too, was checked by changing the scale of the axes in the (α_p, α_u) plane).

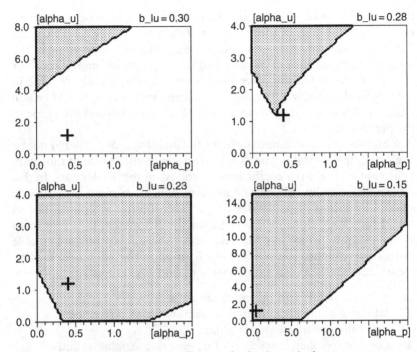

Figure 9.14: Parameter diagrams in the (α_p, α_u) plane

In addition, for every α_p there is a minimum value $\alpha_u^s \geq 0$ such that the equilibrium is stable for all $\alpha_u > \alpha_u^s$, and unstable if $0 \leq \alpha_u < \alpha_u^s$ (in case α_u^s is positive). Though the first finding should not be overrated, as in the two top panels these critical values may indeed be unrealistically high, the output coefficient α_u can in the present context be classified as unambiguously stabilizing.

That property (*b*) does not necessarily carry over to the KMGT model has already been remarked. In figure 9.14 it still applies if the high investment coefficient $\beta_{Iu} = 0.30$ is underlying, but as β_{Iu} decreases and so the stability region enlarges (note the different scaling of the α_u axis), instability drives a wedge between that region and the α_u axis. Accordingly, rising values of α_p produce a reswitching of instability over a certain (reasonable) range of given values of α_u. In particular, the phenomenon is present in our unstable scenario ($\beta_{Iu} = 0.28$) as well as in the stable scenario ($\beta_{Iu} = 0.23$). This kind of reswitching is thus a non-negligible possibility when the central bank responds to the deviations of inflation from its target.

For completeness, we may mention lastly that the stability region in the upper left panel, where it is also the case that the stability frontier is almost a straight line, corresponds well to the stability condition that has been established for the prototype model 4, in chapter 8, section 3, subsection 4. This is easily seen by rewriting the inequality in the corresponding Proposition 4 as $\alpha_u > \beta_p/\alpha_i + (\beta_p/\alpha_i)\alpha_p$. The correspondence is, however, merely qualitative. Using the numerical values $\beta_p = 0.45$ and $\alpha_i = 1.10$ from chapter 8, section 2, subsection 4, the stability condition reads $\alpha_u > 0.41 + 0.41 \cdot \alpha_p$. Hence, because of the low intercept on the α_u axis, the prototype model is normally stable, whereas stability in the upper left parameter diagram of figure 9.14 requires rather extreme values of α_u.

9.4.2   Policy changes and their impact on the dynamics in the stable case

The qualitative distinction between parameter combinations that induce stability or, alternatively, instability covers the most elementary effects to which the policy coefficients may give rise. Other effects, which continuously vary with the parameters, concern the time series characteristics. Appropriately, this question should be addressed separately for stable and unstable systems. Regarding the former, we first return to the impulse–response function in the stable scenario of the KMGT model (where $\beta_{Iu} = 0.23$) and examine how it is affected by changes in the two central coefficients α_p and α_u. The impulse being an adverse shock to expected sales in the steady-state position, the motions of utilization, inflation and the interest rate over the first ten years have already been plotted in figure 9.8, subsection 9.3.2. They are reproduced here as the bold lines in figure 9.15.[31]

The other two lines in figure 9.15 result from a *ceteris paribus* increase in either the output gap coefficient from 1.20 to $\alpha_u = 2.00$ or the inflation gap coefficient from 0.40 to $\alpha_p = 1.00$. The solid line for the first case shows that, as expected, the rise in α_u intensifies the reactions of the interest rate considerably. In contrast, the dynamic effects on utilization and inflation are very weak. If anything, we would say that the greater emphasis on output stabilization accelerates convergence back to the equilibrium values. The effects produced by the increase in α_p are even less pronounced; over long time intervals the dotted lines for u and $\hat{p}$ can hardly be distinguished from the benchmark dynamics. In this

---

[31] Given the parameters of the stable scenario (see chapter 8, section 6, subsection 1), the bold lines result from the estimated policy parameters $\alpha_p = 0.40$, $\alpha_u = 1.20$ (they are reproduced from figure 9.8); the solid lines are generated by $\alpha_p = 0.40$, $\alpha_u = 2.00$, the dotted lines by $\alpha_p = 1.00$, $\alpha_u = 1.20$. The impulse is an (identical) adverse shock to expected sales.

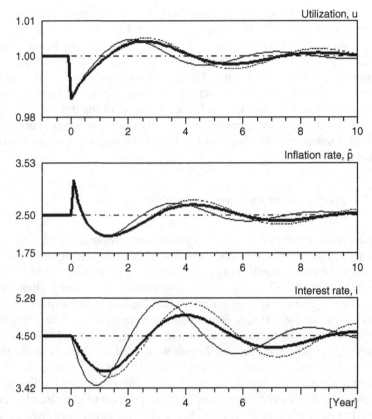

Figure 9.15: Impulse–response functions for different policy parameters

case, convergence takes a little longer, perhaps. The trifling differences between the three time series of u and $\hat{p}$ are all the more remarkable as the increase in the two policy coefficients appears to be fairly strong.

So far it follows that the prospects for the central bank to influence the economy are quite limited. The model – or, at least, the present parameter scenario – might therefore be criticized because of an ineffective interest rate channel. In this respect it is interesting to contrast figure 9.15 with the impulse–response functions that we obtained in the RS model from the same kind of simulation exercise; see figures 8.4 and 8.5 in chapter 8, sections 4, subsection 3. There the similarly strong increase in the two policy coefficients had a similarly weak effect on economic activity to that in figure 9.15. The parameter changes had a greater bearing on the time path of inflation, but the effect was not so much on 'controlling' the immediate reactions of the rate of inflation as on reducing the tenacious persistence in this variable, which we considered to be a rather unfavourable property of the RS model. Since in the KMGT model convergence is already pretty satisfactory, there is no great scope (nor 'need') for monetary policy to improve on this feature. Hence, the weak interest rate channel in our calibrated model is as much, or as little, a point of criticism as it is in the estimated RS model.

Because of the high similarities of the utilization and inflation series in the two upper panels of figure 9.15, it might even be suspected that the differences are completely washed out in a stochastic environment. This question can be readily investigated by adding the quarterly random shocks on the supply and demand side that have been introduced in subsection 9.3.2. 'Stabilization' in this framework means that a suitable choice of the policy coefficients can reduce the variability of some selected variables, where the concept of variability is conveniently represented by the standard deviation of the time series.[32] To obtain significant differences from one parameter combination to another, the law of large numbers needs to be exploited; that is, many stochastic simulation runs must be computed or they must be long enough. If each of the parameter scenarios is associated with the same sequence of random shocks, then for our limited purposes it suffices to run a given economy over 400 years 'only'.

The primary interest, of course, attaches to the standard deviations of utilization and inflation. Often these are the only statistics considered in the literature; occasionally the standard deviation of the first (quarterly) differences of the interest rate are additionally taken into account (see Rudebusch and Svensson, 1999). As we have seen in figure 9.15 that the strongest effect in the impulse–response function comes to bear on the interest rate, we will also have an eye on the standard deviation of the level of the interest rate, while for simplicity the first differences are neglected.[33]

Table 9.2 presents these standard deviation statistics (abbreviated 'sd') for a number of selected combinations of the output gap and inflation

---

[32] In the literature on optimal monetary policy that endows the central bank with a loss function to be minimized, the concern is with the variances of the time series (or quadratic terms of the variables that are discounted over time) rather than with the standard deviations. The reason is habit and the fact that in simpler models the optimization problem can thus still be solved analytically. We refer to the standard deviations, which give a more direct impression of the variability, since we content ourselves with some explorations and do not go into this kind of detail.

[33] Policy changes are very likely to affect the standard deviations of the first differences and the level of interest rate in similar ways. We prefer to consider the levels of the interest rate since this standard deviation can be directly compared to that of the rate of inflation.

Table 9.2: *Standard deviations of time series in alternative stochastic simulations*

	α_p	α_u	sd(u)	sd($\hat{p}$)	sd(i)	λ^*
	0.40	1.00	1.87	1.20	1.73	
	0.40	1.10	1.86	1.18	1.76	
(1)	**0.40**	**1.20**	**1.84**	**1.16**	**1.79**	−0.039
	0.40	1.30	1.82	1.14	1.84	
	0.40	1.40	1.81	1.13	1.88	
	0.40	2.00	1.75	1.06	2.18	
	0.00	1.20	1.72	1.57	2.05	0.011
	0.10	1.20	1.74	1.22	1.72	−0.002
(3)	0.20	1.20	1.77	1.18	1.72	−0.014
(2)	0.30	1.20	1.80	1.16	1.75	−0.027
(1)	**0.40**	**1.20**	**1.84**	**1.16**	**1.79**	−0.039
	0.50	1.20	1.88	1.16	1.85	−0.052
	1.00	1.20	2.14	1.25	2.27	−0.109
	0.30	1.10	1.82	1.19	1.71	
(2)	0.30	1.20	1.80	1.16	1.75	
	0.30	1.30	1.79	1.14	1.79	
	0.20	1.10	1.79	1.20	1.68	
(3)	0.20	1.20	1.77	1.18	1.72	
(4)	0.20	1.30	1.76	1.15	1.75	−0.016
	0.20	1.40	1.75	1.13	1.80	

NB: Based on sample runs over 400 years with identical sequences of quarterly random shocks on supply and demand. sd(u), sd($\hat{p}$) and sd(i) are the resulting standard deviations of u, $\hat{p}$ and i; λ^* is the leading eigenvalue of the Jacobian matrix (they are real). The numbers in brackets in the first column serve for easier reference in the text.

gap coefficients. The results for the estimated parameters $\alpha_p = 0.40$ and $\alpha_u = 1.20$ are given in bold face, in the two lines marked as scenario (1). Starting from this basis, we search for combinations of α_p and α_u that diminish the standard deviations of all three variables u, $\hat{p}$ and i.

The first block begins with *ceteris paribus* variations of α_u. It shows that increasing values of α_u monotonically reduce the variability of both utilization and inflation. In terms of figure 9.15, where the solid line has the coefficient $\alpha_u = 2$ underlying, this can be explained not by the amplitudes of the impulse–response function but by the faster convergence. The reduction goes, however, at the cost of a higher variability of the interest rate, a phenomenon that may also have been predicted from the third panel of figure 9.15. Since the change in sd(i) exceeds the modulus of the changes in sd(u) as well as sd($\hat{p}$), the central bank,

even if it had perfect knowledge, would thus perhaps abstain from raising its responsiveness to utilization. The first two lines in table 9.2, read
upwards from scenario (1) on, make sure that a decrease of α_u produces
the same effects in the opposite direction.

The second block in table 9.2 studies the *ceteris paribus* variations of the
other coefficient α_p. Here it should first be pointed out that an increase of
this responsiveness does *not* lower the variability of inflation but, rather,
amplifies its fluctuations. This applies equally to utilization. Interestingly, for $\alpha_p = 1.00$ the differences in the standard deviations of these
two variables from the benchmark (1) are very measurable, although
the differences in the impulse–response function are minimal and hardly
visible (see the dotted lines in the upper two panels in figure 9.15). That
with α_p the variability of the interest rate also increases will, again, have
been expected from the bottom panel of figure 9.15.

The last column for the second block in the table reports the leading
eigenvalues of the Jacobian, which are all real numbers. A higher modulus of a negative eigenvalue indicates that, eventually, the equilibrium is
approached more quickly. This information can be, however, misleading
for the stochastic dynamics. As a matter of fact, while, with respect to the
eigenvalue criterion, one might be tempted to say that rising values of
α_p are 'stabilizing', we have just seen that their increase is 'destabilizing'
as far as the variabilities of u, $\hat{p}$ and i are concerned.

The last column also tells us (in accordance with the lower left parameter diagram of figure 9.14) that putting $\alpha_p = 0$ induces local instability.
The consequence in purely linear models would be that the variances of
the state variables grow beyond bounds. In contrast, in the present case
sd($\hat{p}$) and sd(i) exceed the standard deviations of the benchmark scenario
significantly, but they are nevertheless still clearly limited; sd(u) has even
fallen. To meet the argument that the limited increase in the variability
is exclusively due to the extrinsic nonlinearity $d_1 = 0.020$, $d_2 = 0.035$
in the investment function (see subsection 9.3.1), we reran the simulation with this mechanism eliminated (which is easily done by assigning
extremely high values to d_1 and d_2). As repeatedly noted, while with this
specification the model is still nonlinear, it is almost linear. Surprisingly,
cancelling the investment nonlinearity even lowers the standard deviations of inflation and the interest rate: sd($\hat{p}$) $= 1.57$, sd(i) $= 1.24$; only
the variability of utilization increases slightly, to sd(u) $= 1.77$.

This finding confirms the conjecture made at the end of subsection 9.2.2 for less plausible parameter values, which was illustrated there
by figure 9.3. If initially after a shock a deterministic system shows a
strong tendency back to the equilibrium values and only in the long run
diverges from them, then a stochastic version of the economy, simply

because of the frequent arrival of shocks, may be stable (at least in practice) and may not explode. To be honest, the statistics in table 9.2 are no
definite proof of the claim. This would require a more extensive study,
from which we refrain at present as it is only a minor theme here.

Back to our concern to improve on the coefficients α_p and α_u such
that all three standard deviations are diminished. Combination (2) in the
second block of table 9.2, obtained from a small *ceteris paribus* decline of
α_p, is in this sense Pareto-superior to scenario (1). The third block in the
table examines whether, by starting from this, a further improvement is
possible by then varying α_u. This attempt is, however, seen to fail.

Though scenario (3) with a stronger reduction of α_p, defined in the
second block of the table as well, does not Pareto-dominate scenario (1),
the rise in sd($\hat{p}$) is relatively moderate in comparison to the decrease
of sd(u) and sd(i). Therefore, one may hope that, subsequently, a suitable variation of α_u can sufficiently lower sd($\hat{p}$) without simultaneously
raising the other two standard deviations too much. This is the motive
for the computations in the fourth block. In relation to (1) as well as
to (2), the outcome is in fact better for $\alpha_p = 0.20$, $\alpha_u = 1.30$ in scenario
(4) (whereas the larger eigenvalue seems to predict the contrary). On
the other hand, (3) itself cannot be improved upon by a change in α_u
alone. It thus follows that, if the variations of α_p, α_u are restricted to
steps of 0.10, then combinations (3) and (4) are both Pareto-efficient
(which, of course, does not rule out there being further Pareto-efficient
pairs α_p, α_u in the neighbourhood of (3) and (4)).

A unique optimal combination of α_p and α_u could be determined if
we set up a loss function L for the central bank and minimize it. In
accordance with the literature on optimal monetary policy rules, a specification referring to the variances of u, $\hat{p}$ and i such as $L = \xi_u \text{Var}(u) +
\xi_p \text{Var}(\hat{p}) + (1 - \xi_u - \xi_p) \text{Var}(i)$ might be proposed, with given weights
$0 \leq \xi_u, \xi_p \leq 1$ (and $\xi_u + \xi_p \leq 1$). However, we do not want to carry the
issue thus far. The few explorations in table 9.2 are already remark-
able enough, for they demonstrate that the results from the estimated
policy coefficients of scenario (1) can be enhanced only moderately.
This is in stark contrast to what the literature suggests (see, for example, Rudebusch and Svensson, 1999), namely that the estimated policy
parameters are rather inefficient, and that (*a*) higher and (*b*) far higher
values would lead to a much better performance by the economy.

Regarding a Pareto-efficient combination of α_p, α_u such as scenario
(4), it is not only the naked time series statistics that should be computed.
We should also have an eye directly on the thus generated time series and
check that they still appear reasonable (though they certainly may not be
required to produce a perfect match to the data). Our enquiry into the

stochastic dynamics of the KMGT model is therefore concluded with a presentation of a sample run of this exemplary scenario. Incidentally, we would like to see more such time series diagrams in the literature on interest rate reaction functions.[34] They would provide additional information and, in particular, may convince the reader that a rule asserted to be optimal does not just establish some formal dynamic system that has lost too much of the model's original economic meaning.

Figure 9.16 shows the evolution of u, $\hat{p}$ and i in a sample run of scenario (4) over the full period of 400 years (inflation in the discretized, monthly model is again computed over twelve months). The changes vis-à-vis the benchmark scenario (1) that these Pareto-efficient coefficients ($\alpha_p = 0.20$, $\alpha_u = 1.30$) induce are not very great; the main qualitative characteristics of figure 9.9 for scenario (1) are maintained. The only potentially undesirable feature is a weak persistence phenomenon for inflation and the interest rate. Remarkable, on the positive side, is the

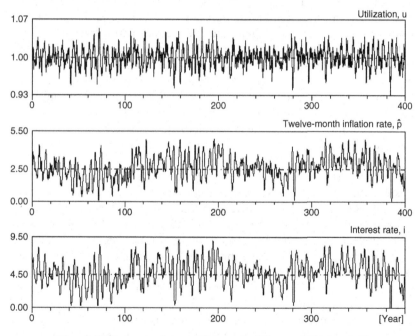

Figure 9.16: A sample run of scenario (4): α_p=0.20, α_u=1.30

---

[34] Personally, none of the three authors of this book has ever seen a time series diagram in published articles or working papers that depicts a stochastic realization of an optimal policy.

narrow range of the fluctuations in both utilization and the rate of inflation. As already observed before, the fluctuations of the interest rate are somewhat wider. Over the whole period there is, nevertheless, only one instance where the rate falls below zero (a few months around $t = 384.75$, where the minimum value $i = -1.00\%$ is attained). In all these respects, even if we do not consider them perfectly satisfactory, the dynamic outcome of the Pareto-improved KMGT model as well is clearly superior to the properties of the Rudebusch–Svensson model (which have been exemplified in figure 8.6, chapter 8, section 4, subsection 3).

9.4.3   Policy changes and their impact on the dynamics in the unstable case

To evaluate the dynamic effects of a change in the policy parameters, the preceding subsection started by studying the induced impulse–response functions. While this is an informative concept for stable systems, it is less appropriate if the steady-state position is locally unstable. The basic idea of an impulse–response function can, however, be easily generalized to these systems when they generate endogenous and persistent cyclical behaviour that takes the form of unique and attractive deterministic limit cycles. It just needs to be borne in mind what, in the two deterministic cases of a stable system and a cyclical system, the natural states of reference are for where to start from and then ignite the impulse: in the first case, this is the point of equilibrium; in the second case, it is the entire limit cycle. For the latter, though, it has to be noted that the response depends not only on the initial shock as such but also on its timing – the stage of the cycle at which it arrives.

The property of a unique limit cycle to which the system's trajectories eventually converge has been established for the calibrated, locally unstable KMGT model of subsection 9.3.3. For the present purpose of examining the changes in the policy coefficients, we do not stick to a strict analogy to the impulse–response function of systems with a stable equilibrium – that is, we leave the effect of a demand shock on a given economy to one side. The shock, so to speak, that we instead choose to impose on the limit cycle is nothing other than the sudden change of one of the policy coefficients themselves.

Let us thus consider the unstable scenario specified in chapter 8, section 6, subsection 1 and put the economy on its stable limit cycle, the characteristics of which are described in chapter 8, section 6, subsection 3. In the first experiment, we want to study the effects from the same increase of the inflation gap coefficient as in the stable scenario in the previous section. At that stage of the limit cycle when inflation has risen above its target and in the past has been experienced to continue rising, the central bank is assumed to take a greater concern in this evolution and so increases α_p from its original value 0.40 to $\alpha_p = 1.00$. The time series of u, $\hat{p}$ and i in figure 9.17[35] show what then happens, in comparison to the time paths that would be obtained if the old policy rule were upheld.

The new coefficient $\alpha_p = 1.00$ is set up at time $t = 9.50$. In comparing the solid line to the dotted line, which still has $\alpha_p = 0.40$ underlying, the policy change is seen to have practically no impact on the further rise of

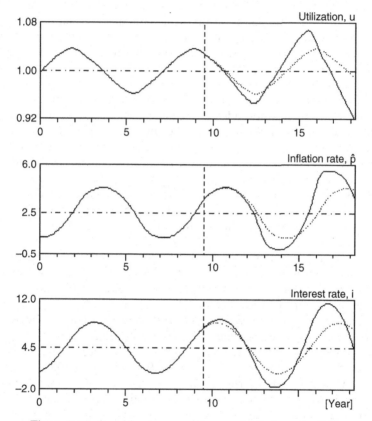

Figure 9.17: A sudden increase of α_p on the limit cycle of the unstable scenario

[35] The solid line until $t = 9.5$ and the dotted line thereafter is the limit cycle generated by the unstable scenario of the KMGT model (see subsection 9.3.3), where $\alpha_p = 0.40$. The solid line after $t = 9.5$ is brought about by the (maintained) change of the policy coefficient to $\alpha_p = 1.00$ at that time.

the rate of inflation over the next eighteen months, although a certain reaction of the rate of interest is visible. In this respect, we get a similar (non-)result to that in the comparison of the impulse–response functions in the stable scenario with $\alpha_p = 0.40$ and $\alpha_p = 1.00$ in figure 9.15. On the output side, one year after the break a weak acceleration in the downturn of utilization can be observed.

It takes a few years for the effects of the central bank's higher responsiveness to work out fully. Regarding output, the impression of, say, the first eighteen months is confirmed and utilization happens to reach its trough earlier. On the other hand, the trough value is also lower than in the reference cycle. The deeper recession causes a deeper fall in the rate of inflation, although it occurs with some delay, when the recovery of economic activity has already set in. The next expansion of output is much stronger than under the old policy, which also holds true for the subsequent rise of inflation. If the reaction intensities in the private sector and, in particular, the nonlinearity in the investment function remain unaltered, then the system converges to a new limit cycle with considerably larger amplitudes of the state variables. In short, it can be said that the effects of the higher coefficient α_p are negligible in the short run, whereas they are unambiguously destabilizing in the longer run.

Figure 9.17 suggests that the central bank, after realizing that its immediate influence on the economy is minimal, may alternatively reduce its responsiveness to the inflation gap in order to dampen the oscillations in the medium term. This hope is fulfilled if the central bank is sufficiently cautious and lowers α_p by not more than 0.17, from 0.40 to 0.23. For $\alpha_p \leq 0.22$, however, we obtain the phenomenon pointed out in subsection 9.2.2: not only do the formal differential equations have second and third stationary points, but without further constraints the system also converges to one of them. In the present case these equilibrium values are not economically meaningful, either. For example, given $\alpha_p = 0.20$ and starting the dynamics with our usual adverse demand shock, the initial oscillations are maintained for several decades, but they gradually shift downwards and, after two or three hundred years, the variables eventually converge to $u = 0.979$, $\hat{p} = -7.99\%$ and $i = -10.62\%$.[36]

On the other hand, it turns out that setting α_p at 0.30 or 0.25 dampens the amplitude of all three key variables. The first block in table 9.3 gives an impression of the quantitative improvement or deterioration brought about by a lower or higher coefficient α_p. The underlying simulations let the economy converge to the new limit cycle and then compute the standard deviations of u, $\hat{p}$ and i on this reference trajectory over the full cycle period T. Besides, T itself is reported.

[36] These limits are different for different values of α_p.

Table 9.3: *Standard deviations of time series in alternative limit cycles*

α_p	α_u	sd(u)	sd($\hat{p}$)	sd(i)	T
0.22	1.20	Convergence towards second equilibrium			
0.30	1.20	2.00	1.10	2.29	7.58
0.40	**1.20**	**2.60**	**1.38**	**2.88**	**7.08**
0.50	1.20	3.33	1.75	3.60	6.50
1.00	1.20	12.49	6.13	11.19	4.75
0.40	1.00	3.37	1.81	3.34	7.17
0.40	**1.20**	**2.60**	**1.38**	**2.88**	**7.08**
0.40	1.50	2.16	1.13	2.73	6.58
0.40	2.00	1.87	0.95	2.79	5.83
0.40	2.50	1.71	0.86	2.96	5.17
0.40	3.00	1.63	0.79	3.13	4.75
0.30	1.20	2.00	1.10	2.29	7.58
0.30	1.50	1.82	0.97	2.34	6.83
0.30	2.00	1.66	0.85	2.51	5.92

NB: T is the period of the limit cycle brought about by the policy coefficients; 'sd' denotes the standard deviations of the time series over a full cycle period.

Comparing the first block in table 9.3 with the second block in table 9.2 for the stochastic simulations in the stable scenario, it is seen that a suitable reduction of α_p now diminishes all three standard deviations, not just sd(u) and sd(i) as in table 9.2. In addition, these statistics change more drastically in table 9.3.

The variations of the second policy parameter α_u are investigated in the same manner. Again, we begin with an inspection of our generalized impulse–response function. The economy is assumed to be on the limit cycle of the unstable reference scenario and the central bank then changes α_u from 1.20 to $\alpha_u = 2.00$. A meaningful time for such a break is the late expansion of output, at $t = 8$ in figure 9.18.[37] A success of the increase in the responsiveness to utilization is already apparent after one year: accumulation falters earlier and the peak value of u (the solid line) is lower than it was on the (dotted) reference cycle. That the rate of inflation is slightly higher in this first year is mentioned only for completeness; the difference is virtually invisible.

[37] The solid line until $t = 8$ and the dotted line thereafter is the limit cycle generated by the unstable scenario of the KMGT model (see subsection 9.3.3), where $\alpha_u = 1.20$. The solid line after $t = 8$ is brought about by the (maintained) change of the policy coefficient to $\alpha_u = 2.00$ at that time.

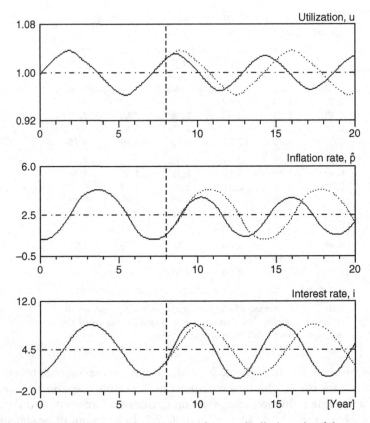

Figure 9.18: A sudden increase of α_u on the limit cycle of the unstable scenario

In the ensuing contraction, it is also the case that the trough of utilization is less deep than on the reference cycle, which subsequently carries over to inflation. On the whole, a new periodic motion is soon reached, with a lower amplitude of both utilization and the rate of inflation. Moreover, after a while the oscillations of the interest rate are slightly dampened. The quantitative reduction of the standard deviations of the three variables is detailed in the second block of table 9.3.

Note the different effects from the *ceteris paribus* increases of α_u in the first block of table 9.2, where sd(u) and sd($\hat{p}$) also decrease, though to a far lesser extent, but sd(i) rises. However, the limit cycle oscillations of the interest rate widen again as α_u is increased further, to values such as $\alpha_u = 2.50$ or $\alpha_u = 3.00$, say. We can thus conclude that a limited increase of the output gap responsiveness from the estimated value $\alpha_u = 1.20$

stabilizes the economy in an unambiguous way; larger increases reinforce the reduction of the amplitudes of utilization and inflation, but now at the cost of a (gently) higher variability of the rate of interest.

The last block of table 9.3 plays around a little with the two policy coefficients and so indicates where additional improvements might be possible. Generally, it may be observed in table 9.3 that the policy effects on the amplitudes are independent of the associated period of the limit cycles. Lower amplitudes brought about by higher values of α_u go along with shorter cycles, while the (moderately) lower values of α_p bring about narrower but also longer oscillations of the three variables.

Just as with table 9.2 in the previous subsection, we could again search for 'Pareto-efficient' combinations of the policy coefficients. Here, however, we are content with pointing out that the variations of α_p and α_u have similarly stabilizing and destabilizing effects on the time series of utilization, inflation and the interest rate, though not in every detail, as in the stable scenario and its stochastic dynamics. There may now be greater scope for improvements by a higher responsiveness to utilization, but these prospects are still limited as the reactions of the interest rate and the increase in the amplitude of the oscillations that are thus generated must not be too strong. The policy effects that we obtain within the Frisch paradigm, on the one hand, and within the framework of self-sustaining endogenous cycles, on the other hand, are therefore broadly compatible. This observation give us further confidence in the approach of the present Keynes–Metzler–Goodwin–Taylor model, that it is also suitable for studying the most common monetary policy rules.

However, before the issue of optimal (in some sense) policy coefficients is pursued in greater depth (which is not our concern here), additional extrinsic nonlinearities in the model's behavioural assumptions should be considered, in order to lend greater robustness to the economy when it moves into the outer regions of the state space. Stronger self-stabilizing forces in the private sector may thus guard against over-interpretations of the efficiency or inefficiency of the measures of monetary policy.

9.5   Towards a landscape of the parameter stability effects in KMGT

9.5.1   Reference to the (β_{Iu}, β_{Iq}) parameter plane

After enquiring into the effects from variations of the policy coefficients in the Taylor rule, we include the other behavioural parameters in the analysis, which represent the disequilibrium adjustments in the private sector. However, we limit ourselves to their impact on the local dynamics around the steady-state position; that is, we examine how the steady state's local asymptotic stability is affected by changes in the calibrated parameters. A study of this kind has already been undertaken for the KMG model in chapter 7, section 5, and so it is only natural that we employ the same procedures for the present KMGT model. Our final aim is to characterize the key parameters as stabilizing destabilizing or ambiguous in this respect. In particular, these results can then be compared to what we have obtained in the KMG model.

As in chapter 7, section 5, subsection 1, we begin our investigation by referring to the stability region in the parameter plane of the two investment coefficients, with β_{Iu} on the horizontal and β_{Iq} on the vertical axis. On the basis of the calibrated parameter values given in (9.19), (9.32), this region is drawn as the dotted area in figure 9.6, subsection 9.3.1. The analysis concerns the other parameters of the model, which are now evaluated in terms of how an exogenous *ceteris paribus* change of them modifies the (β_{Iu}, β_{Iq}) stability region – whether the region is enlarged or reduced, or whether it is enlarged in some parts of the parameter plane and reduced in others. In this section, the expressions 'stabilizing', 'destabilizing' or 'ambiguous' relate to these reactions. Indeed, the concepts can be somewhat refined, and table 9.4 in its summary of the stability effects adopts a few extra symbols. The precise rules for assigning the symbols to the parameters have been laid out in chapter 7, section 5, subsection 1 and they are here reproduced for convenience.

Symbols for the effects of *ceteris paribus* parameter variations in the (β_{Iu}, β_{Iq}) plane (table 9.4):

+: An increase of the exogenously varying parameter (β_{pu}, for example) generally enlarges the stability region in the (β_{Iu}, β_{Iq}) plane (except perhaps for small subsets), such that it strictly contains the original stability region, which has the calibrated value of β_{pu} underlying, as a subset. This also applies the other way round: a decrease of the exogenous parameter reduces the stability region such that it becomes a strict subset of the original one. In this respect the parameter is *stabilizing*.

−: An increase (decrease) of the exogenous parameter (β_{we}, for example) reduces (enlarges) the stability region in the sense just described. Accordingly, the exogenous parameter is characterized as *destabilizing*.

a: This letter denotes *ambiguous* effects. An increase of the parameter noticeably enlarges the stability region in some parts of the (β_{Iu}, β_{Iq}) plane and reduces it in others, so that neither the new stability region nor the original one tends to be a subset of the other; and the same holds true if the exogenous parameter decreases.

Table 9.4: *The impact of parameter variations on the stability region in the* (β_{Iu}, β_{Iq}) *plane*

'Exogenous' parameter	Impact on stability region	Local distance if	
		param.↑	param.↓
$\beta_{pu} (= 0.15)$	+	↓	↑
$\beta_{pv} (= 1.50)$	a	↑	↑
$\kappa_p\ (= 0.00)$	+	↓	–
$\beta_{we} (= 0.55)$	–	↑	↓
$\beta_{wv} (= 0.50)$	(–)	↑	↓
$\kappa_w\ (= 0.00)$	(+)	↓	–
$\beta_\pi\ (= 1.00)$	(a)	↑	↓
$\kappa_\pi\ (= 0.50)$	+	↓	↑
$\beta_y\ (= 8.00)$	–	↑	↓
$\beta_{nn} (= 1.25)$	–	↑	↓
$\alpha_i\ (= 1.10)$	+	↓	↑
$\alpha_p\ (= 0.40)$	a	↑	↑
$\alpha_u\ (= 1.20)$	+	↓	↑

NB: Numbers in parentheses are the calibrated values summarized in (9.19), (9.32). The symbols are explained in the main text.

(+): Though the stabilizing effect is still visible in the parameter diagram, it appears to be rather weak. Correspondingly for (−) and (a).

Local distance: This refers to the two investment coefficients of the unstable scenario, $(\beta_{Iu}, \beta_{Iq}) = (0.280, 0.050)$, and their distance from the stability region, after the exogenous parameter has changed upwards (↑) or downwards (↓), respectively. The reaction is denoted by an upward arrow (↑, in the main body of table 9.4) if the distance thus widens, and by a downward arrow (↓) if the distance narrows. Because (β_{Iu}, β_{Iq}) is originally close to the stability frontier, the latter means that a minor change of the exogenous parameter may already cause $(\beta_{Iu}, \beta_{Iq}) = (0.280, 0.050)$ to be contained in the new stability region (the distance becomes negative, so to speak).

Figure 9.19[38] illustrates these effects for a few selected parameters. The upper left panel shows a shrinking stability region as the slope coefficient of the wage Phillips curve β_{we} is increased to a value $\beta_{we} = 0.70$; hence

---

[38] The dotted areas are the stability regions in the new situation, with *ceteris paribus* $\beta_{we} = 0.70$, etc. The thin lines are the stability frontiers in the unstable scenario, where, as also indicated by the crosses, $(\beta_{Iu}, \beta_{Iq}) = (0.280, 0.050)$.

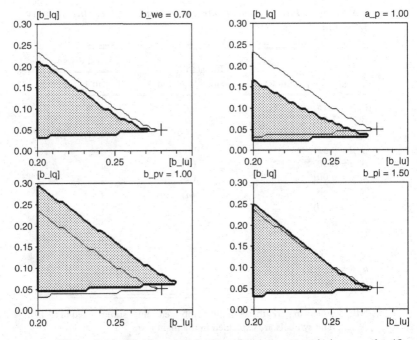

Figure 9.19: The impact of selected parameter variations on the (β_{Iu}, β_{Iq}) stability region

the minus sign in the fourth row of table 9.4. Note, however, that only the north-east stability frontier retreats; in the lower part the new and old frontiers are practically identical. Clearly, the new stability region moves away from the reference coefficients $(\beta_{Iu}, \beta_{Iq}) = (0.280, 0.050)$, which is indicated by the upward arrow ↑ in the fourth row of the table. A decrease of β_{we} (down to $\beta_{we} = 0.40$, say) produces the opposite effects, which, in particular, gives rise to the downward arrow in the last column of that row.

An ambiguous shift of the stability region is brought about by an increase of the inflation gap policy coefficient to $\alpha_p = 1.00$ in the upper right panel of figure 9.19. In the north-east we see a strong retreat of the frontier, while in the southern part pairs (β_{Iu}, β_{Iq}) render the steady state stable that previously, with $\alpha_p = 0.40$, led to instability.

This ambiguity phenomenon is of a different kind from the ambiguity in the upper right panel in figure 9.14, where (over a certain range of given values of α_u) a reswitching of instability is observed as α_p rises from zero. Common to both phenomena, however, is the fact that we cannot make a definite statement as to whether a change of α_p favours or disfavours local stability; it always depends upon the specific combination of the other parameters that we consider. Besides, it may be mentioned that a decrease of α_p causes the entire (β_{Iu}, β_{Iq}) stability region to shift to the north, which explains the upward arrow in table 9.4 for this case as well.

The two bottom panels of figure 9.19 present additional examples of ambiguous stability effects, through a change of β_{pv} and β_{π}, respectively. Given that in the lower right diagram a major increase of the adjustment speed β_{π} from 1.00 to $\beta_{\pi} = 1.50$ is assumed, the impact on the stability region is pretty weak, so for this parameter the *a* symbol is bracketed in table 9.4.

The assessment of the other parameters in the table have been obtained in similar ways. On the whole, table 9.4 can be directly compared to table 7.1 in chapter 7, section 5, subsection 1 – except that in the former the secondary parameters β_{zu}, s_c and τ_w are left to one side, the KMG model's interest elasticity $\eta_{m,i}$ of money demand has no role to play in KMGT and, on the other hand, the present policy coefficients α_i, α_p, α_u do not show up in KMG. We abstain here from pointing out the similarities or differences for the parameters appearing in both tables, but postpone a final and succinct comparison to a later subsection. Lastly, regarding the stabilizing policy coefficients α_i and α_u in table 9.4, we mention that this property is much in line with the results discussed in subsection 9.4.1.

9.5.2   Reference to different stability intervals

To broaden the basis on which the stability effects of the parameters have been evaluated so far, this subsection presents a second battery of experiments. Following the procedure in chapter 7, section 5, subsection 2, five parameters are selected, and then an investigation is carried out to discover how the stability interval of each one of them is affected if the other parameters undergo their *ceteris paribus* variations. The stability interval of such a coefficient β, of course, is the range of values that, given the other numerical parameters of the KMGT model, induce local asymptotic stability. Concerning the variations of a different parameter $\tilde{\beta}$, which is in this context the exogenous parameter, their impact on the stability interval of β can be conveniently studied by means of the $(\tilde{\beta}, \beta)$ parameter diagram; we need only note down how the vertical extension of the stability region changes as we go along the horizontal $\tilde{\beta}$ axis. These parameter diagrams were computed for both the unstable scenario where $\beta_{Iu} = 0.280$, and the stable scenario, with $\beta_{Iu} = 0.230$ – which, however, proved unnecessary since there were no great differences in the qualitative effects.

Table 9.5: *The impact of parameter variations on the stability intervals of five selected ('endogenous') parameters*

Exogenous parameter	Impact on stability interval of				
	α_u	β_{Iu}	β_{Iq}	β_{we}	β_π
β_{Iu}	−	×	−	−	−[~]
β_{Iq}	a	a	×	−[a]	a
β_{pu}	+	(+)	+	+	+
β_{pv}	a	a	(−)	a[−]	a
κ_p	+	(+)	+	+	+
β_{we}	−[~]	−	−	×	−[~]
β_{wv}	−	(−)	(−)	−	(−)
κ_w	+[a]	~[a]	~[a]	+[a]	+[a]
β_π	a	(−)	a	a	×
κ_π	+[a]	(+)[a]	(+)[a]	+[a]	a
β_y	−[~]	(−)	(−)	−	−
β_{nn}	−[~]	−	−	−	−
α_i	+[~]	(+)	+	+[a]	+
α_p	a	a	(−)	a	a
α_u	×	+	+	+	+

NB: The symbols are explained in the main text.

The five selected parameters in chapter 7, section 5, subsection 2 for the KMG model were $\eta_{m,i}$, β_{Iu}, β_{Iq}, β_{we} and β_π. This choice is maintained except for the interest elasticity $\eta_{m,i}$, which is replaced with the utilization policy coefficient α_u.[39] The effects that β_{Iu}, β_{Iq} and the thirteen parameters considered in table 9.4 exert on the stability intervals of these five parameters are summarized in table 9.5. It uses the symbols of table 9.4 in an analogous way, but allows for some additional differentiation. The precise interpretation is as follows.

Symbols for the effects of *ceteris paribus* parameter variations on the stability intervals of selected other parameters (table 9.5)

+: Given the numerical values of all the other parameters of the KMGT model, an increase of the exogenous parameter (β_{pu}, for example) widens the interval of the values of the (single) endogenous parameter under consideration (β_{Iq}, for example) that give rise to local stability. A decrease of the exogenous parameter, on the other hand, diminishes

---

[39] Both coefficients are unambiguous: $\eta_{m,i}$ was destabilizing in the KMG model, while so far α_u has been found to be clearly stabilizing.

this stability interval. As before, an exogenous parameter giving rise to these effects is called *stabilizing*.

−: An increase of the exogenous parameter (β_{we}, for example) reduces the stability interval of the endogenous parameter (β_{Iq}, for example), while a decrease broadens it. The exogenous parameter is accordingly characterized as *destabilizing*.

a: This again stands for *ambiguous* effects. For example, significant subsets of higher values − as well as lower values − of the exogenous parameter widen the stability interval of the endogenous parameter.

(+): Though the stability intervals are visibly enlarged (reduced) by an increase (decrease) of the exogenous parameter, the effect appears to be rather weak. Correspondingly for (−) and (*a*).

∼: Variations of the exogenous parameter have only negligible effects on the stability interval.

[a]: When added to one of the symbols above: there is a certain range of the exogenous parameter further away from the calibrated value where its impact on the stability region of the endogenous parameter is ambiguous. Other combinations of a symbol and a bracketed symbol are to be read correspondingly.

Given these specification, table 9.5 is self-explanatory. For completeness, we add remarks on three cells of the table. Similar notes on the three exogenous parameters (β_{Iq}, κ_w, and κ_π) that they involve may be made for a few other cells, but the three observations reported here are sufficiently representative.

Cell (β_{Iq}, β_π): Parameter β_{iq} acts ambiguously on the stability intervals of β_π if $\beta_{Iq} = 0.230$ is underlying. Total instability prevails if $\beta_{Iq} = 0.280$ is assumed.

Cell (κ_w, β_π): With respect to the stability intervals of β_π, rising values of κ_w are destabilizing only in great distance from the calibrated $\kappa_w = 0$; as a minimum, κ_w must exceed 0.50 for this.

Cell (κ_π, β_{we}): While rising values of κ_π can also have a negative bearing on the stability intervals of β_{we}, this presupposes extreme values, such as $\kappa_\pi > 0.90$, or even $\kappa_\pi > 0.95$.

The counterpart of table 9.5 for the KMG model is table 7.2 in chapter 7, section 5, subsection 2; except for the parameters mentioned above, the entries of the two tables are directly comparable. We will not dwell on the details of such a juxtaposition but, instead, prefer to proceed with the overall characterization of the parameters in the KMGT model vs. the KMG model. This is the subject of the next subsection.

9.5.3   A succinct characterization of the parameters in KMG and KMGT

The aim expressed at the beginning of our numerical stability analysis was to put each parameter under consideration into one of the broad categories 'stabilizing', 'destabilizing' and 'ambiguous'. On the basis of the information collected in tables 9.4 and 9.5, we are now in a position to do this. Of course, such an assignment can never go without some qualification; in particular, for some parameters the stabilizing or destabilizing effects may be stronger than for others. Here, we nevertheless disregard these finer points in order to obtain a clear and concise message, which is of the same kind as our summary for the KMG model. Thus, the parameter characterization on which we settle for the KMGT model is given in table 9.6. Where possible, it is compared directly to the evaluation in the KMG model, which we reproduce from table 7.3 in chapter 7, section 5, subsection 3. As far as the impact of the behavioural parameters on local stability in the two models are concerned, table 9.6 sums up in a nutshell the main result of the book.

The common effects of and differences between the KMG and KMGT models are obvious. We point out a few features that we consider to be noteworthy.

(1) Not only does the KMGT model determine the interest rate in a different way from the KMG model, but the interest rate also appears to respond somewhat differently to the other state variables in the two models. We see this reflected in the fact that the responsiveness β_{Iq} of investment to changes in the return differential $q = r - (i - \pi)$ is no longer generally stabilizing in the KMGT model but becomes ambiguous.

(2) There are three coefficients common to both models that measure the responsiveness to changes in economic activity, which is represented by utilization u in β_{Iu} and β_{pu} or the employment rate e in β_{we}. All three of these coefficients play basically the same role in the two models.

(3) The core coefficients in the two Phillips curves, β_{pu} and β_{we} in the price and the wage Phillips curve, respectively, both act in KMGT in the same way as before, remaining stabilizing in the first case and destabilizing in the second case. We illustrate this by plotting the (β_{we}, β_{pu}) parameter diagram in figure 9.20.[40] Comparing it with the

---

[40] Underlying is the unstable scenario, where, in particular, $\beta_{Iu} = 0.280$. Pairs in the dotted area induce local stability; instability prevails outside. The cross indicates the calibrated values of β_{we} and β_{pu}.

Table 9.6: *A succinct characterization of the parameter stability effects in KMG and KMGT*

Parameter	Theoretical context	In KMG	In KMGT
β_{Iu}	Utilization in fixed investment	Destabilizing	Destabilizing
β_{Iq}	Return differential in investment	Stabilizing	Ambiguous
β_{pu}	Utilization in price Phillips curve	Stabilizing	Stabilizing
β_{pv}	Wage share in price Phillips curve	Ambiguous	Ambiguous
κ_p	Weight of current inflation in price Phillips curve	Stabilizing	Stabilizing
β_{we}	Employment rate in wage Phillips curve	Destabilizing	Destabilizing
β_{wv}	Wage share in wage Phillips curve	Ambiguous	Destabilizing
κ_w	Weight of current inflation in wage Phillips curve	Destabilizing	Stabilizing
β_π	Adjustment speed for inflation climate π	Ambiguous	Ambiguous
κ_π	Weight of adaptive expectations in revisions of π	Ambiguous	Stabilizing
β_y	Adjustment speed for expected sales	Ambiguous	Destabilizing
β_{nn}	Stock adjustment speed	Ambiguous	Destabilizing
$\eta_{m,i}$	Interest elasticity of money demand	Destabilizing	n.a.
α_i	Adjustment speed of i towards Taylor rate	n.a.	Stabilizing
α_p	Inflation gap coefficient in Taylor rule	n.a.	Ambiguous
α_u	Utilization coefficient in Taylor rule	n.a.	Stabilizing

NB: Abbreviation 'n.a.' stands for 'not applicable' i.e. the parameter is absent in the respective model.

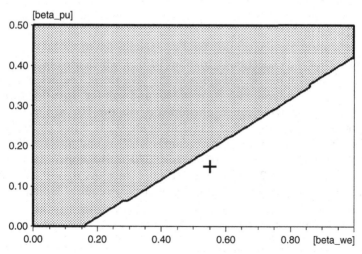

Figure 9.20: The parameter diagram of (β_{we}, β_{pu}) for the KMGT model

two lower parameter diagrams in figure 7.7, chapter 7, section 3, subsection 3, for the KMG model, it is seen that the shapes of the stability regions are indeed fairly similar.[41]

(4) Concerning the finer details of the price and wage Phillips curves, the transition from KMG to KMGT has a different impact on the stability effects from the two curves, which are brought about by the other coefficients. While the two parameters in the price Phillips curve, β_{pv} and κ_p, act similarly in both models, β_{wv} and κ_w in the wage Phillips curve change their role - and, moreover, in a way that would have been hard to predict. A stronger influence of the wage share in KMGT (i.e. a higher coefficient β_{wv}), which is ambiguous in KMG, is destabilizing in KMGT. A higher weight parameter κ_w, which is destabilizing in KMG, now even becomes stabilizing. This finding again underlines the fact that the additional mechanisms in the two Phillips curves, which involve the wage share and the seemingly innocent term representing benchmark inflation, can have quite complicated consequences for the dynamics of the model where they are integrated.

(5) Regarding the adjustments of the inflation climate, it is perhaps surprising that a higher weight κ_π of adaptive expectations (and not of the regressive expectations, with their return-to-normal tendency) proves to be largely stabilizing in KMGT, whereas it is ambiguous in KMG. As in the KMG model, however, the range over which these effects apply is quite sensitive to the variations of other parameters. For the KMG model this was illustrated by the eight plots of the (β_π, κ_π) stability regions under different values of the interest elasticity $\eta_{m,i}$ in figure 7.16, chapter 7, section 4, subsection 4.

Figure 9.21 repeats this kind of exercise for the KMGT model, where for the exogenous variations of $\eta_{m,i}$, which are obsolete here, we substitute minor variations of the investment coefficient β_{Iu}. In the stable scenario with $\beta_{Iu} = 0.230$, and still for $\beta_{Iu} = 0.260$, local stability is a widespread phenomenon in the (β_π, κ_π) parameter plane; see the upper left panel in figure 9.21. Since β_{Iu} is destabilizing, the stability region becomes smaller, and also modifies its general shape, as β_{Iu} increases to 0.270 in the upper right panel, and further to 0.272 in the lower left corner. At $\beta_{Iu} = 0.280$, from the unstable scenario, local stability already requires limited values

---

[41] The two scenarios S1 and S2 alluded to in the title line of figure 7.7 refer to different numerical values for β_y and β_{nn}, which it was meaningful to distinguish between in the simultaneous discussion of the (two-dimensional) wage-price subdynamics in that chapter.

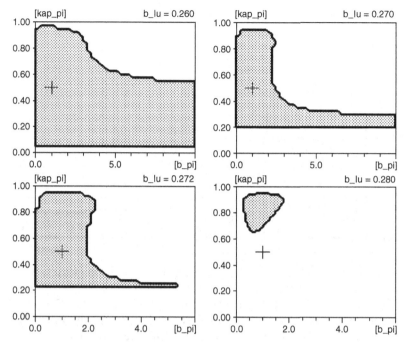

Figure 9.21: Parameter diagrams of (β_π, κ_π) for the KMGT model under variations of β_{lu}

of β_π as well as a relatively small range with relatively high values of the weight parameter κ_π. The phenomenon is qualitatively similar to the above-mentioned figure 7.16 for the KMG model, though the range of β_π and κ_π where stability can prevail is different, apart from the shape of the stability areas themselves.

Increasing β_{lu} slightly above 0.280 in the KMGT model finally causes the stability region of the lower right panel in figure 9.21 to disappear.

(6) The role of the two parameters that characterize the Metzlerian inventory dynamics has changed, too. Both the speed of adjusting sales expectations to current demand, β_y, and the stock adjustment speed with which firms seek to close the gap between desired and actual inventories, β_{nn}, are ambiguous in KMG and destabilizing in KMGT.

The destabilizing effects of the two adjustment speeds are clearly seen in the parameter diagram in figure 9.22, where, again, the unstable scenario with $\beta_{lu} = 0.280$ is taken to be underlying. It is interesting to contrast this diagram with two other figures in the

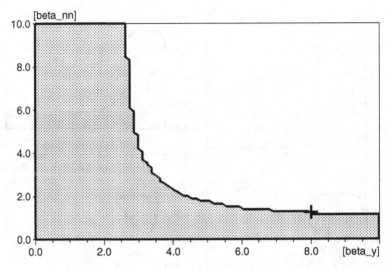

Figure 9.22: The parameter diagram of (β_y, β_{nn}) for the KMGT model

book. On the one hand, figure 7.3 for the KMG model (Chapter 7, section 2, subsection 3) shows that, apart from a thin strip at the left edge of the (β_y, β_{nn}) plane, the stability region is here a narrow island; hence the classification of the coefficients as ambiguous. On the other hand, the numerical study of the two-dimensional Metzlerian subdynamics has yielded figure 7.2 (chapter 7, section 2, subsection 2), in which the stability region, except for the precise 'asymptotes', looks very much like the one in the present figure 9.22. In the discussion of the KMG model we have emphasized the different effects of β_y and β_{nn} from the predictions of the submodel. Now, for the KMGT model, we find that the Metzlerian submodel has regained its explanatory power. This is somewhat bewildering, since the change from KMG to KMGT concerns only the determination of the interest rate, which in turn has no direct bearing on the inventory disequilibrium adjustments but affects only the evolution of aggregate demand.

9.6   Appendix: The detailed Jacobian matrix of the KMGT model

This appendix calculates the full details of the entries of the Jacobian $\mathcal{J}$ in eq. (9.25). We begin by giving some basic partial derivatives with respect to y^e and n, which are used in several places. As usual, here and in the following, the superscript 'o' to designate the steady-state values is omitted.

$$y_y = \partial y / \partial y^e = 1 + (g^o + \beta_{nn})\beta_{ny}$$
$$y_n = \partial y / \partial n = -\beta_{nn}$$
$$u_y = y_y / y^n$$
$$u_n = y_n / y^n$$
$$v_y = -\omega f_z' y_y / y^n \qquad \text{(where } \omega = v)$$
$$v_n = -\omega f_z' y_n / y^n$$
$$e_y = k^s (1 - f_z') y_y$$
$$e_n = k^s (1 - f_z') y_n$$

Referring directly to eq. (9.13) for $\dot{\omega}$, the entries of the first row of $\mathcal{J}$ are given as follows:

$$f_{wi} = f_{w\pi} = 0$$
$$f_{w\omega} = -\beta_{wv} / v$$
$$f_{wy} = [(1 - f_z')\beta_{we} + f_z'\beta_{wv}] y_y / y^n$$
$$f_{wk} = y^n \beta_{we}$$
$$f_{wn} = [(1 - f_z')\beta_{we} + f_z'\beta_{wv}] y_n / y^n$$
$$f_{pi} = f_{pk} = f_{p\pi} = 0$$
$$f_{p\omega} = (1 + \mu)\beta_{pv} = \beta_{pv} / v$$
$$f_{py} = (\beta_{pu} - f_z'\beta_{pv}) y_y / y^n$$
$$f_{pn} = (\beta_{pu} - f_z'\beta_{pv}) y_n / y^n$$

$$j_{11} = \omega\kappa[(1 - \kappa_p)f_{w\omega} - (1 - \kappa_w)f_{p\omega}]$$
$$j_{12} = 0$$
$$j_{13} = \omega\kappa[(1 - \kappa_p)f_{wy} - (1 - \kappa_w)f_{py}]$$
$$j_{14} = \omega\kappa(1 - \kappa_p)f_{wk}$$
$$j_{15} = \omega\kappa[(1 - \kappa_p)f_{wn} - (1 - \kappa_w)f_{pn}]$$
$$j_{16} = 0$$

Regarding the second and sixth row of $\mathcal{J}$, we use the reduced form (9.9) to compute the partial derivatives of the rate of price inflation. Plugging in the above derivatives for f_w and f_p, we get

$$\hat{p}_\omega = \kappa(\beta_{pv} - \kappa_p\beta_{wv})v$$

$$\hat{p}_i = 0$$

$$\hat{p}_y = \kappa[\beta_{pu} - f_z'\beta_{pv} + \kappa_p(1 - f_z')\beta_{we} + \kappa_p f_z'\beta_{wv}]y_y/y^n$$

$$\hat{p}_k = \kappa\kappa_p y^n\beta_{we}$$

$$\hat{p}_n = \kappa[\beta_{pu} - f_z'\beta_{pv} + \kappa_p(1 - f_z')\beta_{we} + \kappa_p f_z'\beta_{wv}]y_n/y^n$$

$$\hat{p}_\pi = 1$$

It remains to substitute these expressions, together with those for u_y and u_n from above, in the second and sixth row of (9.25). For the other three rows, 3, 4 and 5 of $\mathcal{J}$, we need only the partial derivatives of g_k and y^d in (9.11) and (9.12). Using the partial derivatives of q in (9.10), they read

$$g_{k\omega} = -f_{Iq}y^n$$

$$g_{ki} = -f_{Iq}$$

$$g_{ky} = [f_{Iu}/y^n + f_{Iq}(vf_z' + 1 - v)]y_y$$

$$g_{kk} = 0$$

$$g_{kn} = [f_{Iu}/y^n + f_{Iq}(vf_z' + 1 - v)]y_n$$

$$g_{k\pi} = f_{Iq}$$

$$y_\omega^d = (s_c - \tau_w - f_{Iq})y^n$$

$$y_i^d = g_{ki} = -f_{Iq}$$

$$y_y^d = 1 - s_c + (s_c - \tau_w)(1 - f_z')vy_y + g_{ky}$$

$$y_k^d = 0$$

$$y_n^d = (s_c - \tau_w)(1 - f_z')vy_n + g_{kn}$$

$$y_\pi^d = g_{k\pi} = f_{Iq}$$

References

ALEXANDER, J. C., AND J. A. YORKE (1978), 'Global bifurcations of periodic orbits', *American Journal of Mathematics*, 100, 263–92.

AMATO, J. D., AND T. LAUBACH (2003), 'Rule-of-thumb behavior and monetary policy', *European Economic Review*, 47, 791–831.

ASADA, T., C. CHIARELLA, P. FLASCHEL AND R. FRANKE (2003), *Open Economy Macrodynamics: An Integrated Disequilibrium Approach*. Berlin: Springer.

BACKUS, D. K., AND P. J. KEHOE (1992), 'International evidence on the historical properties of business cycles', *American Economic Review*, 82, 864–88.

BALL, L. (1997), *Efficient Rules for Monetary Policy*. Working Paper no. 5952, National Bureau of Economic Research, Cambridge, MA. Published in *International Finance* (1999), 2, 63–83.

BANK FOR INTERNATIONAL SETTLEMENTS (1995), *Financial Structure and the Monetary Policy Transmission Mechanism*. Basle.

BARNETT, W. A., AND Y. HE (1998), *Bifurcations in Continuous-time Macroeconomic Systems*. Mimeo, Department of Economics, Washington University in St Louis.

BARSKY, R., J. PARKER AND G. SOLON (1994), 'Measuring the cyclicality of real wages: how important is the composition bias?', *Quarterly Journal of Economics*, 109, 1–25.

BAXTER, M., AND R. G. KING (1995), *Measuring Business Cycles: Approximate Band-pass Filters for Economic Time Series*. Working Paper no. 5022, National Bureau of Economic Research, Cambridge, MA.

BENHABIB, J., AND T. MIYAO (1981), 'Some new results on the dynamics of the generalized Tobin model', *International Review of Economics*, 22, 589–96.

BERGSTROM, A. R. (1997), 'Gaussian estimation of mixed order continuous time dynamic models with unobservable stochastic trends from mixed stock and flow data', *Econometric Theory*, 13, 467–505.

BERGSTROM, A. R., AND K. B. NOWMAN (1999), *Gaussian Estimation of Continuous Time Macroeconomic Model of the United Kingdom with Unobservable Stochastic Trends*. Mimeo, University of Essex and University of Kent at Canterbury.

BERGSTROM, A. R., K. B. NOWMAN AND C. R. WYMER (1992), 'Gaussian estimation of a second order continuous time macroeconometric model of the United Kingdom', *Economic Modelling*, 9, 313–51.

BERGSTROM, A. R., AND C. R. WYMER (1976), 'A model of disequilibrium neoclassical growth and its application to the United Kingdom', in

A. R. Bergstrom (ed.), *Statistical Inference in Continuous Time Economic Models*. Amsterdam: North-Holland, 267–327.

BERNANKE, B. S., AND I. MIHOV (1997), 'What does the Bundesbank target?', *European Economic Review*, 41, 1025–52.

BLANCHARD, O. J. (1981), 'Output, the stock market, and interest rates', *American Economic Review*, 71, 132–43.

—— (2000), *Macroeconomics* (2nd edn.). Upper Saddle River, NJ: Prentice Hall.

BLANCHARD, O. J., AND S. FISCHER (1989), *Lectures in Macroeconomics*. Cambridge, MA: MIT Press.

BLANCHARD, O. J., AND L. KATZ (1999), *Wage Dynamics: Reconciling Theory and Evidence*. Working Paper no. 6924, National Bureau of Economic Research, Cambridge, MA. Published in *American Economic Review* (2000), 90, 69–74.

BLINDER, A. S. (1998), *Central Banking in Theory and Practice*. Cambridge, MA: MIT Press.

BLINDER, A. S., AND L. J. MACCINI (1991), 'Taking stock: a critical assessment of recent research on inventories', *Journal of Economic Perspectives*, 5, 73–96.

BOORMAN, J. T. (1976), 'The evidence on the demand for money: theoretical formulations and empirical results', in T. M. Havrilesky and J. T. Boorman (eds.), *Current Issues in Monetary Theory and Practice*. Arlington Heights, IL: AHM Publishing Corp., 315–60.

BRAYTON, F., J. M. ROBERTS AND J. C. Williams (1999), *What's Happened to the Phillips Curve?*. Finance and Economics Discussion Series no. 1999–49, Federal Reserve Board, Washington, DC.

BRÜGGEMANN, I., AND D. L. THORNTON (2003), *Interest Rate Smoothing and the Specification of the Taylor Rule*. Diskussionsbeiträge des Fachbereichs Wirtschaftswissenschaft no. 2003/19, Free University of Berlin.

BRYANT, R., P. HOOPER AND C. MANN (1993), *Evaluating Policy Regimes: New Research in Empirical Macroeconomics*. Washington, DC: Brookings Institution.

BURMEISTER, E. (1980), 'On some conceptual issues in rational expectations modelling', *Journal of Money, Credit, and Banking*, 12, 217–28.

CALVO, G. (1983), 'Staggered prices in a utility-maximizing framework', *Journal of Monetary Economics*, 12, 383–98.

CANOVA, F., AND E. ORTEGA (2000), 'Testing calibrated general equilibrium models', in R. Mariano, T. Schvermann and M. Weeks (eds), *Simulation-based Inference in Econometrics*. Cambridge: Cambridge University Press, 400–36.

CASTELNUOVO, E. (2003), 'Taylor rules, omitted variables, and interest rate smoothing in the US', *Economics Letters*, 81, 55–9.

CHEN, P., C. CHIARELLA, P. FLASCHEL AND W. SEMMLER (2004), *Keynesian Dynamics and the Wage Price Spiral: Estimating a Baseline Disequilibrium Approach*. Working paper, School of Finance and Economics, University of Technology, Sydney.

CHIARELLA, C., AND P. FLASCHEL (2000a), *The Dynamics of Keynesian Monetary Growth: Macrofoundations*. Cambridge: Cambridge University Press.

—— (2000b), 'High order disequilibrium growth dynamics: theoretical aspects and numerical features', *Journal of Economic Dynamics and Control*, 24, 935–63.

CHIARELLA, C., P. FLASCHEL, G. GROH AND W. SEMMLER (2000), *Disequilibrium, Growth and Labor Market Dynamics*. Berlin: Springer.

CHRISTIANO, L., M. EICHENBAUM AND C. L. EVANS (1998), 'Monetary policy shocks: what have we learned and to what end?', in J. B. Taylor and M. Woodfor (eds.), *Handbook of Macroeconomics*, Vol. IA. Amsterdam: Elsevier, 65–148.

CLARIDA, R., AND M. GERTLER (1997), 'How the Bundesbank conducts monetary policy', in C. D. Romer and D. H. Romer (eds.), *Reducing Inflation: Motivation and Strategy*. Chicago: University of Chicago Press, 363–406.

COBHAM, D. (2003), 'Why does the Monetary Policy Committee smooth interest rates?', *Oxford Economic Papers*, 55, 467–93.

COOLEY, T. F., AND L. E. OHANIAN (1991), 'The cyclical behavior of prices', *Journal of Monetary Economics*, 28, 25–60.

DEISTLER, M. (2001), 'Comments on the contributions by C. W. J. Granger and J. J. Heckman', *Journal of Econometrics*, 100, 71–2.

DELONG, J. B., AND L. H. SUMMERS (1986), 'Are business cycles symmetrical?', in R. Gordon(ed.), *American Business Cycles: Continuity and Change*. Chicago: University of Chicago Press, 166–79.

DEMIRALP, S., AND O. JORDA (2001), *The Pavlovian Response of Term Rates to Fed Announcements*. Finance and Economics Discussion Series no. 2001–10, Federal Reserve Board, Washington, DC.

DIEBOLD, F. X., AND G. D. RUDEBUSCH (1999), *Business Cycles: Durations, Dynamics, and Forecasting*. Princeton: University Presses of California, Columbia and Princeton.

(2001), 'Five questions about business cycles', Federal Reserve Bank of San Francisco, *Economic Review*, 1–15.

DUNLOP, J. T. (1938), 'The movement of real and money wage rates', *Economic Journal*, 48, 413–34.

EGGERTSSON, G. B., AND M. WOODFORD (2003), *Optimal Monetary Policy in a Liquidity Trap*. Working Paper no. 9968, National Bureau of Economic Research, Cambridge, MA.

ELLINGSEN, T., AND U. SÖDERSTRÖM (2004), *Why are Long Rates Sensitive to Monetary Policy?* Working paper no. 256, Innocenzo Gasparini Institute for Economic Research, Università Bocconi, Milan.

ERCEG, C., D. HENDERSON AND A. LEVIN (2000), 'Optimal monetary policy with staggered wage and price contracts', *Journal of Monetary Economics*, 46, 281–313.

FAY, J. A., AND J. L. MEDOFF (1985), 'Labor and output over the business cycle: some direct evidence', *American Economic Review*, 75, 638–55.

FIORITO, R., AND T. KOLLINTZAS (1994), 'Stylized facts of business cycles in the G7 from a real business cycle perspective', *European Economic Review*, 38, 235–69.

FLASCHEL, P. (1985), 'Macroeconomic dynamics and effective demand: some corrections', *Metroeconomica*, 37, 135–56.

(2000), 'Disequilibrium growth theory with insider–outsider effects', *Structural Change and Economic Dynamics*, 11, 337–54.

FLASCHEL, P., AND R. FRANKE (2000), 'An old-Keynesian note on destabilizing price flexibility', *Review of Political Economy*, 12, 273–83.

FLASCHEL, P., R. FRANKE AND W. SEMMLER (1997), *Dynamic Macroeconomics: Instability, Fluctuations, and Growth in Monetary Economies.* Cambridge, MA: MIT Press.

FLASCHEL, P., G. GONG AND W. SEMMLER (2002), 'A Keynesian macroeconometric framework for the analysis of monetary policy rules', *Journal of Economic Behavior and Organization*, 25, 101–13.

FLASCHEL, P., AND G. GROH (1998), *Textbook Stagflation Theory and Beyond.* Discussion paper, Department of Economics, University of Bielefeld.

FOOTE, C., E. HURST AND J. LEAHY (2000), 'Testing the (S,s) model', *American Economic Review*, 90, 116–19.

FRANKE, R. (1987), *Production Prices and Dynamical Processes of the Gravitation of Market Prices.* Frankfurt: Verlag Peter Lang.

(1992a), 'Stable, unstable, and persistent cyclical behaviour in a Keynes–Wicksell monetary growth model', *Oxford Economic Papers*, 44, 242–56.

(1992b), *A Note on the Relationship between Adaptive Expectations and Extrapolative Regression Forecasts.* Mimeo, Department of Economics, University of Bielefeld.

(1996), 'A Metzlerian model of inventory growth cycles', *Structural Change and Economic Dynamics*, 7, 243–62.

(1999), 'A reappraisal of adaptive expectations', *Political Economy*, 4, 5–29.

FRANKE, R., AND T. ASADA (1994), 'A Keynes–Goodwin model of the business cycle', *Journal of Economic Behavior and Organization*, 24, 273–295.

FRIEDMAN, M. (1953), 'The methodology of positive economics', in *Essays in Positive Economics.* Chicago: University of Chicago Press, 3–43.

FUHRER, J. C. (1997), 'The (un)importance of forward-looking behavior in price specifications', *Journal of Money, Credit, and Banking*, 29, 338–50.

(2000), 'Habit formation in consumption and its implications for monetary policy models', *American Economic Review*, 90, 367–90.

FUHRER, J. C., AND G. R. MOORE (1995), 'Forward-looking behavior and the stability of a conventional monetary policy rule', *Journal of Money, Credit, and Banking*, 27, 1060–70.

GABISCH, G., AND H. -W. LORENZ (1989), *Business Cycle Theory: A Survey of Methods and Concepts.* Berlin: Springer.

GALÌ, J. (2000), 'The return of the Phillips curve and other recent developments in business cycle theory', *Spanish Economic Review*, 2, 1–10.

GALÌ, J., AND M. GERTLER (1999), 'Inflation dynamics: a structural econometric analysis', *Journal of Monetary Economics*, 44, 195–222.

GALÌ, J., M. GERTLER AND J. D. LÓPEZ-SALIDO (2001), 'European inflation dynamics', *European Economic Review*, 45, 1237–70.

GALÌ, J., J. D. LÓPEZ-SALIDO AND J. VALLÉS (2004), 'Rule-of-thumb consumers and the design of interest rates', *Journal of Money, Credit, and Banking*, 36, 739–63.

GITTINGS, T. A. (1989), 'Capacity utilization and inflation', *Economic Perspectives*, 13:3, 2–9.

GOLDFELD, S. (1976), 'The case of the missing money', *Brookings Papers on Economic Activity*, 3, 683–739.

GOODFRIEND, M. (1991), 'Interest rates and the conduct of monetary policy', *Carnegie-Rochester Conference Series on Public Policy*, 34, 7–30.

(2002), 'The phases of U.S. monetary policy: 1987 to 2001', Federal Reserve Bank of Richmond, *Economic Quarterly*, 88:4, 1–17. Published in P. Mizen (ed.), *Central Banking, Monetary Theory and Practice: Essays in Honour of Charles Goodhart*, Vol. I. Cheltenham: Edward Elgar.

GOODWIN, R. M. (1967), 'A growth cycle', in C. H. Feinstein (ed.), *Socialism, Capitalism and Economic Growth*. Cambridge: Cambridge University Press. Revised version in E. K. Hunt and J. G. Schwarz (eds.) (1972), *A Critique of Economic Theory*. Harmondsworth: Penguin, 442–9.

GORDON, D. B., AND E. LEEPER (1994), 'The dynamic impacts of monetary policy: an exercise in tentative identification', *Journal of Political Economy*, 102, 1128–47.

GREGORY, A. W., AND G. W. SMITH (1993), 'Statistical aspects of calibration in macroeconomics', in G. S. Maddala, C. R. Rao and H. D. Vinod (eds.), *Handbook of Statistics*, Vol. XI. Amsterdam: Elsevier, 703–19.

GROTH, C. (1988), 'IS-LM dynamics and the hypothesis of adaptive-forward-looking expectations', in P. Flaschel and M. Krüger (eds), *Recent Approaches to Economic Dynamics*. Frankfurt: Verlag Peter Lang, 251–66.

GUCKENHEIMER, J., AND P. HOLMES (1983), *Nonlinear Oscillations, Dynamical Systems, and Bifurcations of Vector Fields*. New York: Springer.

GUTHRIE, G., AND J. WRIGHT (2000), 'Market implemented monetary policy with open mouth operations', *Journal of Monetary Economics*, 46, 489–516.

HADJIMICHALAKIS, M. G. (1971), 'Money, expectations, and dynamics – an alternative view', *International Review of Economics*, 12, 381–402.

HAYAKAWA, H. (1984), 'A dynamic generalization of the Tobin model', *Journal of Economic Dynamics and Control*, 7, 209–31.

HICKS, J. R. (1950), *A contribution to the Theory of the Trade Cycle*. Oxford: Oxford University Press.

HIRSCH, M. W., AND S. SMALE (1974), *Differential Equations, Dynamical Systems, and Linear Algebra*. New York: Academic Press.

HODRICK, R. J., AND E. C. PRESCOTT (1997), 'Postwar business cycles: an empirical investigation', *Journal of Money, Credit, and Banking*, 29, 1–16.

IRVINE, F. O., JR. (1981), 'Retail inventory investment and the cost of capital', *American Economic Review*, 71, 633–48.

ISSING, O. (1997), 'Monetary targeting in Germany: the stability of monetary policy and of the monetary system', *Journal of Monetary Economics*, 39, 67–79.

JUDD, J. P., AND G. D. RUDEBUSCH (1998), 'Taylor's rule and the Fed: 1970–1997', Federal Reserve Bank of San Francisco, *Economic Review*, 3, 3–16.

KALECKI, M. (1939), *Money and Real Wages*. Polish booklet, reprinted in M. Kalecki (1966), *Studies in the Theory of Business Cycles*. Warsaw and Oxford: Polish Scientific Publishers and Basil Blackwell, 40–71.

(1943), *Costs and Prices*. Final version printed in M. Kalecki (1971), *Selected Essays on the Dynamics of the Capitalist Economy 1933-1972*. Cambridge: Cambridge University Press, 43–61.

KEYNES, J. M. (1936), *The General Theory of Employment, Interest and Money*. London: Macmillan.

KILEY, M. T. (1998), *Monetary Policy under Neoclassical and New-Keynesian Philips Curves, with an Application to Price Level and Inflation Targeting.* Finance and Economics Discussion Series no. 1998–27, Federal Reserve Board, Washington, DC.

KIM, K., AND A. R. PAGAN (1995), 'The econometric analysis of calibrated macroeconomic models', in M. H. Pesaran and M. R. Wickens (eds.), *Handbook of Applied Econometrics in Macroeconomics.* Oxford: Basil Blackwell, 356–90.

KING, R. G., (2000), 'The new IS-LM model: language, logic, and limits', Federal Reserve Bank of Richmond, *Economic Quarterly*, 86:3, 45–103.

KING, R. G., AND S. T. REBELO (1999), 'Resuscitating real business cycles', in J. B. Taylor and M. Woodford (eds.), *Handbook of Macroeconomics*, vol. IB. Amsterdam: Elsevier, 927–1007.

KLOEDEN, P. E., AND J. LORENZ (1986), 'Stable attracting sets in dynamical systems and in their one-step discretizations', *SIAM Journal on Numerical Analysis*, 23, 986–95.

KÖPER, C. (2000), *Stability Analysis of an Extended KMG Growth Dynamics.* Discussion Paper no. 464, Department of Economics, University of Bielefeld.

LANSING, K. J. (2002), 'Real-time estimation of trend output and the illusion of interest rate smoothing', Federal Reserve Bank of San Francisco, *Economic Review*, 17–34.

LANSING, K. J., AND B. TREHAN (2001), *Forward-looking Behavior and the Optimality of the Taylor Rule.* Working Paper no. 01–03, Federal Reserve Bank of San Francisco.

(2003), 'Forward-looking behavior and optimal discretionary monetary policy', *Economics Letters*, 81, 249–56 (abridged version of earlier paper).

LEEPER, E., C. SIMS and T. ZHA (1996), 'What does monetary policy do?', *Brookings Papers on Economic Activity*, 2, 1–63.

LEEPER, E., AND T. ZHA (2001), 'Assessing simple policy rules: a view from a complete macroeconomic model', Federal Reserve Bank of St Louis, *Review*, July/August, 83–110.

LEVIN, A., V. WIELAND AND J. C WILLIAMS (1998), *Robustness of Simple Monetary Rules under Model Uncertainty.* Working Paper no. 6570, National Bureau of Economic Research, Cambridge, MA.

MARSDEN, J. E., AND M. McCRACKEN (1976), *The Hopf Bifurcation and Its Applications.* New York: Springer.

MANKIW, G. (2001), 'The inexorable and mysterious tradeoff between inflation and unemployment', *Economic Journal*, 111, C45–C61.

MCCALLUM, B. T. (1999), 'Solutions to linear rational expectations models: a compact exposition', *Economics Letters*, 61, 143–9.

(2001), *Should Monetary Policy Respond strongly to Output Gaps?* Working Paper no. 8226, National Bureau of Economic Research, Cambridge, MA.

MEHRA, Y. P. (2002), 'Level and growth policy rules and actual Fed policy since 1979', *Journal of Economics and Business*, 54, 575–94.

METZLER, L. A. (1941), 'The nature and stability of inventory cycles', *Review of Economic Statistics*, 23, 113–29.

(1947), 'Factors governing the length of inventory cycles', *Review of Economic Statistics*, 29, 1–15.

MEULENDYKE, A. -M. (1998), *US Monetary Policy and Financial Markets.* Federal Reserve Bank of New York.

MEYER, L. H. (1997), *The Economic Outlook and Challenges for Monetary Policy.* Speech to the Charlotte Economics Club, Charlotte, NC, 16 January.

MISHKIN, F. S. (1999), 'Policy rules for inflation targeting: comment', in J. B. Taylor (ed.), *Monetary Policy Rules.* Chicago: University of Chicago Press, 247–53.

NELSON, C. R., AND C. I. PLOSSER (1982), 'Trends and random walks in macroeconomic time series: some evidence and implications', *Journal of Monetary Economics*, 10, 139–62.

OKUN, A. M. (1980), 'Rational-expectations-with-misperceptions as a theory of the business cycle', *Journal of Money, Credit, and Banking*, 12, 817–25.

ORPHANIDES, A. (2001), 'Commentary', Federal Reserve Bank of St. Louis, *Review*, July/August, 49–57 (relating to the article by J. B. Taylor, 'Expectations, open market operations, and changes in the federal funds rate', 33–47).

OZLALE, U. (2003), 'Price stability vs. output stability: tales of federal reserve administrations', *Journal of Economic Dynamics and Control*, 27, 1595–610.

PHILLIPS, A. W. (1957), 'Stabilisation policy and the time-forms of lagged responses', *Economic Journal*, 67, 265–77.

PLASMANS, J., H. MEERSMAN, A. VAN POECK AND B. MERLEVEDE (1999), *Generosity of the Unemployment Benefit System and Wage Flexibility in EMU: Time-varying Evidence in Five Countries.* Mimeo, Department of Economics, University of Antwerp.

RAZZAK, W. A. (2001), 'Business cycle asymmetries: international evidence', *Review of Economic Dynamics*, 4, 230–43.

REIFSCHNEIDER, D. L., AND J. C. WILLIAMS (2000), 'Three lessons for monetary policy in a low-inflation era', *Journal of Money, Credit, and Banking*, 32, 936–66.

ROBERTS, J. (1995), 'New Keynesian economics and the Phillips curve', *Journal of Money, Credit, and Banking*, 27, 975–84.

ROMER, D. (1999), 'Short-run fluctuations', http://elsa.berkeley.edu/~dromer/index.html.

—— (2000), 'Keynesian macroeconomics without the LM curve', *Journal of Economic Perspectives*, 14:2, 149–69.

RUDD, J., AND K. WHELAN (2001), *New Tests of the New-Keynesian Phillips Curve.* Finance and Economics Discussion Series no. 2001–30, Federal Reserve Board, Washington, DC.

RUDEBUSCH, G. D. (2001), *Term Structure Evidence on Interest Rate Smoothing and Monetary Policy Inertia.* Mimeo, Federal Reserve Bank of San Francisco. Published in *Journal of Monetary Economics*, 49, 1161–87.

RUDEBUSCH, G. D., AND L. E. O. SVENSSON (1999), 'Policy rules for inflation targeting', in J. B. Taylor (ed.), *Monetary Policy Rules.* Chicago: University of Chicago Press, 203–46.

SACK, B., AND V. WIELAND (2000), 'Interest-rate smoothing and optimal monetary policy: a review of recent empirical evidence', *Journal of Economics and Business*, 52, 205–28.

SARGENT, T. (1979), *Macroeconomics.* New York: Academic Press.

—— (1987), *Macroeconomics* (2nd edn.). New York: Academic Press.

SARGENT, T., AND N. WALLACE (1973), 'The stability of models of money and growth with perfect foresight', *Econometrica*, 41, 1043–48.

SCHMALENSEE, R. (1976), 'An experimental study of expectation formation', *Econometrica*, 44, 17–41.

SEYDEL, R. (1988), *From Equilibrium to Chaos: Practical Bifurcation and Stability Analysis*. New York: Elsevier.

SMANT, D. J. C. (1998), 'Modelling trends, expectations and the cyclical behaviour of prices', *Economic Modelling*, 15, 151–61.

SMETS, F., AND R. WOUTERS (2003), *Shocks and Frictions in US Business Cycles: A Bayesian DSGE Approach*. Mimeo, European Central Bank, National Bank of Belgium.

SMITH, G. (1980), 'A dynamic IS-LM simulation model', *Applied Economics*, 12, 131–327.

SOLOW, R. M. (2004), 'Introduction: the Tobin approach to monetary economics', *Journal of Money, Credit, and Banking*, 36, 557–663.

SONTAG, E. D. (1990), *Mathematical Control Theory: Deterministic Finite Dimensional Systems*. New York: Springer.

SROUR, G. (2001), *Why do Central Banks Smooth Interest Rates?* Working Paper no. 2001–17, Bank of Canada.

STEIN, J. L. (1969), 'Neoclassical and Keynes–Wicksell monetary growth models', *Journal of Money, Credit, and Banking*, 1, 153–71.

(1982), *Monetarist, Keynesian and New Classical Economics*. Oxford: Basil Blackwell.

STEINDL, J. (1976), *Maturity and Stagnation in American Capitalism* [reprint of the 1952 edition with a new introduction]. New York: Monthly Review Press.

STIGLITZ, J. E., AND C. WALSH (2000), *Principles of Macroeconomics* (3rd edn.). New York: W. W. Norton.

STOCK, J. H., AND M. W. WATSON (1999), 'Business cycle fluctuations in US macroeconomic time series', in J. B. Taylor and M. Woodford (eds.), *Handbook of Macroeconomics*, Vol. IA. Amsterdam: Elsevier, 3–64.

SUMMERS, L. H. (1991), 'The scientific illusion in empirical macroeconomics', *Scandinavian Journal of Economics*, 93, 129–48.

SVENSSON, L. E. O. (1997), 'Inflation forecast targeting: implementing and monitoring inflation targets', *European Economic Review*, 41, 1111–46.

(2003), 'Escaping from a liquidity trap and deflation: the foolproof way and others', *Journal of Economic Perspectives*, 17:4, 145–66.

TARSHIS, L. (1939), 'Changes in real and money wages', *Economic Journal*, 49, 150–4.

TAYLOR, J. B. (1993a), 'Discretion versus policy rules in practice', *Carnegie-Rochester Conference Series on Public Policy*, 39, 195–214.

(1993b), *Macroeconomic Policy in a World Economy: From Econometric Design to Practical Operation*. New York: W. W. Norton.

(ED.) (1999), *Monetary Policy Rules*. Chicago: University of Chicago Press.

(2000), 'Teaching modern macroeconomics at the Principles level', *American Economic Review*, 90, 90–4.

(2001), *Economics* (3rd edn.). Boston: Houghton Mifflin.

TAYLOR, L. (1989), *Stabilization and Growth in Developing Countries: A Structuralist Approach*. Chur, Switzerland: Harwood Academic Publishers.

THORNTON, D. L. (2000), *The Relationship between the Federal Funds Rate and the Fed's Federal Funds Rate Target: Is it Open Market or Open Mouth Operations?* Working Paper no. 1999-022B, Federal Reserve Bank of St Louis. Published as 'The Fed and short-term rates: is it open market operations, open mouth operations or interest rate smoothing?' in *Journal of Banking and Finance* (2004), 28, 475–98.

TOBIN, J. (1975), 'Keynesian models of recession and depression', *American Economic Review*, 65, 195–202.

(1992), 'An old Keynesian counterattacks', *Eastern Economic Journal*, 18, 387–400.

TURNOVSKY, S. (1995), *Methods of Macroeconomic Dynamics*. Cambridge, MA: MIT Press.

UHLIG, H. (1999), 'A toolkit for analysing nonlinear dynamic stochastic models easily', in R. Marimon and A. Scott (eds.), *Computational Methods for the Study of Dynamic Economies*. New York: Oxford University Press, 30–75.

WALSH, C. E. (2003), *Monetary Theory and Policy* (2nd edn.). Cambridge, MA: MIT Press.

WHITIN, T. M. (1957), *The Theory of Inventory Management*. Princeton: Princeton University Press. Reprinted by Greenwood Press, Westport (1970).

WOODFORD, M. (2003), *Interest and Prices: Foundations of a Theory of Monetary Policy*. Princeton: Princeton University Press.

ZELLNER, A. (1992), 'Statistics, science and public policy', *Journal of the American Statistical Association*, 87, 1–6.

(2002), 'My experience with nonlinear dynamics models in economics', *Studies in Nonlinear Dynamics and Econometrics*, 6:2, 1–18 (www.bepress.com/snde).

Index

Printed in the United States
By Bookmasters